INTERNATIONAL LAW

VOLUME 3

THE LAW OF PEACE

PARTS II–VI

AF711910

INTERNATIONAL LAW

BEING THE COLLECTED PAPERS OF

HERSCH LAUTERPACHT

Q.C., LL.D., F.B.A.

SYSTEMATICALLY ARRANGED AND EDITED BY

E. LAUTERPACHT, Q.C.

VOLUME 3

THE LAW OF PEACE

PARTS II–VI

CAMBRIDGE UNIVERSITY PRESS

CAMBRIDGE

LONDON · NEW YORK · MELBOURNE

CAMBRIDGE UNIVERSITY PRESS
Cambridge, New York, Melbourne, Madrid, Cape Town, Singapore, São Paulo, Delhi

Cambridge University Press
The Edinburgh Building, Cambridge CB2 8RU, UK

Published in the United States of America by Cambridge University Press, New York

www.cambridge.org
Information on this title: www.cambridge.org/9780521109505

© Elihu Lauterpacht 1977

This publication is in copyright. Subject to statutory exception
and to the provisions of relevant collective licensing agreements,
no reproduction of any part may take place without the written
permission of Cambridge University Press.

First published 1977
This digitally printed version 2009

A catalogue record for this publication is available from the British Library

Library of Congress Cataloguing in Publication data

Lauterpacht, Sir Hersch, 1897-1960
International law, being the collected papers of Hersch Lauterpacht.

1. International law. I. Lauterpacht, Elihu, ed.
JX3225.L32 341 70-92250

ISBN 978-0-521-21207-6 hardback
ISBN 978-0-521-10950-5 paperback

CONTENTS

CONTENTS OF PREVIOUS VOLUMES

VOLUME 1

GENERAL WORKS

VOLUME 2

THE LAW OF PEACE
PART I INTERNATIONAL LAW IN GENERAL

PREFACE

As a further step in the presentation of Hersch Lauterpacht's works in systematic form, this volume moves on from Part I, 'International Law in General', to cover a further five Parts falling within the Law of Peace: statehood; territory and territorial jurisdiction; the individual; diplomatic intercourse; and international organization. The fuller titles given to these Parts within the volume correspond with Lauterpacht's own outline.

The volume contains a greater number of Lauterpacht's previously unpublished writings than did the previous volume and will, for that reason, be of special value and interest. Attention may, in particular, be called to the remarkable study of the principles of international organization written, it would appear, some time in 1942–3, which is printed as chapter I of Part VI; to the lectures on 'Sovereignty and federation in international law' (Part II, chapter I), 'State sovereignty and human rights' (Part IV, chapter 4), and 'The League of Nations' (Part VI, chapter 5), all of which, though prepared thirty-five and forty-three years ago respectively, possess a striking degree of contemporary relevance; to four professional opinions of considerable historical significance and, not least, to the dissertation on the Mandates system which Lauterpacht submitted to the University of Vienna in 1922.

It has proved necessary to depart from Lauterpacht's scheme in one respect. The original classification placed 'The Contractual Relations of States: Treaties' after 'State Territory' and before 'The Individual in International Law'. However, because the material on treaties is too great to fit as an undivided Part into its proper place within this volume, it seems better, in the interests of a clearer presentation of this material, to postpone it to the next volume and to advance certain topics which would otherwise have followed it.

This volume contains within the relevant sections one declaration and two separate opinions which Lauterpacht delivered as a judge of the International Court of Justice. His other separate opinions will appear, as appropriate, later. It has not always been easy to classify the separate opinions for, as hardly needs saying, each opinion touches upon a number of topics. The opinions have, therefore, been introduced at the points justified by their principal content. This decision was reached after correspondence with the late Lord McNair, the late Dr C. W. Jenks, Sir Gerald Fitzmaurice, Ambassador Shabtai Rosenne, Professor R. Y. Jennings, Professor R. R. Baxter and Professor S. M. Schwebel, during which two other ways of presenting the judicial materials were considered and finally rejected: one being to publish all the judicial opinions together in a separate volume and the other to divide up each opinion and print its component parts at the appropriate places within the classification.

Those whose names I have just mentioned have given me counsel on many other points connected with these volumes. It is a source of great sorrow to me that I can no longer turn to Lord McNair or to Wilfred Jenks. They were two of my father's closest friends and both of them had shown me, for as long as I could recollect, warm understanding and generous help for which I shall ever remain grateful.

It is fitting, too, that I should recall with deep appreciation the name of the late Mrs Gladys Lyons, B.Sc. (Econ.), who devoted to many of the papers in this volume the same degree of conscientious skill which she showed for more than forty years in relation to so much of my father's other work.

I am most grateful to those who have given their consent to the publication of the various papers. As to hitherto unpublished texts, Part II, chapters 3 and 4, and Part VI, chapter 2 are printed with the permission of the Zionist Archives and Part V, chapter 1 with that of the Swiss Federal Political Department. Permission to reprint the other chapters has been given by the following: the American Society of International Law – Part III, chapter 7; the British Broadcasting Corporation – Part IV, chapter 3; the British Institute of International and Comparative Law – Part III, chapter 8; the Editor of the *Cambridge Law Journal* – Part III, chapters 4 and 6; the International Court of Justice – Part III, chapter 2 and Part VI, chapters 3 and 4; the Editor of the *Jewish Yearbook of International Law* – Part IV, chapter 1; Oxford University Press – Part III, chapters 1, 9 and 10 and Part VI, chapter 6; the Editor of *The Political Quarterly* – Part VI, chapter 7; the Times Publishing Company Ltd – Part II, chapter 5, Part III, chapters 3 and 5 and Part IV, chapter 2.

Ambassador Rosenne, in addition to his advice regarding the judicial materials, assisted me greatly in tracing the opinions which were given to the Jewish Agency. For two major pieces of translation, I must thank Dr K. Skubiszweski and Miss Maureen MacGlashan. Other, no less essential, help has been given to me at various stages in the preparation of this volume by Dr Gillian White, now Professor of International Law at the University of Manchester; Mrs C. A. Hopkins; Mr D. J. Driscoll, Lecturer in Law at the University of Edinburgh; Dr Lyndel Prott, Senior Lecturer in Law at the University of Sydney Law School; and Mr W. M. Bush, of the Department of Foreign Affairs, Canberra.

Mrs S. Rainbow, my secretary in Cambridge – where I began the work on this volume, and Miss J. Koch, my secretary in Canberra – where I have completed the work, have both been pillars of strength.

E. LAUTERPACHT

Department of Foreign Affairs
Canberra
August 1975

TABLE OF CASES

ABBREVIATIONS

OF TITLES OF BOOKS, ETC., QUOTED IN THIS VOLUME

The books referred to in the bibliographies and notes are, as a rule, quoted with their full titles and the date of their publication. But certain books and periodicals which are often referred to in this volume are quoted in an abbreviated form, as follows:

Accioly	Accioly, *Tratado de Direito internacional público*, 3 vols. (1933–5).
A.J.	*American Journal of International Law.*
Annuaire	*Annuaire de l'Institut de Droit International.*
Annual Digest	*Annual Digest and Reports of Public International Law Cases:* 1919–22, edited by Sir John Fischer Williams and H. Lauterpacht (1932); 1923–4, edited by the same (1933); 1925–6, edited by A. D. McNair and H. Lauterpacht (1929); 1927–8, edited by the same (1931); 1929–30 (1935); 1931–2 (1938); 1933–4 (1940); 1935–7 (1941); 1938–40 (1942); 1941–2 (1945); 1919–42 (supplementary volume) (1947); 1943–5 (1949); 1946 (1951); 1947 (1951); 1948 (1953); 1949 (1955)—all edited by H. Lauterpacht.
Anzilotti	Anzilotti, *Corso di diritto internazionale*, vol. I, 3rd ed. (1928), French translation by Gidel (1929); vol. III, part I (1915).
A.S. Proceedings	*Proceedings of the American Society of International Law.*
Balladore Pallieri	Balladore Pallieri, *Diritto internazionale pubblico* (1937).
Baty	Baty, *The Canons of International Law* (1930).
Bibliotheca Visseriana	*Bibliotheca Visseriana Dissertationum Jus Internationale Illustrantium.*
Bittner	Bittner, *Die Lehre von völkerrechtlichen Urkunden* (1924).
Bluntschli	Bluntschli, *Das moderne Völkerrecht der zivilisierten Staaten als Rechtsbuch dargestellt*, 3rd ed. (1878).
Borchard	Borchard, *The Diplomatic Protection of Citizens Abroad* (1915).
Br. and For. St. Papers	*British and Foreign State Papers* (Hertslet), vol. I (1841), continued up to date.
Brierly	Brierly, *The Law of Nations*, 5th ed. (1955).

ABBREVIATIONS OF TITLES OF BOOKS

Bustamante	Bustamante, *Derecho internacional público*, 3 vols. (1933–5).
B.Y.	*British Year Book of International Law.*
Calvo	Calvo, *Le Droit international théorique et pratique*, 5th ed., 6 vols. (1896).
Cavaglieri	Cavaglieri, *Lezioni di diritto internazionale* (general part, 1925).
Clunet	*Journal du droit international.*
Cruchaga	Cruchaga-Tocornal, *Nociones de Derecho internacional*, 3rd ed., 2 vols. (1923–5).
Dicey	Dicey, *Conflict of Laws*, 4th ed. (1927).
Dickinson, *Cases*	Dickinson, *Cases and Other Materials on International Law* (1950).
Documents	*Documents on International Affairs.*
Fauchille	Fauchille, *Traité de droit international public*, 8th ed. of Bonfils' *Manuel de droit international public*, vol. I, part I (1922), vol. I, part 2 (1925), vol. I, part 3 (1926), vol. II (1921).
Fenwick	Fenwick, *International Law*, 3rd ed. (1948).
Fiore	Fiore, *Nouveau droit international public.* French translation by Antoine from the 2nd Italian edition, 3 vols. (1885).
Fiore, *Code*	Fiore, *International Law Codified.* Translation by Borchard from the 5th Italian edition (1918).
Fischer Williams, *Chapters*	Fischer Williams, *Chapters on Current International Law and the League of Nations* (1929).
Fontes Juris Gentium	*Fontes Juris Gentium*, edited by V. Bruns.
Garner, *Developments*	Garner, *Recent Developments in International Law* (1925).
Gemma	Gemma, *Appunti di diritto internazionale* (1923).
Genet	Genet, *Traité de diplomatie et de droit diplomatique*, 3 vols. (1931–2).
Gidel	Gidel, *Le droit international public de la mer, le temps de paix*: vol. I, *Introduction—La haute mer* (1932); vol. II, *Les eaux intérieures* (1932); vol. III, *La mer territoriale et la zone contiguë* (1934).
Grotius	Grotius, *De Jure Belli ac Pacis* (1625).
Grotius Annuaire	*Grotius Annuaire International.*
Grotius Society	*Transactions of the Grotius Society.*
Guggenheim	Guggenheim, *Lehrbuch des Völkerrechts*, Parts I and 2 (1947).
Guggenheim, *Traité*	Guggenheim, *Traité de Droit International Publique*, vol. I (1953); vol. II (1954).
Hackworth	Hackworth, *Digest of International Law*, 7 vols. (1940–3).
Hague Recueil	*Recueil des Cours, Académie de Droit International de La Haye.*

Hall	Hall, *A Treatise on International Law*, 8th ed. (1924), by A. Pearce Higgins.
Harvard Research	*Research in International Law*. Under the Auspices of the Harvard Law School. Draft Conventions Prepared for the Codification of International Law. Directed by M. O. Hudson: (1929) I. *Nationality* (Reporter: Flournoy); II. *Responsibility of States* (Borchard); III. *Territorial Waters* (G. G. Wilson); (1932) I. *Diplomatic Privileges and Immunities* (Reeves); II. *Legal Position and Functions of Consuls* (Quincy Wright); III. *Competence of Courts in regard to Foreign States* (Jessup); IV. *Piracy* (Bingham); V. *A Collection of Piracy Laws of Various Countries* (Morrison); (1935) I. *Extradition* (Burdick); II. *Jurisdiction with respect to Crime* (Dickinson); III. *Treaties* (Garner).
Heffter	Heffter, *Das europäische Völkerrecht der Gegenwart*, 8th ed. by Geffcken (1888).
Heilborn, *System*	Heilborn, *Das System des Völkerrechts entwickelt aus den völkerrechtlichen Begriffen* (1896).
Hertslet's *Commercial Treaties*	Hertslet, *Collection of Treaties and Conventions between Great Britain and Other Powers, so far as they relate to Commerce and Navigation*, vol. I (1820), continued to date.
Higgins and Colombos	Higgins and Colombos, *The International Law of the Sea*, 2nd ed. (1951).
H.L.R.	*Harvard Law Review*.
Holland, *Lectures*	Holland, *Lectures on International Law*, edited by T. A. and W. L. Walker (1933).
Holland, *Studies*	Holland, *Studies in International Law* (1898).
Holtzendorff	Holtzendorff, *Handbuch des Völkerrechts*, 4 vols. (1885–9).
Hudson, *Cases*	Hudson, *Cases and Other Materials on International Law*, 3rd ed. (1951).
Hudson, *Legislation*	Hudson, *International Legislation*: vols. I–XI (1931–50).
Hyde	Hyde, *International Law, chiefly as interpreted and applied by the United States*, 2nd ed., 3 vols. (1945).
I.C.J.	*International Court of Justice*.
I.C.L.Q.	*International and Comparative Law Quarterly*.
I.L.R.	*International Law Reports*, being the continuation of *Annual Digest*, edited by H. Lauterpacht until volume 24 and thereafter by E. Lauterpacht.
J.C.L.	*Journal of Comparative Legislation and International Law*
Keith's Wheaton	*Wheaton's Elements of International Law*, 6th English edition by A. Berriedale Keith, vol. I (1929); vol. II (7th ed., 1944).

Klüber	Klüber, *Europäisches Völkerrecht*, 2nd ed. by Morstadt (1851).
Lapradelle-Politis	Lapradelle-Politis, *Recueil des arbitrages internationaux*, vol. I (1905), vol. II (1924), vol. III (1954).
Lauterpacht, *Analogies*	Lauterpacht, *Private Law Sources and Analogies of International Law* (1927).
Lauterpacht, *The Function of Law*	Lauterpacht, *The Function of Law in the International Community* (1933).
Lawrence	Lawrence, *The Principles of International Law*, 7th ed., revised by P. H. Winfield (1923).
Lindley	Lindley, *The Acquisition and Government of Backward Territory in International Law* (1926).
Liszt	Liszt, *Das Völkerrecht*, 12th ed. by Fleischmann (1925).
L.N.O.J.	*League of Nations, Official Journal.*
L.N.T.S.	*League of Nations Treaty Series.* Publication of Treaties and International Engagements registered with the Secretariat of the League of Nations.
Lorimer	Lorimer, *The Institutes of International Law*, 2 vols. (1883–4).
De Louter	De Louter, *Le droit international public positif*, French translation from the Dutch original, 2 vols. (1920).
L.Q.R.	*Law Quarterly Review.*
McNair	McNair, *The Law of Treaties: British Practice and Opinions* (1938).
McNair, *Opinions*	McNair, *International Law Opinions* (1956).
Maine	Maine, *International Law*, 2nd ed. (1894).
Martens	Martens, *Völkerrecht*, German translation from the Russian original, 2 vols. (1883–6).
Martens, G. F.	G. F. Martens, *Précis du droit des gens moderne de l'Europe*, new edition by Vergé, 2 vols. (1858).
Martens, R. Martens, N. R. Martens, N. S. Martens, N. R. G. Martens, N. R. G., 2nd ser. Martens, N. R. G., 3rd ser.	These are the abbreviated quotations of the different parts of Martens, *Recueil de Traités*, which are in common use.
Martens, *Causes célèbres*	Martens, *Causes célèbres du droit des gens*, 2nd ed., 5 vols. (1858–61).
Mérignhac	Mérignhac, *Traité de droit public international*, vol. I (1905), vol. II (1907), vol. III (1912).
Möller	Möller, *International Law in Peace and War*, English translation from the Danish, vol. I (1931), vol. II (1935).
Moore	Moore, *A Digest of International Law*, 8 vols. (1906).

Moore, *International Arbitrations*	Moore, *History and Digest of the International Arbitrations to which the United States has been a Party*, 6 vols. (1898).
Nordisk T.A.	*Nordisk Tidskrift for International Ret. Acta scandinavica juris gentium.*
Nys	Nys, *Le droit international*, 2nd ed., 3 vols. (1912).
Off. J.	*Official Journal of the League of Nations.*
Oppenheim, I, II	Oppenheim, *International Law*, vol. I, 8th ed. (1955), by H. Lauterpacht; vol. II, 7th ed. (1952), by H. Lauterpacht.
O.Z.ö.R.	*Österreichische Zeitschrift für öffentliches Recht.*
P.C.I.J.	*Publications of the Permanent Court of International Justice*: Series A: Judgments. B: Advisory Opinions. A/B: Cumulative Collection of Judgments and Advisory Opinions given since 1931. C: Acts and Documents relating to Judgments and Advisory Opinions. D: Collection of Texts governing the Jurisdiction of the Court. E: Annual Reports.
Perels	Perels, *Das internationale öffentliche Seerecht der Gegenwart*, 2nd ed. (1903).
Phillimore	Phillimore, *Commentaries upon International Law*, 3rd ed., 4 vols. (1879–88).
Praag	Praag, *Juridiction et droit international public* (1915).
Praag, *Supplément*	Supplement to the above (1935).
Pradier-Fodéré	Pradier-Fodéré, *Traité de droit international public*, 8 vols. (1885–1906).
Pufendorf	Pufendorf, *De Jure Naturae et Gentium* (1672).
Ralston	Ralston, *The Law and Procedure of International Tribunals*, revised ed. (1926). Supplement (1936).
Ray, *Commentaire*	Ray, *Commentaire du Pacte* (1930).
Recueil T.A.M.	*Recueil des décisions des tribunaux arbitraux mixtes.*
Reddie, *Researches*	Reddie, *Researches, Historical and Critical, in Maritime International Law*, 2 vols. (1844).
Répertoire	Lapradelle et Niboyet, *Répertoire de droit international*. Founded by Darras in 1929.
R.G.	*Revue générale de droit international public.*
R.I.	*Revue de droit international et de législation comparée.*
R.I. (*Geneva*)	*Revue de droit international, de sciences diplomatiques, politiques et sociales.*
R.I. (*Paris*)	*Revue de droit international.*
R.I.F.	*Revue internationale française du droit des gens.*
Rivier	Rivier, *Principes du droit des gens*, 2 vols. (1896).
Rivista	*Rivista di diritto internazionale.*

Rousseau	Rousseau, *Principes généraux du droit international public*, vol. I (1944).
Satow	Satow, *A Guide to Diplomatic Practice*, 3rd ed. by Ritchie (1932).
Scelle	Scelle, *Précis de droit des gens*, vol. I (1932), vol. II (1934).
Schücking und Wehberg	Schücking und Wehberg, *Die Satzung des Völkerbundes*, 2nd ed. (1924).
Schwarzenberger	Schwarzenberger, *International Law as Applied by International Courts and Tribunals*, vol. I (1945).
Scott, *Hague Reports*	Scott, *Hague Court Reports* (1916).
Scott, *Hague Reports* (2nd)	Scott, *Hague Court Reports (Second Series)* (1932).
Sibert	Sibert, *Traité du droit international public*, 2 vols. (1951).
Sirey	*Recueil général des lois et des arrêts* (founded by Sirey).
Smith	Smith, *Great Britain and the Law of Nations, a Selection of Documents*, vol. I (1932), vol. II (1935).
Spiropoulos	Spiropoulos, *Traité théorique et pratique du droit international public* (1933).
Stowell	Stowell, *International Law. A Restatement of Principles in Conformity with Actual Practice* (1931).
Strupp, *Éléments*	Strupp, *Éléments du droit international public, universel, européen et américain*, 2nd ed., 3 vols. (1930).
Strupp, *Wört.*	*Wörterbuch des Völkerrechts und der Diplomatie*, ed. by Strupp (begun by Hatschek), 3 vols. (1924–9).
Suarez	Suarez, *Tratado de Derecho internacional público*, 2 vols. (1916).
Temperley	Temperley, *History of the Peace Conference of Paris*, 6 vols. (1920–4).
Testa	Testa, *Le droit public international maritime*, translation from the Portuguese by Boutiron (1886).
Toynbee, *Survey*	Toynbee, *Survey of International Affairs.*
Travers	Travers, *Le droit pénal international*, 5 vols. (1920–2).
Treaty Series	United Kingdom Treaty Series, vol. I (1892), and a volume every year.
Twiss	Twiss, *The Law of Nations*, etc., 2 vols., 2nd ed., vol. I (Peace, 1884), vol. II (War, 1875).
U.N.R.I.A.A.	United Nations, *Reports of International Arbitral Awards.*
U.N.T.S.	*United Nations Treaty Series.*
Vattel	Vattel, *Le droit des gens*, 4 books in 2 vols., new edition (1773).
Verdross	Verdross, *Die Verfassung der Völkerrechtsgemeinschaft* (1926).
Walker	Walker, *A Manual of Public International Law* (1895).

Walker, *History*	Walker, *A History of the Law of Nations*, vol. 1 (1899).
Walker, *Science*	Walker, *The Science of International Law* (1893).
Westlake	Westlake, *International Law*, 2 vols., 2nd ed. (1910–13).
Westlake, *Chapters*	Westlake, *Chapters on the Principles of International Law* (1894).
Westlake, *Papers*	*The Collected Papers of John Westlake on Public International Law*, ed. by L. Oppenheim (1914).
Wharton	Wharton, *A Digest of the International Law of the United States*, 3 vols. (1886).
Wheaton	Wheaton, *Elements of International Law*, 8th American edition by Dana (1866).
Z.I.	*Zeitschrift für internationales Recht.*
Z.ö.R.	*Zeitschrift für öffentliches Recht.*
Z.ö.V.	*Zeitschrift für ausländisches öffentliches Recht und Völkerrecht.*
Z.V.	*Zeitschrift für Völkerrecht.*

PART II

STATES AS SUBJECTS OF INTERNATIONAL LAW

I

ATTRIBUTES OF STATEHOOD IN INTERNATIONAL LAW

CHAPTER I

SOVEREIGNTY AND FEDERATION IN INTERNATIONAL LAW

Editor's note This chapter was found in a file marked by Lauterpacht 'Unpublished incomplete'. Unpublished it is; but incomplete it is not. Certainly it is unpolished; and the text as printed has not been the subject of more than a few minor grammatical and typewriting corrections. But the perennial value of the piece is immediately striking, especially by its relevance to the debate about sovereignty within the European Economic Community. So it seemed that it would be a waste to omit the item simply because Lauterpacht had not refined its style and content in his usual way.

As will be seen, the chapter was written as a lecture. It bears no date. At one point there is a reference to 1940. This is followed by an indication that it was written after 5 December (probably 1939). The general tone of optimism suggests that it could not have been conceived (at any rate in 1940) after the fall of France. Hence, one may conclude that it was prepared in the early spring of 1940. But of the identity of the prospective audience there is no indication.

I

The purpose of this lecture is, in the first instance, to re-state the meaning and the place of sovereignty in international law by reference to the current discussion on the subject of a federation of democratic States. This will include an attempt to show in what way the controversies as to the nature of the federal system have influenced the fortunes of the conception of sovereignty.

My second object will be to review the principal features of the federal system as distinguished from that of a confederation of States. I shall have to draw your attention to the theoretical and practical consequences of the adoption of the federal system as commonly understood, and I shall have to do it for reasons other than mere pedantry. There has always been in the discussion of international affairs a tendency to employ speech which is unreal and wholly divorced from common usage. This is so not only in the matter of obvious abuse of language, as in cases in which a powerful nation invading a weaker neighbour invokes the sacred right of self-defence. That tendency to artificiality finds expression in the use of technical terms which have acquired a definite meaning. We recall how some international lawyers invoked 'prescription' as a reason for the immediate recognition of

Manchukuo and of the conquest of Abyssinia, as if prescription meant the instantaneous validation of every illegality. To give an example directly related to this lecture: when in 1930 the French Government, in a memorandum circulated to the European Members of the League of Nations, proposed the creation of a system of European federal union, they were emphatic that 'in no case and in no degree may the formation of the federal union desired by the European Governments affect in any way the sovereign rights of the States which are members of such an association'. The union, it was said, was to be realized 'on a basis of absolute sovereignty and entire independence'; the federation, it was stated with lucidity, was to be 'founded on the idea of union, not unity'. The last eight words were a literal reproduction, without due acknowledgment, of Dicey's description of the nature of a federal State, but Dicey used the phrase in a quite different connotation. There is reason to believe that in the near future plans for European federation will be put forward in which little will remain of the idea of federation save the name. Such a misuse of language must be opposed, not because we may be in favour of a true and unadulterated federal State – many of us are decidedly not – but because the use of terms stripped of their usual meaning is confusing and wasteful.

The third object of this lecture is to examine the practical possibilities of some of the main requirements of the federal system and to inquire to what extent they may be regarded as capable of realization within the existing confederation of States, namely, the League of Nations.

2. SOVEREIGNTY IN INTERNATIONAL LAW

What, in the first place, is the present position of sovereignty in relation to international law? It is a tempting, but an alarming and inaccurate, simplification of a difficult problem to maintain that international law and sovereignty are incompatible. For in many ways international law seems to give countenance to a conception of sovereignty analogous to that of legal sovereignty within the State – which is the highest power not derived from any superior authority and is absolutely binding upon the agencies administering the law. In fact, a State, in order to be entitled to recognition as a normal subject of international law, must be sovereign not only in the sense of being independent of any other State. It must also possess a sovereign Government exacting and enjoying habitual obedience on the part of the bulk of the population. It must possess legal sovereignty in the accepted meaning of constitutional law. Neither does international law, as at present constituted, claim any right to interfere substantially with sovereignty thus conceived. Within its borders the State's freedom of action is complete save for restrictions to which it may have consented by treaty and subject to the duty to treat aliens in accordance with what has been termed the minimum standard of civilization. (It may be noted, incidentally, that according to the predominant theory that duty is owed not to aliens in their capacity as human beings whose fundamental rights as such are recognized by international law, but only to the States of which these individuals are subjects. The strange result is that the individual may, in his capacity as an alien and while in the territory of a third State, effectively enjoy rights which cease as soon as he enters the territory of the State of which he is a national.)

In the external sphere the position is essentially the same. Although the subjection of the State to international law is both the indispensable hypothesis and an acknowledged principle of the Law of Nations, that subordination is to a large extent purely formal. It has not prevented a far-reaching recognition of rules and principles, often described as the consequences of sovereignty and suggesting that sovereignty in international law is a legal right transcending that of independence in relation to other States. Present-day international law recognizes that each State is independent not only of other States but also of the totality of States acting as organs of what is termed the international community. By virtue of sovereignty thus understood States are under no duty to agree to anything in the nature of international legislation; in the absence of agreement to the contrary, the rule of unanimity is paramount. International society is thus deprived of the essential instrument of any system of law worthy of that name, namely, of the machinery for adapting the law and re-distributing, if necessary, existing rights in accordance with changed conditions. Moreover, to a considerable extent sovereignty claims – and validly claims – freedom of action in relation to existing law. In international law the rule obtains that States are under no duty to submit disputes with other States to obligatory judicial settlement. Every State is, by law, judge in its own cause; it is entitled, in relation to other States, to insist upon its own views of the law. Finally, apart from the ill-fated Kellogg–Briand Pact, every State has a right, seemingly conceded by international law, to seek the annihilation and to destroy the independence of any other State by declaring and waging a successful war. These aspects of sovereignty would seem to indicate that while, in principle, States are subject to international law and therefore are not sovereign, that subjection is accompanied by a practically unlimited recognition of the internal sovereignty of the State and by a measure of freedom of action outside its borders which tends to bring international law to the vanishing point of jurisprudence.

This, of course, is only one side of the picture. It is a clear legal rule recognized by States that in relation to international law they are not sovereign – if by sovereignty is meant the absolute legal supremacy of the will of the State. In so far as they admit the existence and binding force of international law, States acknowledge that they are not sovereign; further, in so far as they can be imagined as rational beings capable of orderly thought, they cannot fail to realize that it is only because of their subjection to international law that their mutual independence and equality can be assured of existence either in juridical logic or, in the long run, in actual fact. Thus viewed, both the internal and external sovereignty of the State is a quality, a competence, conferred by international law.

This is not a theory sadly out of touch with realities, but a legal rule admitted by States through the fact of their recognition of international law and by their submission to its rules flowing from sources independent of their express will. Thus, from the point of view of international law, sovereignty is a delegated bundle of rights. It is a power which is derived from a higher source and therefore divisible, modifiable and elastic. This is so although international law has suffered for a long time from the theory of the indivisibility of sovereignty, with the result that writers were unable, without the assistance of artificial explanations, to comprehend the numerous phenomena in the practice of governments like State servitudes, *condominia*, mandates, and other instances of joint international administration of territory. (The Permanent Court of International Justice has laid down in clear terms that that formidable conception of 'matters of domestic jurisdiction', which some have identified with sovereignty, is a variable notion determined by the progress of international law.)

The conclusions of this cursory survey cannot be summarized in one terse sentence. They seem inconsistent with one another. In fact, they are more mutually exclusive than the perplexing features of the political reality of international relations. That reality shows a picture of the modern world as one of common solidarity and community of interests in the field of economic endeavour and of scientific pursuit of humanitarian assistance – a unity transcending the borders of the sovereign State in a manner which has led many to believe that the exclusive and self-sufficing sovereign State is a challenge to a higher and ever present reality, and that interdependence and not independence is the primary and fundamental fact with which we are inescapably confronted.

But who will deny that the sovereign State exists and that it asserts itself in a decisive manner in law and in fact over the transcending unity of the world and of mankind? That contradiction explains what may appear to be a dialectical and unhelpful summary of the position of sovereignty in relation to international law: firstly, that it is only by dint of a gross inaccuracy of language that we give the same designation of sovereignty to the supreme authority of the State as determined by its constitutional law and to its legal position in international law; secondly, that the rights of sovereignty which international law fully recognizes are nevertheless so extensive in both the internal and the external sphere as to reduce, to a large extent, the regulative and restraining power of international law to a mere formality and as to render its place in jurisprudence purely nominal; thirdly, that, this notwithstanding, the competence of the sovereign State is, by virtue of recognized legal principle, derived from and determined by international law; and that, fourthly, that competence must be thought of as subject to progressive limitation and curtailment.

3. THE THEORY OF FEDERATION AND THE NOTION OF SOVEREIGNTY

We may now, for a while, turn to the further question of the influence which the federal principle has had on the fortunes of the notion of sovereignty. The legal historian cannot fail to be impressed by the fact that one of the principal causes of the modern onslaught upon the notion of sovereignty has been its obstructive influence in the international field. Even when the attack was conducted with weapons taken exclusively from the armoury of national jurisprudence, the hidden springs of its energy were to be found in the resentment against the repercussions of sovereignty in the external relations of States. But it is of special interest for the purposes of this lecture to note that the phenomenon of federation has done almost as much to displace sovereignty from the high seat of exclusive and indivisible authority. It is not only that the federal State was called in to show that a single and undivided sovereign will of Austinian jurisprudence is not essential to the State – where, it was asked, is the sovereign according to the constitution of the United States? The way in which legal writers, largely moved by political motives, juggled with the conceptions of sovereignty in order to find a solution pleasing to themselves has done as much to pave the way for a critical approach to the problem of the sovereign State. The authors of the *Federalist*, anxious to smooth the path of the transition from a confederation to a federal State, developed the theory of the division of sovereignty between the union and the member States. De Tocqueville planted the doctrine in European soil and Waitz adapted it for German consumption with the added embellishment of the distinction between the substance of sovereignty (which, he taught, was indivisible) and the scope of sovereignty (which could be portioned out). This was a moderate theory when contrasted with that of Calhoun (followed in Germany by Seydel), who insisted on the indivisibility of sovereignty, but asserted that the latter was fully retained by the member States and not at all impaired by the delegation of some of its functions to the federal State. The other extreme was represented by those believers in national unity who regarded sovereignty both as indivisible and as essential to the State, with the result that in their view the members of the union could not properly be regarded as States. The pill was in turn sweetened by writers like Laband and Carré de Malberg, who served the causes both of the unity of the exclusively sovereign federation and of the individuality of the members by showing that sovereignty is not at all essential to statehood. They were joined by the high authority of Jellinek, who, while buttressing national unity by insisting on the complete subordination of the member States to the federation and on the absence of any right of secession, flattered the vanity of the members of the federation by arguing that they took part in the life of the union in their capacity as States and that they were not without a status in international law. On the other hand, Duguit, while insisting that the members of the federation are States as distinguished from decentralized provinces, pointed out that that statehood cannot be comprehended with the help of the traditional notion of sovereignty – in which fact he found yet another argument in support of his criticism of the accepted meaning of the sovereign State. But we may be well advised to stop here – not, however, without noting the indirect results of these controversies on the authority of the conception of sovereignty and as an incidental reminder that, in the matter of unions of States, pure theory and rigid classification are not necessarily a reliable guide.

4. THE FEDERAL STATE AND THE CONFEDERATION OF STATES

This reminder is bound to prove useful in relation to the postulated differences between the federal State (the *Bundesstaat*) and the confederation of States (the *Staatenbund*). In the recent discussions concerning the federation of Europe much has been made of a fundamental distinction between a mere confederation of States (a mere 'League', as it is called, for instance, in Mr Streit's book) and a true federal State. That distinction seems to express itself mainly in two directions. In the first instance, it is maintained that in a federal State there is a direct link between the federation and the individual. The federal State exercises in many, although certainly not in all, matters, direct legislative authority over the individual; it has direct powers of taxation; its own courts exercise direct jurisdiction over the citizen; and, last but not least, the individual has a direct share in the creation of the organs of the union. In contrast with the position in a confederation of States, within a federation it is not only the member State but also the individual human being who is a unit of federal law and government. The second difference between a federal State and a confederation of States is due to the fact that, in the first, the component States cease to exist internationally; there is only one international unit, namely, the federal State. In a confederation of States the member States preserve their full international personality, with the concomitant right of conducting a foreign policy of their own. Another distinction, which has established itself in the Continental legal literature, between the two forms of union is based on the view that a confederation rests on a treaty while a federal State owes its existence to a municipal constitutional law. The distinction has been adopted in order to save the federal State from the vicissitudes of international treaties and so to remove any possible legal basis for the right of secession.

It is now being urged that the advance in international organization must be on the lines of a federal State as distinguished from confederations – all of which, beginning with the American confederation and ending with the League of Nations – have, it is said, proved unworkable and have given way to the closer unity of the federal bond.

These two typical features of the two forms of association – the exclusive international personality of the federal State and its direct authority over the citizen – constitute a working test of the distinction between the federal State and a confederation. At the same time, however, closer study shows that the typical characteristics of a federal State may on occasions be found in a confederation; and the converse case is not exceptional. The American confederation did away with the international personality of the State as if it were a federal State; in some matters it exercised direct legislative authority over individuals. The States of the German confederation between 1815 and 1866 were full international persons, although at the same time the confederation was a full subject of international law. On the other hand, the German Federal State of 1871 admitted, and Switzerland, Argentina, Brazil, Venezuela and other federal States still admit, a measure of international status for the member States in the domain of the treaty-making power. And it is significant that the German *Staatsgerichtshof*, prior to the advent of the Third Reich, decided disputes between member States on the basis of international law. This is also a conspicuous feature of the practice of the Supreme Court of the United States and of the Swiss Federal Court. Comparative study and legal analysis both lead to the conclusion that there is no difference in kind between these types of union, and that the only difference is that of the distribution of powers between the federation (or confederation) and the member States.

5. THE SUPPRESSION OF THE INTERNATIONAL PERSONALITY OF MEMBER STATES

This being so, it is advisable to approach the question of any future developments in international organization not in the dogmatic spirit of preconceived choice between two fundamentally opposed forms of organization, but as a matter of weighing the merits of each of them in relation to the fact that the sovereign State as a separate international entity embodies a historic and cultural reality as enduring as the human eye can foresee. It is an attractive but deceptive short-cut of reasoning to assume that the danger to which progress and the very continuance of civilization are exposed as the result of the existing legal position of the sovereign State in the international sphere can or might be removed by the extinction, as distinguished from the limitation, of the sovereign international personality of States. Our task must be – and here the comparative study of institutions will offer substantial assistance – to select from the various forms of State associations those elements of integration which are most suitable to that reality and to reject schemes which because of their crudeness may block the avenue of progress.

Let us consider, for instance, the first of the two principal features of a federal State, namely, the obliteration of the international personality of the member States. It is impracticable to urge a form of European association in which Great Britain, France and Germany, or, for that matter, Holland, Sweden and Switzerland, will disappear as international units; in which they will be deprived of the right to send and receive diplomatic and consular representatives; in which, as in the case of member States of federal States, they will lose the jurisdictional immunities enjoyed by States in foreign courts; in which they will not be permitted to conclude treaties either among themselves or with other States. It is impracticable to urge a form of association in which, internationally, the status of France or Great Britain will be lower than that of Liberia, Ecuador or Panama. In connection with the recent Pan-American Declaration claiming a 300-mile safety zone round the American coasts, the acting President of Panama addressed a telegram of protest to His Britannic Majesty. If a European union were to follow the usual lines of a federal State, Great Britain or any other member of the federation would in relation to Panama cease to be a State with which correspondence could be conducted on a footing of equality. In this respect any future federation of States will have to be much looser than the loose American Articles of Confederation of 1777 which laid down that 'no State without the consent of the United States in Congress assembled, shall send an embassy to, or receive any from, or enter into any conference, agreement, alliance or treaty with any king, prince or state'.

It is unhelpful and irrelevant to point to the existing federal States as showing that separate international personality of member States is not essential and that its absence is borne with equanimity and without a sense of loss of a valuable attribute of statehood or of national dignity. For these member States were not international persons prior to their having been linked by the federal bond. It may be useful to recall in this connection the requisite factual conditions as formulated by Dicey.

There must exist, in the first place, a body of countries such as the cantons of Switzerland, the colonies of America, or the provinces of Canada, so closely connected by locality, by history, by race, or the like, as to be capable of bearing in the eyes of their inhabitants an impress of common nationality. It will also be generally found (if we appeal to experience) that lands which now form part of a federal State were at some stage of their existence bound together by close alliance or by subjection to a common sovereign.

Moreover, the international personality of States with its concomitant rights of sovereignty is not merely a heritage of the past whose main reason for existence lies in its powerful emotional appeal. It is an expression of actual diversity of interest, economic and other, and of disparities in wealth, culture, and standards of life between States. International personality is the legal instrument for the maintenance of that cultural and political separateness of nations which has become one of the central facts of modern civilization. In so far as international sovereignty of States has proved incompatible with other essential postulates of that civilization – and it has become so incompatible to a very considerable extent – it is rational and imperative to urge its further drastic limitation. But the facile dichotomy expressed in such a phrase as 'unless the State destroys sovereignty, sovereignty will destroy the State', does not do justice to the realities and the complexities of the case. The abolition of the international personality and of the concomitant rights of sovereignty of States is impracticable not only for the fully adequate reason that, within the foreseeable future, it is not likely to prove acceptable to the overwhelming majority of persons within the States in question. This is probably the reason why in some recent projects of federal union this aspect of the question is touched on very little, while in others the international personality of the member States is allowed to continue; and while, in others still, the concentration of foreign policy in the federation is combined with the continued freedom of action of the member States in such matters as economic policy and migration. This application of the terminology of the federal system to structures devoid of the essential characteristics of a federation must be regretted.

6. THE LEAGUE OF NATIONS

If we bear in mind that the suppression of the international personality of States and of the entirety of their sovereign rights in the international sphere is neither practicable nor desirable; that for this, if for no other reason, the proposals for a federal system as commonly understood are not acceptable; that the international rights of sovereignty are capable of progressive curtailment; and that the principle of a confederation of States, as distinguished from a federal State, is based on the continued recognition of the international personality of its members – then our eyes must inevitably turn to the existing confederation of States which constitutes the greatest single advance ever made in the way of the political organization of mankind, namely, the League of Nations.

The League is, in this connection, instructive from three points of view. It is, in the first instance, a league of sovereign States. Secondly, the Covenant of the League is an example of an unparalleled and truly revolutionary limitation of the sovereignty of its members. For no other designation can properly be given to the admission of the collective right of intervention on the part of the League in disputes with other States, to the most drastic limitation of the right of war, and to the recognition of the principle of penal sanctions against sovereign States. Thirdly, the Covenant both as adopted and as interpreted in practice shows that these limitations did not go far enough and that this reason, apart from others which may well have proved superior to any purely legal obligation, however rigid and far-reaching, may prove to be one of the principal causes of the temporary collapse of the collective system set up in the Covenant.

In establishing the League, Governments in their wisdom and their caution fell short of their own professions made during the World War and of the expectations of large sections of their peoples. As an instrument for the legal organization of peace the League was defective from the very beginning. Those who framed the Covenant were deliberately obscure in their prohibition of war, and by limiting it to 'resort to war' left the door wide open for abuse and confusion. While introducing the principle of collective enforcement of peace, they limited obligations thereunder to economic action and refrained from providing that the League as a whole should both determine the case of aggression and direct authoritatively the course of collective action aiming at the suppression of aggression. They declined to sanction the principle of obligatory judicial settlement even with regard to disputes which they described as generally suitable for such settlement. They carefully preserved their full freedom of action with regard to any procedure calculated to change the legal *status quo* by common action of the League. Sovereignty, formally enshrined in the rigid principle of unanimity, was made to permeate even the machinery of pacific settlement. The result of that combination of far-reaching restrictions with the maintenance of sovereignty was a flexible instrument of great elasticity – an instrument which, because of its elasticity, has often been described by adherents of the League as the best instrument that could be devised for the purpose for which it was intended. This would have been so if the circumstances had been favourable. But they were not. In consequence, the elasticity of the Covenant has worked one way only. Its potential strength has been allowed to remain in the background; but Governments have often appealed to those of its provisions which left them complete freedom of action and which reduced the Covenant to a mere declaration of principles.

If international sovereignty is regarded as a rigid notion with an indivisible content, then we are tempted to regard ourselves as being under the necessity of making a choice between two abstract and exclusive types of union, i.e. between a federal State in which residuary sovereignty is with the federation and a confederation in which the unimpaired sovereignty rests with the member States. If we pin our action to passionate disapproval of the very form of the sovereign international personality of the State as the *fons et origo mali*, we shall again be confronted with the same rigid alternative. But if we bear in mind the fact that sovereignty in the international sphere is as much, and no more, as international law (as expressed in custom and treaty) determines at any given period, and if we think both of the progress achieved and of the shortcomings revealed by the League of Nations, the most important and significant confederation of States that ever existed, then we are justified in inquiring once more whether there is anything in the present structure of that confederation which prevents the advance which experience has shown to be both necessary and feasible. With the clear affirmation of the principle of obligatory judicial settlement (a principle foreshadowed in Article 12 of the Covenant in terms so emphatic that the authoritative Committee of Jurists who framed the Statute of the Permanent Court of International Justice was of the view that the principle of obligatory judicial settlement had been actually incorporated in the Covenant); with an extension of the scope of Article 19 relating to the revision of existing rights under conventional and customary international law – a problem which many regard as the Cape Horn of inter-State relations – in the direction of the elimination of the power of obstruction on the part of the State (or States) interested in the perpetuation of the *status quo*; with the provision of a procedure more effective than at present for implementing by common action the obligations of Article 16 in the matter of sanctions; with the elimination of the unanimity rule in Article 11 of the Covenant on the lines proposed in the discussions in recent years on the amendment of the Covenant; with the assumption of an obligation to accept as binding the recommendations made by the Council or Assembly in pursuance of Article 15 – such innovations, if widely accepted, would go a long way towards realizing most of the conditions of a progressive political integration of humanity.

These are schemes for changes not devised in the abstract; they have been repeatedly discussed against the background of events and problems that have arisen. To a large extent they have been approved in principle by Governments. They are rooted in existing law and procedures. If adopted, they would go a very long way towards removing the shortcomings of a confederation while retaining its necessary form. Amendments of the Covenant such as those suggested above admittedly imply a further drastic relinquishment of the rights of external sovereignty of the members of the League. Far from being a mere patchwork within the frame of an inherently ineffectual system, they go much further in the direction of subordinating State sovereignty to the requirements of international order than many proposals recently made for the establishment of an international federal system. In some of these proposals, shorn of the essential features of the federal principle, little, apart from the name, remains of the essential principles of federation; others, starting as they do from rigid and exclusive alternatives, must be content with the assumption that the federation will, at least in its initial stages, be limited to a small group of States indistinguishable from a continuation of the war alliance. At the same time, they lack that source of inspiration which is implied in the spiritual conception of the League of Nations as the incipient and potentially universal *civitas maxima*.

It would betray an unwarranted optimism to assume that the suggestions here made for a strengthening of the collective system through a further surrender of sovereignty within the League of Nations have a fair prospect of acceptance. It is probably true to say that in many respects the ground for such changes is less favourable in 1940 than in the concluding stages of the World War, and this for the following reason : the prolonged crisis which preceded the present war consisted not only in the violation of major political treaties imposed by force or voluntarily accepted. It found expression not only in the successful acts of aggression against the very life of independent nations. It manifested itself in the disregard, on a large scale, of many of the accepted rules of international law and comity. This state of affairs was, of necessity, temporary, and those loud questioners who inquire whether there is any international law left may be correctly answered that the fact and the magnitude and the acknowledged meaning of this present struggle are a proper measure of the essential reality of the Law of Nations. At the same time, the successful assertions of force have undermined not only the authority of law, but also the effects of that criticism of sovereignty, both internal and external, which we have learned to regard as a permanent gain of the science of law and of politics in our generation. Some States, in their triumphant departure from established canons of conduct, have proved to be so powerful, and such great power is in turn required to compel them to revert to the channels of legality, that sovereignty, the embodiment of the organized might of the State, has once more come into its own – with a vengeance. This may perhaps be one of the reasons why the authorized spokesman of the British Government, while refusing to define in detail the aims of the war, has not hesitated to put it beyond doubt that at least one thing is clear, namely, that there must be no further abandonment of sovereignty. Lord Halifax was reported to have said on 5 December : 'It was already being said that a new order in Europe could only come through surrender in some measure by nations of their sovereign rights in order to clear the way for some more organic unit. He did not know that he would go quite so far.' There is no compelling ground for assuming that there is any unalterable determination to make these views prevail in the settlement following the liquidation of the war, but the fact is that not only have they been given authoritative expression but also that they are widely shared.

The temporary success of power politics and of defiance of international morality has lent a touch of plausibility to recent attempts to revitalize the doctrine of Frederick the Great, Hegel and Treitschke under the guise of a realist science of international politics in which power, precariously modified by an admixture of a specifically conceived morality of States, is once more acclaimed as being the primary and central factor of international relations. Voices are once more being heard deprecating any suggestion that State sovereignty as such has been the cause of international trouble and maintaining that it is only in the abuse of sovereignty that the root of the evil lies. The fact is that international sovereignty, as fully recognized by existing international law, is, and has in many respects proved to be, inconsistent with the idea of order of which Governments and States are trustees. To say, therefore, that the security of international peace is in inverse ratio to limitations of State sovereignty and to the assumption of binding obligations is to give expression to an inaccurate and frivolous platitude. The same applies to the attempt to support it by reference to the extra-legal but highly effective ties between Great Britain and (by no means all) the Dominions. For such ties do not exist between other States; neither do there exist between Great Britain and the effectively loyal Dominions the potential causes of friction which threaten the peace in the relations of other States. But the fact remains that views of this nature are now being put forward and that they command attention which would have been impatiently denied to them in 1918.

7. THE PRINCIPLE OF IMMEDIATE FEDERAL RULE AND THE LEAGUE OF NATIONS

If, as is submitted here, any scheme of federal association which, in accordance with the theory of the federal State, involves the abandonment of the separate international personality of the member States, is open to objection both in principle and from the point of view of the prospects of its realization, the further question arises whether the other essential feature of the federal principle, with its many beneficial consequences – namely, the principle of direct federal rule over the individual – can be achieved in any other practicable way.

The direct legal relation between the individual and the supranational or international authority manifests itself not only through the fact of federal legislation on a variety of subjects. It finds expression in the direct participation of the individual in the creation of the central legislative organs; in the guarantee by the federal constitution of certain fundamental individual rights as expressed, for instance, in the Constitution of the United States which prohibits States from curtailing the privileges of any citizen of the United States, or from denying to him the right of voting on account of race or colour, or from depriving any person of life, liberty or property without due process of law, or from refusing to any person the equal protection of the laws; in the principle of direct taxation of individuals for the purposes of the federation; and in the existence of federal tribunals accessible to States and individuals alike.

The scope of this lecture does not permit a detailed elaboration of the reasons why these and other aspects of direct relation between the individual and a legal political association wider than the State must be described as beneficent. They help us to realize the principle – which is probably the basic principle of all true jurisprudence – that the individual is the ultimate unit of law and that an international legal order which protects the fundamental rights of the individual from the encroachments of the omnipotent State is therefore a desirable and, indeed, indispensable end of the legal and political development of humanity. In the discussions preceding the establishment of the League that view found expression in the assertion that one of the chief purposes of the League was to make the world safe for democracy. In legal terminology, and on a proper interpretation of the concept of democracy, that would have meant a world in which the fundamental rights of the individual under the rule of law are protected by the organized international society. For this reason the cry about making the world safe for democracy was not a desperate device of war propaganda.

When in 1795 Kant formulated the articles of a federation of peoples for the mutual guarantee of independence and the preservation of peace, he regarded it as essential that the member States should possess a democratic constitution. The League was conceived as a League of democratic States not only because it was thought that democracies are essentially peaceful while dictatorships, for a variety of reasons, tend to regard war, be it by arms or by revolutionary propaganda, not only as a means of achieving political ends but also as part and parcel of the national conception of life. Neither was it postulated as democratic merely for the good reason that ideological affinity, i.e. a community of views on things essential in man's social and political life, was and is not unnaturally regarded as the indispensable condition of a system in which one nation may have to sacrifice what is best and most precious in defence of another. We may have to ally ourselves temporarily with a State whose conceptions of social justice and morality we abhor and whose actions within its borders call forth our indignation and our passionate protest. But to be wedded to it permanently, for good or for evil, for the defence of its inferior statehood is to embark on an artificial and, in the long run, intolerable relationship. For this reason it is true to say that much of the spirit of the League departed from it when it retained the membership of the totalitarian States of Italy and Germany and when it acquiesced in the adhesion of Soviet Russia and, probably, of some States like Abyssinia. In the eyes of many, the League could put up with the membership of these States – but only as a rump of its spiritual self.

The principal reason why the League was contemplated as democratic was that neither peace nor international law, whose firm establishment was described as one of the principal objects of the League, can become a reality until we have recognized the individual human being as the ultimate beneficiary of the law and the ultimate unit of human progress, to be protected by international action, if necessary, from the power of the State. The provisions as to mandates, as to minorities, and as to the protection of labour, and the vast scope of humanitarian action envisaged by the League, bore witness to the view that the general good of the international community cannot be achieved except by the effective acknowledgment of the sanctity of human personality as the final unit of all society. This is the principal explanation why a reformed and strengthened League must necessarily be thought of as assimilating in a more substantial measure than hitherto those tenets of direct federal rule which are intended to secure the freedom and the dignity of human personality.

The direct participation of the individual in the creation of the central deliberative and legislative organs of the association of States is a factor which works in the same direction. In the sphere of peaceful settlement of international disputes such direct participation has the merit of removing disputes from the plane of a contest in which States confront one another in rigid, formal or exclusive solidarity; it introduces neutral and pacifying elements of cross-currents and cross-divisions.

While the suppression of the international personality of the State is in the nature of a revolutionary change, of a surgical operation, the transition in these and other spheres to the directness of the federal principle is a matter of degree. As such it may be capable of accomplishment within the already existing confederation of States, namely, within the League of Nations. Let me mention some examples: the International Labour Organization supplies a valuable instance of the transition from purely governmental representation to that based either on direct voting of individual persons or on nomination by professional or similar bodies. There may be no insuperable or really serious difficulty in the way of adopting a similar and more advanced method with regard to the composition of the Assembly of the League. A modest beginning has already been made by those Members of the League who have followed the practice of sending delegations to the Assembly composed of representatives of the principal parties. With regard to the protection and guarantee of fundamental rights of the individual, an adequate starting point may be found in the generalization of the existing law bearing upon the matter of protection of minorities and its extension to a wider category of individual rights than those covered by the minorities treaties. A further step in the way of establishing a direct link between the League and the individual would be, while leaving the determination of the budget with the Assembly, to tax the nationals of the Member State individually or on the basis of professional groupings. Both the fact of direct taxation and its very insignificant amount would be of considerable value in fostering international loyalty. Finally, the Permanent Court of International Justice, in addition to its normal function, could be given jurisdiction on final appeal in matters involving private rights and arising out of customary international law and treaties, including the obligations of an amended Covenant relating to the respect of the fundamental rights of the individual.

8. THE LEAGUE OF NATIONS AND THE FEDERAL PRINCIPLE

What has been said here is based on the view that the particular form of State association is not critical, and that what is regarded as a distinctive and exclusive feature of a federal State may be achieved in a typical confederation of States. Conversely, what is deemed to be an essential characteristic of a confederation of States, namely, the retention by its members of their full sovereign rights, may, without radical interference with the structure of the confederation, become the subject matter of gradual but far-reaching modifications.

Theoretically, a fully-fledged federal system is more conducive to enhancing the stability of international peace and to reducing the evils and abuses of sovereignty than a looser system of confederation based on the full sovereignty of States. This must be conceded without admitting all the advantages claimed to be linked with the federal system. Thus, for instance, it is perhaps not untimely to utter a warning against regarding a federal constitution as rendering unnecessary or juridically impossible collective enforcement of the federal law as against States. Let us think of the Confederate States during the Civil War and of the collective suffering to which they were brutally exposed for a generation – not to mention the mild Swiss practice of coercing a disobedient canton by quartering in it federal troops at its expense, a sanction which has been described as particularly offensive to the Swiss sense of frugality. The Continental theory of the *Bundesexecution* by no means accepts that enforcement of the law against the rebellious member State is contrary to the idea of the federal system. In the United States the definite abandonment after the Civil War of the doctrine of collective enforcement of the federal law against States as such has been possible only with the assistance of a daring piece of constitutional dialectic, namely, the proposition that an act of a State legislature, or of a State executive, in violation of the constitution or of the acts of the national executive in pursuance of the constitution is an act not of the State Government (which cannot, in law, act against the constitution) but of persons illegally and falsely assuming to act as such Government; and that such persons, but not the State, can and must be coerced individually or as a group.

Neither must we in argumentative excitement commit ourselves to the superficial view that sanctions against collective units are immoral and that men ought to be able to escape the consequences of their criminal conduct in so far as they act as a State. Similarly, it is undesirable to expose the cause of moderation to easy rebuff by arguing that the federal bond is in itself an instrument of civil liberty. It has not promoted democratic freedom in Soviet Russia or in some of the Latin-American Republics. Nor did it in Imperial Germany. Its absence has had no injurious effects on the growth of liberty in European democracies, including bi-national Belgium. Sweden and Norway, after having been linked for a time in a real union, decided after a time to realize in separation their ideals of freedom.

Still, there is, as suggested above, little doubt that if a federal system linking all or some States were feasible and not, in practice, inconsistent with the historical and cultural reality of existing independent States, such a consummation would constitute a better guarantee of peace than a mere confederation in the form of the League of Nations or otherwise. However, these alternatives are not offered for our free and leisured choice. We may not be at liberty to argue that we can afford to wait until public opinion has been educated so as to insist with sustained vigour and consistency on the adoption of the ideal solution.

But these and similar matters cannot be debated in this lecture. Thus, it is beyond the province of this lecture to express an opinion as to the wisdom of a combined effort aiming at securing the co-existence of a reformed and strengthened League and a true federal State as between a limited number of European States (except to the extent of observing that the establishment of a true federal State would imply a different League from that which exists at present; for, in that case, the federation only, and not its units, would be a Member of the League). In particular, it cannot be our task to discuss the question whether from the point of view of economy of effort the attempt to achieve radical progress in two directions may not result in a stultification of both at a time which may be ripe for a far-reaching advance and in which duty bids us to translate into terms of improved law and institutions yet another poignant lesson of history. Nor am I called upon to elaborate the point that the League of Nations as set up in 1919, and even as it has been shaped in the two decades subsequent to its establishment, is more than a valuable experiment in the long process of trial and error in the scheme of international organization: that it has acquired a significant place in the political organization of mankind, and that it may be our duty not to judge it by reference to a brief span of adversity, in circumstances which, in reason and by necessary hypothesis, must be regarded as exceptional. Finally, it is not within our province to offer advice and to suggest that such limited objects of unchallenged importance like economic unity may have a prospect of realization if proceeded with independently rather than as part of schemes aiming at a revolutionary change in the structure of international relations. Thus a treaty whose permanence is fortified by international and constitutional safeguards and which institutes a customs union supplemented by the provision of freedom of migration and organic co-operation in the matter of postal and other communications would achieve most, if not all, economic objects of the federal system.

But if the attitude which underlies this lecture may be put in the form of a practical suggestion, then there appears to be a case for concentrating legal study, alongside of any efforts in other spheres, on an assembly of the League specially convened, after the cessation of the present war, for the sole purpose of adopting reforms of the widest scope, as outlined above, as the principal tangible outcome of the war; an assembly setting a time-limit for the ratification of the changes thus adopted, and thus providing, in conformity with the Covenant, for the speedy cessation of the membership of States abstaining from ratification. Will members of the League acquiesce in a departure so drastic? It would be improper to use this lecture as an occasion for answering this question except to the extent of suggesting that they are more likely to agree to them than to an out and out federation. However, such an assembly could only be a product of a sustained and undivided determination of those imbued with the resolve that good should come out of evil at yet another turning point of history. Such a determination is in turn conditioned by the realization that the experience of the years 1930–40, governed and overshadowed as they have been by the abnormal and transient phenomenon of dictatorships, is not sufficiently persuasive to make us abandon or even doubt the saving virtue of ideals which, embodied in the Covenant, most of us not very long ago regarded as self-evident. It is neither possible nor permissible to think scientifically or constructively of a permanent rational ordering of international society while taking into account forces which by profession, by their nature and by experience have shown themselves to be the very denial of such an ordering.

9. CONCLUSIONS

The general impression created by this lecture will probably be that it is not a plea in favour of the establishment of a European or similar federal system. This would be an accurate impression. But if I may devote the remaining few minutes to straying outside my province I should like to use them for dispelling any lingering feeling that proposals for a federal system embracing a plurality of States are not entitled both to respect and to the closest examination compatible with unrelenting pre-occupation with the urgent tasks of the forthcoming period of reconstruction.

These and similar projects must be regarded as a welcome manifestation of the revolt of the human spirit against the offensive absurdity of civilized communities living in a pure state of nature in their mutual relations. They must be regarded as a constructive protest against the view, insulting to the dignity of man, that the relations of States must for ever remain in a condition of a precarious balance of power, ruthlessness and cunning, and that war – the inevitable upshot of that condition – must for all time be suffered as an enduring factor of human existence and as a decree of blind fate impervious to human will and responsibility. Similar schemes have been put forward in the past, but that is not an argument against them; neither do we do ourselves justice by merely classifying them as utopian. They have been realist schemes in terms of the moral duty of man to challenge the futility of suffering by an active faith in progress.

It is unhistoric to interpret history as teaching that war and power must for ever remain paramount in the relations of States for the reason that they have always been so. Equally, it may be deceptive to succumb to the facile wisdom of the warning that we ought not to create institutions unless they are deeply rooted in the spirit of peoples. For that spirit is the result of the protective and civilizing influence of laws and institutions which intelligent courage and foresight have brought into being 'in advance of public opinion'. The lesson of history is that the idea of the *civitas maxima* of the federation of the world – of which a partial federation may be a necessary stage – is, in the terminology of Emmanuel Kant, the only means of attaining perfect internal government, which in turn is the condition of progress, namely, the realization of the moral and intellectual capacities of mankind. As such it must be regarded as the abiding political idea of humanity.

However, the federation of Kant was not a federal State; it was a confederation, presupposing the continued existence of sovereign States. Whatever may be the future form of the political organization of mankind, its advent will not be promoted by copying existing models of inter-State federations. For these have not been associations of States with a different history, language, culture, traditions and law. The ultimate rational solution of the problem of international organization will be hastened – and this may be submitted as a summary of the conclusions of this lecture – by the acceptance of the view that the differences between the typical forms of unions of States are to a large extent a matter of degree; that none can expect any substantial measure of success in so far as it postulates the disappearance of the international personality of existing sovereign States; that, subject to that condition, there is no practical limit – certainly not in international law – to the abandonment of rights of sovereignty within a State association based on the continued recognition of distinct international personality of sovereign States; and that there is no contradiction between the notion of sovereignty in international law and the gradual approximation of the federation of the world, which must be looked at not as an infinite ideal but as a rational standard of both political action and academic study.

II

PARTICULAR TYPES OF STATEHOOD

CHAPTER 2

THE MANDATE UNDER INTERNATIONAL LAW IN THE COVENANT OF THE LEAGUE OF NATIONS

Editor's note This chapter consists of the dissertation which Lauterpacht submitted to the University of Vienna for the degree of Doctor of Political Science (he was already a 'Dr Jur.'). The dissertation was written in German under the title 'Das völkerrechtliche Mandat in der Satzung des Völkerbundes', with a sub-title 'Zugleich ein Beitrag zur Frage der Anwendung von privatrechtlichen Begriffen in Völkerrechte' ('Being also a contribution to the question of the application of private law concepts in international law'). It bears the date 15 June 1922. It seems to have grown out of some work which Lauterpacht did on mandates during the previous year. Amongst the papers which he brought to England with him in 1923 and subsequently retained is a notebook containing thirty-seven foolscap pages handwritten by him headed 'Das völkerrechtliche Mandat in der Völkerbündsatzüng – Seminararbeit' and dated Vienna, 12 July 1921. This essay, written for a seminar, is not being printed in these *Collected Papers*.

Although it was known that Lauterpacht had submitted a dissertation to Vienna, the text could not be found in the archives of the University there; and there is some ground for the belief that the University's copy was deliberately destroyed during the period of the Nazi occupation. Only by chance was a roughly bound carbon of the original foolscap typescript, together with a volume of appendices containing the texts of relevant documents, found amongst some obscure volumes in Lauterpacht's study in Cambridge.

Notwithstanding the skilful translation from the German made by Miss Maureen MacGlashan, the text does not (and in the nature of things cannot) have the same polish as later works written in English by Lauterpacht and fully prepared by him for publication. Nevertheless, this item is included here principally because it is Lauterpacht's earliest extended work. It shows him as already opening up a subject, the use of private law analogies in international law, which he was to develop later in his first book, *Private Law Sources and Analogies of International Law*. It demonstrates too his early acquaintance with a wide range of European jurisprudential writing, even though the relevant pages in this chapter do not convey the same clear picture of this complex material as do comparable pages in *Private Law Sources* or *The Function of Law in the International Community*. Finally, a number of the substantive observations made in the chapter and written within three years of the inception of the Mandates system show a striking perception of how the system would develop over the next forty years.

PREFACE

The literature on the Mandate under international law in the Covenant of the League of Nations (or – as it tends now to be called – the system of Colonial Mandates) is understandably not yet old. However, the great political and academic interest caused by this new institution of international law has made this literature a voluminous one. But it would be wrong to assume that the abundance of academic treatment has contributed to an unequivocal clarification of the question. On the contrary, the completely disparate results of the legal analyses of Article 22 of the Covenant of the League of Nations are a significant reminder of the traditional weaknesses of research in international law. Whereas German thinking on the Mandates system, based on close analogy with private law, comes to a positive view of this new institution, and part of the English and American literature based on specifically English concepts of law constructs a self-contained theory, the Franco-Belgian literature, with its 'social-dynamic' and 'historic-political' outlook tends towards a complete negation of Article 22 as a new legal concept in international law, thereby giving (it might be said deliberately) scholarly sanction to the widespread view that 'mandate' is but a euphemism for the victors' imperialist annexation policy.

It should be stressed at this point that none of the theories mentioned leaves the solid ground of law as enacted in the League of Nations Covenant and the Peace Treaties. Each is supposed to have followed a strict legal procedure. In dealing with this subject one is therefore left with no choice (if one does not want to confine oneself to a mere digest of others' opinions) but to raise, and strive to answer, the fundamental theoretical questions which are involved. The most important of these questions is the old problem, a live issue since the time of Hugo Grotius, of the application and validity of private law concepts in international law. The derivatory concepts of Article 22, expressed by the words 'mandate', 'mandatory' and 'trust' must be understood and examined for their value in international law.

Directly linked to this task of reviewing the application and validity of private law concepts in international law is a second problem. The historically quite justifiable hestitation about invoking private law analogy has led international lawyers to construe and answer certain questions of international law – such as those concerning entry into treaties, freedom of will and duress, conditions etc., which are only regulated in individual private law systems, or at the most in the general part of the individual private law systems, purely as problems of general legal doctrine. Thus, one arrives repeatedly, albeit with detours, at the forbidden analogy with private law. Is this procedure permissible and, if so, to what extent? This question has to be put in this context, although a detailed attempt at its solution, bordering as it does on the difficult areas of general legal theory and jurisprudence, lies outside the scope of this paper.

Consequently, this paper, which the author originally intended as a thorough exposition of the Mandates system based on official source-material and the relevant literature, has also become an attempt to contribute to legal theory. The original intention of also describing the economic and political conditions and motives of the Mandates system has however remained, for without these the legal implications of this new institution would be less easily understood. Naturally also the plan for the detailed exposition and analysis of the Mandate provisions – the real purpose of this study – has remained unimpaired, all the more as the purely theoretical examination of the problem has rendered this task considerably easier.

The author has endeavoured to examine all the available literature dealing with Mandates, but because of the difficulties in obtaining books from foreign countries, he has been only partly successful. On the other hand official source-material has been available. This has consisted mainly of the individual official draft Mandates and the documents and reports of the League of Nations and of the Mandates Commission established under Article 22.

I. ARTICLE 22 BEFORE, DURING AND AFTER THE VERSAILLES CONFERENCE (HISTORICAL PRESENTATION)

The two main parties to the peace settlement brought the colonies and the non-European territorial possessions of the enemy within their annexation plans long before, as well as during, the Peace Conference. This is certainly true also of the Axis Powers, especially Germany, though here the existence of plans for annexation is less clear since they have not been enshrined in treaties. The enemy foreign countries had certainly noted Germany's tendencies to colonial conquest during the War;[1] indeed to try to deny these tendencies would be wholly to misunderstand one of the most important factors in the history of the origin of the World War. The demand to burst open the closed doors of the world market was too loud.[2] By contrast the Entente's annexation plans leave nothing to be desired in the way of clarity. Nearly all of

[1] *Journal of the African Society* (July 1917), p. 306 (cited in Rolin, 'Le Système des Mandats coloniaux', *R.I.* (1920), no. 3–4).

[2] Dix, *Offene Tür oder Interessensphären, 'die Grenzboten'* (1911), p. 437.

Germany's colonial possessions and nearly the whole of extra-European Turkey were distributed by agreements made between the powers of the Entente months and years before the conclusion of the peace. As examples a few of these agreements may be mentioned here. As early as 19 February 1916 a treaty was concluded between France, England and Russia under which the provinces of Erzerum, Trebisond, Van, Bitlis and the territories of Kurdistan were awarded to Russia, Syria and the Vilayet Adana to France, and Mesopotamia and part of Palestine to Britain. The Entente powers were so confident that they supplemented this treaty with the well known Sykes–Picot Agreement in which the modalities of the distribution were precisely determined. This Agreement not only determined the Syrian–Palestine boundaries but also clearly marked the individual spheres of interest and administrative zones.[1]

These and similar treaties were however overtaken by events. The slogan, 'Peace without Annexation', became such a powerful factor in world opinion and thereby in world policy, that it had, at least on the face of it, to be respected. Woodrow Wilson adopted this slogan with regard to colonies in Point 5 of his speech before Congress on 8 January 1918, by holding out the prospect of sincere and completely impartial settlement of disputes about colonies.[2] The South-African statesman General J. C. Smuts had previously given clear expression to this view.[3] Starting from the presumption that the Central Powers had to lose their colonial possessions, he suggested an international solution to this question, a suggestion which contains the seed of the League of Nations Mandates system. These colonial possessions were to be administered by States appointed as Mandatories of the League of Nations. The principle of unselfish guardianship and of the civilizing task of the Mandatories was clearly expressed here.[4] These ideas were accepted with lively interest by the German side, which in the anxious months of the armistice had resigned itself to the inevitable loss of the colonies and tried to save what could still be saved.[5]

For the victorious powers, who had already solved the colonial

[1] Besson, 'La Syrie de 1921', in *Colonies et Marine* (June 1921), p. 365; *Reports of the Executive of the Zionist Organization to the Twelfth Zionist Congress*, I, 10 and 35.

[2] Schücking–Wehberg, *Die Satzung des Völkerbundes. Kommentar* (1921), p. 15. Cf. also the four principles put forward by Wilson on 11 February 1918, printed in Lansing, *Peace Negotiations*, p. 286.

[3] Smuts, *The League of Nations, A Practical Suggestion* (1918), p. 11.

[4] Schücking–Wehberg, *Die Satzung des Völkerbundes. Kommentar*, p. 422; Smuts, *League of Nations*, points 2–7 of the 21 suggestions.

[5] The draft League of Nations, prepared by the German Society for International Law, Article 32; *The Struggle for a Legal Peace. The Peace Negotiations documents – Remarks of the German Peace Delegation on the Peace Conditions*, published by the German League of Nations Association, p. 193; *The German Government's League of Nations proposal*, published by the German League of Nations Association, p. 20.

problem in a much simpler way between themselves, it seems to have been difficult to adjust even formally to the changed circumstances. The change lay – as already pointed out – in public opinion, which considerably influenced the final Allied statement of war crimes and in the intervention of another ally, the United States which, by virtue of the facts, became another decisive factor in the determination of the fate of the conquered territories. And the new ally showed a completely different interest from the original Allied Powers in the territories conquered 'by their joint struggle and common victory'.[1] At the end of January 1919 the President of the United States presented to the 'Council of Ten' of the five Principal Powers a suggestion for the internationalization of the former German colonies under the supremacy and control of the League of Nations.[2] This plan, which is identical with the draft submitted by Wilson on 10 January 1919 to the American commission, constitutes an almost literal translation of Smuts' 'suggestions'. This thoroughly radical proposal of the President shared the fate of almost all his efforts. It was unable to prevail in the atmosphere of the Versailles Conference. Thus a compromise materialized, which is incorporated in Article 22 of the Covenant of the League of Nations, an Article in which the indisputably new and creative element disappears almost without a trace in an ocean of ambiguity, circumlocution, concealment and generalities.

In the subsequent Peace Treaty, Germany under Articles 118 and 119 renounced all its rights in its overseas possessions in favour of the Principle Allied and Associated Powers and undertook to recognize the arrangements which the Allied and Associated Powers might take, if necessary, in accordance with their powers, to regulate the consequences of this renunciation. The same renunciation was made by Turkey in Articles 94, 95 and 96 of the Treaty of Sèvres of 10 August 1920 with the modification that here – in contrast to the Treaty of Versailles – the right of the Allied and Associated Powers to undertake the choice of Mandatories for Syria, Mesopotamia and Palestine and to determine the conditions for these Mandates was set out expressly.[3] The reason the

[1] Mr Bainbridge Colby to Lord Curzon. Correspondence between H.M.G. and the U.S. Ambassador respecting economic rights in mandated territories, Misc. no. 10 (1921).

[2] Rolin, in *R.I.* (1920), p. 344. The pre-history of the Mandates system at the Peace Conference is currently the object only of suppositions and news reports. It is to be believed only that it was very interesting. In any case the text of Article 22 was strongly influenced by the fear expressed during the negotiations that the colonies might under certain circumstances return to Germany. One of the circumstances, to which acceptance of the Mandates system subscribed, was (as Lansing suspected) that the victorious powers in this way came into possession of the Mandate territories without having to count their acquisition as part of war damages.

[3] Rolin, in *R.I.* (1920), p. 360; Schücking–Wehberg, *Die Satzung des Völkerbundes. Kommentar*, p. 427.

Entente gave for taking away the German colonies was that Germany had shown total incompetence as a colonizing power.[1]

On 7 May 1919 (i.e. before the signing of the Peace Treaty) at a session of the Supreme War Council the Allies distributed amongst themselves the territories to be placed under Mandate. The distribution took place as follows:[2] German East Africa (now Tanganyika) went to England; German South-West Africa to the Union of South Africa; the Samoa islands to New Zealand; the other German possessions south of the equator to Australia; the island of Nauru to England and the German islands north of the equator to Japan. As an agreement concerning Togo and Cameroon could not be reached, it was decided that England and France would later submit a joint recommendation to the League of Nations.[3] The distribution of the territories of the Turkish Empire took place in April 1920 during the meeting of the Supreme Council in San Remo. France took Syria and the Lebanon; England, Mesopotamia and Palestine.[4] At the same time a commission of experts was established with the task of preparing draft Mandates for the individual Mandated territories. The commission met in July and August 1920 and in general reached agreement in respect of the conditions to be applied to the B group (paragraph 5 of Article 22) and the C group (paragraph 6) of Mandates. Only two reservations were expressed: the French Government in respect of conscription in the Mandated territories of Togo and Cameroon, and the Japanese Government regarding the interpretation of the sixth paragraph of Article 22.[5] (The Japanese Government was of the opinion that the provisions on freedom of trade were also to be applied to the C Mandates.)[6]

The initiative for the further development and elaboration of the Mandates system now passed, in accordance with the League of Nations Covenant, to the League of Nations and in particular to its organ capable of action, the Council.[7] The Council seemed to be

[1] *The Entente's Ultimatum*. Text of the covering note and the answer to the German counter-proposal, published by the German League of Nations Association, French text, p. 37.

[2] Document 20/48/161, Annex 2. In this division Belgium was overlooked. Only in August 1919 was Belgium awarded a part of German East Africa and the districts of Ruanda and Urundi.

[3] The Anglo-French negotiations on this question took a fairly long time (see Annex 6 of the same document). They ended only on 10 July 1919. The League of Nations agreed to their results on 17 December 1920 (see draft Mandates for Togoland and the Cameroons. Misc. no. 16 (1921)).

[4] Doc. 20/48/161, Annex 6.

[5] Doc. 20/48/161, Annex 3.

[6] The decisions of the Powers in regard to the division of the Mandated territories and the settlement of their frontiers followed no precise legal form, as the reports of the Council repeatedly emphasized.

[7] In the original version of Article 22 the majority of duties were allotted to the Assembly, cf. Schücking–Wehberg, *Die Satzung des Völkerbundes. Kommentar*, p. 422.

conscious of the responsibility incumbent on it in regard to the Mandate question. On 30 July 1920 the Secretary-General of the League of Nations made a report to the Council in which the rôle of the Council and the steps immediately to be taken by it were officially formulated.[1] The report by the Belgian delegate, Paul Hymans,[2] accepted by the Council of 5 August 1920 represented a substantial step forward. This report is noteworthy not only because of its political content, which became the guideline for the League of Nations and the Mandatory Powers, but it is also of great academic interest. Here the first theoretical, semi-authentic, interpretation of Article 22 can be found. We shall refer to it a number of times in the course of this paper. The Council, in making Hymans' opinion its own, adopted a resolution requesting the Principal Powers to be so good as: (*a*) to name the Powers to whom they have decided to allocate the Mandates provided for in Article 22; (*b*) to inform the Council as to the frontiers of the territories to come under these Mandates; (*c*) to communicate to the Council the terms and the conditions of the Mandates that they propose should be adopted by the Council in accordance with Article 22.[3] The decisions were taken and the Council in the course of the summer and autumn of 1920 repeatedly called upon the Powers urgently to submit to it at least the draft Mandates for groups B and C. Failing this, the Council said it would be compelled to avail itself of its right under Article 22 (8) to determine the Mandate conditions unilaterally.[4] As these steps of the Council remained unsuccessful it concerned itself for the time being with drafting the constitution for the Mandates Commission to be established under paragraphs 7 and 9 of Article 22.[5]

At the first League Assembly in December 1920 it turned out that the A Mandates, for lack of ratification of the Treaty of Sèvres, were not considered,[6] that the B Mandates were not submitted and that only the drafts submitted for the C Mandates could be approved by the Council. This fact induced many Members of the League Assembly, as well as of the sub-committee for Mandate questions established under the presidency of Nansen loudly to manifest their indignation at this state of affairs and to express their apprehension as to the honesty and sincerity attending the execution of the provisions of Article 22.[7] Léon Bourgeois made a conciliatory intervention and the League Assembly contented

[1] Doc. 20/48/161, Annex 3.

[2] *Ibid.* Annex 4.

[3] *Ibid.* Annex 4.

[4] *Ibid.* Annexes 5, 11, 12 and 13.

[5] *Ibid.* Annexes 10 and 14. The Great Powers did not want the Council to discuss the details of the Mandates question until they had settled the question between themselves.

[6] Although the relevant drafts were already in the hands of the Council.

[7] Lord Robert Cecil, in particular, expressed his doubts in a frank and courageous speech.

itself with a few 'requests' in respect of the composition of the Mandates Commission and a few suggestions concerning the A Mandates.[1]

Immediately after the first League Assembly a new difficulty in the definite regulation of the Mandate question arose. The United States denied the right of the Supreme Council, as well as of the League of Nations, to make any decisions concerning the Mandated territories, without having previously obtained the formal consent of the United States. Apart from their determined opposition to the disposition already made of the island of Yap, the United States demanded that all draft Mandates should receive the consent of the Government of the United States before their approval by the Council.[2] The difficulties arising from this attitude, as well as lively exchange of opinions which followed between the League of Nations, the Principal Powers and the United States,[3] made it impossible for the Council to bring the Mandate question any nearer to a settlement.

So the second League Assembly, which met in September 1921, found itself confronted with a similar situation to the first League Assembly. The sub-committee for Mandates questions however did not content itself with deciding that the blame for the delay did not lie with the Council; it endeavoured to suggest to the League a provisional régime in order to prove to the world 'the earnestness of the League in pressing for the speedy realization of the aims of Article 22 of the Covenant'.[4]

Regardless of these facts, the Mandates Commission established by the Council of the League under paragraphs 7 and 9 of Article 22 commenced its work. With the consent of the Mandatory Powers it subjected five annual reports from various Mandated territories to a non-compulsory but nevertheless thorough examination. The purely factual nature of the Commission's deliberations shows its seriousness and goodwill in fulfilling a politically very delicate and difficult task.[5] The Commission, in order to facilitate the preparation of the annual reports by the Mandatory Powers, prepared a detailed questionnaire.[6]

Thus we come to the end of this historical account. In the first half of

[1] It was decided, for example, that members of the Mandates Commission could be relieved of their office only by a majority decision of the League Assembly; further, at least one place on the Mandates Commission was to be reserved for a woman. The Assembly expressed, *inter alia*, its wish that the Group A Mandatories should not be permitted to use their position to enlarge their military forces.

[2] Annexes 154 and 154b of the record of the 12th session of the Council.

[3] *Ibid.* Annexes 154a and 154c (League of Nations Doc. C. 122, M. 71 (1921), VI).

[4] League of Nations Doc. Ass. A. 105 (1921). Decision of the Commission, no. 6.

[5] Permanent Mandates Commission (League of Nations Doc. C. 416, M. 296 (1921), VI); procès-verbaux of the first session held at Geneva, 4–8 October 1921 (League of Nations Doc. C. 395, M. 294 (1921)); Permanent Mandates Commission. Rules of procedure (League of Nations Doc. C. 404, M. 295 (1921), VI).

[6] B Mandates questionnaire (League of Nations Doc. C. 396, M. 298 (1921), VI); C Mandates questionnaire (League of Nations Doc. C. 397, M. 299 (1921)).

1922 no essential change has occurred. The Council of the League of Nations is at the time of writing (May–June 1922) concerned with this question.

2. THE HISTORICAL, ECONOMIC AND POLITICAL CONDITIONS OF THE MANDATE SYSTEMS

Examination of part 1 of this study could easily lead to the conclusion that the Mandates system owes its coming into existence to a passing conjunction of political circumstances and that it is, as it were, a subspecies of the concealed cessions listed in the international law books[1] and accomplished by a clever compromise. Robert Lansing's sceptical remarks on the true character of Article 22 of the Covenant of the League of Nations[2] show that this impression is liable to be made not only on the reader of the reports but also on those better acquainted with the secrets of the origin of the Peace Treaties. I would not deny that the Mandates system breathes much of the spirit of the Versailles Peace Treaty, but it would be quite wrong and unhistorical to attribute it solely to this spirit. Such an approach would be unhistorical – and excusable only on psychological grounds – because it completely misunderstands the interaction and variety of the causes and motivations which lie behind historical events. It also makes an understanding of the Mandates system impossible. Its peculiar and most essential provisions have their explanation far away from peace conference politics: they are the end-product of a long historical development.

A cursory glance at the provisions of Article 22 is sufficient to show that the Mandates system – apart from its legal description – contrasts sharply with previous colonial systems. The freedom of the administering power is here limited in binding form and under far-reaching safeguards in two respects: first, in respect of the native population, second, in respect of other States, Members of the League of Nations. It is the purpose of this section to illustrate the historical reasons for this limitation.

One of the most characteristic features of the political and politico-economic history of European States in the last century is imperialism. Born against the background of the only true 'world' empire, the *Imperium Romanum*, it ended up in an attempt by certain States to gain territorial, economic and political strongholds as large and important as possible in all parts of the world in order to have a decisive voice in all

[1] For example, Liszt, *Das Völkerrecht* (11th ed.), p. 91.
[2] Lansing, *Peace Negotiations*, p. 139.

questions of world policy and world economy.[1] Colonial policy was the most important expression of these endeavours. And so Hasse is ultimately right in saying: 'To enter into this area [colonial policy] would mean covering most of contemporary history and politics.'[2] At the same time he characterizes this period by adding: 'In approaching the present, one would have to touch on numerous delicate questions of practical foreign policy.'[3] Apart from minor exceptions, efforts to colonize really had at all times been a national affair.[4] The colonies were and have remained 'external areas of administration of a State for world-economic and world-political purposes'.[5] But in becoming one of the most important political factors of modern times, they became at the same time the source of continuous international conflicts and quarrels. There is a consistent line[6] from the Hispano-Portuguese delimitation of spheres of interests[7] to the eighteenth-century Anglo-French colonial war[8] and to the violent struggle for Morocco, Tunis, Abyssinia etc.

This struggle would certainly have been less violent if the victors in the competition had not abused their position by affecting world economic markets through protectionist tariff policies and limiting concessions and privileges to their own nationals. In a number of colonies the system of preferential tariffs, which sometimes took the form of a more or less complete customs union with the mother country, was adopted.[9] This was particularly so in the case of France. It was, however, also adopted by Portugal, Spain, Italy, the United States and Japan.[10] The British dominions too, notwithstanding the mother country's free trade policy, gradually adopted a consistent practice of preferential tariffs.[11] This tendency to a 'closed door' policy – for it would have to be called that – was characteristic of modern imperialism in the realm of colonial policy; it was also decisive for the formation of the economic and international law concept of the 'spheres of interest', which – in sharp contrast to the 'open door' theory – is based upon the principle of exclusiveness and priority.[12] And thus the time from 1880 to 1914 saw one of the most violent peacetime struggles for territories and

[1] Kobatsch, *Internationale Wirtschaftspolitik* (1907), p. 364.
[2] *Handwörterbuch der Staatswissenschaften* (1909), V, 939.
[3] *Ibid.* [4] Rolin, in *R.I.* (1920), p. 353.
[5] Hasse, *Handwörterbuch der Staatswissenschaften*, p. 930.
[6] Kobatsch, *Internationale Wirtschaftspolitik*, p. 375.
[7] Hasse, *Handwörterbuch der Staatswissenschaften*, p. 939.
[8] Woolf, *Mandates and Empire* (1920), p. 6.
[9] Trescher, *Vorzugszölle. Ihre Geschichte und Wirkung im Internationalen Warenaustausch* (1908), p. 122. [10] Trescher, *Vorzugszölle*, p. 125. [11] *Ibid.*, pp. 7, 11 and 35.
[12] Dix, *Offene Tür oder Interessensphären*, p. 435. In this connection, England, for example, has gone through important changes. Originally a defender of the 'open door' it has gone over gradually to a policy of spheres of interest (e.g. the Anglo-Russian action in Persia). In view of this policy there was an ever louder demand in Germany for the locked doors of the world market to be burst open by force.

spheres of interest so as to reserve to the victors' nationals (and to the exclusion of foreign nationals) the more far-reaching economic opportunities. This was the inflammable material in the fire of world war.

The Berlin Congress of 1885 and its 'declaration concerning the freedom of trade in the Congo basin, its estuary and in the adjacent countries'[1] proves that the Powers were aware of the dangers of such a situation. But, even in its limited application to the Congo, the principle of freedom of trade for all nations found little respect, because the Congo Government managed to evade it by a clever interpretation of the provisions of the Berlin Congress.[2] Article 22 revives the free trade concept which has been shown here to be the result of a long development. The simple provision: 'secure equal opportunities for the trade and commerce of other Members of the League' is an important part of the peace-order of the League of Nations.

No less important are the limitations of the Mandatory Power in relation to the native population. Here they go far beyond the provisions of the Congo Congress, not so much in the extent of obligations as in the guarantees incorporated into the Covenant to safeguard their execution.[3] The reason for these limitations and for these guarantees is deeply rooted in the history of the colonizing activity of the European States. It lies in the fact that of the two kinds of colonizing activity (by which is meant the settlement of colonies and their exploitation) the latter has won the day.[4] The humanitarian, cultural and cosmopolitan aspects have been constantly repressed not only by considerations of national policy but also of private commerce and the capitalists. 'Le monde colonial moderne', says Rolin,[5] 'est issu de l'amour du gain et de la puissance.'

The history of the colonial conquests of the European Powers has in fact been a history of the most ruthless economic exploitation of native peoples, maintained by the despotic rule of military administrations.[6] From time to time during the last twenty years the so-called colonial revelations have shocked the public opinion of Europe. One need only be reminded of the reports on the cruelties and acts of violence in the colonies which reached the public through questions in the English House of Commons, in the French and Belgian Chambers and in the

[1] General Act of the Berlin Conference, 26 February 1885 (printed in Liszt, *Das Völkerrecht*, p. 401; Christ-Socin, 'Der Berliner Kongo-Vertrag vom 26 Februar 1885', *Zeitschrift für Kolonialpolitik und Kolonialwirtschaft*, 13, 672; Ferdinand Lentner, *Das internationale Kolonialrecht im 19. Jahrhundert* (1886), p. 97.

[2] The Government of the Congo interpreted the expression 'freedom of trade' only in the normal sense of traffic in goods (Rueger, 'Privatrechtliche Begriffe im Völkerrecht', *Z.I.* 28, 447).

[3] General Act of the Berlin Conference, Art. 6.

[4] Hasse, *Handwörterbuch der Staatswissenschaften*, p. 934.

[5] Rolin, in *R.I.* (1920), p. 354.

[6] Woolf, *Mandates and Empire*, p. 7.

German Reichstag. When the Europeans, for example, set foot in Africa they found an agricultural system there which knew nothing of the private ownership of land, money was unknown and commercial intercourse did not go beyond a system of barter. Without any ado the economic system of the colonizing State was imposed upon this economically backward society. The land was taken away from the natives and sold to European settlers and companies. Bloody and cruel acts of violence by the administrations followed in order to force the natives to work on this land. Added to all this was the neglect of the most basic cultural and health obligations towards the native population.

In the long run, public opinion in a democratic age could not put up with such a state of affairs. And only the fact that it is still States and not peoples which determine policies explains why public opinion has contented itself with spontaneous outbursts of passionate protest.[1] Public opinion did not have sufficient power to help realize the clear provisions of the Congo Act. The radical attempt to solve this problem, with guarantees and safeguards, thus lay not only in the passing political circumstances of the Peace Conference, and in the conceptions of Wilson, Smuts and others, but also in the spirit of the time and its demands. And one would be wrong to think, in spite of the Berlin Congress and a few similar treaties, that Article 22 contained nothing new.[2] For there the relevant provisions of the treaty constituted but one of its parts, while here an instrument was created for them alone, a new institution of international law, the Mandate under international law.

ARTICLE 22: AN ANALYSIS OF THE INDIVIDUAL PROVISIONS

A few observations should be made before the presentation and analysis of the individual provisions of Article 22. The complaint is made over and over again that the wording of this Article is misleading and unclear and that the unnatural solemnity of expression barely conceals the inherent difficulties and incompleteness of the text. This is indeed so. One has, however, to take into consideration the fact that this Article is the result of a compromise between a cultural–ethical requirement and the pure principle of power. One must reconcile oneself to this, and take

[1] Christ-Socin, in *Zeitschrift für Kolonialpolitik und Kolonialwirtschaft*, 13, p. 578. Before the war the Social Democratic Party of Germany supported the force and its theories but at the same time, on the grounds of the requirements of the class struggle, had included in their programme the fight against the exploitation of the colonies. At the 1907 International Socialist Congress in Stuttgart, however, the revisionist wing took a positive position towards colonization and even then expressed thoughts of guardianship.

[2] Cf. e.g. the Brussels Anti-Slavery Treaty of 2 July 1890.

it as the starting point for legal research. It is true that the nucleus of this cultural-ethical requirement has been retained – that is just what the Mandates system is – but only at the price of considerable concessions to the power principle. And these concessions expressed themselves in the form of euphemisms, vagueness, contortions, limitations and partial contradictions to the essence of the Mandates system itself. But still they have become part of the Covenant of the League of Nations and one has to accept them as such. Any other procedure weakens the position of those who fight with scientific methods against expressions of power which may evolve even after the conclusion of peace.

It may be added that the general presentation of the Mandates system which follows, though based on Article 22 as its main source, still draws for illustration of the individual provisions upon the draft Mandates which have appeared since. For the time being, only the positive and undisputed contents of the Article are illustrated; the controversial issues will be but briefly touched on and pointed out as such. They will be dealt with only after discussion of the basic legal-historical problem which is under consideration here.

Article 22 provides as follows:

1. To those colonies and territories which as a consequence of the late war have ceased to be under the sovereignty of the States which formerly governed them and which are inhabited by peoples not yet able to stand by themselves under the strenuous conditions of the modern world, there should be applied the principle that the well-being and development of such peoples form a sacred trust of civilization and that securities for the performance of this trust should be embodied in this Covenant.

2. The best method of giving practical effect to this principle is that the tutelage of such peoples should be entrusted to advanced nations who by reason of their resources, their experience or their geographical position can best undertake this responsibility, and who are willing to accept it, and that this tutelage should be exercised by them as Mandatories on behalf of the League.

3. The character of the mandate must differ according to the stage of the development of the people, the geographical situation of the territory, its economic conditions and other similar circumstances.

4. Certain communities formerly belonging to the Turkish Empire have reached a stage of development where their existence as independent nations can be provisionally recognized subject to the rendering of administrative advice and assistance by a Mandatory until such time as they are able to stand alone. The wishes of these communities must be a principal consideration in the selection of the Mandatory.

5. Other peoples, especially those of Central Africa, are at such a stage that the Mandatory must be responsible for the administration of the territory

under conditions which will guarantee freedom of conscience and religion, subject only to the maintenance of public order and morals, the prohibition of abuse such as the slave trade, the arms traffic and the liquor traffic, and the prevention of the establishment of fortifications or military and naval bases and of military training of the natives for other than police purposes and the defence of territory, and will also secure equal opportunities for the trade and commerce of other Members of the League.

6. There are territories, such as South-West Africa and certain of the South Pacific Islands, which, owing to the sparseness of their population, or their small size, or their remoteness from the centres of civilisation, or their geographical contiguity to the territory of the Mandatory, and other circumstances, can be best administered under the laws of the Mandatory as integral portions of its territory, subject to the safeguards above mentioned in the interests of the indigenous population.

7. In every case of mandate, the Mandatory shall render to the Council an annual report in reference to the territory committed to its charge.

8. The degree of authority, control, or administration to be exercised by the Mandatory shall, if not previously agreed upon by the Members of the League, be explicitly defined in each case by the Council.

9. A permanent Commission shall be constituted to receive and examine the annual reports of the Mandatories and to advise the Council on all matters relating to the observance of the mandates.

The nine paragraphs of the Article can be divided into three groups. The first (paragraphs 1–3) contains the reasons for the Mandates system and the general provisions on the character and the functions of the Mandate; the second group (paragraphs 4–6) contains the division of the Mandated territories into three categories of A, B and C Mandates; finally, the third group (paragraphs 7–9) deals with the organization of the Mandates system, e.g. the Mandatory's duty to report, supervision by the League, etc.

Paragraph 1 expresses the concept of the high humanitarian task of the civilized nations towards peoples in a culturally lower position. It is not the rights but the duties of the nations to be entrusted with this task which are mentioned here. Not they and their interests are the starting point, but the native populations 'not yet able to stand by themselves'.

Thus the provisional and temporary nature of the system is indirectly expressed. An historical obligation is imposed upon the civilized nations. They have to care not only for the well-being but also for the development of those entrusted to their protection. The political aim and the duration of this stage of development are indirectly expressed in the Covenant: until they are able to stand by themselves. And it is not only a positive provision but also an historical judgment over the past when the paragraph speaks of the necessity 'that securities for the performance of this trust should be embodied in this Covenant'.[1]

Specific attention has to be given to the word *Aufgabe* – 'a sacred trust of civilization', 'the performance of this trust'. It is an accurate translation of the French *mission*, but an imprecise rendering of the English 'trust'. By means of this translation the word is – justifiably – deprived of the possibility of any specific legal content. In the course of our examination we will however look at the English attitude, which places the emphasis of the system on exactly this word, claiming that it is identical with the traditional concept of the equitable 'trust'.[2] The word 'trust', according to this view, is not a vague phrase, but has a clearly determined and precise legal meaning. We will not for the time being pursue this question but will revert to it, after discussing the admissibility of dealing with problems in international law on the basis of private law concepts and legal provisions.

In the second paragraph the legal nucleus of the Mandates system is formally stated and paraphrased as follows: advanced nations shall be entrusted with the tutelage of peoples in the territories and colonies under consideration and shall exercise this tutelage as Mandatories of the League and in its name. Of these two concepts – i.e. tutelage and mandate – only the latter is of formal legal relevance to us. Tutelage is the substance of the mandate but is of little importance in the legal construction of this institution. On the other hand the concept of the mandate remains at the centre of our consideration. The only question to be answered is, how is this concept to be understood and what consequences flow from it? Here opinions are diametrically opposed to one another. The German (and, in part, the English and official American) attitude[3] clings to the full private law implications of the wording, namely that the mandator is always and in every way superior, that he and only he has the right to appoint the mandatory and to dismiss him, and that he, and only he has the right to determine the conditions of the mandate and to amend them at any time, being always able actively to intervene. Even the rule, antiquated as it is in private law, of the gratuitous nature of the mandate is claimed to have

[1] The fate of the Congo Act has shown how little value such arrangements have if their execution is not at the same time secured by far reaching guarantees. Cf. Christ-Socin, in *Zeitschrift für Kolonialpolitik und Kolonialwirtschaft*, 13.

[2] Karplus, *Handbuch des englischen Privatrechtes*, pp. 23 *et seq.*; Campbell-Lee, *The Mandate for Mesopotamia and the Principle of Trusteeship in English Law*, p. 17.

[3] E.g. Schücking–Wehberg, *Die Satzung des Völkerbundes. Kommentar*; Bileski, 'Das Mandat des Völkerbundes', *Z.V.* 12, 66; *Die Denkschrift der deutschen Regierung an die erste Völkerbundversammlung*, Doc. no. 106; Campbell-Lee, *The Mandate for Mesopotamia*; Harris, *The Challenge of Mandates* (1920), pp. 6 *et seq.*; Woolf, *Mandates and Empire*, p. 11; the same, *Scope of the Mandates under the League of Nations*, p. 5; the Anglo-American correspondence (see above, p. 33 n. 1).

unqualified application. A quite different interpretation is given to the concept of mandate by the 'western' side, and partly also by the theoretical decisions of the Council and by the practice of the League of Nations.[1] There, every civil law analogy is harshly rejected, this dissociation from private law foundations going so far as to lead to the view that the complete transfer of sovereignty to the mandatory is possible, or even the only correct solution. The mandate is thus irrevocable and its conditions cannot be amended by the unilateral act of the mandator; it is non-gratuitous by reason of the absolute powers acquired by the mandatory. Thus two opinions sharply confront each other, but it is clear that the difference can be reduced to the problem of the application of private law concepts, a problem which must be solved. Only the solution of this question will enable us to take a definite stance.[2]

The third paragraph formulates the principles according to which the division of the Mandates into the various categories takes place. However, because of the clause: '... and other similar circumstances', the provision becomes so flexible that it is almost deprived of its value. It was as a result of it for example that the island of Nauru was given to Great Britain.[3] It is also only in this way, as will be shown later, that one can explain why Togo and Cameroon were dealt with in direct contradiction to the provisions of the Covenant. The 'similar circumstances' were decisive here too.

In the second sub-group of the Article (paragraphs 4–6) we have the familiar division of the Mandated territories into the categories A, B and C. This comprises, in a significant gradation, communities (A), peoples (B) and territories (C).[4]

The fourth paragraph is concerned with the A class of Mandates. Certain communities formerly belonging to the Turkish Empire which have reached a stage of development where their existence as independent nations can be provisionally recognized belong here. They administer their country themselves and the Mandatory Authorities are limited to giving advice and other assistance to the autonomous administration. The duration of the Mandatory Authority is explicitly limited to such time 'as they are able to stand alone', but this provision also remains subject to arbitrary interpretation.[5] The recognition of these

[1] Rolin, in *R.I.* (1920), p. 329; *Documents of the 1st Assembly*, 161 (20/48/161), Annexes 3 and 4; Sir Eric Drummond's explanations in an interview – communicated by the English League of Nations Association.

[2] Discussion of this question follows in the next section.

[3] Schücking–Wehberg, *Die Satzung des Völkerbundes. Kommentar*, p. 429.

[4] Rolin, in *R.I.* (1920), p. 340.

[5] *Temps* newspaper of 4 April 1921 reported the answer which Winston Churchill, the English Minister for Colonies gave to a Muslim delegation: '...la forme actuelle du gouv-

communities as independent nations has also been taken into account in the provision that their wishes must be a principal consideration in the selection of the Mandatory.[1]

Syria, Lebanon, Mesopotamia and Palestine belong to this group. It would however be wrong to think that they are uniform entities in international, constitutional and administrative law. This provisional independence is – as expressed by Hymans – 'une notion susceptible d'une infinité de nuances'; he even thinks that that kind of administration will have to adjust itself not only to the degree of civilization of the community in question, but also to the administrative system and principles of the Mandatory Power itself.[2] As is immediately apparent from an examination of the draft Mandate for Palestine, it would be wrong to demand uniform handling of these areas.[3] While in the draft Mandate for Mesopotamia the independence of the country is expressly recognized in accordance with paragraph 14 of Article 22, this declaration is absent from the Palestine draft. The administration here is expressly transferred to the Mandatory Power; the draft also – in contrast to the Mesopotamian draft – nowhere speaks of a Palestine 'Government', but only of an 'Administration'. Thus Palestine appears as an intermediate step between the A and B Mandates. There is all the more basis for this view in that paragraph 4 does not speak of all territories that previously belonged to Turkey but only of certain communities.

ernement continuera pendant de longues années. Peu à peu, nous établirons des institutions epresentatives, qui conduiront à un gouvernement autonome; mais les enfants de nos enfants seront morts avant que cette œuvre soit accomplie'. The drafts for Mesopotamia and Palestine contain provisions for the case of termination of the Mandate. (Article 20, Mesopotamia; Article 28, Palestine.)

The Times newspaper of 16 August 1920 reported on the first steps towards the organization of self-government in Mesopotamia.

[1] This provision was, however, completely disregarded. But basically it could not be carried out because the principle Arab tribes of these lands repeatedly expressed their wish not to have any mandatory whatsoever over them. See, e.g., the memorandom of the representatives of the Baghdad and Mosul Departments to the Secretary-General of the League of Nations dated 26 February 1921: '...la nation mesop. exprima à maintes reprises et par des moyens divers son désir de vivre complètement indépendante'. (*Temps* newspaper of 22 March 1921.) It could also not be executed in conformity with the basic considerations of the creator of the mandate system where the heterogeneous condition of populations made an authoritative expression of will impossible (cf. Smuts, *The League of Nations*, p. 17).

[2] Doc. 20/48/161, Hymans' Report; W. Ormsby-Gore, 'Art. XXII (Mandates)', *The Covenant* (July 1920), pp. 482 and 485.

[3] The special position of Palestine arises beause of the differences of the nationalities living there (of the Arab majority and the Jewish minority) and because of the familiar Balfour Declaration of 2 November 1917 which envisaged the re-establishment of a national home for the Jewish people in Palestine. This Declaration was imposed as an obligation on the English Government by the Supreme Council in San Remo and the relative provisions of the Palestine Mandate annexed. Cf. Bileski, in *Z.I.* 12, 75; Ormsby-Gore, in *The Covenant* 1920), p. 485; Smuts, *The League of Nations*, p. 17; Final Draft of the Mandate for Palestine (Articles 1, 11 and 17).

However, even in areas which undoubtedly belong to the A group and whose independence is expressly recognized, the legal position is insufficiently clear. For how far should the 'advice' and 'assistance' of the Mandatory go? Does this not open the door to extreme arbitrariness? The apprehension is obvious but still not quite justified. The arbitrariness is limited not only by the general provisions of the Article, but also by the wording of paragraph 4 itself. Does the Mandatory exercise the administration? No. One cannot 'assist' oneself, one cannot render oneself advice. The logical conclusion is therefore that the provisions of paragraph 4 undoubtedly require 'self-administration'.[1] On the other hand it has not been disputed by anybody that external representation – a necessary consequence of the idea of guardianship – remains reserved to the Mandatory Power.[2] It follows from this that the question of the position of the Mandated territories of group A under international law can be answered fairly simply. There is almost complete unanimity on the point that the areas in this category are to be described as protectorates under international law.[3] In reality the qualities of the protectorate, as e.g. Liszt gives them, correspond with the circumstances in the Mandated territories of the A group; for they are after all States, which 'in certain international relationships are represented by another State' and which 'are not members of the international community with full rights'. This specification is all the more acceptable, as it is very flexible and contains a number of possibilities. 'These are transitional steps in historical development, either from complete dependence to unlimited independence or the reverse.'[4] The statement is also important in that the powers of the protector State in relation to the administration may very well differ from one to another. If, for example, we refer for comparison to the draft Mandate for Mesopotamia, we see that the 'protector' (here the 'Mandatory'), is clearly distinguished from the Government of the country. The inhabitants of these areas have their own nationality and not that of the Mandatory Power. But the decisive say in certain branches of administration is reserved to the Mandatory, while in foreign affairs, on the other hand, it takes complete charge. It has the right to issue exequaturs

[1] Ormsby-Gore, in *The Covenant* (1920), p. 482; Woolf, *Scope of Mandates*, p. 9; Campbell-Lee, *The Mandate for Mesopotamia*, p. 16; Rolin, in *R.I.* (1920), p. 340.

[2] Here and there it was demanded that the 'independent Nations' of the A Mandates should be admitted straightaway to the League of Nations. Cf. Woolf, *Scope of Mandates*, p. 430.

[3] Rolin, in *R.I.* (1920), p. 340; Scelle, *Le Pacte des Nations et sa liaison avec le Traité de Paix*, p. 198; Schücking-Wehberg, *Die Satzung des Völkerbundes. Kommentar*, p. 430.

[4] Liszt, *Das Völkerrecht*, pp. 51 *et seq.*; Rivier, *Lehrbuch des Völkerrechtes* (2nd ed.), p. 103; Ullmann, *Völkerrecht* (1908), p. 105; Kohler, *Grundlage des Völkerrechtes* (1918), p. 56 ('Ein Staat übernimmt die vormundschaftliche Verwaltung über einen un-oder halbmündigen Staat'); De Luter, *Le droit international public positif* (1920), pp. 177 *et seq.*; Martens, p. 250.

to foreign consuls and to grant diplomatic and consular protection to the citizens of Mesopotamia outside its borders.[1]

Of course, the relationship of protection as described above is not conceptually at odds with the idea of the Mandate. It is only a kind of execution of the latter, which in the case of the B Mandates (and to some extent in Palestine) amounts to administration by the Mandatory, and in the C group to the almost complete assimilation of the territory to the territory and the legislation of the Mandatory. The theoretical question, whether this protectorate is in a relationship of protection or one of 'divided sovereignty' (half-sovereignty) cannot be pursued further at this stage.[2] It is still for discussion whether the freedom of trade enacted for the B group also refers to the A Mandates. It is not given a single mention in paragraph 4. It is difficult to assume that there is a drafting mistake here. The duty of the Mandatory to introduce freedom of trade can hardly be deduced from the general provisions of the Article. The interest of the population – and it is the primary obligation of the Mandatory to provide for the latter – is not always identical with a system of free trade.[3] The argument, moreover, that the Mandatory should not draw any benefit at all from its office is merely a naive *petitio principii* – unless this altruistic concept has a claim to recognition by reason of a positive provision in the Covenant. This provision is, however, missing from Article 22, paragraph 4. But important political reasons – especially consideration towards the United States – have led the first League Assembly as well as the relevant draft Mandates to declare that the provision of paragraph 5 on freedom of trade is also applicable to the A Mandates.[4]

The Mandates over those peoples who 'are at such a stage that the

[1] Cf. final draft, Mandate for Mesopotamia. The system of Protectorates had actually been suggested during the peace negotiations by people who were totally sceptical of the Mandates system and preferred to stick to well-tried methods.

[2] If one wanted to discuss this question more closely it would mean examining some of the most difficult material of international law and of the theory of the State. The problem of divided sovereignty and its possibility in theory is, particularly in Germany, sufficiently dealt with in the extensive literature on the federal State. 'Divided sovereignty' has been rejected almost unanimously as a logical non-thing. (Cf. Jellinek, *Die Lehre von Staatenverbindungen*; Kelsen, *Das Problem der Souveränitat und die Theorie des Völkerrechtes*; particularly, however, Nawiasky, *Der Bundesstaat als Rechtsbegriff*; cf. also De Louter.) However it seems to me that this reasoning which, in the case of Kelsen, leads in strict logic to a denial of State sovereignty in general is of little practical value. It shows itself completely incapable of registering the many-sidedness of the legal structure. And so writers can almost unanimously use the expression 'half-sovereignty' even though they describe it as 'nonsense' (Martens) or 'évidemment fausse' (De Louter).

[3] Christ-Socin, in *Zeitschrift für Kolonialpolitik und Kolonialwirtschaft*, 13, p. 570.

[4] Cf. Article 11 of the draft Mandate for Mesopotamia and Article 18 of the draft Mandate for Palestine; correspondence between H.M.G. and the U.S. Ambassador respecting economic rights in mandated territories; Campbell-Lee, *The Mandate for Mesopotamia*, pp. 21 *et seq*. The binding character of the 'wish' of the Assembly in the Mandate question is, moreover, very doubtful.

Mandatory must be responsible for the administration of the territory' belong to category B (paragraph 5). They are in particular the Central African peoples. This transfer in principle of the exercise of sovereign rights is subject to 'conditions'. That is to say, abuses like the slave trade, arms and liquor traffic are to be abolished; and freedom of conscience and religion, subject to certain limitations, are to be guaranteed. These regulations, which in essence remind one of the analogous decisions of the Berlin Congress of 1885 and of similar conventions (Brussels 1890), are quite unequivocal, even though their execution in practice meets with great difficulties.[1] Even though the abolition of forced labour in principle is not mentioned in the Covenant, the pertinent provision was nonetheless incorporated into the draft Mandates.[2] This shows the enormous influence of public opinion in general and of the English Society for the League of Nations in particular. The same spirit is expressed by the provisions, incorporated into the draft Mandates, that the Mandatory has to take local laws and customs into account in legislating for the Mandated territory, and must respect the rights of the native population and safeguard their interests.[3] There is also an express prohibition of any reinforcement of the armed forces of the Mandatory. There must also be guarantees against 'the establishment of fortifications or military and naval bases and of military training of the natives for other than police purposes and the defence of territory'. This prohibition seems to have been accepted only after a long struggle. In particular France showed a great interest in the conscription of troops among the natives. This resistance has tried subsequently to make itself felt by a decidedly far-fetched interpretation.[4] Thus the formulation of the respective points in the draft Mandate not unintentionally leaves much to be desired in the way of clarity.[5] The freedom of trade provision in this paragraph refers only to League Members, a fact which

[1] Cf. the Protocol of the Permanent Mandates Commission (League of Nations Doc. C. 416, M. 296).

[2] Nor is this question to be solved at a stroke, as is shown by the interesting differences of opinion of the Mandates Commission in the presence of the representatives of the International Labour Office (pp. 36 and 37 of the Protocol).

[3] Draft Mandates for Togoland and the Cameroons, Articles 4 and 5; Leys, *A Plan for Government in Africa* (1921), p. 8; Woolf, *Scope of the Mandates*, p. 11.

[4] Harris, *The Challenge of the Mandates* (1921), p. 8, who maintains that the form of the relevant sentence in the 5th paragraph ('. . . and the defence of the territory', as well as the absence of the definite article) permits the use of troops also outside the mandate area. Cf. *Temps* newspaper of 24 June 1921 on the draft French Mandate for Togo and Cameroon: 'il est toute fois entendu que les troupes indigènes pourront, en cas de guerre générale, être employées dans un but défensif en dehors de la région soumise au mandat'. See also the report of Sub-Committee VI, *Journal* of the 2nd Assembly, no. 18 for Lord Cecil's remarks on this question; Doc. 20/48/161 (Hymans' Report). Article 3(2) of the draft French Mandate for Cameroon permits the use of native troops outside the Mandated territory.

[5] Cf. the English draft Mandate for Togo and Cameroon, Art. 3. Cf. also the Protocol of the Mandates Commission.

is mainly responsible for the subsequent refusal of the United States to accept any Mandates, and has created the need for special treaties regulating this question between the United States and the individual Mandatory Powers.

The position of these Mandated territories under constitutional and international law is that, even though the administration and the exercise of all sovereign rights belong to the Mandatory, the Mandated territory nonetheless is not part of the territory of the Mandatory and its inhabitants enjoy their own nationality. However, this point is not regulated in the draft Mandates.[1] The question with whom lies real sovereignty over these areas can be answered only after a fundamental legal appraisal of the Mandates system.

It would, however, on the other hand,[2] be wrong to talk of the areas of the B Mandates as uniform entities. They are not so. And if Hymans was of the opinion that one could draw up the drafts for the B Mandates, on the basis of a stock draft he has been taught better. One always assumed, for example, that Togo and Cameroon, by virtue of Article 22, belonged to the B group because it is, after all, mainly Central African countries that paragraph 5 mentions. Oddly enough, however, the literature on the subject does not bother to study carefully the draft Mandate for Togo and Cameroon, or it would have observed that according to these drafts these territories no longer belong to the B group, but constitute at most (like Palestine with the A Mandates) an intermediate step between the B and C Mandates.[3] On the one hand, these drafts contain the important B Mandate clauses such as the provisions on military forces, on the abolition of abuses and guaranteed freedom of religion and conscience. On the other hand, they include also the materially most important provision of the C Mandates, namely, that these Mandated territories are to be administered under the laws of the Mandatory and as an integral part of its territory.[4] Thus, here too, we deal with intermediate steps, which constitute new types of Mandates, not provided for in the Covenant of the League of Nations.

[1] Cf. Schatzel, 'Die Staatsangehörigkeit bei Gebietsveränderungen', *Z.I.* (1921), p. 115.

[2] Cf. above on the Palestine Mandate.

[3] The event is set out in the joint proposals which England and France submitted to the League on Togo and Cameroon. In the Supreme Council's session, on 7 May 1919, it was decided, in regard to the allocation of the Mandates, that France and England should submit a joint proposal regarding these two territories. The Powers also thought that it might be believed that Togo and Cameroon should be excluded from the application of the Mandates system. On the other hand it seems beyond doubt that Article 22 applies the Mandates system to all German overseas possessions. The fact that these countries are, contrary to paragraph 5, placed in the C group is justified in the proposal by reference to the interests of the population and the administrative difficulties which must otherwise arise. This explanation was submitted to the League Council on 17 December 1920 (Misc. no. 16 (1921)).

[4] Draft Mandates for Togoland and the Cameroons, Misc. no. 16 (1921). Cf. also Ormsby-Gore, in *The Covenant* (1920), p. 483.

Paragraph 6 contains arrangements for the C group of Mandates. For various reasons, set out individually by the Covenant, these territories 'can be best administered under the laws of the Mandatory as integral portions of its territory'. We are here confronted with a regulation which shows features characteristic of annexation. Rolin has for instance categorically asserted that we are dealing here with annexation.[1] According to him the laws of the Mandatory are the very embodiment of sovereignty; and the description 'as integral portions of its territory' expresses everything but a straightforward annexation. This opinion must be here rebutted. If it is asserted that the C Mandate provisions have resulted from a desire for annexation and that they must therefore be regarded as annexation, then this reasoning must be shown to be false. The very fact that the idea of the Mandate – even in an extremely weakened form – was able to maintain itself against claims of annexation by the Powers, makes the above-mentioned argumentation appear as a non-juristic interpretation of something which does not require interpretation. For there is no doubt that the general provisions of the Mandates system contained in Article 22 also apply to the C Mandates.[2] One can only justify a claim of full sovereignty for the Mandatory in the C areas by showing that the Mandate under international law not only permits the complete transfer of sovereignty but also automatically brings it about. However, it would be completely wrong to derive this transfer of sovereignty from the words 'under the laws of the Mandatory as integral portions of its territory', since they constitute no more than an administrative, though admittedly far-reaching, modification of a type of Mandate which is in other respects very flexible. The C Mandates – as the Covenant expresses it – 'can be best administered [etc.]'. Thus the basic legal structure of this Mandate is not altered. The wide powers of the Mandatory are of a purely administrative nature. That a complete transfer of the exercise of supreme authority is not identical with annexation can be clearly established by reference to the example of Bosnia and Herzegovina.[3]

Certain limitations of the Mandatory Power can, however, also be found in the C Mandates. They are those which have been enacted, in the case of the B Mandates, in the interest of the native population.

[1] In *R.I.* (1920), pp. 347 *et seq.*

[2] Woolf, *Scope of the Mandates*, p. 10.

[3] The question of the citizenship of the inhabitants of these areas is not yet definitely settled. For example, in respect of Samoa, a committee of jurists has expressed the opinion that the inhabitants are to be considered as citizens of Samoa. Outside the area they enjoy the protection of the British consular service. (Cf. the Protocol of the Permanent Mandates Commission, *Journal* (1921), p. 41.) Cf. also the report of the same Commission to the Council (League of Nations Doc. C. 395, M. 294 (1921), VI, p. 4, Annex); Schatzel, in *Z.I.* (1921), pp. 115 *et seq.*

Here the question arises whether the remaining provisions of paragraph 5, imposing limitations on the Mandatory, are to be applied in respect of the C Mandates. After all, the prohibition of the establishment of fortifications or military and naval bases, and of the suppression of freedom of religion and conscience in respect of foreigners is not said to be in the exclusive interest of the natives.[1] The draft Mandates of the C areas have also incorporated these provisions. On the other hand the provisions for freedom of trade and equal treatment of the nationals of all League Members are missing from paragraph 6 of Article 22 as well as from the draft Mandates. The absence of this provision is deliberate and therefore, despite the protest of the Japanese Government, it was not incorporated into the draft Mandates.[2] This procedure is easy to explain and has its roots in purely practical considerations. The C Mandates constitute integral portions of the territory of the Mandatory Power and it is impossible to divide a uniform administrative area into two spheres in which different economic-political systems prevail.[3]

The third part of Article 22 – paragraphs 7 to 9 – contains 'the guarantees' for the execution of the Mandates system: the rights of supervision and examination by the League, in whose name the Mandate is exercised. The contents of this part, as well as the controversial questions connected with it, will constitute the subject of the sixth part of this paper.

4. PRIVATE LAW CONCEPTS AND PRIVATE LAW ANALOGY IN INTERNATIONAL LAW

From the predecessors of Hugo Grotius, who answered questions of international law by reference to Roman law, and from the great founder of international law himself, who used Roman law as the natural law foundation of his system, to the constant struggle between the naturalist and positivist attitude to the newest developments in international law, an important tendency is apparent – a tendency to autarky, to the complete independence of international law, and to its liberation from the influence of private law concepts, analogies and attitudes which govern and impede it in its development as positive law.[4] This tendency

[1] Schücking–Wehberg, *Die Satzung des Völkerbundes. Kommentar*, p. 433.

[2] Cf. Doc. 20/48/161, p. 14 (Hymans' Report); statement of the Japanese Government on the question of the C Mandate (Doc. 20/31/96 F). It is interesting that in the question of the island of Yap, Japan rejected the 'open door' position. Cf. Gregory on the long controversy on this matter, 'The Mandate over Yap', *A.J.* 15 (1921), 419.

[3] Cf. on all C Mandate questions, the drafts for Samoa (20/31/96B), Nauru (20/31/96C), the other German overseas possessions south of the Equator (20/31/96II) and north of the Equator (21/31/14E).

[4] Cf. on this Triepel, *Völkerrecht und Landrecht*, § 8, pp. 211 *et seq.*; Nippold, *Der Völkerrechtliche Vertrag, seine Stellung im Rechtssystem und seine Bedeutung für das internationale Recht* (1894),

has, however, never come to full realization, for what theory with one hand endeavoured to reject as private law, it grasped in modified form with the other; what had been rejected as private law was accepted as 'general legal doctrine', as 'arising from the nature of the matter' or as 'necessary international law'. It was, in particular, Roman law which, as the recognized natural law, repeatedly took possession of the doctrines of international law. Scholars are aware of this wavering and inconsistency. But they have not gone beyond fragmentary or rapid general attempts at the solution of this problem. In particular, they have paid little attention to the fact that there can be an important methodological difference between private law analogy and the various forms of private law formulation of concepts.[1] Nowhere have I, therefore, found a solution to help me in my task.

It is advisable to adduce a few typical examples to show how this problem has been treated in international law. I have chosen Nippold's *Der Völkerrechtliche Vertrag, seine Stellung im Rechtssystem und seine Bedeutung für das internationale Recht* (*The Treaty under International Law, its Position in the System of Law and its Significance for International Law*), a much quoted book, even though it is frequently attacked for self-contradictions and for deviating from prevailing doctrine. Just as in the eighteenth century the struggle against Roman law analogy and concepts was still a struggle of positive against natural law methods, so here Nippold takes up the struggle with 'the weed of natural law, in whatever form and disguise it may appear'. Only positive law, as the embodiment of those norms which have actual validity because they are the declared will of the law-creating authority,[2] only this law is binding also in the realm of international law. This basic attitude is not the only one which causes Nippold – and others too – *inter alia* to declare war on private law in international law. Nippold thinks that as a consequence of the private law attitude, the construction of international law as a law becomes impossible. The strict conceptual separation between the source of law and the contract is typical of private law. 'In private law the norm is something which necessarily lies outside the contract.' This is a conception which, transferred into international law, prevents its being considered as positive law based on treaty as its source. It is these two facts, the need for international law to be 'positive' and the impossibility of constructing international law and the relationships to

§ 5, p. 80; Ruegger, in *Z.I.* 28, 426–502; Neumeyer, 'Ein Beitrag zum internationalen Wasserecht, in the *Festschrift für George Cohn* (1915); Jellinek, *Die rechtliche Natur der Staatsverträge* (1880).

[1] By 'private law analogy' is to be understood here and elsewhere in this paper the (analagous) application in international law of private law legal principles. So here 'private law formulation of concepts' means the application of private law concepts in international law.

[2] Nippold, *Der Völkerrechtliche Vertrag*, p. 18 (also pp. 2, 12, 15 and 19).

be regulated by it on the basis of private law, which produce the theoretical aversion to the process of analogy.

Nippold does not content himself with warning against over-hasty analogy, as do Ernst Meier, Bergbohm, Jellinek and others. Though he is generally against any process of analogy he tries to show, with reference to Jellinek, that many cases of so-called analogy are not a product of this artificial process, but a necessary consequence of the basic legal nature of the relationships to be regulated and the concepts to be used. In comparison with the imposing structure of private law, international law is very incompletely developed. This fact, as well as the absence of a general doctrine of legal positivism, explains why international law constantly 'glances across' to private law thus being deprived of its independence and positiveness. On this basis a plea is later made for a general doctrine of legal positivism, a doctrine which should be the rallying point for the basic legal concepts of all legal systems.[1]

We must now examine this line of thought carefully because it is characteristic of prevailing doctrine. It takes as its starting point Jellinek's proposition that 'analogies from a self-contained legal system must not be advanced as *jus cogens* in a totally different system'.[2] Nonetheless, the concepts and forms of private law are incorporated into international law. How do scholars cope with this difficulty? Nippold and many others declare that these are not forms and concepts belonging exclusively to private law but to general legal doctrine as for instance is the case with agreements.[3] We will revert later to the incompleteness and inherent contradictions of this line of argument. For the time being we shall stick to the proposition quoted from Jellinek as a thoroughly correct one and show that it is robbed of its content by this line of argument.

'Analogies from a self-contained legal system must not be advanced as *jus cogens* in a totally different system.' This remark by Jellinek strongly limiting the application of analogy, assumes particular importance in its application to international law. Nowhere is the need for analogy to fill the *lacunae* so great, even if one, as suggested by Stammler, limits the use of *lacunae* to cases where the existing law is silent on a particular question, and disregards the second category of *lacunae*, i.e. where there is a discrepancy between existing and 'correct' law.[4]

A gap is 'the absence, despite the fact that there is a need for it, of an

[1] Nippold, *Der Völkerrechtliche Vertrag*, pp. 87 *et seq.*

[2] Jellinek, *Die Rechtliche Natur der Staatsverträge*, p. 51.

[3] E.g., Ullmann, *Völkerrecht*, p. 48; Ernst Meier, *Ueber den Abschluss von Staatsverträgen* (1874), p. 34.

[4] Stammler, *Theorie der Rechtswissenschaft*, p. 641.

evaluation, directly executed in positive law, of a legally relevant set of facts with a legal consequence'.[1] This evaluation is achieved by an inference by analogy. Certain legal consequences of a legally regulated premise are stated to be authoritative for a similar premise not regulated in positive law. When are the premises of two legal principles similar? Stammler replies: When the same basic legal concepts can be observed in them in a sort of partial meshing together.[2] When there are three known elements, i.e. the premises and consequences of one legal problem and the premises of a second legal problem, there then can be inferred a fourth element, namely the same legal consequences in both legal considerations. The formula runs: $a+b:f = a+c:x+f$ where a is, according to the first basic concept, of substantially the same nature in both premises.[3] In accepting this model for example, Joerges answers the question whether private law rules can be applied by analogy to public law, in the sense that this is then only permissible where the legal idea having authoritative private law legal consequences is not limited to private law by the character of the legal circumstances.[4]

In principle the question of the application of private law and international law will have to be answered in the same way. Here, however, the circle of possibilities of analogy will have to be drawn very tightly, since these two legal systems, their sources, their subject and object, are so different that 'the decisive factor in private law', when looked at in terms of international law, is nearly always so much affected by 'private law' considerations that it is not relevant to the analogy. It is all the more important to emphasize this assertion since the admissibility of analogy is substantiated on the ground that States in their intercourse with each other are in the same position as individuals under the rule of municipal law.[5] This statement turns up again and again, although experience shows that wherever private law concepts are used in international law, for technical, constructive and other reasons, they undergo a formulation and development that departs almost completely from private law (unless positive international law specifically, in a particular case, provides for conformity with a private law regulation).

International law offers many examples of this process. The development of the concept of territorial supremacy from *dominium* to *imperium*, from a profitable real right under private law in a geographical area to public authority over human beings within that area, is for instance

[1] Joerges, 'Können privatrechtliche Vorschriften analog in öffentlichen Rechte angewendet werden?', in *Zeitschrift für Rechtsphilosophie*, 3, 290.

[2] Stammler, *Theorie der Rechtswissenschaft*, p. 637.

[3] *Ibid.*, pp. 639 *et seq.*

[4] Joerges, in *Zeitschrift für Rechtsphilosophie*, 3, 295.

[5] Triepel, *Völkerrecht und Landrecht*, p. 212; Heilborn, *System*, p. 413.

very instructive for the history of the private law analogy in the theory of international law generally[1] and of the private law concept of property in particular. Even though it lingers on in the doctrine of State servitudes, doctrine seems, by and large, to be dispensing with the concept of *ius in rem*.[2] And even if it sticks by the concept, it rejects the idea of using private law principles to determine public legal relationships. This appears in particular with Clauss.[3] The doctrine of freedom of will and of duress in international law is a clear example of the heterogeneity of the two legal systems. A concept of private law is adopted, but continues still, by a crude fiction, to be maintained within the system, although, as a result of the operation of customary law it is completely divested of its content. Although it is quite clearly realized that to apply analogy here would mean to pursue a natural law philosophy, the concept is retained and applied to State organs.[4] A further example is offered by international law modes of acquisition. Doctrine has followed Hugo Grotius and accepted the modes of acquisition of Roman law, i.e. cession, occupation, accretion, prescription as modes of acquisition in international law, although any analogy seems very doubtful, because of the unlimited validity of the rule in international law 'that to possess is to have the legal right to possess'. These private law modes of acquisition have therefore here lost their legal and have retained only their factual character.[5] However, as far as prescription is concerned, recognition of this point leads to a complete denial of the concept.[6]

Other examples could be given if the narrow scope of this paper permitted. These two were adduced – and this must be reiterated – to show that even where international law runs the risk of civil law analogy by accepting civil law concepts, its own special nature transforms these concepts and even robs them of their content. In practical terms, therefore, there is no analogy.

I have already mentioned that, in answering certain questions of international law, one tries to evade the formal process of analogy by relying on the general doctrine of law. Thus, for instance, Liszt says:[7] '. . . this does not exclude use being made in international law of the rich intellectual structure of private law'. However, this is really a

[1] Heilborn, *System*, § 1; Clauss, *Die Lehre von den Staatsdienstbarkeiten*, p. 135; Ullmann *Völkerrecht*, p. 288.

[2] Liszt, *Das Völkerrecht*, p. 70, n. 8.

[3] Clauss, *Die Lehre von den Staatsdienstbarkeiten*, p. 127.

[4] Cf. F. K. Neubecker, *Zwang und Notstand in rechtsvergleichender Darstellung*, § III, p. 134; Cf also Liszt, Ullmann, Heilborn, Rivier, Heffner, and many others.

[5] Jerusalem, 'Ueber völkerrechtliche Erwerbsgründe', 1911, in the *Festgabe für Augus Thon*, p. 413.

[6] Liszt, *Das Völkerrecht*, p. 156; Ullmann, *Völkerrecht*, p. 309.

[7] *Das Völkerrecht*, p. 38.

matter of drawing on general concepts and principles common to every law. Liszt reverts to the question of general legal doctrine several times (for instance, the conditions and causes of termination of agreements). So, among many others, do Ullmann, Heilborn[1] and Nippold. The latter's opinion in this case also is typical. He knows how to distinguish exactly between private law analogy and general legal doctrine. He even reproves his predecessors, who answer the question of the rôle of duress, mistake, fraud, of the admissible cause and of the rule *pacta sunt servanda* etc. by reference to private law analogy. These, he says, are recognized rules of general legal doctrine.[2]

This procedure must be regarded as mistaken. If 'general legal doctrine' is not to lose its character as an empirical study of all positive legal systems, it must naturally limit itself to the basic questions : what is the nature of law, its formation and its sources ; what are its subject and object ; and finally, how are we to comprehend it ?[3] Thus, in answering other questions, for instance on the law of treaties, by relying on so-called general legal doctrine, a kind of transformation takes place almost unnoticeably. For these questions are answered not on the basis of general legal doctrine but on the basis of the general principles of private law, and still it is thought that private law has been brushed aside. Heilborn, for example, continually refers to general legal doctrine by quoting Savigny, Windscheid and Dernburg. Thus general legal doctrine ceases to be an empirical science of positive law in general and becomes instead the general part of a specific legal system, although it is supposed to disregard 'the subjective formation of concepts and definitions that take place in any particular legal system'.[4] If, therefore, Nippold talks of general principles[5] which cannot be repealed by any positive provision in international law, then on no account are we dealing with general legal doctrine in the sense described above but with private law or with legal philosophy.[6] It should be clear that, just because, for example, treaty law has the doctrines of *pacta sunt servanda* (a 'general' principle) and *rebus sic stantibus*, doctrines which are exactly paralleled in 'the principles of general legal doctrine' governing the denunciation of contracts (principles which include also the rule that non-fulfilment of a contract by one contracting party entitles the other to

[1] Especially in *System*, p. 419.

[2] *Der Völkerrechtliche Vertrag*, pp. 177, 179 and 182. On the other hand, not in the case of *laesio enormis* (p. 189).

[3] *Arnds v Arnesberg, Juristische Enzyklopädie und Methodologie* (8th ed.), pp. 10, 12 and 19; Merkel, *Juristische Enzyklopädie*.

[4] Ignatz Kornfeld, *Allgemeine Rechtslehre und Jurisprudenz*, § 1.

[5] *Der Völkerrechtliche Vertrag*, p. 168.

[6] This sort of mixing of the two disciplines is found for example in Merkel, 'Ueber das Verhaltnis der Rechtsphilosophie zur "positiven" Rechtswissenschaft', *Collected Papers*, II, 308.

withdraw from it), there is no such thing as 'general legal doctrine' to be relied upon.[1]

We have seen that the procedure described brings about two evils: (*a*) it destroys the concept of 'general legal doctrine', by turning it into legal philosophy or into an ideal 'law of law'; (*b*) it reintroduces by a roundabout route private law analogy which endangers the independence of international law and fails to recognize its peculiarity. In considering generally the rôle of private law in international law, it is necessary to lay emphasis on this less appreciated point.

Private law formulation of concepts as a matter of legal construction has to be distinguished from private law analogy. While I have rejected the latter in any shape or form, in conformity with doctrinal tendencies, it is necessary with the private law formulation of concepts in international law to make a distinction, which seems to be important for the solution of the whole question. For private law formulation of concepts flows from a double source: it is either a product of the learned work of international lawyers, juristic construction, or of positive international law, a treaty-regulated rule. This twofold mode of origin is of such great importance that it has to be closely examined here.

The transfer of private law concepts to international law by way of (let us not hesitate to say it) subsequent construction[2] takes place as follows. Rules governing inter-State relationships, which are in fact laid down by treaty or custom are, for the sake of order and categorization and for easier understanding and interpretation, attributed *ex post facto* to an already existing and well-developed private law concept. The search for legal harmony, which constitutes the real purpose of legal definition, here transgresses the boundaries of one legal system and seeks points of contact in another. To obtain an insight into their true nature, it is useful now to give a few examples of this kind of private law formulation of concepts. In the Vienna Treaty of 30 October 1864 the Duchy of Schleswig was ceded to the Emperor of Austria and the King of Prussia to hold in common. After the former had renounced his rights in this connection to the latter, under Article v of the Peace of Prague, Prussia in a clause annexed to the Article in question undertook to restore the northern districts of Schleswig to Denmark should its population opt for union in a free plebiscite.[3] This clause is now

[1] Bruno Schmidt, for example, indicates a methodologically correct way ('Ueber die völkerrechtliche *clausula rebus sic stantibus* sowie einige verwandte Völkerrechtsnormen', in *Staats- und völkerrechtlichen Abhandlungen*, 6, no. 1, 1–4, 201, 210, 226). Starting from the special question of international law he reaches results important for general legal doctrine. The upside-down, incorrect procedure lies in the fact that one seeks in general legal doctrine the source material for individual legal rules.

[2] A juristic construction, cf. Stammler, *Theorie der Rechtswissenschaft*, pp. 336–63.

[3] Schmidt, *Der schwedisch-mecklenburgische Pfandvertrag über Stadt und Herrschaft Wismar*, p. 5.

construed, on the basis of private law, as a so-called 'treaty in favour of a third party'. As it is of a purely formal character, such a construction would be permissible if it did not contain a far reaching private law analogy. But the civil law contract in favour of a third party has a specific significance: the third party has a claim arising directly out of the contract – something which writers on international law resolutely refuse to accept.[1] State servitudes are another example. They are the result of legal formulation subsequent to a treaty. In the treaty texts this expression is regularly avoided and it is therefore always left to interpretation to determine whether an obligatory legal relationship or a State servitude is involved.[2] The inherent weakness of this procedure is shown, incidentally, by the fact that the whole institution is rejected by a considerable number of authors as being incompatible with the principles of international law.[3] A further example related to the last is offered by the development of the *nudum jus*, which was established in connection with – or to put it more correctly in opposition to – the well-known concept of 'concealed cession'.[4] Despite the great authority of its originators this development, derived from private law (the servitude), is also rejected by many authors on account of the peculiar structure of international law where the usufructuary lives forever.[5]

These examples may suffice for the time being to establish that this method of concept formulation is not essentially different from private law analogy. Even though, in origin, it is a question purely of form, it leads easily to analogy in substance. Thus the method ceases, as Stammler points out, to be exclusively imitative but results in the formation of a legal rule different in substance from that which it wished, lock, stock and barrel to embrace. The differences between legal systems are disregarded and the fact forgotten that legal institutions must be construed within the context of their own legal systems. This kind of reasoning is therefore to be rejected – it stands in contradiction, not only to the positive nature of international law, but also to the nature and functions of legal construction.

The position is, however, quite different where positive international treaty law itself undertakes the legal evaluation and construction, where it speaks itself of an agreement for purchase, lease or pledge, or of a servitude, or of a mandate, etc. Here we deal with the case where international law enriches itself directly (and, one would like to say,

[1] Heffter-Geffcken, *Europaisches Völkerrecht.*

[2] Clauss, *Die Lehre von den Staatsdienstbarkeiten*, p. 197.

[3] Liszt, *Das Völkerrecht*, p. 70, n. 8.

[4] Jellinek, *Die Staatenverbindungen*, p. 53; Bluntschli, 'Le congrès de Berlin', *R.I.* 13, 585.

[5] B. Krunsky, *L'Annexion de la Bosnie et de L'Herzégovine en 1908*, p. 49; in part, Liszt, *Das Völkerrecht*, p. 92.

authentically) from private law. The process here is clear. Positive international law itself adopts concepts and institutions which have already specific implications in one or more legal systems. It adopts them explicitly, and thus by 'the transfer of particular rules of private law in a naive manner a new general category of international law is created'.[1]

A few examples will make this process clear. In 1803 the City and Domain of Wismar were, by the Treaty of Malmo, transferred to Mecklenburg-Schwerin by their previous owner, Sweden, as a pledge in real security for the grant of a loan of 1,250,000 Reichsthaler. The modalities of interest, and the time and conditions of the eventual redemption were laid down exactly. It was a typical mortgage-deed.[2] The legal facts are unequivocal. Positive law has decided the construction and equated the completed legal transaction to one which is exactly defined in private law. The function of interpretation is quite precisely limited in this case; it has always to operate within the specific mortgage-deed. Consequently the private law concept is not forced upon international law from outside; there is no question of analogy.

Another example: the so-called territorial leases of the last decade of the nineteenth century have attracted general attention. A similar case gave occasion to Jellinek and others for theoretical consideration of this question.[3] This was the German–Chinese Treaty of 6 March 1898. In this treaty China ceded to Germany 'on lease, provisionally for 99 years, both sides of the entrance to the Bay of Kiautshou'. In order to avoid conflict, China renounced the exercise of sovereign rights in the leased area for the duration of the lease and left their exercise to Germany. Under Article 5 Germany undertook never to sub-lease this area to another power. Provisions (e.g. in respect of the repayment of expenditure) were laid down in case of termination of the lease. In this and all similar cases, the legal principle behind the transaction has been pronounced upon by positive international law itself in close reliance on a private law relationship. Here in particular – as Jellinek points out – an institution developed within a specific legal system (the English 'lease') was of decisive relevance. In this case, too, there can be no question of analogy. Article 22 of the Covenant of the League of Nations provides for the transfer of the exercise of sovereign rights over areas which 'as a consequence of the war have ceased to be under the sovereignty of the States which formerly governed them' to individual

[1] Jellinek, 'Die Staats- und völkerrechtliche Stellung Kiautschous', *Deutsche Juristenzeitung* (1898), p. 254.

[2] According to Schmidt, *Der schwedisch-mecklenburgische Pfandvertrag*, p. 13.

[3] In *Deutsche Juristenzeitung*, p. 253. Gerard gives a more precise summary of these leases: *Des sessions déguisées de territoires en droit international public*, pp. 255, 259, 280 and 312.

States who are to exercise their sovereign rights to a more or less limited extent as Mandatories on behalf of the League. Here too a concept of Roman law, accepted by all systems of private law, is raised to an institution of international law. The Mandate under international law, as expressed in Article 22, is therefore now a formulation of the jurisprudence of international law. It is a positive creation of law.

The great relevance of this and similar cases for the development of international law has been, in part deliberately, ignored by the literature.[1] In complete disregard of the fact that the legal character of the new legal institution has been definitively and authentically fixed, some writers have tried, by unnecessary and impermissible interpretation, to improve upon the formulation set out in the source of law, i.e. the relevant treaties. Thus, for instance, the lease agreements mentioned were construed as a veiled form of derivative acquisition; they were conceived as sham transactions, in which the need to consider the covetousness of other powers, the sensitivity of the lessor State and other reasons 'pour sauver la face' were said to have dictated their ostensible form. A compulsory lease agreement, a duty legally imposed on the victim incapacitated by a war, was considered as a cession; and the law as laid down was corrected by an interpretation guided by dubious political considerations. Thus some of the literature in international law has completely closed its mind to the significance and understanding of this new concept by making so bold as to apply to the object of its research a standard other than a purely legal one.[2]

This procedure, which made itself felt in deliberations on the legal character of the 'occupation and administration' of Bosnia and Herzogovina by Austria–Hungary in 1878 and the occupation of Cyprus by England in the same year, has not remained uncontradicted. In addition to the positive efforts of Jellinek, Ullmann for instance has with desirable clarity opposed this point of view. He emphasizes that in all these cases the practical significance and the political purpose cannot be decisive

[1] Liszt, *Das Völkerrecht*, p. 93 and n. 16; Rivier, *Lehrbuch des Völkerrechtes*, p. 151; De Louter, p. 368. Here also the idea of the concealed cession is defended – ostensibly because such a juristic structure 'conduisent parmi les practiciens du droit international aux idées et aux déductions les plus contradictoires' (p. 371). Certainly it is very easy with the 'concealed cession' to cut this Gordian knot. However, the correctness of a solution is not established by its clarity alone.

[2] Cf. Martin, 'Zum deutschfranzösischen Kamerun-Abkommen', *Deutsche Juristenzeitung*, 18, 917. Here a sharp position is taken against the process described. 'Die Scheingeschfte haben die Eigentümlichkeit, das der unbefangene Dritte ihnen nicht ansehen kann und soll, das sie Scheingeschäfte sind. Wer also von einem völkerrechtlichen Pachtvertrag behauptet, er sei ein Scheinvertrag, weis offenbar mehr, als er nach dem Wunsche der Vertragsparteien eigentlich wissen sollte.' Schonborn partly agrees: 'Der deutsch-französische Pachtvertrag auf Grund des Kamerun-Abkommens von 1911. Zugleich ein Beitrag zur Lehre vom völkerrechtlichen Pachtvertrag überhaupt.' *Z.V.* 8.

for evaluating their legal character. The type of private law contract and its consequences cannot be ignored.[1]

The principle of the positiveness of international law requires that the factual contents of its provisions must not be undermined. If international law adopts a private law institution and if it goes so far as to adopt also the technical term, then one is dealing with the clear will of the 'legislator' which does not require any further interpretation. The importance and significance of this procedure is in no way prejudiced by the fact that it is sometimes unclear which specific system of private law is to be applied. This difficulty is of a secondary nature and can be resolved. Private international law has taken the lead on this point[1] and the doctrine of interpretation is no longer confronted helplessly with this problem. Often treaties dispense with the need for a decision of this sort by expressly taking the private law concept in question from a specific legal system, or by defining it themselves. This applies mainly in respect of Roman law concepts. This idea is for instance expressed thus by Paul Ruegger: 'A definition of the adopted legal provisions is not required, as they are known and treated as of Roman law origin in all anguage districts. An agreement, by appropriating concepts of Roman law, implicitly leaves their interpretation to Roman law.'[2] This is quite correct. Let me mention only for the sake of completeness that, even though the quotation applies only to those private law concepts which regulate private law relationships, there is no reason to create different rules of interpretation for 'public' international law.[3]

Let me now briefly recapitulate the conclusions of this section. I have rejected the idea of private law analogy in any form and I have referred to the roundabout ways by which the theory – against its own logic – slips back into the tabooed procedure. As against this I have pointed out cases in which the development of concepts in private law terms even though strongly reminiscent of certain kinds of private law analogy, is still in reality a positive disposition of international law. This is of decisive importance for the subject to be dealt with here.

5. THE BASIC PROBLEMS OF THE MANDATES SYSTEM

Only on the basis of the results reached in the preceding section are we in a position to embark upon the basic problems of the Mandates system. I have drawn a firm distinction between private law analogy and the application of rules of international law which are taken from

[1] *Völkerrecht*, p. 297.
[2] Ruegger, *Z.I.* 28, paras. 5 and 6.
[3] *Ibid.* p. 478.

private law by way of positive legal enactment. This result now has decisive importance.

1. *The legal character of the Mandate in international law*

In Article 22 international law adopts an institution which originated and was fully developed in Roman law, and which entered into modern legislation by way of the *gemeine Recht*.[1] However, this was not the end of the matter. Individual legal systems have considerably modified the institution, or have substantially limited its range of application, as a result of the development of similar institutions.[2] In Roman law the mandate was originally a legal transaction entered into in good faith and based on friendship, in which one contracting party at the behest of another undertook to carry out legal or practical business. Originally directed only to the interest of the mandator, it gradually developed to include various combinations of the formula *mea, tua et aliena gratia*; its strictly gratuitous character was preserved to the end, although there were exceptions in the *extraordinaria cognitio*. In European legislation the mandate has, as I have said, undergone various modifications.[3] Its gratuitous nature, for instance, which still constituted an essential of the contract under old French law, has, in the *Code civil* (§1986) given way to the provision that 'the mandate is gratuitous, unless a provision to the contrary has been made'. Under §1004 of the *abGB*, for instance, consideration for the mandate has almost become a rule. Furthermore, in French law the mandate contract has been limited to acts of a legal nature only. In England, even though the concept of the mandate as non-gratuitous was early recognized through the doctrine of consideration, the significance of this institution was reduced by the development of the law of 'agency' and of 'trust'.[4]

We see therefore that legal systems differ. The question is: to which private law system are we to look for guidance? Ruegger's opinion mentioned above (that an agreement, by adopting concepts of Roman law, implicitly leaves their interpretation to Roman law) cannot in this case be approved without qualification, for the development has here in some respects gone quite a way beyond Roman law. The theory of the mandate in international law has to adjust itself to these modifications; an easy task, if one considers that the changes are not many and do not

[1] *Translator's note: Gemeine Recht* is the Roman-based common law of the German Empire as it was before codification.

[2] An attempt at a comparison of the Roman mandate with the international Mandate is made by Professor Goudy, 'On mandatory government in the law of nations', *J.C.L.* 3rd series, 1, 175. He also warns against an uncritical analogy with private law (p. 182).

[3] Goudy, in *J.C.L.* 1, 179; Campbell-Lee, *The Mandate for Mesopotomia*, p. 12; Rolin, in *R.I.* (1920), p. 334; Holtzendorf, *Enzyklopädie der Rechtswissenschaft*, 2, 703.

[4] Goudy, in *J.C.L.* 1.

differ much in the individual systems of private law. The essence of the mandate has been maintained in all private law systems and this essence has to be considered constantly if one is not to do violence to positive law.[1]

On the other hand, however, it has been emphasized that it is not private law alone which has adopted this legal institution, and private law, therefore, is not by itself decisive for its interpretation. Thus Rolin, for instance, points out that in commercial law and in public law (in the electoral system of delegation) the mandate has undergone a far-reaching development and transformation.[2] In view of this, it is necessary to state that when the word 'mandate' appears one is not always dealing with a specifically private law institution. In Rome itself this word served in Imperial times to denote the Emperor's order to the provincial governors. One should also consider the use of this term in the old English court procedure, in canon law, in the appeals procedure of the United States, in the Austrian criminal procedure and in administrative law.[3] In all these cases it is immediately evident that there is no contractual relationship in a mandate; the word 'mandate' is meant to indicate the unilateral will of a superior – a relationship which is fundamentally different from the contractual mandate of private law. Only where the characteristic of contract, of agreement is present, can one trace the legal institution back to a private law origin. This is the case, for instance, in commercial law which adopts this type of contract – although without taking over the terminology. Here we also have evidence for the nature of such adoption. Let us look at the commission business (*Kommissionsgeschaft*). There can be no doubt that in its legal core it is 'a kind of special contractual "mandate"'. This fact did not prevent commercial law developing and altering it; thus the characteristic of reward, an incidental feature of the civil law mandate, becomes an essential one in commission transactions. 'It is not presumed to be gratuitous without a specific agreement so providing. In this respect the opposite rule from the civil law mandate applies.'[4] Thus the adopted forms of private law are amended by positive provisions where the requirements of intercourse and the peculiarity of the adopting law so demand. But otherwise the rule applies in commercial law – just as the contract of commission is subject to the principles of the mandate – that 'concepts of this kind, which, even though they are peculiar to commercial law, are but adaptations of a more general

[1] Only with their reservation can Ruegger's opinion, quoted above, on the value of Roman concepts be accepted.

[2] In *R.I.* (1920), p. 333.

[3] Cf. also Campbell-Lee, *The Mandate for Mesopotomia*, p. 9.

[4] *Handbuch des deutschen Handels-See- und Wasserrechtes* (1885), III, 163.

institution developed in civil law, are subject to the rules of this specific concept as well as to the general rules of civil law, insofar as this is not contrary to their manifest character'.[1]

Without disregarding either the great difference which exists between the relationship to one another of two areas of municipal law or the relationship of international law to concepts developed in the municipal legal system, the above rule has to be applied *mutatis mutandis* when private law concepts are taken into international law. It is of a purely legal-logical character and arises from the general rules of interpretation of technical terms.[2] It is for international law to determine whether it will adopt the private law mandate. It is also entirely for international law to determine whether to amend or abolish the individual provisions of the institution when adopted. If, however, it does not do so, the matter rests with the basic concepts and basic provisions of the accepted legal rule. Thus we came to the following result: The Mandate in international law, under Article 22, is comparable to the legal concept of the private law mandate, whose principles are overriding insofar as they have not been amended or abolished by this same Article, by the Covenant of the League of Nations, by the relevant Peace Treaties or by other agreements concluded between the contracting parties.

Again, depending closely on the wording of the Covenant of the League of Nations, attempts have been made to derive the Mandates system from a different source and thus to construe it in a different manner. It has been maintained that it was not the concept of the mandate, as originated and developed on the continent, which lay behind the international law institution, but the English concept of the 'trust'.[3] This conception of the Mandates system is all the more important in that it is not only a privately held English view. It appears that the Government of the United States too is not averse to such a concept.[4] The institution of 'trust' was the first to which the law of equity came to apply and it has lost nothing in importance over the centuries. Indeed, it still remains one of the most widespread institutions of English law. However, it seems to me very questionable to take this institution, which constitutes a sort of combination of mandate and deposit of property for the purpose of guardianship, as a basis for the mandate in international law.[5] The words 'sacred trust' and 'this trust' in Article 22 paragraph 1, obviously have no legal character and

[1] Goldschmidt, *Handbuch des Völkerrechtes*, para. 37.

[2] Ullmann, *Völkerrecht*, p. 282.

[3] 'This dominion will be wholly misconceived, not to say abused, if there is even the slightest deviation from the spirit and the exclusive purpose of a trusteeship as strict as it is comprehensive' (from the letters of the U.S. Secretary of State to Lord Curzon, Misc. no. 10 (1921)).

[4] Campbell-Lee, *The Mandate for Mesopotamia*, p. 13.

[5] Similarly Goudy, in *J.C.L.* 1, 177.

as with the word 'tutelage' serve only to indicate the purpose of the system. Nor are they repeated in Article 22, while the word 'Mandate' and, in particular, 'Mandatory' appears in every paragraph. Smuts also couched his proposals in the legal form of the 'mandate' or 'agency', while the word 'trust' is only used in phrases like 'a great trust and honour' or 'prolonged abuse of this trust'.[1] The word is also missing from Wilson's 10 January 1919 draft for the League of Nations,[2] while the words 'agent', 'agency', 'mandatory' are used interchangeably. The word 'trustee', however, appears, though only in application to the League of Nations. These are not the only reasons why the 'trust'-interpretation must be rejected. This English relationship of trust is based on the strict principle of absence of consideration and of unselfishness of the trustee.[3] It is exaggerated and unnecessary enthusiasm to force a relationship under international law into such a frame. But it should not be denied that certain peculiarities of the 'trust' (for instance, that the trustee, as far as the donor is concerned, is unable to revoke the trust, or that he is the legal owner of the property, the beneficiary having only an equitable ownership) could be of relevance for an understanding of the Mandates system.

For these reasons and the ones indicated in the preceding section I also have to reject the interpretation of mandates as State servitudes, a theory mentioned by Rolin but only partly adopted by him.[4] This is not because I reject the broad concept of the State servitude 'as a continuous and general limitation of sovereignty as against another State',[5] nor because I want to lend validity to the principle *servitus in faciendo consistere nequit*, nor because I consider the premise for such an interpretation namely, the sovereignty of the Mandatory – as wrong, although all these reasons certainly have to be considered. For me the one decisive fact is that the concept one is seeking to establish has already been unequivocally and clearly set forth in Article 22.

For the same reason, I have to reject the interpretation which conceives the Mandates system as an open or veiled cession or annexation. Though in substance incorrect,[6] such a procedure was, for instance, from the point of view of methodology, permissible in the case of

[1] Smuts, *The League of Nations*, p. 21.

[2] Lansing, *Peace Negotiations*, appendix I. The President's original draft of the Covenant of the League of Nations, laid before the American Commission on 10 January 1919, p. 262.

[3] Karplus, *Handbuch des englischen privatrechtes*, § 1; Birrell, *The Duties and Liabilities of Trustees* (1920).

[4] Rolin, in *R.I.* (1920), p. 350.

[5] Clauss, *Die Lehre von den Staatsdienstbarkeiten*, p. 133.

[6] Gérard, *Des sessions déguisées*, p. 313, § 7; Liszt, *Das Völkerrecht*, p. 92; Blociszewski, 'L'Annexation de la Bosnie et de l'Herzegovine', *R.G.* 17, 432. Certainly 'annexation' as a basis of construction of the Berlin Treaty was here first rejected and instead the description 'occupation of unlimited duration' was chosen; but a few pages later this unlimited occupation was described as a fiction which was removed by the successful annexation of 1908.

Bosnia-Herzegovina or Cyprus. There the treaty, as Stammler points out, did not base the legal transaction in question on a fundamental principle of law. It was thus impossible for academic research, confronted with a completely new situation in international law, to resist interpretations and constructions which pursued a merely political purpose.[1] But here not only has the will of the contracting parties been clearly expressed by defining itself in legal terms; it has also disposed in part of the academic problem. Thus, on these technical grounds alone, we can abstain from proving the incorrectness of this interpretation on individual points. Incidentally, I shall still have to cope with it when considering the question of sovereignty.

2. *Sovereignty over the Mandated territories*

This question is not simply of theoretical interest, as Hymans seems to believe in his report.[2] Nor is it of purely practical significance for the solution of the various problems raised by the Mandates system. It is the problem which lies at the very heart of the Mandates system and is thus of decisive political significance.

Here, too, opinions are strongly opposed to one another. According to one, sovereignty over the Mandated territories lies in the Mandatory; according to another, it lies with the League of Nations. I am not going to consider here other solutions to the problem, for instance, the suggestion that sovereignty is divided between the Mandatory and the League of Nations, or, in the case of the A group of Mandates, that external sovereignty lies with the Mandatory State and internal sovereignty with the autonomous national Government, or, that sovereignty remains 'in suspense' until these areas have achieved full independence.[3]

The theoretical impossibility of these suggestions is immediately evident. According to the first theory,[4] the Mandatory is entitled to sovereignty over the Mandated territories. This is particularly so in the case of the B and C group. The term 'Mandate' is given a completely new and peculiar significance, which is compatible with the complete annexation of the Mandated territory and to which none of the provisions of the mandate under civil law can be applied. It is morally and conventionally only a polite linguistic recognition of the noble ideas of the President of the United States. This applies in particular to the C group, where, after all, it is expressly provided that they 'can be best administered under the laws of the Mandatory as integral portions of

[1] Linguistic usage has also here brought about a 'construction' by spreading the use of the word 'mandate'. [2] Doc. 20/48/161, p. 17.

[3] Campbell-Lee, *The Mandate for Mesopotamia*, p. 19.

[4] Rolin, in *R.I.* (1920), pp. 335, 338–53.

its territory'. This is a straightforward annexation. It is true that this provision is not to be found in the case of the B Mandates, but there is no reason not to extend it to the B group, because the concept of the 'Mandate' under Article 22 is not based on civil law and therefore does not exclude annexation. Besides it is impossible to attribute sovereignty to the League of Nations which has no personality distinct from that of its Members and also because it has no means of exercising sovereignty. I have set out this line of argument at length, in order to show how difficult it is in individual cases to discriminate precisely between the political and the strictly legal approach. A refutation of this reasoning can be found in the general considerations covered in this and the preceding sections. The C Mandates will be dealt with in more detail in section 3.

However, there is a line of thought in the argument that deserves attention. This is the consideration that it is not the Mandated territories and the sum of the sovereign rights appertaining to them which are the object of the Mandate, but only the exercise of tutelage over the peoples of the Mandated territories in accordance with the provisions of Article 22 paragraphs 4, 5 and 6. In paragraph 2 the wording runs: '. . . this tutelage should be exercised by them as Mandatories on behalf of the League'. It would not be possible simply to ignore objections arising on this count, which would see the individual Mandate provisions as a condition imposed by international law on the occasion of a division or cession of territory. Nevertheless, these objections stand in contradiction to the contents of the Article as a whole, as well as of its spirit and the expressed intentions of the Mandate's creators, which must be relied on as aids to interpretation.[1] Article 22 regulates the entirety of the Mandated territories. In paragraph 1 it speaks of the position of these territories in international law hitherto (under the sovereignty of the vanquished powers) and contrasts it with their new position under the Mandates system. It thereby differs basically from previous treaties, which dealt only with the question of the colonial peoples at individual points, for instance, the General Act of the Berlin Congress of 1885 and the Brussels Anti-Slavery Acts of 1890. It appears from the Wilson draft of 10 January 1919 that the individual provisions of paragraphs 4–6 were intended only as an enumeration of individual and particularly important rules. There it says: '. . . the League of Nations shall be regarded as the residuary trustee with sovereign right of ultimate disposal or of continued administration in accordance with certain fundamental principles hereinafter set forth; and this reversion and control shall exclude all rights or privileges of annexation on the

[1] Cf. Schücking–Wehberg, *Die Satzung des Völkerbundes. Kommentar*, p. 423.

part of any power'; or: 'Any authority control, or administration which might be necessary in respect of these peoples or territories . . . shall be the exclusive function of and shall be vested in the League of Nations and exercised or undertaken by or on behalf of it.' Article 22 covers the same ground, although in a deliberately obscure and blurred language, which nonetheless escapes total incomprehensibility. If, for example, paragraph 6 for various reasons permits the C Mandates to be administered 'under the laws of the Mandatory as integral portions of its territory', there is nothing here incompatible with paragraph 1. In the case of the C areas there are administrative and other practical reasons which, while not denying the Mandate principle, require the Mandated territory to be more closely connected with the territory of the Mandatory.[1] The other types of Mandated territory do not constitute part of the territory of the Mandatory Power. In view of this it may be pointed out here that the purpose of the Mandate is tutelage, not in the sense of a limitation of the acknowledged sovereignty of the Mandatories, but as the exercise, on behalf of the League of Nations, of some sovereign rights over the Mandated territory and its population.

Therefore sovereignty lies with the League of Nations and is derived from it. This assertion is based, however, only on legal-logical reasoning. An explicit and formal transfer of sovereign rights to the League of Nations can not be found either in the Covenant of the League of Nations or in the Peace Treaties. By virtue of Article 119 of the Treaty of Versailles sovereignty over the German overseas possessions is transferred to the Allied and Associated Powers. Between this Article and Article 22 there is a gap which can be filled only by assuming a tacit transfer by the Principal Powers to the League of Nations.[2] From this tacit transfer the League of Nations derives its legal title to sovereignty.

In this context it is necessary to deal briefly with the question of the legal title of the Mandatory, for the reason that it is often and without justification regarded as decisive for the question of sovereignty.[3] In his well-known report, Hymans lays stress on circumscribing exactly the Mandatory's legal title. Basing himself on the fact that, on one hand, the Principal Powers grant the Mandate and that, on the other, it is exercised on behalf of the League of Nations, he states that the legal title is twofold because it originates both from the League of Nations

[1] Lansing, *Peace Negotiations*, appendix, p. 263; Smuts, *The League of Nations*, p. 22; Scelle, *Le Pacte des Nations*, p. 197.

[2] Rolin would fill this gap by depriving Article 22 of all its specific legal content and reducing the whole Mandates system to the reporting obligation of the Mandatory (in *R.I.* (1920), p. 343).

[3] Bileski, in *Z.V.* 12, 67; Schücking–Wehberg, *Die Satzung des Völkerbundes. Kommentar*, p. 426.

and from the Principal Powers.[1] Anticipating later argument, I would note here that this statement is correct, but that it is not of any importance for the question of sovereignty. The valid title is the legal cause appropriate for the acquisition of a right;[2] but it has, as it were, only a law-creating and not a law-maintaining effect. The Principal Powers distribute the Mandated territories, choose the Mandatory and have a decisive influence in determining the conditions of the Mandate. By these acts their right is, however, consumed; they no longer retain any part of the sovereignty.

Only the League of Nations is sovereign, and this by virtue of the fact that the Mandated territories are administered under its authority and on its behalf. This sovereignty is not, of course, impaired by the fact that its exercise is delegated to the Mandatory Powers. It could theoretically exist simply by virtue of the wording of the second paragraph of Article 22, even if there were not far-reaching conditions and limitations on the Mandatory Power.[3] These limitations are, however, so great (considering the provisions of paragraphs 4, 5 and 6, particularly in respect of military powers, the obligation of the Mandatory to render reports, the right of every League Member, as expressed in the Mandate provisions, to bring the Mandatory State before the Permanent Court of International Justice for non-fulfilment of the Mandate obligations, etc.) that the idea of the *nudum jus*, which has become so popular, has no place here.

3. *The nomination and removal of the Mandatory*

With this question, which we have already had to answer in anticipation when dealing with the problem of sovereignty, we come to the heart of one of the most disputed points of the Mandates system. While Smuts and Wilson dealt with the problem unequivocally (by providing that 'it shall be lawful for the League of Nations to delegate its authority, control, or administration of any such people or territory to some single state or organized agency which it may designate and appoint as its agent or Mandatory'),[4] the diplomatic negotiations as reflected in Article 22 produced silence. Before academics got down to work on the question, before the League of Nations was offered an opportunity to express an opinion, before even the Peace Treaty was signed, the Principal Powers, in their decision of 7 May 1919, proceeded with the distribution of the Mandated territories.[5] Did this process, as is asserted

[1] Doc. 20/48/161, p. 14.

[2] Paragraph 316 of the Austrian Civil Code.

[3] On the limits of restrictions on sovereignty, see Jellinek, *Die Lehre von den Staatenverbindungen*.

[4] Lansing, *Peace Negotiations*, p. 263; similarly Smuts, *The League of Nations*, p. 21.

[5] Doc. 20/48/161, p. 7.

on the German side, do violence to the Peace Treaty or strictly carry it out?

The latter view is advocated by Hymans in his report.[1] That is, the gap, created at this point by the silence of Article 22, is completely filled, first, by Article 119 of the Peace Treaty of Versailles, in which Germany renounces, in favour of the Principal Allied and Associated Powers, all her rights and titles over her overseas possessions and, second, by Article 118(b) of the same treaty, in which Germany undertakes to recognize and conform to the measures which may be taken by these Powers in order to carry the consequences of that renunciation into effect. Thus the Principal Powers have the right to nominate the Mandatories. In applying the earlier mentioned rule of the twofold legal title, Hymans recommends the following procedure:

(1) the Principal Allied and Associated Powers grant a Mandate to one of them or to a third power;

(2) the Principal Powers officially notify the Council that a particular Power has been appointed Mandatory of a specific territory;

(3) the Council of the League of Nations takes official cognizance of the appointment of the Mandatory Power; notifies the Mandatory that the Council considers it as vested with a Mandate; and informs the Mandatory of the conditions of the Mandate, after having checked that these conform with the provisions of the Covenant.

So much for the report to the Council, which actually became decisive for the practice of the League of Nations. The English and French Governments have repeatedly and quite resolutely rejected the view that the League of Nations is entitled to appoint the Mandatories.[2] This opinion is shared by Rolin in his article which has been quoted many times in this paper.

The German Government and German commentators on the Covenant start from the simple assumption that only the true Mandator can appoint the Mandatory. As Article 22 in no way whatsoever relieves the League of Nations of this duty, any other procedure is impermissible and illegal.[3]

A short consideration leads to the conclusion that this last point of view is untenable. Neither the sovereignty of the League of Nations nor

[1] Doc. 20/48/161, p. 14.

[2] The English Prime Minister said in the House of Commons on 23 June 1920: 'I repudiate entirely the suggestion that it is for the League of Nations to determine who shall be the Mandatories of these countries.' Similarly, Lord Curzon on 25 June 1920: 'It is quite a mistake to suppose ... that under the Covenant of the League, or under any instruction, the gift of the Mandate rests with the League of Nations. It does not do so. It rests with the powers who have conquered the territories which it falls to them to distribute.' (Cited in Ormsby-Gore, *The Covenant* (1920), p. 486.)

[3] The German Government memorandum to the First Assembly, Doc. 106; Schücking-Wehberg, *Die Satzung des Völkerbundes. Kommentar*, p. 426; Bileski, in *Z.V.* 12.

the nature of the Mandate require that the Mandatory should be appointed by the Mandator to hold permanent rights of sovereignty. Just as in a purchase the contracting parties can decide to transfer the right to determine the price of the purchase or other conditions to a third party, so it is easily conceivable that the Mandator, while reserving to himself the other Mandatory rights of authority, transfers the right of nominating the Mandatory to a third party. The connection which has to be made between Articles 118(b) and 119 of the Treaty of Versailles and Article 22 can mean only that the Principal Powers are limited in their rights of disposition of the Mandated territories. Are they however so far limited in this right that without any more ado they are bound to transfer sovereignty to the League of Nations? Apparently not, because otherwise Article 118(b) would have no meaning – at east in respect of the colonies.[1] But in interpreting the Treaty one must seek not to deprive any part of it of its content. In this case the Principal Powers are limited only in three respects: (*a*) by the sovereignty of the League of Nations, which is enacted in Article 22; (*b*) by the nature of the Mandate; (*c*) by the individual provisions of Article 22. Otherwise they can avail themselves of their right of disposition at discretion. And they actually do so. They transfer their sovereign rights to the League of Nations on the condition that they themselves choose the Mandatory, that they themselves determine the Mandate clauses etc. This condition, as has been mentioned, is not incompatible with the concept of the Mandate; it is also clear that its operation does not impair the sovereignty of the League of Nations; nor does it violate the provisions of Article 22. The right of appointment of the Mandatory lies with the Allied and Associated Powers, not with the League of Nations.

The question of the dismissal of the Mandatory is for the time being a purely theoretical one. Nevertheless, here too, opinions are completely divergent. On the one hand, the Mandate is said to be irrevocable; on the other, the League of Nations is said to have the right at any time to substitute one Mandatory Power for another. Article 22 contains no elucidation of this controversial matter. The draft Mandates and the already confirmed C Mandates contain no provisions on this point. The most obvious answer, considering the sovereignty of the League of Nations and the nature of the Mandate, would be to recognize the possibility of revocation in principle.[2] In private law an irrevocable

[1] Schücking–Wehberg (*Die Satzung des Völkerbundes. Kommentar*, p. 427) puts forward the view that Article 118, para. 2, 'certainly has a meaning if one does not think at all of territorial separation'. Certainly, this Article contains a part of the meaning also in this case – but is it not rather arbitrary simply to 'think away' the rest of the content?

[2] To this effect, see Schücking–Wehberg, p. 426 and Bileski, in *Z.V.* 12, 81.

authority is impermissible.[1] This would have to be so even without a positive provision to that effect, because it is in logical contradiction to the nature of authority. The same thing applies to the Mandate in international law. But there is here, as in private law, the possibility of a limited waiver of the right to revoke. This waiver is expressed tacitly by the contractual determination of the duration of the Mandate relationship. The duration of the Mandate is circumscribed in Article 22 not by a time provision, but by its purpose. It is a question of tutelage over 'peoples not yet able to stand by themselves under the strenuous conditions of the modern world'. Paragraph 4 regulating the A Mandates contains even more articulate language: 'the rendering of administrative advice and assistance by a Mandatory until such time as they are able to stand alone'. The Mandate of Article 22 is accordingly not totally irrevocable, particularly if one thinks of it as belonging to the type of *mandatum mea, tua et aliena gratia*. Naturally for the distant future a forum will need to be established with the right to pronounce that the Mandate (after fulfilling its task) is herewith terminated. This forum could be either the League Assembly or the Permanent Court of International Justice. It is also to be presumed that in the case of an established non-fulfilment (under the draft Mandates this would be within the competence of the Permanent Court of International Justice), the Mandate can be revoked by the League. This eventuality (even though theoretically acceptable) is of little practical importance in view of the requirement that decisions of the Council and the League Assembly[2] be unanimous.

4. *Determination and amendment of the terms of the Mandate*

This question too has been subject to various interpretations. Who is competent to determine the terms of the Mandate: the League of Nations or the Principal Allied and Associated Powers?[3] Those who advocate the first alternative do not have to depend on legal assumptions which are of questionable value, such as the proposition that as a rule the grantor of authority determines the terms of the authority (although also this argument is put forward every now and then).

[1] Schuster von Bonnot: *Grundriß des Obligationenrechtes*, p. 157.

[2] The possibility of the discharge of the mandatory and his replacement by another is expressly envisaged in Wilson's original draft. (Lansing, *Peace Negotiations*, p. 263; Smuts, *The League of Nations*, p. 21.)

[3] The vigorous battle on this subject is explained by its great importance. As Lord Cecil wrote in *The Times* newspaper of 24 June 1920: 'It is on the conditions of the Mandates that the whole efficacy of the system depends. I venture to urge that . . . no attempt shall be made by the Supreme Council to send to the Council a cut-and-dried Mesopotamia Mandate to be obediently confirmed by the latter – that in short the Mandatory provisions of the Covenant shall be treated seriously and not as a "scrap of paper".'

Paragraph 8 says expressly: 'The degree of authority, control or administration to be exercised by the Mandatory shall, if not previously agreed upon by the Members of the League, be explicitly defined in each case by the Council'.

In the report approved by the Council Hymans admits that if one wanted to interpret paragraph 8 literally, this would mean that the League Assembly would normally be competent to lay down the terms of the Mandate since it alone unites all Members of the League.[1] Hymans declares himself against this view (advocated *inter alia* by Lord Robert Cecil), for the following reasons: (*a*) in such a case the Covenant would expressly speak of the League Assembly, instead of using a vague phrase; (*b*) a few months after the drafting of Article 22, but before the ratification of the Treaty of Versailles, a committee of colonial experts set up by the Principal Powers met in London in order to draw up drafts for the various kinds of Mandates; (*c*) it is not likely that such a difficult and complicated task would have been entrusted to a corporate body as numerous and hard pressed as the League Assembly. For these reasons, and because during the drafting of Article 22 in 1919 it was thought that only the Allied and Associated Powers would be considered as original Members of the League of Nations, Hymans felt himself drawn to the following interpretation of paragraph 8: 'The degree of authority, control or administration to be exercised by the Mandatory shall, if not previously agreed upon by the signatories of the Treaty of Versailles which are Members of the League, be explicitly defined in each case by the Council.'

An examination of Hymans' arguments soon reveals that the reasons adduced for (*b*) and (*c*) are not sound. The meeting of colonial experts for the purpose of drawing up Mandate provisions can be of little importance in determining the intention of the contracting parties, since it is in any case a one-sided interpretation. The other contracting party, Germany, has no part in this interpretation. In any case the experts could be regarded as being engaged in the preparation of suggestions for the League Assembly. The argument that the League Assembly is clumsy can also be safely rejected. The organization of the Assembly and its division into committees and sub-committees offers the safeguard that it will be able to tackle the most difficult tasks.

However, the first objection cannot be rejected out of hand. Paragraph 8 indeed speaks not of the League Assembly but of the Members of the League. Is the conclusion of the German Government,[2] of Lord

[1] Doc. 20/48/161, p. 15.

[2] Documents of the First Assembly, Doc. 106.

Cecil[1] and of other commentators on the Covenant[2] that the 'Members of the League' means the League Assembly, really so compelling? Is Lord Cecil's question justified: 'I venture to ask Lord Curzon what there is in the context of Article 22 to alter the plain grammatical meaning of the words?' Article 22 is not the only article in the Covenant of the League of Nations which raises this question. Article 14 provides: 'The Council shall formulate and submit to the Members of the League for adoption plans for the establishment of a Permanent Court of International Justice. The Court . . . may also give an advisory opinion upon any dispute or question referred to it by the Council or by the Assembly.' The Council has to submit the plan to the Members of the League. Does one understand 'Members of the League' here to mean 'League Assembly'? For technical reasons the Council has adopted this interpretation and has submitted the draft to the Assembly. It seems to have proceeded on the basis that it would be impracticable to submit the report to the individual Members.[3] However, it is clear that this interpretation was not a definitive one since the League Assembly, in considering precisely the special wording of the Article, did not regard even the unanimous acceptance of the draft as sufficient but considered necessary the subsequent ratification by the individual Members of the League. It would seem, therefore, that the League Assembly did not want to declare itself as quite identical with the 'Members of the League'. Article 15 of the Covenant of the League of Nations also speaks several times of the 'Members of the League'. Yet here it is clear that only some of the Members are intended.

Thus the true meaning of paragraph 8 remains open for the time being. The obscurity of expression is here obviously intentional;[4] it is certainly insufficient to establish beyond question the right of the Principal Powers to determine the terms of the Mandate. This seems to have been taken for granted not only in Hymans' Report but also by the Principal Powers, which in official Government statements have expressed their intention voluntarily (and not under any Covenant obligation) to submit the draft Mandates to the Council of the League of Nations for examination and confirmation.[5] On the other hand the

[1] His letter to *The Times* newspaper of 1 July 1920.

[2] E.g., Schücking–Wehberg and Bileski.

[3] Schücking–Wehberg, *Die Satzung des Völkerbundes. Kommentar*, pp. 62 and 348.

[4] It is the more significant in that the formulation in Smuts and Wilson was quite clear. ('The degree of authority, control, or administration to be exercised by the Mandatory State or agency shall in each case be explicitly defined by the League in a special Act or Charter which shall reserve to the League complete power of supervision and of intimate control.') The Smuts and Wilson texts are almost identical. The first joint League draft of 14 February 1919 speaks in this matter not of 'League Members' but of the 'High Contracting Parties'.

[5] Lord Curzon on 25 June 1920: '. . . we have even given in excess of what was demanded from us by the Covenant of the League'.

competence of the Council should the interested Powers fail to reach agreement, to proceed independently to the determination of the terms is undisputed. This right became a question of moment when the Powers, despite reiterated admonitions by the Council, hesitated with the submission of their draft Mandates. But the Council has not made use of this right and has preferred for practical reasons to wait for suggestions from the Powers.[1]

In asking who is entitled to determine the conditions of the Mandate we are thus confronted with three attempts at an interpretation of Article 22. The first view (held by the Germans, Lord Cecil and the English League of Nations Association) claims this right for the League Assembly. The second (held by the Council of the League of Nations) asserts the right of the signatories of the Peace Treaty (except for the defeated Powers) and, in the absence of an agreement between them, the Council of the League of Nations. The third (held by the Governments of the Principal Powers), favours the position of the Principal Allied and Associated Powers. We have seen that none of these opinions can fully rely on the wording of paragraph 8 of Article 22. Which solution, then, is the correct one? I refrain from an unequivocal interpretation of this provision of the Covenant of the League of Nations, because it seems to me that, because of the doubtlessly deliberately unclear and misleading phrasing of the Covenant at this point, we are here confronted with a task of interpretation which cannot be undertaken without resort to arbitrary value judgments and appeals to the 'spirit' of the Covenant of the League of Nations. I have therefore confined myself to pointing out and correcting the obvious errors in the various arguments. It is also clear from what actually happened that the Principal Powers were neither willing nor able to claim unqualified support for their opinion. Hymans' Report to the Council laboriously attempts an interpretation which grants the right of deciding the terms of the Mandate to all the Versailles signatory States (except Germany) and for 'reasons of practicability' turns to the Principal Powers with the request that they should draw up the relevant proposals. The Principal Powers claim the competence in question for themselves as their exclusive right and submit their proposals (quite voluntarily) to the Council for approval.

However, the question whether the Mandator – the League of Nations – can unilaterally amend the terms of the Mandate remains entirely unanswered in Article 22. The question must be answered in the negative for the following reasons: Acceptance of the Mandate takes the form of a treaty (to be approved by the Council), between the

[1] The precise basis for this is in Hymans' Report, Doc. 20/46/161, p. 16.

Principal Powers and the Mandatory Power. This treaty which is concluded by the Principal Powers, in effect as representatives of the League of Nations, is binding on the League, particularly after it has approved it. The League cannot, therefore, unilaterally change the Mandate provisions. (Nor, of course, do the Mandatories have this right.) But in order that change might not from the outset be excluded, Article 18 of the draft Mandate for Mesopotamia, for instance, contains the following provision: 'The consent of the Council of the League of Nations is required for any modification of the terms of the present Mandate provided that in the case of any modification proposed by the Mandatory, such consent can be given by a majority of the Council.'[1] As England (in this case the Mandatory) is permanently represented on the Council, and given the need for unanimity in Council decisions, there can be no amendment of the terms of the Mandate against its will. This arrangement is in no way at odds with either the sovereignty of the League of Nations or the principles of the Mandate.

I hope that in these sections I have thrown light in a systematic fashion upon the most important problems of the Mandates system. Writings on this subject usually take one of two courses; either they base themselves on private law analogy and by ruthlessly applying it, entirely disregard positive law as expressed in the treaties; or they proceed on purely practical grounds and thereby go counter to the positive law as well as to the decisive principles of the Mandates system. It was impossible to adopt either of these methods here. On the basis of the fundamental distinction between private law analogy and positive formation of concepts in international law from private law sources, I have opted for the Article 22 approach, a construction which bases this new institution of international law on a type of contract 'mandate'. At the same time I have tried to claim validity for this construction only insofar as it has not been modified by the Covenant of the League of Nations or by the other contemporary treaties. I believe that this is the only way to deal with 'the principle of power'.[2] It also appears to me to be the one that fits in with the need for a positive law.

[1] The same provision is also to be found in the other draft Mandates for the A and B Mandates. It is puzzling why in the C Mandates only the first part of this provision is included. There is thus no mention of the possibility of a majority decision.

[2] See Bileski, in *Z.V.* 12, 81; Schücking–Wehberg, *Die Satzung des Völkerbundes. Kommentar*, p. 431.

6. THE ORGANIZATION OF THE MANDATES SYSTEM

In presenting the organization of the Mandates system it is necessary, first of all, to deal with the question of competence. In questions appertaining to the Mandate is the Council of the League of Nations or the League of Nations Assembly supreme ? The answer can be found partly in Article 22 and partly in other provisions of the League of Nations Covenant. Individual decisions of the League Assembly and of the Council are also relevant in this context.[1] Under the Covenant, both the League Council and the League Assembly have overall competence, unless one of these organs is specifically given exclusive competence. However, if this is the case, the other organ has no right to deal with the matter in question ; it has moreover to comply with the decision made by the first organ.[2]

The centre of gravity in Mandate matters lies without doubt with the Council. This has the right to receive the reports of the Mandatory Powers, to have them examined by the Permanent Mandates Commission and to exercise general control over the administration of the Mandated territories on the basis of the Mandates Commission's report. The Council has the right to lay down the terms of the Mandate if not previously agreed upon by the Members of the League ; it elects the permanent Mandates Commission, approves its constitution and supervises its work. The Mandate provisions enlarged the scope of the Council's competence still further. It has for instance the right to approve the constitution for Mesopotamia to be enacted by the Mandatory Power.[3] It appoints the chairman of the Commission which is to inquire into and settle questions concerning the different religious communities in Palestine.[4] The most important Mandate affairs are therefore referred to the Council.

There is no matter on which the League Assembly has exclusive competence. Cases in which a joint competence would have to be assumed, can naturally arise only rarely. The League Assembly has to content itself with receipt of the report, its examination and with eventual *voeux*. These *voeux*, if they relate to cases within the exclusive competence of the Council, which means nearly all cases, bear the character of a recommendation not binding on the Council. As however the members of the Council are at the same time members of the League Assembly, the *voeux* are in practice of no small significance as an

[1] Cf. Bileski, in *Z.V.* 12, 80.
[2] Schücking–Wehberg, *Die Satzung des Völkerbundes. Kommentar*, pp. 190 and 211.
[3] Article 2 of the draft Mandate for Mesopotamia.
[4] Article 14 of the draft Mandate for Palestine.

expression of the will of the entirety of the members and as a means of interpreting the Covenant.[1]

In general the League of Nations is alone competent in Mandates questions. The Principal Powers have no right of interference deriving from their former sovereignty over the Mandated territories. From the moment the Council approves a Mandate agreement concluded between the Principal Powers, their rights are extinct. From then on they are regarded formally like any other League Member. Even though they distribute the Mandates, they are in no sense Mandators. The Mandator is the one in whose name and on whose behalf the Mandate is exercised and who has the right of supervision and control.[2]

Under paragraph 7 of Article 22 the Mandatory is required to render to the Council an annual report on the territories committed to its charge. Under paragraph 9 a permanent Commission is to be constituted to receive and examine these annual reports, and at the same time to advise the Council on all matters relating to the observance of the Mandates. The examination of the Mandate reports and the subsequent giving of advice on administration is so far the only means for the exercise by the League of Nations of its right of control.[3] It is probably for this reason that Hymans in his report favours an exclusive interpretation of paragraph 9 of Article 22.[4] The Council should not content itself with the statement that the Mandatory has not exceeded its authority. Rather it should take as a starting point the Mandatory's obligation to care generally for the well-being and the development of the peoples of the Mandated territories and go on from there to examine the whole administration. This interpretation was also accepted by the Mandates Commission when it met for the first time from 4–8 October 1921. As the majority of the Mandates had not at that time been approved, the Commission was unable to deal with the Mandate reports proper and had to accept as the basis for its deliberations the reports of the individual administrations of the Mandated territories to their central Government.[5] It has nevertheless discharged its task scrupulously, considering in particular detail the question of the participation of the indigenous population in the administration, the questions of finance, duties (freedom of trade), taxes and import duties (alcohol tax and prohibition of alcohol), the land system, natural

[1] The moral effect of the attitude of the Assembly and its influence on public opinion is particularly to be emphasized.

[2] Nor has 'the double title' any effect whatsoever for the duration of the mandate relationship.

[3] Cf. Rappard's statement at the opening of the sitting of the Permanent Mandates Commission. (Protocol, p. 6.)

[4] Doc. 20/48/161, p. 17.

[5] Protocol of the first session of the Permanent Mandates Commission (*League of Nations* Doc. C. 416, M. 296 (1921), VI, 3 and 6).

resources (concessions), forced labour, education, and hygiene and sanitary arrangements.

The fact that the report and its examination is the only link between the League of Nations and the Mandatory Power has also induced the Council to pay greater attention to the organization of the Permanent Mandates Commission, which by virtue of paragraph 9 of Article 22 is entrusted with the relevant responsibilities.[1] The most important principles for the Commission have already been laid down in Hymans' Report. Each Mandatory State is to be represented by one delegate. The objection that the Mandatory State is, in this way, both judge and party is countered by Hymans with the argument that the Commission does not judge but examines and gives an opinion. But steps should be taken to safeguard the full objectivity of the Commission. For example, no member of the Commission should participate in a vote on an opinion on his own Government's report and the Commission should be composed in such a way that the representatives of the Mandatory States hold only a minority of seats.

The statute was finally adopted by the Council on 1 December 1920. The most important points may be set out here. The Commission is to consist of nine members, the majority of which should come from non-Mandatory States. The members are to be elected by the Council solely on the basis of their personal qualifications. As long as they are members of the Commission they may not hold an office which puts them in a position of direct dependence on their governments. The International Labour Organization has the right to appoint a member with an advisory function (on labour matters). The Mandatory States are to send their annual report to the Mandate Commission through duly authorized representatives ready to give explanations to the Commission and to supply supplementary information. The reports of their Governments are to be examined in their presence. After the termination of the discussion the Commission will decide, in the absence of the Mandatory Power's representative, on the opinion to be submitted to the Council together with the report of the Mandatory Power and the final statements of its representative. If the Council publishes the report and the Commission's opinion, it has also to publish the comments of the Mandatory Power's representative, if he so requests. In agreement with the accredited representatives of the Mandatory Power the Commission will hold a plenary meeting for the purpose of studying the reports and drawing conclusions from them. It is to meet once in a year in Geneva. It has the right to consult experts. Its autonomous rules of procedure are subject to approval by the Council.

[1] Doc. 20/48/161, pp. 17, 24, 28, 34.

So much for the Commission's constitution. It is understandable that the task of the Commission is quite a difficult one, requiring much tact, patience and political insight. The Commission is limited in its scope for activity, not only by the modesty of its powers, but also, to an even greater extent, by consideration for the sensitivity of the Powers, who are inclined to see in even the smallest indiscretion an obstacle to their task of colonization. The Commission, in fact, obviously tried hard during its first meeting to show the Powers and the Council that it was not over-eager but was moved rather by a wish to facilitate the task of the Mandatory Powers.[1] When, for instance, during the deliberations on the French report on Cameroon, the question of the correspondence of the respective draft Mandate with Article 22 was raised, the Commission hastened to avert a possible reproach of exceeding its powers by adopting the following resolution: the Mandate Commission is of opinion that it is not its duty to render any judgment on the conditions of the Mandate, and that its powers are limited by the last paragraph of Article 22. Similar understanding was shown by the Commission in the deliberations on the question whether it was allowed to receive petitions and complaints. In a few questions in which important doubts of a political nature have arisen the Commission has contented itself with asking the Council for elucidation and a decision, e.g. on the question of citizenship in the Mandated territories, on a customs-union between a B group territory and the Mandatory Power's neighbouring territory (violation of the freedom of trade), on forced labour (different wording of the corresponding English and French drafts) and so forth.[2] These tactics of the Mandates Commission, based on political as well as on legal considerations, have a good chance of proving themselves the right ones.

The objectivity and thoroughness of the Commission's work are not impaired by these tactics. They are indeed helped by the removal of points of friction. The questionnaire for the B and C Mandates, which was drawn up for the purpose of facilitating the preparation of the annual reports, may serve as an example of this.[3]

Finally, the Permanent Court of International Justice should be mentioned as an important element in the organization of the Mandates

[1] Protocol of the first session, pp. 11, 20, 28, 33 and 46. During the debate on whether it was necessary to make a report to the Council on the work of the Commission, the French representative said he was in favour, on the ground that it would be advisable to persuade the Powers and the Council 'que la commission . . . n'a pas fait preuve d'un zèle excessif et qu'elle s'est tenue dans les grandes lignes de sa tache'.

[2] Report of the Permanent Mandates Commission presented to the Council of the League of Nations. Report and Appendix. (*League of Nations* Doc. C. 395, M. 294 (1921), VI; Internal regulation, *League of Nations* Doc. C. 404, M. 295 (1921), VI.)

[3] For the B Mandates, see *League of Nations* Doc. C. 396, M. 298 (1921), VI. For the C Mandates, see *League of Nations* Doc. C. 397, M. 299 (1921), VI.

system. In the course of the Mandate relationship, disagreements can arise between the League or its individual members on one side and the Mandatory Power on the other. The revocation of the Mandate because of violation of the treaty obligation, although theoretically possible, is in practice out of the question for the reasons mentioned in the previous chapter. Are the League Members and the League as such therefore powerless if the Mandatory acts contrary to the treaty? No. The wording of Articles 13 and 14 of the League of Nations Covenant always provides the possibility for appeal to the Permanent Court of International Justice in Mandate matters. In the draft Mandates the admissibility of an action before the Permanent Court of International Justice is explicitly recognized: 'If any dispute whatever should arise between the Members of the League of Nations relating to the interpretation or application of these provisions which cannot be settled by negotiations, this dispute shall be submitted to the Permanent Court of International Justice as provided for by Article 14 of the Covenant of the League of Nations.'[1] Each Member of the League of Nations by itself – or several together – can bring an action before the Permanent Court of International Justice for violation of their rights (for instance for impairment of the freedom of trade) or for non-compliance with other conditions of the Mandate. In this way the rigid principle of unanimity in League of Nations decisions is circumvented and the execution of the obligations under the Mandate is safeguarded.

7. CONCLUSION

The three year history of the Mandates system is so instructive that it already permits an evaluation of what has happened in the years following the Peace Treaty of Versailles, for this is a period of construction of the new international law institution created by Article 22. For of the nine paragraphs of this Article, none is so clear and undisputed that one could claim that it has facilitated the formulation of theory and practice for the Mandates system. But the new institution had to struggle not only against the misleading wording of the legal formula which established it. It had also to maintain itself against the conservatism of the traditional concepts of cession and protectorates, against the influence deriving from the superiority of the victorious powers and, in part also, against attempts at scholarly interpretation.

Now that the result of this struggle is seen to a large extent in the

[1] E.g. Article 25 of the draft Mandate for Palestine. It is to be noted that for the C Mandates the relevant article reads as follows: 'The Mandatory agrees that in the event of any difference of opinion . . .'

Mandate provisions which have been drawn up for all the Mandated territories and an insight has been granted into the mode of operation of this institution, it is safe to say that the system has proved itself practicable. I reject the contention that the principle of power has dominated its realization. The factor of power has certainly been of consequence – but mainly in the drafting of Article 22 and of the Peace Treaties generally. True, it was the factor of power which created the institution of the Mandate, but the modifications contained in the Covenant of the League of Nations and in the Peace Treaties have been so far-reaching that one has to try hard to find a mandate relationship in it. An assignment in which not the assignor but a third party chooses the assignee, and in which this third party decides on the terms of the assignment; an assignment which even though it is in principle revocable comes very close to being irrevocable because of its duration is conclusively determined by the statement of the purpose of the assignment and because of the requirement of unanimity in the decisions of the League of Nations – such an assignment leads to the conclusion that the specific legal context of this institution has been completely lost, and that, quite simply, the content has spilled out of the form. This disfigurement of the Mandate principle is however – one may repeat again – already contained in Article 22 and in the Peace Treaties. But it only showed itself when the Mandate provisions came to be carried out. As the victorious Powers have also secured for themselves a decisive rôle in the carrying out of the Mandates, the opinion that they forcibly warp the law is psychologically understandable. This is not the case. They only carry out enacted law – law which was, however, formed by the victor's claim to power.

I am, therefore, of opinion that those who deny any legal quality to the Mandate under international law because of these limitations and modifications, or even say that the inherently meaningful Mandates system has now become useless because of encroachments by the Administering authority, are mistaken both politically and legally. The facts that it is not the League of Nations which chooses the Mandatory or that it does not have full freedom to end the Mandate, or that the League does not decide the terms of the Mandate – these are certainly more than aesthetic shortcomings in the Mandates system. It is however incorrect to think of them as decisive. There are other essentials: the waiver of sovereignty, albeit indirectly expressed in the drafts (as a consequence of the reliance on Article 22 and the recognition of the fact that the supreme rights of the Mandatory are exercised in the name of the League of Nations); the acknowledgment of the transitory character of the Mandate relationship in the A Mandates; the acceptance of a number of positive and negative obligations in respect of other Mandated territories which not only contain far-reaching limitations of the Mandatory Power's freedom, but also principles of a new policy of colonization; the recognition of the right of every League Member actively to intervene should the Mandatory Power not comply with its obligations; the obligation periodically to submit reports; and the connected right of control of the League of Nations. Only the material content of the Mandate provisions themselves and their external legal form are of decisive significance here – not the lack of irrelevant, though normal, characteristics of a contract mandate. Therefore, the assertion must be made here – though in contradiction to the greater part of academic and non-academic opinion – that the execution of the Mandates system has so far by and large moved along the lines laid down by the Covenant of the League of Nations and the Peace Treaties.

This statement, however, has one important exception – an exception which, though not easily grasped, still contravenes the spirit as well as the wording of Article 22. The Mandates system, in the minds of its creators, was conceived as a counter to the system of annexation – not only in the unofficial suggestions of Smuts but also in the official draft submitted by Wilson to the American commission on 10 January 1919. There was to be no allocation of booty. Though the absolute character of this requirement gave way to the 'qualifications' of the political and diplomatic circumstances at the Peace Conference, its essential core has still found its way into Article 22. The letter and the spirit of this Article exclude the right to annex, the 'right of seizure' of the victorious States. The Principal Powers have not taken this fact into account. The selection of the Mandatories and the delimitation of the Mandated territories took place on the basis of general plans of conquest and of treaties of division. The 'holy mission' became the 'well-founded right' of the Principal Powers. Thus Lloyd George in the House of Commons defended the moral and material right of England in the Mandate for Mesopotamia and referred to the bountiful supplies which would be capable of covering the costs of administration; thus Belgium, which was originally not awarded a Mandate, demanded as compensation for participation in the military operations in Africa, that the holy mission of tutelage of the areas Ruanda and Urundi should be entrusted to it; thus France claimed its rights in Togo and Cameroon with great emphasis. In the case of the island of Yap, its importance as a cable communications centre in the Pacific, and in the case of Nauru its phosphorus plants were decisive – and not the 'well-being and development' of its peoples. Thus it was that no Mandatory could be found for hard-pressed Armenia because, as a member of the House of Commons dramatically expressed it, 'there is no oil there'. In this point, therefore, the Mandatories have disregarded an important provision of Article 22. However, it must here be said that the Principal Powers are not entirely to blame for this; the time has not yet come, when States, in the name of civilization and in abandonment of their immediate interests, will be willing and able to bear permanent sacrifices.

Nevertheless – or, perhaps, therefore – it would be quite wrong, for this reason, to assert the failure of the Mandate system and proclaim the victory of force. For we have already mentioned that the Mandate of the League of Nations, despite its far-reaching discrepancy from the normal type, shows rich and positive content. The prospects of the Mandates system are too important lightly to be abandoned by reference to extra-legal considerations. The Mandates system has to protect the populations of extensive areas from misuses of previous colonial policy and to further the development of these peoples; it has to erect the independent Arab State of Mesopotamia and to put into practice the re-establishment of a Jewish national home in Palestine; it has to found independent communities in Syria and in the Lebanon; it has to carry out, with minor exceptions, the open-door principle. In this way not only is the possibility of free activity in the lost possession to be guaranteed for the defeated States, but at the same time one of the most dangerous points of friction in the relationship of States to each other is to be removed. The Mandates system is after all one of the most important supports of the League of Nations and consequently of the idea of world sovereignty of the international legal order. To abandon the Mandates system – and the constant reiteration of the victory of sheer power amounts to abandoning it – would mean the rejection of all these possibilities. One should therefore stop talking of the 'power' principle and of its encroachments; one should stop trying to tell those who are charged with operating the Mandates system that they constantly and consciously warp the law. *Virtutem credant habere et habebunt.* The Mandates system has become a legal institution. One should therefore treat it as a matter of jurisprudence in international law. Only in this way can it be elevated from the world of politics and power into the realm of the positive legal norm.

CHAPTER 3

THE INTERPRETATION OF ARTICLE 18 OF THE MANDATE FOR PALESTINE

Editor's Note This chapter consists of an opinion completed by Lauterpacht on 24 August 1939. It was sought by the Jewish Agency for Palestine and in fact covered two questions: the participation of Palestine in the scheme of Imperial Preferences as well as the interpretation of Article 18 of the Mandate.

This is the first of Lauterpacht's professional (as opposed to academic) writings to find a place in these *Collected Papers*. It also happens, so far as I can make out, to be the first substantial opinion which he wrote – though he may have assisted the Chinese Government with a memorandum (of which I have not found any trace) at the time of the Manchurian crisis. In any event, the present item demonstrates Lauterpacht's ability to tackle a practical problem in a direct and constructive manner. The method of interpretation applied to Article 18 of the Mandate is an early illustration of Lauterpacht's willingness to go behind the strict words of the treaty provision in order to determine its true purpose.

Paragraph 16 of the opinion is incomplete. On the carbon copy found amongst Lauterpacht's papers there is a blank space equal to about five and a half lines of typescript. The copy bears no attempt to fill the blank or to note what is missing, but from the context the omission appears to relate to the rôle which the Jewish Agency might play in making representations to the Mandates Commission. It does not seem to affect the principal content of the opinion.

§1 I was asked originally to give an opinion on the following two questions:

(1) Is the Palestine Administration permitted, under the terms of Article 18 of the Palestine Mandate, to introduce such a system of differential custom tariffs on goods imported into Palestine as would enable countries or groups of countries buying more in Palestine to be favourably treated from a tariff point of view?

(2) Can Palestine as a Mandated Territory be brought or held to be within the scope of Imperial Preference, or otherwise benefit from any of the custom tariff advantages enjoyed by the British Dominions or the Crown Colonies, and if the latter, from which of such advantages may it so benefit?

It appeared from the subsequent correspondence with the Jewish Agency that the latter are particularly interested in the first of these questions. The present opinion is, accordingly, largely devoted to the question of Article 18.

§2 The two questions as formulated are distinct, but, as suggested below (§17), they are connected in one important respect which renders their joint treatment advantageous. As a result of the interpretation hitherto adopted by the Mandatory authorities and by the Mandates Commission Palestine has, in the matter of Article 18, been deprived of one of the principal prerogatives of independent statehood, namely, of the power of independent economic policy on a footing of equality with other States in the matter of external trade. At the same time, as a result of the interpretation of the legal position as adopted by British authorities in the matter of the extension to Palestine of the benefits of Imperial Preference, Palestine has been treated as a foreign independent State. These two results are not easily reconcilable, and the advantage of raising the two questions together may well be to show that at least one of the interpretations hitherto adopted cannot be maintained. Palestine cannot at the same time be a foreign independent State (for the purposes of Imperial Preference) and a country deprived of an essential attribute of State independence (for the purposes of Article 18).

§3 Article 18 of the Mandate for Palestine provides as follows:

> The Mandatory shall see that there is no discrimination in Palestine against the nationals of any State Member of the League of Nations (including companies incorporated under its laws) as compared with those of the Mandatory or of any foreign State in matters concerning taxation, commerce or navigation, the exercise of industries or professions, or in the treatment of merchant vessels or civil aircraft. Similarly, there shall be no discrimination in Palestine against goods originating in or destined for any of the said States, and there shall be freedom of transit under equitable conditions across the Mandated area.
>
> Subject as aforesaid and to the other provisions of this Mandate, the Administration of Palestine may, on the advice of the Mandatory, impose such taxes and customs duties as it may consider necessary, and take such steps as it may think best to promote the development of the natural resources of the country and to safeguard the interests of the population. It may also, on the advice of the Mandatory, conclude a special customs agreement with any State the territory of which in 1914 was wholly included in Asiatic Turkey or Arabia.

There are a number of indications which suggest that both the Mandatory Power and the Mandates Commission have hitherto adhered to the view that the terms of Article 18 are peremptory and that they do not permit the introduction of a system of differential tariffs on goods imported into Palestine so as to favour countries which take a correspondingly larger share of Palestinian goods. In the course of the frequent discussions on the subject before the Mandates Commission the representative of the Palestine Administration has never questioned that view. Moreover, the Administration has on occasions expressed the opinion that discrimination may have economically deplorable results inasmuch as it tends to increase the cost of living. This was the sense of the relevant Observations in the Report of 1936 to the Mandates Commission (p. 265). This must still be regarded as the predominant and official view, as may be seen, for instance, from the attitude of the Mandatory with regard to the Memorandum of the Citrus Export Federation presented in 1936 to the Mandates Commission (*Minutes of the 32nd Session* (1937), p. 219). The Peel Commission, while submitting that Article 18 was out of date and required amendment, was clearly of the opinion that as that Article now stands it is not compatible with a policy of differentiation, however equitable in the circumstances (Cmd. 5479 of 1937, p. 217). The Mandates Commission as such has not, so far, formally departed from that view. In 1930 its response to the action of the Jewish Agency in the matter was to suggest that other Members of the League should voluntarily agree to extend to Palestine the advantages of the most-favoured-nation clause and of similar benefits enjoyed by the Mandatory. Poland and some other countries have acted on that suggestion. When in 1937 the matter was once more formally brought before the Mandates Commission they advanced only slightly from their position. While recalling the terms of the recommendations of 1930, they drew attention to the terms of the petition pointing to the disadvantages of a unilateral system of economic equality. In 1935, M. Rappard, a not-unfavourably disposed member of the Commission, expressed the view that the application of a differential system would be contrary to the provisions of the Mandate (*Minutes of the 27th Session of the Commission* (1935), p. 56). On the whole, subject to what is said below (§4), the incompatibility of a differential system of quotas with the terms of Article 18 must still be regarded as the official view.

§4 On the other hand, the past history of the administration of the Palestine Mandate shows that there has been no tendency either on the part of the Mandatory or on the part of the Mandates Commission to interpret Article 18 in a rigid and uncompromising manner. Thus, to mention a minor example, the majority of the Mandates Commission have declined to associate themselves with the view expressed in a report of one of its members that it was contrary to the principle of economic equality that the rates applicable in territories under A and B Mandates to postal matter destined for the territory of the Mandatory Power, or its colonies, should be fixed at a lower level than the rates applicable to similar matter destined for other countries. That member thought that the differential postal rates 'unconsciously directed the attention of traders' to the country of the Mandatory (Report of M. Kastl, *Minutes of the 16th Session* (1929), p. 131). Persuasive reasons for the contrary view were adduced by M. van Rees, who pointed out that in this matter the Mandatory treated all inhabitants of Palestine on a footing equal with his nationals (*ibid.* p. 195), by M. Rappard (p. 132), and by Lord Lugard (*ibid.*), who observed that differential rates facilitated the execution of the Mandate. When in 1929 and in subsequent years the Commission was confronted with the equality clause in the matter of purchase of materials for the execution of public works, the general view was that, while the interests of the Mandated Territory were the paramount consideration, the Mandatory was free to organize public works as he thought fit and that he was entitled to dispense with public tender. By way of a clearly extensive interpretation it was thought that the clause in the B Mandates providing that the Mandatory was free to organize on such conditions as he thought fit essential public works meant that he was free to organize *all* public works, and that that clause applied also to A Mandates (Report of M. van Rees, *Minutes of the 16th Session* (1929), p. 195; *ibid.* pp. 148–53; *Minutes of the 22nd Session* (1932), p. 360).

For these reasons no serious objection was raised when the Palestine Government contracted and utilized a loan under the Colonial Development Act, 1929, section 1 (2), according to which it may be a condition of the loan that whenever possible purchases of materials should be made in the United Kingdom. The view prevailed in the Mandates Commission and with the British authorities that if the loan could be obtained on conditions more favourable than any obtainable from other sources and if throughout the transaction the vital test was adhered to, namely, the essential interests of the Mandated Territory, the provisions of Article 18 were not infringed as the result of the provision of preference for materials from the United Kingdom.

In 1928, in connection with the Haifa works, the view of the British authorities was that there would be no infringement of the equality clause if it were decided that the interests of Palestine and the efficient execution of the work required that in a particular case British goods should be given preference.

The Mandatory has also acted on the view that the granting of exemption from import duty on certain raw materials and the increase of import duties for protective purposes on certain manufactured articles, so long as these measures were general in character, did not in any way violate the economic equality clause of the Mandate. This was so although as a result some countries might have been injuriously affected more than others (*Minutes of the 29th Session* (1936), p. 153).

Finally, reference may be made to individual pronouncements of some of the members of the Commission on the question as to how far discrimination is generally compatible with the provisions of Article 18 of the Mandate. In 1936 we find M. Rappard, who, a year before, expressed a different view (see above, §3), stating that it was obviously detrimental to Mandated Territories that they possess no power of negotiation and that this could not have been the intention of those who drafted the Mandate. He pointed out that economic equality did not mean equality of imports; that it would not be contrary to the principle of economic equality to allow all countries equal imports up to 50 per cent of their own imports from Palestine; and that a country which buys nothing from Palestine ought not to be treated on the same footing as a country which is one of its best customers (*Minutes of the 29th Session* (1936), p. 155). Another member of the Commission suggested significantly that an attempt might be made to introduce specific as distinguished from *ad valorem* duties. Those cognizant with the machinery of governmental trade restrictions will readily realize that the institution of specific duties, although nominally affecting a plurality of countries, may in effect operate as against certain countries only.

§5 It seems from what has been said above that the attitude of the Administration of Palestine and of the Mandates Commission, although still officially based on an unconditional interpretation of the principle of economic equality as laid down in Article 18, is not sufficiently crystallized to preclude a re-examination of the legal position. Apart from the view so far adopted by both these agencies, it appears that the insistence on absolute equality in the matter of imports, unqualified by any condition of reciprocity, constitutes a purely formal interpretation of the Article in question – an interpretation which cannot be easily reconciled with the intention of its authors and with the essential purpose of the Mandates system. The accepted principles of interpretation of treaties and the previous practice of the Permanent Court of International Justice suggest that that Tribunal might feel considerable hesitation in endorsing the official interpretation which underlies the practice followed in the matter.

§6 The interpretation hitherto officially followed in the matter of Article 18 cannot be regarded as sound inasmuch as it fails to take into consideration the circumstances which led to its adoption and the object which it was intended to fulfil. The main if not exclusive object of Article 18 – and, generally, of the principle of equality of opportunity enshrined in corresponding provisions of other Mandates – was to give effect to one of the principal features of the idea of trusteeship. That idea is that the Mandatory must be discouraged from deriving exclusive economic and other advantages from the performance of his task. The second purpose of Article 18 was to remove a cause of international friction which consisted in the monopolization of the commerce and resources of territories subject to the rule of the colonizing State. It is generally admitted and it appears clearly from the so-called *travaux préparatoires* preceding the drafting of the Covenant of the League of Nations and of the individual Mandates that these were the objects of the restrictive clauses of Article 18. They were admittedly modelled after the pattern of the Berlin Treaty of 1885 relating to the Congo and the Treaty of St Germain of 1919 which revised it. To that extent the idea of equality of economic opportunity introduced the principle of the 'open door'. But it was a principle different from that adopted at the end of the nineteenth century in China and elsewhere, where the principle of the 'open door' signified not only equality of opportunity for Western Powers, but also a position of unilateral advantage for the latter and a pronounced degree of economic inequality for the State whose territory was affected by the provisions in question. Any interpretation which transforms the prohibition of non-discrimination contained in Article 18 into a consecration of the permanent inequality of the Mandated Territory in the field of international trade must therefore be rejected as unrelated to the purpose of the Mandate and as contrary to the intention of the framers of the Mandate. The régime of Mandates was not conceived as a system of economic exploitation of the Mandated Territories by all Members of the League as distinguished from exploitation by the Mandatory only.

The true object, as suggested here, of the equality provisions in the Covenant and in Article 18 appears clearly from what is generally regarded as the inspiration of the Mandates system, namely, General Smuts' *The League of Nations. A Practical Suggestion* (1918). The relevant passage may be quoted verbatim:

> It must be part of this suggested scheme of mandatory control that the Mandatory shall in no case adopt an economic or military policy which will lead to its special national advantage. In fact, for all territories which are not completely independent States the policy of the open door, or equal economic opportunity for all, must be laid down. In this way a fruitful source of rivalry and friction between the Powers will be removed (p. 22).

For these, and no other, reasons he suggested that 'the Mandatory State shall in each case be bound to maintain the policy of the open door, or equal economic opportunity for all' (p. 23). This suggestion was in that form incorporated in Article 22 (5) of the Covenant with regard to B Mandates; it was subsequently extended to cover A Mandates as being in conformity with the Mandates system. This was also the view of the Assembly and of other organs of the League prior to the drafting of the individual Mandates. Thus we read in a recommendation to the Council adopted by the First Assembly on 18 December 1920, with special reference to A Mandates: 'The Mandatory should not be allowed to make use of its position to increase its military strength . . . or to use its power under the Mandate to exploit for itself or its friends the national resources of the Mandated Territory.'

This object of Article 18 was clearly expressed in the opening and principal passage of the Article. As one of the most authoritative members of the Mandates Commission has said: 'What these authors desired, in conformity with the Convention of St Germain, was equality of treatment for all the nationals of State Members of the League of Nations as regards activities within the territory for the development of the territory' (M. van Rees, *Minutes of the 16th Session* (1929), p. 195). The Article was intended to cover primarily activities within Palestine. The crucial passage of the second sentence of Article 18 – 'Similarly, there shall be no discrimination in Palestine against goods originating in or destined for any of the said States' – must be read as developing the same idea, and not as introducing, by way of elaboration of the preceding sentence, a new principle of vast comprehensiveness alien to the purpose and the spirit of the Mandate. The intention, it may reasonably be assumed, was to make it impossible for the Mandatory to achieve by means of a system of tariffs exclusive advantages ruled out by the opening sentence of the Article. There is no indication either in the history of the provisions in question or in the whole economy of the Mandates system to substantiate the view that there was an intention to render it impossible for the Mandatory to authorize measures of discrimination not directed specifically against any one nation or groups of nations with a view to his own exclusive advantage and merely calculated to promote the well-being of the inhabitants of the Mandated territory.

§7 Neither can any interpretation of Article 18 be regarded as acceptable which proves to be inconsistent with an essential postulate of the system of Mandatory government. Every clause of the Mandate must be interpreted subject to the fundamental principle that the well-being and the interests of the Mandated Territory and of its population are the governing and overriding considerations in the execution of the Mandate. The well-being of the population is the decisive test. This consideration, it may be assumed, underlay the decision of the British authorities in the matter of the Colonial Development Act when they came to the conclusion that there was no violation of the principle of economic equality if as a condition of receiving a loan on specially advantageous terms it was necessary to accept undertakings reserving special benefits for the British market (see above, §4). The same consideration underlay the view of the Mandates Commission when it interpreted liberally and extended to other Mandates the provisions of the B Mandates concerning the freedom of action of the Mandatory in the matter of public works (*ibid.*). Both the spirit and the purpose of the Mandate would be disregarded by an interpretation which, while rendering inadmissible the exploitation of the Mandated Territory for the exclusive benefit of the Mandatory, would nevertheless sanction a substantial measure of unilateral advantage for the benefit of all Members of the League at the cost of crippling the economic development of the Mandated Territory.

§8 It must be noted that Article 18 does not refer *expressis verbis* to equality of opportunity. It provides that there shall be no discrimination. While admittedly equality of opportunity is a consequence of non-discrimination, the emphasis on the principle of equality may create – and to a large extent has created – the unwarrantable impression that economic equality is a rigid and formal principle irrespective of the purpose of the Mandate and of accepted canons of interpretation.

§9 The true purpose and the origin of the non-discrimination clause as outlined above (§6), as well as the essential purpose of the principle of trusteeship of the interests of the Mandated Territory (§7), add special weight to the view that the term 'discrimination' used in Article 18 cannot properly be interpreted in its literal meaning. It is not believed that an international tribunal, if called upon to interpret the equality clause in an international instrument of a kind similar to that of a Mandate, would feel at liberty to adopt a purely literal interpretation of that provision. The Permanent Court of International Justice has repeatedly held that a formal interpretation of the term 'equality' is not admissible. The Court has held that there must be equality not only in law but also in fact; it has similarly held that the formal absence of discrimination is not sufficient justification of injurious conduct. (See, for instance, Advisory Opinion concerning *German Settlers in Poland*, *P.C.I.J.* Series B, no. 6, p. 24; Advisory Opinion concerning the *Treatment of Polish Nationals in Danzig Territory*, *ibid.* Series A/B, no. 44, p. 28.) These decisions had reference to the obligations of a State to grant equal treatment to minorities. Article 18 is concerned with the right of a State to equal treatment. But the essential problem is the same in both cases. In both cases the claim protected by law is not to formal equality, but to factual, substantive equality. A State burdened by the obligation to grant equal treatment is entitled to insist that the absence of discrimination thus claimed should be a substantive one. In the present case it would be consistent with the principle of equality as enunciated by the Permanent Court of International Justice that a State which does not admit Palestine products or admits them subject to restriction should not be entitled to claim treatment identical with that enjoyed by a State which is a good commercial customer of the State bound by the duty of non-discrimination.

There are decisions of international and national tribunals bearing on the construction of economic equality clauses in treaties and showing that there has been no inclination to give to these clauses a formal and literal interpretation. Thus in the *Chinn* case, decided on 12 December 1934, by the Permanent Court of International Justice, it was held that the provisions of the Treaty of St Germain providing for complete commercial equality did not imply absolute equality in results in every respect. The Court said: 'The form of discrimination which is forbidden is therefore discrimination based upon nationality and involving differential treatment by reason of their nationality as between persons belonging to different national groups' (*P.C.I.J.* Series A/B, no. 63, p. 87). In a case decided in the same year by the Supreme Court of the United States, it was held that the provisions of the Webster–Ashburton Treaty of 1842 between the United States and Great Britain, laying down that all water communications from Lake Superior to the Lake of the Woods 'shall be free and open to the use of the citizens and subjects of both countries' (291 U.S. 138), did not prohibit the raising of tolls and charges for the use of improvements on the waterways in question. These are merely examples. Should the question of Article 18 come for judicial determination, it would not be difficult to produce an imposing body of judicial decisions showing that provisions for equality of treatment must be interpreted in a liberal and elastic spirit having regard to the nature and the purpose of the instrument in question.

§10 The operation of a clause providing for equality of treatment is not as rigid and automatic as that of a most-favoured-nation clause. With regard to the latter, most States, including Great Britain (but not, as a rule, the United States), have adopted an unconditional interpretation, namely, that the treatment equal to that to be granted to the most-favoured nation is not conditioned by an additional grant of advantages co-extensive with those accorded by that nation. The position is not the same for the reason that the particular interpretation put by Great Britain and other countries upon the most-favoured-nation clause has now acquired a pronounced degree of consistency and is well understood abroad. Moreover, Article 18, as compared with a most-favoured-nation clause, does not admit of an automatic and rigid interpretation for the reasons: (*a*) that the grant of equality of treatment was, on the part of the Mandated Territory, without any reciprocal advantage; and (*b*) that in the case of Mandates there is a particular reason, grounded in the principle of trusteeship, why the country bound by the provision in question should not be exposed to an interpretation resulting in sanctioning a permanent and inequitable disadvantage to that country.

§11 It is possible that an international tribunal may arrive at the conclusion that the provisions of Article 18 must be interpreted according to its plain meaning as distinguished from an interpretation based on the origin of the provisions in question and the essential purpose of the Mandates system. It is also possible that an international tribunal would attach importance to the fact that Members of the League and the Mandates Commission have, for a considerable period, put a practical interpretation on that Article in the sense that according to the intention of the authors of the Mandate no discrimination of any kind whatsoever was to be permissible. Even if this should happen, there would still remain the question whether conditions which obtained at the time when the Article was drafted have not changed in such a manner as to make its continued application inconsistent with what must reasonably be presumed to have been the intention of the Mandate and of the authors both of the Mandates system and of the Mandate for Palestine.

§12 Assuming that the intention of the authors of the Mandate was to introduce a system of unconditional economic equality, there arises the further question of the effect of the fundamental change in economic conditions which has taken place in the meantime. When the Mandate was drafted the tendency was to assume that the economic relations of States would develop in the direction of free trade and of absence of artificial State restrictions, as contemplated in Article 23(e) of the Covenant in which Members of the League agreed to 'make provision to secure and maintain . . . equitable treatment for the commerce of all Members of the League'. In the intervening fifteen years there had taken place a radical change in the field of international commerce. Exchange restrictions, high and prohibitive tariffs, restrictions upon and prohibition of imports, State subsidies, and the like, have become the typical and not abnormal manifestations of inter-state economic intercourse. What in 1922 might have been a reasonable concession in anticipation of equal benefits in a world of economic free trade, has become fifteen years hence a restriction seriously and inequitably hampering the economic development of the country. This is a result which raises in a prominent manner the question whether an international court would not hold that the particular provision of the Mandate has ceased to be operative or whether it does not require modification as the result of the operation of the so-called doctrine *rebus sic stantibus* – the legal doctrine, that is to say, which recognizes a vital change of circumstances as a sufficient reason for terminating, wholly or in part, the obligations of international treaties.

It is difficult to assess what are in the present case the chances of invoking the legal principle embodied in that doctrine. On former occasions international tribunals have been reluctant to give effect to it. They have not denied that it has a place in international law, but they have found almost invariably that it did not apply to the particular case before them. This, for instance, was the case in 1933 in the case of the *Free Zones of Gex and Upper Savoy* between Switzerland and France. If this were the only ground relied on in favour of an interpretation of Article 18 different from the one adopted hitherto, the chances of an appeal to an international tribunal would be slender. However, when taken in conjunction with the other grounds referred to above, this aspect of the question is a factor of legal significance which may well decide the issue.

§13 It would appear from what has been said before that the position is such as to render not without prospects the interpretation of Article 18 by a judicial tribunal. The legal case for an interpretation of Article 18 in the sense contended for by the Jewish Agency rests, as has been shown, on four propositions: (*a*) that the purpose of the provision in the matter of equality was not to impose a unilateral burden upon the Mandated territory for the benefit of all Members of the League, but to prevent the Mandatory from turning the administration of the Mandate to his own exclusive advantage; (*b*) that the governing principle which must underlie the interpretation of the Mandate is that the well-being of the population is the guiding consideration and that no interpretation ought lightly to be adopted which results in a permanent obstacle in the way of the development of the Mandated Territory; (*c*) that the terms 'equality' and 'discrimination' must, following a practice now sanctioned by the Permanent Court of International Justice and other tribunals, be interpreted as implying a substantive as distinguished from a merely formal equality of rights and obligations; and (*d*) that in any case the provision in question must be applied in the light of the radical changes in the economic conditions of the world since the establishment of the Mandate.

While the force of each of these four legal contentions may not be decisive, their cumulative effect is such as to render it doubtful whether an international tribunal would find it possible to adopt without qualifications the official interpretation acted upon hitherto.

§14 It is not believed that the matter can be brought before the Permanent Court of International Justice without the concurrence of the Mandatory Power. It would therefore seem advisable to put the legal position before the authorities of the Mandatory on the lines suggested above and to urge the propriety of bringing the matter for a judicial decision. Once the consent of the Mandatory Power to that course has been secured, the actual method of submission would be a matter of arrangement. A pronouncement of the Permanent Court of International Justice might be brought about either as the result of a request for an advisory opinion or through the contentious procedure by way of a judgment in pursuance of Article 26 of the Mandate or by way of a special arbitration agreement between the Mandatory and a third State concluded with a view to clarifying the situation. It is almost certain that no advisory opinion could or would be asked for without the consent of the Mandatory.

Whatever may be the form of the submission to the Court it will be of importance that the request for an advisory opinion or the special agreement for a judicial decision should be in the form of alternative questions: (1) as to the interpretation of Article 18; (2) in case the Court should feel impelled to give an interpretation of that Article which affirms the view of absolute and formal equality, the Court should pronounce whether, having regard to the intention of the parties and to the purpose of the Mandate, the maintenance of the principle of absolute equality is consistent with the new developments in the sphere of international economic relations. International practice, both before and after the establishment of the Permanent Court of International Justice, shows frequent instances of recommendations of this nature.

§15 It is, however, possible that the Mandatory will not be disposed to consent to an elucidation of the matter by the Permanent Court of International Justice on the ground that a procedure of this nature may set an undesirable precedent in other spheres. In that case the Mandatory might still be agreeable to an interpretative resolution of the Council of the League laying down that the establishment of a system of differential tariffs, within the framework of a system of substantive equality, would be consistent with the terms and the purpose of Article 18. But it must be a matter for serious consideration by the Jewish Agency whether, having regard to circumstances, it is politic to solicit an interpretative resolution of this kind on the part of the Council. By the same token, it would appear that a solicitude shown by the Jewish Agency for a judicial interpretation of Article 18 might be of advantage in matters of wider import.

§16 Neither an interpretative resolution of the Council nor a judicial pronouncement can in fact be passed against the considered view of the Mandatory or even without his active support. This being so, it is advisable to initiate any further action in the matter by approaching in the first instance the authorities of the Mandatory with the legal presentation of the case. These are not so strongly committed to the existing official interpretation as to render impractical any expectation of support. An inquiry, accompanied by such full legal presentation of the case, ought to be made whether His Majesty's Government would be prepared, in view of the new arguments adduced, to make arrangements for or facilitate the submission of the matter for a pronouncement of the Permanent Court of International Justice by advisory opinion in pursuance of a request by the Council of the League or by way of a judgment. It might be a matter for consideration whether a Palestine body or bodies representing the economic interests involved should accompany an inquiry of this kind by an offer to bear the whole or part of the costs of the proceedings before the Court. A similar inquiry could be made with regard to obtaining an interpretative resolution of the Council – a course which, as indicated, may be fraught with danger from the political point of view. The danger will be less pronounced if the Council were seized with the matter in pursuance of a favourable recommendation on the part of the Mandates Commission. This being so, and should the Mandatory authorities give a negative or discouraging answer, the proper course would be to bring the matter, on the lines here suggested, before the Mandates Commission as a first step in the direction of creating a body of legal opinion in favour of a more reasonable and equitable interpretation of Article 18 than has been the case hitherto. Such submission before the Mandates Commission from a body more general and representative than a particular economic association in Palestine...

§17 It must be a matter for consideration, from the political point of view, whether the moment is opportune for raising demands or making requests which imply acquiescence in a development in the direction of Palestine being treated or regarded as an integral part of the Empire. From the legal point of view, it may not be quite feasible to insist, with regard to Article 18, that Palestine is entitled to be allowed the full prerogatives of sovereignty in the economic sphere, and at the same time to claim a position implying, as will be shown later, that Palestine is a subordinate and non-sovereign unit of the larger entity of the British Empire. However, the answer to this objection may well be that the British Dominions whose external independence for all practical purposes is not in question nevertheless enjoy the advantages of Imperial Preference.

§18 The question of Imperial Preference is entirely one between Great Britain and the administration of Palestine. It is not a question which is within the purview of the Mandates Commission or which involves the principles of Mandatory government. Individual members of the Mandates Commission have encouraged the idea of unilateral Imperial Preferences being granted to Palestine (see, e.g., the Observations of M. van Rees at the 22nd Session of the Commission (1932), p. 93, and at the 23rd Session (1933), p. 99). There has been no suggestion that such Preference might be interpreted as involving a degree of assimilation or annexation contrary to the Mandates system.

§19 Neither is the question of Imperial Preference one of legal right and duty as between the British Government and Palestine. It is on the part of Great Britain a matter of undoubted concession. The only relevant question is whether Great Britain is in a position to grant that concession to Palestine having regard to existing commercial treaties between Great Britain and other countries. These treaties provide that the other Contracting Party shall be entitled to benefits and advantages which Great Britain grants to any 'foreign State' or 'other State' or 'third State'. The question with which the British authorities have been confronted is whether Palestine is in relation to Great Britain a 'third State' or 'foreign State' or 'other State'. If she is, then any State with which Great Britain has concluded a treaty providing for most-favoured-nation treatment may ask for the same preferential treatment as is accorded to Palestine – which means the same preferential treatment as is accorded to Colonies and Dominions. This risk the British authorities have so far been unwilling to take.

§20 It appears that the Government of the United Kingdom, as advised by legal authorities, has so far taken the view that Palestine is in relation to Great Britain a foreign country in the meaning of the relevant commercial treaties and most-favoured-nation clauses. Importance has apparently been attached to the facts that Article 22(4) refers to A Mandates as those whose 'existence as independent nations can be provisionally recognized'; that under the Palestine Order in Council, 1922, Palestine is administered by virtue of the powers under the Foreign Jurisdiction Act, 1890 – an enactment which concerns countries which are not technically British territory; that an international tribunal would not be likely to give an interpretation assimilating a Mandate of an advanced type to British territory; and that the result may be a judgment of an international court to the effect that by granting preferential treatment to Palestine without granting it to countries entitled to most-favoured-nation treatment Great Britain has infringed her international obligations to the countries concerned and, in addition to being liable in damages, is bound to grant to them such preference in the future.

§21 It is doubtful whether an international tribunal would find that Palestine is a 'third State' or 'other State' or 'foreign country' in relation to the United Kingdom in this connection. It is probable that it would attach considerable importance to such facts and arguments as that the 'other State' or 'foreign State' or 'third State' must be an independent sovereign State not only by way of formal designation but in substance – a condition which is far from being fulfilled in Palestine; that Palestine is not recognized as an independent State and that Article 22 of the Covenant merely provides that it can be so recognized; that the circumstance of Palestine being governed under the Foreign Jurisdiction Act is not decisive seeing that the British Crown Protectorates, although formally foreign territory and governed under the provisions of the Foreign Jurisdiction Act, have benefited from the advantages of Imperial Preference without any claim to identical advantages having been raised by any foreign State; that as by virtue of the Palestine Order in Council, 1922, which established the constitutional basis of the Palestine Mandate, that country is administered by His Majesty, it is unreasonable to maintain that His Majesty in his capacity as the sovereign of the United Kingdom is foreign to himself in respect of the administration of Palestine; that in section 8 of the Finance Act of 1919 it was expressly contemplated that Palestine may by an Order in Council be brought within the scope of Imperial Preference; that it has been held that Palestine is not a foreign country for the purposes of section 13 of the British Nationality and Status of Aliens Act of 1914, with the result that a British subject acquiring Palestinian nationality does not automatically lose his British nationality; that B and C Mandates have been granted the benefits of Imperial Preference without any 'third State' or 'foreign State' having raised claims to identical treatment and that it is therefore inadmissible to regard Palestine as being a foreign country for the sole reason that it is a Mandated territory; that Palestine cannot be regarded as a foreign State simpliciter seeing that full powers of administration have been granted to the Mandatory in the Mandate for Palestine in contradistinction to the Mandate for Syria; that it is not inconsistent with the spirit of trusteeship that for certain purposes beneficial for the Mandated territory the latter should be treated as not being a foreign country in relation to the Mandatory; that that interpretation has special force in a situation in which as the result of the operation of other provisions, as in the case of Article 18 of the Mandate for Palestine, the territory in question has been deprived of one of the principal rights of independent Statehood by having been deprived of the advantages of economic equality and of buying capacity in the field of international economic relations; and that it is purely artificial to regard Palestine as being more in the nature of an independent foreign State than a self-governing Dominion whose independence is for most practical purposes indistinguishable from that of a fully sovereign State and whose inclusion within the system of Imperial Preference has not given rise to claims or complaints on the part of other States.

§22 It is not unlikely that the Government of the United Kingdom have carefully considered these arguments in favour of either view. They had before them in 1932 a legal opinion signed by Sir John Simon and Lord Erleigh in favour of the view contended for by the Jewish Agency. That opinion, although short and general, was of such a nature as to carry weight. But that opinion did not apparently influence the conclusion previously reached that Palestine *was* a third, independent, State for the purposes of the most-favoured-nation clause. The reasons for that legal conclusion have never been published, but – unless there is a strong disinclination against any judicial interpretation of the Mandate – it is possible that the British Government might be disposed to have the matter tested by means of a judicial pronouncement.

§23 The matter can be brought before the Permanent Court of International Justice by an arrangement between Great Britain and any foreign State submitting the question for a decision either in the form of a claim for damages following upon a refusal to grant most-favoured-nation treatment on the lines of a grant of benefits identical with those extended to Palestine or in the form of a request for a declaratory judgment even before the question of damages has arisen. There is nothing in the Statute of the Court militating against giving a declaratory judgment; and there are pronouncements of the Court in favour of such a possibility. In that case the only risk attendant upon the initiation of judicial proceedings would be that of cost. This being so, it might facilitate matters if the Jewish Agency or the Administration of Palestine were to offer to compensate His Majesty's Government for any costs incurred in connection with the proceedings before the Permanent Court of International Justice.

CHAPTER 4

ARTICLE 18 OF THE MANDATE FOR PALESTINE AND THE DISSOLUTION OF THE LEAGUE OF NATIONS

Editor's note This chapter consists of an opinion dated 22 November 1946 written by Lauterpacht at the request of the Jewish Agency. In it he takes the view that the requirement of non-discriminatory treatment of Members of the League of Nations in matters of trade contained in Article 18 of the Mandate did not survive the dissolution of the League of Nations.

For many, the interest of the opinion will lie in the manner in which Lauterpacht developed the view that, after the dissolution of the League, such rights and obligations under the Mandate survived as could continue to operate independently of the League. From this he concluded that clearly the Mandates Commission could no longer function. But, he went on in the next sentence, and without further reasoning, to say: 'Similarly, there is no room for any rights of States grounded in their membership of the League of Nations.' Within this body of rights he included those prescribed in Article 18 of the Mandate. This conclusion must now be compared with the views expressed by the International Court of Justice in 1950 in the Advisory Opinion on the *International Status of South-West Africa* (*I.C.J. Reports* 1950, p. 128) and in the judgment of 1962 in the *South-West Africa* cases (*I.C.J. Reports* 1962, p. 319). On the other hand, a few pages later in this opinion, Lauterpacht treats Article 26 of the Mandate, which confers jurisdiction upon the Permanent Court of International Justice, as remaining operative for contentious cases. Lauterpacht does not advert to the apparent inconsistency between these two expressions of view.

§1 I have been asked to give an opinion on the question to what extent, if any, the dissolution of the League of Nations and the adoption of the Charter of the United Nations have affected the continued validity of Article 18 of the Mandate for Palestine. The first paragraph of that Article provides as follows:

> The Mandatory shall see that there is no discrimination in Palestine against the nationals of any State Member of the League of Nations (including companies incorporated under its laws) as compared with those of the Mandatory or of any foreign State in matters concerning taxation, commerce or navigation, the exercise of industries or professions, or in the treatment of merchant vessels or civil aircraft. Similarly, there shall be no discrimination in Palestine against goods originating in or destined for any of the said

States, and there shall be freedom of transit under equitable conditions across the Mandated area.

§2 According to Article 76 (d) of the Charter of the United Nations the objects of the Trusteeship System should be, *inter alia*:

(d) To ensure equal treatment in social, economic and commercial matters for all Members of the United Nations and their nationals, and also equal treatment for the latter in the administration of justice, without prejudice to the attainment of the foregoing objectives and subject to the provisions of Article 80.

Article 80 (1) of the Charter of the United Nations provides as follows:

1. Except as may be agreed upon in individual Trusteeship agreements, made under Articles 77, 79 and 81, placing each territory under the Trusteeship system, and until such agreements have been concluded, nothing in this chapter shall be construed in or of itself to alter in any manner the rights whatsoever of any State or any peoples or the terms of existing international instruments to which Members of the United Nations may respectively be parties.

§3 In April 1946 the League of Nations was declared to be dissolved by a Resolution adopted by its last Assembly. The Assembly also adopted a resolution relating to Mandates which provided, *inter alia*, as follows:

The Assembly . . .

(3) Recognizes that, on the termination of the League's existence, its functions with respect to the Mandated territories will come to an end, but notes that Chapters XI, XII and XIII of the Charter of the United Nations embody principles corresponding to those declared in Article 22 of the Covenant of the League;

(4) Takes note of the expressed intentions of the Members of the League now administering territories under Mandate to continue to administer them for the well-being and development of the peoples concerned in accordance with the obligations contained in the respective Mandates, until other arrangements have been agreed between the United Nations and the respective Mandatory Powers.

The Resolution was preceded by a series of declarations made by the representatives of various Mandatories and announcing their intention of continuing the administration of the Mandate in accordance with the general obligation to ensure the protection and the advancement of the interests of the population of the Mandated territories.

§4 In a memorandum which has been submitted to me and which is signed by the Head of the Department for Trade and Industry of the Jewish Agency it is suggested: (*a*) that as the result of dissolution of the

League of Nations Article 18 of the Mandate has lost its validity; (*b*) that while, having regard to Articles 76 and 80 of the Charter, the benefits of Article 18 can still be claimed by some Members of the United Nations, they cannot be claimed: (i) by States which, while Members of the United Nations, were not Members of the League 'at the critical time', namely: Russia, Brazil, Byelorussia, Costa Rica, El Salvador, Guatemala, Haiti, Honduras, Lebanon, Philippines, Saudi Arabia, Syria, Turkey, Ukrainian S.S.R., Venezuela, United States of America; (ii) by States which, although they were Members of the League of Nations 'at the time in question', do not belong to the United Nations, namely: Sweden, Switzerland, Italy, Spain, Portugal, Bulgaria, Roumania, Austria, Hungary, Finland, Transjordan, Japan, Afghanistan, Siam, Chile, Colonies of the United Kingdom (including Cyprus, Burma, Rhodesia, etc.), Colonies of France (including Morocco, Algeria and Tunis), Colonies of Belgium, Colonies of Holland, Colonies of Spain, Colonies of Portugal, Eire, Germany.

It is not clear from the Memorandum what is the meaning of the expression 'at the critical time' or 'at the time in question'. It is difficult to assume that it refers to the time of the adoption of the Charter for, with regard to (i), Turkey was a Member of the League at that time and, with regard to (ii), Italy, Spain, Hungary, Roumania, Austria, Transjordan, etc. were not Members of the League at that time. Neither apparently do the lists refer to the time of the signature of the Covenant or of the dissolution of the League of Nations. However that may be, it is submitted below that the suggested distinction is not relevant for the purpose of the matter under consideration.

§5 It must be regarded as axiomatic that the general obligations of the system of Mandates continue, notwithstanding the dissolution of the League of Nations, until such time as the individual Mandates have been replaced by agreements concluded in connection with the system of Trusteeship. This follows clearly from the Resolutions of the Assembly which dissolved the League of Nations (see above, §3), from the declarations made by the representatives of the Mandatories in the course of the last Assembly of the League (see below, §6) and from similar declarations made by them in the course of the First General Assembly of the United Nations. The affirmation of that principle is also the main object of Article 80 of the Charter of the United Nations, which constitutes a legal obligation of the Members of the United Nations in the matter of Mandates. That aspect of the legal position admits of no doubt, and, in view of this, it is not necessary to inquire further into the legal basis of the continued validity of the general obligations of the Mandates system.

The question which is material is the following: What are the general rights and obligations of the Mandates system which continue to operate notwithstanding the dissolution of the League of Nations? These, it is believed, are the rights and obligations the continued existence of which is independent of the continued existence of the League of Nations and its organs entrusted with the supervision of the system of Mandates. It is clear, for instance, that there is no longer room for the activity of the Mandates Commission, with all that it implies, or for reports of that Commission to the Council of the League of Nations. Similarly there is no room for any rights of States grounded in their membership of the League of Nations.

§6 It follows from what has been said above that no rights can be derived from the membership of the League after the League of Nations has ceased to exist. This applies also to the rights enjoyed by Members of the League of Nations under Article 18 of the Mandate for Palestine. For these reasons I am of the opinion that, subject to Article 80 of the Charter of the United Nations – which, it will be submitted presently, is not applicable to the matter here discussed – Article 18 of the Mandate for Palestine ceased to be operative on 18 April 1946, i.e. with the dissolution of the League of Nations. The only method by which the rights under Article 18 could have been preserved would have been to provide for their continuation in the agreement – i.e. in the Resolution of 18 April 1946 – dissolving the League of Nations. But, it will be noted, the Resolution of 18 April 1946, in the matter of Mandates was limited to putting on record the expressed intention of the Mandatories to administer the Mandated territories 'for the well-being and development of the people concerned in accordance with the obligations contained in the respective Mandates'. There was, significantly, no reference to any rights enjoyed by other Members of the League under the various Mandates. Similarly no reference to any such rights was contained in the various declarations of the Mandatories made in April 1946 at Geneva in connection with the dissolution of the League of Nations. Stress was laid on the intention of the Governments concerned to continue the administration of the areas in question, pending the conclusion of Trusteeship agreements, in accordance with the interests of the peoples of these territories. (For the text of these declarations see *The League Hands Over*, *League of Nations Publications*, *General* (1946), 1, 67–72.)

I am of the opinion that, but for the doubts introduced by what has been described as the 'conservatory clause' of Article 80 of the Charter, the effect of the dissolution of the League of Nations would be to terminate rights grounded in the membership of the League.

§7 The question which must now be considerd is whether Article 80 of the Charter of the United Nations has affected the legal position with regard to Article 18 of the Palestine Mandate. Article 80 of the Charter lays down that 'nothing in this Chapter shall be construed *in or of itself* to alter in any manner the rights whatsoever of any States or any peoples or the terms of existing international instruments to which members of the United Nations may respectively be parties'. The Charter does not say – and probably it could not say – that no event whatsoever and no agreement whatsoever shall have the result of affecting rights created by any international instrument or agreement in force at the time of the adoption of the Charter. It merely lays down that nothing in the provisions and the principles of chapter XII of the Charter relating to the 'International Trusteeship System' shall be construed '*in or of itself*' to alter rights under existing international instruments – including the rights under various instruments relating to Mandates. Thus nothing in the Charter is intended 'in or of itself' to affect the rights under Article 18 of the Palestine Mandate. This does not mean that other events, such as the dissolution of the League of Nations, cannot legally affect the rights in question.

It would be inaccurate to suggest that the effect of Article 80 of the Charter is to preserve all the clauses of the Palestine Mandate (such as Article 24 relating to submission of annual reports to the Council of the League of Nations) or the clauses of Article 22 of the Covenant relating to the supervision of the Mandate system. It is equally improbable that it preserves rights arising out of the membership of the dissolved League of Nations.

As this is the principal legal submission of the present opinion, it may be emphasized once more that the Charter does not say generally that pending the conclusion of the Trusteeship agreements there shall be no change whatsoever in the rights of any State or people under existing international agreements. It merely says that 'nothing in this chapter' (i.e. the chapter on the International Trusteeship System) shall be construed as having '*in or of itself*' that effect. There is no warrant for giving an extensive interpretation of that provision.

§8 Possibly the conservatory clause could have had some indirect bearing upon Article 18 in the period between the adoption (or the ratification) of the Charter and the dissolution of the League of Nations in April 1946. In that period, but for the conservatory clause, it might have been possible to assert – though with doubtful accuracy – that the conservatory clause was intended to exclude the operation of the provisions of the Charter which modified the principle of the 'open door' and which might be construed as having a bearing upon the continued validity of Article 18 of the Palestinian Mandate. No such connection can be deemed to exist subsequent to the dissolution of the League.

§9 While it thus appears that a textual interpretation of the relevant documents leads to the conclusion that Article 18 of the Palestine Mandate has ceased to be valid and that Article 80 of the Charter does not affect the result thus reached, it is proper to ascertain to what extent the circumstances preceding the adoption of the Charter and the dissolution of the League substantiate that conclusion. In particular, it is permissible, in the attempt to elucidate the intention of Article 80 of the Charter in relation to the rights under Article 18 of the Palestine Mandate, to recall the views entertained by the principal States concerned as to the adequacy and justice of the clause of that Article providing for unconditional equality of economic opportunity. For it cannot be assumed that the States concerned would have made a special effort to perpetuate – or would have agreed to a perpetuation of – what they considered to be an anomaly.

It is a matter of general knowledge that prior to the Conference at San Francisco, the Mandatory Power and the successive Royal Commissions on Palestine gave expression to the view that the provisions of Article 18 have had an effect not foreseen by the States which adopted it and that their operation has been inequitable and harmful to the interests of Palestine. The relevant passages of the Report of the Royal Commission on Palestine of 1937 and of the Palestine Partition Commission of 1938 may suitably be quoted:

Report of the Palestine Royal Commission (1937), chapter VIII (20), p. 214:
. . . Italy, Spain, the United States and other citrus-producing countries can make their bargains and commercial treaties, while Palestine alone is stretched on the rack of the non-discriminating injunction of the Mandate – bound by a rigid adherence to the policy of the open door . . .

Chapter VIII (28), p. 217:
We take the view that the provisions of Article 18 are out of date. Opinion may differ as to the value of economic nationalism: but its principles are wholly inconsistent with non-discrimination and the open door. The application of the principle of the open door to Mandated territories was certainly never intended to have an injurious effect on their 'well-being and development'. We think it is clear that without an amendment of Article 18 Palestine must continue to suffer from the restrictions which hamper international trade and we recommend that negotiations should be opened without delay to put the Palestine trade upon a fairer basis.

Chapter XIX (Conclusions and Recommendations) (10), 9, p. 368:
We recommend that steps should be taken to secure the amendment of Article 18 of the Mandate and place the external trade of Palestine upon a fairer basis.

Report of the Palestine Partition Commission (1938), para. 435, p. 212:
The Royal Commission took the view that the provisions of Article 18 are out of date; and it is certain that the Jews, who have long pressed for an alteration of that Article, would hold that their industrial development in the new State was being unfairly hampered if they are given no greater measure of freedom under the new conditions than the Palestine Government now possesses under the Mandate. It would therefore seem to be a necessary condition of the formation of a customs union including the Mandated territories that under the new Mandate those territories should be given the same freedom as other countries to make their own commercial bargains with the rest of the world.

At the Conference at San Francisco the British delegation opposed in strong terms the principle of the 'open door' conceived as a unilateral concession. Lord Cranborne said:

Our experience, as a result of the twenty-five years of administration of these territories, is that non-discriminatory provisions do not operate in the interests of the inhabitants. If I were to ask the delegates of the forty-nine nations that they should repeal all legislation in their own countries which contained any discriminatory provisions either against goods or materials of other countries, I feel confident that there would not be a single member present who would not immediately protest, that such a step would be fraught with grave dangers to the interest of his fellow-countrymen. If that is true of the sovereign States capable of standing by themselves in the conditions of the modern world, how much more is it true of the dependent territories which could not. (Committee II/4, 4th Meeting, 14 May 1945; *Proceedings of the Conference*, 10, 440.)

Other delegations voiced the same view. As a result, the Charter, in Article 76 (d), qualified the principle of economic opportunity by subordinating it to the interests of the population of the Trust Territories.

It is not suggested that the general and uniform rejection of the principle of the 'open door' would be sufficient to override any clear intention of the conservatory clause of Article 80 of the Charter. However, Article 80 does not evidence such intention. In fact it has been suggested above that Article 80 is not relevant to the legal situation which has arisen, in the matter of Article 18 of the Palestine Mandate, as the result of the dissolution of the League of Nations. Yet, in so far as there is an element of doubt in the interpretation here submitted, it is of some importance for the construction of Article 80 to bear in mind the attitude of the Powers concerned, both before and during the Conference at San Francisco, to the question of the 'open door'. The applicable rules of international law fully authorize recourse to so-called 'preparatory work' and to accompanying historical circumstances for the interpretation of controversial provisions of treaties.

§10 There is in the proceedings of the San Francisco Conference no support for the suggestion that the intention to preserve the economic rights of non-Mandatory States was a factor in the adoption of the 'conservatory clause'. The 'conservatory clause' was intended to prevent any application or misapplication of the provisions of the Charter for the purpose of upsetting the regime of Mandatory Government either in general or in relation to any particular Mandatory territory in advance of the conclusion of Trusteeship agreements. Thus in relation to A Mandates the delegate of the United States said: 'Among the "rights whatsoever of any States or any peoples" mentioned in the proposed amendment there were included any rights set forth in para. 4 of Article 22 of the Covenant' – an observation clearly directed towards Palestine, the only remaining Mandate of Class A (Committee II/4, 13th Meeting, *Proceedings of the Conference*, 8, 513. This observation was included in the rapporteur's report to the full Commission, vol. 10, pp. 607 and 610, and in the Commission rapporteur's report to the Plenary Session, vol. 8, p. 235.)

The kind of subject which was in the minds of some delegates as coming potentially within the scope of the 'conservatory clause' may be surmised from the proposals made by the delegations of Egypt, Syria and Iraq and intended to formulate the wording of the 'conservatory clause' in such a manner as to throw doubts on the continued validity of the provisions of the Palestine Mandate in so far as it relates to the National Home for the Jewish people (see Egyptian amendment, Committee II/4, 10th meeting, 24 May 1945, 10, 485; Syrian amendment, *ibid.* p. 487; amendment of Iraq, 13th meeting, 8 June 1945, 10, 575). These proposals were defeated. The delegate of Guatemala proposed amendments, which were not adopted, calculated to meet some remote contingencies with regard to British Honduras (8th meeting, 22 May 1945, 10, 470). No evidence can be found in the *travaux préparatoires* of the Conference to suggest any clear relation between the 'conservatory clause' and the continuance of provisions such as those of Article 18.

§11 If Article 18 of the Mandate for Palestine has ceased to be operative on the ground that, with the dissolution of the League of Nations, there are no longer Members of the League to which it can apply, then, for the purposes of the present opinion, there is no room for drawing a distinction between States which are Members of the United Nations and those which are not. The Charter of the United Nations and membership of the United Nations cannot 'in and of themselves' confer any rights in respect of Mandated territories independently of particular Trust agreements. This is one of the indirect results of the 'conservatory clause'. The position would, of course, be the same even without the 'conservatory clause'.

If, on the other hand, the view should prevail and be acted upon by the Government of Palestine to the effect that Article 18 of the Mandate continues to operate, then, in any case, it would not operate in relation to States which either were never Members of the League of Nations or, although they were so for a time, were not Members of the League in April 1946 because of previous withdrawal or for some other reason. These States include: Brazil (cessation of membership: 13 June 1928); Chile (1 June 1940); Costa Rica (1 January 1929); Germany (1 October 1935); Honduras (9 July 1938); Hungary (10 April 1941); Italy (10 December 1939); Japan (26 March 1936); Nicaragua (26 June 1938); Peru (8 April 1941); Roumania (10 June 1942); El Salvador (9 August 1939); Spain (8 May 1941); Venezuela (10 June 1940); Soviet Russia (1940); and (probably) Paraguay (1937) and Austria (1940).

§12 The position of the United States requires special consideration inasmuch as the United States was never a Member of the League of Nations and as the rights of 'open door' enjoyed by it derived not from its membership of the League but from a special agreement concluded with Great Britain as the Mandatory Power, namely, the Convention of 3 December 1924 respecting Rights in Palestine (Treaty Series (1925), no. 24; United States, Treaty Series no. 728).

However, it is not believed that the actual legal position in respect of the United States is different from that of other interested States. For Article 2 of the Convention in question provided that the United States 'shall have and enjoy all the rights and benefits secured under the terms of the Mandate to Members of the League of Nations and their nationals notwithstanding the fact that the United States is not a Member of the League of Nations'. The effect of this article is to secure to the United States the same treatment, but no more, which is enjoyed by other Members of the League of Nations.

§13 Although what is believed to be the correct interpretation of the relevant documents leads to the conclusion that the provisions of Article 18 of the Palestine Mandate have lost their validity in consequence of the dissolution of the League I do not consider that the legal position is so free of doubt as to permit the Palestine Government to act unilaterally on the interpretation here suggested. In a matter involving both an international trust and the interests of other States it is desirable to avoid anything open to the reproach of arbitrary *ex parte* proceedings. It is believed, therefore, that there are two courses open to the Government of Palestine in the matter in case it should be in agreement with the view expressed in the present opinion, namely, that Article 18 is no longer valid:

(1) One course is to approach the Governments of those States which were Members of the League of Nations at the time of the dissolution of the League (as well as the Government of the United States), to put before them the view of the Palestine Government as to the legal situation consequent upon the dissolution of the League of Nations, and to ask for their formal acquiescence in the resulting measures of the Palestine Administration in the direction of resuming the freedom of action denied to it by Article 18.

(2) Should all or some of these Governments be unwilling to accede to the view of the Administration of Palestine, it would be proper – and practicable – for the latter to attempt to obtain a ruling of the International Court of Justice either by way of an advisory opinion or by way of a judgment rendered in pursuance of Article 26 of the Mandate for Palestine. An advisory opinion could be asked for by the General Assembly or the Security Council at the request of Great Britain by virtue of Article 96 of the Charter. The Court could also render a judgment, in the course of contentious proceedings instituted in accordance with Article 26 of the Mandate, by a State which was a Member of the League of Nations at the time of its dissolution. These would be proceedings in the nature of a test case brought by one State affected by a decision of the Government of Palestine to adopt discriminating economic measures against it.

§14 Should the Government of Palestine feel unable to accede to or to act upon the view expressed in the present opinion as to the legal position which has arisen with respect to Article 18 of the Palestine Mandate as the result of the dissolution of the League of Nations, it would still be open to it to approach the interested Governments with a request for a voluntary renunciation of the benefits hitherto unilaterally enjoyed under Article 18 of the Mandate. In deciding upon a step of this nature, the Government of Palestine could submit that, in the light of experience and of weighty official pronouncements, Article 18 has operated in a way which is inequitable and, in its cumulative effect, iniquitous; that the principle of a unilateral 'open door' system in what used to be Mandated territories has been abandoned in the Charter of the United Nations; and that, therefore, the renunciation of that one-sided privilege in the period of transition would be indicated and proper.

III
REPRESENTATION OF STATES

CHAPTER 5

RECOGNITION OF GOVERNMENTS

Editor's note Lauterpacht's extensive work on the law of recognition was done principally in the period before 1947. Before the outbreak of the Second World War he had already largely completed the manuscript of the volume which appeared, after revision, as *Recognition in International Law*, published by the Cambridge University Press in 1947.

The work was stimulated by the investigations which Lauterpacht had made in the late 1920s into the opinions of the Law Officers of the Crown, amongst which he found many dealing with the various aspects of recognition. He drew the whole source to the attention of Professor H. A. Smith (1885–1961), who was then professor of international law at the London School of Economics. On 22 November 1929, Smith wrote to Dr Hugh Dalton, who was serving as Parliamentary Under-Secretary of State in the Labour Government, but had been previously, and was again later to be, a member of the staff of the L.S.E., as follows:

22 November 1929

Dear Dalton,

I am going to suggest to you that you should add lustre to your term of office by inaugurating a work which will be of outstanding importance in the history of International Law. To shorten this letter I will ask you to glance briefly at the title page and preface of Moore's *Digest of International Law* (8 volumes), published by the Government Printing Office at Washington in 1906. As Malkin and his colleagues will tell you, this is an indispensable work of reference for all who are concerned in any way either with the teaching or with the practice of international law. What I am suggesting is that we should prepare a corresponding publication for this country.

Lauterpacht has discovered an immense mass of unpublished material in the Record Office, much of it being of the highest value, e.g. the opinions of Lord Stowell as a Law Officer. In your own office there is a great deal more. Obviously, therefore, the work can only be done under official sanction. Moore's *Digest* has had a very large sale, so the publication, if not actually profitable, will only be a very small charge on the public purse.

As Moore points out (Preface, p. iv) the work cannot be done properly without a certain amount of editorial exposition, and this involves the expression of opinions on controversial questions. It should therefore be made clear that the Foreign Office accepts no responsibility for such opinions. A paragraph to this effect appears in the preface to Hull's *Digest of British Prize Cases* published by the Stationery Office in 1927. It is therefore desirable that the editors and compilers should be unofficial persons, the responsibility of the Foreign Office being limited to providing facilities and money.

I am prepared, having consulted my colleagues, to say that we would undertake the work here, and probably this would be the cheapest and most convenient way of doing it. But we claim no copyright in the idea, the credit for which is due to Lauterpacht, and this suggestion is not intended to limit your freedom of choice. When you have talked the matter over with Malkin, I should like to know as soon as possible what you think of it.

Sincerely yours
H. A. Smith

A carbon of the letter amongst Lauterpacht's papers is marked in his hand 'the answer to this was in the end negative'.

Subsequently, however, the Law Officers' opinions were used and in part printed, first, by H. A. Smith in his two volumes, *Great Britain and the Law of Nations* (vol. I (1932); vol. II (1935)), then by Arnold McNair in *The Law of Treaties* (of which the first edition appeared in 1938) and finally by Lauterpacht in *Recognition in International Law*. Later, McNair published a much fuller selection under the title *International Law Opinions*, in three volumes (1956). Since then the whole collection of Law Officers' opinions up to 1860 in their original manuscript form has been photographically reproduced in 95 volumes.

In the period 1939–45 Lauterpacht published the following articles on or related to recognition:

'The Form of Foreign Office Certificates', *B.Y.* 20 (1939), 125–8

'The Principle of Non-Recognition in International Law', *Legal Problems in the Far Eastern Conflict* (1941), 129–56

'Recognition of States in International Law', *Yale Law Journal*, 53 (1944), 385–458

'Recognition of Governments, I and II', *Columbia Law Review*, 45 (1945), 815–64, and 46 (1946), 37–68

'Recognition of Insurgents as a *de facto* Government', *Modern Law Review*, 3 (1939–40), 1–20

'Insurrection et Piraterie', *R.G.* (1939), 513–49

'Implied Recognition', *B.Y.* 21 (1944), 123–50

'*De facto* Recognition, Withdrawal of Recognition, and Conditional Recognition', *B.Y.* 22 (1945), 164–90

These reappeared as parts of *Recognition in International Law*. A reprint of that volume, with a substantial introduction by Sir Gerald Fitzmaurice and Professor Gillian White, is now in preparation. It is, therefore, unnecessary to reproduce in these *Collected Papers* the articles listed above.

The item of which the present chapter consists was, however, published after the appearance of *Recognition in International Law* – the concepts of which, particularly as regards the legal duty to recognize a Government which has acquired effective control of a country and enjoys the habitual obedience of the bulk of the population, were soon invoked by the British Government as an academic exposition of its own approach to the subject.

So much was this so that as the moment approached when recognition of the displacement of the Nationalist Government of China by the Communist Government became necessary, Lauterpacht was asked by the Foreign Office to write an article for *The Times* newspaper summarizing the legal position. The article appeared on 6 January 1950, on the morning of the announcement by the British Government of the recognition of the Government of the People's Republic of China.

It may be helpful, at a time when his Majesty's Government are faced [in China] with the necessity of taking a decision of great moment, to state the rule of international law in the matter of recognition of Governments. Such action as is about to be taken must be based on legal principles capable of general application and rooted in the practice of this and other States. It must not be open to the charge that it is being adopted exclusively for the sake of advantages which may be immediate and tangible but which are insignificant when weighed in the balance of the enduring interests of this country and of the peace of the world.

The problem of recognition of Governments is one of the crucial issues of international law. It touches the independence of States at one of its most vital points. To decline to recognize a Government is to withhold from the community which it governs most of the advantages of international law. It involves, among other things, a refusal to acknowledge the validity of its legislative and judicial acts; and the denial to it and its organs of the ordinary jurisdictional immunities. On the other side, it involves the Government refusing recognition in a series of difficulties since *ex hypothesi* it is unable to use the ordinary international methods of protecting its own nationals and interests in territory controlled by the Governments which it refuses to recognize.

There are some who maintain that, all this notwithstanding, recognition is a purely discretionary act of policy – act of grace which may be withheld at pleasure and may legitimately be used as a weapon of political intervention or of economic pressure. There is no support for any such view in the bulk of the practice of this and other countries. On the contrary, overwhelming authority points to the view that, provided that the conditions presented by international law are fulfilled, there is a legal duty to recognize.

The principles of international law, which, in the absence of an international authority, States have by and large observed, are, stated as briefly as the subject permits, as follows:

(1) Recognition is a declaration of an existing fact. Whenever the requisite conditions of governmental capacity exist recognition is due as a matter of right. Once the revolutionary Government may fairly be

held to enjoy, with a reasonable prospect of permanency, the obedience of the mass of the population, and once it is in effective control of the bulk of the national territory, it is entitled to recognition. Its revolutionary origin or the method of the revolutionary change is irrelevant.

The United States of America, which more than any other country has had occasion to formulate an attitude on the subject, has given emphatic and repeated expression to that view. As President van Buren said in 1829, 'that which is the Government *de facto* is equally so *de jure*', or, as Secretary of State Fish said in 1875, 'the practice of the United States in recognizing that Government of a people which is a *de facto* one, is founded on the only true and wise principle and policy'.

(2) International law prohibits premature recognition of the revolutionary Government. So long as the lawful Government has a reasonable prospect of reasserting its authority, recognition is an unfriendly act and a violation of international law. The presumption is in favour of the established Government. As Sir William Harcourt, who was the first Whewell Professor of International Law in the University of Cambridge, put it in a letter to *The Times* during the American Civil War, 'a friendly State is bound to exact very conclusive and indisputable evidence that sovereignty of a Government with which it has existing relations over any part of its former dominions has been finally and permanently divested'. On the other hand, if I may quote from my book written in 1947, 'to maintain that the lawful Government holding out in one isolated fortress is entitled to continued recognition *de jure* is to strain to breaking point an otherwise unimpeachable rule'. It is a question of fact, to be ascertained in good faith, whether the authority of the lawful Government has become purely nominal.

(3) Can recognition properly be given to a revolutionary Government the support of which by the people is not evidenced by, to use a phrase of Jefferson's, 'the will of the nation substantially declared'? Is effectiveness pure and simple the decisive test or is a subsequent legitimation of the revolutionary change by a freely expressed popular approval an essential requirement of recognition? That was a condition of recognition sometimes insisted upon by Great Britain until the First World War. That was also the practice of the United States, especially under President Wilson. But that practice, rational and desirable as it may be, was abandoned after the First World War and is not at present part of the law. It may be revived when the right of man to government by consent has become part of the positive law of nations suitably guaranteed and enforced. That day is not as yet.

In the meantime, constitutional legitimation through democratic process as understood by the western nations is not a condition of recognition according to existing international law. Professor Hyde, the leading American authority, has summarized in the following words the recent attitude of his country: 'It [the United States] does not seek by the withholding of acknowledgment of the achievements of insurgents to invoke a fiction that would identify a technically existing Government, however decrepit, with the foreign State concerned, so as to succor that Government in its extremity. In a word, the policy of the United States in relation to the recognition of new Governments appears to be no longer associated with, or made the handmaiden of, intervention'. (*International Law*, 2nd ed. (1945), 2, 182.)

(4) There is, finally, the question of the willingness to fulfil international obligations and of assurances to be given to that effect by the Government recognition of which is under consideration. That particular test of recognition has been often resorted to, and has recently loomed large in public discussion, including leading articles in *The Times*. But it is extremely doubtful whether it is a sound test and whether it forms part of international law. It was absent from British practice in the nineteenth century. It is a condition of recognition which has often been abused, in relation to weak Governments, for the purpose of extracting unilateral advantages and concessions. In relation to the Government of a large State its futility is obvious, for it is a clear rule of international law that a newly recognized Government is bound by the obligations of its predecessor and of international law generally.

No special assurances are required. Neither can it be expected that the Government of a great State will be induced to give them unless on a basis of mutuality and equality. The value of any such assurance, if not accompanied by good will, is insignificant. The proper course is to assume that the Government of a sovereign State will fulfil its obligations in good faith. Failing that, it is open to other States to adapt since methods of persuasion as circumstances and international law permit.

The distinction must be asserted between recognizing a Government and entering into diplomatic relations with it. No State is legally obliged to enter into and maintain diplomatic relations with a State or Government which it recognizes. On the other hand, it cannot enter into full and normal diplomatic relations with a State or Government which it does not recognize.

Recognition of a new governmental authority, accompanied as it must be by automatic withdrawal of recognition from its predecessor, necessitates an invidious decision which, in relation to old friends, may be distasteful and not free from anxiety. But decisions of this nature are unavoidable. They do not become easier by dint of being postponed. It may be of importance, in the case now before His Majesty's Government, to reassure public opinion that the decision at which they have arrived is not arbitrary or intended to minister to what may be a transient advantage, but that it is in accordance with principle and with the practice of enlightened nations, including that of our closest friend and ally.

IV

EFFECT OF TOTAL OR PARTIAL EXTINCTION OF STATE PERSONALITY. STATE SUCCESSION

CHAPTER 6

SUCCESSION OF STATES WITH RESPECT TO PRIVATE LAW OBLIGATIONS

Editor's note This article appeared in a Polish periodical, *Glos Prawa*, 5 (1928), no. 5–6 (May–June), p. 18. It has been translated from the Polish by Dr K. Skubiszweski, Lecturer in International Law at Poznan University and *Associé* of the *Institut de Droit International.*

The editor of *Glos Prawa* attached the following note to the indication of Lauterpacht's authorship at the beginning of the article:

> It is thanks to the initiative taken by Professor Julian Makowski that we owe the contact with the author of the present paper, our compatriot from Lwow, occupying today, in spite of his young age, an outstanding position in the English world of learning. After having spent the first two years of legal studies at the Jan Kazimierz University in Lwow, Dr Lauterpacht studied in Vienna, where he received the doctor's degrees in law and in political science. Thereafter he obtained his LL.D. degree from the University of London. In view of his outstanding scholarly writings in international law he was appointed Lecturer at the London School of Economics and Political Science, where he is a teacher of recognized authority. The principal work of Dr Lauterpacht is his book on *Private Law Sources and Analogies of International Law.* In addition, he regularly contributes to the principal English and American periodicals on international law. Off-prints of his two recent contributions, which the author sent to us, viz. 'Spinoza and International Law', *B.Y.* 8 (1927), 89, and 'Revolutionary Activities by Private Persons against Foreign States', published in *A.J.* 22 (1928), 105, both show the extent of his scholarly interest.
>
> The present article, written on the invitation of the Editor, though it treats its subject from a higher or general point of view, nevertheless indirectly supplies the reader with substantial scholarly and practical criteria helpful in deciding the important and topical problem with which the *Glos Prawa* has dealt on several occasions in connection with the decisions of the Supreme Court, namely, the problem of the responsibility of the Polish State for private law obligations undertaken by the former Austrian State. We are pleased to state that the final conclusions of the distinguished author are in line with the attitude that we have adopted, cf. contributions published in *Glos Prawa* by Dr Lutwak, 1925, nos. 17–20, pp. 388–96; Professor Allerhand, 1926, no. 2, pp. 69 *et seq.*; and Dr Weinberg, 1927, no. 12, p. 437; for the opposite view see Professor Julian Makowski, 1925, no. 23–4, pp. 487 *et seq.*

I

If there existed on the European continent the Anglo-American habit of frequently identifying the more important lawsuits by using the names of the parties, the ladies Niedzielskie would undoubtedly acquire a certain fame among Polish international lawyers. Their case was the occasion of divergent decisions which once again made the problem of State succession a matter of legal discussion. The course of the case was more animated probably in view of the fact that the Court of Appeal in Lwów, departing here from the constant practice of Polish courts on this question, tended to adopt an attitude which some consider both progressive and equitable. But the Supreme Court quickly and in an unequivocal manner quelled this attempt at independence. In a decision of 13 October 1925 the Third Division of the Supreme Court of the Polish Republic repeated its position in the following words:

> It is true that the older science of the Law of Nations applied, by analogy, the principles of private law on succession and inheritance of property to the taking over of the territory of the predecessor State by the new State: the newly created State or the State taking possession of a part of the territory of another State also assumed all such obligations and debts of the former State as were connected with the area involved. In modern times this view of the law underwent a change. The new State is now legal successor with respect to the extinct State and takes over the latter's burdens and debts only in so far as it has explicitly accepted them.[1]

There was nothing strikingly new in this decision. The plaintiffs, who requested payment for certain construction work ordered by the former Austrian authorities and carried out in several Government buildings, were not taken by surprise because a long series of decisions rendered by the Supreme Court and other tribunals has bestowed on the legal principle expressed in the *Niedzielskie* case the character of a clear and categorical rule which, though subject from time to time to attack on grounds of interest, common sense, or ethics, does not contain anything that would amount to unjustified arbitrariness or deviation from the attitude heretofore adopted by the highest Polish judges. Decisions of the Supreme Administrative Tribunal in the *Ludwig* case in 1924, or the judgment of the Supreme Court in *Graffowa and Wolanowski* v. *Ministry of Agriculture* in 1923, are examples of a clear and unequivocal formulation of the attitude taken by the highest judicial instances. The number of such decisions is legion.[2]

[1] L. cz. III. Rw. 1485/26, *Glos Prawa* (1927), no. 12, p. 444. (The decision is digested in *Annual Digest*, 3 (1925–6), 74: *Niedzielskie* v. (*Polish*) *Treasury*.)

[2] These judgments, as well as some further ones which adopt a similar attitude, are quoted in the excellent treatise by Professor Ehrlich, *Prawa Narodów* (1927), pp. 272–9, which apparently approves of the position taken by the courts.

It would be neither justified nor in line with the respect due to the supreme judges of the Republic to attribute this attitude to so-called fiscal patriotism. A glance at the judicial decisions of other States before and after the World War shows that in the question of State succession municipal courts were not inclined to be too liberal. In 1871 the Court of Appeal in Florence adopted the view that State succession with respect to private law claims is a matter of morality rather than of law. In 1905 the King's Bench Division of the English High Court, in *West Rand Central Gold Mining Company* v. *The King*,[1] a case which has frequently been cited, expressed a similar opinion in relation to certain claims arising out of measures of requisition taken by the former Government of South Africa. In the same year, the Supreme Court of South Africa, in *Postmaster-General* v. *Taute*, handed down a similar decision, the contents of which were repeated twenty years later, in 1925, by the same Court in *Shingler* v. *Union Government*.[2] In deciding on concession claims arising in relation to the obligations of the Spanish Government in Cuba, American courts took an identical position in 1912.[3] The Supreme Court of Poland will undoubtedly find, in the practice of other States after the World War, numerous judgments which coincide with its own attitude. In cases involving State succession, Czechoslovak courts simply ask whether the claim is based on any provision of Czechoslovak law and, if not, they dismiss the action. As a rule, Austrian courts decline to consider Austria as the universal successor of the former Austrian Empire and recognize only those obligations for which express provision was made in the Treaty of St Germain. These involve not only such claims as, for instance, a request for the payment of a pension connected with a war decoration awarded by the former Austrian State,[4] but also pensions payable by the Administration of the Imperial Railways.[5] The practice of Roumanian[6] and German courts is similar. The latter denied in recent years the principle of succession, with the exception of cases where such a negative attitude could be harmful to the Reich Treasury. Quite recently, in a case

[1] [1905] 2 K.B. 498.

[2] South African Law Reports (1925), Supreme Court, Appellate Division 556: *Annual Digest*, 3 (1925–6), 77. It should be emphasized that the above attitude of the Anglo-American courts follows from the notion, peculiar to these countries, of annexation as an Act of State not subject to the jurisdiction and control of ordinary courts.

[3] *The Eastern Extension, Australasia and China Telegraph Co.* v. *The United States* (1912) 48 Ct. Cls. 33.

[4] Judgment of 15 March 1926; *Sammlung der Erkenntnisse des Verfassungsgerichtshofs* (new ed., 1926), 6, no. 542, 24–5.

[5] Judgment of 23 June 1925: *Entscheidungen des österr. Obersten Gerichtshofes in Zivil- und Justizverwaltungssachen*, 7 (1925), no. 223, 561–4.

[6] Cf. judgments of the Roumanian Tribunal of Appeal, digested and commented on in *Clunet*, 54 (1921), 1166.

involving the deposit of money with the Court at Windhuk in that part of South Africa transferred to the British Empire as a Mandate, the Reichsgericht decided that the obligation devolved on the Mandatory in spite of the absence of relevant provisions in the Treaty of Versailles.[1]

Thus, on the face of it, the Supreme Court of the Polish Republic is not alone in expressing the opinion expressed above.[2] Nor has the Court contradicted any of its former judgments. It is also clear that its view does not technically encroach upon any written rule of the Polish law in force. However, this is all that can be said in defence of the Court's attitude.

Against this attitude it can and should be emphatically stated that, in so far as the Court intends to base its position on international law, this attitude is unfounded, and the way in which the Supreme Court invokes international law is inexact and, in consequence, erroneous. Some lawyers have become so much accustomed to see in international law a typical example of a 'weak' law and of discrepancy between law and ethics that they have recourse to the Law of Nations as the authoritative source of legal arguments which, *de lege ferenda*, would not stand for a single moment in municipal private law.

It is true that two hundred or three hundred years ago rulers kept lawyers at their courts specially trained in finding, in the Law of Nations, justifications for necessities which were dictated, in fact or seemingly, by *raison d'état*. But the spirit and atmosphere of those times has vanished for ever. Today the Law of Nations is not an obedient *ancilla regnorum*, and the less courts invoke that law as the source of arguments which are highly dubious from the point of view of equity and justice, the better the situation will be.

Nevertheless, the very fact that the Supreme Court invoked international law indicates considerable progress towards the recognition of certain rights of the individual independently of municipal law. This well-justified attitude is followed by the courts of justice of almost the whole world. For let us imagine that the plaintiff in these cases involving succession be not a Polish national but an alien who remains, in case of unjust treatment, under the protection of his State, or an individual belonging to a national minority the rights of which are internationally guaranteed, as happened in the case of the *German Settlers in Poland*,

[1] Judgment of 27 April 1926: *Entscheidungen des Reichsgerichts in Zivilsachen*, 113, 281.

[2] The similarity to the decisions of other courts is more apparent than real. The cases cited concern to a large extent claims either arising under concessions or claiming recognition of future rights and are frequently not devoid of a profiteering character. On the other hand, the unconditional attitude taken by the Polish courts covers, without exception, *all* kinds of claims.

whose claims against the Polish State have been upheld in an advisory opinion of the Permanent Court of International Justice.[1] In such cases there would be no doubt that the rights of the persons involved are in principle guaranteed by international law and that fundamentally such rights could be the object of international proceedings regardless of whether or not the individual claim was actually based on international law.

The contention that, in the realm of international law, relationships involving succession arise only between States is at variance with the international legal writings on succession (in particular, those writings dealing primarily with the rights which private persons have against the successor State), with the practice of municipal courts which invoke international law even when they deny particular claims, and with judgments of international tribunals.[2] It is true that the individual cannot assert these rights on the international plane, but this fact does not deprive such rights of their international character. This character becomes visible and effective when the home State espouses the claim.

Accordingly, the intention of the present article is to treat the subject only from the standpoint of general international law. We do not examine the question whether one or another category of claims finds justification in the Treaty of St Germain or in the provisions of Polish law.

2

The problem of succession in international law is highly complicated in its details and application, but it is very simple as a basic legal problem. In so far as the details are concerned, it is generally known that the succession of States assumes a different complexion depending on whether one is dealing with a case of cession, annexation, or complete dismemberment. With respect to each of these cases there exist rules regulating specific rights and duties, e.g. obligations under international treaties, different kinds of public debt, concessions and contracts, damages for torts of the former State, taking over of functionaries, salaries and pensions, mortgage debts, and so forth. One could write separate treatises on the application of the general principle to each of these cases.

But as a basic legal problem the question of succession which results from legal occurrences following upon territorial changes between

[1] *P.C.I.J.*, Series B, no. 6.

[2] Cf. however, the opposite view by Professor Makowski (*Glos Prawa*, 2 (1925), 488), who states that 'there is room for succession only within the framework of one and the same system of objective legal rules and only among subjects belonging to such system'. I admit that I can hardly understand this categorical and general statement of the distinguished scholar.

States is relatively simple. This question is analogous to or, rather, identical with, the problem of succession in private law. In both spheres the purpose of the law should be, and in fact is, to preserve acquired rights and maintain the continuity of law, independent of the physical or legal death of the natural or juridical person concerned.

In his work on the use of private law analogies in international law the present writer has discussed this problem more fully in the context of the questions which necessarily arise here.[1] Is the international legal system strong enough to regulate facts connected with changes involving territorial sovereignty, or do these changes take place in a legal vacuum? What is the source of rights acquired by the new sovereign: his sovereign will or international law? What determines the extent of the new State's obligations: its will and immediate needs, or a rule of international law? 'Between the death of the former State and the taking over of its constituent elements by the new State or a State which already exists there is a hiatus which the law does not succeed in filling'[2] – such is the opinion of a distinguished Italian writer, in which he expresses, with laconic brevity, his conviction as to the anarchical character of the Law of Nations, that law being unable to regulate changes which arise in connection with one of the most important turning points in international life. However, this opinion does not find corroboration in either the theory or the practice of the Law of Nations. The opinion has been quoted only to illustrate the basis of the theory which denies State succession. In fact, the Law of Nations cannot strip itself of a function which is common to all law, namely, the protection of established rights and the continuity of law. Private law performs this task within the various legal systems not only through the institution of succession, but also by recognizing the validity of foreign judicial decisions based on independent and different systems of rules. International law does it through the institution of State succession, which is expressive of the fact that international law is a higher system which co-ordinates the divergencies and fills in the gaps.

Law, like physics, does not tolerate a vacuum. Apart from the question of succession, international law supplies us with a convincing example of its function of filling the gaps and securing continuity. Internal revolutions are without significance both for the continuity of international obligations and the existence of the State in the Law of Nations. From the point of view of municipal law a new revolutionary system of government is a totally new legal creation separated from its

[1] Lauterpacht, *Analogies*, pp. 125–33.

[2] Cavaglieri, in *Rivista*, 16 (1924), 33. A similar attitude has been adopted by the same writer in his treatise, *La dottrina della Successione di Stato a Stato* (1910), and by Keith, *The Theory of State Succession* (1901), and Schönborn, *Staatensukzessionen* (1913).

legal predecessor by the abyss of the revolutionary phenomenon. Here the Law of Nations is the uniting factor, a kind of legal bridge. Similarly, with respect to territorial changes, rules of State succession are the factor which, in eliminating anarchy from the inter-State life, bestows on it the character of law. The contention that in cases of cession or annexation the will of the State is the only law-creating factor is not valid. In both these cases international law is the source of rights; it attaches certain consequences to certain facts, for example, to the will of the ceding State, or to the objective situation which makes conquest and annexation possible. Even the legal title based on conquest is regulated by and duly defined in the Law of Nations.

An exaggerated emphasis on the will of the State as the law-creating factor in the sphere of State succession explains the overstatement of the supposed difference between succession in private law and succession in international law. Professor Huber, followed in this respect by many writers, is of the opinion that whereas in private law succession emphasis is placed on continuation, that is, on universal succession, in international law the heart of the matter lies in substitution. In fact, the problem is not so simple. Private law, both Roman and modern, does not know continuation pure and simple in case of succession; obligations which are strictly personal, obligations arising out of crimes, limitations of succession following from the so-called *beneficium inventarii* – these are all examples which show how elastic is the notion of succession in private law. Identical or analogous limitations on succession have been, or could be, accepted in the Law of Nations with respect to political and and commercial treaties, war debts, debts incurred *in detrimentum* of certain parts of the population, etc. One may generally say, however, that in principle the opinion of Grotius is still valid today: 'heredis personam, quoad dominii tam publici quam privati continuationem, pro eadem censeri cum defuncti persona, certi est iuris'.[1]

Below we try to show that the practice of States and the writings on international law are much closer to this fundamental attitude than would appear at first glance. But the lawyer should proceed to explore these sources with his eyes wide open, especially in relation to two questions. The first concerns the unfair and suspicious treatment, during the past fifty years, of private law as the source of international law. The second concerns the influence of notions of morality on the problem of State succession. As to the latter problem, it may be suggested that the view according to which reasons of morality are irrelevant is erroneous.

Undoubtedly, law is not identical with morality, if only because morality regulates behaviour which is often not a matter of legal

[1] Book II, ch. IX, § xii.

concern, while law frequently establishes requirements which lie completely beyond the realm of ethics. It is also true that law does not often satisfy us on the ethical side in cases where both categories of rules govern the same object. However, it does not follow therefrom that any legal system could bear, for a longer period of time and to a large measure, the obvious discrepancies between law and morality. Law is not a spiritless and self-sufficient mechanism. Moreover, law is being put into motion by people of flesh and blood – by moral beings. The impact of ethical postulates and opinions is especially great when law is *in statu nascendi* and has not yet crystallized. This concerns international law as a whole, and in particular those parts thereof which have not yet attained the form of well-established rules. Such a part of the Law of Nations is that dealing with State succession. In discussing the views of writers we shall see how much the ethical way of looking at our problem imprinted itself in this section of the Law of Nations. Charles Cheney Hyde, author of the best general treatise on international law in this century,[1] states that the ethical point of view tends in the direction of recognizing, possibly to quite a large degree, the principle of succession in the relations between States, that the practice of States tends in the same direction, and that a formal merger between ethics and law in this domain is only a question of time, although this practice has not yet acquired the character of *necessitatis iuris*.

Another difficulty which should be overcome is the deeply embedded prejudice about the complete independence of international law from private law.

3

Under the influence of the exaggerated positivism of the last fifty years there has been established among writers of authority the belief that international law, for the sake of its independence and self-sufficiency, ought to liberate itself from the influence of private law; that the two systems are essentially different with regard to their structure, subjects, and substance; and that the Law of Nations has heretofore been fettered in its development by the unoriginal and slavish imitation of private law – a tendency from which it ought to free itself as soon as possible.[2] This negative attitude towards the great source of legal experience and tradition provided by private law, constituting as it does a legal system in which principles of justice have been embodied to such

[1] *International Law Chiefly as Interpreted and Applied by the United States*, I (1922), 205.

[2] See, especially, Nippold, *Der völkerrechtliche Vertrag* (1894), p. 91, chapter on the relation between private and international law, and Triepel, *Völkerrecht und Landesrecht* (1899), pp. 211–25. The position of British authors is quite different, e.g. Phillimore, I, 34; Westlake, I, 16 and Lorimer, *Studies* (1890), pp. 148–63.

a high degree, has become one of the hall-marks of contemporary positivist thought, similar to the doctrines of sovereignty, of equality of States, of 'exclusively domestic' matters, etc.

However, the practice of States and the science of the Law of Nations both distinctly suggest that this rejection of private law is erroneous and unfounded. The whole structure of international law is permeated with private law. This is as true in modern times as it was in the classical period of the development of international law in the century of Grotius. In the theory of State territory the private law point of view, which looks at territory as the object of State authority, withstood with much force the impact of competing theories of space and competence. Sale, exchange, and lease of territory were, in the past hundred years, neither less frequent nor less rare than two or three centuries ago. The principle of occupation based on the requirements of *animus et corpus* has from the very beginning been and still is today the governing principle affecting the acquisition of title to territory. It was that principle which decisively influenced the theory of territorial waters and the freedom of the high seas. The rule that only effective possession gives a right to acquire title is still in force today. The private law institutions of prescription and of periods of limitation gain more and more recognition in international law, while the theory of State servitudes is today no less strong than fifty years ago. The private law theory of responsibility based on fault (*dolus* or *culpa*) is in process of regaining its significance in international law after attempts at introducing the principle of absolute responsibility into the practice of States have failed. Private law principles relating to measure of damages and payment of interest are increasingly gaining ground, despite the writers who declare that international law sanctions only direct damages and does not recognize the institution of interest. There was recourse to the analogy with the *mandatum* of Roman law in the recent Peace Treaties with respect to certain territories ceded by Germany and Turkey. That international treaties are legally analogous to, because they are identical with, contracts of private law, is generally recognized. And slowly the belief gains acceptance that at the very point where there is a break in the chain of analogies, namely, in the rejection of the invalidating effect of compulsion in the case of international treaties, this fault does not reflect the specific character of the Law of Nations but shows rather the insufficient development of international law as a legal system.

This constant use of and reliance upon private law becomes even more conspicuous in connection with judicial settlement of international disputes, both in the arguments of representatives of States as well as in the decisions of the tribunals. Thus, for instance, in the case of the

Alabama and other vessels between the United States and Great Britain in 1871, it was clear that private law notions influenced the definition of the duty of 'due diligence' resting upon neutral States in the context of war at sea, as also the recognition of consequential damages. The same is true of the *Behring Sea* arbitration in 1893 (questions involving the ownership and possession by States of animals *ferae naturae* in the high seas); the boundary dispute between Great Britain and Venezuela in 1899 (possession, discovery, and prescription in relation to title to territory); the *Pious Fund* case in Mexico in 1902 (extinctive prescription, *res iudicata*); the dispute in 1904 involving priority to custom revenues in Venezuela (mortgage, bankruptcy, *negotiorum gestio*); and the *Newfoundland Fishery* dispute (servitudes in international law). One could multiply such examples at will.

In fact, one could say with much force that in judicial practice the cases are rare in which recourse to private law analogies is not necessary.

The practice of States clearly recognizes that in the great majority of cases the narrow and undeveloped rules of international law do not suffice in order to settle disputes. In almost all treaties in which States agree to submit a specific dispute or a certain category of future disputes to judicial settlement by international judges, the articles that deal with the sources of law which the judges must follow do not limit themselves to international law as such but mention rules of 'justice', 'equity', 'general principles of law', etc. Article 38(3) of the Statute of the Permanent Court of International Justice provides that judges must decide cases, *inter alia*, on the basis of the general principles of law recognized by civilized nations. Practice shows that these general principles of law are essentially nothing more than the generally recognized rules of private law. On the other hand, both the practice of States and a critical appreciation of the science of the Law of Nations show that in the great majority of cases, and where there exists a formal identity of legal relationship, the extent to which international law approaches private law is also the extent to which the former is strengthened as a system of law, justice, and common sense.

State succession is thus a classic example of the problem of analogy. The above discussion of the much-disputed question of the relation between the two systems of law is intended to remind the reader that the fact that State succession is an analogy of private law is a *prima facie* argument not against the institution of succession between States, but in its favour.

4

The Supreme Court is undoubtedly right when it states that the older science of the Law of Nations recognized the principle of State succession. But when the Supreme Court proceeds to say no more than that the modern science of the Law of Nations 'abandoned' this attitude, then – if one may with due respect say so – the said statement contains both *suppressio veri* as well as *suggestio falsi*. What does the Supreme Court mean by the 'modern science of the Law of Nations'? Has the Court in mind the writers of the last thirty years?

Huber, who was the first to introduce the notion of the supposed right of victorious States to destroy and incorporate other State entities, and of the ensuing right to regulate the details of succession, concludes nevertheless that there exists a real duty of succession.[1] During the last twenty-five years several authors – Keith,[2] Cavaglieri,[3] Schönborn,[4] and to some extent Gidel[5] – denied the principle of succession. They did so (*a*) under the influence of a general prejudice against the use of private law notions and (*b*) under the influence of the consequences, understood in a peculiar way, of positivism and the doctrine of State sovereignty. The principal proposition of these writers is that the sovereign will of the State, unfettered by rules of international law, is the source of the law on succession. Thus, when the State, in a specific case, did not expressly recognize the obligation to take over debts, then, according to those writers, that alleged obligation is devoid of any legal basis. The question of the extent to which the theoretical premises on which this attitude is founded may be sound, has been touched upon in the preceding sections. We are not concerned with it now. Of more decisive significance is the fact that, in the last resort, when they draw their concrete conclusions these writers arrive at results diametrically opposed to those which the Supreme Court appears inclined to attribute them. In fact, they reach the conclusion that – apart from the absence of a relevant provision of international law – the rejection of duties following from succession is in most cases contrary to general principles of law, the rule of law, justice, and last but not least the practice of States. Thus, for instance, Schönborn admitted fifteen years ago that the practice of States during the last two hundred years universally recognized the obligation to take over debts;[6] he admitted it again a few years ago when he drew unavoidable conclusions from the provisions of the Peace Treaties.[7]

[1] *Die Staatensukzession* (1898).
[2] *Theory of State Succession.*
[3] In *Rivista*, 16, 33.
[4] *Staatensukzessionen.*
[5] *Des effets de l'annexion sur les concessions* (1904).
[6] *Staatensukzessionen*, p. 100.
[7] In Strupp, *Wört*, II, 580.

The attitude of Arrigo Cavaglieri, one of the most distinguished Italian writers in this field, is both characteristic and instructive. In 1910 his attitude to the principle of succession as being analogous to private law was simply negative. Nevertheless, even before that date he had expressed the view that civil courts should apply the principle of unjust enrichment whenever a State persistently declined to recognize the consequences that ensue from moral duties or from such principles as *bona non intelliguntur nisi deducto aere alieno, res transit cum onere suo,* and *qui habet commoda ferre debet onera.* Cavaglieri has continued his studies on succession and though, as we have previously seen, he still defends his original theoretical proposition, in his last treatise he quite clearly recognizes the duty to assume debts as a duty arising under customary international law. This duty is subject to modification with respect to war debts or debts contracted for purposes which are radically contrary to the political interests of the new State: 'ma dove non sussita una particolare, essezionale legitimazzione del rifiuto, l'obbligo di assunzione è inderogabile' (the duty to take over the debt is unavoidable where there is no particular or exceptional reason for not incurring the obligation).[1] We call special attention to the present opinion of this writer because it originates with a representative of a doctrine which no doubt the Supreme Court had in mind in its judgment. Two authors who after the War dealt thoroughly with the problem of State succession took clearly and decidedly the position that acquisition of territory involves the duty to take over the debts connected with the territory. The first is Guggenheim, who wrote a monograph entitled *Beiträge zur völkerrechtlichen Lehre vom Staatenwechsel* (1925); the second is Sack, author of an extremely detailed and painstaking treatise on the continuity of public debts, *Les effets des transformations des États sur leurs dettes publiques et autres obligations financières* (1927), volume I. Other scholars who in the last thirty years have strengthened international law with general treatises do not generally deny the duty to take over debts. Indeed, such denials are exceptional. Although the framework of the present article does not permit extensive quotations, one cannot, however, forbear to mention the names of those authors whose general treatises have been published within the past ten years. They are Kohler (one of the greatest jurists of the twentieth century),[2] Hatschek,[3] Fenwick,[4] Hyde,[5] and Fleischmann (in his edition of Liszt),[6] not to speak of Cavaglieri. All these writers emphasize the objective duty to recognize private law obligations. On what basis, then, does the Supreme Court of the Polish

[1] Cavaglieri, p. 216.

[2] *Grundlagen des Völkerrechts* (1918), p. 99.

[3] *Völkerrecht* (1923), p. 172.

[4] *International Law* (1924), p. 117.

[5] *International Law*, I.

[6] Liszt, p. 277.

Republic state that the modern science of the Law of Nations 'abandoned' the principle of succession? This must remain a riddle for anybody who tries to find support in writings on international law for the impression which the members of the Supreme Court gained from their studies in this branch of the Law of Nations.

5

Limitations of space do not permit a more thorough discussion of the practice of States as reflected in international treaties. Such discussion should no doubt deal with the theoretical problem involved, namely, that because an authoritative rule of international law is lacking, it is difficult to decide in individual cases whether a treaty positively providing for succession with regard to obligations simply regulates the details of an undeniable fundamental duty, or whether such a treaty is only a constitutive (not declaratory) act of 'good will' which is independent of a hitherto non-existent provision of international law.

Fortunately, the research done by others relieves us from the necessity of studying the practice of States. Testimony borne by those others is at least impartial. For it comes from authors who in theory adopt the attitude that international law does not recognize the objective duty to take over debts. We have seen how Schönborn and Cavaglieri, willingly or unwillingly, arrive in a manner which is both clear and emphatic at the conclusion that the practice of States accepts succession with respect to obligations. Our research led us to the same conclusion.

It is sufficient to glance at the extensive, detailed, and complicated provisions in the Peace Treaties concluded after the World War – provisions by virtue of which heavy burdens have been assumed by the victors to a large extent out of good will – in order to understand how strongly this practice found confirmation even in the atmosphere of a complete triumph of the sword. Whether one considers Article 254 of the Treaty of Versailles, or Article 203 of the Treaty of St Germain, or Articles 186–8 of the Treaty of Trianon, or Article 141 of the Treaty of Neuilly, or Article 46 of the Treaty of Lausanne – the fact remains that in no earlier peace treaty had the taking over of a large part of the public debt been regulated in greater detail. Even concessions and economic privileges – a rather frail and undefined category of rights – have been respected and protected. The now famous Protocol no. XII to the Treaty of Lausanne, or the Annex to chapter 5 of part 10 of the Treaty of Versailles, or Article 4 of the Treaty of 15 May 1922, between Poland and Germany, may serve as examples.

It is true that in these and other treaties there are no separate provisions dealing, for instance, with the continuity of obligations arising under contracts which have already been performed by one party. However, only superficial and rather unconvincing reasoning could infer therefrom that such silence is identical with the exclusion of such obligations. International law, as well as the statesmen responsible for the drafting of the Treaties, have their faults, but these faults do not make it legitimate to insinuate that both the law and the statesmen wholly lack legal logic and legal common sense – a failure consisting in our case in the proposition that international conventions which recognize the principle of succession with respect to extensive categories of public debt, and regulate the precise details of the mechanism of the taking over and distribution of such debt, might be inclined to exclude this duty with respect to other and lesser burdens.

Whoever reads Advisory Opinion no. 6 and Judgment no. 7 of the Permanent Court – both rendered in disputes between Poland and Germany – must see how unconditionally the highest international tribunal took the position that the Peace Treaties of 1919 sanction in full measure the principle of respect for acquired rights. These decisions of the Permanent Court do not concern explicitly the category of claims which became the starting point for the present article. However, this is less important than the fact that these supreme judges decidedly and consistently expressed the opinion not only that the said treaties generally recognized the principle of respect for acquired rights, but also that one cannot hesitate to apply it broadly by way of analogy. Nothing characterizes this attitude better than Advisory Opinion no. 6, in which the Court decided the question involving the duty of the Polish State to recognize certain rights of a kind intermediate between *jura in rem* and *jura in personam* – rights which were rooted in the Germanization policies of the Prussian Government before the War and which were perfected after the suspension of hostilities but before the entry into force of the Peace Treaty.

If the doctrine of State succession sanctions exceptions to the obligation of recognizing rights not yet crystallized as property rights, such exceptions relate first of all to rights rooted in political purposes and situations which cannot always be maintained for reasons dictated by justice and the *raison d'État* of the successor State. The reason for the difference, formulated by Huber, between continuity and substitution consists precisely in the opportunity, given to the new State, of not recognizing debts and rights the further existence of which is contrary to that State's history and *raison d'État*. Nevertheless, the Permanent Court, in spite of the convincing argument on the subject presented by Professor Rostworowski and his colleagues, on two occasions in the same opinion explicitly decided that the political motive behind the rights of the German colonists was of no significance. The Court paid attention to the detailed provisions of the Treaty of Versailles which, in a manner that was both extensive and far from negative, regulated obligations arising out of succession between France and Germany, and it pointed out that if such were the treaty stipulations on relations between former enemies, the same obligation applied even more to one's own citizens.

The decisions of the Permanent Court are the most authoritative and an almost unique source for ascertaining the views of international tribunals on the question of State succession. Apart from them, there are only two awards, of the American–British Claims Arbitration Tribunal established by virtue of the Convention of 1910, which indirectly throw some light on the problem of succession. In *Brown's* case and in the *Hawaiian Claims* case the claims were made in respect of torts of the former State. In both cases the Tribunal rejected the claims because in each case the Tribunal found that even private law did not, as a rule, sanction succession to torts or delicts.[1]

6

Neither general considerations on the relation between international law and municipal law nor the views of writers of authority nor the practice of international courts warrant the view that international law does not recognize the existence of an obligation to respect the debts of the predecessor State. Indeed, they rather suggest the contrary. It only remains, therefore, to draw some conclusions from the material discussed above and to answer a few questions arising from it.

(*a*) If it is not established that international law does not sanction obligations connected with succession, can it be said that there exists an explicit and categorical provision of international law which does recognize such obligations? Such provision exists if the international practice of States, interpreted by writers in a spirit conforming to the general principles of law and justice, is considered as a source of the Law of Nations. If, on the other hand, only explicit and written rules (which exclude any reference to particular cases) are the sole source of the Law of Nations, there is no such provision. However, one may safely say that today there is no international lawyer who would favour such a limited conception of the sources of international law.

(*b*) Does the passive succession discussed above embrace all kinds of obligations? Law regulates complicated relations among people and therefore it cannot adjust wide categories of relationships with a simple

[1] The two awards have been published in *A.J.* 19 (1925), 193, and *ibid.* 20 (1926), 381.

'yes' or 'no'. We know, for instance, that in the later Roman law (and, in general, in contemporary private law) the principle of universal succession with respect to obligations *ex delicto* was and has been limited to strictly personal obligations. The same is true of the *beneficium inventarii*. These are limitations which follow from general principles of law and they are valid in all legal systems. In international law there must be added to these exceptions the category of so-called *dettes odieuses*, that is, debts contracted in an unjust and undemocratic manner and against the interests of the local population now living in the new State. War debts also fall into this category – an exception which, *de lege ferenda*, certainly commends itself to our support. The fact that a war debt will not be paid off in case of the debtor's defeat may become an important element contributing to the pacification of relations between States.

But, besides the above exceptions, the great principle of the rule of law and respect for the individual – the principle of respect for acquired rights – remains unbroken. Such acquired rights may involve different categories of property rights or contract rights : there is no fundamental difference between them. The right to payment for services rendered stands legally on an equal footing with property registered in public books. An acquired right is any right which, were there no territorial changes, would be protected by the courts in a lawful State. The principle of recognizing acquired rights is so generally binding that the rule *res transit cum onere suo*, though it adds to the authority of the principle, does not increase its legal force. The latter rule is mentioned here because it concerns specifically the case referred to at the beginning of the present article. Even those writers who recommend care in drawing rules and analogies from private law admit that the rule *res transit cum onere suo* is a general legal notion not limited to one system but binding everywhere and in all circumstances.

(*c*) That reasons of justice, ethics, and security dictate recognition of such obligations is admitted even by those who deny that there exists a passive duty of succession. That within a State morality and law cannot remain any longer in striking discrepancy has been already pointed out. That such discrepancy can less easily be tolerated when its source lies in the supposed interest of the State – the very State whose purpose is to realize morality in so far as the latter can be brought about through the medium of legal institutions – is also clear. The discrepancy is even less acceptable when the supposed interests of the State are small, insignificant and out of all proportion to the amount of individual harm which such cleavage between law and morality causes. The total amount of claims arising from benefits in fact obtained by the former State and now accrued to the new State is usually not so large as to cause fear of a serious shock to the national budget. An indifferent shrug of the shoulders, even if the shoulders involved are those of the supreme judges, and the statement that 'no one can help the creditor since the preceding debtor became bankrupt', must be objected to as a purely dialectical treatment of the problem.[1] The declaration that there has, in truth, been no enrichment of the State because it took over a part of the public debt of the former State is, to be sure, comforting, in that the Court recognizes that even a State might be unjustly enriched. Nevertheless such a declaration involves an awkward arithmetical calculation which does not convince anyone and is not meant to be convincing.

Such a state of things should not be tolerated by municipal law. There is always time for taking the initiative in this direction. But this is up to municipal law. The international lawyer can make his modest help available in putting an end to a situation which is not characterized by the dignity and majesty of law. His help consists in testifying that the doctrine of succession in international law is based, as far as private law obligations are concerned, on an unconditional respect for acquired rights. The Law of Nations is not the source that should be cited by courts which consider it their duty to ignore the acquired rights of the nationals of the State.

[1] One of the arguments frequently adduced to support the negative attitude of the Polish courts with respect to private law obligations of the former Austrian treasury is the fact that Poland acquired new territories by cession, and not by annexation, accompanying the complete dismemberment and extinction of a previously existing subject of law. Apparently this argument is used in view of the fact that in the science of the Law of Nations some writers, who are inclined to recognize the duty to take over debts in the latter case, require that there be specific treaty stipulations in cases of cession where the subject of law continues to exist. It is a matter of dispute whether the renunciation of territories on the part of Austria in the Treaty of St Germain was technically a cession; it is even more disputed whether present-day Austria is the continuation of the former Austrian Empire. The majority of authors give a negative answer to the latter question. But while that discussion is highly theoretical and fruitless, it becomes annoying when courts draw therefrom conclusions the purpose of which is to free the State from certain morally and factually justified claims. The purely legal point of view shows that the Treaty of Peace considered the Austria of today as a continuation of the former Austria with respect to certain matters, while this was not the intention of the Treaty in other matters. The Treaty apparently did not have this intention in matters of succession, because it divided the public debt among the several successor States. Those who are inclined to arrive, in regard to the present problem, at quick and over-simple conclusions are recommended to recall the prudent words of Anzilotti, now President of the Permanent Court, in his *Corso di diritto internazionale* (1923), part I, p. 102: 'La questione se l'Austria attuale sia o non lo stesso subietto giuridico che preesisteva al trattato di S. Germain, è questione che, per tutti gli Stati i quali hanno ratificato il detto trattato, va anzitutto posta o discussa sulla base delle norme in esso contenute.'

I

NATURE OF STATE TERRITORY

PART III

STATE TERRITORY AND TERRITORIAL JURISDICTION

CHAPTER I

SOVEREIGNTY OVER SUBMARINE AREAS

Editor's note Some explanation may be required as to why an article on the continental shelf has been inserted in a section entitled 'Nature of State Territory'. In formal terms the answer is that in the outline which Lauterpacht prepared for his projected treatise and which provides the main headings for these *Collected Papers* (see Preface to volume 1) there is, surprisingly, no entry for the continental shelf or even, indeed, for the high seas. In substantive terms the answer lies in the approach and content of the article. Its main theme (which, it must be remembered, was developed in 1949) is that the continental shelf is, and always has been, part of the territory of the adjacent coastal State. This theme is developed by reference to basic concepts regarding the nature and acquisition of State territory.

The article was an outgrowth of Lauterpacht's professional involvement in problems connected with the continental shelf in the Gulf area – Kuwait, Qatar, Dubai and Abu Dhabi. The question arose in relation to each as to whether oil concessions expressed to extend to, e.g., all the territory, islands and waters of a State also covered that State's adjacent continental shelf. Lauterpacht's affirmative answer to this question rested on his view, stated above, that the continental shelf is *ipso jure* subject to the sovereignty of the coastal State. A contrary view was developed by Sir Humphrey Waldock in his article on 'The Legal Basis of Claims to the Continental Shelf', in *Grotius Society*, 36 (1950), 115. The issue was twice arbitrated. In *Petroleum Development Corporation Ltd.* v. *Sheikh of Abu Dhabi*, *I.L.R.* 18 (1950), 144, Lord Asquith of Bishopstone rejected Lauterpacht's thesis, not so much in favour of Sir Humphrey Waldock's view as on the basis that the doctrine of the continental shelf had not as yet assumed the hard lineaments of a rule of law. Lord Radcliffe in *Petroleum Development Corporation Ltd* v. *The Ruler of Qatar*, *I.L.R.* 18 (1950), 161, reached a comparable conclusion, but gave an award in formal terms unaccompanied by reasons.

However, within the decade Lauterpacht's view was reflected in the provisions on the continental shelf included in the draft Articles on the Law of the Sea completed by the International Law Commission in 1956 and later included in Article 2(3) of the Continental Shelf Convention concluded at Geneva in 1958, which provided that 'the rights of the coastal State over the continental shelf do not depend on occupation, effective or notional, or on any express proclamation'.

The article appeared in *B.Y.* 27 (1950), 376–433.

I

Seldom has an apparent major change in international law been accomplished by peaceful means more rapidly and amidst more general acquiescence and approval than in the case of the claims to submarine areas – the sea-bed and its subsoil – adjacent to the coast of littoral States. These areas have been generally described as the continental shelf. The latter term will be occasionally used in the present article for the sake of both convenience and abbreviation, although the two expressions are by no means identical. The continental shelf is a submarine area adjacent to the coast of the State. But the converse proposition is not necessarily true. In a great number of proclamations and enactments relating to the matter the term 'continental shelf' does not occur at all. In so far as that term has a well-defined geographical connotation – a question which is somewhat controversial[1] – it cannot be regarded as covering all situations arising out of the claim of States to exclusive jurisdiction and control over the sea-bed and its subsoil in the seas adjacent to their territories.

The latter consideration brings into relief the fact, which it is proposed to elaborate here in greater detail, that the problems raised by the proclamations of the continental shelf cannot be resolved by reference to technical notions in the field of geography. Nor, being entirely novel in their nature, can they be satisfactorily explained by exclusive reference to some traditional concepts connected with acquisition of territorial sovereignty. Essentially, the problem which has arisen in connection with the continental shelf raises not only the question of application of existing international law but also of its adaptation to a situation which at the beginning of the twentieth century was not considered – if it was considered at all – to be within the realm of practical possibility. Accordingly, while account must be taken of such law as there is on the subject, the latter is only one factor in the situation. The other, equally essential, factor is that of legitimate interests of States, viewed in the light of reasonableness and fairness, and of the requirements of the international community at large. It will be submitted in this article that the application of these tests leads to the result that there is no existing principle or rule of international law which is opposed to what, for the sake of brevity, may be called here the doctrine and the practice of the continental shelf, and that the latter has now, in any case, become part of international law by unequivocal positive acts of some States, including the leading maritime Powers, and by general acquiescence on the part of others. The main business of international lawyers is therefore

[1] See below, p. 151.

to explain the nature of the rights claimed and acquired under the new practice; to formulate its philosophy, in a manner capable of general application, in terms both of application and of development of the law as distinguished from a mere unilateral assertion of power; to elaborate principles likely to assist in the solution of problems which result from the assertion or assumption of rights over submarine areas, such as the delimitation of the respective spheres of the neighbouring States or the status of installations erected on the high seas superincumbent upon the submarine areas; to examine possible solutions of the difficulties arising out of any conflict between the actual appropriation of the submarine areas and the reasonable emanations of the conception of the freedom of the seas; and to discourage attempts to rely on claims to submarine areas as a screen for exaggerated pretensions alien to the apparent occasion which gave rise to them and inimical to what is the essence of the still beneficent and valid principle of the freedom of the seas.

For it is possible that what may appear to many the excessive interest of international lawyers in the 'continental shelf' is due not so much to the intrinsic importance of the subject from the economic or political point of view as to its association with the development and the present position of the law relating to the freedom of the seas. In the exhaustive Memorandum on the Régime of the High Seas prepared under the auspices of the Secretariat of the United Nations in connection with the work of the International Law Commission, the discussion of the continental shelf occupies more than one half of the entire work.[1] In the course of the discussion of the subject in the International Law Commission during its session in 1950 it was freely stated that this was the most important matter that had come before the Commission – possibly second only in importance to the formulation of the principles of the Nuremberg Charter. Several members of the Commission were inclined to share the sanguine estimate of some writers, who have compared the assertion of the claims to the continental shelf with the discovery of America.[2] No opinion can be here expressed on the question as to the

[1] Doc. A/CN.4/32, pp. 48–112.

[2] In his Report to the International Law Association, written in 1948, Jonkheer P. R. Feith refers to an article by Professors Clark and Renner in *The Saturday Evening Post* of 14 April 1946 in which the Proclamation of President Truman (see below, p. 148) in the matter of the continental shelf is described as 'one of the decisive acts in history, ranking with the discoveries of Columbus as a turning point in human destiny' (*Report of the 43rd Conference*, Brussels, 1948, p. 195). For an expression of the views of some members of the International Law Commission at its Session in 1950 see A/CN.4/S.R. 66, in particular pp. 23 and 24 for the statement of Professor Hudson, who voiced the prediction that 'fantastic deposits of oil would certainly be discovered in the subsoil of the Persian Gulf'. Professor Scelle, the Chairman of the Commission, said that Professor Hudson's 'statement reminded him of the discovery of America by Columbus; it had to be conceived in order to be transformed into reality'. Professor Spiropoulos expressed the view that the continental shelf 'was undoubtedly the most important question with which they had to deal' (at p. 26).

extent to which such estimates are likely to correspond to the economic potentialities of submarine resources, but there is little doubt that the subject has proved to be of considerable attraction for international lawyers. The reason for that, as already submitted, is, in the first instance, that it has become identified – and will continue to be so – with the major problem of the freedom of the seas. It is in this connection that the view was expressed, in the Memorandum of the Secretary-General of the United Nations, that 'the Grotian idea of the freedom of the high seas is losing the paramountcy[1] which, generally speaking, has survived fairly well down to the present day'.[2]

In so far as the original conception of the freedom of the seas, as it came to full fruition in the nineteenth century, acquired a rigidity impervious to the needs of the international community and to a régime of an effective order on the high seas, that 'loss of paramountcy' provides no occasion for anxiety. However, that 'loss of paramountcy' must constitute a justifiable cause for apprehension in so far as it threatens to affect adversely what is the essence of the notion of the freedom of the seas, namely, the reasonably conceived principle of freedom of navigation and exploitation of the riches of the sea not dependent for their protection and preservation upon the exclusive efforts of the coastal State. It is unlikely that any purely doctrinal opposition of lawyers – even if otherwise well-founded – would be able to stem the hitherto uniform progress of claims and developments, which are not intrinsically unreasonable, in the matter of the 'continental shelf'. But the attitude of international lawyers may be of assistance not only in containing such developments within the channels of moderation and order, but also in demonstrating that there is little or nothing in the properly conceived notion of the freedom of the seas which stands in the way of such developments. If that is done, then the principle of the freedom of the seas, shown to be able to withstand the impact of contingencies unforeseen at the time of its adoption, will emerge from the trial strengthened and revitalized. If that course is not adopted there may be a danger that the restraints, actual or assumed, of the principle of the freedom of the seas will be disregarded in any case and its general authority impaired by excess and abuse spuriously attaching themselves to the idea of the continental shelf. These considerations explain the importance which the question of the continental shelf has acquired in legal discussion. For it is probable that the issue raised by the proclamations and enactments on the continental shelf is even wider than that of the principle of the freedom of the seas itself.

[1] A somewhat free translation of *le caractère primordial* in the original French text.

[2] Doc. A/CN.4/32, p. 55.

It is the more general issue of the adaptation of international law, labouring as it does under the absence of effective machinery for creating and changing the law, to fresh needs and conditions of the international community. In comparison with that wider issue the problem of the continental shelf is of limited compass. The work of the two bodies – the International Law Association[1] and the International Law Commission[2] – which have studied the question in its principal aspects justifies the expectation that international lawyers may be fully alive to the implications of that responsibility.

The preceding observations indicate the method which it is proposed to adopt in this article. It will be useful, in the first instance, to survey the various instruments proclaiming rights in the 'continental shelf' in order to ascertain (*a*) to what extent they are based on the geographical concept of that term and (*b*) the nature – in the alternative terms of sovereignty and exclusive control and jurisdiction – of the authority claimed under them. Secondly, it is necessary to consider the question of the extent to which the doctrine of the 'continental shelf' has become, irrespective of its intrinsic merits, part of the law by virtue of the affirmative conduct of some States and the acquiescence of others. Thirdly, it is intended to inquire, in relation to the fundamental principle of the freedom of the seas, into the legal validity of acquisition of exclusive rights over the sea-bed and its subsoil outside territorial waters. Finally, there will be examined the legal basis of the claims to adjacent submarine areas by reference to the accepted notions of occupation and contiguity in the matter of acquisition of territorial sovereignty.

2. THE PROCLAMATIONS AND OTHER INSTRUMENTS RELATING TO SUBMARINE AREAS

It may be convenient, before drawing attention to the principal types and features of the proclamations and other instruments relating to submarine areas and the continental shelf, to give what is no more than a bare list of these instruments, commencing with the Submarine Areas

[1] See *Report of the 43rd Conference* at Brussels (1948), pp. 168–206, for the Report of Jonkheer P. R. Feith and the discussion thereon. In preparation for the Conference of 1950 the Committee on 'Rights to the Sea-bed and its Subsoil' submitted a statesmanlike Report which, although inconclusive in some of its aspects, constitutes a major contribution to the problem. It was relied upon, to a large extent, by the International Law Commission at its Session in 1950 (see below, pp. 154, 182, n. 1).

[2] The International Law Commission discussed the matter in connection with the Report prepared by Professor François on the Régime of the High Seas (A/CN.4/17). For the discussion of the Commission see the procès-verbal of its meetings in 1950 (A/CN.4/S.R. 66–69). See also the Report of the Commission to the General Assembly (*United Nations, General Assembly, Official Records*, Fifth Session, Supplement no. 12 (A/1316)) for some provisional conclusions on the question of the continental shelf (p. 22).

of the Gulf of Paria (Annexation) Order issued by the United Kingdom on 6 August 1942. While the various instances, prior to that date, of attempts at exploitation of the subsoil of the sea outside territorial waters and of references in official documents to the continental shelf or submarine areas generally are of some historical interest,[1] the Paria Annexation Order may be regarded as the starting point of the development. Like the Treaty of 26 February 1942[2] between the United Kingdom and Venezuela relating to the Submarine Areas of the Gulf of Paria, in which each of the parties agreed to recognize 'any rights of sovereignty or control which have been or may hereafter be lawfully acquired' by the other party, the Order does not refer *eo nomine* to the continental shelf. Neither does it delimit the frontiers of the annexed area by reference to the conventional depth of the continental shelf (for the reason, apparently, that the Gulf as a whole does not reach that depth). However, like practically all other subsequent instruments appropriating the continental shelf, it expressly discards any claim to territory above the surface of the sea or any part of the high seas and disclaims any intention to prejudice rights of passage or navigation on the surface of the sea. The Order instructed the Governor of the Island of Trinidad, to which the areas in question were annexed, to issue regulations for ensuring that these areas should not be closed to navigation and that any works or installations should be so constructed and lighted as not to constitute an obstruction or danger to shipping.[3]

It was not, however, until 1945 that the terminology and the attempt to provide a philosophy of the doctrine of the continental shelf made their appearance in official instruments. Both formed part of the Proclamation of the President of the United States[4] of 28 September 1945. The latter, in turn, was the starting point for a series of Proclamations by Latin-American and other States. Thus the proclamation of the United States was followed by a Declaration by Mexico of 29 October 1945,[5] and a Declaration by Argentina of 9 October 1946, proclaiming

[1] See below, pp. 168–71, 197. See also Mateesco, *Vers un nouveau droit international de la mer* (1950), pp. 99–102. For a reference to the continental shelf see the Report submitted in 1927 by M. Suarez to the League of Nations Committee of Experts on Progressive Codification of International Law in the matter of the Exploitation of the Products of the Sea (C. 196, M. 70. 1927. v, pp. 63, 122). And see Young in *A.J.* 42 (1948), 848–55, and Borchard, *ibid.* 40 (1946), 53–63.

[2] Treaty Series no. 10 (1942), Cmd. 6400. For an analysis of the Treaty see Vallat, in *B.Y.* 23 (1946), 334–6.

[3] The Submarine Areas of the Gulf of Paria (Annexation) Order, 1942.

[4] For the text of the Proclamation of 28 September 1945 and the Executive Order of the same day, see *A.J.* 40 (1946), Suppl., 45–8.

[5] See also the Presidential Decree of 25 February 1949, incorporating the property of 'Petroleos Mexicanos', the subsoil of the lands covered by the territorial waters of the Gulf of Mexico, and other lands expressly specified.

sovereignty over 'the epicontinental sea and the continental shelf'.[1] Similar, but more far-reaching, were the Declarations by Chile of June 1947,[2] by Peru of 1 August 1947,[3] and by Costa Rica of 27 July 1948.[4] On 26 November of the same year Great Britain issued the Bahamas (Alteration of Boundaries) Order in Council[5] and the Jamaica (Alteration of Boundaries) Order in Council.[6] In 1949 the Rulers of the territories in the Middle East followed suit with a series of proclamations. These included the proclamation by the King of Saudi Arabia of 28 May 1949,[7] and by the following Sheikhdoms, all under British protection, in the Persian Gulf: Bahrein (5 June),[8] Qatar (8 June), Abu Dhabi (10 June), Kuwait (12 June), Dubai (14 June), Shayah (16 June), Umm al Qeiwain (20 June), Ajman (20 June), and Ras el Khaima.[9] On 19 May of the same year a Bill relating to the subsoil resources of the Persian Gulf was approved by the Council of Ministers and laid before the Iranian Parliament.[10] On 2 November 1949 Costa Rica issued a Decree-Law concerning the continental and insular shelf.[11] In 1949 the Senate and Chamber of Deputies of Nicaragua adopted a Declaration laying down that, in conformity with Article 2 of the Constitution adopted in 1948, the continental shelf is that part of the territory which is covered by the sea up to a depth of 200 metres and that in cases in which the continental shelf extends to the coast of another State the line of demarcation shall be established by agreement on the basis of equity. In Article 5 of the Constitution as formally adopted in 1950 the 'continental platform and the submarine shelves' (*zocalas*) were enumerated, together with the adjacent islands, the subsoil of the territorial waters, the air space and the stratosphere as forming part of national territory.[12]

The following year saw further additions to the instruments asserting rights in submarine areas. Thus on 7 March 1950 the National Congress of Honduras decreed an amendment to Article 4 of the Constitution which laid down that 'the submarine platform or continental and insular shelf, and the waters which cover it, in both the Atlantic and Pacific Oceans, whatever be its depth and however far it extends, form part of the national territory'.[13] On 9 March the Government of Pakistan

[1] For the text see *A.J.* 41 (1947), Suppl., 11.
[2] *I.L.Q.* 2 (1948), 135.
[3] *Ibid.* p. 137.
[4] See below, p. 182.
[5] *Statutory Instruments* (1948), no. 2514.
[6] *Ibid.* no. 2574.
[7] See *A.J.* 43 (1949), Suppl., 156.
[8] See *ibid.* p. 185.
[9] The text of all these proclamations is practically identical with that of Bahrein.
[10] For the text see *Revue égyptienne de droit international*, 5 (1949), 347.
[11] Decree-Law no. 803.
[12] For the text see Azcáraga in *Revista Española de Derecho Internacional*, 2 (1949), 64. See also Mateesco, *Vers un nouveau droit*, p. 121.
[13] Honduras Legislative Decree no. 102. Legislative Decree no. 103 of the same date made consequential amendments in the Agrarian Law.

published a Declaration stating that 'the sea bed along the coasts of Pakistan extending to the one hundred fathom contour into the open sea should, with effect from the date of this declaration, be included in the territories of Pakistan'.[1] On 9 October 1950 the British Honduras (Alteration of Boundaries) Order in Council was issued.[2] It was followed on 21 December 1950 by the Falkland Islands (Continental Shelf) Order in Council.[3] The two Orders extended the boundaries, respectively, of Honduras and the Falkland Islands to include the area of the continental shelf contiguous to their coasts. On 18 November a Brazilian Decree 'expressly recognized that the part of the sea-bed which corresponds to the continental and insular territory of Brazil is incorporated in the said territory, under the exclusive jurisdiction and dominion of the Federal Union'.[4] Finally, Article 7 of the Political Constitution of El Salvador of 1950 declared that the territory of the Republic 'includes the adjacent seas to a distance of two hundred marine miles from low-water mark and comprises the corresponding aerial space, subsoil and continental shelf' – a truly sweeping assertion which was promptly followed by protests on the part of Great Britain and the United States.[5] Reference may also be made in this connection to the Icelandic Law of 1948 concerning the scientific conservation of the continental shelf fisheries,[6] the Guatemalan Petroleum Law of 1949,[7] and the Philippines Petroleum Act of 1949.[8]

The above bare recital of the various instruments asserting title to submarine areas unavoidably fails to bring into relief significant differences between them. While some of the proclamations and enactments invoke the claim – or the right – to exclusive jurisdiction and control, others speak of sovereignty or of unqualified incorporation into national territory by dint of extension of boundary or otherwise. While some refer to the continental shelf, others speak of the sea-bed and its subsoil (or only of the sea-bed) adjacent to national territory. Some define the area of the continental shelf by reference to the depth of the sea or otherwise; others are silent on the subject or leave the extent of the areas in question to be determined by future agreement. While some purport to extend national sovereignty or jurisdiction by what appears to be a constitutive act of annexation, the majority are couched in language consistent only with a declaration of an already existing title.

[1] *Gazette of Pakistan, Extraordinary*, 14 March 1950.
[2] *Statutory Instruments* (1950), no. 1649.
[3] *Ibid.* no. 2100.
[4] Decree no. 28,840.
[5] See below, p. 183. For a survey of most of these instruments see also the Memorandum of the Secretary-General (referred to above, at p. 145), pp. 58–64, and Azcáraga, in *Rivista Española de Derecho Internacional*, 2, 43–99.
[6] Law no. 44 of 5 April 1948.
[7] Law no. 649 of 30 August 1949.
[8] Act no. 387 of 18 June 1949.

Some deem it expedient to adduce the reasons for the apparently new departure in the realm of the law of the sea – the philosophy, as it were, of the continental shelf; others confine themselves to a bare announcement of the measures taken or proposed. Above all, while some are limited to a statement of claims and principles in the matter of the continental shelf (or, where there is no continental shelf, of submarine areas generally), others combine such announcement with a claim to jurisdiction or sovereignty over the superincumbent sea and air space.[1]

There are only two features – both of them of significance – which these instruments have in common. In the first instance, they all disclaim any intention of interfering with the principle of the freedom of navigation on the high seas as established by the accepted principles of international law.[2] Secondly – though this is extrinsic to the contents of these instruments – none of them has drawn upon itself the protest of any State except in cases in which the proclamation of rights over the submarine areas has been used for asserting exorbitant claims lacking any foundation in law and alien to the apparent occasion which prompted them.[3]

These features of the proclamations and other instruments relating to the continental shelf or submarine areas generally will now be considered in relation to the relevant principles of international law. Before that, however, it is necessary to inquire into the significance of the fact that these instruments do not invariably refer to the continental shelf *eo nomine*; that those which refer to it do not necessarily use it in the same meaning; and that the expression 'continental shelf' has become no more than a convenient formula covering a diversity of titles or claims to the sea-bed and its subsoil adjacent to the territorial waters of the State.

3. THE NOTION OF THE CONTINENTAL SHELF

A survey of the various proclamations and instruments announcing the rights in or claims to what passes by the name of the continental shelf shows: (*a*) that in some of them the term 'continental shelf' does not appear at all, and (*b*) that in others, apart from the Falkland Islands Order in Council and the Gulf of Paria (Annexation) Order, which define in some detail the boundaries extended by the inclusion of the continental shelf, there is no attempt to delimit the area in question except, in some cases, by reference to the 100-fathom depth.[4] The frequent absence of definition corresponds to the now generally admitted

[1] See above, p. 149 and below, p. 183.

[2] See below, p. 172.

[3] See below, pp. 161, 183–4.

[4] 'One hundred fathoms' and '600 feet' are used interchangeably. They represent th same depth: 200 metres equals 109 fathoms; 100 fathoms equals 180 metres.

elasticity of the notion of the continental shelf viewed as a geographical concept denoting the platform – the base, the pedestal – on which the continent rests and which gradually slopes towards the sea until, at points where the latter is about 600 feet deep, it descends rapidly towards the depths of the ocean. Geographers now seem to recognize that the contour line of 200 metres is a mere approximation; that there are often a number of successive sharp descents before the ocean depths are reached; and that, as suggested by the author of one of the most authoritative works on the subject, 'the only accurate method of defining the continental shelf is to consider it as lying between the shore and the first substantial fall-off – on the seaward side – whatever its depths'.[1] That 'substantial fall-off' begins in some cases, such as the western coast of North and South America or practically the entire coast of Africa, at a small distance from the coast; in other countries, such as Great Britain, the continental shelf extends in some directions for several hundred miles before the 'substantial fall-off' begins. The continental shelf of the eastern coast of Great Britain extends for nearly 300 miles in the direction of the southern coast of Norway and reaches practically the Norwegian coast before encountering the 'substantial fall-off'. Similarly, there seems to be no continental shelf, in the technical meaning of the term, between Great Britain and Denmark[2] or Great Britain and France. In some important areas there is no 'continental shelf' in the sense indicated. Thus in the Persian Gulf there is nowhere either a rapid drop or a depth of 600 feet. To these areas the geographical concept, even in its general connotation, of the continental shelf does not seem to be applicable at all. That circumstance explains why there is no reference to the continental shelf in the proclamations issued by the rulers of the Sheikhdoms in the Persian Gulf and why in other proclamations, such as those of Peru and Chile, which refer expressly to the continental shelf, that term is used without even remote reference to its approximate geographical meaning. These and similar proclamations invoke the continental shelf regardless of its depth and extent.[3] It is also

[1] Bourcart, *Géographie du fond des mers. Étude du relief des océans* (1949), p. 130 (as quoted in the Memorandum of the Secretary-General, A/CN. 4/32, p. 50). The French expression for 'substantial fall-off' is 'la première rupture de pente importante'.

[2] In Denmark, where, at the time of writing, a Commission appointed by the Government is investigating the problem, the position seems to be that while there is a continental shelf proper round Greenland and the Faroe Islands, and between Denmark and Norway, there is no continental shelf in relation to other countries. See Cohn in *Jus gentium*, 20 (1950), 21–31.

[3] It may be noted in this connection that the idea, usually associated with the continental shelf, of a flat, gently-sloping plateau applies only to some submarine areas, such as those adjacent to the arctic Russo-Siberian plateau, while in areas such as the Appalachian mountain system in the United States, in which chains of mountains run parallel to the shore, the structure of the adjacent submarine area often follows the pattern of broken valleys and ridges. Unless the contrary is expressly stated in the particular proclamation or instrument, i.e.

clear that, for the reasons stated, the alternative and more general description of the continental shelf as the platform – the base – upon which the continent is supposed to rest, is no more than a figure of speech.

It would appear, accordingly, that, so far as most of the relevant proclamations and enactments are concerned, the expression 'continental shelf' is no more than a general indication of title to areas of indeterminate extent. This is so for the reason that the concept of the continental shelf, viewed as a term of geography, is itself unsatisfactory and somewhat arbitrary inasmuch as it is limited to the depth of 600 feet. Even if this were not so, the usefulness of the concept of the continental shelf, thus limited, would be impaired for the additional reason that its literal application would result in some States having no continental shelf at all, or practically none, while the continental shelf of others might extend for hundreds of miles almost up to the immediate vicinity of the territorial waters of other States. It may be – and has been – suggested that, by international agreement or regulation, States with a very narrow continental shelf should be allotted an extended 'contiguous zone' with regard to their adjacent sea-bed and subsoil, and that disproportionately large areas of the continental shelf of other States should be artificially limited. To say that is to admit that the notion of the continental shelf is of only relative usefulness. It is not surprising therefore that, in its provisional report on the subject to the General Assembly, the International Law Commission found it sufficient to refer to the sea-bed and subsoil of submarine areas.[1] In the course of its deliberations it adopted a formula laying down that 'control and jurisdiction over the sea-bed and subsoil of submarine areas outside the marginal sea may be exercised by a littoral State for the exploration and exploitation of the natural resources therein contained'. It added that 'the area for such control and jurisdiction will need definition, but it need not depend on the existence of a continental shelf'.[2]

The considerations here set forth are not intended to suggest that the

unless there is an explicit reference to a definite depth of sea as limiting the extent of the continental shelf, there is no warrant for the assumption that it has accepted the rough estimate of 600 feet. In the case of the proclamation of the United States of 28 September 1945 a press release issued on the same day referred to the 100-fathom depth.

[1] *United Nations, General Assembly, Official Records*, Fifth Session, Supplement no. 12 (A/1316), p. 22.

[2] A/CN. 4/SR. 67, pp. 16, 24. The latter part of the formula was adopted on the proposal of Professor Brierly, who pointed out that 'legally speaking, the presence or absence of a continental shelf was of no importance'. He instanced Chile as an example of a State which possesses no continental shelf, and added that if a State wished to explore or exploit the subsoil of the sea and was able to do so, 'there was nothing against it from the legal standpoint' (p. 18). For an exhaustive, though somewhat inconclusive, discussion of the subject see pp. 49–52 and, especially, pp. 102–7 of the Memorandum of the Secretary-General referred to above (at p. 145).

notion of the continental shelf was devoid of usefulness from its very inception or that it can no longer fulfil any useful purpose whatever. It served as a rallying point for a new complex of ideas by giving it the authority of a natural geographical phenomenon. This it may continue to do. Moreover, whatever may be the merit of the 600-foot limit, it has the advantage of setting *some* limit. That limit, conceived as a rebuttable presumption of practicability of exploitation, is neither unreasonable nor one arbitrarily arrived at. It signifies an approximation, which probably errs on the side of optimism, to the practical possibilities of the exploitation of the sea-bed and the subsoil. It may thus provide a convenient starting point for future regulation and agreement. But it must not be more than that. Inasmuch as it makes the law on the subject rigidly dependent upon the hazards of a geographical phenomenon and of natural configuration, it has little likelihood of or claim to acceptance. After all, the attempts at exploitation of the sea-bed and the subsoil are in themselves an assertion of the supremacy of man over a purely natural phenomenon. This approach apparently underlay the provisional report of the International Law Commission to the General Assembly in 1950, when it expressed the view that where the depth of the waters permits exploitation the rights of States to control and jurisdiction shall not be dependent on the existence of a continental shelf; and that any other solution would be unjust to countries having no continental shelf.[1] It is reasonable to assert that if such rights do not depend upon the existence of the continental shelf they cannot also be dependent upon its configuration in any particular case. The coastal State cannot properly be expected to submit to the appropriation or exploitation by a foreign State of relatively shallow areas of the adjacent sea-bed and subsoil for no better reason than that these areas are separated from the continental shelf proper (if there be any) by a drop the depth of which exceeds 600 feet.[2] However, there may be room, in any final solution that may be adopted, for attaching some weight to the view that any absence of equality resulting from hard facts of geography cannot altogether be ignored.

The various proclamations and enactments relating to submarine areas give expression to these difficulties. Their cumulative result is that

[1] *United Nations, General Assembly, Official Records*, Fifth Session (1950), Supplement no. 12 (A/1316), p. 22. This was also the view of the rapporteur, Professor François (A/CN. 4/17, p. 40). But see the remarks, in a contrary sense, of Professor Hudson (A/CN. 4/SR. 66, p. 28). It appears that in the end the view as formulated by the Commission in its report secured general agreement (A/CN. 4/SR. 67, pp. 6–11).

[2] For this reason, in cases in which (in States with a narrow continental shelf) the substantial fall-off is followed by an elevation which is less than 600 feet deep there would appear to be no cogent or plausible reason for denying to the coastal State the right of appropriation, within a reasonable distance, as in the case of the continental shelf proper.

in relation to the subject matter of these instruments the expression 'continental shelf', whether it occurs there or not, need not be regarded as necessarily bound up with such ordinary geographical connotation as it otherwise possesses. The same applies probably to any future developments in this field. That expression has served a useful function in the formative period of the adoption of the idea of the exclusive control and jurisdiction of the State over the adjacent sea-bed and subsoil. In so far as it supplies a graphic description of the essential unity of the bed and subsoil of the adjacent sea and of the territory on which it rests, its usefulness is not yet spent. But its continued utility will depend to a large extent on the degree of its emancipation from the technicalities and the designation of its geographical prototype and on its becoming interchangeable with – and, in proper cases, on its being replaced by – some such expressions as 'the adjacent submarine area of the State' or 'the contiguous submarine area of the State'. There may be a disadvantage in referring uniformly to these areas as the 'continental shelf' even when they do not in fact exhibit the characteristics of the continental shelf. On the other hand, there is an advantage in using terms in their accepted meaning in the sphere with which they are normally associated and in assisting in freeing the terminology of international law from the reproach, often justified, of using terms in a peculiar – and therefore artificial – connotation.[1] The expressions 'adjacent submarine areas' or 'contiguous submarine areas' may also tend to emphasize the fact, the implications of which will now be considered, that there is no essential difference between the rights of sovereignty which the State exercises over its territory and its exclusive control and jurisdiction over the submarine areas contiguous to it.

4. THE NATURE OF THE RIGHTS OVER SUBMARINE AREAS

The language of the proclamations and other instruments and enactments relating to appropriation of or assertion of claims over submarine areas does not supply a clear answer to the question whether these rights are rights of sovereignty, or merely rights of jurisdiction and control, or – whether it be 'sovereignty' or merely 'jurisdiction and control' – whether they are rights over the submarine areas or over their resources. The purely British proclamations, such as those embodied in the Orders in Council relating to the Gulf of Paria and to the continental shelves of the Bahamas, Jamaica, and the Falkland Islands, amount, by clear implication, to an assumption of rights of full sovereignty. No other

[1] See below, pp. 185 and 191, as to 'effective occupation' and 'inchoate title'.

interpretation can be put on the announcement that the 'boundaries' of the territories in question are 'extended' so as to include the continental shelf or that the Gulf of Paria is annexed. This result is not inconsistent with the repeated acknowledgement of the overriding duty and determination to respect the principle of freedom of navigation on the high seas. For the same principle applies to territorial waters; yet the sovereignty of the State over them is now an undisputed part of international law. Full sovereignty over the continental shelf is claimed explicitly in some proclamations, such as those of Argentina, Chile, Peru, Costa Rica, Nicaragua, Honduras and El Salvador. The same applies to the Brazilian Decree of 1950, which 'declares the incorporation in the national territory of that part of the sea-bed which corresponds to that territory'. The absence of intention to distinguish between 'exclusive control and jurisdiction' on the one hand and sovereignty on the other is shown in the recitals of the Brazilian Decree, which speaks of the 'interest in the declaration of sovereignty or of the dominion and jurisdiction of States over the region thus accruing to the national territory'. The same trend of thought is expressed in the operative Article 1 of the Decree, in which 'it is expressly recognized that the part of the sea-bed which corresponds to the continental and insular territory of Brazil is incorporated in the said territory, under the exclusive jurisdiction and dominion of the Federal Union'. This is also the effect of the Pakistanian Declaration of 1950, which, in pursuance of Section 5 of the Government of India Act, 1935, relating to accession of new States to the Indian Union, declares the sea-bed along the coast of Pakistan 'extending to the one hundred fathom contour into the open sea' to 'be included in the territories of Pakistan'. The Mexican Proclamation of 1945, while declaring that 'it is not reasonable, wise or possible that Mexico should ignore jurisdiction, exploitation and control' over the continental shelf, proceeds to state that 'the Government of Mexico claim the whole of the continental platform or base adjacent to its coast'.

With these claims to full sovereignty there may be contrasted the proclamation issued by the United States in 1945. It declared that 'the Government of the United States regards the natural resources of the subsoil and sea-bed of the continental shelf beneath the high seas but contiguous to the coast of the United States as appertaining to the United States, subject to its jurisdiction and control'. It would seem not only that the assumption of 'control and jurisdiction' was preferred to assumption of 'sovereignty', but also that the 'control and jurisdiction' thus claimed had reference not to the sea-bed and subsoil of the continental shelf as such but merely to the resources of the continental shelf. That nuance of language was, it appears, intentional. It may have been due, in the first instance, to the fact that according to the Constitution of the United States formal annexation or acquisition of territory requires legislative approval and cannot be accomplished by Presidential proclamation. Secondly, in view of the persistent attitude of the United States in the matter of acquisition of sovereignty over arctic and antarctic regions – an attitude based on a rigid insistence on effective occupation as a condition of acquisition of a valid title – it was deemed preferable to give a somewhat different and less emphatic formulation to a claim based on the fact of contiguity.[1] As pointed out below,[2] such caution was probably unnecessary seeing that the situations are hardly comparable. However that may be, that attachment to consistency may explain not only the reluctance to adopt the terminology of sovereignty but also the decision to assert the claim by means of a Presidential proclamation. Finally, it is possible that some importance was attached to the theory that 'sovereignty and ownership go together' and that in view of domestic controversies in the United States concerning the ownership of the subsoil of the continental shelf[3] the express assumption of sovereignty was deemed to be prejudicial to an as yet unresolved issue.

Be that as it may, the cautious formulation by the United States of its title over the continental shelf has not been followed by other States. Thus in the proclamation of 1949 by Saudi Arabia the 'subsoil and the sea-bed of those areas of the Persian Gulf seaward from the coastal sea of Saudi Arabia but contiguous to its coasts, are declared to appertain to the Kingdom of Saudi Arabia and to be subject to its jurisdiction and control'. It is no longer the *resources* of the subsoil and the sea-bed, but those areas themselves which are declared to *appertain* and to be subject to the exclusive jurisdiction and control of the State. The proclamations issued by the rulers of the British protected States in the Persian Gulf adopted the same wording.

There remains the question whether there is any difference between declaring that the sea-bed and the subsoil appertain – belong – to the State and declaring that they are under its sovereignty. The difference, it is believed, is merely one of words.[4] An area which is under a State's exclusive control and jurisdiction, not delegated by or accountable to a foreign Government or authority,[5] is under the sovereignty of that State It is part of that State. An area declared to be henceforth within the

[1] See below, pp. 194–200. [2] See p. 186.

[3] See below, p. 160, n. 3.

[4] See, to the same effect, Sir Cecil Hurst in *Grotius Society*, 34 (1948), 161, and Vallat in *B.Y.* 23 (1946), 337.

[5] Undoubtedly, on occasions, States exercise jurisdictional rights over territory – rights of 'jurisdiction or control' or 'exclusive jurisdiction and control' – although they do not possess or claim sovereignty. This is so in all cases in which the exercise of sovereignty is divorced from residuary sovereignty vested with and delegated by a higher authority (as in the case of

exclusive jurisdiction and control of a State becomes part of its territory. As such it benefits from rights accruing to the State by virtue of the treaties previously concluded by it; similarly, it is subject to obligations arising from such treaties. For exclusive jurisdiction and control *is* sovereignty. This is so necessarily, seeing that State territory 'is the space within which the State exercises its supreme authority'.[1]

It is probable that while for reasons of its constitutional law and of attachment to consistency in its diplomatic practice the United States may have resorted to a terminology intended to dispel the appearance of assumption of sovereignty, it used words and assumed powers which in fact can have no other result. To say that the State has acquired an exclusive right of control and jurisdiction over the resources of the submarine areas but not over the submarine areas themselves may be as artificial as saying that the coastal State has no right to the submarine areas by virtue of a proclamation or otherwise, but that it acquires as the result of such a proclamation an exclusive right of occupation of the sea-bed and subsoil of the submarine areas (or of the resources of the subsoil). In a sense, so far as the actual practice of States is concerned, the question whether the relevant proclamations or enactments amount to assumption of sovereignty is answered by the terms of these instruments. They – in the majority – either refer expressly to the assumption of sovereignty or do so by stating that the adjacent submarine areas 'belong' or 'appertain' to the States. This, it has been suggested, is also in essence the position with regard to the proclamation of the United States. Accordingly, to the extent to which these proclamations and enactments have not encountered protest and must therefore be regarded as not inconsistent with international law,[2] the question whether the authority of the coastal State over the adjacent submarine areas is one of sovereignty must be regarded as having received a conclusive answer. For these proclamations and enactments have, in law and in fact, assumed sovereignty. In the course of the deliberations of the International Law Commission those members who voiced a reasoned opinion on the subject expressed themselves in favour of the view that the powers of the State in the adjacent submarine areas are those of sovereignty.[3] The provisional report of the Commission to the Fifth

the mandates of the League of Nations or trust territories under the Charter of the United Nations) or by another State (as in the case of leases, grants in perpetuity, and the like). None of these broad contingencies occurs in relation to submarine areas. There is no authority or State which is entitled to or claims residuary sovereignty over them.

[1] Oppenheim, *International Law* (7th ed. by Lauterpacht, 1948), I, § 170.

[2] See below, pp. 161–7.

[3] This, in particular, was the view of Professor Brierly and the Rapporteur (Professor François), who described the view formally expressed by the Commission as amounting to admitting sovereignty (*Minutes*, A/CN. 4/SR. 68, pp. 6–8).

Session of the General Assembly of 1950[1] used language of studied restraint which, perhaps, was not fully in keeping with the views expressed in the course of its deliberations. It stated that 'the sea-bed and subsoil were subject to the exercise, by the littoral States, of control and jurisdiction for the purposes of their exploration and exploitation'. In so far as the use of such language can be interpreted as deprecating the idea of the sovereignty of the coastal State over the adjacent submarine area, it is at variance, apart from the single exception of the proclamation of the United States, with the relevant proclamations and enactments of all other States, which have claimed sovereignty either expressly or by obvious implication (inasmuch as they included these areas within their boundaries or declared them to belong – to appertain – to their States).

It is not believed that such a claim to sovereignty, pure and simple, over submarine areas is improper or – assuming that it is not otherwise contrary to international law in general or to the principle of the freedom of the seas in particular[2] – that it does not provide the best solution. Sovereignty over the adjacent submarine areas – like sovereignty over territory in general – is not incompatible with restrictions imposed by customary international law or undertaken by treaty. Thus although the rights acquired, or claimed, by States over submarine areas are rights of sovereignty, this does not mean that they are not subject to such limitations as follow from international law and, especially, from any reasonable requirements of the principle of the freedom of the seas. In particular, the normal extent of territorial sovereignty as expressed in the principle *usque ad coelum* does not apply in this case either in relation to the superincumbent sea or to the air above it. Similarly, the general rule of freedom of navigation, in so far as it has a practical meaning in relation to the bed of the sea, may be fully applicable, as in the case of the right to lay cables and, probably, pipe-lines.[3]

[1] Special Supplement no. 12 (A/1316), p. 22. The proposals submitted in 1950 to the Conference of the International Law Association by its Committee on 'Rights to the Sea-bed and its Subsoil' referred throughout to the *control and jurisdiction*, by the coastal State, over the sea-bed and the subsoil of the continental shelf. In the course of the deliberations of the International Law Commission in 1950 Professor François made the interesting suggestion that there existed a substantial distinction between sovereignty on the one hand and jurisdiction and control on the other. He submitted that while in regard to the first the powers of the State were limited only to the extent of obligations specifically undertaken, with regard to the second its powers extended only to the extent to which they have been expressly conceded (A/CN. 4/SR. 68, p. 7). There seems to be no warrant for that distinction in accepted terminology.

[2] See below, pp. 167, 171–3.

[3] See below, pp. 172, 184. International practice shows the feasibility of a combination of rights of passage more complicated than that resulting from an accumulation of pipe-lines. See, for instance, the arrangement of 1936 between the United States and Panama providing for a corridor in favour of Panama across the United States zone and for a right of transit for the United States across the corridor created for Panama (*A. J.* 34 (1940), Suppl. p. 144).

There is therefore little point in limiting the right of States over the submarine areas to control and jurisdiction and confining the latter, in turn, to control and jurisdiction for the purpose of exploration and exploitation only. There is no other use to which such control and jurisdiction could be put. Such exceptions as those relating to the superincumbent sea and air and to freedom to lay cables and pipe-lines on the sea-bed can, without difficulty, be accommodated within the orbit of the traditional conception of territorial sovereignty. Thus the sovereignty of the State over its territorial waters is not inconsistent with the generally-accepted principle of innocent passage.

In fact, through the entire branch of international law relating to State territory and territorial sovereignty there runs as a constant theme the phenomenon of limitation of sovereignty in various spheres and directions. This is not confined to so-called State servitudes or to those instances in which the exercise of sovereignty – actual control and jurisdiction – is divorced from residuary sovereignty as in the case of so-called political leases or grants in perpetuity. It is sufficient to mention the less sweeping limitations resulting from express treaty stipulations, such as the air bases granted in 1941 by Great Britain to the United States, or from rules of general international law such as the prohibition of nuisance or the limitations upon the State's freedom of action in respect of the use of non-national rivers. It follows from this capacity of territorial sovereignty to adaptation and modification that the sovereignty of the coastal State over the adjacent submarine areas is fully compatible with its obligations in respect of freedom of navigation on the high seas and of passage, on and through the bed of the sea, of cables and pipe-lines.[1] 'Sovereignty' has adverse and, for some, justifiably, sinister connotations. But it is an established term of a clarity transcending that of 'control and jurisdiction'. In particular it implies not only rights but also international responsibility – an aspect of the situation which is of particular importance in relation to a problem of conspicuous novelty within federal States and which in the United States has led the Supreme Court, in face of considerable authority to the contrary and weighty dissents, to affirm the ownership of the United States over the subsoil of the sea-bed both under the territorial waters[2] and outside them.[3] In this matter – as in many

[1] See below, pp. 172, 184.

[2] *United States* v. *State of California* (1947), 332 U.S. 19: *Annual Digest*, 14 (1947), 56.

[3] *United States* v. *Texas* (1950), 339 U.S. 707; *I.L.R.* 17 (1950), 126. See also, to the same effect, *United States* v. *Louisiana* (1950), 339 U.S. 699; *I.L.R.* 17 (1950), 131. The main reason, in *United States* v. *California*, for distinguishing the principle established in *Pollard's Lessees* v. *Hagan*, 3 How. 212, that a State title prevailed over federal ownership with respect to 'internal waters' (i.e. land between low-water and high-water mark) was the paramount factor of the fulfilment of the international responsibilities of the United States. The Court said:

others – the proper method is not to attempt to solve the difficulties inherent in a novel situation by choosing terms of studied vagueness and elasticity but by using language which, for the very reason that it has an accepted connotation, lends itself to qualification and modification with the view to meeting the exigencies of new problems.

As already suggested, the question of the nature of the right over the adjacent submarine areas is to a large extent an academic question inasmuch as it has been resolved by the practically unanimous practice of the coastal States concerned – a practice which has not been followed by protests by other interested States or by States in general. It is now necessary to consider the question of the relevance of the absence of protest with regard to both the claim to adjacent submarine areas and to the nature of the right, conceived as a right of territorial sovereignty, as generally advanced.

5. SOVEREIGNTY OVER SUBMARINE AREAS AS PART OF CUSTOMARY INTERNATIONAL LAW. THE RELEVANCE OF ABSENCE OF PROTEST

A conspicuous and significant feature of the various proclamations and other formal assertions of the right to adjacent submarine areas has been the degree of general acquiescence in what at first sight appeared to be a startling innovation. That acquiescence has expressed itself in an entire absence of protest, except in isolated cases in which the

'The ocean, even its three-mile belt, is thus of vital consequence to the nation in its desire to engage in commerce and to live in peace with the world; it also becomes of crucial importance should it ever again become impossible to preserve that peace. . . . The State is not equipped in our constitutional system with the powers or the facilities for exercising the responsibilities which would be concomitant with the dominion which it seeks. . . . Consequently, we are not persuaded to transplant the *Pollard* rule of ownership as an incident of State sovereignty in relation to internal waters out into the soil beneath the ocean, so much more a matter of national concern'. The opinion of the majority of the Court was in keeping with its series of pronouncements since the First World War in which, in deference to the international responsibilities of the Union, the Supreme Court affirmed in various ways the paramountcy of federal action over the Constitutions of the States and their rights and even over certain constitutional conventions of the United States itself. See, e.g., *Missouri* v. *Holland* (1920), 252 U.S. 416: *Annual Digest*, 1 (1919–22), 4; *United States* v. *Curtiss-Wright Export Corporation* (1936), 299 U.S. 304: *Annual Digest*, 8 (1935–7), 48; *United States* v. *Belmont* (1937), 301 U.S. 324: *Annual Digest*, 3 (1935–7), 34; *Hines* v. *Davidowitz* (1941), 312 U.S. 52: *Annual Digest*, 10 (1941–2), 295; *United States* v. *Pink* (1942), 315 U.S. 203: *Annual Digest*, 10 (1941–2), 48. No opinion is here expressed as to the cogency, in relation to submarine areas, of the argument based on the international responsibilities of the Union. The case of *United States* v. *Texas*, based to a large extent on the decision in *United States* v. *California*, was decided by reference to the terms of the admission of Texas into the Union 'on an equal footing with the existing States'. It must remain a matter of speculation whether a less literal interpretation of the equality clause, for which impressive precedents can be found in international practice and – it is submitted with some diffidence – in the constitutional practice of the United States, would have led to a different conclusion. See also Illig, 'Tidelands – an Unsolved Problem', in *Tulane Law Review*, 24 (1950), 51 *et seq.*

proclamation of rights over the adjacent submarine areas has been combined with or has served as a cloak for the assertion of claims to sovereignty over the high seas.[1] When in 1949 the rulers of some territories in the Persian Gulf, acting under what is in law and in fact the international responsibility of Great Britain, issued proclamations declaring the adjacent submarine areas to be subject to their 'exclusive jurisdictional control', they asserted – apparently having regard to similar proclamations issued in the four preceding years – that a right of that nature 'has been established in international practice by the action of other States'.[2] Four years in international relations is on the face of it too brief a period to make possible the creation of a new rule of customary law. However, assuming – an assumption which, it will be submitted, is unnecessary – that the emergence of the doctrine of sovereignty over the adjacent areas constituted a radical change in pre-existing international law, the length of time within which the customary rule of international law comes to fruition is irrelevant. For customary international law is not yet another expression for prescription. A 'consistent and uniform usage practised by the States in question' – to use the language of the International Court of Justice in the *Asylum* case[3] – can be packed within a short space of years. The 'evidence of a general practice as law' – in the words of Article 38 of the Statute – need not be spread over decades. Any tendency to exact a prolonged period for the crystallization of custom must be proportionate to the degree and intensity of the change that it purports, or is asserted, to effect. With regard to the submarine areas adjacent to the coast, the assertion of sovereignty over them would constitute a drastic change in the law only if it could be shown that the international law of the sea – as distinguished from the deductions made by writers on the consequences of the principles of the freedom of the sea – actually prohibited, instead of being merely silent on the matter, the appropriation of the sea-bed and the subsoil outside territorial waters. This, as will be submitted, is not the case. There is no significance in the circumstance that rights in submarine areas have been expressly asserted by some States only – by a minority of States. For it is apparent that most of the other States may have felt no need to put forward what, in the circumstances of the case, would be no more than a gesture. They can do it at any time. The issue of a proclamation is an act wholly dependent upon the will of the State in

[1] See below, p. 183.

[2] Already in 1947 Peru, in the recitals of her Decree regarding national sovereignty and jurisdiction over the continental and insular shelf, asserted that such right 'has been claimed by other countries and practically admitted in international law' (see below, p. 194).

[3] *I.C.J. Reports* 1950, p. 276.

question. This is so whether we do or do not accept the view that rights in submarine areas which are a contiguous part of the territory of the State belong to it *ipso jure* without the necessity of issuing a proclamation declaratory of its rights.

Moreover, assuming that we are confronted here with the creation of new international law by custom, what matters is not so much the number of States participating in its creation and the length of the period within which that change takes place, as the relative importance, in any particular sphere, of the States inaugurating the change. In a matter closely related to the principle of the freedom of the seas the conduct of two principal maritime Powers – such as Great Britain and the United States – is of special importance. With regard to the continental shelf and submarine areas generally, these two States inaugurated the development and their initiative was treated as authoritative almost as a matter of course from the outset. This was so particularly having regard to the traditional attachment of these States to the principle of the freedom of the seas and the customary limit of territorial waters.[1]

At the same time, the very fact that the apparent change was introduced by the two leading maritime Powers firmly – and, on occasions, rigidly[2] – wedded to the principle of the freedom of the seas raises the question whether the change thus effected was not more apparent than real. As will be submitted in the next section, it is doubtful whether the practice of these – and other – States in the matter of the continental shelf, and submarine areas generally, amounts to a drastic change in the law. Its initiation did no violence to any established prohibition – or proposition – of international law. In that sense the various proclamations and enactments relating to the continental shelf constitute, in the language of Article 38 of the Statute of the International Court of Justice, 'international custom, as evidence of a general practice accepted as law'. In that sense the inauguration and the reception of the 'new' law relating to the continental shelf and other submarine areas throw instructive light on the mysterious phenomenon of customary law, which is deemed to be a source of law only on condition that it is in accordance with law. To that extent custom is both a source of law and evidence of it – a suggestive reminder that the difference between a source of law and evidence of it is only a matter of degree. Unilateral declarations by traditionally law-abiding States, within a

[1] See, (e.g.), the judgment of the Mixed Tribunal of Port Said, reported in *Annual Digest* 3 (1925–6), 3, in which it was held that although Egypt was not among the Powers which signed the Brussels Convention of 1910 on Salvage, that Convention, which was signed by nearly all maritime Powers, was applicable by the Mixed Courts of Egypt (*Crichton* v. *Samos Navigation Company*).

[2] See below, pp. 173–5.

province which is particularly their own, when partaking of a pronounced degree of uniformity and frequency and when not followed by protests of other States, may properly be regarded as providing such proof of conformity with law as is both creative of custom and constituting evidence of it.[1]

Similar considerations are relevant to the fact that the proclamations and declarations of rights in the adjacent submarine areas have not been followed by protests. The significance of that fact – as of protest in the international sphere generally – shows itself in various directions. In the first instance, the absence of protest on the part of other States may be fairly interpreted as meaning that *they* 'accepted as law' – i.e. as being in conformity with the existing law – the practice of other States relating to submarine areas. While that practice may justly have created the appearance of novelty, it does not follow that the law on which it is based is new. To that extent the absence of protest, in face of an apparently new departure publicly proclaimed, provides evidence of the essential conformity of the new practice with the principles of international law.

However, in addition to providing evidence as to the views of Governments on the existing legal position, the absence of protest on the part of interested States – for in the case of most proclamations and other instruments in the matter of submarine areas there must have been States actually or potentially directly affected – may in itself bring about legal effects. For the absence of protest in the past can be adduced not only as showing that in the view of a complaining State itself the act which is now being made the subject of challenge was not inconsistent with international law. The absence of protest may, in addition, in itself become a source of legal right inasmuch as it is related to – or forms a constituent element of – estoppel or prescription. Like these two generally-recognized legal principles, the far-reaching effect of the failure to protest is not a mere artificiality of the law. It is an essential requirement of stability – a requirement even more important in the international than in other spheres; it is a precept of fair dealing inasmuch as it prevents States from playing fast and loose with situations affecting others; and it is in accordance with equity inasmuch as it protects a State from the contingency of incurring responsibilities and expense, in reliance on the apparent acquiescence of others,

[1] For some indirect discussion of the authority of unilateral declarations as a source of international law see Pflüger, *Die einseitigen Rechtsgeschäfte im Völkerrecht* (1936). The Memorandum of the Secretary-General (see above, p. 145) draws attention to the following passage in *The Scotia* (1871), 14 Wall. 170; Hudson, *Cases* (2nd ed. 1936), p. 672: 'Many of the usages which prevail, and which have the force of law, doubtless originated in the positive prescriptions of some single State, which were at first of limited effect, but which when generally accepted became of universal obligation.'

and being subsequently confronted with a challenge on the part of those very States.

The juxtaposition of these elements reveals the close connection between prescription, protest, and estoppel in the international sphere. The duty to protest, and the relevance of the failure to protest, are especially conspicuous in the international sphere, where the normal avenues for ascertaining disputed rights through the compulsory jurisdiction of tribunals are not always available. Thus there may exist a clear cause of action on account of an international wrong and yet a protest may be for the time being the only appropriate course, for the reason that the offending State is not bound by any commitment of obligatory judicial or arbitral settlement and refuses voluntarily to submit to international adjudication. Or there may have taken place a legislative or administrative act in the nature of a proclamation of intention and assertion of a right, and yet, unless an actual attempt has been made to apply the law or decree in question and until an injury has actually occurred, it is probable that no judicial remedy will lie.[1] In that instance, too, a protest may be both proper and necessary for the reservation of a right. The same applies to cases in which the remedy of appeal to a political agency such as the United Nations is not available for the reason that, according to its constitution, the controversy is not of sufficient importance in terms of preservation of international peace to warrant action, even of a conciliatory nature, in relation to the subject-matter of the dispute. Thus, as the case of the Finnish ship-owners showed, the Council of the League of Nations interpreted rigidly the provision of Article 11 of the Covenant which, apparently, did not confer upon it jurisdiction to entertain complaints in matters other than those relating to 'any war or threat of war'.

[1] This principle was expressed with clarity by Mr Beckett (as he then was) in the Third Committee of the Hague Conference of 1930 for the Codification of International Law. He said: 'It is not the enactment of the law which produces the breach of an international obligation, but its application, and, until the court has applied the law, it cannot definitely be said if there has been a breach of international law' (*Minutes*, p. 71). The British Reply to the Questionnaire of the Committee of Jurists on the subject was in practically identical terms (*Bases of Discussion, Responsibility of States*, p. 27). See also *ibid.* p. 29, for the Swiss reply. See also Anzilotti, *Cours de droit international* (French transl., 1929), pp. 474, 475. The matter is of some difficulty. Although prior to the application of the law no actual injury can, as a rule, be deemed to have occurred, the legislation can at least be regarded as a manifestation of intention to commit an international wrong and as such calling for protest. Moreover, it is possible that legislation as such may, because of resulting uncertainty, have injurious effects. In connection with the Panama Canal controversy arising out of the Canal Tolls Act of 1912 it was maintained by the United States that the British protest against the Act was inadmissible as no action had yet been taken on the Act (see Wright, in *A.J.* 32 (1938), 530). See p. 23 of the Judgment of the Permanent Court of International Justice in the *Lotus* case, where the Court seems to have attached importance to the fact that States had omitted to protest against the criminal law of other States which contained provisions asserting jurisdiction over foreigners for acts committed abroad (*P.C.I.J.* Series A, no. 10).

The same applies to the provisions of chapter VI of the Charter of the United Nations, which is confined to disputes 'the continuance of which is likely to endanger international peace and security'. These circumstances enhance the importance, in the international sphere, both of protest and of failure to protest. That factor figured conspicuously among the reasons underlying the judgment of the Permanent Court of International Justice in the case of the *Lotus*. The Court referred to the several instances, quoted in argument, of criminal proceedings in respect of collisions before the courts of a country other than that of the flag of the vessel concerned, and stressed the fact that in these cases the States affected did not object and refrained from protesting. The Court said:

> This fact is directly opposed to the existence of a tacit consent on the part of States to the exclusive jurisdiction of the State whose flag is flown . . . It seems hardly probable, and it would not have been in accordance with international practice, that the French Government in the *Ortigia–Oncle Joseph* case and the same Government in the *Ekbatana–West-Hinder* case would have omitted to protest against the exercise of criminal jurisdiction by the Italian and Belgian Courts, if they had really thought that this was a violation of international law.[1]

It follows from what has been said above that such a duty to protest is especially incumbent upon States directly interested – in the case of the proclamations relating to submarine areas, in particular upon neighbouring States – though there would be nothing improper, and it might be prudent, for other States to assert their legitimate interest in upholding, through protest, a legal principle of general application. The international law of both peace and war provides numerous examples of such protests.[2]

On the other hand, it is probably true to say that the absence of protest is irrelevant if the action of the State claiming to acquire title is so wrongful in relation to any particular State or so patently at variance with general international law as to render it wholly incapable of becoming the source of a legal right. This would be so even if the

[1] *P.C.I.J.* Series A, no. 10, p. 29. See also, on the relevance of the absence of protest in the case of declarations of sovereignty by other States, the award, given in 1933, in the *Guatemala–Honduras Boundary* arbitration: *Annual Digest*, 7 (1933–4), 115; *U.N.R.I.A.A.* II, 1397. And see, to the same effect, *U.N.R.I.A.A.* I, 250, 262, 280 (award of 1922 in *Colombia–Venezuela* arbitration). See also, for an affirmation of the relevance of the absence of protest as barring prescription, the award of 1911 in the *Chamizal* arbitration between the United States and Mexico (*A.J.* 5 (1911), 785–812, at p. 807); and the *Walfisch Bay* arbitration in 1911 between Great Britain and Germany (Hertslet's *Commercial Treaties*, 26, 187–250, at p. 249). And see Johnson in *B.Y.* 27 (1950), 332–54.

[2] See Oppenheim, I, § 135(4); II (6th ed. by Lauterpacht, revised 1944), § 246. See also Bernard, *Neutrality of Great Britain during the American Civil War* (1870), pp. 199 *et seq.* for the protests of Germany, Austria and France against the seizure of Messrs Mason and Slidell from the Trent.

illegal action in question were formally announced to the world and even if it directly affected the interests of a particular State. In such cases a protest might be advisable; it would not be essential. Thus, for instance, if a State were to proclaim an exclusive right of navigation, jurisdiction or exploitation on what is regarded by the generality of States as part of the high seas, the absence of protest would hardly make any difference to the legal position – in the same way as the manifest illegality of any other action would preclude it from becoming a valid basis for precedent. *Ab injuria jus non oritur.* There are acts which are so tainted with nullity *ab initio* that no mere negligence of the interested State will cure it.[1] For reasons which have been given and which will be developed presently, this is not the situation with regard to the proclamation – or assumption – of sovereignty over submarine areas. In these cases the absence of protest was expressive of the fact that, in the view both of the States declaring the title and of the States which have acquiesced in it, that action was not inconsistent with existing law, and that although it may have inaugurated a new practice it did not inaugurate new law. However, the conformity of that action with the pre-existing principles of international law in the matter of the freedom of the seas is controversial and that aspect of the question must now be considered in some detail.

6. THE FREEDOM OF THE SEAS AND SOVEREIGNTY OVER SUBMARINE AREAS

In answering the question of the compatibility of the assumption of sovereignty over adjacent coastal areas with the principle of the freedom of the seas, it must be borne in mind that the problem involved is novel in character and that in examining it we can derive no substantial assistance from any previous articulate practice of States in relation to the bed of the sea and its subsoil. Apart from the isolated and somewhat exotic instances of pearl and oyster fisheries and the like, there is, as will be seen[2], no such practice. There exists a voluminous body of opinions of writers applying to these questions their interpretation of and deductions from the conception of the freedom of the seas. Although such opinion is not altogether unanimous, it merits, in so far as it proceeds from the principle of the freedom of the seas, careful consideration. On the other hand, while the conception of the freedom of the seas represents a venerable and almost universally accepted part of international law and although its force is far from spent, there

[1] See on the whole subject Guggenheim, in *Hague Recueil*, 74 (1949) (i), 195–263.

[2] See below, p. 171.

is no such immutability about it as to preclude investigation into the possibilities of its adaptation to new circumstances and problems. Clearly, a great deal of the historic argument on which it was founded is no longer applicable. Grotius's explanation that what cannot be effectively occupied cannot become subject to the sovereignty of a single State no longer carries conviction. If effective occupation means the physical power of excluding and eventually controlling the conduct of any person whatsoever within the area in question, then large portions of the high seas lend themselves to effective occupation not only by means of guns, with their present range, along the coast of the State, but also by other means. We recall the – not irrelevant – British argument, in the course of the prolonged correspondence with the United States during the First World War, on the undoubted effectiveness of the so-called long-distance blockade. The second explanation given by Grotius, namely, that that which by nature can be used by all without its substance being exhausted ought not to be subject to the exclusive dominion of a single State, hardly applies in modern conditions without far-reaching modifications. For experience has shown that some of the resources of the high seas may not be inexhaustible unless wisely husbanded by international agreement and co-operation. However, the principle of the freedom of the seas has now become part of international law irrespective of the legal arguments which assisted at its birth. It still provides the proper and convenient starting point in any consideration of problems arising out of its application.

At the same time, the principle of the freedom of the seas cannot be treated as a rigid dogma incapable of adaptation to situations which were outside the realm of practical possibilities in the period when that principle first became part of international law. In that period the notion of the exploitation of the resources of the subsoil of the sea was too remote from reality to call for or to admit of serious consideration. At the end of the nineteenth century the subject acquired a certain – essentially still theoretical – importance in connection with some English enactments (such as the Cornwall Submarine Mines Act, 1858)[1] and with the plans to construct a tunnel under the Channel between Great Britain and France. On the part of the great majority of writers there

[1] The Act provided that 'all mines and minerals lying below low-water mark under the open sea adjacent to, but not being part of the County of Cornwall, are vested in Her Majesty the Queen in right of her Crown as part of the soil and territorial possessions of the Crown'. See also the Norfolk Estuary Act, 1846, and the Lincoln Estuary Act, 1851. Professor François, Rapporteur of the International Law Commission in 1950, had no hesitation in admitting that occupation of the subsoil of the high sea was permissible at least so long as its exploitation was possible without touching the surface of the sea-bed (A/CN. 4/17, p. 33). See also, to the same effect, his observations and those of Professor Brierly at the Session of the Commission in 1950 (A/CN. 4/SR. 66, pp. 20–2).

was no disposition to deny the lawfulness of such appropriation of the subsoil of the sea, especially if the operations for that purpose started from the territorial waters of the coastal State. Writers did not as a rule expressly exclude the possibility of acquisition or assumption of title over the subsoil of the sea as the result or for the purpose of operations commencing from the surface of the high seas. With isolated – though not unimportant[1] – exceptions, they were not prepared to permit any abstract deductions from the principle of the freedom of the seas to stand in the way of any future developments.[2] Professor Hyde, writing in 1945 without any apparent hesitation, said: 'The subsoil appurtenant to the coast of a State and *extending therefrom* into an area beneath the high sea is doubtless susceptible to acquisition by that State. Accordingly, by appropriate processes indicative of the assertion of control, a right of sovereignty therein may be brought into being.'[3] He added: 'It is not understood, however, that the United States has found occasion to endeavour to exercise such a privilege.' The italicized words in the passage quoted above probably were not intended to indicate that the right of acquisition is dependent upon whether it starts from the territorial waters. But the clarity of the statement is expressive of the change which had taken place since 1918, when the Department of State of the United States gave a somewhat hesitating – though, in fact, not negative – reply to a question put to it by some citizens of the United States who purported to have discovered a large oil pool in the Gulf of Mexico about forty miles from land on a reef where the water was less than a hundred feet deep. The State Department was asked whether it would be possible to acquire property or leaseholds, and consequent protection, over that part of the bottom of the ocean. It was also suggested that an artificial island might be erected and the question was put whether such island could be brought under the jurisdiction of the United States. The answer given was that the United States has no jurisdiction over the ocean bottom of the Gulf of Mexico beyond the territorial waters and has therefore no right to grant leaseholds or other property rights in respect of the areas in question. At the same time the petitioners were informed that: '(*a*) unless the creation of an artificial island interfered with the rights of the United States or of its citizens, or formed the subject

[1] See, in particular, Gidel, I, 502, 508. Nevertheless, Professor Gidel did not altogether deny the right to erect installations on the surface of the sea for that purpose: 'Leur création', he said, 'doit être subordonné à l'agrément, exprès ou tacite, des autres États.' However, see below, p. 178, for a substantial modification of Professor Gidel's views.

[2] This was, very emphatically, the view of Fauchille. See Fauchille, I, Part II, 18, 19, 61. The literature on the subject is surveyed in some detail in the illuminating Report of Jonkheer P. R. Feith, presented in 1948 to the 43rd Conference of the International Law Association (*Report*, pp. 184–92).

[3] Hyde, I, § 145A.

matter of a complaint made upon apparently good grounds by a foreign Government', it was not likely that the Government of the United States would object to the creation of the proposed island; (*b*) it was not likely that any foreign Government would interfere with the plan unless its rights or those of its citizens were injuriously affected; and (*c*) if the island were created it was possible that the United States would exercise 'some sort of control over it'.[1] Though the direct relevance of this incident to the question of the subsoil of the sea may be uncertain, it is indicative of the attitude – already at that time not wholly negative – of the United States.

While with regard to the subsoil of the sea-bed the possibility of interference with the freedom of the seas appeared remote (at a time when underwater drilling starting from the surface of the sea, as distinguished from exploitation through activities proceeding from territorial waters was hardly contemplated), this was not altogether so with regard to the bed of the sea. As to the latter, historic examples of pearl, oyster, and other sedentary fisheries, with occasional accompanying attempts at the exclusion of aliens or at least controlling their activities, made writers more inclined to question the possibility of its future occupation and appropriation – although they were prepared in any case to recognize title acquired in this sphere by prescription. This was the opinion of Professor Gidel,[2] but not, perhaps, of Sir Cecil Hurst, who does not seem to have denied the possibility of future occupations.[3] A similar view was expressed in Oppenheim's *International Law*, where, however, the import of the new developments has caused a somewhat perplexing cumulation of apparently contradictory views on the subject.[4]

[1] Hackworth, II, 680.

[2] I, 498–500, 507 *et seq.* See also Higgins and Colombos, *The International Law of the Sea* (1943), p. 541.

[3] In his article in *B.Y.* 4 (1923–4), 34 *et seq.* Sir Cecil Hurst, after surveying in some detail the practice of States, arrived at the conclusion that, so far as Great Britain was concerned, her claims to sedentary fisheries were a survival of more extensive claims, since abandoned, to sovereignty over the bed of the sea and that in so far as they were based on effective occupation of the bed of the sea they were valid and entitled to recognition. There is nothing to indicate that in Sir Cecil's view such occupation was inadmissible in the future. The concluding passage of his article is as follows: 'The claim to the exclusive ownership of a portion of the bed of the sea and the wealth which it produces in the form of pearl oysters, chanks, corals, sponges or other fructus of the soil is not inconsistent with the universal right of navigation in the open sea or with the common right of the public to fish in the high seas.' See also, to the same effect, his report to the Institute of International Law, *Annuaire*, 32 (1935), 160.

[4] Thus, on p. 508 (§ 221) of vol. I it is stated that 'the bed of the sea cannot be an object of occupation'; on pp. 575 and 576 (§ 287*bb*) a substantially different view is expressed. It is stated there that 'when regard is had to the arguments which brought about the abandonment of the former claims to occupy the waters of the open sea . . . it must surely be conceded that these reasons do not apply to the surface of the sea-bed or to its subsoil. . . . Although it is traditional to base these cases on the ground of prescription, it is submitted that it would not be inconsistent with principle, and would be more in accord with practice, to recognize

It is apparent that the views of writers on the question of the occupation and appropriation of the bed of the sea and its subsoil, in so far as they were voiced prior to the proclamations and declarations in the matter of submarine areas, must be regarded as being of distinctly limited importance for the reason that in the nature of things they are not evidence, on this subject, of the practice of States. There was no such practice save for the odd cases of the sedentary fisheries of Ceylon, Madras, Tunis, Bahrein, and, probably, in some parts of Western Australia.[1] The opinions of writers were based on their deductions from and their interpretation of the principle of the freedom of the seas at a time when problems such as those which prompted the appropriation of submarine areas in the middle of the twentieth century had not yet arisen. With few exceptions, they agreed that submarine areas – the sea-bed and the subsoil – were a legitimate object of appropriation and that they did not partake of the nature and of the legal régime of the high seas. But they were thinking in terms of appropriation, through actual use and occupation, of limited portions of the submarine areas – in the case of the subsoil by operations emanating from national territory and territorial waters. They did not discuss – and the necessity for such discussion did not occur to them – the question of appropriation of submarine areas by virtue of some other title and other considerations, determined by economic necessities and scientific progress, which were beyond the reach of their vision or interest. That question, it will be shown, can be answered – and in fact it has been answered – in the affirmative.

However, even if submarine areas can, *per se*, be subject to appropriation – by virtue of occupation or otherwise – for the reason that, unlike the high seas, they are not *res omnium communis*, the question still remains whether they can be so appropriated consistently with the fundamental rule of international law embodied in the principle of the freedom of the seas. If their being part of the territorial domain of States is not in itself contrary to international law, the question remains – and to that major question we must now address ourselves – whether the concomitant of their exploitation and utilization is not such as to conflict with the freedom of the seas.

frankly that, as a matter of law, a State may by strictly local occupation acquire, for sedentary fisheries and other purposes, sovereignty and property in the surface of the sea-bed provided that in so doing it in no way interferes with freedom of navigation and, perhaps we should add, with the breeding of free-swimming fish.' With regard to the subsoil, the statement of the law is emphatic: 'There is no reason whatever for extending this freedom of the open sea to the subsoil beneath its bed. On the contrary, there are practical reasons – taking into consideration the building of mines, tunnels, and the like – which compel recognition of the fact that this subsoil can be acquired through occupation' (at p. 577).

[1] See Hackworth, II, 677.

If the activities and control connected with the subsoil of the sea and the sea-bed could be confined to those areas and spaces, any objections, by reference to an abstract principle of the freedom of the seas, to acquisition of exclusive rights over them would be merely pedantic. However, it is clear that they cannot be so confined. The exploitation of the subsoil of the sea-bed involves – apart from the possibility of exploiting it by means of tunnels proceeding from under the territorial waters – exploitation by means of works and installations appearing above the surface of the sea. These must constitute some obstacle in the way of unimpaired navigation both by their actual presence and by the necessity of protecting them from negligence or malicious design of passing or approaching vessels. If such installations increase in size and density, it may be necessary to prescribe lines of traffic. The various instruments proclaiming rights of sovereignty or exclusive jurisdiction and control over submarine areas include almost invariably the substance of the final proviso in the proclamation of the United States of 1945, which declares that 'the character as high seas of the waters above the Continental Shelf and the right to their free and unimpeded navigation are in no way thus affected'. There is no reason to doubt the sincerity of these assurances.[1] They are not an empty phrase – though they must be read subject to reasonable interpretation, without which these instruments would be deprived of much of their purpose and effect. For the undoubted possibility of interference with navigation on the high seas as the result of installations (and of the necessity to protect them), connected with the exploitation of the resources of the subsoil is, essentially, of a limited character. Unless abused, they may offend against the theory but not the true object of the freedom of the seas. Imagination may be tempted to conjure alarming vistas of the high seas crowded with installations impeding navigation and of crippling regulations intended to protect these installations. It may be wise to resist the temptation to picture these perturbing possibilities or to elaborate the legal relevance of methods calculated to minimize the anticipated dangers, such as the provision of radar facilities for approaching ships. The essential insignificance of such apprehended dangers reveals itself as soon as we abandon the notion of the freedom of the seas as implying an absolute right to absolutely unimpeded navigation – a conception which, when rigidly applied, may be as obnoxious as the uncompromising doctrine of absolute sovereignty. The possibility of interference with the high seas

[1] Professor François in his *Report on the Régime of the High Seas* submitted to the International Law Commission (A/CN. 4/17, p. 37) seems to share the scepticism, voiced by the Rapporteur of the International Law Commission, as to the value of these assurances. And see his observations at the Session of the Commission in 1950 (A/CN. 4/SR. 66, p. 22).

is disturbing and provides a cause for apprehension only when viewed against the background of a rigid conception of the freedom of the seas impervious to reasonable requirements of economic life and scientific progress. It is in this context that the question of the continental shelf – of submarine areas – raises issues of wider significance for international law and the method of its development and adaptation to new conditions. The subject of the freedom of the seas which, next to diplomatic immunities, is the most typical example of customary international law, is particularly well calculated to shed light on this general problem of international law.

For there are two parallel streams, both clearly discernible, in the history of the freedom of the seas in the last three centuries. The course of the first has been determined by insistence, averse to compromise, on the full right of freedom from any kind of interference. Governments have resisted attempts to extend the right of visit and search by foreign warships in time of peace even when the concession of such right was necessary to render effective the object of international conventions in matters such as the prevention of trade in slaves or the protection of fisheries. Thus, with regard to the first, the Brussels General Anti-Slavery Act of 1890 did not merely circumscribe narrowly the area of its operation and the type of vessels, the tonnage of which should not exceed five hundred, to which it applied. The part of warships authorized to assist in the execution of the Treaty was limited to verification of the flag and, in cases of suspicion, to bringing the arrested vessel before a court of her own jurisdiction. Similarly, with regard to policing of fisheries, as in the case of the North Sea Fisheries Convention of 1882, the powers of the supervising warships were severely limited. The governing rule, with regard to verification and search by warships in time of peace, is still that any interference by a man-of-war with a vessel flying the flag of a foreign country takes place at the risk and subject to the strict accountability of the State to which the warship in question belongs. The right of hot pursuit, without which the enforcement by the State of its protective jurisdiction within its territorial waters tends to become nugatory, was not finally established without substantial opposition and qualifications. In the *Behring Sea* arbitration Sir Charles Russell still referred to hot pursuit as being 'not a strict right by International Law, but which is something which nations will stand by and see done, and not interpose if they think that the particular person has been endeavouring to commit a fraud against the laws of a friendly nation'.[1] As late as 1902, Dr Asser, arbitrator in the case of the *James Hamilton Lewis* and the *C. H. White* between the

[1] *Proceedings of the Aritration* (American ed.), 13, 300.

United States and Russia, used language to all appearance questioning the existence of the right[1] of hot pursuit. In 1935, in the case of the *I'm Alone*,[2] it was given a limited – according to some, unduly limited – interpretation which diminished the apparent value, for the United States, of the Anti-Liquor Treaty of 1924. Even in the matter of piracy it was denied by a distinguished jurist, the French representative at the League of Nations Committee of Experts on Codification of International Law, that a State had a right to try a piratical ship flying the flag of a foreign State.[3] When in connection with the enforcement of the 18th Amendment the United States, in 1922 and 1923, approached a number of countries with the request to agree to the boarding and searching of their ships within a specified limit outside the territorial waters of the United States, some of them resisted the request. It was only when, after the decision of the Supreme Court in *Cunard* v. *Mellon*,[4] the United States proceeded to enforce its law in relation to ships bringing liquor, even if under seal, into the ports of the United States, that an attitude of accommodation made possible arrangements of the nature desired by that country. These arrangements took the form of a number of treaties – the so-called Liquor Treaties – in which the various States, while upholding the principle of the three-mile limit of territorial waters, undertook to raise no objection against the boarding and searching of their ships within a zone coterminous with the distance capable of being traversed by the suspected vessel in one hour. Although Great Britain was originally among the Powers which somewhat rigidly resisted the proposed extension of the jurisdiction of the United States,[5] she subsequently gave, in connection with the attempts to codify the law on the subject, weighty expression to a principle of accommodation and reasonableness indicating in an enlightened manner the possibilities of future development.[6] The Behring Sea controversy between the two countries provided another instructive

[1] Moore, I, 929.

[2] *Annual Digest*, 7 (1933–4), 203.

[3] *Minutes of the Third Session* (1927), p. 45.

[4] (1923), 262 U.S. 100: *Annual Digest*, 2 (1923–4), 112.

[5] For the history of the rejection by Great Britain of the original proposals of the United States see Jessup, *The Law of Territorial Waters and Maritime Jurisdiction* (1927), pp. 281–7. In 1923 Lord Curzon stated in the House of Lords that 'there is no chance of our agreeing in any circumstances whatsoever to the proposal for a twelve-mile limit' (*H.L. Deb.* 5s., 54, cols. 728, 729).

[6] In her reply to the questionnaire of the Committee of Experts on the Codification of International Law in 1929 Great Britain accepted 'the view that no State can be expected to tolerate with equanimity circumstances arising under which, owing to peculiar local circumstances, the absence of jurisdiction over foreign vessels on the high seas immediately contiguous to its territorial waters may prejudice gravely the enforcement of the laws or the well-being of the community within its territory'. She stated that 'where such circumstances arise, it is the duty of any foreign State to come to an agreement enabling the State concerned to exercise such rights of control over the merchant vessels of the foreign State concluding the agreement as may be necessary' and that 'for a State to refuse to enter into an agreement of

example of legitimate though rigid resistance to what was believed to be – and was so found in 1893 by the Arbitration Tribunal – an unlawful encroachment upon the freedom of the seas. Yet it is possible that both the arbitration and the findings of the Tribunal were made feasible only because it was given the power to make recommendations, subsequently accepted by the parties, with regard to a situation in which uncompromising reliance upon the principle of the freedom of the seas was bound to be productive of a disregard of the equitable interests of the coastal State and of the resulting danger of unilateral action.

It is this phenomenon of unilateral action, apparently or actually in conflict with the principle of the freedom of the seas, which constitutes the second, parallel, stream in the practice of States in this sphere. It has found expression in measures which on the face of it are not unreasonable, such as the assumption of protective jurisdiction for customs and revenue purposes, for the enforcement of health and sanitation laws, and, to a limited extent, for safeguarding the security of the State in time of emergency. These encroachments upon the principle of the absolute freedom of the seas have met with no persistent protests. They have been crystallized in what are generally referred to as claims to the contiguous zone. In contradistinction to the formal extension of the limit of territorial waters, there is now – with some weighty exceptions including, to some extent, Great Britain[1] – a general disposition to recognize the justification of the claim to the contiguous zone for the purposes outlined above – as distinguished from the assertion of exclusive jurisdiction for the economic benefit of the nationals of the State. Within these limits the conception of the contiguous zone is now in the stage of approximation to a customary rule of international law. It is essentially grounded in unilateral action. Occasionally, unilateral action – for the very reason that it is unilateral – tends, notwithstanding its intrinsic reasonableness, to assume the form of an innovation so startling as to lay itself open to initial criticism. This was probably, to some extent, the case with regard to the Anti-Smuggling Act adopted by the United States in 1935 and the proclamation issued by it in 1945 in the matter of fisheries (concurrently with that on the continental shelf). The first contained, *inter alia*, provisions for a

this kind would be to show an entire absence of the consideration for the rights of other States upon which the solidarity of nations depends' (*Territorial Waters, Bases of Discussion*, pp. 28, 29). In the *Behring Sea* arbitration Sir Charles Russell, while agreeing that in similar circumstances other States would probably acquiesce in the enforcement of the law of the coastal State outside the territorial waters, insisted that such enforcement could not be claimed as a matter of right against an objecting State (Moore, *International Arbitrations*, I, 903).

[1] But only to some extent. See above, p. 174. See also the British 'Hovering Acts', allowed to lapse in 1853. And see for an affirmation, in wide terms, of the principle of contiguous zones *Croft* v. *Dunphy*, [1933] A.C. 156: *Annual Digest*, 6 (1931–2), 157.

'customs enforcement area' which gave the President the power to proclaim an area extending one hundred nautical miles north and south from the point in which a suspected foreign ship is hovering and including all of the waters 62 miles from the coast within the area of 200 miles thus designated. Within that area, subject to existing treaty obligations, foreign vessels could be boarded and seized.[1] It appears that no protests have been made against the adoption of the Act – a circumstance which is not in itself decisive seeing that, for the purpose of safeguarding rights, a protest is essential at the time of the application of the enactment as distinguished from its adoption.[2] Similarly, there were no protests when in 1945 the United States issued the proclamation establishing, in principle, conservation zones for fisheries in the high seas contiguous to the coasts of the United States. In that proclamation the United States claimed the right to establish 'explicitly bounded conservation zones in which fishing activities shall be subject to the regulation and control of the United States' in all areas in which fishing activities 'have been or shall thereafter be developed and maintained by its nationals alone'.[3] With regard to areas in which foreign nationals participated in the fishing activities, the regulation and control within the conservation zones was made subject to agreements with the foreign States concerned. The significance of that unilateral action – the manner and propriety of which are referred to below[4] – was enhanced by the declared readiness of the United States to recognize similar action on the part of other States. In a different sphere, the practice of courts of many countries in assuming jurisdiction in the matter of collisions occurring on the high seas irrespective of the nationality of the vessel amounts, to some extent,[5] to a claim of jurisdiction in respect of the high seas – a claim which amounts to an affirmation of the common interest in the maintenance of a régime of order in an area of international concern. At the same time, the very character of unilateral action tends to encourage claims, under the colour of general principle, which are unjustified *per se* and occasionally extravagant to the point of irresponsibility. The student of international law will find no difficulty in recalling examples of such action.

A comparison of these two parallel streams – the insistence, in reliance on established international law, on full freedom from interference by other States with respect to events occurring on the high seas and the unilateral assertion of such jurisdiction – helps to draw atten-

[1] For an analysis of the provisions of the Act see Jessup in *A.J.* 31 (1937), 101–6.

[2] See above, p. 165.

[3] For the text of the proclamation see *A.J.* 40 (1946), 46.

[4] See p. 184.

[5] But only to some extent. In certain circumstances English courts exercise jurisdiction in the matter of torts occurring in foreign territory.

tion to a persistent problem (as revealed by the claims to sovereignty over submarine areas adjacent to the coast) of the traditional conception of the freedom of the seas. Its authority and continued usefulness can be safeguarded only if it is acted upon in accordance with its true purpose and the ever-valid test of reasonableness. Its true purpose is to ensure freedom of navigation, unhampered by exclusive claims of individual States, and freedom of utilization of the resources of the sea to a degree to which they can be equitably utilized by all. The resources of the submarine areas adjacent to the coast of the State cannot be feasibly and reasonably utilized by all. They can be so utilized mainly by the adjacent coastal State. Similarly the true object of the freedom of the seas is not invariably to prevent its use for the purpose of securing the individual interest of any particular State – provided that that interest is not incompatible with the two essential purposes of the principle of freedom of the seas as here formulated. Neither can it be interpreted as demanding an absolute prohibition of jurisdiction on the part of foreign States or of the community of nations. For that reason, unilateral acts such as the proclamation of the United States of 1945 in the matter of fisheries, although amounting in some way to a claim to exercise jurisdiction on the high seas in areas in which fishery rights have hitherto been exercised only by citizens of the United States, may not necessarily be inconsistent with a rational interpretation of the principle of the freedom of the seas so long as its primary object is not the exclusion of nationals of foreign States. The same applies to the assertion of jurisdiction, even though exercised by individual States, for the purpose of safeguarding a general interest. The future development of the law of contiguous zones may, from this point of view, provide a test of enlightened and far-seeing statesmanship of Governments. If the freedom of the seas is interpreted so as to result either in a régime of waste or disorder on the high seas – such as must follow from the absence of effective agreement in the matter of protection of fisheries or of pollution of the sea – or in the stifling of properly conceived interests of individual States, its authority will disappear and it will be increasingly flouted by unilateral assertions of selfish and monopolistic interest. The same, with reference to the subject here under discussion, would be the effect of resistance, in reliance on supposed rules of international law, to a limited – and relatively trifling – use of parts of the high seas for the purpose of erecting installations or to reasonable measures of protection of such installations. Writers who speak with special authority on the subject of the law of the sea and who in the past were inclined to look with disapproval at any possible tendency to encroach upon the freedom of the seas are now emphatic in warning against the exaggerations of the 'tyranny' of the traditional conception.[1]

Once the principle permitting the use of parts of the sea for erecting or placing permanent installations for operations on the sea-bed or its subsoil is admitted as valid, its application becomes to a large extent a matter of machinery and procedure. That principle has been acted upon by States which have been responsible for the instruments proclaiming rights in submarine areas and which re-affirmed, in those very instruments, their determination to abstain from action which may impede freedom of navigation. Such affirmation cannot be brushed aside as a meaningless promise incapable of fulfilment and not intended to be fulfilled. It must be regarded as the basis of future development. Undoubtedly, the question of providing the requisite procedure for applying the test of reasonableness in relation to limited encroachments upon the freedom of the seas may not lend itself to an easy solution. The forms of such machinery are a proper object of study by international lawyers. There would appear to be no reason why, as between States bound by or willing to accept the obligations of the jurisdiction of the International Court of Justice, that tribunal should not, at least in the initial stages, decide any controversies that may arise and, in so doing, lay down general principles applicable to any similar situations. On the other hand, in case developments should make such disputes a phenomenon both normal and frequent, other organs, partly judicial and partly administrative and expert in character, could properly fulfil that function. Some such organs have in fact been proposed in the past.[2] Machinery of that nature may make possible the evaluation and judicious balancing of the interests involved – for instance, in relation to the question of the admissibility of interference with navigation for the purpose of protecting installations on the high seas. Such organs may be given the power to decide, in any given case, that there is justification for a limited diversion of shipping in order to make possible the exploitation of what may be a valuable oil-field. Evaluation of conflicting interests and the effective recognition of those which, on balance, are entitled to protection is a constant feature of judicial activity, as, indeed, of law in general. Witness, for

[1] See Gidel, *La Plataforma continental ante del derecho* (Lectures delivered in the University of Valladolid, 1951), p. 161. He says: 'The concept of the freedom of the high seas has now lost the absolute and tyrannical character imposed upon it by its origin as a reaction against claims to territorial sovereignty over the high seas.' These and similar passages are a literal translation of the corresponding passages in the Memorandum of the Secretary-General of the United Nations (referred to above, p. 145) and they permit therefore an inference as to the authorship of that Memorandum. For the more conservative views of Professor Gidel prior to the rise of the problem of submarine areas see above, p. 169.

[2] For a survey of some of these proposals see Higgins and Colombos, *The International Law of the Sea*, pp. 282, 283.

example, the manner in which the Supreme Court of the United States affirmed the right of the State of Massachusetts to make use of the waters of the tributaries of the Connecticut river on the ground that the purpose of the action complained of – namely, the installation of a modern water-supply system in the city of Boston – was superior to the more limited interest of the State of Connecticut in the unimpaired use of its share of the waters of the tributaries in question.[1]

Machinery as indicated may also be useful – though it is not essential – for the solution of the problems connected with the determination of the submarine areas either between directly adjacent States sharing the same coast-line, as in the case of Mexico and the United States in the Gulf of Mexico, or in the case of States on opposite coasts, such as Saudi Arabia and Iran in the Persian Gulf. As between the former, the problem is to a large extent similar to that involved in the delimitation of territorial waters between neighbouring States.[2] As between the latter, the analogy of boundary lakes rather than of boundary rivers – i.e. the emphasis on the middle distance rather than the mid-channel (the *thalweg*) – may be helpful as embodying a solution dictated by common sense. However, for that very reason, such analogy can be no more than of initial usefulness with respect to what is essentially a novel situation. As adumbrated in the various proclamations, the delimitation can properly be effected by reference to equitable considerations, and any formula based on a system of median[3] and lateral lines[4] ought to be no more than the starting point in the search for an equitable solution – except that for reasons both of convenience and established principle[5] the low-water mark may properly be deemed to be the basis for the determination of the boundary. The problems involved may become particularly complicated if islands belonging to one State are situated within the area of the continental shelf (or of appropriated submarine areas generally) of another State. For such islands, or groups of islands, have not only territorial waters of their own; the State to which they belong may claim the continental shelf (or its

[1] *Connecticut* v. *Massachusetts* (1931), 282 U.S. 660: *Annual Digest*, 6 (1931–2), 119.

[2] See, on boundaries through territorial waters, Boggs, *International Boundaries* (1940), pp. 184–91. See also, with regard to the continental shelf, the Memorandum of the Secretary-General (cited above, p. 145), pp. 101, 108, and Vallat in *B.Y.* 23 (1946), 336. For an instance of regulation of the boundary in territorial waters see 18 and 19 Geo. V, c. 23, approving the agreement with the Sultan of Johore with regard to territorial waters between the Straits Settlement and the State of Johore.

[3] I.e. a line of which every point is equidistant from the low-water mark (see below, n. 5) of the coast of the littoral States concerned.

[4] I.e. a line extending from the termination of the land boundary of the coastal State. For a valuable study of the subject see Boggs, in *A.J.* 45 (1951), 240–66.

[5] See, e.g., Oppenheim, *International Law*, 1, § 199 (3), where it is stated: 'It is . . . certain that the boundary line runs not nearer to the shore than three miles, or one marine league, from the *low-water mark*'.

equivalent) appurtenant to the islands in question. A further technical problem of considerable potential importance and complexity, requiring adjustment and regulation, will arise in connection with the existence of pools of deposits situated across the surface boundaries of the respective submarine areas.[1] However, these are not problems directly connected with the question of the freedom of the seas in relation to submarine areas. But there are two aspects of the question which bear intimately upon the subject here discussed.

The first is that of the legal status of the installations erected on the high seas for the purpose of exploring and exploiting the sea-bed and the subsoil. While no dogmatic interpretation of the principle of the freedom of the seas ought to be permitted to prevent the erection and protection of such works and installations, care must be taken lest they, in turn, become an occasion for wide claims derogatory to the freedom of the seas. This might, in particular, be the result of attempts to treat such installations as assimilated to islands and as such entitled to territorial waters (and possibly also to surrounding submarine areas) of their own. The question of territorial waters around artificial islands and lighthouses is far from settled.[2] Whatever may be the existing or future law on the subject, it is clear that works and installations erected on the surface of the sea in connection with the exploration and exploitation of the sea-bed and subsoil are not entitled – and properly ought not to be entitled – to territorial waters (and, *a fortiori*, to submarine areas) of their own. They are on the high seas as licensees, as it

[1] The problem has arisen repeatedly in the United States in the relations of adjoining owners of oil deposits. It has found expression, among others, in the so-called 'rule of capture' according to which the owner of a tract of land acquires title to the oil or gas which he produces from wells drilled there even if it can be proved that part of such oil or gas migrated from adjoining lands. The rule as originally applied was based on the principle that an owner of a well had the privilege of using and wasting the product as he saw fit regardless of injury to his neighbour or of depletion of valuable natural resources. That principle does not recognize correlative rights in an underground reservoir, but accords to each well-owner an unlimited right of exploitation. It was only gradually and after irretrievable harm had been done to the industry that courts enunciated limiting principles such as that there must be no deliberate waste to the injury of the neighbour and that the owner must not wantonly perform acts injurious to the common reservoir or calculated to destroy it. Administrative regulation has worked in the same direction. Attempts have been made to pass compulsory unitization statutes according to which all surface lessees over a given reservoir agree to treat their properties as a single unit. These have been not wholly ineffective in stemming the irresponsibility of unbridled competition. An authoritative writer has summarized in the following passage the results of the situation which is bound to arise in regard to such boundary areas within a State which has no machinery for the public regulation of problems of this nature: 'It may be impossible for our successors to believe that in the space of less than a century our system of laws allowed the loss of an essential resource and a resort to substitutes; that our people voluntarily submitted to the process; and that the industry was helpless to avoid it' (Northcutt Ely, 'The Conservation of Oil', in *H.L.R.* 51 (1937–8), 1244)). It will be noted that the phenomenon of common pools independent of political boundaries is relied upon in the recitals of the proclamation of the United States of 1945.

[2] See Johnson, in *I.L.Q.* 4 (1951), 203–15.

were, by dint of a liberal interpretation of a hitherto rigid principle. They are normally in any case in a category different from that of artificial islands created in shallow waters by means of walls surrounding the projected elevation.[1] To some extent any controversy in this connection as to artificial islands may in itself be unreal. For in so far as they are thought of as being within the area of the continental shelf of any State, they cannot properly be constructed there without interfering with the existing continental shelf, which includes the bed of the sea, of that foreign State. In so far as they are situated in proximity to the coast within the area of the continental shelf of the coastal State, they can make no difference in the legal situation. They may become relevant if they are thought of as situated on the outward fringe of the submarine area, i.e. at a great distance from the coast – a problem of distinctly limited practical importance. In any case, it seems inadmissible that artificial installations, the authorization for which is based on an exception, should become the starting point for appropriation, in the literal sense, of parts of the high seas.[2] If the submarine areas in question are large and the installations numerous and scattered, the territorial waters round them might cover substantial parts of the sea. Undoubtedly, such installations must be protected and there may, on that account, ensue limited interference with the freedom of navigation. However, there is all the difference between that incidental result and the subjection of large portions of the high seas to the territorial

[1] For an example of such islands see the inquiry, referred to above on p. 169, addressed in 1918 to the Department of State. It is difficult to assess the degree of probability of such structures being erected to an extent warranting their detailed examination. In general it would seem that the considerations adduced in the text above in the matter of artificial installations must apply to artificial islands. With regard to the delimitation of the continental shelf, considerations both of equity and of convenience would seem to require that such artificial islands should be disregarded not only when they are situated within the continental shelf of another State but also in so far as they are calculated to impinge upon the legitimate continental shelf of a foreign State or States.

[2] For this, and other reasons, such installations are even less entitled to territorial waters of their own than lighthouses, with regard to which the better and almost generally accepted opinion is that they are not entitled to territorial waters. See Oppenheim, *International Law*, I, § 190*a*: 'Just as a State may not claim sovereignty over a maritime belt around an anchored light-ship, so it may not make such a claim in the case of a lighthouse in the open sea.' See also Westlake, *International Law*, I (1st ed., 1904), 186, for a criticism of Sir Charles Russell's suggestion, in the contrary sense, made in the course of the *Behring Sea* arbitration in 1899; Gidel, III, 696; Jessup, *The Law of Territorial Waters*, p. 69; Hyde, I, 485, who points out that the erection of a lighthouse on a submerged rock in the high seas 'does not confer upon the State that erects and maintains it the privilege of making valid claims to the surrounding waters as territorial'. See, however, Johnson, referred to above (p. 180, n. 2). It is understood that the British legal and other authorities regarded, and still regard, the Eddystone lighthouse as entitled to territorial waters of its own. It is not believed that installations for underwater drilling would, in any case, come within the observation made by Sub-Committee No. 2 at the Hague Codification Conference in 1930 which stated that 'the definition of the term "island" does not exclude artificial islands provided these are true portions of the territory and not merely floating works, anchored buoys, etc.' (*Acts of the Conference*, III, 219).

sovereignty of the State in question. The International Law Commission had no difficulty in discarding such a solution. In its provisional report to the General Assembly in 1950 it stated that 'for works and installations established in the waters of the high seas for working the sea-bed and subsoil, special security zones might be set up, but they could not be classed as territorial waters.'[1] Artificial installations on the high seas for the purpose of exploiting the resources of the bed of the sea are not artificial islands partaking of the nature of territory. An authoritative affirmation of that rule may serve the useful purpose of discouraging the abuse of the notion of the continental shelf and submarine areas for objects alien to their legitimate purpose.

Secondly, the claim to sovereignty over submarine areas may be – and has been – abused for the purpose of advancing pretensions to sovereignty over the high seas as such or the exclusive exploitation of their resources. Pretensions of that nature are wholly external to the apparent occasion which prompted them. It was perhaps unfortunate that the United States, on the day on which it issued the proclamation as to the continental shelf, also issued the proclamation relating to the conservation zones in the matter of fisheries.[2] Whatever may have been the propriety of the latter, it was independent of the claim to the continental shelf. Yet some States, in following the apparent example of the United States, have combined in the same instrument the claim to the adjacent submarine areas with sweeping assertions of sovereignty over the high seas. While Mexico did no more than join in one proclamation the substance of the two separate proclamations of the United States, some other States went substantially beyond that. Thus Chile, in addition to proclaiming sovereignty over the continental shelf, 'confirmed' and 'proclaimed' national sovereignty over the adjacent seas of whatever depth to 'within the limits necessary in order to reserve, protect, preserve and exploit the natural resources of whatever nature found on, within and below the said seas'. The proclamations of Peru and of Costa Rica were to the same effect and in almost identical language. In the case of those countries the only connection between the assumption of sovereignty over the continental shelf and the assertion of sovereignty over the adjacent sea is that both are contained in the same instrument. It will also be noted that, in the case of those States, the claim to sovereignty over the high seas is limited to the

[1] *General Assembly, Fifth Session* (1950), Supplement no. 12 (A/1316), p. 22. The Commission followed in this report the recommendations contained in the Report submitted in 1950 to the Copenhagen Conference of the International Law Association by its Committee on Rights to the Sea-bed and its Subsoil. See *Summary Record* of the Meeting of the Commission of 17 July 1950 (A/CN. 4/SR. 69, pp. 11, 12).

[1] See above, p. 177.

protection and exploitation of its natural resources. The problems raised by the inconsistency with international law – which inconsistency is not open to doubt – of these claims to sovereignty over the high seas, even if only for limited purposes, fall outside the scope of the present article. They are referred to here as an example of action which by the extravagance of the underlying claim – even if explained by the differing importance attached in various countries to emphasis of language – tends to cast doubt upon the reasonableness and justification of the claim to submarine areas. Some other countries have gone beyond these proclamations and have asserted sovereignty over the adjacent seas generally and not merely for limited purposes. Thus Article 7 of the Constitution of El Salvador of 1950 provides, in language of some simplicity, that the territory of the Republic 'includes the adjacent seas to a distance of two hundred nautical miles from low-water mark and comprises the corresponding aerial space, subsoil and continental shelf'. Although the same article expressly laid down that its provisions 'do not affect freedom of navigation in conformity with the accepted principles of international law', it is clear that the claim thus made was contrary to international law. For the freedom of the seas comprises other freedoms in addition to that of navigation. Moreover, as stated in the communication of the Government of the United States addressed to the Government of El Salvador and expressing the former's 'deep concern' at the implications of this provision of the Constitution, the disclaimer of the intention to interfere with the freedom of navigation, when coupled with an assertion of sovereignty, 'might be claimed to be a privilege granted by El Salvador rather than based on a right derived from international law'.[1]

As stated, this association of the assumption of title over submarine areas with sweeping claims to sovereignty over the high seas is mischievous in its results and must therefore be a cause for regret. This is so not only because these claims are in themselves contrary to international law, but also because they tend to cast doubt upon the justification of the claim to submarine areas and its essential conformity with international law. For, it has been shown, there is no principle of international law – and certainly no principle of international practice – which makes the submarine areas share automatically the status of the high seas. Unlike the latter, they are not *res omnium communis*. To that extent they can, consistently with the rules of international law in the matter of acquisition of territorial title,[2] become subject to the sovereignty of the State – though not of every State. They are not *res*

[1] Communication of 12 December 1950 addressed to El Salvador (*Department of State Bulletin*, 24 (1950), 24).

[2] See below, pp. 185–92.

nullius. The more difficult question, namely, whether their exploitation, when originating from the surface of the sea, unavoidably necessitates activities which are inconsistent with the freedom of the seas, must be answered in the negative. There is no difficulty in reaching that answer once we abandon a conception of the freedom of the seas which is both rigid and pedantic.

However, that very factor as well as the apparent novelty of the claim to submarine areas make it incumbent upon States which have asserted such a claim to explain, in all requisite detail, the propriety of the action taken. The proclamation of the United States in the matter of the continental shelf went a long way in the direction of supplying what may be called the philosophy of the new doctrine in terms of national and international interest, of modern scientific progress, and of geographical propinquity which make the utilization of the resources of the submarine areas by the coastal State feasible and essential. The recitals of the proclamation gave lucid expression to these considerations. The proclamations of other States followed the example of the United States in explaining to the world the considerations which led to the new departure. In thus giving an explanation for their action they appealed to the test which is decisive in relation to the freedom of the seas, namely, the test of reasonableness and of legitimate common and particular interest. For unless the exploitation of submarine resources is to become a source of friction, disorder, and uncertainty, it must be placed in the hands of the coastal State. This is also the solution most consistent, as a rule, with economic considerations. Moreover, it is the only solution compatible with the security of the coastal State. The coastal State cannot be expected to tolerate permanent installations, of potential military importance, erected by any State, however distant, in the neighbourhood of its maritime frontier. All these factors are of importance as great as the circumstance that the appropriation of submarine areas has become part of international practice – including that of the two principal maritime States – accompanied by general acquiescence. To that extent the admissibility of sovereignty over submarine areas is no longer a matter to be determined by purely doctrinal considerations. Such sovereignty has been declared by international practice to be part of the law, and international lawyers can no more prevent – or retard[1] – the consequential developments than they were able to impede the adoption of the principle of the full sovereignty of the State over the air above its

[1] There may perhaps have been an element of exaggeration of the power of lawyers in Professor Hudson's observation at the Session of the International Law Commission in 1950 that 'lawyers had no right to prevent the exploitation of those resources for the benefit of mankind' (A/CN. 4/SR. 66, p. 24).

territory. Nor is it necessary for them to adopt an attitude of obstruction or discouragement or circumlocution, for example by suggesting that what has been acquired as the result of the proclamations in the matter of submarine areas is not a right over them but an exclusive right to occupy them.[1] For international law, reasonably interpreted, is not inimical to these developments. At the same time its principles, unhampered in their efficacy by an endeavour to obstruct changes consistent with the freedom of the sea, may continue to fulfil the useful function of checking abuses and excessive claims divorced from the true purpose and the true justification of these developments.

7. 'OCCUPATION' OF SUBMARINE AREAS

It has been suggested that, regardless of the form of words used, the rights of exclusive control and jurisdiction claimed in the submarine areas are rights indistinguishable from sovereignty.[2] It has also been submitted that such rights are not inconsistent with the reasonably interpreted conception of the freedom of the seas. We may now inquire what, in addition to the decisive test of reasonableness[3] and the fact of its having become part of the practice of States, is the legal basis of the asserted title, conceived as a territorial title, to submarine areas. The main argument, other than that based on the freedom of the seas, which has been raised against the acquisition of title over submarine areas is that international law requires effective occupation as a condition of valid acquisition of territorial title, and that no such effective occupation is possible with regard to submarine areas. That argument is based on two assumptions. The first is that the principles applicable with regard to acquisition of title over territory apply, automatically and without modification, to the novel case of the submarine areas. The second is that effective occupation is, according to international law, invariably and rigidly a condition of acquisition of territorial sovereignty. Both these assumptions are unwarranted.

Any attempt to base the title to submarine areas on the accepted notion of effective occupation must result either in a denial of the legality of the title thus claimed or in depriving the notion of effective occupation of its natural meaning. For it is clear that in all cases in which the title to submarine areas has been proclaimed there has been no approximation to effective occupation. There has been only a proclamation and, in some cases, a conferment of concessions in respect of the areas in question. This absence of effective occupation is in no

[1] See below, p. 190.
[2] See above, pp. 155 et seq.
[3] See above, p. 184.

way fatal to acquisition of territorial title over submarine areas. For modern international practice does not invariably consider effective occupation to be a condition of acquisition of title. As it is occasionally put in a more circuitous fashion, the requirement of effectiveness of occupation is a matter of degree. Even that attenuated condition of effectiveness represents an over-simplification of the true legal position. What is true is that, *all other things being equal*, effective occupation constitutes, except as against the lawful sovereign, a title superior to any competing title. To that extent – but to that extent only – is it possible to consider as accurate the statement that international law has discarded discovery, purely symbolic occupation (which does not differ in nature from pretensions based on mere discovery), and similar claims, including that of contiguity, as a valid source of territorial title. Thus in modern international judicial practice the border-line between the attenuated conditions of effectiveness of occupation and the total relinquishment of the requirement of effectiveness has become shadowy to the point of obliteration. In the judgment given in 1933 in the case between Denmark and Norway concerning the *Legal Status of Eastern Greenland*, the Permanent Court of International Justice, after laying down the general principle that a claim to territorial title based upon continued display of authority must show 'the intention and will to act as sovereign, and some actual exercise or display of such sovereignty', proceeded to qualify very substantially the requirement of 'some actual exercise or display' of authority. It said:

It is impossible to read the records of the decisions in cases as to territorial sovereignty without observing that in many cases the tribunal has been satisfied with very little in the way of the actual exercise of sovereign rights, provided that the other State could not make out a superior claim. This is particularly true in the case of claims to sovereignty over areas in thinly populated or unsettled countries.[1]

The principle that the requirement of 'some display of authority' may be reduced to the bare existence of a claim was shown clearly in the way in which the Court dealt with the title of Norwegian Kings in the sixteenth century, from which the Danish title was subsequently derived:

That the King's claims amounted merely to pretensions is clear, for he had no permanent contact with the country, he was exercising no authority there. The claims, however, were not disputed. No other Power was putting forward any claim to territorial sovereignty in Greenland, and in the absence of any competing claim the King's pretensions to be the sovereign of Greenland subsisted.[2]

[1] *P.C.I.J.* Series A/B, no. 53, at pp. 45–6.

[2] *Ibid.* at p. 48.

Moreover, the Court held, with regard to the much later period between 1721 and 1814, that as there had been no claim to sovereignty by any other Power, and in view of the arctic and inaccessible character of the uncolonized part of the country, mere acts of legislation were sufficient evidence of effectiveness. Neither was the Court prepared to exact a substantially higher degree of effectiveness with regard to the modern period covering the nineteenth and twentieth centuries and immediately preceding the dispute. It considered as sufficient such manifestations of display of sovereignty as acts of legislation concerning navigation in the seas round Greenland and the conclusion of commercial agreements referring to Greenland.

Even less exacting, if possible, in the matter of the requirement of effectiveness was the award by the King of Italy, acting as Sole Arbitrator, in the *Clipperton Island* case between France and Mexico in 1931. That case is occasionally referred to as an example of the elasticity of the notion of occupation. Upon analysis, it is an instance of a situation in which international law dispenses altogether with the requirement of effectiveness. In that case the actual display of State activity by France consisted in the drawing up, by a Lieutenant of the French Navy acting upon instructions of the French Minister of Marine, of a proclamation of French sovereignty over the island; in taking geographical notes; in an unsuccessful attempt to reach the shore; and, in 1897, in an inquiry addressed to the Government of the United States as to the activities of certain American citizens in connection with the island. The Arbitrator decided that the island belonged to France. After holding that 'the actual, and not the nominal, taking of Possession is a necessary condition of occupation', he proceeded to base his decision on the rule that 'if a territory, by virtue of the fact that it was completely uninhabited, is, from the first moment when the occupying State makes its appearance there, at the absolute and undisputed disposition of that State, from that moment the taking of possession must be considered as accomplished, and the occupation is thereby completed'.[1] Yet it is clear that there was in this case nothing in the nature of an initial taking of possession in the ordinary sense of the word. There was a symbolic act, a proclamation. Such symbolic act cannot, without doing violence to language, be regarded as occupation. The *Clipperton Island* case shows that the notion of occupation, as traditionally understood, may be valueless, in relation to some areas, for the purpose of acquiring title.[2] Such areas are not only

[1] *Annual Digest*, 6 (1931–2), 105, at p. 107.

[2] As Professor Dickinson put it, in 1933, in his analysis of the award: this retention of the term 'occupation' in such cases provides 'adequate criteria for determining the ownership

those which are uninhabited, but also those which are normally uninhabitable.

The judicial and arbitral decisions referred to above demonstrate the advisability of viewing the principle of effectiveness against the background of the historic circumstances which gave rise to it. It was conceived as a check upon the fanciful arbitrariness of pretensions inimical to a reasonable apportionment of the normally inhabitable territorial domain of the world and productive, by their very excess, of uncertainty and friction. But it is not a magic formula applicable to all situations. If so applied it can be maintained only by dint of being used, in the end, in a sense contrary to its natural connotation. The futility of the mechanical application of the notion of effectiveness was demonstrated in an instructive manner in the discussions preceding the general recognition of the sovereignty of States over the air. It was argued by international lawyers of distinction that as the air was incapable of effective occupation it was incapable of appropriation. To speak of occupation of submarine areas is to use language even more unreal than that referring to occupation, as a basis of territorial title, of arctic and antarctic regions. States have indeed put forward claims – not altogether uncontroverted – to the latter, but they have not based them on any principle germane to occupation, effective or fictitious.[1] In doing so they have by implication rejected the notion of occupation as an invariable basis of title. The same applies to the various proclamations relating to submarine areas. There is no element of occupation, in a sense consistent with the ordinary meaning of the word, in the British proclamations concerning the continental shelf in the Bahamas, Honduras, Jamaica, and the Falkland Islands. To say that a proclamation amounts to occupation, or that it constitutes the first step to occupation giving an 'inchoate title'[2] is, in fact, to deny that occupation is necessary. A proclamation is a means by which a title, claimed or acquired, is announced. It is not a *source* of a title or a means of acquiring it. That does not mean that it is meaningless or unnecessary. When the rulers of various Sheikdoms in the Persian Gulf were advised in 1949 by the British authorities that the issue of a proclamation is a prerequisite of their effective assertion of rights over the adjacent submarine areas, the advice was given in deference to an obvious

of such parts of the earth as still remain unclaimed and unexploited'. Among these parts of the earth he included 'the unexploited lands that lie under the sea' (*A.J.* 27 (1933), 133). For modern examples of claims by Great Britain and the United States based on purely symbolic occupation see the interesting article of Orent and Reinsch, *ibid.* 35 (1941), 443–61. The late Professor Decencière-Ferrandière came to the conclusion, in an exhaustive study, that 'la limitation de l'effet des occupations au territoire effectivement occupé . . . ne fait plus partie du droit international positif' (*R.I.* 3rd ser. 18 (1937), 662).

[1] See below, p. 197.

[2] As to which see below, p. 191.

proposition of order and orderliness which requires that a person – or a State – asserting a claim, however inherently valid, must make his claim known by a formal pronouncement or notification. This is so especially if the subject of the claim in question is novel in character, undefined in extent, and likely to require determination in relation to similar claims by other persons or States. Accordingly, the issue of the proclamations of the continental shelf in no way militates against the view that they were of a declaratory character in relation to what was considered to be a title claimed or acquired by or belonging to the State by reference to a legal basis other than occupation.

The International Law Commission not only put on record, in its Report to the General Assembly in 1950, its view that the exercise of control and jurisdiction over the continental shelf 'was independent of the concept of occupation'.[1] It had previously adopted a text stating that 'the submarine area (sea-bed and subsoil) of the continental shelf off the coast of a littoral State and outside the area of its territorial waters is subject *ipso jure* [*sc.* without a proclamation] to the control and jurisdiction of the littoral State'.[2] The Commission had no difficulty in thus disposing of the idea of 'notional occupation', which in effect amounts to a denial of the necessity of occupation. In the long run little purpose is served by adhering to words deprived of their content. Those who, apprehensive of the seemingly limitless comprehensiveness of the rival doctrine of contiguity,[3] are inclined to see in occupation the only legitimate mode of acquiring title to submarine areas, find themselves in a dilemma which can be solved only by dint of a verbal nicety. As no effective acts of occupation (in the ordinary sense of the word), concurrently with the act of proclamation of title or at any ascertainable period in the foreseeable future, are possible in relation to contiguous submarine areas, it is found necessary to fall back upon the barest minimum of occupation which reduces occupation to a shadow of its natural meaning, namely, to a proclamation and,

[1] *General Assembly, Fifth Session* (1950), Supplement no. 12 (A/1316), p. 22.

[2] A/CN. 4/SR. 68, p. 13. Professor Brierly expressed the correct position in clear terms: 'If this right [of sovereignty] belonged *ipso jure* to the littoral State, there was no necessity for the latter to make any claim or annexation. Such a proclamation or annexation might of course serve to indicate that a State had begun to work its zone of control, but legally it was not necessary' (*ibid.* p. 6). On this point, apparently, the Commission was not prepared to share the indecision of the Report of the Committee of the International Law Association in 1950. That Report stated, in the text, that 'control and jurisdiction over the sea-bed and subsoil of the continental shelf outside territorial waters can be vested in the coastal State by effective occupation'. However, a footnote attached to the text stated that 'it is not the intention of the Committee that affirmation of this principle should be interpreted as a rejection of the possibility that control and jurisdiction over the sea-bed and subsoil of the continental shelf outside territorial waters vest *ipso jure* in the coastal State or that they can be vested in the coastal State by a proclamation to this effect'.

[3] See below, p. 201.

possibly, the granting of concessions. But this is the very question which is at issue, namely, whether the State is in the position to rely on a valid legal basis and title for issuing the proclamation and granting concessions. There is little persuasive force in an attempt at juridical analysis which proceeds, in effect, as follows: 'The State is entitled to issue the proclamation annexing the continental shelf and to grant concessions over it if it occupies it to the extent of issuing the proclamation and granting concessions.' The tautologous nature of the solution emphasizes its essential unhelpfulness. For the same reason it seems unhelpful to answer the question whether a State is entitled to exercise sovereignty, i.e. display State activities, by explaining that it is entitled to do so if it displays State activities, by legislating, granting concessions, and concluding treaties.[1] There would be an element of consistency – though, it is believed, of misguided consistency – in the view that as the occupation of submarine areas is impossible there can be no title over them. But there is probably no more than dialectics in the attempt to combine the requirement of occupation with a denial of it by reducing it to a formal claim in the form of a proclamation.

However, the defect of the attempt to base the title to submarine areas on occupation is not only one of logic. If 'occupation' thus conceived were the true basis of the legal claim to the adjacent submarine areas then there would be nothing – save the extra-legal remedies of intervention or self-preservation on the part of the coastal State – to prevent distant and strategically and economically powerful States from 'occupying' the adjacent submarine areas of other States by proclaiming their annexation and by emphasizing the 'effectiveness' of the title thus claimed to have been acquired by granting concessions, by legislating in respect of them, by concluding treaties – with States willing to do so – relating to the submarine areas thus acquired, and, eventually and after a long period of uncertainty, from proceeding to the actual exploitation, possibly in active competition with other States, of the submarine areas in question. Wide and disturbing possibilities of friction would thus be opened not only as between the coastal State and its more or less distant neighbours, but also between the neighbours themselves. These possibilities are probably present to the minds of the adherents of the 'occupation doctrine'; for eventually they fall back upon contiguity. However, there may be an element of

[1] It may perhaps be deceptive to rely, in support of that view, on the judgment, referred to above, of the Permanent Court in the *Eastern Greenland* case. There is all the difference between the Court holding, retrospectively, that legislation, conclusion of treaties relating to the territory, and the granting of concessions constituted, *in the absence of an adverse claim*, sufficient evidence of effectiveness, and relying on such manifestations of State activity as conferring title, *pro futuro*, in respect of a controversial situation.

artificiality in an argument which starts from the proposition that 'contiguity is a dangerous doctrine unless confined within the principle of effective occupation'[1] and ends by reducing the 'effective occupation' to a proclamation which, however, can be issued only by the coastal, the contiguous, State. It may be essentially unhelpful to rely, as a check upon exorbitant claims of contiguity, on the doctrine of occupation – of effective occupation – and to proceed to argue that the effectiveness required is the effectiveness of 'a symbolic act of appropriation in the form of a proclamation' which can issue only from the coastal State. It may be tempting, in that predicament, to invoke the authority of the Permanent Court of International Justice in the case of the *Legal Status of Eastern Greenland*, as well as the award in the *Clipperton Island* case, as supporting the proposition that full effectiveness of occupation is not essential. Actually these decisions demonstrate more than that. They show that there are situations in which occupation, in the normal meaning of the word, is not required at all and in which the conception of occupation is a more or less deceptive figure of speech. If this is so with regard to inhabited or sparsely inhabited territory, it is particularly true in relation to uninhabitable areas such as the sea-bed and its subsoil.

Neither can the difficulty be obviated by relying on the somewhat nebulous notion of 'inchoate title' as applied to claims based on discovery. The latter, it has often been said, gives an 'inchoate title' which must be confirmed by use and settlement[2] and which is lost if not thus confirmed. The doctrine of 'inchoate title' has often been invoked in diplomatic correspondence and arbitral proceedings[3] and has been the subject of an occasional judicial *dictum*. In the only arbitral decision in which it was directly applied – namely, in the *Island of Palmas* arbitration – it was applied in the sense that the 'inchoate title' was held to have lapsed in view of the proved adverse claim based on effective occupation.[4] In the nature of things there can be no question, in the matter of submarine areas, of any loss of the

[1] Waldock, 'The Legal Basis of Claims to the Continental Shelf' – a paper read before the Grotius Society in April 1950 and published in *Grotius Society*, 36 (1950), 115. This paper, which is an important contribution to the subject, was also published as an annex to the Report of the Committee of the International Law Association in 1950.

[2] See Moore, I, 258.

[3] For some references see Moore, pp. 259–61, and Lindley, pp. 136–8.

[4] The Arbitrator said 'Throughout the nineteenth century there prevailed the principle that an inchoate title of discovery must, in order to be productive of definite title, be completed within a reasonable period by effective occupation. . . . No act of occupation nor any exercise of sovereignty by Spain at Palmas Island had been alleged. Even if it were possible to admit that the Spanish title still existed as an inchoate title in 1898 and as such passed over to the United States, such inchoate title could not prevail over continuous and peaceful display of authority by Holland' (*Annual Digest*, 4 (1927–8), 4).

'inchoate title' by adverse occupation by another State. The very object of the proclamation is to make such adverse occupation impossible. Can it be said that 'inchoate title' over the submarine areas will be lost if it is not followed by actual exploitation or exploration? To whom will it be lost? What is the reasonable period within which such exploitation or exploration must materialize? With regard to 'inchoate title' generally, writers have discussed the question whether a period such as twenty-five years is sufficient.[1] Hall, in a careful treatment of the subject, suggested that an 'inchoate title' is good, as against another occupying State, for such time as 'allowing for accidental circumstances or moderate negligence, might elapse before a force or a colony are sent out to some part of the land intended to be occupied'[2] and that 'in the course of a few years the presumption of permanent intention afforded by such act dies away'. The quotation shows the degree of applicability of the doctrine of inchoate title to submarine areas. Will the granting of concessions – a measure easy of accomplishment – suffice to perfect or keep alive the title? If not, within what period must the concession be followed by operations which are not purely nominal? That question can be put even more pertinently in relation to 'exploration' conceived as a manifestation of an effective exercise of the right of occupation. What international or national authority will exercise the power of exacting the penalty for inefficiency or failure?[3] These questions could be multiplied. They are sufficient to show the inadequacy of the notion of 'inchoate title', conceived for entirely different circumstances, in regard to a situation in which international law, if it is to be of assistance, must supply the necessary element of precision and stability as distinguished from an infusion of uncertainty and potentialities for conflict.

On the other hand, it is possible to use in this connection the term 'inchoate title' in a specific connotation different from that with which it is usually associated. It is possible to say that the littoral State is entitled *ipso jure* to the adjacent submarine areas, but that so long as it has not perfected its title by claiming it formally through the issue of a proclamation, declaratory of an existing right, the title is merely 'inchoate'. The language thus used may not be wholly devoid of artificiality inasmuch as it identifies the dividing line between a full

[1] See Von der Heydte, in *A.J.* 29 (1933), 461–2, for a survey of some of the periods suggested.

[2] Hall, *A Treatise on International Law* (3rd ed. 1890), p. 106.

[3] In the course of the deliberations of the International Law Commission in 1950 Professor Hudson expressed the opinion that the rights over the continental shelf should not belong to the State *ipso jure*, but 'should be subject to the exercise of the right for the purposes of exploring and exploiting the continental shelf' (A/CN. 4/SR. 68, p. 14). The Commission did not adopt that view.

and an 'inchoate' title with a purely formal act which can be accomplished with a stroke of the pen. However, there is room for the argument that there is no compelling necessity in relation to an entirely novel situation to use terms in full conformity with their accepted meaning. Moreover, the formula may be useful inasmuch as it emphasizes the importance of and necessity for an express declaration even if conceived as a purely formal act.[1]

The theory of occupation as the legal basis of the claim to submarine areas has been favoured largely for the reason that it supplies an alternative to exorbitant and altogether undefinable claims based on contiguity and continuity. However, it may be a mistake to attempt to provide a legal basis for new problems in international law in such a way as to eliminate all possibility of abuse. No legal doctrine can by itself do away with that possibility. There is no compelling necessity to conjure dangerous vistas of unchecked nationalistic expansion following in the wake of the principle of contiguity. Such expansion – which, in terms of law, must remain a *brutum fulmen* – can equally well take place on the purported basis of fictitious and nominal, of 'notional', occupation. The claim to sovereignty or to exclusive rights over the high seas is unlawful whether it is put forward under the colour of contiguity or occupation accomplished by an act of appropriation in the form of a proclamation or enactment. The claim to territories already occupied or administered by another State is as groundless when put forward by reference to contiguity as it is when advanced by reference to notional occupation in the form of a proclamation or a prior title based on discovery. In so far as occupation means effective occupation – and that is its only natural meaning – it is not applicable to the continental shelf and to submarine areas generally.[2] In so far as it is used in a figurative sense, i.e. as a mere claim to be substantiated by no more than a proclamation or a similarly nominal act such as the granting of concessions, it is as elastic and as open to abuse as the doctrine of the contiguity of the coastal State. The latter, at least, has the merit of using terms in their ordinary connotation. It will now be considered to what extent that doctrine has in actual practice been made the basis of the assumption of title to submarine areas and to what extent such practice can find support in the notion of contiguity and continuity as reasonably adapted to the circumstances of the case.

[1] See above, pp. 188–9.

[2] The view here put forward is confirmed in an authoritative article by Young – who has made this subject particularly his own – in *A.J.* 45 (1951), 228 *et seq.*

8. CONTIGUITY AS THE LEGAL BASIS OF SOVEREIGNTY OVER SUBMARINE AREAS

The inadequacy of the notion of occupation as the basis of the legal right to the submarine areas brings into prominence the alternative solution, namely, that of the principle of contiguity or, which is probably the same, of continuity.[1] In so far as the various proclamations and enactments have attempted to specify the legal grounds on which they are based, most of them have invoked, in addition to other reasons, the principle – or the fact – of contiguity and geographical unity. There is in this respect no difference between the proclamations of the United States of America, of many Latin-American States, and of the rulers in the Persian Gulf acting under the international responsibility of Great Britain. The proclamation of the United States spoke of the continental shelf as 'an extension of the land mass of the coastal nation and thus naturally appurtenant to it' – a unity emphasized by the fact that 'these resources frequently form a seaward extension or a pool or deposit lying within the territory'. The Mexican Declaration of the same year was even more specific : 'As is well known, the lands which constitute continental masses do not as a rule rise steeply from the great ocean depths, but rest upon a submarine base called the continental platform. . . . This platform obviously constitutes an integral part of the continental countries.' The Argentine Declaration of 1946 began by reciting that 'the submarine platform, known also as the submarine plateau or continental shelf, is closely united to the mainland both in a morphological and in a geological sense'. The Peruvian Decree of 1947 opened with the statement that 'the continental submerged shelf forms one entire morphological and geological unit with the continent'. Similarly, the introductory passage of the Brazilian Decree of 1950 asserted that 'the sea-bed which borders continents and islands and extends under the high seas is a veritable submerged territory and constitutes, with the land to which it is adjacent, one single geographical unit'.

In the passages quoted, the basis of the title appears to be not contiguity in the accepted sense, i.e. as connoting horizontal prolongation of the already occupied territory, but a different, and apparently more intense, degree of unity – a unity provided by the fact that the shelf is supposed to constitute the base, the platform, on which the continent rests. It is possible to imagine that kind of unity also in relation to sub-

[1] Attempts are occasionally made to distinguish between 'continuity' as referring to territory directly co-terminous, and 'contiguity' as referring to islands or other territory separated by water. There is probably no warrant for that distinction in accepted usage.

marine areas – such as those in the Persian Gulf – which do not constitute a continental shelf in the technical meaning of the term. However that may be, it is probable that the difference between the two types of submarine areas is one of emphasis. On the one hand, the conception of the continent resting on the shelf visualized as a platform may partake to some degree of a figure of speech; on the other hand, the relation of the mainland to the submarine area where there is no continental shelf proper is different from that of mere horizontal prolongation as in the normal case of contiguity. Nevertheless, although there is probably more than a geographical nicety in the various hypotheses which gave substance to the words of the American and other proclamations that 'the continental shelf may be regarded as an extension of the land mass of the coastal nation',[1] it is more convenient, in the first instance, to view the true relation as one of contiguity.

The principle of contiguity as the basis of the title to submarine areas has encountered opposition on two grounds: The first is that the doctrine of contiguity, although occasionally enunciated, has never become part of international law and has been rejected by international tribunals. The second, already referred to,[2] is that contiguity represents a theory which, because of its vagueness and comprehensiveness, is full of dangerous implications and ought therefore to be discouraged. Neither of these two objections can be regarded as valid.

To say that the principle of continuity – or contiguity – has no place in international law, is to state a proposition of doubtful accuracy. The principle of contiguity played a useful part in the period when some compromise between the fanciful assertions of pure discovery and effective occupation best fulfilled the needs of the time. This applies to the rule, which is no more than a variant of the principle of contiguity, that the occupation of the portion of the shore confers title to inferior territory up to the limit of the watershed or that the occupation of the coast carries with it a right, in reasonable proportion to the extent of the occupied area, to the entire territory drained by the rivers emptying their waters within its line. The latter rule Hall[3] described as unobjectionable, although in an opinion given in 1821 Lord Stowell doubted its accuracy except, possibly, in relation to islands.[4] Sir Travers Twiss was emphatic that 'there is no dispute amongst nations as to it'.[5] Some conception of contiguity underlay the early British Colonial Charters, such as that of Massachusetts Bay of 1628, which

[1] See above, p. 194. [2] See above, p. 190.

[3] Hall, *International Law* (3rd ed.), p. 109.

[4] The opinion is reproduced in Smith, II, 3. Thus Lord Palmerston seems to have suggested in 1834 that the proximity of Lobos Island to Peru gave to the latter a *prima facie* title to it (*Br. and For. St. Papers*, 31, 1097). [5] Twiss, I, 209.

purported to operate 'from the Atlantick and Westerne Sea and Ocean on the east parte to the South Sea on the west parte'.[1] In connection with the Oregon controversy, the United States Secretary of State wrote in 1844: 'That continuity furnishes a just foundation for a claim of territory, in connection with those of discovery and occupation, would seem unquestionable.'[2] He was echoing, in a different form, the frequently quoted words uttered in 1827 by Mr Gallatin, the American Commissioner in the same controversy:

> It will not be denied that the extent of contiguous territory to which an actual settlement gives a prior right, must depend, to a considerable degree, on the magnitude and population of that settlement, and on the facility with which the vacant adjoining land may, within a short time, be occupied, settled, and cultivated by such population, as compared with the probability of its being occupied and settled from another quarter.[3]

This cautious statement was described by Westlake as still leaving the 'pseudo-scientific principle of contiguity in a position of near equivalence to the "manifest destiny" of rhetoricians'.[4] Sir Travers Twiss had previously described the doctrine of contiguity as being 'but a disguised appeal to the principle of *vis major*' and as striking 'at the root of the fundamental axiom of international law, that all nations are upon a footing of perfect equality as to their obligations and rights'.[5] Yet in his treatise on the *Law of Nations* he formulated other principles of contiguity such as that of the watershed, of the middle distance, and of the rule that 'when a nation has discovered a country and notified its discovery, it is presumed to intend to take possession of the whole country within those natural boundaries which are essential to the independence and security of its settlement'.[6] In 1852, not many years after the Oregon controversy, in the dispute with Peru concerning Lobos Island and with Haiti concerning Navassa Island in 1873, the United States asserted the virtues of effective occupation over 'the facts of contiguity'.[7] But in the Note of Mr Olney, Secretary of State, to Sir Julian Pauncefote in connection with the British Guiana controversy with Venezuela in 1896, there was once more a pointed reference to mere constructive occupation being 'kept within bounds by the doctrine of contiguity'.[8]

In the arbitration between Great Britain and Portugal in 1870 concerning the Island of Bulama the Arbitrator, in awarding the island

[1] See Twiss, *The Oregon Question Examined* (1846), p. 311; Westlake, *Papers*, p. 73.
[2] Moore, I, 264.
[3] See Twiss, *The Oregon Question*, p. 310.
[4] Westlake, *Papers*, p. 173.
[5] *Ibid.* p. 312.
[6] Twiss, I, 209, 216.
[7] Moore, I, 266, 267.
[8] *Ibid.* p. 269.

to Portugal,[1] relied to a substantial extent on the fact of contiguity – a view not shared by an authoritative commentator in the *Recueil* of Lapradelle and Politis on the ground that 'contiguity in the case both of adjacent islands and of the watershed, cannot, like discovery, provide more than an inchoate title'.[2] When in the course of the arbitration in 1865 between Holland and Venezuela the latter relied on the doctrine of contiguity, she did so on the ground that that doctrine was 'well established in the relations of the United States and Great Britain'.[3] Some of the argument of Great Britain in the course of the *British Guiana* arbitration was couched in terms closely approaching the doctrine of contiguity. She urged that 'great weight must be given to the relative importance and presumable power of expansion in the direction of the vacant territory of the settlements, between which it is to be divided'.[4] Venezuela opposed that principle of division of territory although in the same arbitration she, too, put forward claims which were in effect closely akin to those of contiguity inasmuch as they were based on the natural and geographical features of the contested territories. In 1883 Great Britain put forward a claim, based on contiguity, to what subsequently became German South-West Africa.[5] She subsequently abandoned that claim. It is not clear whether the reasons for that step were of a political or a legal nature. Similarly, it is difficult to distinguish between the legal and political significance of the recognition of the relevance of geographical propinquity in relation to the *hinterland* doctrine in arrangements such as those of the Franco-British Agreement of 1904 concerning Morocco and French interests in Syria; the Anglo-Japanese Treaty of 1905 in so far as it concerned Korea; the Anglo-Russian Agreement of 1907 relating to spheres of influence in Persia;[6] and the Agreement of 1917 between the United States and Japan concerning China.[7]

Some aspects of the doctrine of contiguity also underlie the claims to Arctic and Antarctic regions put forward by a number of States – such as Great Britain, Canada, New Zealand, France, Russia, and Norway[8] – in so far as it is based on the so-called sector principle. By virtue of that principle areas have been claimed which are embraced by the projection northwards or southwards, as the case may be, of the areas bordering the respective maritime territories. While with regard to the Arctic these areas are, in a sense, contiguous to the territories of the

[1] *Br. and For. St. Papers*, 61, 1102; Herslet's *Commercial Treaties*, 13, 963.

[2] Lapradelle-Politis, II, 616.

[3] *Ibid.* p. 411.

[4] As quoted by Lindley, p. 220.

[5] Lindley, p. 230.

[6] *Ibid.* p. 331.

[7] As to which see Wright, in *A.J.* 12 (1918), 519–22.

[8] That country originally opposed the 'sector' principle, but seems to have relied upon it since 1939. See Hackworth, II, 460.

States concerned, in the case of the Antarctic the contiguity is distinctly symbolic. In some cases an element of uncertainty is added to the situation by the fact that the territory claimed as the base of the sector is claimed by virtue of discovery. This applies, for instance, to Adélie Land claimed by France. While New Zealand has dissented from the suggestion that the Ross Dependency is claimed by virtue of discovery alone, the 'effective settlement' of it has taken place largely by 'display of State activity' in the wider sense, such as the issue of licences and the appointment of magistrates.[1] Essentially, notwithstanding the controversial differences of the geographical features of the Arctic and Antarctic in relation to the mainland from which they project,[2] the claims to them are based – in so far as they are based on legal grounds – on some as yet undefined kind of contiguity, variously referred to also as proximity, region of attraction, and continuity. It is of interest to note that when the Russian claim to Arctic islands was first put forward in 1916, it referred to them as constituting 'an extension northward of the continental tableland [shelf] of Siberia'.

The award of Dr Huber in the case of the *Island of Palmas* has occasionally been cited as proving the assertion that international law does not recognize the title of contiguity.[3] Even if that were the correct interpretation of the award it is doubtful whether, notwithstanding the high authority of the Arbitrator, it could dispose of a doctrine which has figured prominently in the practice of States. However, it is doubtful whether this is the intended effect of the award. The Arbitrator, it is true, held that 'it is impossible to show the existence of a rule of positive international law to the effect that islands situated outside territorial waters should belong to a State from the fact that its territory forms the *terra firma*'.[4] However, it must be borne in mind that the award related only to islands; that, in a sense, it was *obiter* inasmuch as the claim of the United States was not based mainly on contiguity;[5] that the Arbitrator admitted that a group of islands may form 'in law a unit, and that the fate of the principal part may involve the rest'; and that he held in effect, with regard to occupation of territories which form a geographical unit, that the appropriation must be presumed, in the initial stages, to extend to the whole unit (a rule which is one of the main aspects of the doctrine of contiguity) and that the only considera-

[1] See Hackworth, II, 456–8 for the correspondence on the subject.

[2] See Hyde, I, 350, and Waldock, in *B.Y.* 25 (1948), 340 *et seq.*, where the variants of the doctrine of contiguity are discussed in detail in relation to claims to the Polar regions. See also Hyde, in *Iowa Law Review*, 19 (1934), 293.

[3] See Waldock, in *B.Y.* 25, 342.

[4] *Annual Digest*, 4 (1927–8), 111.

[5] See Jessup, in *A.J.* 22 (1928), 743.

tion to which contiguity must cede is that of actual adverse display of sovereignty by the competing State.

The relevance – which is of special importance in relation to submarine areas – of the geographical unity of the main and contiguous territory is also illustrated by the arbitral award given in 1904 by the King of Italy in the controversy concerning the boundary between British Guiana and Brazil. He held that 'the effective possession of a part of a region, although it may be held to confer a right to the acquisition of the sovereignty of the whole of a region which constitutes a single organic whole, cannot confer a right to the acquisition of the whole of a region which, owing either to its size or to its physical configuration, cannot be deemed to be a single organic whole *de facto*'.[1] Similarly, it is difficult to understand fully the judgment of the Permanent Court of International Justice in the case of the *Legal Status of Eastern Greenland* unless due weight is given to that part of the pronouncement of the Court which extended the legal consequences of a display of sovereignty to uninhabited and uncolonized parts of Greenland forming an integral part of the territories which the Court considered to have been occupied by means of the display of some State activity.[2]

In fact, the apparent antinomy of effectiveness and contiguity begins to wear thin as soon as we realize – and the award in the case of the *Island of Palmas* and other cases clearly urge that consideration – that effectiveness need not be as complete as appears at first sight and that contiguity is not as theoretical and arbitrary as may appear at first sight. This explains why those who are sceptical of contiguity as a title occasionally suggest that a mere proclamation may satisfy the requirement of effectiveness – provided that it has the support of contiguity. The fact is that as a rule the conceptions of effectiveness and contiguity often provide no more than an argumentative starting point. There is a sound core in both, though in case of conflicting claims mere contiguity when confronted with effective occupation which is not *per se* illegal must yield to the latter as representing a superior title. But effectiveness is not a magic formula which can be applied with mathematical precision. It is effectiveness relative to the situation and to the circumstances.[3] It may range from the requirement of intensive administration in every 'nook and corner' in a densely populated and developed area to mere 'State activity' manifesting itself in the conclusion of

[1] *Br. and For. St. Papers*, 49 (1905), 930 (Cmd. 2166) (1904).

[2] To that extent, but only to that extent, Professor Ross's interpretation of the judgment of the Court as having 'relinquished all demands of effectiveness' is believed accurately to express the legal position (*A Textbook of International Law* (English transl. 1947), p. 147).

[3] See above, p. 186.

treaties and conferment of concessions by an authority situated in a narrowly circumscribed part of the territory, or even outside it; and it may even assume the form of a mere proclamation. When that point is reached there is little to choose between contiguity and 'effectiveness' of occupation. Contiguity in such cases may be an essential condition which gives the only element of substance to such otherwise abstract occupation. In that sense contiguity is a factor more potent than effectiveness reduced to the very shadow of its natural self. Conversely, the claim of contiguity is *pro tanto* much stronger when there is only a remote prospect of occupation by rival States to oppose it – as is the case in the matter of submarine areas. While effectiveness in the shape of 'notional' occupation exhibits a somewhat formal and nebulous complexion, contiguity assumes, in comparison, a distinct degree of reality.[1] As already suggested, the conceptions of effective occupation and contiguity, being relative, are but a starting point. It is within the legitimate province of the judicial function – and of statesmanship – to use them with such discretion as the equities of the case and considerations of stability require.

The second objection against the principle of contiguity as the basis of the claim to submarine areas is partly of a political and partly of a legal nature. It is that the conception of contiguity may be so vague in its comprehensiveness and elasticity as to lend itself to abuse in the form of exorbitant and eccentric claims, including those to remote territories effectively occupied by other States for prolonged periods, bordering on absurdity. As already intimated,[2] the answer to that objection is that no device can prevent the abuse of a rule or principle, however otherwise useful and reasonable, by unilateral claims of States which refuse to submit disputed issues to impartial adjudication. For, as has been shown, even more pertinent criticism can be levied in this respect against 'notional' occupation. Thus, although the apparent precision of the principle of effectiveness of occupation seems to make it preferable to the uncertain vagueness of contiguity, it lends itself to interpretations which deprive it of its natural meaning. The supposedly dangerous doctrine of contiguity becomes in effect the governing condition of 'occupation', while occupation is reduced to a declaration which is saved from being a purely nominal act only by dint of being supported by contiguity. In fact, both practice and principle suggest

[1] It is of interest to note that when in 1885 Great Britain, Germany, and Spain concluded a treaty in which the two former Powers recognized, apparently in reliance upon propinquity, the Spanish sovereignty over the Sulu Archipelago including 'the places effectively occupied as well as those places not yet occupied', Holtzendorff, the German international lawyer, regarded this as a recognition of the principle of effective possession (*Holtzendorff*, II, 266, n. 12).

[2] See above, p. 189.

that, unless we fall back upon 'notional' occupation, contiguity, in particular such as that which occurs in relation to submarine areas, constitutes a proper basis of law and reasonableness[1] for the assumption of title over them. Contiguity may be, on occasion, a transparently eccentric figure of speech when made the basis of claims to distant territories. It may in the past have served retrogressive purposes under the guise of monopolistic claims to entire continents. This does not mean that in a case such as that of adjacent submarine areas it does not represent the only solution consonant with convenience, economic necessities, and requirements of international peace. There is therefore no inconsistency in the action of a State which rejects it in one sphere and adopts it in another.

While the doctrine – and the fact – of contiguity provide the natural foundation for the principle that the adjacent submarine areas belong to the littoral State, that principle may receive a substantial accession of strength from the view that the relation is one not only of contiguity and proximity but also of physical identity. That view underlies the conception, referred to above, of the submarine area in general and the continental shelf in particular, as being the platform – the base, as it were – on which the continent rests. This conception of unity, as distinguished from mere contiguity, underlies also the principal geographical explanations of the phenomenon of the continental shelf. One of these explanations is that the continental shelf originally formed part of the territorial domain of the littoral State, from which it has been detached by maritime attrition.[2] Under that view the formal appropriation of the continental shelf is no more than a case of restitution *in integrum* in favour of the State asserting its pre-existing right over its own territory. The second theory explains the continental shelf by reference to the reverse process of accretion or accession, i.e. of the continental shelf having been formed by gradual sedimentation from the territory contiguous to it. Accession and accretion are recognized modes of original acquisition of territory,[3] and some authors have attempted to base the appropriation of the continental shelf on that particular phenomenon.[4] Thirdly, it has been suggested that the continental shelf may be due to marine transgression over areas which were

[1] See above, p. 184.

[2] This, and the other geographical explanations of the continental shelf are analysed in the leading work on the subject by Bourcart (see above, p. 152). They are examined from the legal point of view in the Memorandum of the Secretary-General of the United Nations on the *Régime of the High Seas* (A/CN. 4/32, pp. 66–70).

[3] See Oppenheim, *International Law*, I, § 229. For an emphatic approval of the 'accession' theory in the matter of the continental shelf before the International Law Commission see the observation of M. Yepes (A/CN. 4/SR. 67, pp. 66, 67).

[4] See, for example, Jonkheer Feith, in *Report*, p. 400 (cited above, p. 169).

previously continental. This view, which does not differ substantially from the first explanation, is favoured in the most authoritative exposition of the subject.[1] It is most in accord with the wording of the proclamation of the United States in its reference to the continental shelf as 'an extension of the land mass of the coastal nation'.

It is not intended here to express a preference for any of these hypotheses. In so far as any of them can be accepted, they add to the fact of contiguity without replacing it. It is in that fact of contiguity, in addition to other factors such as general acquiescence, that there must be sought the legal and rational explanation of the title, of which the proclamations and enactments of the littoral States are declaratory, to the adjacent submarine areas. That fact is given expression in most of the relevant instruments. It provides a legal basis of utility and reasonableness which is most consistent with the technical realities of the situation, with the security of States, and with the requirement of international stability.[2]

All these considerations explain why, independently of any legal doctrine, the appropriation – or, which is essentially the same, the right of appropriation – of the adjacent submarine areas have become part of international law by custom initiated by the leading maritime Powers and acquiesced in by the generality of States. The law-creating – or law-revealing – effect of that practice and of the absence of protest against it are emphasized by the circumstance that, as has been submitted, that practice is not only in conformity with a reasonably conceived notion of the freedom of the seas, but also that it adds vitality to it by demonstrating its capacity for adaptation to new problems and conditions. The practical demonstration of the possibility of reconciling the principle of the freedom of the seas with the justifiable claims inherent in the new developments connected with submarine areas can alone prevent their abuse by exorbitant pretensions violative of the freedom of the seas and wholly alien to the apparent occasion which has given rise to them. Such demonstration can also, on a wider plane, act as a reminder that, pending the establishment of an effective system of international legislation, unilateral action need not necessarily be disdainful of legality and reasonableness.

It is within the legitimate province of the science of international law to draw attention to the general and specific implications, in the above sense, of the new doctrine, essentially rooted in established law, of the continental shelf and of adjacent submarine areas generally. Thus the

[1] See Bourcart, *Géographie du fond des mers*, pp. 142–6, 160.
[2] See above, p. 193.

circumstance that the sovereignty over these areas can be fully reconciled with the restrictions and obligations following from the principle of the freedom of the seas confirms the lesson – amply illustrated by practice but still in need of emphasis – of the elasticity, adaptability, and divisibility of territorial sovereignty. Similarly, international law may be of assistance in devising procedures for the solution of difficulties arising out of any conflict between the rules safeguarding freedom of navigation on the high seas and the actual operation of the new developments. Such assistance may also be required for the settlement of problems connected with the delimitation of the submarine areas either in general or as between competing States. For that purpose there may be a tendency to provide the adjudicating agencies with a body of law in the form of general rules. Such a tendency may be justified to a large extent. At the same time, international law may have to steer in this matter a middle course between initiative and restraint. For while it may be important to guide and facilitate, through general rules, the progress of new development, it is probable that much of that guidance must be the cumulative result of arbitral decisions given on equitable grounds or of special agreements between the interested Governments. A general international conference may not always constitute the best machinery. On some questions, such as the exact delimitation of the submarine areas outward to the sea, it may be preferable to await actual proof of the necessity for a concrete solution. Such necessity may never arise. Facts of geography may conclusively reveal lack of urgency in the imaginative zeal of lawyers. In other matters, such as the affirmation of the principle that artificial structures erected on the high seas for the purpose of exploiting submarine areas cannot be permitted to encroach on the freedom of the seas by any claim to territorial waters of their own, clear-cut international regulation may be called for at the very outset. Circumstances have brought about the affirmation by means of unilateral action of the principle of the right to adjacent submarine areas. That principle, it has been shown, is not contrary to any basic rule of international law. There still remains the task of ensuring that its application takes place in conformity with the established law, reasonably interpreted, relating to the freedom of the seas and with the legitimate interests of the States concerned. The successful fulfilment of that task may in itself constitute a significant contribution to the enduring problem of peaceful change in international society.

II

BOUNDARIES OF STATE TERRITORY

CHAPTER 2

SOVEREIGNTY OVER CERTAIN FRONTIER LAND

Editor's note This chapter consists of a declaration made by Lauterpacht in the *Case concerning Sovereignty over certain Frontier Land* between Belgium and the Netherlands (*I.C.J. Reports* 1959, p. 209, at pp. 230–2), recording his dissent from the judgment of the Court. The majority of the Court consisted of the President (M. Klaestad), the Vice-President (Sir M. Zafrullah Khan) and Judges Basdevant, Hackworth, Winiarski, Badawi, Kojevnikov, Cordova and Sir Percy Spender; the other dissenting judges were Judges Armand-Ugon, Moreno Quintana and Spiropoulos.

Although the declaration is mainly concerned with a question of title to territory, it contains a brief and intriguing observation regarding the law of treaties. At the end of the second paragraph Lauterpacht expresses the opinion that 'the relevant provisions of the Convention must be considered as void and inapplicable on account of uncertainty and unresolved discrepancy'. These grounds for the invalidity of a treaty are not mentioned in the leading textbooks of international law, e.g. Oppenheim's *International Law* which Lauterpacht himself edited. Nor are they mentioned in either the Vienna Convention on the Law of Treaties or, again, Lauterpacht's own drafts on the Law of Treaties prepared when he was rapporteur on this subject during his period of membership of the International Law Commission (see the materials in volume 4 of these *Collected Papers*). It is tantalizing, therefore, that Lauterpacht should not have developed at greater length in the declaration his views on this subject.

I have voted in favour of a decision determining that the sovereignty over the plots in dispute belongs to the Netherlands.

Article 90 of the Descriptive Minute of the Boundary Convention of 1843, in assigning these plots to *Belgium*, purports to transcribe word for word the Communal Minute between Baerle-Duc and Baarle-Nassau which assigns these plots to the *Netherlands*. The Netherlands has produced before the Court what it described as one of the two original copies of the latter Minute. No other copy of the original Minute has been produced before the Court. The authenticity of the Minute produced by the Netherlands has not been challenged – though it has been alleged by Belgium that a mistake had occurred in the course of transcribing it. On the other hand, it has been alleged by the Netherlands that a mistake, in the contrary direction, had occurred in the process of transcribing that document when the Descriptive

Minute was adopted in 1843. In the words of Counsel for Belgium, the accumulation of errors in this case was such 'as though some evil genius had presided over the whole affair'. I have formed the view that the evidence submitted to the Court in the shape of the formal Minutes, succinct in the extreme, of the Boundary Commission and of fragmentary correspondence lacking in sequence has not wholly dispelled the impact of the confused situation thus created. The circumstances of the adoption, in 1843, of the Descriptive Minute must, to some extent, be in the nature of conjecture. In particular, it has not been proved possible to state a direct conclusion as to the authenticity or otherwise of the cardinal piece of evidence, namely, of the only existing copy of the Communal Minute produced by the Netherlands. Moreover, while the Commissioners who drafted the Descriptive Minute enjoyed wide powers, they had no power to endow with legal efficacy a document in which they purported to transcribe word for word the Communal Minute and to observe the *status quo* but in which they actually modified the Communal Minute and departed from the *status quo*. The law knows of no such power. For these reasons, I am of the opinion that the relevant provisions of the Convention must be considered as void and inapplicable on account of uncertainty and unresolved discrepancy.

The Special Agreement of 26 November 1957 submitting the dispute to the Court is by design so phrased as not to confine its function to giving a decision based exclusively on the Convention of 1843. By the generality of its terms it leaves it open to the Court to determine the question of sovereignty by reference to all relevant considerations – whether based on the Convention or not. Accordingly, in the circumstances, it seems proper that a decision be rendered by reference to the fact, which is not disputed, that at least during the fifty years following the adoption of the Convention there had been no challenge to the exercise, by the Government of the Netherlands and its officials, of normal administrative authority with regard to the plots in question. In my opinion, there is no room here for applying the exacting rules of prescription in relation to a title acquired by a clear and unequivocal treaty; there is no such treaty. It has been contended that the uninterrupted administrative activity of the Netherlands was due not to any recognition of Netherlands sovereignty on the part of Belgium but to the fact that the plots in question are an enclave within Netherlands territory and that, therefore, it was natural that Netherlands administrative acts should have been performed there in the ordinary course of affairs. However, the fact that local conditions have necessitated the normal and unchallenged exercise of Netherlands administrative activity provides an additional reason why, in the absence of clear provisions of a treaty, there is no necessity to disturb the existing state of affairs and to perpetuate a geographical anomaly.

III

TERRITORIAL WATERS

CHAPTER 3

IMPLICATIONS OF THE *NORWEGIAN FISHERIES* CASE

Editor's note On 18 December 1951 the International Court of Justice delivered its judgment in the *Fisheries* case brought by the United Kingdom against Norway (*I.C.J. Reports* 1951, p. 116). The present chapter consists of a turn-over article about this judgment which Lauterpacht wrote in *The Times* newspaper on 8 January 1952.

The article reflects some of the disappointment and concern felt in England after the Court's judgment. (Another, much more detailed and critical reaction may be found in the article by Sir Humphrey Waldock on 'The Anglo-Norwegian Fisheries Case' in *B.Y.* 28 (1951), 112.) But it is typical of Lauterpacht's approach to problems that even within three weeks of an event which at the time was seen as a major setback to British fishery and more general maritime interests, he was able to present the Court's judgment in a constructive as well as a critical light. In this he was to some extent anticipating the work of the International Law Commission which, as will be recalled, incorporated into the first drafts of its articles on the territorial sea, provisions which followed very closely the principal elements in the Court's exposition of the rules for drawing the base-lines of territorial waters. Those provisions were carried through into the Commission's final draft articles on the law of the sea in 1956 and were adopted without alteration in paragraphs 1 to 4 of Article 4 of the Convention on the Territorial Sea and Contiguous Zone adopted at Geneva in 1958.

The judgment delivered on 18 December [1951] by the International Court of Justice in the case of the Norwegian fisheries is likely to rank among the most significant pronouncements of that high tribunal. It brought to a close a protracted dispute between two nations bound by a firm tradition of friendship. It gave a ruling on questions directly affecting the principle of the freedom of the seas. Inasmuch as it may create, with some, the impression of a daring piece of judicial legislation in the sphere of the law of the sea and in disregard of the historic attitude of the great maritime Powers, it raises issues which transcend the economic importance of the problem directly before the Court. These issues affect the future of international judicial settlement, of which this country has been one of the staunchest supporters in the past; and, judging from the dignified and statesmanlike acceptance of the decision of the Court by the British representative, of which it wishes to remain a firm supporter.

The question which the Court was called upon to decide was whether the Norwegian decree of 12 July 1935, which delimited the Norwegian fisheries zone, was in accordance with international law. That decree, which purported to be in accordance with earlier Norwegian decrees dating back to 1812, laid down that the outer limit of Norwegian territorial waters 'shall run parallel with straight base-lines drawn between fixed points on the mainland, on islands or rocks'. In international law, as understood by the majority of States prior to the judgment of the Court, the 'base-line' – i.e., the line at which the territorial waters of a State begin – runs along the low-water mark, following generally the sinuosities of the coast. In the case of bays (other than so-called historic bays which may cover vast stretches of the sea) the general, though not universal, consensus of opinion and practice has been that the base-line is formed by a straight line drawn across the bay at a point at which it is not more than ten miles wide. The decree of 1935 departed from that principle. It selected forty-eight fixed points either on the mainland or on islands or rocks, some of which are at a considerable distance from the mainland.

These points were connected by straight lines of lengths ranging from eighteen to forty-four miles. The sea enclosed by these lines, as well as the adjoining four-mile belt of territorial waters, was to constitute the Norwegian fisheries zone. The Court found, by a majority of ten votes to two, that the method which the decree employed for the delimitation of the fisheries zones was not contrary to international law. It also held, by eight votes to four, that the lines fixed by the decree in application of that method were not contrary to international law.

The salient points of the judgment may be summarized as follows:– The ten-mile rule for the determination of the base-line in the case of bays has not acquired the authority of a general rule of international law. In any event, it was not applicable to Norway, who had always resisted attempts to apply it to the Norwegian coast. Subject to restrictions of international law and the overriding test of reasonableness, the littoral State is entitled to determine the method of selection of base-lines. The base-line must follow the general direction of the coast rather than the low-water mark along the coast. That principle is particularly applicable to the peculiar geographical configuration of the Norwegian coast. In the case of Norway it is sanctioned by long and, on the whole, consistent usage which, until recently, was unopposed by other States, including the United Kingdom. The base-lines as fixed by the decree of 1935 'have been kept within the bounds of what is moderate and reasonable'.

Sir Arnold McNair and Judge Read delivered dissenting opinions, in which, on all these points, they expressed views opposed to those enunciated by the Court. It may be deceptive to gauge the authority of that dissent by reference to its numerical strength. The meticulous scholarship and the elaboration of detail make the dissenting opinions a weighty and lucid contribution to international law on the subject. Their exhaustiveness is in contrast with the judgment of the Court as a whole which, in its formulation of the applicable principles of law, is remarkable for its brevity.

In many cases decided by it in the past, the Court has been fully alive to the fact that its proper function is not only to decide disputes but to clarify and to develop international law in a manner likely to enlighten and convince public opinion. Needless to say, the ability and impartiality of the Court are not in question. But no tribunal in the world has greater need to justify, by full and careful reasoning, by detailed reference to available authorities and precedent, and by an exhaustive examination of the arguments of the parties, the confidence placed in it by Governments. It may be added that Judge Hackworth agreed with the judgment only on the ground that, in his view, Norway had established a historic title to the disputed maritime areas, and that Judge Hsu Mo dissented from the judgment of the Court in respect of the base-lines of two areas of very considerable extent.

It is natural that the judgment of the Court should have caused some disappointment in this country, and that the innovation – for an innovation it is – implied in the express judicial recognition of straight base-lines should be viewed with some anxiety. However, it is probable that, essentially, the judgment amounts to no more than an affirmation that in view of the absence of general agreement on the subject of base-lines their selection is in the first instance within the province of the littoral State; that such selection is a matter of law and not of arbitrary discretion; that in case of dispute it is for an international tribunal to determine the reasonableness and justification of the principle and of the method of selection adopted by the State concerned; and that such determination must be made in the light of various relevant factors, including prescriptive title, acquiescence by other – and particularly the complaining – States, 'geographical realities', and the economic and social equities of the situation.

Thus circumscribed, the judgment of the Court ought perhaps to give less cause for apprehension than may appear at first sight – although the fact remains that the various tests as laid down by the Court, being of a subjective nature, are necessarily vague and elastic and may make it difficult for legal advisers to advise Governments as to the correct legal position in any particular case.

There are ample indications in the judgment that what it conceived to be the equities of the case made a deep impression on the Court, and that, to a large extent, those equities formed the by no means inarticulate major premise of its decision. Thus we find the Court stating, at the very commencement of the exposition of the reasons of its judgment, that 'what matters, what really constitutes the Norwegian coast line, is the outer line of the "skjäergaard"' (the 'rock rampart' which includes the islands, islets, rocks, and reefs); that these areas were exploited by Norwegian fishermen from 'time immemorial'; that 'in these barren regions the inhabitants of the coastal zone derive their livelihood essentially from fishing'; and that 'such are the realities which must be borne in mind' in appraising the validity, under international law, of the decree of 1935.

It is perhaps not unnatural that the dissenting judges should have considered such 'realities' to be irrelevant for the purposes of a legal decision. On the other hand, there is now the impressive authority of the overwhelming majority of the Court in support of the view that international law on the subject of base-lines and, generally, of the maritime frontiers of States has shown no such approximation to a generally agreed rule as to preclude the Court from taking these factors into consideration.

It is possible that the Court was influenced by the fact that recent developments in international practice have paved the way for a measure of adaptation of a rigidly conceived notion of the freedom of the sea to the requirements of the legitimate interests of the littoral State. These developments include the proclamation, on the part of a number of States (including the United Kingdom and some of its dependencies in the Persian Gulf), of exclusive control and jurisdiction over submarine areas adjacent to their coasts. However, in these proclamations the States concerned have attached importance to leaving intact the overriding principle of freedom of navigation on the high seas.

The full implications of the judgment of the Court on the general issue before it are not beyond doubt. But there are some factors which clearly limit the apparently alarming comprehensiveness of the judgment. The base-lines must, generally, represent the line of the coast. Accordingly, straight lines, when used, must not depart appreciably from the general direction of the coast. Moreover, the Court, while upholding the Norwegian system of straight lines, repeatedly emphasized the special circumstances of the case, such as the exceptional configuration of the coast of Norway, her economic interests, and her historic claims.

These considerations suggest that there is perhaps no sufficient reason for the assumption that the judgment has caused irreparable injury to the principle of the freedom of the sea or that it has left the door wide open to exorbitant claims in the future. That principle still constitutes part of international law, and its beneficence is not yet spent. The practice of enlightened States, aided by a judicial determination of the test of reasonableness, may evolve a rational compromise between rigid insistence on the status of the high seas as being, without limitations, *res omnium communis* in all its manifestations, and unilateral assertions of extravagant national claims inimical to the wider aspects of the principle of the freedom of the sea. It is only such judicial ascertainment of the reasonableness of the delimitation effected by the littoral State that can prevent the principle as now formulated by the Court from becoming a source of abuse.

IV

RIGHTS OF TERRITORIAL JURISDICTION

CHAPTER 4

ALLEGIANCE, DIPLOMATIC PROTECTION AND CRIMINAL JURISDICTION OVER ALIENS

Editor's note This chapter consists, as its second footnote indicates, of the substance of a lecture delivered by Lauterpacht in Cambridge in the Lent Term, 1946. It was Lauterpacht's practice to introduce into his general course of two lectures a week on public international law an occasional departure from the main line of the syllabus when he was specially interested or involved in a particular subject. The present lecture was one of those. It reflected his participation at the request of the then Attorney-General, Sir Hartley Shawcross, Q.C., M.P., in the preparation of the case for the prosecution for treason of William Joyce ('Lord Haw-Haw'). When the *Trial of William Joyce* was included in the 'Notable British Trial Series', Sir Hartley sent a copy to Lauterpacht inscribed 'To Professor Lauterpacht whose assistance contributed so largely to the success of the legal argument.'

The article appeared in the *Cambridge Law Journal*, 9 (1947), 330–48. The same journal subsequently published an article by Professor Glanville L. Williams, entitled 'The Correlation of Allegiance and Protection', *ibid.* 10 (1948), 54, which differed strongly from Lauterpacht's view.

The *cause célèbre* of *King* v. *William Joyce*, subsequently reported as *Joyce* v. *Director of Public Prosecutions*,[1] was concerned to a large extent with matters of interest for international law, and it is mainly from this point of view that it is proposed to discuss it in the present article.[2] Obviously, the case is also of considerable importance both for criminal law – in so far as it is concerned with the crime of treason – and for constitutional law – inasmuch as it bears directly on the question of the nature and the obligations of allegiance. However, it is probable that the case books which will claim it most insistently will be those of international law. For the decision in *Rex* v. *Joyce* is not only an authority on certain aspects of allegiance owed by aliens and of the right of a State to assume jurisdiction over acts committed by aliens abroad. It sheds light on such questions as the nature of diplomatic protection of citizens, the right of a State to protect diplomatically persons who are not its citizens, the obligation of allegiance of so-called protected

[1] [1945] W.N. 220; 173 L.T. 377 (Court of Appeal); [1946] A.C. 347 (House of Lords).

[2] This article is the substance of a lecture delivered in the Law School of the University of Cambridge in the Lent Term, 1946. I have expanded the lecture by the addition of footnotes and otherwise, but I have retained some passages as delivered on that occasion.

persons, and some others. Not all of these questions were judicially answered, but they loomed large in argument and imparted to the proceedings the complexion of a case concerned predominantly with international law. In view of this it may be pertinent to preface this article by drawing attention to a point which appears to be a mere matter of terminology but which, it is believed, raises an issue of wider significance.

I. 'COMITY OF NATIONS'

Throughout the proceedings in the *Joyce* case the principal argument put forward on behalf of the accused was that it would be contrary to the 'comity of nations' for an English court to assume jurisdiction over an alien for a crime committed abroad. The House of Lords held that 'no principle of comity demands that a State should ignore the crime of treason committed against it outside its territory'.[1] The reference to 'comity of nations' when what the Court really has in mind is 'the Law of Nations' or 'international law' has been a somewhat persistent feature of recent English (and, at times, American) judicial practice. It seems to have gained currency following upon the judgment in the *Parlement Belge*, the well-known case concerned with the jurisdictional immunity of foreign State-owned ships. In that case Brett L. J. formulated the principle of jurisdictional immunity as being 'the consequence of the absolute independence of every sovereign authority, and of the international comity which induces every sovereign State to respect the independence and dignity of every other sovereign State'.[2] Prior to that decision the courts, in relevant cases, referred as a rule without ambiguity to 'the Law of Nations' or to 'international law'.[3]

This is not the proper occasion for inquiring in detail into the reasons for the fascination which the term 'comity of nations' has exercised over judges and practising lawyers. It is possible that the lingering influence of Austinian positivism, which rejects the claim of the Law of Nations to be law 'properly so-called', may have given added attraction to a vague, non-committal and somewhat pretentious form of words which is on occasions strangely out of keeping with the reality of international relations. However that may be, it is suggested that the term 'comity of nations' is misleading and that there is no such anti-

[1] [1946] A.C. at p. 372.

[2] (1880) 5 L.R.P.D. 197, at p. 214.

[3] See, e.g., *Viveash* v. *Becker* (1814), 3 M. & S. 284; *De Wutz* v. *Hendricks* (1824) S.C., 9 Moore, 586, where Best C.J. held 'that it was contrary to the Law of Nations (which in all cases of international law is adopted into the municipal code of every civilized country)' to raise money in England in support of a rebellion in a foreign country; *The Emperor of Austria* v. *Day and Kossuth* (1861) 2 Giff. 628; and many others.

quity about it as to make its abandonment impracticable. Essentially,[1] the term 'comity of nations' refers to considerations of courtesy, amity, neighbourly feeling and reciprocity. Such considerations are not, on the face of it, germane to any distinct element of legal obligation.[2] Yet the rules which English courts administer in deference to 'comity of nations' in such matters as diplomatic privileges or immunities of foreign States and of their property are rules which are binding by reason of international law proper, not by virtue of vague considerations of 'comity'. An English court could not properly refuse to apply such rules with respect to a State with which Great Britain entertains normal diplomatic intercourse but with which it has no relations amounting in any true sense to 'comity'.

The expression 'comity of nations' is often used in the sphere of 'conflict of laws', especially in connection with the enforcement of foreign judgments. Even in the limited province of 'conflict of laws' writers are practically unanimous that the notion of 'comity of nations' is at best unhelpful and at worst wholly inaccurate.[3] In the sphere of public international law it suffers from the same – and additional – drawbacks. For in the practice of States there exist rules which are followed habitually but not *opinione necessitatis juris*, i.e. as a matter of legal obligation. Thus, for instance, Great Britain, the United States of America, and other States grant to foreign diplomats certain facilities and exemptions in connection with customs duties and customs examination. These facilities are conceded not because of any duty owed by virtue of international law, but as a matter of courtesy. Similarly, while as a matter of international law, as interpreted by her courts, Great Britain has full jurisdiction over foreign merchant vessels in British ports and territorial waters, as a matter of 'comity' that jurisdiction is in fact exercised only in certain categories of cases.[4] There is thus in these matters a clear and practical distinction between 'comity' and law, and, if the current laxity of terminology is persisted in, judges might find it necessary in the same case to use the same word to express two essentially different ideas. Moreover, if the habit

[1] For the various meanings of 'comity of nations' see Oppenheim, *International Law*, I (6th ed. by Lauterpacht), § 19*c*.

[2] Unless, of course, what is meant, by way of a somewhat confusing circumlocution, is that the rule applied is one of law though *originating* in 'comity'. See, for instance, *Russian Socialist Federated Soviet Republic* v. *Cibrario* (an American case): *Annual Digest*, 2 (1923–4), case no. 17; 235 N.Y. 255; 139 N.E. 259, where the Court said: 'Comity may be defined as the reciprocal courtesy which one member of the family of nations owes to the others. It presupposes friendship... Rules of comity are a portion of the law that they [courts] enforce.'

[3] See Cheshire, *Private International Law* (2nd ed. 1938), pp. 6, 581; Wolff, *Private International Law* (1945), pp. 14, 15.

[4] See also Phillimore, I, 552, where he points out that extradition of criminals is a matter of comity, not of right.

continues of referring to 'comity' when 'law' is meant, there is a danger, which some decided cases have brought home, of law being in fact treated as if it were mere 'comity'. Thus in the *El Neptuno*,[1] a case involving jurisdictional immunities of a vessel claimed by two recognized Governments, Mr Justice Langton remarked that 'the whole of this doctrine of immunity from arrest is a matter that rests upon the comity of nations' and exhorted both parties not to strain the obligation of courtesy, 'resting as that obligation does upon that slender point'.[2] It is an interesting gloss upon the existing confusion of terminology that that 'slender point' of comity of nations was described, in a case decided in 1946, as a 'paramount rule of law'.[3] In view of this it is suggested that it would be conducive to both clarity and accuracy if, in cases involving the application of the Law of Nations, lawyers would revert to the practice which was followed for a century since Lord Mansfield and Blackstone and which dispensed with the solemn and benevolent reference to 'comity of nations'. The doctrine that international law is part of the law of the land is one of the major and beneficent contributions of the common law to modern jurisprudence, and this fact provides an additional reason for referring to international law when international law is at issue.

2. CORRELATION OF PROTECTION AND ALLEGIANCE

It is convenient, at this stage, to give a brief account of the facts in the case of *Joyce* v. *Director of Public Prosecutions*. William Joyce was born in 1906 in the United States of America. His father was a British subject by birth, but later, before William Joyce was born, he acquired American citizenship by naturalization. William Joyce thus became a natural-born citizen of the United States, born of an American father. In 1909 he was brought to Ireland, where he stayed until 1921. In that year he came to England and settled there. On various occasions he described himself as a British subject. In 1933 he applied for a British passport. In the application he described himself as a British subject by birth, born in Galway, Ireland. He was granted the passport, for the purpose of holiday, valid for various European countries. In September 1938, and in August 1939, he applied for, and was granted, a renewal of the passport. On 24 August 1939 he left England, leaving in the country his parents, his brothers and his sister. On 18 September

[1] *Lloyd's List Law Reports*, 62 (1938), 7.

[2] At p. 9.

[3] *The Tolten* [1946] P. 135, at p. 151 (*per* Scott L.J.). And see *Foster* v. *Driscoll* [1929] 1 K.B. 470, where Lawrence L.J. based the decision on 'obligations' of 'international comity' the disregard of which 'would furnish a just cause for complaint by the United States Government'.

1939 – at a time when Great Britain and Germany were at war – he accepted a post as an announcer of English news in the German radio company of Berlin and continued in that capacity until 1945, when he was arrested in Germany by British authorities. His passport was not found on him. It appeared that in 1940 he had acquired German nationality. When brought to England he was indicted for high treason under the Treason Act, 1351. In the Central Criminal Court Tucker J. directed the jury that 'on 24 August 1939, when the passport was applied for, the prisoner beyond a shadow of doubt owed allegiance to the Crown of this country and that, on the evidence given, if they accept it, nothing happened at the material time thereafter to put an end to the allegiance that he then owed'. The jury found Joyce guilty, and he was sentenced to death. He appealed. The Court of Appeal unanimously dismissed the appeal. After the Attorney-General certified that the decision of the Court of Appeal involved a point of law of exceptional public importance and that it was desirable in the public interest that a further appeal should be brought, Joyce appealed to the House of Lords. The House of Lords, by a majority of four to one, dismissed the appeal. On the matter of substantive law the Law Lords were unanimous that, in the words of Lord Porter's dissenting judgment, 'if an alien is under British protection he occupies the same position when abroad as he would occupy if he were a British subject' and that 'each of them owes allegiance, and in so doing each is subject to the jurisdiction of the British Crown'.[1] The reasons, which are more of a procedural nature, of Lord Porter's dissent are discussed below.[2]

The rule of English law in the matter of the obligations of allegiance owed by an alien residing within the realm is clear and fully in conformity with the existing international practice in the matter. An alien owes allegiance to and is subject to the law of the country, including the law of treason, in respect of acts committed within the territory in which he resides. This subjection to the law of the State – and, in particular, to the law relating to treason – is, in principle, an obligation limited to the alien while present in the country and while receiving the protection of its laws; it ceases with the termination of the corporeal presence of the alien within the territory and the cessation of the protection of the laws of the State of his residence. This is a somewhat elaborate statement of the law, but it is a more accurate statement than the simple proposition that an alien owes allegiance to the Crown only while he is in this country. As far back as 1707 it was laid down in a rule adopted 'by all the Judges assembled at the Queen's command'

[1] At pp. 375, 376.

[2] See p. 230, n. 3.

that if such an 'Alien seeking the Protection of the Crown having a Family and Effects here, should during a War with his Native Country, go thither and there Adhere to the King's Enemies for purposes of Hostility, He might be dealt with as a Traitor. For He came and settled here under the Protection of the Crown. And though his Person was removed for a time, his Effects and Family continued still under the same Protection'.[1] The case is somewhat apocryphal, but the House of Lords, which did not doubt its authenticity – as well as the Courts below – relied on it in the *Joyce* case as an illustration of the underlying major principle rather than as a direct authority fully covering the details of the case before them. What are these principles?

The first is of a general character. There may be cogent reasons in the case of the law of treason, which has often been used as an instrument of despotism and oppression, for viewing with suspicion anything in the nature of judicial legislation. On the other hand, this is a branch of law in which the security and the highest interests of the State require that the purpose of the law should not be defeated by an inability to adapt, in a spirit of justice and common sense, established principles to new circumstances and conditions. Thus by a consistent judicial interpretation of the statute of 1351, which was by its terms limited to acts committed in England, it had been established that treason, under the statute, may be committed by a British subject both within the realm and abroad. There was no disposition, in *R.* v. *Casement*,[2] to challenge the soundness of that interpretation of the statute. In *De Jager* v. *Attorney-General of Natal* it was held, by way of a seemingly striking innovation, that the alien's duty of allegiance, as established by the relation of protection, was not affected by the circumstance that owing to enemy occupation the authority of the Crown had been temporarily displaced.[3]

The second principle illustrated by the Resolution of the Judges in 1707 and more directly related to the case at issue is the correlation between allegiance and protection. This principle was formulated in *Calvin's* case in the maxim: *Protectio trahit subjectionem, et subjectio protectionem.* It expresses a feudal doctrine of much antiquity and much moral force. The protection given by the lord had as a necessary corollary the obligation of fidelity. That reciprocity of benefit and duty, of allegiance and protection, is not, of course, an artificial and obsolete formula of a past period. It is expressive of a compelling principle of political ethics and, above all, of the security of the State. The alien

[1] Foster's *Crown Cases* (1762 ed.), p. 185.

[2] [1917] 1 K.B. 98.

[3] [1907] A.C. 326. A striking illustration of the same principle will be found in the American case of *Carlisle* v. *United States* (1872), 16 Wall. 147.

resident in a foreign country continues to owe allegiance to the sovereign of his own State. That allegiance expresses itself in his continued subjection to the laws of his own country – though, more often than not, the home State considers it convenient to limit its claims to jurisdiction with regard to the acts of its nationals when abroad. But, while continuing to be bound by allegiance to his own State, the alien becomes subject to another allegiance – that concomitant with the protection of the law which shelters him. There is nothing technical or mercenary about that reciprocity of allegiance and protection. That reciprocity is a formal relation only in the sense that it is of no legal relevance whether there is at any given moment an equivalence of duty and benefit, of allegiance and protection, of an actual disposition to fidelity and actual capacity to afford protection. The *De Jager* case[1] showed that the duty of allegiance is not affected by the temporary and involuntary absence of protection. In *Johnstone* v. *Pedlar*[2] the Court brushed aside the suggestion that the plaintiff, an American citizen of Irish revolutionary sympathies, was not entitled to the full protection of the law because of his active sympathies with the cause of the Irish revolution.

It was the overriding principle of the correlation of allegiance and protection on which the Crown based its case in *R.* v. *Joyce* and which is the *ratio decidendi* of the judgments of the Court of Appeal and the House of Lords. In leaving the country armed with a British passport obtained at his request and as the result of his own representations – 'wrapped in the Union Jack', to use the picturesque phrase of the Attorney-General – Joyce caused the continuation, in a different sphere, of the protection hitherto extended to him by the law. In the view of the prosecution, fully adopted by all three Courts, that protection was, *in posse*, of a substantial character. The diplomatic protection of citizens abroad is one of the most important functions of the foreign services of the modern State. This applies in particular to a country such as Great Britain, with far-flung interests and considerable foreign investments. Lord Palmerston's great speech in the case of *Don Pacifico* – one of the frequently-cited examples of pacific blockade and reprisals undertaken as a measure of protection of a British subject abroad – reveals impressively this aspect of the foreign relations of the modern State.[3] The South African War, the (somewhat nominal) war with Venezuela in 1903, and a number of others had their origin in the necessity to protect the interests of British subjects in foreign countries.

[1] See above. [2] [1921] 2 A.C. 262.

[3] For a general appreciation of its importance see Dunn, *The Protection of Nationals* (1932), pp. 27–71. See also Jessup, in *Columbia Law Review*, 46 (1946), 903–09.

The great majority of cases which have come before international tribunals – including those before the Permanent Court of International Justice – have been cases arising out of an alleged injury suffered by a national abroad. In a recent case the Supreme Court of the United States gave vivid expression to this aspect of the foreign relations of the State.[1]

The significance and value of diplomatic intercession lie not only in the actual instances – numerous as they are – of representations, complaints, formal claims and other methods of intercession. They lie in the availability of that protection, in the power which lies behind it, and in the resulting respect and security enjoyed by the subject as a normal accompaniment of his stay abroad. That protection extends – and is to a large extent effective – to citizens in the territory of a country with which a State is at war. They are protected, against treatment in violation of international law, by the threat of reprisals against enemy nationals, and, in favourable circumstances, of compensation exacted after the war. For these reasons there was probably little persuasive force in the suggestion, put forward on behalf of the accused in the *Joyce* case, that the kind of protection which, in the past, was the basis and the cause of the duty of allegiance was protection by the law – i.e., by the ordinary processes enforceable by the courts of law – as distinguished from what was described as administrative protection, namely, in the present case, protection by the officers of the State abroad. The House of Lords rejected that distinction largely on the ground that, historically, the protection enjoyed by the alien within the realm was also an 'administrative' protection exercised as part of the royal prerogative. An equally persuasive answer could have been founded on the fact that in so far as allegiance is a corollary of the duties of protection assumed by the State, such duties are more onerous and more exacting in the external sphere than within the State where the protection of the alien is part of the ordinary machinery of the administration of the law.

3. DIPLOMATIC PROTECTION OF NON-NATIONALS

The correlation of allegiance and protection is of such basic and compelling character that no determined attempt was made in *R.* v. *Joyce*

[1] *Hines* v. *Davidowitz* (1941), 312 U.S. 52. The Court said: 'One of the most important and delicate of all international relationships, recognized immemorially as a responsibility of Government, has to do with the protection of the just rights of a country's own nationals when those nationals are in another country. Experience has shown that international controversies of the gravest moment, sometimes even leading to war, may arise from real or imagined wrongs to another's subjects inflicted, or permitted, by a Government.'

to challenge it as a major principle of law. However, it was sought to limit its operation by reference both to the case at issue and to the nature of protection in general. This aspect of the case raises issues of international law of considerable interest. It was contended on behalf of the accused that in the case before the Court there was no basis in law for the establishment of the relation of protection (with the corresponding duty of allegiance) on the ground that a State is not entitled to issue a passport to a non-national; that it is, in any case, not entitled to extend diplomatic protection to a person who is not one of its nationals; and that, in view of this, as well as of the fraudulent nature of the representation by which the passport had been obtained, that document was not calculated to afford effective protection abroad.

For the purposes of the case before the Court the question whether a State can issue a passport to a person who is not its national was, largely, irrelevant. For the passport had been issued to an individual representing himself and believed by the authorities to be a British subject. In general, the question whether a State is entitled to issue a passport to a non-national is one of the municipal law of that State.[1] A passport is primarily a means of identification, and foreign States are concerned with it only to the extent that, in relation to them, a person holding a passport and described there as a national (or, probably, as a protected person) of a State is entitled to treatment as such and to the recognition of his right to be diplomatically protected by his own State. Undoubtedly, the foreign State in question is entitled to challenge his right to such treatment and to diplomatic protection on the ground that, contrary to the allegation of the passport, he is not in fact a national of the State concerned. The frequent controversies in which the United States has been concerned on this subject provide some illustration of the difficulties involved. The uniform practice of the United States has been that although a foreign Government may traverse, on the ground of fraud or illegality, the American nationality of the holder of an American passport, the Government of the United States has

[1] So far as international law is concerned there is probably nothing to prevent a State from issuing a passport (or similar instrument of identity) to a person who is described there as not being its national – except that in such cases the passport will not provide a basis for diplomatic protection. The case of passports issued to so-called protected persons is discussed below, p. 231. The United States claimed for a time the right to issue passports and to afford diplomatic protection to aliens who declared their intention to become citizens of the United States. The latter claim was repeatedly challenged by other States, and the relevant statute, enacted in 1907, was repealed in 1920 (see Hackworth, III, § 266). On one occasion the United States invoked for a person in this category treaty benefits conferred upon citizens of the United States: see *United States* (*Edward A. Hilson*) v. *Germany*, decided in 1925 by the American–German Mixed Claims Commission (*Annual Digest*, 3 (1925–6), case no. 198). This was a case of a seaman, a British subject, who had filed a declaration of intention to become an American citizen. The Commission rejected his claim.

alone the right to determine whether the person concerned is in fact an American citizen.[1] The controversies have arisen largely in connection with cases in which a foreign Government has challenged the legality, according to the law of the United States, of a naturalization of one of its nationals in the United States. It is unlikely that other countries would show a similar sensitiveness in the matter or that they could do so consistently either with the practice of international tribunals or with the rules relating to nationality of claims. International tribunals have uniformly asserted jurisdiction to determine whether a person does in fact, according to the law of the country granting the passport, possess the nationality of that country.[2] As a matter of wider principle, the subject is governed by the somewhat technical but essentially reasonable rule, usually referred to as the rule of nationality of claims, according to which an international tribunal has jurisdiction to entertain a claim put forward by a State on behalf of a private person only if that person was a national of that State continuously from the time of the occurrence of the injury until the actual commencement of the proceedings (or, probably, even until the rendering of the award). This means necessarily that the question whether the person concerned is its national or not cannot be left to the exclusive determination of the State claiming the right of protection. On the other hand, until an international tribunal has found that the person in question is not a national of the State issuing the passport and asserting the right of protection, that State is entitled to insist that the passport constitutes *prima facie* evidence of nationality.

With reference to the matter directly before the Court in the *Joyce* case, the position was, therefore, as follows: (*a*) by virtue of the relationship evidenced by the issue of the passport, Joyce enjoyed the protection of the Crown for the duration of the validity of the passport so long as it was not revoked by the competent British authority;[3]

[1] See, for a detailed account, Borchard, pp. 517–19.

[2] For references to these cases see Borchard, p. 522.

[3] The passport, though fraudulently obtained, was a valid document, until its validity expired or until it was revoked by the authorities. The position in this respect was the same as in the case of a certificate of naturalization obtained by fraudulent representations. So long as the certificate has not been revoked by the Secretary of State it is conclusive as to the status of the person naturalized. The effects of a fraudulent naturalization may go even beyond that. There is an interesting opinion of the Law Officers of the Crown of 6 July 1906, to the effect that a person who had obtained American naturalization by fraud and whose naturalization was subsequently cancelled could not nevertheless recover his British nationality which he had lost as a result of the original naturalization.

It may be convenient to refer in this connection to Lord Porter's dissenting judgment in the *Joyce* case. The learned Law Lord held that there was no evidence before the jury on the strength of which they could – or, indeed, were invited to – hold that the accused in fact retained the passport for the duration of its validity. He was of the opinion that that question was one for the jury to decide. For if the passport had been discarded, there would have been (*b*) although during that time it was open to a foreign State to challenge the attestation of British nationality as shown in the passport, Joyce would, until an adverse decision of an international tribunal, enjoy British diplomatic protection. Actually, unless he had himself raised the issue, no foreign State would have had reason for questioning his nationality.

At the same time, the issue before the Court in the *Joyce* case drew attention to the necessity for a somewhat revised formulation of the rule of nationality of claims and of diplomatic protection generally. The test of nationality is probably too narrow for the purpose even if we discard the now practically obsolete relic of *protégés* – i.e., persons employed in the legations and consulates of the protecting State – in certain Oriental countries. A number of States, including Great Britain, grant diplomatic protection abroad to natives of territories over which they exercise the functions of protection in various forms. Thus there are at least four classes of persons – often referred to as British protected persons – who, though not British subjects, receive British passports and enjoy British consular and diplomatic protection. These persons are the inhabitants of British protectorates, of British protected States, of Indian native States, and of various other territories such as Bahrein and the Anglo-Egyptian Sudan, and, finally, the inhabitants of the

an end to the relation of protection and, with it, of the obligations of allegiance (at pp. 374 81). It is submitted that if the accused had actually destroyed the passport, that circumstance would not have materially affected the legal position. The passport, conceived as a document with words written and printed on it, is but a piece of evidence. It may be replaced by a duplicate. What matters is the relationship established by the document. That relationship would not cease as the result of the physical loss or destruction of the paper which evidences it. If Joyce, after having deliberately destroyed the passport, after having served Germany for a period, and after having gained experience of the methods and of the true purposes of her rulers, decided, at grave peril to his life and liberty, to sever his connection with what he had come to consider a régime of evil, he would have been in the same position as if he had never discarded the passport. If imprisoned in Germany, he would have been entitled to British diplomatic protection. If he had succeeded in escaping and in reaching neutral territory, he would have come there under the protection of British diplomatic and consular representatives. It is probable that nothing short of a formal and public act of renunciation of protection – a renunciation effected by a revelation of his true nationality – would have been sufficient to put an end to the mutuality of protection and allegiance. Of this there was no indication. On the contrary, it was not denied that, until the collapse of Germany, Joyce kept up the pretence of being a British subject. In an interesting opinion given on 13 November 1861 the Law Officers advised Earl Russell that although certain British subjects lost the right to British protection as the result of enlisting in the army of the Pope, on leaving the service as the result of discharge or desertion they could claim British protection outside the Papal territory (F.O. 83/2296). See also the opinion of 25 February 1862 admitting the right of protection enjoyed by a person who renounced his allegiance to the Crown 'though prospectively, and not in an irrevocable manner' – apparently as the result of a declaration of intention to become naturalized in the United States (F.O. 83/2213). And see the opinion of 11 March 1865 for the acknowledgment of the principle that 'the sons of British-born subjects are bound by the obligations of allegiance, and, *therefore*, entitled to the protection of Her Majesty' (F.O. 83/2296).

Quaere, does the principle of *R.* v. *Lynch* [1903] 1 K.B. 444 apply to the termination of the allegiance, during war, of a protected person who is not a British subject?

Mandated territories and, in due course, of the territories under the system of trusteeship.[1] Thus Great Britain, as the Mandatory, affords diplomatic and consular protection to Palestinian citizens outside Palestine, who, for this purpose, are in the same position as other British protected persons. At the same time Palestinian citizens are aliens in the contemplation of the British Nationality and Status of Aliens Act.[2]

International law recognizes the right of a State to grant diplomatic protection to persons in these and similar categories. International tribunals have held that some of these protected persons are British nationals (*ressortissants*) – though not British subjects – within the meaning of the Peace Treaties of 1919 and that for that reason they were entitled to the benefits of those Treaties.[3] In a different sphere, in the *Muscat Dhows* case between France and Great Britain, decided in 1905 by the Permanent Court of Arbitration, it was held that a State is entitled to grant the protection of its flag to the ships of any other nation.[4]

To what extent does the existing rule as to nationality of claims require modification in view of the fact that international law permits diplomatic protection of persons other than the State's own nationals? The correct answer is probably that international tribunals have jurisdiction to entertain claims by the protecting State on behalf of such persons provided that they are not nationals of any other State. This is so especially when the particular relationship of the protecting State to the territory in question has been internationally recognized. The same principle applies to diplomatic protection.[5]

[1] For a discussion of the subject see Mervyn Jones, in *B.Y.* 22 (1945), 122–9.

[2] *R.* v. *Ketter* [1940] 1 K.B. 787. For a case on the status of an Egyptian who was a British protected person by virtue of the British protectorate over Egypt see *R.* v. *Campbell* [1921] 2 K.B. 473. Interesting information on the diplomatic protection of British protected persons will be found in the opinions of the Law Officers of 8 June 1893 and 17 February 1905.

[3] *National Bank of Egypt* v. *German Government* (decision of the Anglo-German Mixed Arbitral Tribunal of 31 May 1924: *Annual Digest*, 2 (1923–4), case no. 9), and *National Bank of Egypt* v. *Austro-Hungarian Bank* (decision of the Anglo-Austrian Mixed Arbitral Tribunal of 13 July 1923: *ibid.* case no. 10).

[4] In this particular case the Tribunal held that the right of France to grant to the subjects of the Sultan of Muscat the right to fly the French flag had been restricted by a previous Treaty. The award of the Tribunal is discussed by Westlake, in *L.Q.R.* 23 (1907), 83–7.

[5] There may well be other exceptions to the rule of nationality of claims as generally propounded. See, for instance, the dissenting opinion of Judge Van Eysinga in the *Panevezys-Saldutiskis Railway* case, decided by the Permanent Court of International Justice on 28 February 1939 (*P.C.I.J.* Series A/B, no. 76, at p. 16). There is probably no room for the rule of nationality of claims in the case of a treaty regulating the condition of stateless persons. Any signatory of the treaty is entitled to raise the case of an infraction of the treaty – although it is arguable that this does not amount to an espousal of a claim of a private person.

4. THE DUTY OF ALLEGIANCE OF PROTECTED PERSONS

The principle, seemingly adopted in the *Joyce* case, that an alien receiving diplomatic protection abroad is, because of that fact, bound by the obligations of allegiance, leads on the face of it to consequences so far-reaching as to make us pause before accepting it in its entirety. Does such a principle mean that the inhabitants of British protectorates, of British Protected States, of the native States of India, and of British Mandated (and trust) territories owe allegiance to the Crown either generally or when they are abroad? These territories are foreign territory in the contemplation of English law. Thus in *Sobhuza II* v. *Miller*[1] it was held, in effect, that the Protectorate of Swaziland was foreign territory and its inhabitants aliens, and that the Crown was entitled to plead in relation to them the defence of 'Act of State' – a defence available only with regard to acts done outside the dominions of the Crown in relation to persons who are not British subjects. It is, of course, arguable that, apart from the question of diplomatic protection abroad, such persons owe, indirectly, allegiance to the Crown. They owe direct allegiance to their ruler, who, in turn, owes some kind of allegiance to the suzerain or the Protecting State. The oath of allegiance of a national of Palestine is not to the King, but to the Government of Palestine. Yet the Government of Palestine is one appointed under the authority of the King and probably owes allegiance to him. The South African case of *Rex* v. *Christian*[2] showed that the full international sovereignty of the administering Power or the requirement of a formal status as a British subject are not essential for maintaining the charge of treason.

In the *Joyce* case the defence did not fail to draw attention to the consequences which, it was alleged, would follow with regard to the various categories of protected persons if the Court were to accept the main proposition of the prosecution, namely, that the duty of allegiance is established by protection not only inside but also outside the State. This, it was suggested, would amount to an assertion that all British protected persons owe allegiance to the Crown, at least when they are abroad. Before the House of Lords the Attorney-General appears to

[1] [1926] A.C. 518.

[2] *South African Law Reports* [1924] Appell. Div. 101. In this case the indictment recited that the accused as an inhabitant of the Mandated territory of South-West Africa 'owed allegiance to His Majesty King George the Fifth in his Government of the Union of South Africa as the Mandatory thereof under the Mandate conferred in pursuance of the Treaty of Peace with Germany, signed at Versailles on the 28th day of June, 1919, upon His Britannic Majesty for and on behalf of the aforesaid Government of the Union of South Africa'. In *Rex* v. *Earl of Crewe* [1910] 2 K.B. 576, counsel expressed doubt whether Chief Sekgome owed allegiance to the King, but the suggestion was not pressed.

have admitted that there was some such connection. It was not necessary for the House of Lords to pronounce on the matter. In fact it is not certain that the suggested connection is inevitable and that the decision of the House of Lords in *Joyce* v. *Director of Public Prosecutions* amounts to more than establishing that an alien already subject to the duty of allegiance because of his residence within the realm continues to owe allegiance if on leaving the realm he applies for and obtains the continued protection of the Crown. In the case of 'protected persons' – such as those from a protectorate or mandated territory – the diplomatic protection which they obtain is not due to any voluntary act of their own (which alone in the case of aliens is an adequate reason for bringing about a duty of individual allegiance), but to a situation which is in the nature of an internationally-recognized arrangement in respect of territories which have no *locus standi* of their own in the international sphere. In the case of an alien in the position of Joyce, the consequential duty of allegiance is the result of his voluntary act in asking for a continuation abroad of the protection hitherto enjoyed within the realm. In fact the contention by reference to which the House of Lords held Joyce to be guilty of treason was that 'by the holding of a passport he asserts and maintains the relation in which he formerly stood, claiming the continued protection of the Crown and thereby pledging the continuance of his fidelity'.[1] For this reason it does not necessarily follow from the *Joyce* case that a foreigner who receives the diplomatic protection of Great Britain by reason of a special arrangement made with his State[2] owes allegiance to Great Britain. On the other hand, although an inference of this nature is not inevitable, it could not properly be regarded as an unreasonable conclusion. For this is not only a question of reciprocity of benefits and obligation. The alien who receives protection is, as a rule, placed in a particularly advantageous position, because of the assumed relation of confidence, for causing injury to the protecting State if he is so minded. So far as international law is concerned, the case would be amply covered by the protective principle, discussed below, which permits jurisdiction over aliens in the matter of crimes committed abroad and seriously affecting the security of the State.

[1] [1946] A.C. at p. 371.

[2] As would be the case, for instance, if Great Britain were to undertake the diplomatic protection of Dutch subjects in a country in which, because of a state of war or for other reasons, Holland has no diplomatic or consular representative.

5. CRIMINAL JURISDICTION OVER ALIENS FOR ACTS COMMITTED ABROAD

Assuming that, as the Court held in the *Joyce* case, an alien who, while abroad, continues to enjoy the protection extended to him within the realm, owes allegiance to the Crown with the result that he may be tried for treason, has an English court jurisdiction to try him? The main contention for the defence in *Joyce* v. *Director of Public Prosecutions* was that to assume jurisdiction over an alien with regard to a crime committed abroad would be contrary to international law at least as understood by English courts. This aspect of the case constituted the central issue in the pleadings and in the successive judgments. In view of its general importance, it will be considered here in some detail.

In general, English courts have adhered in the past to the principle of territoriality in the matter of jurisdiction with regard to crimes committed by aliens abroad. In *Reg.* v. *Keyn*[1] the Court of Crown Cases Reserved held, by a majority, that there was even no jurisdiction in respect of offences committed by aliens in British territorial waters. The view of some of the majority of the Court was clearly influenced by the belief, for which there was no foundation, that international law does not confer such jurisdiction.[2] In *Reg.* v. *Jameson* the Court, in laying down the rule that 'an Act will not be construed as applying to foreigners in respect of acts done by them outside the dominion of the sovereign enacting' the statute, based that rule on considerations of 'international law by which one sovereign power is bound to respect the subjects and the rights of all other sovereign powers outside its own jurisdiction'.[3] Whatever may have been the rule of international law on the subject in 1896, there is little doubt that present day international law contains no such absolute prohibition of exercising jurisdiction over aliens for offences committed abroad. What is believed to be the correct legal position is stated in the following terms in the sixth edition of Oppenheim's *International Law* published in 1937, to the effect that the prohibition of the exercise of such jurisdiction 'cannot cover acts done abroad in preparation of and participation in common crimes committed or attempted to be committed in the country claiming jurisdiction; neither can it cover crimes injuring its subjects or serious crimes against its own safety'.[4] This statement expresses also some of the difficulties which confront this branch of the law and which are discussed below.[5] In fact, in the previous editions of Oppenheim's

[1] (1876) 2 Ex.D. 63.
[2] See, in particular, the observation of Cockburn C.J., 2 Ex. Div. at pp. 238–41.
[3] [1896] 2 Q.B. 425, 430.
[4] I, § 147.
[5] See pp. 238–44.

treatise the contrary view was stated, in the sense that the exercise of such jurisdiction is prohibited altogether. However, recent judicial authority and, in particular, the practically uniform trend of municipal legislation in this matter no longer permit adherence to what has become clearly an obsolete view. In 1927 the Permanent Court of International Justice, in the case of the *Lotus*,[1] held that there is no rule of international law which prohibits a State from exercising jurisdiction over a foreigner in respect of an offence committed outside its territory. The Court said: 'The territoriality of criminal law is . . . not an absolute principle of international law, and by no means coincides with territorial sovereignty.'

There is general agreement that international law recognizes the right of every State to assume protective jurisdiction when its security is concerned and to punish foreigners for serious crimes against its interests, its peace, and its institutions. Most States, in Europe and elsewhere, have enacted express legislation to that effect.[2] Courts of the United States, which otherwise adhere to the territorial conception of jurisdiction, have increasingly stressed and acted upon the doctrine of protective jurisdiction.[3] The Permanent Court of International Justice, in the *Lotus* case, declared the exercise of such protective jurisdiction to be consistent with international law. The Institute of International Law adopted in 1931 a Resolution according to which every State has the right to punish acts committed outside its territory if such acts constitute an attack upon its security, even if they have been committed by aliens and even if they are not punishable by the law of the country where they have been committed.[4] In view of this it is almost an understatement to hold, as did the House of Lords, that 'no principle of comity demands that a State should ignore the crime of treason committed against it outside its territory'.[5] There is no doubt that if Joyce had been the citizen of a State capable of challenging the action of English courts in the matter and if such a challenge had been attempted, an international court would have held that the assumption, in such circumstances, of jurisdiction for treason committed abroad by an alien was fully in conformity with international law. 'In such circumstances' – for it is not suggested that a State is entitled to extend in all circumstances its law of treason to aliens abroad and to treat them, at will, as bound by obligations of allegiance. What is submitted

[1] *P.C.I.J.* Series A, no. 10

[2] For a survey of the relevant legislation see Harvard Research in International Law, *Jurisdiction in Respect of Crime* (1935), Comment on Article 7.

[3] See, in particular, *United States* v. *Bowman*, 260 U.S. 94, 98.

[4] *Annuaire* (1931) (2), p. 128.

[5] [1946] A.C., at p. 372.

is that if there are adequate reasons for holding an alien to duties of allegiance – for instance, in the case of an alien continuing outside the realm the relation of protection which he enjoyed there – international law will attach no importance to the principle of territoriality of crimes and will not deny to a State the right to exercise jurisdiction over an alien with regard to acts committed abroad.

The issue might have been more doubtful at the end of the nineteenth century, when the principle that a State may assume what is occasionally described as protective jurisdiction over aliens for crimes committed against the security of the State was not as widely adopted and as generally acknowledged as it is now.[1] This change of emphasis is due, among other reasons, to the fact that with the technical developments in the field of communications and of transmission of news and sound by telegram, telephone and wireless, the importance of mere physical distance – and, therefore, of the territorial principle – has correspondingly diminished. In the *Joyce* case the Lord Chancellor alluded to the implications of that change. He said: 'It would, I think, be strangely inconsistent with the robust and vigorous commonsense of the common law to suppose that an alien quitting his residence in this country and temporarily on the high seas beyond territorial waters or at some even [? more] distant spot now brought within speedy reach and there adhering and giving aid to the King's enemies could do so with impunity'.[2]

The impact of the technical changes referred to above is such that much of the object of protective jurisdiction with regard to acts committed by aliens abroad may be achieved, in a somewhat unexpected way, through the doctrine of the locality of the act as determined not by the place of its causation but by the *situs* of its effect. This applies, in particular, to offences committed by means of broadcasting. There is abundant authority, in decisions of English courts, to the effect that, for the purpose of jurisdiction in the sphere of criminal law, the decisive factor is not the place where the offence was commenced but the place where it was consummated. That principle, acknowledged by Coke[3] and acted upon in a number of early cases,[4] was first made applicable to the question of venue. Later on, mostly in cases relating to extradition, the same principle was applied in the international sphere in the

[1] In Lord Macmillan's judgment in *The Cristina* [1938] A.C., at pp. 496–8, there will be found an interesting exposition of the view that English doctrines in matters related to international law ought to take into account the various developments in the international sphere.

[2] [1946] A.C., at p. 369.

[3] *Instit.* 2, 318.

[4] In *Coombes'* case (1 Leach 338) it was held that a person standing on the shore and shooting and killing another person, who died on board a ship, was within the jurisdiction of the Admiralty. In *Reg.* v. *Keyn* (L.R. 2 Exch. Div. 63) some of the judges – in particular Denman J. and Lord Coleridge – relied on that principle.

form of the proposition that a person may commit a crime in a country without being physically present there.[1] This practice is not a peculiarity of English law. In the words of a leading authority on the subject, 'the principle that a man who outside of a country wilfully puts in motion a force to take effect in it is answerable at the place where the evil is done, is recognized in the criminal jurisprudence of all countries'.[2] In particular, the courts of the United States have applied it repeatedly and on an increasing scale.[3] The courts of Germany have acted upon it with characteristic thoroughness – a practice which includes a case of the conviction of a person who shouted 'Vive la France' in France near the German border and who was found guilty of sedition on the ground that the cry was heard in Germany and, accordingly, took effect there.[4] Legislation in numerous countries, including various States of the American Union, has expressly adopted that principle. There is international authority – in the judgment of the Permanent Court of International Justice in the *Lotus* case – in support of the extension, by reference to the place of effect, of the territorial principle. In that case the Court accepted as a valid proposition of law that 'it is certain that the courts of many countries, even of countries which have given their criminal legislation a strictly territorial character, interpret criminal law in the sense that offences, the authors of which at the moment of commission are in the territory of another State, are nevertheless to be regarded as having been committed in the national territory, if one of the constituent elements of the offence, and more especially its effects, have taken place there'.[5] Broadcasting is an instance of an act which is inoperative and meaningless unless consummated, through appropriate

[1] *R.* v. *Nillins* (1884), 53 L.J.M.C. 157; *R.* v. *Godfrey* [1923] 1 K.B. 24. See also *R.* v. *Oliphant* [1905] 2 K.B. 67, and other cases cited in Russell on *Crimes*, 1 (8th ed.), 55. There is also a number of Scottish and Irish cases. As to the latter see *County Council of Fermanaugh* v. *Farrendon* [1923] 2 Ir. Rep. 180 (with references to English cases). And see Beckett in *B.Y.* 6 (1925), 44–60.

[2] Moore, *Report on Extraterritorial Crime and the Cutting Case* (1887), p. 23; *U.S. For. Rel.* (1887), p. 771.

[3] *People* v. *Adams* (1846), 3 Den. (N.Y.) 198; 1848, 1 Comst. (N.Y.) 173 – a leading case – where the accused had made false representations in Ohio through an innocent agent in New York whereby money was obtained fraudulently in New York; *Simpson* v. *State* (1893), 92 Ga. 41, where the accused stood on the South Carolina bank of the Savannah river and shot at a person in a boat on a part of the river within the boundaries of Georgia (the Court said: 'The well-established theory of the law is that, where one puts in force an agency for the commission of crime, he, in legal contemplation, accompanies the same to the point where it becomes effectual'); *Ford* v. *United States* (1927), 273 U.S. 593 – aliens prosecuted in the United States for conspiring abroad with persons inside the United States to violate the United States prohibition and tariff laws; *Strassheim* v. *Dailey*, 221 U.S. 280, 285 ('Acts done outside a jurisdiction, but intended to produce or producing deterimental effects within it, justify a state in punishing the cause of the harm as if he had been present at the effect, if the state should succeed in getting him within its power': *per* Mr Justice Holmes); and many others.

[4] *Decisions of the German Supreme Court in Criminal Matters*, 20, 146.

[5] *P.C.I.J.* Series A, no. 10, p. 23.

mechanical devices, in the country where it is intended to be heard.[1] To refuse to apply to broadcasting the principle of the locality of the offence as a test of jurisdiction would mean to render the State and its subjects unprotected against new instrumentalities of science. It is at this point that there may be noted a suggestive convergence of the two independent grounds of jurisdiction – that of protective jurisdiction and that based on the locality of the effect of the act. It did not prove necessary for the Crown in the *Joyce* case to invoke that latter basis of jurisdiction.[2] However, its implications are worth noting.

6

While the position in international law – the main point relied upon by the defence in the *Joyce* case – is fully in accordance with the decision of the House of Lords, it is proper to attempt to answer the more limited question, namely, whether so far as English law is concerned the judgment did not amount to an assumption, by way of judicial legislation, of a hitherto dormant or non-existent jurisdiction. It may not be sufficient to say that although Great Britain has in the past, in deference to what English courts believed to be a rule of international law, declined to exercise jurisdiction in the case of offences committed by aliens abroad, the position in international law has changed and that, therefore, if an English court were now to express an opinion that it has no jurisdiction over an alien for an act committed abroad and affecting the security of the realm it would be expressing a view clearly out of keeping with generally recognized practice and opinion. For there may be a strong suspicion of dialectics in the insistence that what has changed is not the attitude of the courts but international law on the subject and that, as in the past so also in the *Joyce* case, the courts merely gave

[1] The nature of radio communication was considered in *In re Regulation and Control of Radio Communication in Canada* [1932] A.C. 304. See also *Horwitz* v. *United States* (1923), 63 F. (2d.) 716, in which, apparently, the defendant had operated a wireless station in a place in Mexico from which were broadcast to listeners in the United States solicitations to participate in a lottery. And see McCain in *Air Law Review*, 11 (1940), 144–153. Some aspects of this question are lucidly discussed by Professor Preuss in *Grotius Society*, 30 (1944), 184–208.

[2] It was probably by reference to that latter ground of jurisdiction that the alternative count of the indictment, based on the Treachery Act, 1940, was drafted. On the instruction of Mr Justice Tucker in the Central Criminal Court, that count was not proceeded with pending the hearing of the case under the Treason Act, 1351: see p. 144 of the official transcript of the proceedings. The Treachery Act, 1940, applies to activities calculated, by their effect in the United Kingdom, to assist the military, naval or air forces of the enemy, to impede British forces, or to cause loss of life. The offence, wherever begun, must, according to the Act, be committed in the United Kingdom. The indictment under the Treachery Act would have proceeded on the lines of the argument that the act of broadcasting from Germany was consummated and, therefore, committed in the United Kingdom. It must remain a matter of speculation whether, if the result of the indictment under the Treason Act had been different, the Crown would have proceeded with the indictment under the Treachery Act.

effect to international law. This may be true, but the explanation may be somewhat ingenious when adduced in relation to what may appear to some a judicial innovation in the sphere of criminal law.

A more convincing answer is that the *Joyce* case is not a case of assumption of jurisdiction over an alien pure and simple, but over an alien who, by reason of the relation of protection in which he had placed himself, acquired a status in many ways indistinguishable from that of a subject. It has been shown that, so far as English law is concerned, there is no innovation implied in the assimilation, for the purpose of allegiance, of an alien enjoying the protection of the State to a national. This is a case of an application of the well-established principle of correlation of allegiance and protection to a somewhat novel set of facts. There was no question here of an imprudent man being caught within the meshes of a technicality. The Resolution of the Judges of 1707 was not the source of the decision; it was resorted to as an illustration of a wider principle. The Court expressly declined to adhere to what would have been a somewhat technical rule of law, namely, acquisition of British nationality (and of the corresponding obligation of allegiance) by estoppel.[1] Formal principles of law are a questionable ground for proceedings in State trials, even if the accused may be driven to base his case on the letter of the law. Yet, though it is not believed that the decision in the *Joyce* case is open to criticism on the ground either of retroactive judicial legislation or of reliance on technicalities, there is probably no reason to deplore unduly the volume of criticism to which it gave rise. Suspicion of judicial legislation in treason trials – where more than anywhere else the relentless machine of the State and of 'reason of State' has been used to crush human freedom – is a healthy sign of that eternal vigilance on the part of public opinion which is the sole guarantee of the maintenance of a true rule of law. In the long run, the inherent merits of a sound judicial decision will assert themselves over criticism, both factious and well-intentioned.[2]

What is more important, both generally and for the purposes of the present article, is the question of the exact extent of the decision in the *Joyce* case in the matter of territoriality of jurisdiction in relation to

[1] See F.O. 83/2216 for an opinion of the Law Officers of the Crown of 31 January 1863 approving of the view that the claimants were 'morally estopped from denying their citizenship, for the purpose of evading liabilities, to which they would be legally subject if the profession of citizenship, on the faith of which they have enjoyed political franchises, had been true'.

[2] On the other hand, there is room for the view that ultimately the authority of the law depends on the support given to it by public opinion, and that criticism must therefore be studiously and painstakingly informed – especially in face of a practically unanimous decision of the judges in all three instances. It will be noted that the dissenting judgment of Lord Porter expressed agreement with the major principle on which the decision of the House of Lords was based.

crimes committed by aliens abroad. That decision, it is well to bear in mind, cannot be adduced in support of the proposition that a State has unlimited jurisdiction over an alien for acts which have been committed abroad and which it considers to be prejudicial to its safety.[1] There is no warrant in international law for a rule of such alarming comprehensiveness. An individual in one State cannot be expected to exhibit scrupulous care in respecting the interests of other States or to incur the dangers of criminal prosecution in case he should, voluntarily or involuntarily, come into the power of those States. On the other hand, if a person acts in such a manner as seriously to threaten the security of another State, he must be deemed to act at his peril – for instance, if he is an active party to a revolutionary conspiracy or to military espionage. The test cannot properly be whether such acts are permitted by the law of the State where he resides.[2] For States are not, as a rule, in the habit of penalizing acts prejudicial to the safety of other States except in the case of active participation in a hostile expedition.[3] The test is whether such acts constitute a *serious* injury or threat of injury to the State or its citizens. It must be a matter for judicial agencies, national and international, to determine in particular cases whether that test has been complied with.[4]

[1] It may be emphasized once more that in *R.* v. *Joyce* the Court was not confronted with the case of an alien *tout court.*

[2] A test suggested in the Harvard Research Draft, *Jurisdiction in Respect of Crime*, p. 543.

[3] See the writer's article in *A.J.* 22 (1928), 105–30.

[4] It would be in accordance with an enlightened principle of justice – a principle which has not as yet become part of the Law of Nations – if, in the absence of effective extradition, the courts of a State were to assume jurisdiction over common crimes, by whomsoever and wherever committed, of a heinous character. Territoriality of jurisdiction is a rule of convenience in the sphere of the law of evidence. It is not a requirement of justice or even a necessary postulate of the sovereignty of the State.

CHAPTER 5

TESTING THE LEGALITY OF PERSIAN POLICY

Editor's note Lauterpacht's involvement in the legal consequences of the Iranian nationalization in 1951 of the Anglo-Iranian Oil Company, of which the main aspect was his preparation of the legal argument in the British Memorial in the proceedings commenced before the International Court of Justice in 1951 (see volume 4 of these *Collected Papers*), also led to his being consulted on the steps which might be taken within national jurisdictions to assert the rights of the Company. Beyond that, he was not professionally concerned with the 'pursuit' litigation commenced by the Company in Aden, Italy and Japan. But the present chapter, the note on the *Rose Mary* which forms the next chapter and paragraph 115 *ab* of his eighth edition of Oppenheim's *International Law* express his general approval of the doctrine that the courts of one State ought not to recognize or give effect to such legislation of another State as violates public international law.

This chapter consists of the second part of an article published in *The Times* newspaper in two parts on 30 and 31 July 1952. Both parts carried as their principal title 'The Hague Judgment' – a reference to the decision of the International Court of Justice on 22 July 1952 in the *Anglo-Iranian Oil Company* case (*I.C.J. Reports* 1952, p. 93). The first part, however, dealt with the substantive part of the Court's judgment, in which the Court held that it did not possess compulsory jurisdiction in the proceedings brought by the United Kingdom against Iran. It will, therefore, be printed in a later volume containing Lauterpacht's papers on the International Court of Justice. But the second part of the article, which bears the sub-title appearing at the head of this chapter, examined the possibility of proceedings in national courts to test the legality of the Iranian action. It is therefore included here.

Another question which has been brought into prominence by the declaration of the International Court of Justice that it is not competent to adjudicate upon the legality, under international law, of the fact and the manner of the nationalization of the property of the Anglo-Iranian Oil Company in Persia is this: What courts, if any, are now in the position to do so? It is the question which is likely to come before the courts of various countries, including this country, in connection with the claim of the Anglo-Iranian Oil Company that the oil of which it has been deprived by a Persian Act of Parliament is still the property of the company.

English courts have held in some cases arising out of the confiscatory decrees of Soviet Russia passed in and after 1917 that 'the validity of the acts of an independent sovereign Government with respect to property and persons within its jurisdiction cannot be questioned in the Courts of this country' (*per* Lord Justice Warrington in *A. M. Luther Company* v. *James Sagor and Co.* (37 *The Times* L.R. 777; [1921] 3 K. B. 532, at p. 548)). They have held that 'our Courts are bound to give effect to the laws and acts of [the foreign recognized] Government so far as they relate to property within that jurisdiction when it was affected by those laws and acts' (*per* Lord Justice Scrutton in *Princess Paley Olga* v. *Weisz* (45 *The Times* L.R. 365; [1929] 1 K. B. 718, at p. 725)).

Similar decisions, in a different sphere, have been given by courts of some other countries – though not of all countries. Thus French courts have held that they would not recognize, as being contrary to French conceptions of *ordre public*, title claimed to have been acquired as the result of expropriation not accompanied by fair compensation.

The issue with which English courts will be faced in the matter will be of a novel character. In the Russian cases English courts were not confronted with the question whether they would recognize, as conferring title upon the confiscating State, foreign legislation which was contrary to international law and which deprived British subjects of their rights. But it is exactly this type of problem which will confront them in the case of the Anglo-Iranian Oil Company – assuming always that they will come to the conclusion, which must not be taken for granted, that the action of Persia was contrary to international law. In the Russian cases, it must be noted, they were called upon to decide – and they decided the question in the negative – whether they would apply English conceptions of public policy to the acts of a foreign State affecting in the first instance foreign nationals. But is there a rule of international or municipal law which obliges – or, indeed, permits – the courts of a State to recognize title acquired by another State in violation of international law?

That question becomes particularly pertinent in countries in which, by virtue of an unwritten law (as in England and the United States) or an express constitutional provision, international law forms part of the law of the land. It is by reference to this question that courts may be called upon to re-examine the widely held view that if a State through its legislation deprives aliens of their rights in violation of international law it incurs international responsibility, but that such legislation, being the legislation of a foreign sovereign State, must be given effect in respect of title claimed to have been acquired over property situated in that foreign State. In the absence of effective international remedies – and the United Kingdom may have none in its claim against Persia – international responsibility may be but a *brutum fulmen.*

In such cases, it may be argued, national courts ought, in so far as within their limited sphere they may be in a position to do so, to make their contribution to securing at least partial observance of international law. They may come to the conclusion that unqualified respect for the sovereignty of foreign States as expressed in their legislation, however arbitrary and internationally illegal, may be a rule as obsolete as that of the absolute jurisdictional immunity of foreign States and their agencies.

English courts are subject to the sovereignty of Parliament. It does not follow that they are subject to the sovereignty of every foreign Parliament and that they must recognize the legal effect of its decrees with regard to property corporeally within its jurisdiction even if such decrees are violative of international law. There thus arises the interesting possibility that, as the result of the judgment of the International Court of 22 July, English – and other – courts will be faced with a question which is of considerable jurisprudential interest and for which the precedent of the Russian cases affords no obvious guidance.

With regard to its immediate legal consequences, it would appear that the judgment given on 22 July by the International Court of Justice has affected but little – if at all – the legal position and the interests of the Anglo-Iranian Oil Company. Assuming the disposition of the Persian Government to respect the authority of the Court, the effect of the judgment will be merely to shift to another tribunal the task of determining the legal issue involved in the dispute. Instead of being determined by the Court itself, it will have to be decided by the arbitrator to be appointed by the President – or the Vice-President – of the Court in conformity with the Concession Agreement of 1933 between Persia and the company.

In that year, in pursuance of a request made by the British and Persian Governments, the Permanent Court of International Justice gave in effect its consent to the acceptance by its President of the task of appointing the arbitrator. When in due course that appointment – postponed by the proceedings brought before the Court by the Government of the United Kingdom in 1951 and now brought to a close by the judgment of the Court – is made by the President or Vice-President of the Court, the arbitrator thus appointed will constitute a tribunal competent to decide on the claims of the company. There is no reason to assume that the Government of Persia will treat the decision appointing the arbitrator, made under the aegis of the Court, with less respect than it would have treated the decision of the Court to assume jurisdiction on the merits.

CHAPTER 6

THE ROSE MARY

Editor's note The background to this case-note is set out in the Editor's note to the previous chapter.

The appeal in the *Rose Mary*, referred to in the note, was lodged in the East African Court of Appeal, but was dismissed for want of prosecution in December 1954.

The note was published in the *Cambridge Law Journal*, 12 (1954), 22–3.

Since the decision of the Court of Appeal in *Luther* v. *Sagor*,[1] it has been regarded as an unquestioned principle of English law that courts will not examine or question the validity of legislative acts of a recognized foreign State, at least in so far as they affect title to property within the territory of that foreign State. That principle was considered in *Luther* v. *Sagor* to follow from an international obligation binding upon this country. This was also believed to be the attitude of the courts of the United States in a number of decisions relied upon in *Luther* v. *Sagor*. Yet, a British court, sitting in Aden in 1953, held that as the Iranian Oil nationalization law amounted to expropriation without compensation, it was contrary to international law; that the court must refuse validity to that law in so far as it related to nationaized property of the plaintiffs within its territorial jurisdiction; and that, therefore, the oil in dispute was still the property of the plaintiffs, the Anglo-Iranian Oil Company: the *Rose Mary*.[2] Notice of appeal was lodged.

At the time of writing, the question is *sub judice* and only some tentative observations are appropriate. The main question is to what extent, if any, the judgment in the *Rose Mary* departs from the wide principle laid down in *Luther* v. *Sagor*. Some of the judgments in the latter case were couched in general and emphatic terms, and on a number of occasions it has been found necessary, in judicial decisions and elsewhere, to explain or qualify their apparent comprehensiveness.[3] It is possible that some such qualification, which may prove not to be inconsistent with the basic principle of *Luther* v. *Sagor*, underlies the decision in the *Rose Mary*. The reason for that may be found in the following statement in Sir Arnold McNair's *Legal Effects of War*: 'It is

[1] [1921] 3 K.B. 532. [2] [1953] 1 W.L.R. 246.

[3] See *Haile Selasse* v. *Cable and Wireless Ltd.* (*No.* 2) [1939] Ch.D., at pp. 187–94. And see Sir Arnold McNair's observations on *Bank of Ethiopia* v. *National Bank of Egypt and Liguori* [1937] Ch. 513, in *Legal Effects of War* (3rd ed. 1948), pp. 340–3.

usual for our courts to give effect to the acts of foreign Governments within the sphere of their competence, subject to certain exceptions such as penal, revenue and political laws and *provided that these acts do not conflict* with rules of international law.'[1] The words as here italicized seem to indicate that the general principle in *Luther* v. *Sagor* does not apply – and probably was not intended to apply – to such legislative acts of foreign States as are contrary to international law. In *Luther* v. *Sagor* there was no allegation that the confiscatory Soviet legislation amounted to a breach of international law. There is, therefore, room for the suggestion that what was decided in *Luther* v. *Sagor* was no more than that where a State, through legislation, confiscates without compensation the property of *its own nationals*,[2] the courts of other States may not, by reference to their own conceptions of morality or public policy, question such legislation and deny recognition to legal title which, in pursuance thereof, has been acquired within the territory of the confiscating State. Neither was there any question of international law involved in the American decisions relied upon in *Luther* v. *Sagor*.[3]

It is thus possible that the clarification of the issue raised by the judgment in the *Rose Mary* may take place not by way of confirmation of or departure from the decision, thus interpreted, in *Luther* v. *Sagor*, but by reference to the wider issue expressed in the following question: Does international law impose upon a State the duty to ensure that its courts give effect to such foreign legislation as is contrary to international law? It has been asserted that such English judicial authority as exists on the subject inclines to a negative answer to that question.[4] Such negative answer is likely to receive an accession of strength if the argument – which is controversial – is admitted that no other attitude can properly be taken by the courts of a country in which customary rules of international law are recognized as part of the law of the land. The paramount doctrine of the sovereignty of Parliament may compel courts in this country to give effect to British legislation which is contrary to international law, but, it may be said, no such compulsion imposes itself upon them in respect of legislative acts of foreign countries. At the same time, it is difficult to leave out of account the view that as States are not bound to submit to international jurisdiction the question whether their legislation is in conformity with international

[1] At p. 322.

[2] See the qualifying statement by Russell L.J. in *Princess Olga Paley* v. *Weisz* [1929] 1 K.B., at p. 736. A number of American cases take that qualification into account. But see McNair, *Legal Effects of War*, p. 362.

[3] *Underhill* v. *Hernandez* (1897), 168 U.S. 250; *Oetjen* v. *Central Leather Co.* (1917), 246 U.S. 397; *Ricaud* v. *American Metal Co.* (1917), 246 U.S. 304.

[4] See case cited by Sir Arnold McNair, *Legal Effects of War*, p. 362, and Fachiri in *B.Y.* 12 (1931), 101–4.

law, a competence of that nature cannot properly be attributed to domestic tribunals of a foreign country and that the assumption of any such power may not be conducive to the maintenance of friendly international relations. On the other hand, it may be said that friendly relations are likely to suffer if the courts of a country are constrained to lend their assistance to perpetrating a legal wrong committed either against its nationals or the nationals of another State (other than the confiscating State itself). Neither is the argument based on sovereignty conclusive. There may be force in the suggestion that there is a denial of the sovereignty of the State if foreign courts take it upon themselves to examine its legislation and to refuse to give effect to it as being contrary to international law. There may be no less force in the view that respect for the sovereignty of a State is put under strain if its courts are compelled to give effect to foreign legislation which inflicts grievous injury upon its nationals in violation of international law.

It may be noted that the decision in the *Rose Mary* was not followed, in the same year, either by the Court of Venice, in *Anglo-Iranian Oil Co.* v. *Supor Oil Co.*[1], or by the Tokyo Court in the *Nissho Maru*.[2] However, in both cases the courts – while doubting their right to review foreign legislation – examined the Iranian nationalization law from the point of view of its consistency with international law. Unlike the Court of Aden, they found that compensation offered by the Iranian law was sufficient to enable them to hold that the expropriation was not of a confiscatory character. There may be significance in the circumstance that, notwithstanding incantations to the contrary, the two Courts did in fact examine the foreign legislation in question. French courts have shown no hesitation, over a long period of years, in reviewing foreign legislation and denying to it effect, extraterritorial and other, if deemed contrary to the French conception of public policy (which includes respect for international law). The same applies to courts of some other countries. In this country there has been no disposition to decline to review foreign legislation and, in proper cases, to deny to it extraterritorial effect on the ground of its confiscatory or penal nature. It also seems reasonable to assume that the courts have power to examine foreign legislation from the point of view of its formal validity.

It is selfish to voice the apprehension that on account of any settlement of the controversy with Iran an opportunity may be lost to obtain an elucidation of the main issue thus raised by the decision in the *Rose Mary*.

[1] *Foro Italiano*, 78 (1953), I, p. 719.

[2] See *I.L.R.* 20 (1953), 305, *sub nom. Anglo-Iranian Oil Company* v. *Idemitsu Kosan Kabushiki Kaisha*.

V

DUTIES OF TERRITORIAL JURISDICTION

CHAPTER 7

REVOLUTIONARY ACTIVITIES BY PRIVATE PERSONS AGAINST FOREIGN STATES

Editor's note This article was first submitted to the *American Journal of International Law* in May 1927 under the title of 'Fomenting and Preparing Revolutions in Foreign Countries'. As the then managing editor of the *Journal*, Dr George A. Finch, wrote, the article was 'considered favourably', but was about twice the acceptable length. Lauterpacht then reduced it by half, mainly by omitting the section dealing with revolutionary activities originating from the government of a State itself. (This section was probably then incorporated in the paper on 'Revolutionary Propaganda by Governments' which forms chapter 8 below.)

If it is wondered why the present chapter and the one which follows have been introduced at this point in these *Collected Papers*, rather than under the heading of 'State Responsibility' to which they may be thought more directly to relate, the answer lies in the rough classification for his projected treatise which Lauterpacht left behind. The Part on 'State Territory and Territorial Jurisdiction' contains a chapter entitled 'Duties of Territorial Jurisdiction' of which two of the three sections specifically named are, respectively, 'Hostile Acts against Foreign States' and 'Hostile Propaganda against Foreign States'.

The article was published in *A.J.*22 (1928), 105–30.

Revolutionary acts[1] and preparations are liable to punishment by the

[1] The problem of State responsibility for revolutionary activities by private persons against foreign States has in the years following the World War become, once more, a matter of international importance. One of the consequences of the substitution, in a number of countries, of the democratic form of government for different types of dictatorship has been the growth of revolutionary activities conducted from abroad against the régimes thus established and, as a result, a series of demands put before foreign States and calculated to safeguard the security of the menaced Governments. As will be shown later, many European States and the United States of America have in the last hundred years been confronted with similar demands. However, the present situation is to a large extent complicated by the fact that, alongside revolutionary activities of private persons, another problem has come to the foreground, namely, that of revolutionary acts and propaganda originating directly from a Government and aimed at a foreign State – a problem which lies outside the scope of the present article. There is a possibility that the severity of condemnation which naturally attaches to this latter kind of illegal interference with the independence and the constitution of foreign States might warp the judgment of the international lawyer when engaged in determining the extent of State responsibility for revolutionary acts of private persons. The danger of being misled by a superficial analogy is the greater as text-book writers either pass lightly over this subject or indulge in vague generalities. It is intended to present in this article the theoretical argument and to collect the relevant facts as a starting point for a future detailed enquiry into this rather neglected branch of the doctrine of State responsibility.

It will also be observed that the question dealt with in this article covers only one aspect criminal law of the community against which they are directed, and belong as such to the domain of municipal law. They become a matter of direct importance to international law when the menaced State finds that the efficacy of its laws and the possibilities of peaceful internal development are being frustrated by revolutionary propaganda or by acts of rebellion coming from abroad. Such acts may, when brought to consummation within its territory, be punished with all the rigour of the law. But the probability of their suppression is diminished and the chances of their success are enhanced as a result of their being hatched out and prepared under cover of the territorial supremacy of another State. It happens thus that what one State believes to be its internationally recognized right of peaceful existence is put in danger in consequence of another State's right to exclusive jurisdiction over its territory, a right, in turn, fully protected by international law. We get over the difficulty, for a while, by bringing to our mind the fact that territorial supremacy being a sum of rights granted by international law, the very conception of the Law of Nations requires that it should be made use of in a manner compatible with the respect due to equally recognized rights of others. However, 'respect' is a word capable of a variety of meanings. It may range from the abstract duty of non-interference to a positive duty of protection. Is it the formal right to choose and to retain, while free from interference *by other States*, such a constitution and such a Government as the nation pleases that is recognized by international law, or is it the right to protection against *whomsoever* of the existing Government and constitution? Accordingly, is the duty of respect incumbent only upon the State as such, or does reciprocal recognition go so far as to impose upon it the duty to prevent all treasonable acts against a State with which it is at peace? This distinction is not a purely theoretical one. For while the duty of respect extends to the State solely and exclusively, that of protection carries with it the obligation to restrain private individuals from a certain line of conduct. Respect and protection thus conceived are not interchangeable terms. There are interests which international law safeguards only to the extent of imposing restrictions upon the freedom of the State's own action without in any way obliging it to exact a similar measure of restraint from its subjects. Indeed, the entire law of neutrality is based on a differentiation of this kind.

It would seem, therefore, that the right to protection as against

of the vaster subject usually referred to as delicts against foreign States and embracing such topics as violations of neutrality, libelling foreign sovereigns, acts of violence against heads of foreign States and foreign diplomatic envoys, insults to the flag of friendly States, and the like. These offences are here referred to only so far as they bear directly on the subject under discussion.

private individuals cannot be deduced from the rights inherent in the international personality of States, but only from the principle, if there be such one, that the legal system embodied in the constitution of a particular State is part of the international legal order and, accordingly, an interest which States are under a duty actively to defend against all attacks. Such a principle, however, is a postulate which, far from being a generally accepted rule of international law, must still be proved by reasons more cogent than theoretical deductions from the fundamental rights of States. For it will be observed that although the growing solidarity, legal and otherwise, of the international community requires that what is stamped in one State as a crime should not be left unpunished within the borders of its neighbour, there are nevertheless weighty exceptions to this rule, the most important flowing from the attitude of modern States with regard to political offences against foreign Governments. The legal consequences of the postulated unity of law are limited in extent and of doubtful application to treasonable acts against foreign States.

On the other hand, it is equally clear that a State is entitled to expect that the exclusiveness of other States' jurisdiction over their territory will not result, even indirectly, in a serious menace to its existence and safety. For it is only and alone the respect for the sovereignty of the neighbouring State that induces the menaced State to refrain from invading the territory of its neighbour in order to put an end to an impending danger. But it will, in the long run, be impossible to maintain that attitude of self-restraint, if the neighbour shows no consideration for the vital interests of the threatened State. A menace of this kind constitutes, according to an almost unanimous consensus of opinion, a perfectly good ground for intervention.

The above considerations, showing as they do the difficulties involved in the question, suggest at the same time the way in which its solution should be approached. It consists in the possibly exact determination of the nature of acts which may give just cause for complaint or for a demand for redress. American publicists, while pointing to the clear rules of that part of the neutrality laws of the United States and of Great Britain which relate to hostile expeditions, express the opinion that the laws of other countries fall short, in this respect, of the fulfilment of a clear international duty. And yet hostile expeditions constitute only one class of possible hostile acts of a revolutionary character, and Continental writers, far from admitting the inferiority of their own laws, express the view that the common law countries have remained, so far as the protection of foreign Governments is concerned, in a rudimentary stage of law incompatible with the requirements of international solidarity. In fact, it is by no means certain that of all revolutionary acts coming from abroad hostile expeditions constitute the greatest danger. At least, they present an open menace which, given the means, can be repelled by force. But the menaced State is to a considerable degree powerless against revolutionary propaganda generated abroad, possibly spread from the air by means of publications or broadcast by wireless, inciting its population to armed revolt and its troops to rebellion; against revolutionary organizations formed abroad with the view to assisting an actual or impending revolt in their mother country; against moneys being subscribed or lent, or other assistance given, for such purposes. What protection, if any, from such acts falling short of hostile expeditions does international law afford, and what duties, if any, does it impose upon the State from whose territory such acts originate? The sweeping statement, so frequently encountered, to the effect that international law imposes upon States the duty to prevent, within their territory, *all* acts injurious to their neighbours, is superficial and misleading. It must necessarily result in the answer to the question being determined by purely political factors, e.g. by the enforced submissiveness of weak States or by opportunistic arrangements of mutual insurance between reactionary States or between revolutionary Governments of precarious standing.

The answer must be sought in the practice of States, both internal, as evidenced in that part of their municipal law which deals with offences against foreign States, and external, as shown in international incidents and negotiations. The municipal legislation which protects foreign Governments and constitutions does so, so far as it goes, with the view to avoiding conflicts with other States. But the principle of preservation of peace is, when taken as a measure of international obligation, both defective and highly relative. Different countries pay a different price for their peace. A State will usually succeed in exacting from a weak country a measure of vigilance the mere demand for which would be rejected by its more powerful neighbour as an act of intolerable interference. And a reactionary Government will be prone to see a danger of external complications in activities which a more progressive Government will hardly regard as meriting attention. Here lies the reason why different criminal codes, although starting from the same premises, arrive at solutions diametrically opposed to one another. There is a curious kind of *renvoi* in this matter. The international lawyer looks, as he is bound to do, to municipal legislation as showing what is the legal conviction of States on this matter. But the laws of different countries obviously start from the consideration that acts should be prohibited which might bring about a declaration of war, or expose the country or its citizens to reprisals, or embroil it with other Powers, and, generally speaking, all such acts as are contrary to international law. He is thus brought back to the beginning of his search, seeing that it is for international law to decide which acts may legitimately cause a declaration of war or give just offence to other States.

I. REVIEW OF AUTHORITIES

Text-books and treatises on international law do not as a rule refer specifically to the question of State responsibility for revolutionary acts by private persons against foreign States.[1] They mention it incidentally when discussing problems of neutrality, of intervention, of fundamental rights and duties of States, or of non-extradition of political criminals. There is a tendency, or rather a habit, to include revolutionary activities within the more general designation of hostile acts against foreign Powers, and to speak indiscriminately of international law as imposing upon States the duty to prevent the commission of such acts within their territory.[2]

Nevertheless, the student inquiring what, in the opinion of those writers, is the meaning of 'hostile acts' will be able to distinguish two sets of opinions. According to one view, the duty of prevention and suppression extends to all acts injurious to other States; according to the other, the circle of such acts is strictly limited and embraces mainly organized acts of force.

Thus we find Liszt expressing the opinion that every member of the family of nations is under a duty to oppose within its territory *all* attempts, by its own subjects or by foreigners, against the interests of

[1] On the other hand, valuable references to the subject will be found in monographs and articles dealing with hostile acts against foreign States in general, or, within a more restricted scope, with the question of hostile expeditions. The more important may here be mentioned: Lewis, *On Foreign Jurisdiction and Extradition of Criminals* (1859), pp. 70 *et seq.*; Heinze, in *Archiv für preussisches Strafrecht*, 17 (1869), esp. 743–50; Lammasch, in *Zeitschrift für die gesamte Strafrechtswissenschaft*, 3 (1883), 376–440; Clunet, *Offenses et actes hostiles commis par des particuliers contre un Etat étranger* (1887), and in *Journal de droit international privé*, 14 (1887), 5–21; Craies, *ibid.* 16 (1889), 357–80; *Gastfreundschaft und Hausrecht der Schweiz* (1889); Wheeler, *Foreign Enlistment Act*, 1870, with Notes on the Leading Cases of this and the American Act (1896); Olivart, *R.G.* 5 (1898), 499–518; Perrinjaquet, *ibid.* 18 (1911), 666–75, and 19 (1912), 344–9; Fenwick, *The Neutrality Laws of the United States* (1912), pp. 81–8, 124–5; Curtis, *A.J.* 8 (1914), 1–37, 224–52; Fick, *Gerichtssaal*, 87 (1919), 76–97; and, above all, Gerland, 'Feindliche Handlungen gegen befreundete Staaten', in *Vergleichende Darstellung des deutschen und ausländischen Strafrechts* (1906), Part I, pp. 113–255. For the literature dealing with the relevant parts of the criminal law in individual countries see the works referred to in the following section.

[2] See, for instance, Oppenheim, *International Law* (3rd ed. 1920), I, § 124 (duties resulting from territorial independence), § 164 (State responsibility), § 316 (right of asylum).

foreign States.[1] Calvo asserts categorically that international law imposes upon the State the duty to prevent its subjects from committing acts prejudicial to the interests of friendly nations, and to oppose plots and conspiracies of any nature whatsoever likely to disturb their security.[2] Rivier is emphatically of the view that mere toleration of propaganda against the political institutions and the territorial integrity of friendly States constitutes a violation of a clear rule of international law.[3] This is also the opinion of Pradier-Fodéré.[4] Fauchille's comprehensive treatise bristles with general statements to the effect that it is the duty of the State 'to prevent within its territory plots, conspiracies and in general all attempts against a foreign Power'.[5] De Louter's view is no less sweeping.[6] Recently, in his enumeration of the fundamental juridical duties of States, Alvarez emphasized the duty to prevent conspiracies against the security and the public order of other States.[7] And Redslob goes the length of construing as a measure of authoritative intervention the mere toleration of such attempts.[8]

On the other hand, British and American writers mention less frequently the duty to protect the Government and the public order of foreign States. They too speak of hostile attempts, but it is obvious that they refer here mainly to organized acts of force directed against foreign territory. This appears clearly from Phillimore's treatment of the subject in his chapter on self-preservation. It is only actual invasion or threat of invasion by rebel forces which must be prevented, and it is only in cases like those that the menaced State is justified in having recourse to measures flowing from the right of self-preservation.[9] Hall speaks of the State's duty not to lend 'the shelter of its independence to persons organising armed attack upon the political or social order elsewhere established'.[10] Moore's statement is even more guarded. Referring to the duty of obedience to the law which political refugees owe to the country granting asylum, he points out that they are subject to such measures 'as the Government may lawfully adopt to prevent the national territory from being used by any persons as a base for

[1] Liszt, p. 118. This view is shared by almost all German writers. Cf. especially Bluntschli, *Das moderne Völkerrecht* (1868), §§ 396, 398; Heffter, § 63a; Triepel, *Völkerrecht und Landesrecht* (1899), p. 340. But see Schön, *Die völkerrechtliche Haftung der Staaten aus unerlaubten Handlungen* (1917), p. 69, 70.

[2] Calvo, III, § 1298; also I, § 108. See also Olivart, in *R.G.* 5.

[3] Rivier, I, 266.

[4] Pradier-Fodéré, I, §§ 238, 260.

[5] Fauchille, I, Part I (1922), no. 255; see also nos. 245, 256, 295, 295 (1), 441 (24), 472.

[6] De Louter, I, 244.

[7] Quoted by Fauchille, no. 295.

[8] *Histoire des grands principes du droit des gens* (1923), p. 511. See also Hettlage, in *Z.V.* 37 (1926), 25.

[9] Phillimore, I, §§ 214–20. See also § 369 which, however, should be read subject to the above interpretation of 'hostile attempts.'

[10] Hall, § 8. See also *ibid.* §§ 13 and 63.

criminal or hostile enterprises'.[1] But it will be seen later that the scope of measures which the Government of the United States may lawfully adopt in this connection is not too wide, and that the conception of 'criminal enterprises' is here subject to a specifically restricted interpretation. It may be said at this stage that the very dearth of British-American authority, so far as text-books are concerned, is indicative of the general attitude of the two countries on this matter.

The Institute of International Law adopted in 1900 a Resolution on the Rights and Duties of Foreign Powers as regards the Established and Recognized Governments in case of Insurrection.[2] Section 3 of Article II of the resolution laid down that it is forbidden for foreign Powers to allow a hostile military expedition against an established and recognized Government to be organized within its territory.

It appears that only once was an international tribunal confronted with this problem. In the first case which came before the Central American Court of Justice (created in 1907 between the five Central American Republics), Honduras and Nicaragua charged Guatemala and Salvador with fomenting revolution in Honduras and with unneutral conduct in respect of the insurrection which had broken out in that country. Both charges were alleged to have been in violation of the conventions concluded in 1907 between the five republics. In July 1908 the court issued an interlocutory decree instructing the defendant Governments to refrain from acts which might imply direct or indirect interference with the revolution in Honduras and to confine in one place emigrants suspected of a hostile attitude towards the Honduran Government.[3] In the final judgment, given in December 1908 the Court held, by a majority of votes, that neither Salvador nor Guatemala were guilty of the charge brought against them.[4] In particular, the Court held that the mere fact of a prejudice to the interests of the foreign State is not sufficient to create responsibility. It demanded a proof of either intentional malice or culpable negligence.[5]

2. MUNICIPAL REGULATIONS

The wide divergence of opinion between international publicists is to a large extent due to the fact that the criminal laws of various countries

[1] Moore, II, § 221; see also his *Treatise on Extradition* (1891), p. 7, and Field, *Code* (1872), § 207.

[2] *Annuaire*, 18 (1900), 227; *Resolutions of the Institute* (ed. by J. B. Scott, 1916), p. 157.

[3] *A.J.* 2 (1908), 838.

[4] Martens, N.R.G., 3rd ser., 5, 325–58. The final conclusions of the judgment are printed in the *A.J.* 3 (1909), 434–6.

[5] See also the award of the American and British Claims Commission under the Treaty of May 1871 (Moore, *International Arbitrations*, IV, 4042–54).

differ widely on this point. And yet at first sight it is rather surprising that any considerable divergence of legislative practice should have taken place at all. For the relevant provisions in different legislations can be traced to one common source, namely, to the wish to preserve the external peace and safety of the legislator's own country. The Roman law punished any one 'cujusve opera dolo malo . . . ex amicis hostes populi Romani fiant'.[1] In the formative period of international law, that consideration was given additional weight as a result of the then prevailing practice based on the principle of collective responsibility. The unfriendly act of the alien individual was imputed to the foreign community or to any of its members. This state of affairs constituted a powerful obstacle in the way of peaceful intercourse, and frequent attempts were made to put an end to it. International publicists contributed their share by introducing the Roman law doctrine of culpability as a condition of international responsibility, a doctrine which, first propounded by Grotius, remains today the basis of this branch of international law, notwithstanding the attempts at its replacement by the modern positivist theory of absolute responsibility. In addition, numerous treaties regulated or forbade altogether the use of reprisals as based on the principle of collective responsibility.[2] But one of the most efficacious remedies lay in enacting laws providing for punishment of individuals committing acts injurious to foreign States. We find at the end of the seventeenth century orders issued by the King of England forbidding English subjects to enlist in the service of foreign rulers or to assist the rebels of a foreign prince.[3] It is the interest of commerce and peace that lies at the origin of the old rule of common law which stamps as a criminal offence the commission of acts calculated to disturb the amity between England and a foreign Power. This motive is frequently referred to in judicial decisions, in formal indictments before courts of justice, and in utterances of statesmen.[4] The same applies to other countries. The Criminal Code of Maria Theresa enacted that higher punishment should be meted out to those responsible for such libellous publications as tended to disturb the external peace of the State.[5] In the Dutch Act of 1816 which introduced penalties for acts injurious to foreign States, the main motive which inspired the legislator was described as 'l'intérêt . . . qu'il y a de prévenir tout

[1] *A Dig. ad L. Jul. Maj.* (48, 4).

[2] Cf. Article 14 of the Treaty of 8 July 1670 between Great Britain and Spain (Hertslet's *Commercial Treaties*, 2, 198).

[3] Cf. Holdsworth, *A History of English Law* (1924), 6, 308.

[4] Cf. the judgments in *R.* v. *Peltier*, *R.* v. *Vint*, *Reg* v. *Jameson*, *R.* v. *Antonelli and Barberi* – all referred to below; Sir G. Grey, 115 *H.C. Deb.* 1s., p. 885; Lord Lyndhurst, 124 *H.C. Deb.* 1s., p. 1046; Attorney-General, 148 *H.C. Deb.* 1s., p. 1823; Gladstone, 215 *H.C. Deb.* 3s., pp. 634, 891.

[5] Article 101, § 8.

ce qui pouvait causer de l'animosité ou de l'aigreur entre les puissances'.[1] Passages of this kind will be found in the numerous German Codes at the beginning of the nineteenth century which provided for penalties for such offences.[2] When, after the French Revolution, the non-extradition of political offenders became a general rule, the same considerations of peace acted as an additional reason for introducing legislation against refugees using the territory of the State granting asylum as a base for designs likely to engage its international responsibility.

The reason why, out of this common origin of protection granted to foreign States, rules have evolved varying so largely from country to country lies in the circumstance that their *rationale*, namely, the considerations of peace, has worked in a different way in relation to different countries. In fact, as a measure of international obligation this reason is now of purely historical importance. Born out of the uncertainties of international life in the formative period of international law, it has been subsequently defined in more detail, and partly deprived of its original character, as a result both of a clearer conception of international duties of the State and of the working of several other important factors. Some of these factors may be mentioned here: States with advanced institutions and with a democratic and progressive form of government will not and have not been eager to protect foreign Governments and constitutions more than is absolutely necessary. On the other hand, reactionary Governments are ready, with characteristic solidarity, to offer a large measure of protection in order to ensure by reciprocal arrangements equal security for themselves and to inculcate in their subjects the principles of legitimacy and constitutionalism. Revolutionary Governments of precarious standing, menaced in turn by subversive designs, will be apt to demand and willing to concede an extended protection, while countries with a well-established Government will remain foreign to such considerations. Powerful States will successfully resist exaggerated foreign demands for repressing plots and conspiracies against their neighbours; weak communities, otherwise of a democratic and tolerant disposition, will be driven by threats and pressure to a submissive attitude of repression and to excessive vigilance both in legislation and in practice.

As a result of the operation of these divergent factors, the following three systems have been evolved:

(*a*) The Anglo-American group based on the principle of neutrality;

(*b*) The German-Austrian-Russian system (partly applied in South and Central America) closely resembling a system of mutual insurance;

[1] Quoted after Fick, *Gerrichtssaal*, p. 82.

[2] Cf. for instance, *Allgemeines Preussisches Landrecht*, Part II, 20, §§ 135, 136.

(*c*) The Latin group, which may be described as a reference back to international law.

(1) *The principle of neutrality*

In this group, the duty of the State is assimilated to that arising out of the position of neutrality. Two fundamental consequences flow from this principle. One is the rigid distinction between the duties of the State as such and those of its subjects. This means that whereas the State itself is prohibited by international law from committing acts amounting to assisting revolutionary movements abroad, its subjects are not, with one exception, so prohibited. The second is that, in consequence of that exception, private persons are forbidden by municipal law, enacted in performance of a clear international duty, from committing such acts as amount to making the national territory a base for military or naval operations against a friendly State. Further than this the international duty of the State does not go, with the exception, of course, of the obligation to prevent and to punish certain common crimes which will be mentioned later; further than this the duties of the subject under municipal law do not go.

Great Britain

Conspiracies, plots and treasonable practices against foreign States are not punishable under the law of England, except when they are related in certain special ways to the common crime of murder, or when they amount to levying war against a Power at amity with this country, i.e., unless they fall within the scope of sections 11 and 12 of the Foreign Enlistment Act of 1870. This Act, which is an amended and enlarged restatement of the Act of 1819,[1] is described as 'An Act to regulate the Conduct of Her Majesty's Subjects during the Existence of Hostilities between Foreign States with which Her Majesty is at Peace.' Although it is primarily a measure of neutrality in wars between third Powers, section 11, which constitutes a new feature of the Act of 1870, relates equally to times of peace and war. It provides that any person engaged in fitting out or in the preparation of a naval or military expedition to proceed against the dominions of any friendly State, or assisting therein or employed in any capacity in such expedition, shall be guilty of an offence against the Act and shall be punishable by fine and imprisonment. According to section 12, any person who aids, abets, counsels or procures the commission of any offence against the Act shall be punished as a principal offender. It appears from the two cases decided

[1] For a history of the British Neutrality and Foreign Enlistment Acts, see Phillimore, III, § 146, and Wheeler, *Foreign Enlistment Act, 1870*, pp. 15–18, 22–6.

subsequent to the passing of the Act that the courts do not shrink from giving an extensive interpretation to this section in the interest, as they repeatedly point out, of the maintenance of friendly relations with foreign Powers. Thus it has been held that it is not necessary that the expedition should be completed in this country, and that it is sufficient if the offence originated here;[1] that the offence is completed whether the expedition has or has not in fact proceeded;[2] and that it is even not necessary that an attempt should be made to overthrow the Government, and that an expedition within the meaning of the Act is one which intends either by actual force or by show of force to interfere with the constitution, government, law or administration of a foreign State.[3] Apart, however, from hostile expeditions, the criminal law does not prohibit subscriptions and loans in aid of revolutions in foreign countries, although it appears that contracts arising out of transactions of this kind are illegal and incapable of enforcement in an English court.[4]

With regard to such activities of a revolutionary character as assume the form of attacks in print against the person of foreign sovereigns, it was laid down in several cases at the end of the eighteenth and at the beginning of the nineteenth century that publications tending to degrade, to revile and to defame persons 'in considerable situations of power and dignity in foreign countries' may, as calculated to embroil this country with foreign Powers, be taken and treated as libels.[5] However, it is believed that the rule enunciated in these cases and now rather indiscriminately referred to in text-books as expressive of the existing law, should be read in the light both of the special circumstances of its origin and of the now obtaining conceptions of the freedom of the press and of expression of opinion. It was stated in a comparatively recent case[6] that not all publications against foreign

[1] *R.* v. *Sandoval*, 3 T.L.R. 411, 436. See also, before the passing of this Act, *Reg.* v. *Granatelli* (1849), 7 State Trials, new series, p. 1026.

[2] *Reg.* v. *Sandoval*, quoted above.

[3] *Reg.* v. *Jameson*, 12 T.L.R. 551.

[4] *Demetrius de Wütz* v. *Hendricks* (1824), 9 Moo. 586; *Thompson* v. *Barclay* (1831), Coop. Pr. C. 501; *Thompson* v. *Powles*, 25 Sim. 194; and the American case *Kennett, et al.* v. *Chambers*, 14 How. 38, and Scott, *Cases* (1922), p. 893. The limited scope of this article does not permit an examination of the legal bases of this rule, whose origin is obscure. The writer believes that the effect of the two first-mentioned cases has been frequently overestimated, and that it owes its origin to an unduly extensive interpretation of the rule that an unrecognized foreign Government cannot sue before an English court: *City of Berne* v. *Bank of England* (1804), 9 Ves. Jr. 347; *Jones* v. *Garcia del Rio* (1823), Turn & R. 296. Cf. here also Scott, *Cases*, p. 901, note; Pitt Cobbett, *Cases* (4th ed. by Bellot, 1924), II, 498; Westlake, I, 252. For a more correct statement of the law see the speech of Gladstone, as advised by the Law Officers (215 *H.C. Deb.* 3s., pp. 634, 897) in the matter of subscriptions in aid of Spanish Carlist revolutionaries. Cf. also the Law Officers' opinion in 1823 (printed in Phillimore, III, appendix x).

[5] *R.* v. *Peltier* (1803), 28 State Trials, p. 529; *R.* v. *Vint* (1799), 22 State Trials, p. 627.

[6] *R.* v. *Antonelli and Barberi* (1905), 70 J.P. 4.

Governments constitute criminal libel. Phillimore J. (as he then was) delivering judgment in this case, said:

> Seditious libels are such as tend to disturb the government of this country, and in my opinion a document published here, which was calculated to disturb the government of some foreign country, is not a seditious libel, nor punishable as libel at all . . . To hold otherwise . . . would make our great statesmen guilty of seditious libel, and those persons also who espoused the cause of Italian liberty.

Revolutionary activities frequently assume the form of preparations aiming at assassination of the head or the members of the Government of a foreign State. The law of England does not countenance this kind of revolutionary action. According to section 4 of the Offences against the Person Act of 1861,[1] 'all persons who shall conspire, confederate, and agree to murder any person, whether he be a subject of her Majesty or not, and whether he be within the Queen's dominions or not, and whosoever shall solicit, encourage, persuade or endeavour to persuade, or shall propose to any person, to murder any other person, whether he be a subject of her Majesty or not, and whether he be within the Queen's dominions or not', shall be guilty of a misdemeanor and, on conviction, punished by penal servitude. There are instances of prosecution and conviction under this section.[2] The same Act affirmed the well-established statutory rule that a British subject who is an accessory before or after the fact to murder committed abroad may be tried and punished as for the principal offence (section 9). And it appears, both on principle and according to clear judicial pronouncements, that the term 'subject' is here meant to signify persons owing permanent as well as temporary allegiance to the Crown.[3]

The United States of America

The law of the United States is, with regard to the subject under discussion, confined almost exclusively to hostile expeditions. Similarly as in Great Britain, it forms part of the neutrality law; and the expression 'Neutrality Act' does not, here also, necessarily imply the existence of a state of belligerency. The Act of 1917 gave the following formulation to the relevant provision of the criminal law of the United States:

> Whoever, within the territory or jurisdiction of the United States or any of its possessions, knowingly begins or sets on foot or provides or prepares a means for or furnishes the money for, or who takes part in, any military or naval expedition or enterprise to be carried on from thence against the

[1] 24 & 25 Vict. c. 100.

[2] *Reg.* v. *Most* (1881), 7 Q.B.D. 244; *R.* v. *Antonelli and Barberi* (1905), 70 J.P. 4.

[3] *Reg.* v. *Sandoval,* 3 T.L.R. 411.

territory or dominion of any foreign prince or State, or of any colony, district or people with whom the United States is at peace, shall be fined not more than $3,000 or imprisoned not more than three years or both.[1]

The gist of this section was incorporated in the Neutrality laws of 1794 and 1818, and amended several times in the course of the last century. In applying the law relating to hostile expeditions, American courts have not, on the whole, shown an inclination to extend unduly the restrictions placed upon American citizens.[2] They insist on strict proof that the purpose of the alleged offence was some attack or invasion, *from the territory of the United States*, of another country as a military force. It has been repeatedly held that assistance rendered to expeditions proceeding from other countries is not illegal, and that the existence of an expedition from the United States is a condition precedent to the existence of accessories.[3] This seems to be the main characteristic feature of the obtaining law. However, the presence of this requirement once established, the law is strictly applied to different kinds of participation in criminal offences of this kind.[4] But the courts will refuse to suppress revolutionary activities so long as they are confined to moral agitation,[5] or to interfere with publications criticizing foreign Governments or encouraging revolt against them. Neither have the federal courts the power to punish libels or seditious publications against foreign sovereigns or incitement to assassination of persons residing abroad.[6] But it appears that, at least in some of the States, the courts will take cognizance of conspiracies to commit common crimes abroad.[7]

[1] Section 8 of the Act of 15 June 1917 (*A.J.* 11 (1917), Suppl., 186).

[2] The law of the United States is exhaustively treated in the scholarly monographs of Fenwick and Curtis (referred to above), and it is therefore not necessary to discuss it here in detail.

[3] *U.S.* v. *O'Sullivan*, Fed. Cas. 15975; *U.S.* v. *Ybanez*, 53 Fed. 536; *U.S.* v. *Nunez*, 82 Fed. 599; *U.S.* v. *Trumbull*, 48 Fed. 99, 103; *The Itata*, 49 Fed. 646. See also H. Ex. Doc. no. 74, 25th Cong., 2nd Sess., p. 7, and Cushing, Attorney-General in 8 *Op. Att. Gen.*, 216. Neither does the Neutrality Act prohibit the shipping of arms or ammunition to a foreign country or forbid individuals from leaving the United States, singly or in unarmed associations, to join in any military operations: *U.S.* v. *Pena* (1895), 69 Fed. 983. The laws of the United States make it a penal offence secretly to transport any explosive from the United States to any foreign country (see Moore, II, § 221). See also the Joint Resolution of the Congress of 14 March 1912 empowering the President to declare unlawful the exportation of arms to any American country where 'conditions of domestic violence exist which are prompted by the use of arms and munitions of war procured from the United States'.

[4] Some cases which came before the American courts in the course of the Cuban insurrection offer interesting instances of frustrated attempts at defeating by ingenious devices the ends of the neutrality law. See, e.g., the much cited case of *The Horsa* (*Wiborg* v. *U.S.*, 163 U.S. 632, 655).

[5] *United States* v. *Lumsden*, 1 Bond 5.

[6] Wharton, I, § 56; III, § 389.

[7] Moore, II, § 221.

(2) *The system of mutual insurance*

In the States which have adopted this system, revolutionary acts of a treasonable character against a foreign Government are treated as criminal offences. Here also writers and legislators refer to the necessity of preserving the external peace of the State as the main motive underlying the enactments in question, while some appeal to sentiments of international solidarity. However, to judge from the historical antecedents and the individual provisions of the relevant codes, especially from the requirement of reciprocity, this attitude appears to be the product of a policy calculated to ensure the stability of the particular State's own Government.

According to Article 102 of the German Penal Code, a German who either at home or abroad, or a foreigner who during his residence in Germany, undertakes an act against a State not belonging to the German Empire which if committed against the German Empire or a federal State would be punished as treason in the meaning of the code, shall be liable to imprisonment up to ten years. The range of these treasonable acts is certainly a wide one. For according to Articles 81 and 85 of the code, it is not only assassination or attempts at assassination of crowned persons, or attempts to alter by force the constitution of the Empire or of a federal State that rank as treason, but also direct incitement, by speech or publications, to committing such acts.[1] The operation of these provisions is made contingent upon the fulfilment of three conditions: Firstly, there must be a reciprocal arrangement of the foreign State with Germany; secondly, proceedings only take place at the request of the foreign Government; thirdly, the request, which may be withdrawn, must be maintained up to the end of the proceedings.[2] The provisions of the Austrian Penal Code of 1852 are of a similar character.[3] This code is still binding in Austria and, it appears, in some of the new States composed wholly or in part of territories formerly belonging to the Austrian Empire. The Russian Penal Code of 1903 was the most reactionary of all.[4] It threatened with punishment not only all attempts, in Russian territory, to overthrow a foreign Government, but also conspiracies and preparations leading up to such attempts, and even participation in organizations working for such objects. And it is not without interest to note that the principle under-

[1] Cf. Liszt, *Lehrbuch des deutschen Strafrechts* (18th ed. 1911), § 170.

[2] The writer is not aware of any movement in favour of altering this part of the code. It appears that the draft codes of 1919 published by the Federal Ministry of Justice follow closely the wording of Article 102. See *Entwürfe zu einem deutschen Strafgesetzbuch* (1920).

[3] Article 66.

[4] § 135. It was a reproduction of § 260 of the Criminal Code of 1858.

lying this kind of legislation has now been introduced into the criminal law of Soviet Russia. In a decree promulgated on 25 February 1927, defining offences against the State and anti-revolutionary crimes, such acts are included in the latter designation as are directed against a State of workers even if that State does not belong to the Union of Soviet Socialist Republics.[1] The provisions of the old Russian code are still binding in several States formerly constituting a part of the Russian Empire, especially in Poland.[2]

Some of the South and Central American Republics, much troubled as they were by internal revolutions, approach this type of legislation. Thus the Penal Code of Peru, of 1924, makes it an offence not only to violate the territorial sovereignty of a foreign State by performing there acts of sovereignty and by invading it in violation of international law (§297), but also to commit acts calculated to alter by force the political order of other States.

(3) *Reference back to international law*

The criminal codes of the countries belonging to this group do not state *expressis verbis* what are the acts which are deemed likely to disturb the external peace of the State and which are accordingly prohibited by law. They content themselves with stigmatizing as crimes such acts as are described as being against international law, or as exposing the country to the danger of war or reprisals, or, in general, as compromising its foreign relations. Whatever may be the propriety of describing certain acts of individuals as 'offences against the Law of Nations', there is no doubt that the municipal law of States belonging to this group views them as such, and that it thus offers a typical example of the adoption, for certain specific purposes, of rules of international law as a part of the law of the land. On the other hand, it seems that this altogether general reference to an extraneous and largely undefined system of law is liable to render very difficult the enforcement of the legal rules in question.

The French Criminal Code may be taken as a good illustration of this group. Articles 84 and 85 of the *Code Pénal* provide that a person shall be liable to punishment who by a hostile act not approved by the Government has exposed the State to a declaration of war, or the State

[1] See Ljublinski, in *Zeitschrift für Ostrecht*, I (1927), 325. On the other hand, Article 21 of the Soviet Constitution of 10 July 1918 and Article 12 of the Soviet Constitution of 11 May 1925 open the doors of Soviet Russia to foreigners prosecuted for political and religious crimes.

[2] Makowski, *Kodeks karny, etc.* (1921), II, 140. Belgium, yielding in part to foreign pressure, enacted in 1858 a law by which she adopted to a large extent the principles underlying the corresponding provisions of the codes in Germany, Austria and Russia.

or a French citizen to reprisals. There is, so far as these two articles are concerned, no case of conviction on record,[1] and only in one case was the prosecution proceeded with. It is a matter of controversy whether these articles relate at all to offences against foreign States, and if they do, whether the expression 'hostile acts' applies only to overt acts connected with the organization of military attacks,[2] or to revolutionary propaganda and conspiracies in general. Writers of authority express the opinion that the two articles are without practical application and that they are bound to remain a dead letter.[3] This position was clearly illustrated in November 1926 by the occurrences arising out of an attempted revolutionary expedition of about 400 Spaniards and Italians into Spain. After the French authorities had speedily and efficiently frustrated the plan and arrested about 130 persons, it transpired that they were uncertain as to what charge should be proffered against the arrested filibusters. Of those arrested, about one hundred were subsequently expelled from France, whereas against twenty-six legal proceedings were taken under a law of 1834 which makes it a criminal offence unlawfully to manufacture, possess or distribute arms or munitions of war, and under a law of 1893 which extended that offence to explosives or lethal engines acting by explosion.[4] Very critical also are the Italian writers in their comments upon their own code.[5] It provides, in Article 113, that any person shall be liable to punishment who by enlistment or other hostile acts unauthorized by the Government exposes the State to the danger of war or reprisals, or, in general, who disturbs the friendly relations between the Italian Government and a foreign State. The Spanish Criminal Code punishes such acts as compromise the external peace of the State or as violate the Law of Nations.[6] The provisions of the Norwegian and Swiss Criminal Codes are of a similar character.[7]

[1] For an account of several cases of abortive prosecution cf. appendix 4 to the Report of the Neutrality Law Commissioners, Great Britain, *Reports from Commissions*, 32 (1867–8), 45; Garraud, quoted below, nos. 837 and 839, and Clunet in *Journal*, quoted above, pp. 13, 14.

[2] This appears to be the almost unanimous opinion of French writers. See, for instance, Garraud, *Traité du droit pénal français* (1899), III, § 841.

[3] *Ibid.* § 837; Clunet, in *Journal*, and Pradier-Fodéré, I, § 238.

[4] *The Times* newspaper, 15 November 1926.

[5] Cf. Manzini, *Trattato di diritto penale italiano* (1911), IV, nos. 1014 *et seq.*, where the matter is treated exhaustively and with great learning.

[6] §§ 148, 153, 154.

[7] Articles 85 and 41 respectively. As to the Swiss legislation and practice see Stooss, *Die Grundzüge des schweizerischen Strafrechts* (1893), II, § 125, who criticizes the vagueness of Article 41; Fleiner, *Schweizerisches Bundesstaatsrecht* (1923), p. 748, and Salis, *Schweizerisches Bundesrecht* (2nd ed. 1903), IV, nos. 2044–66 (revolutionary propaganda against foreign States) and nos. 2048, 2050, 2066, 2075, 2078 (approval of assassination).

3. INTERNATIONAL CONVENTIONS

A survey of conventional international law bearing upon the subject shows that treaties providing for an extensive measure of protection, a measure wider than that which is put forward in this article as the accepted standard of international obligation, are few and of an altogether exceptional character. They are mainly conventions concluded by revolutionary Governments or Governments of countries suffering chronically from revolutionary commotions, both seeking, for an adequate *quid pro quo*, to attain additional security from revolutionary designs coming from abroad.

The treaties concluded by the revolutionary British Government under Cromwell offer an early illustration of this type of compact. In the Treaty of 11 April 1654 between Great Britain and Sweden the contracting parties bound themselves to 'take care of, and promote the welfare of each other; and . . . advertise each other, upon knowledge thereof, of all imminent dangers, plots and conspiracies of enemies against the other; and, as much as in them lies, oppose and hinder the same'.[1] Similar obligations were assumed at that period in the treaties of Great Britain with Denmark,[2] Portugal,[3] and Spain.[4]

Victorious Napoleonic France was anxious to insert in her treaties detailed provisions intended to protect her from conspiracies on the part of her royalist subjects abroad. Thus the Treaty of Paris, of 8 October 1801, between France and Russia provided in Article III:

> The two Contracting Parties . . . engage not to suffer their respective subjects to maintain any correspondence, direct or indirect, with the enemies of the present Government of the two States, or to propagate principles contrary to their respective constitutions, or to foment disturbances, and that in consequence of this Agreement, every subject of one of those Powers inhabiting the states of the other, who shall do anything to its safety, shall be removed from the said country and transported beyond its frontiers without having any claim to the protection of its own Government.[5]

In the course of the nineteenth and twentieth centuries, the South and Central American States, suffering acutely on account of frequent revolutions, enriched conventional international law on this subject by numerous treaties calculated to prevent the territories of neighbouring

[1] Article II; Hertslet's *Commercial Treaties*, 2, 310.
[2] Article V of the Treaty of 13 February 1660; *ibid.* 1, 179.
[3] Article I of the Treaty of 19 July 1654; *ibid.* 2, 9.
[4] Article II of the Treaty of 13 May 1667; *ibid.* 2, 140.
[5] Article I, Martens, R., VII, 386.

States from becoming a basis for hostile expeditions or hostile attempts in general.[1]

After the World War, Soviet Russia, presenting in this respect a close analogy to revolutionary France, concluded a series of treaties with a view to curbing the revolutionary activities of the opponents of the Soviet Government residing abroad, as well as to affording to the other contracting party some assurance as to the revolutionary propaganda emanating from the territory of Soviet Russia. Thus Article VII of the Peace Treaty of 2 February 1920, between Soviet Russia and Esthonia provides that both parties undertake 'to prohibit the creation and presence in their territories of organizations and groups which claim to be the Government of the territory, or a part of the territory of the other contracting party, or of representations and officials of such groups and organizations as aim at the overthrow of the Government of the other contracting party'.[2] Similar provisions are contained in the treaties concluded by Soviet Russia with Latvia,[3] Mongolia,[4] Persia,[5] Turkey,[6] and Japan.[7] But it appears that the Soviets are not prepared to enter into such engagements with other Powers.[8]

It is believed that the treaties to which attention has been drawn in this section are entirely outside the circle of those contractual relations which are the outcome of normal intercourse between nations. They tend to confirm the proposition that there is nothing, so far as conventional international law is concerned, to warrant the assertion that States have assumed the obligation to protect their neighbours from every conceivable kind of revolutionary design directed against them.

[1] See the Treaty between Peru and Ecuador of 16 March 1853 and between Peru and Bolivia of 19 April 1840 (both referred to by Pradier-Fodéré, I, § 238). More recent treaties are, however, less exacting. The duties of the contracting parties are here confined to prevention of hostile expeditions proper and recruitments. See, e.g., the Treaty between Bolivia, Colombia, Ecuador, Peru and Venezuela of 18 July 1911, in *R.G.* 19 (1912), 345. The considerations of mutual insurance which frequently underlie these treaties are well expressed in Article XVI of the General Treaty of Peace and Amity of 20 December 1907 concluded between the five Central American Republics (*A.J.* 2 (1908), Suppl., 226).

[2] The Treaty is printed in *Russlands Friedens- und Handelsverträge* (ed. by Freund, 1924), p. 49.

[3] Article IV (2) of the Treaty of 11 August 1920, *ibid.* p. 99.

[4] Article III of the Treaty of 3 November 1921, *ibid.* p. 130.

[5] Article IV of the Treaty of 25 February 1921, *ibid.* p. 144.

[6] Article VIII of the Treaty of 16 March 1921, *ibid.* p. 190.

[7] Article V of the Treaty of 20 January 1925, Martens, N.R.G., 3rd ser., XV, 324.

[8] When, at the International Economic Conference at Genoa in 1922, Russia was asked to suppress the attempts to assist revolutionary movements in other countries, the Russian delegation replied that the Soviets are not willing to curb the activities of political parties and workers. Cf. 1922 (Cmd. 1667). Similar treaties concluded by Soviet Russia with other states – e.g., the Preliminary Treaty of Peace between Poland and Russia of October, 1920 (*L.N.T.S.* 4, 35), or the unratified General Treaty between Great Britain and Russia signed at London on 8 August 1924 (1924) Cmd. 2260 – relate to subversive activities originating from the Government itself, from its organs, or persons and organizations assisted and subsidized by it. They are outside the scope of the present article.

4. INTERNATIONAL INCIDENTS

While the obligation of the State to prevent its territory from becoming a base for organized armed insurrection against foreign countries has never been seriously challenged, the claim to protection from revolutionary propaganda and conspiracies in general has been constantly repudiated by States whose constitutional principles did not allow an excessive measure of compliance with the requirements of the safety of foreign Governments, and which were at the same time in a position to resist political pressure from abroad. Reasons of space permit to mention here only a few instances illustrating this proposition. They are taken from the history of the three States which came into closer grips with this problem, i.e., Great Britain, the United States and Switzerland.

Great Britain

To judge from the bulk of the correspondence which preceded the British and French declarations of war in 1803, the complaints of France on account of the activities of the French royalists in England were one of the principal reasons which contributed to the estrangement of relations between the two Governments.[1] France complained that royalist refugees caused seditious publications to be distributed in that country, and that French bishops counteracted, from the safe soil of England, the ecclesiastical reforms introduced by the Emperor. Indignation was even expressed at the royalists being allowed openly to wear French orders which no longer existed.[2] As to the attacks on the French Government in the press and in political pamphlets, it was maintained that, although the liberty of the press with regard to internal affairs may be unlimited, it is the duty of the Government to punish and to repress such publications as cause injury to the interests and to the honor of foreign States. Throughout the controversy, the British Government refused to admit that the Law of Nations countenances demands of this kind. It was emphatic in pointing out that, being itself frequently exposed to abuse in prints which it had neither the power nor the desire to punish, it was not willing to depart from this policy in deference to the interests or wishes of a foreign Power.[3] As to the suggestion that the recently passed Aliens Act gave to it the power to expel aliens at discretion, the characteristic reply was that the Act was passed for the protection of Great Britain, and not for that of other countries.

[1] Cf. the official *Moniteur* of 9 August 1802.

[2] Dispatch of Mr Merry to Lord Hawkesbury on 4 June 1802, *Annual Register* (1803), p. 656, and note of M. Otto to Lord Hawkesbury on 25 June 1802, *ibid.* p. 660.

[3] Lord Hawkesbury to Mr Merry on 17 June 1802, *ibid.* p. 658; the same to M. Otto, on 17 August 1802, *ibid.* p. 661, and on 28 August 1802, *ibid.* p. 664.

Even more instructive is the correspondence which took place in 1852 between the British Government, on one side, and Austria, France, Prussia, Russia, the German Confederation and the Kingdom of the Two Sicilies, on the other. The Continental Powers demanded that Great Britain should repress the revolutionary activities of the numerous bodies of foreign political refugees organized in this country. This the British Government consistently refused to do unless it could be shown that these activities amounted to the common law offence of levying war against a friendly Power, i.e., to organizing a hostile expedition. The complaining Powers urged that there were other undertakings against the security of foreign States than levying war against them. They illustrated this by pointing to the fact that Italian refugees issued in London a loan the produce of which was destined to purchase arms and munitions with the avowed purpose of fomenting civil war in Italy; that proclamations had been issued in London calling the Continental peoples to arms; and that the refugees attempted to spread among the armies of the Powers seditious writings with the view to shaking the allegiance of troops.[1] The British Government, however, did not recede from the position originally adopted, and the British note which concluded the correspondence contained an affirmation, wrapped in language of sympathetic understanding, of the original British attitude. It undertook to discourage and to repress the revolutionary activities so far as law and constitution warrant.[2] A year later Lord Palmerston gave expression, in a form even less ambiguous, to the sentiments of the British Government on the matter: 'The British Government has never undertaken to provide for the internal security of other countries; it is sufficient for them to have the power to provide for the internal security of their own.'[3] The consistency with which this attitude was maintained by Great Britain is the more instructive as a different practice would have enabled successive British Governments to press with more vigour their complaints with the United States on account of the Irish and Fenian activities conducted from that country. It seems that Great Britain, in her correspondence with the United States, was prepared to admit that so far as hostile propaganda and revolutionary activities

[1] Correspondence between Great Britain, France etc., respecting Foreign Refugees in London (1851, 1852), *Br. and For. St. Papers*, 42, 401–5, 430 *et seq.*

[2] The Earl of Malmesbury to Count Buol, *ibid.* p. 439.

[3] In the House of Commons on 1 March 1853 (124 *H.C. Deb.* 3s., p. 815). The opinion may be ventured that the statement of the law on the subject as laid down a few days later by Lord Lyndhurst, supported by Lord Brougham and Lord Truro, and defining in very wide terms the duty of private persons to refrain from revolutionary attempts against foreign States (*ibid.* p. 1046) was made with the view to influencing the political refugees and strengthening the hands of the Government, and that its contents and spirit find no confirmation either in the judicial or political practice of Great Britain.

falling short of preparations for a hostile expedition are concerned, a State is not bound to accede to requests the fulfilment of which is incompatible with its laws and constitution.[1]

The United States

The practice of the United States resembles that of Great Britain. In answering complaints, the Department of State refers as a rule to the municipal law of the United States which does not punish revolutionary proceedings until they have reached their natural consummation, namely, interference or overt attempts at interference in the affairs of other countries by organized acts of force. The British inquiry in 1885 as to the legality in the United States of participating in the Irish National League, an organization to promote insurrection in Ireland, was answered to the effect that the United States punished treason only against its own country, but not against other countries.[2] A similar answer was made to the complaints of Spain in the same year: 'It (the United States) does not assume to visit with penalty conduct, which if committed within a foreign jurisdiction, might be punished therein.'[3]

[1] See Lord Palmerston's note of 30 September 1848 (Ex. Doc. no. 19. House of Repr., 30th Cong., 2nd Sess., 4, 21). As to the activities in London after 1848 of the sundry revolutionary bodies, like the Committee of Central European Democracy, the Central Democratic European Committee, the Central National Italian Committee, and the Central Committee of Italian Refugees, see memorandum to the note of Count Walewski, of October 1851, House of Commons, *Bills and Papers* (1852) LIV, 49 *et seq.* There should also be noted the attempted expeditions in 1846 and 1847 against Ecuador and Portugal respectively (see Report of the Neutrality Law Commissioners, appendix no. 3, p. 38, *Reports from Commissions* (1867–8), XXXII, 24); the frustrated expeditions against Spain from England and Gibraltar in 1830 (*Br. and For. St. Papers*, 24, 812 *et seq.*); the much quoted Terceira affair in 1827 (the entire correspondence is reprinted in the *Annual Register* (1829), pp. 435–71); the Carlist activities in 1874 (see 215 *H.C. Deb.* 3s., p. 634); and the preparations of the Portuguese royalists in 1911 (Fauchille, I, Part I, no. 295).

[2] Secretary Bayard to the British representative on 2 April 1885; Moore, II § 221.

[3] Secretary Bayard to Mr Valera on 31 July 1885; For. Rel. (1885), p. 776. See also President Cleveland's fourth Annual Message to the Congress referring to the Spanish demands arising out of the revolutionary activities of the supporters of the Cuban insurrection: 'Many Cubans reside in this country and indirectly promote the insurrection through the press, by public meetings, by the purchase and shipment of arms, by the raising of funds, and by other means which the spirit of our institutions and the tenor of our laws do not permit to be made the subject of criminal prosecution' (Richardson, *Messages*, IX, p. 718).

Valuable references, especially with regard to cases which came before the courts of the United States, will be found in the monographs of Fenwick and Curtis referred to above. Apart from this, the following references to some of the incidents which gave rise to diplomatic correspondence may be found useful: the United States were involved in 1835 in diplomatic correspondence with Mexico in consequence of the support given by American citizens to revolutionaries in Texas (H. Ex. Doc. no. 74, 25th Cong., 2nd Sess.); with Great Britain in connection with the Canadian rebellion in 1837 and the activities of Fenian societies and Irish insurgents: Curtis, in *A.J.* 8, 1–37, 224–52, pp. 25, 242; For. Rel. (1865–6), I, 572; *ibid.* II, 96, 103; *ibid.* (1866–7), I, 25, 69–97; Moore, II, § 221; with Spain in consequence of the hostile expeditions to Cuba from 1849 to 1851, in 1868, in 1873 and from 1884 up to the Spanish-American War: Fenwick, *The Neutrality Laws*, p. 45; H. Ex. Doc. no. 160, 41st Cong., 2nd Sess., p. 133; For. Rel. (1871), pp. 778–91; *ibid.* (1874), pp. 117 *et seq.*; *ibid.* (1875), pp. 1158–256; *ibid.* (1884), pp. 493–521; *ibid.* (1885), pp. 767–73; *ibid.* (1887),

Switzerland

The practice of Switzerland is different from that of the United States and Great Britain. There is here no departure from the principle of granting asylum to political offenders, but hospitality is afforded subject to the condition that the alien refugee will abstain from such revolutionary activities as may compromise the international relations of Switzerland. Thus we find the Swiss federal authorities expelling in 1879 a German journalist for having published in a Socialist paper an article reproaching the German Socialists on account of their inactivity and exhorting them to more energetic propaganda.[1] The same fate, for a similar offence, befell in 1888 four editors of the organ of the German Socialist Party published in Switzerland.[2] These are only two instances of the regular practice followed by Swiss judicial and administrative authorities.[3] The final adoption of this policy was brought about mainly by two factors. The first is that, apart from the vague provision of Article 41 of the Penal Code, Switzerland possesses no laws dealing with hostile expeditions proper, and that the penalty of expulsion was applied alike to all kinds of hostile action, from a hostile expedition *stricto sensu* to the publication of a relatively innocuous pamphlet. The unusually lenient treatment of the former offence was balanced by harsh interference with mere expression of opinion and propaganda. The second factor was that Switzerland, being politically and economically dependent upon her neighbours, was frequently driven by external pressure to measures foreign to the spirit of her institutions. What, however, was originally acquiesced in only with considerable reluctance, had by the end of the nineteenth century developed with many Swiss writers into an *opinio necessitatis*.[4] While disclaiming any intention of relinquishing

pp. 1026, 1029, 1471–3; Olivart, in *R.G.* 5, 499–518; with Nicaragua in 1885: Moore, VII, § 1300; with Honduras and Nicaragua in 1866: For. Rel. (1868), II, pp. 536–45; again with Mexico in 1868, 1872, 1877, 1878, 1893 and 1912: For. Rel. (1868–9), II, pp. 534, 574, 633–9; *ibid.* (1877), p. 405; *ibid.* (1878), pp. 674–84; *ibid.* (1893), pp. 425–35, 440–8; as to the insurrection in 1912, see Fenwick, *The Neutrality Laws*, pp. 56–8 and, in particular, For. Rel. (1912), pp. 240–2; with Colombia in 1885: For. Rel. (1885), pp. 23, 275; with Haiti in 1888 and 1889: *ibid.* (1888), pp. 988–90; with Chile in 1891: *ibid.* (1891), pp. 314–17; with Venezuela in 1892: *ibid.* (1892), pp. 624–34, 645–8; and with Honduras in 1885 and 1889: *ibid.* (1885), pp. 138–43 and 1899, pp. 364–70.

[1] The *Gehlsen* case, Salis, *Schweizerisches Bundesrecht*, IV, no. 2049.

[2] *Ibid.* no. 2064.

[3] For numerous cases from 1874 upwards, see *ibid.*, nos. 2035–88. For details as to diplomatic incidents arising out of revolutionary activities against France at the end of the eighteenth and at the beginning of the nineteenth century, see Danliker, *Geschichte der Schweiz*, III, 517–19, 585–7; for later instances up to 1870 see *Gastfreundschaft und Hausrecht der Schweiz* (1881), pp. 25, 26, 44–7, 57, 58. As to the activities, after the Congress at Vienna, of the democratic societies of 'Young Europe', 'Young Germany', 'Young Austria', and the like, see *Die geheimen deutschen Verbindungen in der Schweiz seit 1829* (Basle, 1823).

[4] See *Gastfreundschaft, etc.*, *passim*; Fleiner, *Schweizerisches Bundesstaatsrecht*, p. 49; Salis, *Schweizerisches Bundesrecht*, no. 2040.

the much cherished right of granting asylum to foreign political offenders, Swiss statesmen and publicists exhibit a marked apprehension – justified, no doubt, by the experiences of the past – lest the hospitality granted to foreigners be abused in a manner likely to embroil Switzerland with other Powers. However, beyond general statements of this kind, there is no attempt to define the exact measure of the international obligations of Switzerland in this respect. Much stress is laid on the necessity of avoiding friction with foreign Powers; the question is not gone into what kind of hostile acts may in law give cause for complaint.

It was only after prolonged resistance that Switzerland, yielding in 1823 to the pressure of Austria and of the Powers forming the Holy Alliance, enacted the first alien decree in which the Cantons were instructed to expel such refugees as abuse the right of asylum by engaging in machinations against the legitimate Governments of friendly States. The decree was repealed in 1829, but again introduced in 1836 as a result of the concerted action of Sardinia, Austria, France and the South German States on account of manifest preparations for the invasion of the territory of the latter, as well as of an unsuccessful raid of several hundred refugees into Savoy. Switzerland, acting under the threat of reprisals, had to comply with the demand of these Powers to the effect that not only actual accomplices should be expelled, but also all persons likely to disturb in the future their security or tranquillity.[1] In these alien decrees lies the origin of that elastic provision of the Federal constitution which threatens with expulsion aliens who endanger the external security of Switzerland. The Powers did not fail to take advantage of the latitude of this provision. France and Austria demanded in 1853 that Switzerland should undertake to expel such refugees as the diplomatic representatives of these countries may designate. Austria backed her demand by closing her Swiss frontier and by recalling her envoy. Although the Federation refused this particular request, it had to give assurances which again had the effect of extending the scope of its obligations.[2] No attempts were afterwards made to frame more detailed laws relating to hostile expeditions, and when in 1898 armed revolutionary groups of Italian subjects tried to invade from Switzerland the northern provinces of their country, 249 of these

[1] The entire correspondence in this matter between Switzerland and the Continental Powers is printed in *Br. and For. St. Papers*, 24 (1835–6), 979–1063, where instructive references will be found on what the Powers believed to be the rule of international law on the subject. 'Le Directoire Fédéral doit sentire que le premier des devoirs d'un Etat envers ses voisins est de ne pas devenir pour eux un objet d'inquiétude' – thus wrote Count Metternich in 1834.

[2] *Gastfreundschaft, etc.*, pp. 57–65.

insurgents were actually arrested and handed over to Italian troops guarding the frontier.[1]

5. CONCLUSIONS

The examination of the internal and international practice of States has shown that there is no common measure of agreement on the question as to the scope of state responsibility for preventing and repressing revolutionary acts of private persons against foreign States. What, then, is there, in default of a concordant practice, to guide our steps in extracting a working rule? It is the consideration that, there being no agreement on all the aspects of the problem, the rule of international law must necessarily be deduced from such minimum of concordant opinion and practice as exists on the matter. This rule could be formulated as follows:

International law imposes upon the State the duty of restraining persons resident within its territory from engaging in such revolutionary activities against friendly States as amount to organized acts of force in the form of hostile expeditions against the territory of those States. It also obliges the State to repress and to discourage activities in which attempts against the life of political opponents are regarded as a proper means of revolutionary action.

Apart from this, States are not bound to prohibit, on their territory, the commission of acts injurious to other States. In particular, revolutionary propaganda does not fall within the scope of revolutionary acts which a State is bound to prevent. The circumstance that even such States as prohibit in their penal codes *all* kinds of treasonable practice against foreign Powers do so subject to reciprocal arrangements with those Powers, is sufficient to show that the enactment of these penal provisions is not regarded as directly following from a precept of international law. States do not make the fulfilment of fundamental international obligations contingent upon express assurances of reciprocity.

The nearest approach to what is believed to be the true juridical construction of the State's duty to prevent organized hostile expeditions from proceeding in times of peace against a friendly State will be found in the law of neutrality. The law of neutrality, while enjoining upon the State itself absolute impartiality and abstention from assisting either belligerent, does not impose upon it the duty of securing an identical line of conduct on the part of its subjects. They may assist individually one or both belligerents in a variety of ways, as, for instance, by enlisting

[1] The Federal Assembly expressed its disapproval of the action of the Federal Council at whose instance this measure was taken. See Hilty in *Politisches Jahrbuch*, 12 (1898), 346 *et seq.*; Kebedgy in *R.G.* 5 (1898), 480–92; Salis, *Schweizerisches Bundesrecht*, no. 2082.

in their armies, by selling ships, munitions and provisions, by managing for them factories and depots, by transporting their goods and munitions, by supplying them with loans, etc. There is, however, one important exception to the liberty which the State may accord to its citizens: it must prevent them from committing such acts as would result in the neutral territory becoming directly a base for the military operations of either party. They must not build or fit out ships to the order of belligerents; they must not supply the belligerents' war vessels with coal and provisions in such a manner as to make the neutral ports a naval base of that belligerent; they must not leave the neutral territory in organized military units. In these two features of the law of neutrality – the distinction between the duties of States and those of their subjects, and the exclusion of neutral territory as a base for military or naval operations against a friendly State – lies also the main characteristic of the duty of States with regard to hostile expeditions in time of peace. This duty is not a consequence of the other State's right of independence which cannot, logically, in any way be interfered with or impaired by acts of individuals. It is the result of the well-established customary rule that the territory of a State must not be allowed to serve as a base for military or naval operations against another State. The two situations being closely analogous, it is only natural that they are regulated in Great Britain and in the United States in the same legal enactments. The law of hostile expeditions is nothing else than the law of neutrality in relation to an actual or impending civil war.

With regard to preparations and conspiracies to murder, it is believed that a State is fully entitled to claim from other members of the international community a reasonable measure of protection from this particular kind of revolutionary activity. In fact, most municipal systems of criminal law provide for punishment of conspiracies to assassinate persons abroad, or of incitement to assassination, or of participation in murders committed abroad. No unreasonable burden of specially protecting the life of foreigners abroad is thereby imposed upon a State. Its sole duty is to give to foreigners abroad, without distinction of person, the same security from assassination, not a greater or a special one, which it affords to those resident within its territory. This is a duty imposed by considerations higher than international solidarity. For assassination is, in international law, a crime even as between regular belligerents.

It will, of course, be observed that the rule that the State is responsible for such revolutionary acts of private individuals as it is bound to prevent is terminologically not quite exact. For the State is responsible for its own acts or omissions. It is originally responsible for having culpably omitted to prevent certain acts on the part of private persons. And it is vicariously responsible when, notwithstanding due diligence having been exercised by its authorities – for culpability is here as elsewhere a *conditio sine qua non* of liability, injurious acts have been perpetrated and the duty of the State is reduced to apprehending and meting out punishment to guilty individuals. But hostile acts having been committed, it is for the State to establish that no guilt can be attributed to it. Especially, it will not escape liability if its Government has failed to cause such laws to be enacted as would enable the administrative and judicial authorities effectively to prevent or repress the criminal act. International law is not concerned with the manner in which states elect to meet this particular duty of theirs. Great Britain and the United States may do it by means of well-defined rules relating to hostile expeditions; Germany may meet this particular obligation with the help of the very comprehensive provision punishing treasonable acts against foreign States; France may perform that duty by relying on her laws against unlawfully possessing and distributing arms and explosives. So long as these laws are reasonably sufficient to prevent hostile acts or to punish them after they have occurred, the State has performed its duty. But should it visit such offences by small fines, or, with regard to foreigners, by expulsion only, or should its laws be of such a nature that, notwithstanding their theoretical comprehensiveness, they are in fact incapable of enforcement, then again it will find it difficult to escape liability for hostile acts rendered more probable as a result of the leniency or technical shortcomings of its laws.

Apart from the two kinds of revolutionary action referred to above, international law imposes no further obligations. All other forms of revolutionary activity cannot, if coming solely from private individuals, furnish a legitimate cause of complaint. This being the state of the law, it may now be asked whether it is a satisfactory one. It is pointed out on the part of the advocates of a more vigorous protection of foreign Governments and constitutions that the unity of law and the growing solidarity between the members of the international community necessarily imply such a course. To this the answer must be that the international community is not, to use Westlake's expression, one of mutual insurance for the maintenance of established Governments. Treason is not an international crime. An active enemy of his Government is not an enemy of mankind. The principle of legitimacy introduced by the Holy Alliance is not part of modern international law, although it may have survived to a certain extent in one or two penal codes, and although some American republics may have recently found it necessary to revive it, to a limited extent, in a series of conventions and declarations based on the so-called Tabor doctrine. Neither does international law treat as outlaws individuals who, in a civil war, rise in arms against their Government. It grants them, under certain conditions, the status of belligerency and, according to the better opinion, stamps as unlawful intervention in aid of the established Government. International law flowing from international solidarity cannot mean that a State is bound to prevent anything which constitutes a danger to foreign States. Not every injury done to the interests of a foreign country constitutes a breach of international law. As between individuals, there must be not only *damnum*, but also *injuria*. A State must not be forced into the impossible position, dangerously approaching intervention, of a guardian of other States' constitutions and tranquillity. Foreign Governments themselves should secure this end, either by adequately enforcing their own laws or else by creating reasonable conditions for their firm establishment. A State cannot be saddled with the duty of actively protecting, to an extent in excess of the irreducible minimum, a constitution or a régime which may be either distasteful to the overwhelming majority of its own citizens, or a matter of complete indifference to them. The constitution is the first and highest law for the country in which it is in force, and it lies in the nature of things that acts and attempts calculated to overthrow it by unlawful means are visited by severe punishment. But it would be difficult to adduce reasons of equity or of law in favor of the contention that a country is bound to ensure the continued existence of Governments and constitutions, frequently ephemeral, other than its own. In the course of eighty years France changed her form of government seven times, but there was nothing, except her own laws which successive régimes were enforcing at different times, to suggest that any particular form of government in France was an interest protected by international law. What international law protects is the right of the State to possess, free from interference on the part of other States, such constitution or Government as its citizens choose or tolerate. The duty of respect which a State owes, in international law, to the constitution and Government of another country is a negative one, a *non facere*; it is not a duty of active protection. If there were such a duty, many States might frequently become exposed to international complications in consequence of the impossibility of securing a conviction by their juries and other judicial organs. It is better that the scope of this kind of law should be a limited one, than that its comprehensiveness should eventually give rise to complaints and remonstrances. Undoubtedly, a State may go beyond its international obligations and, in its own interest, put a check upon such revolutionary activities as it is not in international law bound to prevent. Many States may not, from a variety of reasons, be disposed to tolerate within their borders revolutionary propaganda, even if not directed against their own Government. But such repressive measures, dictated as they may be by reasons of international comity or internal police, cannot be invoked as constituting a test of international obligation.

It is believed that a systematic treatment, with the view to formulating clear rules of international law on the subject of this branch of the doctrine of State responsibility, may do much to remove the question from the realm of politics and purely momentary considerations. Above all, it would supply the much needed test for municipal legislation and administration of justice, which will thus be relieved of the necessity of relying upon the vague, much abused and ever-changing conception of preservation of peace, a remnant of a rudimentary stage of international law. It is for international law to lay down clear principles as to what acts and omissions will, in strict law, endanger a country's peace. No doubt, the measure of protection thus defined will be a modest one, but it will be all that healthy and progressive States are likely to concede or apt to demand. By eliminating exaggerated and never-conceded claims of protection, the rule thus formulated is bound to bring into relief those obligations grounded in the responsibility for revolutionary acts of private persons which no civilized State may disregard with impunity. On the other hand, the very limitation of the scope of State responsibility for revolutionary acts of private persons will accentuate its undoubted and unlimited responsibility for such revolutionary propaganda and other acts of revolutionary character as originate from its own Government or from persons or institutions in receipt of governmental subsidy or assistance.

CHAPTER 8

REVOLUTIONARY PROPAGANDA BY GOVERNMENTS

Editor's note The content of this chapter probably incorporates much of the material which Lauterpacht removed from the article which he submitted to the *American Journal of International Law* in May 1927 and which, after shortening, was sent back to the *Journal* in August 1927 and then published in the form in which it appears as chapter 7 above.

The chapter was originally read as a paper by Lauterpacht before the Grotius Society on Tuesday 12 July 1927 and subsequently published in *Grotius Society*, 13 (1928), 143–63.

I. ACTS OF GOVERNMENTS AS DISTINGUISHED FROM ACTS OF PRIVATE PERSONS

The subject of this paper is the question of the international responsibility of States for such revolutionary propaganda as originates directly from their Governments or other State organs acting in their official capacity. It is not intended to discuss here the responsibility of States for revolutionary acts of private individuals. Of course, international law being a law between States only and exclusively, the ultimate responsibility is also in the latter case borne by the State itself. The distinction is, nevertheless, justified both in fact and in law. Thus a neutral State is not bound to prevent persons resident within its territory from committing acts of any nature whatsoever injurious to the interests of either belligerent. It is bound to prevent only certain of those acts. But the neutral State as such is under a strict duty to refrain from assisting the cause of either of the belligerent parties. The legal position in regard to the subject under discussion is a similar one. An act or an utterance emanating from an individual will here as a rule pass unnoticed. In the majority of cases it will not engage the legal responsibility of the State within the territory of which it took place. But the same act or utterance when emanating from the State as such, from its agents, or from bodies assisted by it, will constitute a clear violation of international law.

In the last ten years, the world has been confronted by both aspects of the question. First, the rise of several revolutionary Governments opposed to principles of democracy and suppressing all political opposition resulted in large numbers of refugees plotting abroad against the dictatorial régimes established in their countries. Secondly, a powerful revolutionary Government has been accused of being wedded to and acting upon the doctrine that its success or even its continued existence is to a large extent dependent upon the possibly universal spread of the principles and the form of Government peculiar to itself. Thirdly, the establishment of dictatorial régimes in several countries and the ensuing concentration in the hands of the State of functions otherwise fulfilled by private agencies have necessarily tended to saddle them with responsibilities from which other States are free. This circumstance has resulted in the obliteration of the important distinction between official acts and those of a private character, and, as a consequence, in a further complication of a difficult international problem.

As already mentioned, we are not concerned here with acts of individuals like revolutionary propaganda, hostile expeditions, or perpetration of terroristic acts against members of foreign Governments or foreign Sovereigns.[1] However, in order to make clearer the question of responsibility of States for their own acts, it may be convenient to devote a few remarks to the legal position in respect of individuals. Authors of text-books and treatises either do not mention this question at all or indulge in inaccurate and sweeping generalizations. Thus we find authoritative writers declaring in very comprehensive terms that a State is bound to prevent the commission, within its territory, of all acts injurious to another State. Rivier, for instance, is clearly of the opinion that mere toleration of revolutionary propaganda against friendly States is a violation of international law.[2] Calvo,[3] Pradier-Fodéré,[4] Liszt,[5] De Louter[6] and many others express the same view. However, there is nothing either in the general practice of States as evidenced in their municipal legislation or in the principles of international law that would justify such a contention. The law of England, for instance, does not punish revolutionary activities against foreign States unless: (*a*) they fall within the scope of section 11 of the Foreign Enlistment Act of 1870,[7] which deals with hostile expeditions, in times both of peace and war, against a State at amity with this country; or (*b*) they are connected in certain ways with the crime of murder, i.e., when they amount to conspiracies to murder or to soliciting or encouraging that crime.[8] Apart from this, revolutionary activities, and

[1] See on this aspect of the question Lauterpacht, 'Revolutionary Activities by Private Persons against Foreign States', in *A.J.* 22 (1928), 105.

[2] Rivier, I, 266.

[3] Calvo, III, § 1298, and I, § 108.

[4] Pradier-Fodéré, I, §§ 238, 260.

[5] Liszt, p. 118.

[6] De Louter, I, 244.

[7] Cf. here *R.* v. *Sandoval*, 3 T.L.R. 411, 436, and *R.* v. *Jameson*, 12 T.L.R. 551.

[8] See section 4 of the Offences Against the Person Act, 1861; *R.* v. *Most* (1881), 7 Q.B.D. 244; and *R.* v. *Antonelli and Barberi* (1905), 70 J.P. 4.

especially revolutionary propaganda, are not punishable in this country. 'Seditious libels are such as tend to disturb the Government of this country', said Phillimore J. in *R.* v. *Antonelli and Barberi*,[1] 'and in my opinion a document published here, which was calculated to disturb the Government of some foreign country, is not a seditious libel, nor punishable as libel at all. . . . To hold otherwise would make many of our statesmen guilty of seditious libel, and those persons also who espoused the cause of Italian liberty.' The law of the United States is even more pronounced in that direction. It is true that the legislation of other countries[2] differs from the Anglo-American law in this respect, but the very divergence of municipal practice shows that there is no generally recognized international duty to restrain private persons from committing acts prejudicial to foreign States except those circumscribed in the analogous case of neutrality or involving common crimes, especially murder.[3]

On the other hand, general considerations of international law seem to force the conclusion that revolutionary propaganda, when originating from the Government itself, constitutes a clear international delinquency. On general principles of international law there appears to be no doubt that: (*a*) a revolutionary hostile expedition organized by a foreign Government is an act of war pure and simple, aggravated by the absence of a formal declaration of war; (*b*) an attempt to interfere, by hostile propaganda and active incursion in political party strife, with the Constitution and internal public order of a friendly State is nothing short of an attack against the international personality of that State, against its internal sovereignty and external independence. The State's right to determine, free from external interference, its own Constitution is the gist of independence, as is freedom from interference with the choice of its Government. International law does not protect so much the actual constitution of the State and its actual Government as its right to determine both by its own free will. The constitution and the Government of a State may be swept aside at any time by an internal revolution causing a complete break in legal continuity, but as long as they continue as law they are the manifestation of the existence of a community as a State and as an indepen-

[1] *Loc. cit.*

[2] See, for instance, Article 102 of the German Penal Code, according to which persons committing against a foreign State an act which if committed against a German Federal State would be punished for treason shall be liable to imprisonment for up to ten years. The Russian Decree of 25 February 1927 punishes acts directed against any State of workers even if that State does not belong to the Union of Soviet Socialist Republics (Ljublinski, in *Zeitschrift für Ostrecht*, 1 (1927), 325).

[3] The provisions of the municipal law of various countries as well as the practice of States in this respect are discussed in Lauterpacht, in *A.J.* vol. 22.

dent unit in the international society. The protection of that international personality is the main object of the Law of Nations. The rest is a superstructure which, however necessary, is easily distinguishable from that primary function of international law. Amidst the controversy occasioned in recent years by the attitude of certain revolutionary organizations, this truth has been frequently lost sight of, and a fundamental principle of international law has been re-affirmed in mutual contractual undertakings as if fundamental rights and duties of nations could properly be made the object of a *quid pro quo* relation. It may therefore be not without advantage to re-state the principles underlying this question, so troublesome in relations between States, and to examine it in the light of international practice and of the science of international law.

2. THE PRACTICE OF STATES

(1) *Incidents after the World War*

In the period following the World War, the problem of revolutionary propaganda and revolutionary preparations fomented and directly aided by a foreign Government frequently occupied diplomats and statesmen in many countries. The relation of the present Government of Russia to the activities of the so-called Third International will be discussed later in the course of this paper. Here it is sufficient to refer to analogous problems which have arisen in other parts of the world. Thus, at the beginning of the year 1927, the United States, while anxious not to allow its territory to be used as a basis of hostile expeditions against Mexico, at that time menaced by an internal revolution, felt compelled to bring against the latter country grave charges of directly aiding the revolutionary armies in Nicaragua. In January of that year President Coolidge addressed to Congress a message in which the Mexican Government was officially charged with shipping arms and munitions to revolutionists in Nicaragua.[1] The Balkan States have of late been raising against one another accusations of fostering revolutionary and irredentist attempts against their respective territories. The various military organizations having as their main object the liberation of territories detached from Bulgaria as a result of the World War gave rise to repeated complaints and charges, as against the Bulgarian authorities, of toleration of and complicity in the activities of these bodies directed against the neighbouring States. In August 1926 the Governments of Greece, Roumania and Yugoslavia addressed to Bulgaria a collective note emphasizing the necessity of putting an

[1] *The Times* newspaper, 11 January 1927.

end to the plottings of the irredentist organizations.[1] In October 1927 Yugoslavia sent to the Bulgarian Government a strongly-worded ultimatum following an outrage said to have been committed by members of those organizations. On the other hand, in the spring of 1927, European diplomacy was seriously perturbed by a circular note addressed by Italy, as the protecting State of Albania, to the main European Powers. In this note Yugoslavia was charged with tolerating and aiding within her territory organized Albanian forces intent upon overthrowing the Government of their country.[2] Following the assassination of her envoy in Warsaw in June 1927, Soviet Russia charged Polish authorities not only with tolerating the Russian counter-revolutionary organizations, but also with directly supporting them in their activities.[3] Finally, to cut short the enumeration of instances in the much troubled post-War period, the French and Belgian authorities in charge of the occupied German territories on the right bank of the Rhine were reported to have fomented and assisted from 1920 to 1923 the revolutionary separatist movement which culminated, in August 1923, in the proclamation of the short-lived Rhineland Republic.[4]

(2) *The seventeenth and eighteenth centuries*

In regard to the frequency of this form of hostile action in the course of the three preceding centuries, a distinction must be drawn between the formative period of international law and the nineteenth century representing a more mature stage in the development of the Law of Nations. In the formative period of international law, the characteristic feature of which is the frequent absence of a clear line of demarcation between the state of war and the state of peace between nations, recourse by Governments to revolutionary propaganda abroad was not an uncommon occurrence. It is sufficient to mention the persistent machinations of Philip II of Spain against Queen Elizabeth, and his attempts to cover Scotland and Ireland with plotting emissaries inciting to rebellion.[5] And in several text-books of international law, in chapters dealing with diplomatic immunities, exhaustive accounts will be found of revolutionary or dynastic conspiracies instigated by foreign ambassadors.[6] But it soon became apparent that such activities were incon-

[1] See *Bulletin de l'Institut Intermédiaire International*, 15 (1926), 339.

[2] *The Times* newspaper, 10 October 1927.

[3] *The Times* newspaper, 8 and 13 June 1927.

[4] There appears now to be no reason to doubt the accuracy of these reports. See Toynbee, *Survey, 1924* (1926), pp. 300–22. See also Springer, *Loslösungsbestrebungen am Rhein, 1918–24* (1924), especially pp. 150–65, where the secret report of the French High Commissioner is printed. See also Allen (Commander of the United States occupational forces), *My Rhineland Journal* (1924), pp. 412, 413.

[5] See, for instance, Calendar of State Papers, Foreign Series, Elizabeth, 1581–2, no. 712.

[6] See especially Phillimore, II, §§ 159–64, 170.

Nevertheless, it took the National Convention only a short time to recognize that the position created by the somewhat rash act of November was incompatible not only with the public law of Europe, but also with the interests of France and, in the long run, with her position as a member of the European community of nations. In a resolution of 13 April 1793, while denouncing strongly the attempts at foreign interference the National Convention declared solemnly on behalf of the people of France that henceforth it would not interfere in any way with the government of other Powers. Danton, with a characteristic understanding of the practical side of things, praised the resolution as showing that the Convention had now learned to reconcile politics with republican virtues. And the Constitution of June 1793 again expressly declared that the people of France did not wish to interfere with the government of other nations.[1]

How general was the condemnation by international publicists of the attitude originally adopted by the Convention may be gauged from the fact that Phillimore, writing over half a century later, called that Decree a barbarous and unprecedented proclamation. He expressed the opinion that it is not possible to conceive a grosser violation of the principle that 'No State has a right to establish a form of government which is built upon professed principles of hostility to the government of other nations.' A declaration, he says, like the foregoing justifies other nations in intervening and demanding, and if necessary by force of arms compelling, the abolition of a Government avowing a *principle* of hostility to the existing Governments of all nations'.[2] However, this strong condemnation hardly added in substance to the admission of the National Convention itself.

(4) *Revolutionary propaganda in time of war*

While the question of revolutionary propaganda in time of peace was thus settled for the next hundred and twenty-five years, the relations of belligerents in this respect necessarily remained unaffected by considerations of mutual respect of sovereignty which States owe one another. Before the World War international lawyers used to discuss the question whether the Law of Nations permitted a belligerent to promote his ends by inducing the subjects of his opponents to treason and by counselling the overthrow of his Government. Some writers thought that the relation of sovereignty between the State and its subjects should in no circumstances be tampered with, and even that deserters should be handed over by one belligerent to another.[3] How-

[1] *Moniteur* (21 June 1793).

[2] Phillimore, I, § 396.

[3] See Basdevant, *La révolution française*, p. 161.

ever, this opinion was by no means unanimously held. It was difficult to maintain it in view of the fact that international law permitted even the total annihilation of the enemy. Vattel, for instance, was of the opinion that there was nothing in strict law to prevent a belligerent from sowing disaffection and treason among the armies of his opponent and his population.[1] But he thought that such a course would not be compatible with good conscience. Modern writers were apt to condemn recourse to revolutionary propaganda as a means of warfare.[2] This disapprobation cannot, it appears, be supported by reference to the practice of States.

It was only natural that the revolutionary armies of the French National Convention availed themselves of that means of warfare in their campaign against the European coalition. While the Convention withdrew its propagandist Decree as against States at peace with France, it asserted to the very end the legitimacy of such action as against belligerents. In the enemy territories occupied by the troops of the Republic, legal and constitutional changes were being effected immediately upon the arrival of the armies of occupation.[3] Entire regiments were created composed of political refugees from enemy countries, and deserters were put on liberal pay.[4] Great Britain retorted in the next war by applying similar measures. When in 1803 and 1804, following the reopening of the war with France, Great Britain engaged the services of several thousand French royalist refugees, France entered a vigorous protest. In its answer, the British Government did not go further than to assert that belligerents had the right to avail themselves of discontent existing in countries with which they happened to be at war[5] – a cautiously-worded statement which should be read in conjunction with the widely-held opinion that although the belligerent might not himself foment a revolt among the subjects of his opponent, he might avail himself of a rebellion which had already broken out. France in 1859, and Prussia in 1866, tried to organize armed forces of Hungarian revolutionaries; and in 1870 France had to protest

[1] Vattel, book III, ch. x, § 180.

[2] See Pillet, *Les lois actuelles de la guerre* (1898), p. 99; Martens G.F., II, 208; Despagnet, *Cours de droit international public* (4th ed. 1910), § 526; Mérignhac, III, 150 (but see, for a significant change of opinion, Spaight, *Air Power and War Rights* (1924), p. 300). See also Hyde, *International Law* (1st ed. 1922), II, § 665; and Oppenheim, *International Law* (4th ed. by McNair, 1926), II, § 162.

[3] See Decree of 15 December 1792 (*Moniteur*, 17 December), containing detailed instructions on this matter. It was said in that Decree: 'The object of this war is the annihilation of all privilege. War to castles, peace to cottages. The privileged and the despots ought to be treated as enemies in the countries which you enter . . . otherwise our own liberties will be in danger.'

[4] See Basdevant, *La révolution française*, pp. 168, 169.

[5] Circular Note by Lord Hawkesbury to foreign Ministers resident at the Court at London, 30 April 1804 (printed separately).

against German attempts to foment rebellion in Algeria. But if prior to 1914 publicists were still in doubt as to what weight to attribute to the practice of some States and to the protests of others, the World War – and, in fact, the character of modern warfare – have settled the controversy in a final manner. Revolutionary propaganda was not only resorted to but systematically organized and pursued. The propaganda of the Allies among the oppressed nationalities in the German, Austro-Hungarian and Turkish Empires, and the part played by the Central Powers in Ireland and India and in the overthrow of the Russian Government by the Bolshevik party in 1917, constituted a characteristic feature of the World War.[1] The armed forces of Czechoslovaks and Poles were recognized as 'allied belligerent armies' before the official recognition of the Governments of those States. However, the fact that before the last war the great majority of writers held the view that revolutionary propaganda was prohibited even as between States waging war against one another is highly significant. It shows how fundamental and well-recognized is that aspect of the duty of non-interference which relates to fomenting revolutions in foreign countries.

(5) *International treaties*

The self-evident character of the duty not to interfere with the affairs of other States by the drastic means of inciting their subjects to revolt is by no means shaken by the fact that in some treaties the contracting parties deemed it necessary to insert express provisions to that effect. In abnormal times and in abnormal situations obligations are frequently accepted in treaties which are otherwise expressive of generally-recognized principles of international law.[2] The period after the World War is rich in treaties of this type in consequence of the attitude said to have been adopted by the Russian Soviet Government in connection both with its general policy and with the original character of the Bolshevik revolution, purporting, as it did, to assume protection over the oppressed proletariat in all countries outside Russia. Thus the Trade Agreement between Great Britain and Russia of 6 March 1921 provided in its first Article that 'each party refrains from hostile action or undertakings against the other and from conducting outside its borders any official propaganda, direct or indirect, against the institutions of the British Empire or the Russian Republics respectively'.[3]

[1] See Spaight, *Air Power*, p. 309, and Fauchille, no. 1088 (1). See also Sir Campbell Stuart, *Secrets of Crewe House* (1920), and Stowell, *Intervention in International Law* (1921), p. 353.

[2] The Supreme Allied Council at Cannes in 1922 found it necessary to adopt the following resolution as one of the bases of the proposed Genoa Conference: 'Nations can claim no right to dictate to each other regarding the principles on which they are to regulate their system of ownership, internal economy and government.' See Cmd. 1821 (1922).

[3] See Hertslet's *Commercial Treaties*, 30, 977.

In the Preliminary Treaty of Peace of October 1920 between Poland and Russia, it was laid down that 'each of the contracting parties reciprocally undertakes to respect the national sovereignty of the other and to abstain from any intervention in the internal affairs of the other, and not to form or lend support to organizations having as their object the promotion of armed action against the other contracting party, the abolition of its political and social régime or the violation of its territorial integrity'.[1] In the Provisional Agreement of 26 December 1921 between Italy and Soviet Russia both parties undertook to refrain from direct or indirect propaganda within their territories against each other.[2] In order to find a parallel to undertakings of this character, it would be necessary to go back to the seventeenth century when international law was only in its beginning.[3] There is no doubt that they are merely declaratory of existing rules of international law, and that the fulfilment of the international duties which they envisage is not dependent upon the continued existence of the treaties in question.

(6) *Conclusions*

Reasons of space do not allow a more detailed examination of the above instances taken from the practice of States. They are, however, sufficient for the purpose of formulating the following provisional conclusions: (*a*) the recourse, by a Government of a State, to revolutionary propaganda abroad is not a frequent occurrence in the history of international relations; (*b*) it was confined mainly to the primitive stage of the development of international law; (*c*) when resorted to in modern times, it is either an incident of an actual state of war, or a measure preceding a state of war, or an act of reprisals; (*d*) when resorted to apart from an actual state of belligerency (in which case no illegality attaches to it), it inevitably tends to obliterate the border-line between the state of peace and the state of war, and as such is incompatible with the maintenance of orderly intercourse between nations.

3. THE RULE OF INTERNATIONAL LAW

The science of international law, so far as it busies itself with this question, furnishes a good illustration of the development of ideas entertained on the subject. Vattel, for instance, was emphatic in condemning 'evil practices tending to produce disturbances in other States to keep

[1] *L.N.T.S.* 4, 35.

[2] See *Russland's Friedens- und Handelsverträge* (ed. by Freund, 1924), p. 49.

[3] See, for instance, the Treaties concluded by Cromwell in 1654 and the following years with Sweden (Hertslet's *Commercial Treaties*, 2, 310), with Denmark (*ibid.* 1, 179), with Portugal (*ibid.* 2, 9), and with Spain (*ibid.* p. 140).

up dissensions therein, to corrupt the citizens'.[1] But the same writer when discussing the legality of the assistance given by the United Provinces to the Prince of Orange justified their attitude with equal emphasis: 'When a people from good reasons takes up arms against an oppressor, it is but an act of justice and generosity, to assist brave men in the defence of their liberties'.[2] Grotius himself regarded it as a duty of a foreign nation not to stand aloof when 'a tyrant practises atrocities towards his subjects'.[3] He was followed in this regard by Pufendorf.[4] It is possible that they thought of this kind of interference as what is termed today 'intervention in defence of humanity'.[5] But be that as it may, no such oscillation will be found in the writings of modern publicists. Hall, for instance, is clearly of the opinion that one of the grounds on which intervention may be said to be allowed is when a Government foments revolution abroad.[6]

No elaborate argument is necessary, in the present stage of international law, in order to arrive at a condemnation, as a clear violation of the Law of Nations, of this form of intervention. There is, in international law, no right (and no corresponding duty) more absolute, more rigid or more formal than freedom from external interference. If any clear inference at all may be drawn from the duty to respect the independence of other States, then it is the duty to abstain from interference with the internal affairs of a recognized Power with which a State is not at war. It is not customary for Governments, unless expressly invited, to offer friendly advice to other States on political matters pending within their territories, except when such a right is stipulated for in special treaties. A Government may not receive officially subjects of a friendly Power claiming to represent political interests in opposition to the Government of their State.[7] Whatever may be thought of the haste with which the United States acted in 1898 in terminating the mission of Lord Sackville, the British Minister at Washington, for having privately advised an American citizen how to vote on the occasion of a presidential election, the incident is a good illustration of the weight which States attach to freedom from external

[1] Vattel, book II, ch. V, § 64. He says in another place (book II, ch. IV, § 53): 'If there should be found a restless and unprincipled nation, ever ready to do harm to others, to thwart their purposes, and to stir up civil strife among their citizens, there is no doubt that all others would have the right to unite together to subdue such a nation, to discipline it, and even to disable it from doing further harm.'

[2] Book II, ch. IV, § 56. This passage was quoted with approval by Lord Russell in a dispatch defending the action of the King of Sardinia in rendering assistance to the revolutionaries in Naples (*Annual Register* (1860), p. 294).

[3] Grotius, book II, ch. XXV, § 8 (2).

[4] Book VIII, ch. VI (14), *in fine*.

[5] See Oppenheim, *International Law* (3rd ed. 1920), I, § 137.

[6] § 91.

[7] See Wharton, I, § 91.

interference.[1] In September 1927 the Russian plenipotentiary representative at Paris affixed his signature to a manifesto urging soldiers in the armies of capitalist countries to desert to the Red Army in the event of a war against the Soviet Republic. His recall was demanded, insisted upon, and obtained.[2] As may be seen from these instances, such interference need not necessarily assume the form of demands addressed to the foreign Government. It may be exercised by propaganda or by intervening in the political party strife in the foreign country. The violation of the duty of non-interference becomes more conspicuous and intolerable when interference assumes the form of inciting the subjects of another State to criminal acts of treason against their lawfully constituted authorities. There are, according to an opinion generally held, few cases in which intervention is more justified than when it is undertaken in order to remove a Government which thus menaces the internal order of other countries.[3] How fundamental and well-recognized is especially that aspect of the duty of non-interference which relates to fomenting revolutions may be gauged from the fact that, as we have seen, such acts are, in the opinion of many writers, prohibited even as between belligerents.

It is only of academic interest to establish what kind of international delinquency is created by fomenting revolutions abroad. Possibly 'intervention' would be the most suitable term, seeing that intervention need not necessarily be accompanied by an act of force,[4] and that it need not take the form of an express demand addressed to a Government. But, as said, the exact classification of that international delinquency is of minor importance when compared with the fact that the delinquency strikes at the roots of international law and that it is in the long run incompatible with the maintenance of a state of peace between the delinquent and the attacked nation. The history of British-Russian relations in the years 1922–1927 afforded an instructive instance of how the mere fact that a Government was charged with that violation of international law resulted, long before diplomatic relations were broken off, in a state of mutual relations which from the point of view of accepted forms of intercourse between Governments did not differ appreciably from that obtaining between nations at war with each other. The unusual spectacle of members of the two Governments

[1] See *Br. and For. St. Papers*, 81, 479–508. See also *ibid.* 505 *et seq.*, on the case of Sir Henry Bulwer, British Envoy to Spain in 1848, who was handed his passports for recommending, at the instruction of Lord Palmerston, to the Spanish Government a more legal and constitutional course of administration.

[2] See *The Times* newspaper, 10 October 1927.

[3] See Westlake, I, 318; Fauchille, no. 303 (4).

[4] See Fauchille, no. 303 (4), and Gemma, in *Hague Recueil*, 4 (1924) (iii), 365. Thus it is frequently maintained, not without good reason, that premature recognition of a new State or Government constitutes intervention.

addressing each other in terms of common abuse was nothing else than a popular expression of the fact that such an alleged violation of an essential principle of international law, even if not followed by a declaration of war, inevitably results in what may be termed the obliteration of the border-line between the state of peace and the state of war. This is a position which is in many respects as disastrous as a state of actual hostilities inasmuch as it signifies the return to a typically primitive stage of international law.

4. THE BORDER-LINE CASES

The main theoretical and practical difficulty of the problem under discussion lies in elaborating a working rule governing the border-line cases, that is to say, situations in which acts of Governments become indistinguishable from acts of private persons, and *vice versa*. As altogether different principles have been shown to apply to the two classes of acts, it appears necessary to devote the closing remarks to a consideration of this question.

The duty of non-interference (especially by not fomenting revolution), is a fundamental one. Accordingly, the obligations of Governments in this matter must needs be subject to a rigid and exacting interpretation. In the first instance, it is clear that what is meant by a Government is not only members of the Government and of the official hierarchy of the State, but also its institutions and resources. Acts of bodies maintained, controlled or subsidized by the State must of necessity be attributed to the State as such. It cannot escape responsibility except by relinquishing its control or withdrawing its assistance. Naturally, the more centralized a State and the smaller the degree of autonomy afforded by it to its component geographical or functional units, the greater will be the probability of its international responsibility becoming engaged. This increased responsibility is one of the unavoidable incidents of a political system in which the range of functions directly performed by the State is much wider than in States governed in a different manner. A State which has chosen this particular form of government may, by this very fact, find itself compelled to follow a considerably higher standard of formal and substantive respect for the dignity, susceptibilities and interests of its neighbours; a standard which frequently will have to be higher than that observed by nations the constitutions of which leave to individuals and to associations within their territories a wider scope of economic initiative, of freedom of opinion, and of liberty of organization. Such a centralized Government has in many respects deprived itself of the power – which other States may frequently find so convenient – to act *per alium*, namely, through its citizens and private organizations. International law will not countenance any ignoring of this increased responsibility. This point is well illustrated by the controversy between Great Britain and Soviet Russia, in February 1927, as to (*inter alia*) the appeals to revolutionary action addressed to certain classes of the population in Great Britain and printed in the official organ of the Soviet Government. In reply to the British note, it was admitted that the organ complained of was an official publication of the central authority of the Soviets, but responsibility was disclaimed on the ground that 'this paper has one of the largest circulations and caters for hundreds of thousands of readers, who must be given all the information interesting them, including manifestos and resolutions of the Soviet, as well as of party institutions'.[1] The inadequacy of this answer is obvious. For the formal distinction between State responsibility for acts of private individuals and acts of Governments and their organs has now become well recognized in international law, and to jettison it, even if it were juridically possible, would be disastrous. It would for all practical purposes destroy the basis of State responsibility in the field of international law.

On the other hand, the fact that the State is in the position to exercise influence over private institutions and undertakings, for instance over the organs of the press, is not in itself sufficient to saddle it with responsibility for their acts and utterances.[2] Thus, although a Government may have suppressed all other organs of expression of public opinion except those of its own party, it will not be responsible for revolutionary propaganda conducted by the latter unless they are officially controlled by the Government or in receipt of assistance from public funds. The correct legal formulation of this aspect of the question will, it is believed, be found in the Convention of January 1925 between Japan and Soviet Russia in which the contracting parties undertook 'to refrain and restrain all persons in any governmental service for them and all organizations in receipt of any financial assistance from them, from any act overt or covert liable in any way whatever to endanger the order and security' in any part of their respective territories.[3] With

[1] See the Russian Note of 26 February 1927 (*The Times* newspaper, 28 February 1927). The British Note of 23 February 1927 is printed in *The Times* of 24 February 1927.

[2] When the Serbian Government, in reply to the Austrian ultimatum in 1924, pointed out that it could not be held responsible for utterances of a private character such as newspaper articles, the official, and obviously misguided, Austrian comment on this part of the reply was that the contention of Serbia was contrary to the modern practice of States, especially considering that Serbia was actually exercising control over her newspapers (see *A.J.* 8 (1914), Suppl., 387).

[3] Martens, N.R.G., 3rd ser., xv, 324. Similar provisions were contained in Article 16 of the unratified General Treaty between Great Britain and Soviet Russia, signed in London on 8 August 1924; Cmd. 2260 of 1924. See also the correspondence, in 1923, between these two

regard to the civil service and the armed forces of the State, it is both necessary and convenient to apply the general principles governing the responsibility of States for the acts of their organs. So far as the members of the Government and such higher officials for whom the State bears original responsibility are concerned, it is in practice impossible to draw a line between their official attitude and their acts as private persons, and to absolve the State from responsibility for the latter. However, it would be difficult to exact an equal measure of self-restraint from officials with an inferior status. Their position approaches that of private individuals, provided always that their sympathies with the revolutionary cause abroad do not result in abuse of their official authority and in making governmental and State institutions serve the purposes of that cause.[1] In any case, the State should whenever possible dissociate itself from such acts of its minor officials, for instance by insisting that when engaged in such activities they should not appear in uniform or official dress likely to invest their proceedings with an appearance of official action. Thus in March 1921 the military authorities in Boston, in the United States, forbade men in uniform to take part in a demonstration organized by the American Association for the Recognition of the Irish Republic.[2]

The vexed question as to the responsibility of the Soviet Government of Russia for the revolutionary propaganda conducted by the so-called Third International will have to be answered by reference to the principles stated above. Two relevant questions must be asked and answered : (*a*) Is that organization receiving financial or other assistance from the Government ? (*b*) Do leading members of that organization occupy leading positions in the civil service or in the armed forces of the Russian State ? It is not necessary, for the purpose of this paper, to examine the details of Russian constitutional law or to inquire how far other facts tend to give an affirmative or a negative answer to these two questions.[3]

countries respecting revolutionary propaganda and assistance; Cmds. 1846, 1869, 1874, 1890 of 1923. In the Note of 9 June 1923 the Russian Government undertook, in conformity with the demand of Great Britain, not to support with funds or in any other form persons or institutions whose aim was to spread discontent or to foment rebellion in any part of the British Empire.

[1] Thus, for instance, so far as the Austrian complaints in 1914 on account of the aid received by Bosnian irredentists from Serbian officials were based on facts, it is believed that the Serbian Government could justly be called upon to put an end to such abuses.

[2] See Stowell, *Intervention in International Law* (1921), p. 383. However, when, in 1865, the British Government complained that officers of the United States Army attended Fenian meetings, the Government of the United States refused to take action; *U.S. For. Rel.* (1865), II, 96 and 103.

[3] For a full and impartial account of the activities of the Third International and of their bearing upon the foreign relations of the Union of the Soviet Socialist Republics up to December 1924, see Toynbee, *Survey, 1924* (1926), pp. 161–265, and especially pp. 163–75, 199–206, 215–24, 247–9.

The problem of broadcasting by wireless must also it is believed, be answered in a like manner. In countries where the broadcasting stations are managed or controlled by the Government, any attempt on their part to spread revolutionary propaganda abroad or to interfere in the internal affairs of other countries will, as coming from a governmental institution, immediately engage the international responsibility of the State concerned. The situation is entirely different where broadcasting is left to private initiative and competition, as is the case in the United States of America. No remedy will here be available to the aggrieved State unless it can substantiate the allegation that it is the foreign State itself which, through the medium of the private station, indulges in objectionable propaganda. It may appeal to the courtesy of the foreign Government and request it in a friendly way to put pressure on its private stations. Should, however, such appeals remain without effect, the State thus menaced will be left with no alternative but to trust to the good sense and the discretion of its citizens or to repel, by such mechanical means as science may put at its disposal, the nuisance coming from abroad.[1]

5

It is not necessary to append the usual summary of conclusions to a paper the main theme of which has been the elaboration of what is only a necessary deduction from a fundamental principle of international law. Instead, attention may be drawn to three tasks of a formal character which accrue to the international lawyer in connection with this matter:

Firstly, it is essential that the strictly legal aspect of the problem should be brought into relief and kept in the foreground. Freedom from interference by way of revolutionary propaganda conducted by a foreign Government should not be put forward as a political demand, but as a legal right flowing from one of the most uncontroverted principles of international law. A State may obstinately adhere to a certain line of conduct so long as the character of impropriety attaching to it is merely a political one. But it will find it increasingly difficult to maintain this attitude in the teeth of its general condemnation, as striking at the very roots of international law, by impartial scientific opinion.

[1] The Institute of International Law adopted, at its meeting in 1927, a resolution on radio-telegraphic communication which, in its fifth article, declares that the State is responsible 'if it does not employ the means at its disposal to prevent radio-telegraphic emissions which, by their contents, are of a nature to disturb the public order of another State, when similar emissions have already been called to its attention by the latter'. It is believed that this article is only so far expressive of existing international law as it applies to broadcasting stations managed by the State itself. See also Cereti, in *Rivista*, 18 (1926), 17, who adopts a view similar to that expressed by the Institute.

Secondly, in order that the legal inquiry may be productive of working results, it is necessary to remember that different rules of international law apply according to whether fomenting rebellion abroad originates from governmental agencies or from private individuals. The two aspects of the problem must be studied one alongside the other.

Thirdly, it will be the duty of international jurists patiently to analyse the legal position in cases where these two kinds of responsibility tend to merge into one as the result of a dictatorship or another form of absolute Government.

CHAPTER 9

BOYCOTT IN INTERNATIONAL RELATIONS

Editor's note This chapter, like the two preceding it, might more appropriately be printed in the part of these *Collected Papers* devoted to 'State Responsibility' (which will appear in volume 4). But unlike the two earlier chapters, its contents were not expressly identified in Lauterpacht's rough classification for his projected treatise. Nonetheless, its subject matter is so closely related to chapters 6 and 7 that it seems right to print all three chapters together within this section.

There is reason to believe (though no documents evidencing the belief can be found) that Lauterpacht was in some way involved in the preparation of China's appeal to the Lytton Commission, which is referred to in the first lines of the chapter.

The chapter consists of the article under this title which appeared in *B.Y.* 14 (1933), 125–40.

I

The Report of the Lytton Commission appointed by the Council of the League of Nations to inquire into the dispute between China and Japan contains a long chapter on the boycott of Japanese goods by China as one of the essential factors of the dispute.[1] The Commission found that although the boycott had its origin in a spontaneous popular movement it was organized and largely directed and controlled by a powerful party closely associated with the Government. It also questioned whether the Chinese Government could be absolved from responsibility both for isolated acts of direct support of the boycott movement by governmental departments and for indirect assistance as the result of the failure to suppress acts punishable under Chinese law. On the question of responsibility for the boycott movement as a whole, the Commission showed some degree of hesitation. It did not deny the right of individual Chinese to decline to have commercial relations with Japanese subjects or to make propaganda, in a lawful manner, for the idea of the boycott. At the same time the Commission preferred to dissociate itself from any intention of pronouncing authoritatively on the subject. In doing so, it seemed to imply that it is controversial from the point of view of international law whether 'the

[1] League of Nations. Appeal by the Chinese Government. *Report of the Commission of Inquiry*, Doc. C, 663, M. 320, 1932, VII, 112–21.

organized application of the boycott to the trade of one particular country is consistent with friendly relations or in conformity with treaty obligations'.[1] Accordingly, the Commission expressed the hope that 'in the interest of all States, this problem should be considered at an early date and regulated by international agreement'.[2] It will be submitted in the present article that the matter is already covered by existing principles of State responsibility and by rules of international law relating to the treatment of aliens; that the creation of a specific international delinquency in connection with the boycott of foreign goods is not feasible in practice; and that, even if it were practically possible, it is not desirable that it should be introduced.

The participation of the population of a State in matters of foreign policy by means of refusal of commercial intercourse, in particular of purchase of goods[3] coming from a foreign State charged with an unfriendly attitude, is not a new phenomenon in international life. It is a weapon which has been resorted to on a number of occasions in the last thirty years. It was used in 1908 by large parts of the population of Turkey as a protest against the annexation of Bosnia and Herzogovina by Austria–Hungary.[4] In 1909 there was a boycott in Turkey of Greek

[1] *Ibid.* p. 120. Apparently the Commission had in mind treaty obligations of ordinary commercial treaties.

[2] *Ibid.* p. 120. The Report of the Assembly under Article 15, para. 4 – a report which embodied the substance of the Report of the Commission of Inquiry – did not make the matter clearer. It stated (at p. 17) that 'the use of the boycott by the Chinese previous to the events of 18 September 1931 to express their indignation at certain incidents or to support certain claims, could not fail to make a situation which was already tense still more tense', but that 'the use of the boycott by China, subsequent to the events of 18 September 1931 falls under the category of reprisals'. While the first statement refers to the 'Chinese', the second refers to China. If the word 'reprisals' is used in its technical sense – and there is a strong presumption that this is the use of a term in an international instrument of this importance – then the statement would imply that, at least since 18 September 1931 the Chinese Government was responsible for the boycott; that the boycott was contrary to international law; and that if, subsequent to 18 September 1931, the boycott could not be regarded as contrary to international law, this was only on account of the illegality of the Japanese action. It is doubtful whether it was the intention of the Assembly to commit itself to the view of the initial illegality of the boycott. The confusion is probably due to the manner in which China presented her case. See *Memorandum on the Boycott*, presented in June 1932 to the Lytton Commission. While arguing that under international law no responsibility attached to the Chinese Government for the acts of boycott, the author of the *Memorandum* insisted that the boycott was in the nature of reprisals which had been rendered legitimate by various Japanese acts in Corea, Manchuria, and Shanghai (see pp. 26–31 of the *Memorandum*).

[3] The refusal to buy goods is the principal but not the only manifestation of boycott. The recent Chinese boycott directed against Japan included the following measures: (*a*) refusal to purchase, use, or carry Japanese goods; (*b*) refusal to use Japanese ships, banks, or warehouses; (*c*) refusal to offer labour or services to Japanese subjects; (*d*) refusal to supply Japanese subjects with foodstuffs and other necessities of daily life; (*e*) abstention from social intercourse with Japanese subjects. See on the methods and scope of this boycott *Supplementary Documents to the Report of the Lytton Commission*, Part III, Study no. 8, pp. 220 *et seq.* See also *British Encyclopaedia* for the origin of the term 'boycott'.

[4] For details of this boycott see Laferrière, in *R.G.* 17 (1910), 301–9. See also Baty, *International Law* (1909), pp. 66–70.

goods in order to induce Greece to abstain from assisting the Cretan insurrection.[1] Since 1924 there have taken place in Egypt sporadic attempts to boycott British goods. However, it is in China that the practice and the technique of boycott have developed with particular intensity and frequency. In China the boycott has for a long time been almost a national institution. The existence in that country of disciplined guilds of merchants capable of being used as a directing, co-ordinating, and enforcing agency has tended to constitute the boycott a weapon of considerable efficiency. The weak position of China in the international sphere, combined with the policy of pacific penetration on the part of foreign Powers and their insistence on obtaining special privileges in Chinese territory, has been an additional factor in constituting the boycott a weapon of national action. In 1905 the restrictions upon Chinese immigration into the United States called forth a commercial boycott of the United States.[2] In 1908 Japanese goods were boycotted when, as the result of the apparently justified seizure of the Japanese steamer *Tatsu Maru*, suspected of smuggling, the Chinese Government was compelled to offer apologies and to pay compensation. In 1915 the Japanese ultimatum to China, presented in the form of the well-known twenty-one demands, resulted in another boycott. The same instrument was used in 1923 in order to induce Japan to restore to its original term the lease of the Kwantung Territory prolonged as the result of the twenty-one demands. In 1925 a disturbance, in which a number of Chinese were killed or wounded by a police detachment commanded by a British officer, in the course of a labour dispute at Shanghai, brought about a widespread boycott of British and Japanese goods in China. In 1927 and 1929 there followed further boycotts in connection with the dispatch of Japanese troops to Shantung. What has been described as 'the most extensive, best organized and probably most efficient movement of its kind'[3] is the boycott launched in 1931 following upon the massacre of a number of Chinese in Corea. That movement, which has had an unprecedented accession of strength as the result of the occupation of the three Manchurian provinces and of Jehol, is still in unabated vigour at the time of writing.

[1] See Laferrière, in *R.G.* 17, 309–11.

[2] For the diplomatic correspondence relating to this boycott see *U.S. For. Rel.* (1905), pp. 204–34.

[3] For details of this and other Chinese boycotts see *Supplementary Documents to the Report of the Commission of Inquiry*, Study no. 8, pp. 212–17. And see Fauchille, I, nos. 985 (1)–985 (5), for an account of numerous instances of boycott.

2

As a matter of broad principle, it is difficult to see how a State can be made internationally responsible for the private boycott of the goods of a foreign country. This principle is subject to the qualification – part of which is, as we shall see, controversial – that the boycott does not originate with the Government, that it is not supported by it directly or indirectly, and that nothing is done in pursuance of it which results in the disregard of the State's international duty to respect and protect the life and property of aliens. Subject to these qualifications, the proposition is too obvious to require detailed elaboration. As a matter of international duty, a Government cannot be expected to dictate to private individuals from whom they shall buy the goods they need. The position might be different if a State undertook in a treaty to guarantee to the other contracting party, now affected by the boycott, that a definite quantity or proportion of goods would be purchased from it. An ordinary treaty of commerce and establishment does not, of course, have this effect. It provides the legal basis and guarantees of commercial intercourse on the assumption that the subjects of the contracting parties will be prepared to enter into such intercourse with one another.

Undoubtedly, a Government may go beyond its international duties and suppress acts of private individuals which threaten to disturb international relations by embroiling it with a foreign State. The municipal law of various States abounds in examples of this nature. The British Foreign Enlistment Act of 1870[1] – by prohibiting enlisting in the service of the belligerent and the supplying of coal and provisions to a belligerent fleet – goes much beyond the duties of neutrality which international law imposes upon a State. The criminal law of many countries prohibits high treason and revolutionary propaganda against foreign States although no such duty of repression is laid down in international law.[2] Some municipal systems punish acts which may embroil the State with foreign States[3] – thus adopting a criterion which is more political

[1] 33 and 34 Vict., c. 90.

[2] According to Article 102 of the German Penal Code persons committing in Germany against a foreign State an act which if committed against Germany would be punished as high treason within the meaning of the Penal Code shall be liable to imprisonment for a period up to ten years. A Decree promulgated on 25 February 1927 in Soviet Russia described as anti-revolutionary crimes acts directed against a State of workers even if that State does not belong to the Union of Socialist Soviet Republics.

[3] See, for instance, Articles 84 and 85 of the French Penal Code; Article 113 of the former Italian Criminal Code; Article 41 of the Swiss Criminal Code. And see *R.* v. *Peltier* (1803), 28 *State Trials*, p. 529, to the effect that publications tending to degrade, to revile, and to defame persons 'in considerable situations of power and dignity in foreign countries' are calculated to embroil this country with foreign Powers and may, therefore, be treated as libels. See also *R.* v. *Vint* (1799), 22 *State Trials*, p. 627. But see Phillimore J. in *R.* v. *Antonelli and Barberi* (1905), 70 J.P. 4.

than legal. For a State, especially a weak State, may become embroiled with foreign States on account of events for which there is normally no responsibility in international law. Also, a State may deem it wise to suppress a movement which although in itself not giving rise to international responsibility may lead to acts for which the State bears responsibility. In 1905 the United States, in protesting against the boycott, drew the attention of the Chinese Government to the possibility of the acts of boycott assuming the dimensions of attacks against the life and property of aliens.[1] The non-suppression of a boycott may possibly be regarded as a failure to use due diligence to prevent the subsequent losses of life and property of aliens and may therefore give rise to international responsibility. But it is clear that in such cases the toleration of the boycott is not a specific international wrong, just as the toleration of propaganda against or criticism of a foreign State do not in themselves constitute a separate international delinquency.

Such practice of States as exists on the matter cannot be regarded as disproving the somewhat obvious view set forth above.[2] When protesting in 1905 against the boycott of their goods in China, the United States seemed to assume the existence of a wider duty than the one here defined. However, a study of the correspondence suggests that on the whole the protest of the United States was based on the alleged support of the movement by the Chinese Government[3] and officials, and also, as shown, on the apprehension that the boycott might lead to disturbances of a serious character. In so far as the complaints of the United States went beyond these demands, their attitude was one which, it may safely be assumed, they would not have tolerated had the rôles been reversed.[4] During the boycott of Austro-Hungarian goods in Turkey in 1908, Austria-Hungary complained not on account of the boycott as such but because the usual port facilities were withheld from Austrian shipping, because Turkish customs officials refused to handle Austrian goods, and

[1] 'We have long realized the gravity and even the danger of the situation and endeavoured to bring your Government to a sense of the perils involved in permitting the growth of the anti-foreign sentiment, which, ostensibly limited to a single phase of China's relation to an outside Power, is ready to overleap all bounds and to lead at any time to the recurrence of the dreadful atrocities of Lienchow' (Secretary Root to the Chinese Minister, 14 November 1905; *U.S. For. Rel.* (1905), p. 232).

[2] See, to the same effect, Laferrière, in *R.G.* 17, 310–26; Baty, *International Law*, p. 70; Hyde and Wehle, in *A.J.* 27 (1933), 1–4.

[3] See *U.S. For. Rel.* (1905), pp. 214, 223. In the course of the correspondence the Chinese Government expressed the view that the boycott would never have taken place but for the United States immigration laws which the Chinese people regarded as oppressive. The United States Minister felt justified in inferring from this statement that the boycott movement had a certain amount of sympathy from the Chinese Government.

[4] The United States Minister referred to 'an unwarranted attempt of the ignorant people to assume the functions of government and to meddle with international relations' (*ibid.* p. 223).

because no action was taken against persons forcibly preventing intending customers from entering Austrian stores.[1]

The view has been stressed so far that so long as the State as such is not connected with the boycott movement by way of initiating it or by supporting it directly or indirectly, its responsibility is not involved. But does not even this qualifying admission of State responsibility go too far? Is there a good reason for assuming that, in the absence of a commercial treaty and without infringing the rules of international law as to the protection of the life and property of aliens, a State is liable for initiating and supporting a boycott of goods from another country? It is difficult to see on what grounds international responsibility could in such cases be based. In the absence of explicit conventional obligations, particularly those laid down in commercial treaties, a State is entitled to prevent altogether goods from a foreign State from coming into its territory. It may – and frequently does – do so under the guise of a protective tariff or of sanitary precautions or in some other manner. The foreign State may treat such an attitude as an unfriendly act and retort accordingly. But it cannot legitimately regard it as a breach of international law.

The further question must be asked: What is the position pending the duration of a commercial treaty? Is the responsibility of the State involved if a Government bound by a commercial treaty, while conforming with the rules of international law relating to the respect for the life and property of aliens and while placing no legal or administrative obstacles in the way of foreign goods, at the same time makes it clear that it approves of the boycott as a measure of justifiable national action and even promotes the boycott in various ways? The Lytton Commission of Inquiry found that the boycott of Japanese goods in China was promoted, *inter alia*, by slogans printed on currency notes and on letters and telegram-forms.[2] This was a direct form of governmental assistance. It has been submitted that such and similar assistance is not necessarily contrary to the duties of customary international law in regard to the treatment of aliens and their property. Aliens are not by international law entitled to absolute equality of rights as compared with nationals. They are entitled to an equal protection of such rights as they possess. But they do not enjoy all the rights which are enjoyed by nationals. Does the existence of a commercial treaty make a difference? Or does the answer to the question depend upon the content of the relevant provisions of the commercial treaty? A survey of treaties of commerce shows some variations in the

[1] See Austrian note of 14 December 1908 in Laferrière, in *R.G.* 17, 317.

[2] *Report of the Commission*, p. 116.

relevant provisions. The treaty of commerce between the United States and China of 1858 (to which the United States frequently appealed in the course of the boycott in 1905) laid down in Article 15 that

> at each of the ports open to commerce, citizens of the United States shall be permitted to import from abroad and sell, purchase, and export all merchandise of which the importation is not prohibited by the laws of the Empire.

The Treaty of commerce and navigation between China and Japan of 21 July 1896 provides in Article 4 that

> Japanese subjects may, with families, employees and servants, frequent, reside and carry on trade, industries and manufactures or pursue any other lawful vocations in all the ports, cities and towns of China, which are now, or may hereafter be, opened to foreign residence and trade.

The terms of other treaties of commerce and navigation are wider. Thus the Treaty of 2 December 1924 between the United Kingdom and Germany provides in Article 1 that

> the subjects or citizens of each of the two contracting parties shall have liberty freely to come, with their ships and cargoes, to all places and ports in the territories of the other to which subjects or citizens of that contracting party are or may be permitted to come, and shall enjoy the same rights, privileges, liberties, favours, immunities and exemptions in matters of commerce and navigation as are or may be enjoyed by subjects or citizens of that contracting party.

The Treaty of commerce between the United Kingdom and the United States of 3 July 1815 provides in Article 1, *inter alia*, that

> the merchants and traders of each nation respectively shall enjoy the most complete protection and security for their commerce.

Is the fulfilment of obligations under these and similar provisions compatible with the open encouragement and support of a boycott movement by the Government of a State? The commercial treaty obviously implies that the State cannot prohibit generally the importation and sale of goods coming from the territory of the other contracting party. But does it mean that it may not exhort its citizens not to buy the goods of the State with which it has a commercial treaty and that it must not place its governmental departments at the disposal of the boycott propaganda? It may be and has been argued that the protection and granting of equal favours relates only to such goods as have been actually imported and to such commercial intercourse as has in fact materialized; that the provisions of the commercial treaty do not imply the duty of commercial intercourse, but merely favourable treatment of such intercourse as actually takes place; and that by the conclusion of a commercial treaty States do not intend to abandon generally their freedom of action in matters of commerce.[1] These arguments cannot be accepted as containing a fair interpretation of commercial treaties. If a State promises to another State to grant to its merchants 'complete protection and security for their commerce' then it ill becomes it to exhort its citizens to suppress such commerce and to make its governmental services available for propaganda to this end. By no stretch of interpretation could such an attitude be squared with the undertaking to confer upon foreign merchants the same 'privileges, liberties and favours' as are enjoyed by the State's own citizens. The same, it is believed, applies to treaties such as the above-quoted commercial treaties between Japan and China or the United States and China, in which the provisions of the treaty are merely of a permissive character. It is submitted that the only way left open in such cases to a State determined not to put itself in conflict with its treaty obligations is either to denounce the treaty if this is possible[2] or else to trust that the patriotic sentiment of the population favouring the boycott will assert itself without governmental aid.

This view seems to be substantiated by some of the diplomatic correspondence on the matter, which shows a tendency to dissociate the Governments in question from the boycott. In the actual conduct of boycotts Governments have been equally anxious to do nothing which might enable a foreign State to charge them with active participation in the boycott. In the extended anti-Japanese boycott in China since 1931, diligent researches have produced only four not very persuasive instances of governmental participation or condonation.[3]

The fact that the responsibility of the Government as such for

[1] This is to some extent the view of Hyde and Wehle, quoted above.

[2] It will be noted that the State's freedom of action is less hampered by commercial treaties than is generally assumed. Treaties of commerce are as a rule liable to comparatively short notice; commercial treaties concluded without any fixed time limit are probably terminable at reasonable notice by one of the contracting parties.

[3] These instances are enumerated in the above-mentioned Study no. 8 (*Supplementary Documents to the Report of the Commission of Inquiry*, pp. 230–2). One referred to a secret document issued by the President of the Executive Yuan (one of the chief Government departments) transmitting to the municipal and provincial authorities the Kuomintang plan of action against Japan. The document transmitted contained no reference to the boycott (see *ibid.* p. 218). The second was a circular of the Chinese Minister of Railways to the administrations of some Chinese railways referring to the necessity of bringing about 'at any price the rupture of economic relations with Japan' and exhorting the railways to take effective measures for promoting the national industry by granting facilities to the transport of Chinese goods. The third document was a minute issued by the Chinese Ministry of Communications and informing those concerned of a resolution passed by a mass meeting at Nanking and pointing to the necessity of recovering the right of coastal navigation by refusing to board Japanese steamers. The fourth instance was the registration by the Chinese Ministry of Industry and Agriculture of two trade-marks with anti-Japanese slogans.

participating in the boycott is to some extent a matter of controversy constitutes an additional reason for proceeding cautiously in attributing to a State responsibility for acts of bodies and individuals more or less closely associated with it. What is meant by 'the State' in connection with this and other instances of State responsibility? 'The State' means the Government and other organs of the State regardless of rank and position in the State hierarchy. It extends from the Government to the lowest official in a provincial post office or to a private in the army or to an ordinary seaman in the navy[1] – the only difference being that the responsibility of the former is direct whereas in regard to the latter the State is responsible only if it does not disavow and remedy the injurious action. The same applies to a large extent to private bodies in receipt of governmental financial assistance. The activities of such bodies do not directly engage the responsibility of the State, but the foreign State is entitled to expect that the Government will make continued financial support dependent upon the cessation of activities which if conducted by the Government as such would create international responsibility on the part of the State.

But what is the position in regard to bodies closely associated with the Government but not in receipt of direct financial assistance from the resources of the State? The problem involves such questions as the responsibility of the Russian Government for the activities of the Communist Party, or of the Italian Government for the activities of the Fascist Party, or of the Government of China for the activities of the Kuomintang. In countries like these the composition and the activities of the Government are to a large extent influenced by the party actually wielding the supreme power in the State. Although in such cases the Government and the party behind the Government are frequently indistinguishable, it is extremely doubtful whether the State can be made responsible for the acts of the party. In most States the composition of the Government and, frequently, its acts, are determined by one or more parties which command a majority in the legislative assemblies and which either as a matter of constitutional machinery or of actual fact have a distinct place in the working of the Government. To make the latter responsible for the acts of the party would mean to play havoc with the established rules of State responsibility. The standards of restraint and mutual respect in intergovernmental relations are more rigorous than in the relations of individuals. To require the same standard from private persons and associations would mean to expect from

[1] In March 1921 the American military authorities in Boston prohibited men in uniform from taking part in a demonstration organized by the American Association for the Recognition of the Irish Republic. See Stowell, *Intervention in International Law* (1921), p. 383.

them a degree of diligence and restraint which may be in excess of that required from them in relation to their own Government. Rules of international law on the matter of State responsibility are based on the separation of the State from the individuals and associations of which it is composed. This may at times enable a State to do through individuals and private bodies what it is not allowed to do itself. But the advantages of this state of affairs have, in the present stage of international organization, been found greater than the concomitant disadvantages of the possibility of evading international duties. In any case this is the present position of international law. The fact that a boycott is directed and controlled by a political party associated with, influencing, and, possibly, appointing the Government is not sufficient to saddle the State with international responsibility.[1]

3

Direct participation in and encouragement of a boycott does not exhaust the range of State responsibility. The international responsibility of a State may become engaged if it furthers indirectly the boycott movement by failing to enact adequate laws, or properly to interpret or to enforce existing laws in cases in which their enforcement is necessary for the effective protection of rights of aliens recognized by international law. In particular, aliens are entitled to expect that where their interests are concerned there shall be no relaxation in the application of the law even if the parties directly affected are subjects of the State within whose territory the boycott is conducted and even if the aliens affected by the boycott are injured only indirectly.

In the first instance there is a duty of repression, of the State's own accord and without waiting for a private complaint, of such acts of interference with personal freedom or property rights as constitute a breach of the criminal law of the country. Such duty includes the enactment of criminal laws sufficient to meet the obligation and a reasonable interpretation of the existing law. Thus a State must be expected to possess adequate penal provision against unauthorized taking away of property of others. But, to quote a recent instance, according to the Chinese Criminal Code seizure of property is not regarded as robbery liable to punishment if the act is not done with the intention of bringing profit to the person responsible for the seizure or to third persons. Such

[1] The Lytton Commission and its experts were, it seems, inclined to accept a wider measure of responsibility in this matter. See Study no. 8 (quoted above), pp. 229, 230. On the responsibility of Soviet Russia for the activities of the Third International, see Lauterpacht, in *Grotius Society*, 13 (1928), 160 *et seq.*; Verdross, in *Z.ö.R.* 9 (1930), 577–82; Mannzen, *Sowjetunion und Völkerrecht* (1932), pp. 42–56.

acts escape punishment unless the seizure is accompanied by violence against the person (Article 318 of the Penal Code). This, at least, was the way in which Chinese courts interpreted the existing law. In a case which came before the Shanghai District Court in November 1931, they further mitigated the rigour of the Penal Code by deciding that 'leniency should be granted to the defendants because they committed a crime due to the over-expression of patriotism'.[1] But a State cannot be held responsible if in some cases criminal prosecution is at the instance of the injured person and if such prosecution never takes place because for the person affected to institute proceedings is to expose himself to a public discussion of acts undertaken in disregard of a strong national sentiment.

In the second instance, apart from the criminal law, there is a duty of impartial enforcement of the private law of torts and generally of the relevant private law. This duty is obvious and without qualifications so far as the aliens are the direct object of the illegal act. But does it apply in relations *inter se* between the subjects of the State? The Chinese assessor before the Lytton Commission vigorously maintained that the answer to this question must be in the negative. He said:

> A foreign nation is not authorized to raise a question of internal law. In fact we find ourselves confronted with acts denounced as unlawful but committed by Chinese nationals in prejudice to other Chinese nationals. Their suppression is a matter for the Chinese authorities and it seems to us that nobody has the right of calling into account the manner in which the Chinese penal law is applied in matters where both offenders and sufferers belong to our own nationality. No State has the right of intervention in the administration of exclusively domestic affairs of another State. This is what the principle of mutual respect for each other's sovereignty and independence means.[2]

The Lytton Commission was not, it seems, prepared to accept this view. The Japanese complaint, it said, was not that Chinese subjects committed with impunity illegal acts against other Chinese, but that no action was taken to repress violations of the law injurious to Japanese subjects. It is submitted that this is the only correct view. It is a well-recognized rule of municipal law of most countries that in cases of conspiracy and intimidation in which illegal action is taken to the detriment of a third party, that third party is entitled to a legal remedy.

In most countries the law provides some measure of protection, in the domain of the law of torts, against such acts of boycott as are achieved by illegal or immoral means. In English law many an act of

[1] *In re Ko Yun-ting and Others*, printed as an appendix to the *Memorandum on the Boycott* submitted to the Lytton Commission of Inquiry, p. 33.

[2] *Memorandum on the Boycott*, p. 21.

boycott will constitute a wrong actionable at the instance of the party against whom the boycott is directed.[1] Intimidation through physical violence or any other illegal act is actionable regardless of whether or not conspiracy exists; and intimidation by way of conspiracy is actionable if effected without lawful justification and with an intention to injure. The conception of what is lawful justification, i.e. what is a just and lawful defence of one's own rights and interests, is an elastic one and leaves sufficient scope for the consideration of the special conditions under which the boycott takes place.[2] But its elasticity is modified by the principle that in any case the use of unlawful means, such as violence or the threat of violence or fraud, constitutes a good cause of action. German law reaches the same result in a different way. German courts have interpreted Articles 823 and 826 of the Civil Code to the effect that a boycott is actionable when the proclamation of it contravenes the criminal law, i.e. when it involves libels or threats, or when it is immoral having regard either to the means used or the purpose aimed at. The means are immoral when, for example, the recital of the facts in the proclamation of the boycott is incomplete or incorrect. The purpose of the boycott is immoral when it aims at or results in ruining the opponent, or when the object pursued is so small as to be out of proportion to the magnitude of the injury inflicted upon the boycotted party.[3] The position in France is, on the whole, similar.[4]

The protection, in the domain of the law of torts, which the municipal law of many countries affords against certain manifestations of boycott, is available to the nationals both of the boycotting and the boycotted State. It is available to the latter if they are individually injured as the result of such acts of boycott as are actionable. If, for instance, in Great Britain, in the course of a boycott against a foreign State, unlawful means are used to induce a British firm to abstain from business with a national of that foreign State, the alien in question

[1] *Sorrell* v. *Smith* [1925] A.C. 700 contains a sufficiently clear exposition of the existing law in the matter. It does not attempt to reconcile the inconsistencies between the previous leading cases such as *Allen* v. *Flood* [1898] A.C. 1; *Mogul Steamship Co.* v. *McGregor Gow* [1892] A.C. 25; *Quinn* v. *Leatham* [1901] A.C. 495. And see the recent decision of the High Court of Australia in *McKernan* v. *Fraser and Another*, 46 *C.L.R.* 343. See also conflicting decisions, in the matter of so-called 'stop-lists', of the Court of Criminal Appeal in *R.* v. *Denyer* [1926] 2 K.B. 258, and of the Court of Appeal in *Hardie & Lane, Ltd.* v. *Chilton* [1928] 1 K.B. 663.

[2] See below, p. 309.

[3] See the decision of the *Oberlandesgericht* (Upper District Court) in Karlsruhe of 9 December 1926 (*Juristische Wochenschrift* (1927), p. 2832); of the *Reichsarbeitgericht* (Federal Labour Court) of 23 December 1927 concerning the legality of a lock-out; *International Survey of Legal Decisions on Labour Law* (1928), p. 177.

[4] See, for instance, the case of *Brune, Brussac and Others*, decided by the Bordeaux Court of Appeal on 24 February 1929 (*Semaine Juridique* (1929), p. 856)), in which the Court adopted a more severe view than that adopted in *Allen* v. *Flood*. And see the cases reported in the *International Survey of Legal Decisions on Labour Law* (1929), pp. 42–5, and (1930), pp. 59–61, 102–5, 109.

would be in a position to bring a successful action against the persons responsible. The same remedy would be available to a British firm dealing with a firm of a boycotted country if that British firm had suffered because persons had been induced by illegal means not to transact business with it. But this remedy is on the whole of limited scope. If the boycott is the result of an intense national movement, it is probable that persons charged with flouting the national sentiment may deem it wiser not to pursue their grievance before a court of law. Individual foreign traders may indeed be in a position to appeal to courts in such cases, but as a rule private persons or individual firms will not be able to point to a concrete loss directly attributable to the boycott. The loss will be suffered by the foreign traders as a whole.[1] Also it will be noted that – to limit the inquiry to English law, which is not backward in defending individual rights menaced by a boycott – apart from the question of conspiracy, only such acts of boycott are illegal as are performed by unlawful means. As to boycott by means of conspiracy – and that is, of course, the normal type of boycott – when the means used are lawful much will depend on whether there will be found to be lawful justification for the intentional causing of injury to others. The conception of lawful justification is, as pointed out before, an elastic one. It is possible that in time of national resentment courts may, without disregarding the law, be inclined to see a lawful justification for acts of boycott done in defence of what the defendant deemed to be a collective national interest not of a commercial character, provided always that patriotic action does not assume the form of illegal coercion or intimidation punishable by criminal law.

It will thus be seen that the protection afforded by municipal law against acts of boycott is of a limited scope. So long as the means used are not otherwise unlawful, it would be possible for a boycott of foreign goods to be conducted without contravening the law of the land. Against the toleration of such a boycott the foreign State is not entitled to protest. The situation is different when means are applied which are otherwise punishable by criminal law. The non-enforcement of the criminal law – even if the parties directly concerned are nationals – is in such cases nothing short of denial of the right of protection of the property of foreign subjects, and there ought to be little doubt that it involves the international responsibility of the State. However, effective boycotts may be possible without violations of the criminal law of the

[1] *Quaere*, could any of these bring a so-called representative action ? See Order 16, Rule 9, of the Orders of the Supreme Court: 'Where there are numerous persons having the same interest in one cause or matter, one or more of such persons may sue or be sued, or may be authorized by the Court or a judge to defend in such cause or matter, on behalf or for the benefit of all persons so interested.'

country and, generally, without committing acts which are contrary to the law. If the popular sentiment is genuine and widespread and if the national grievance is obvious and overwhelming, the object of the boycott can be achieved by refusal of commercial intercourse on the part of each member of the community without there being any necessity for coercion and intimidation ordinarily punishable by criminal law.

4

It has been submitted at the beginning of this article that the international responsibility of the State is not involved if the boycott of the goods of a foreign country is pursued by the population by legal methods. There are acts of private individuals against a foreign State which a Government must not tolerate. It must not, for instance, tolerate the preparation of a hostile expedition against a foreign State or, when neutral, direct military aid to the units of the fleet of a belligerent. The boycott of foreign goods does not belong to this category. There appears to be no good reason for a change in the existing law by way of imposing upon States the duty to suppress boycotts of this nature. No international agreement can effectively compel the population of a country to buy goods from a foreign State whose policy has become the object of deep resentment and indignation. An international agreement might prescribe the duty to prohibit an *organized* boycott or public propaganda to this end by printed or spoken word. Such an agreement would compel a State to suppress individual freedom in a manner which many States would find distasteful to their traditions and political institutions.

Neither is there a good reason for a summary condemnation of boycotts peacefully conducted by the population of a State on the ground that such boycotts are contrary to the idea of pacific settlement of international disputes. The view that a boycott is an act of economic force identical or comparable with military force in the shape of war is based on a mere manner of speech. Undoubtedly an economic boycott is an instrument of struggle. But it is a peaceful contest as compared with the physical violence of international or civil war. To apply to it the term 'war' by juxtaposition with international war in its technical meaning is as misleading as to apply that term to industrial disputes within the State in the form of a strike or lock-out. A strike or lock-out is normally a lawful exercise of a person's right not to enter into a contract. Such withdrawal of work or employment may take place in the course of what is at times called industrial warfare. But industrial warfare is normally a pacific form of contest conducted within the orbit of the law. Equally in regard to economic boycott in the international sphere, we must not be misled by a juxtaposition and implicit equal condemnation of economic and military force. In a world in which physical violence through wars proper has not become a matter of the past, there is an obvious element of exaggeration in the attempts to treat a peaceful form of struggle or resistance as war. Peace, in the sense of the absence of any form of competition, friction, or struggle, is a superficial idea – both within the State and outside it. International peace does not mean absence of international friction, or rivalries, or conflicting ambitions for the realization of men's will to power. It means that competition and conflicts of interests must find a solution by means other than war in its technical legal meaning. International peace does not mean that States will not behave in their mutual relations in a foolish, unfair, or immoral manner, or that such conduct will not be visited by retaliation of a similar nature. In a community from which war in its technical sense has been eliminated and which has not reached the stage of moral perfection, pacific means of pressure are unavoidable. To prohibit them would mean to court the more radical remedy of war. Finally, in a world in which the powerful States are still in a position to impose their will upon weaker members of the international community, a boycott may frequently be the only means of national defence of any degree of effectiveness. It may frequently be the only means of protest and retaliation against a State which finds in its military strength the source of its alleged rights and refuses to the other the benefit of judicial settlement. Certainly, the stronger State may be powerful enough to insist on and obtain the suppression of the retaliatory measure of boycott, but such action will constitute an addition to the original wrong, and not the removal of an action condemned by international law. It follows that, even if it were possible to impose upon States the duty to suppress peaceful boycott of foreign goods, such an innovation would be open to objection on general grounds. This is not a case in which the separation of the duties of the State from those of the individuals composing it is necessarily productive of injustice.

VI

LIMITATIONS UPON AND EXEMPTIONS FROM TERRITORIAL JURISDICTION

CHAPTER 10

THE PROBLEM OF JURISDICTIONAL IMMUNITIES OF FOREIGN STATES

Editor's note In 1950 the British Government set up an Interdepartmental Committee on State Immunity under the chairmanship of Lord Justice Somervell to examine the law of both State and diplomatic immunity and to report as to whether English law on these subjects conferred a more extensive immunity than was required by international law. Lauterpacht was appointed a member of the Committee and contributed to it a substantial study on State immunity. It is this study which, after some revision, became the article which forms the present chapter.

The possibilities for change in the law opened up by Lauterpacht's paper do not appear to have been acceptable in 1951. The only published outcome of the Committee's work was a Report on Diplomatic Immunity (Cmd. 8460), the recommendations in which formed the basis of the Diplomatic Immunities Act, 1955. The Committee also produced an interim report on State immunity, which was not published.

The situation has changed since then and the suggestion for the abolition of State immunity by way of international agreement made in section 6 of Lauterpacht's article was undoubtedly influential in the movement which led to the adoption by the Council of Europe on 16 May 1972 of the European Convention on State Immunity (Miscellaneous no. 31(1972), Cmnd. 5081).

Lauterpacht adopted the unusual course of attaching to the article a substantial appendix containing a summary of national decisions on immunity. The purpose of this analysis was to demonstrate that the concept of absolute immunity was much less widely accepted than had previously been thought.

The article was published in *B.Y.* 28 (1951), 220–72.

Almost concurrently with the work of the Committee on State Immunity, a commission of the *Institut de Droit International*, of which M. Ernest Lémonon was the rapporteur, was also examining this topic. Lauterpacht was a member of this Commission. His comments on M. Lémonon's Report and draft Resolutions appear in *Annuaire* (1952), I, 111–24, in the form of a letter to M. Lémonon dated 8 October 1951. As the content of the letter covers relatively briefly some of the ground already covered at length in this chapter and was prepared at almost the same time as this chapter, I have not thought it necessary to reprint the letter in these *Collected Papers*.

The reasons for the tendency, which has been on the increase since the end of the First World War, to do away with the doctrine of jurisdictional immunity of foreign States have been repeatedly stated. It is unnecessary, in this essay, to elaborate them in detail. The main – and articulate – source of the opposition to it has been the realization that the principle of immunity as originally applied by courts was intended to cover the political activities of the State as a sovereign entity in the strict sense of the word and that it has become obsolete and productive of injustice and inconvenience at a time when the operations of the State are increasingly extending into the commercial, industrial – and similar[1] – spheres. However, the growing opposition to the jurisdictional immunities of foreign States has drawn its strength from factors more significant than modern developments in the economic sphere. These factors arise to a large extent from the challenge to the prerogatives of the sovereign State, which denies to the individual legal remedies for the vindication of his rights as against the State in the matter both of contract and of tort, and which asserts a privileged position for the State in the procedural sphere. That challenge has been largely successful in most States under the rule of law. In France, a country which has led the way in the recognition of the responsibility of the State, occasionally even to the point of making it accountable for the acts of its legislative organs, the connection between the denial of the immunity of the State and the ideas of the Declaration of 1789 has been conscious and acknowledged – though for reasons peculiar to that country these principles failed to secure full recognition in relation to the immunities of foreign States.[2] In Great Britain, the immunity of the Crown, which was a survival of the personal immunity of the Sovereign, continued to assert itself with some tenacity. It yielded substantially, in the contractual sphere, even before the Crown Proceedings Act of 1947, to the dual impact of the implications of the rule of law and of the growing activities of the State in the economic and social spheres. The Crown Proceedings Act completed that process for most – though not all – purposes. Similar changes have taken place in the United States of America and other countries.[3] In that climate of legal development the maintenance of the immunity of foreign States requires special justification. Public opinion and practical considerations do not permit too wide a gap between the law governing the immunities of the home State and the law – which many regard as increasingly artificial, unjust, and archaic – relating to the immunities of foreign States. It is against this background – not altogether unre-

[1] For, as was shown in the case of *Krajina* v. *The Tass Agency* (see below, p. 372), the problem is not limited to purely commercial and contractual relations. In the *Conclusions* of the rapporteur of the relevant sub-committee of the League of Nations Committee on Codification there was enumerated among the questions requiring elucidation in connection with implied waiver of immunity the question of 'actions for damages for a tort or quasi-tort committed in the territory' (Doc. A (1928), v, 54)).

[2] See below, p. 330.

[3] See below, pp. 330–1.

lated to the incipient recognition of human freedoms as part of positive international law – that it may be opportune to re-examine the problem of jurisdictional immunities of foreign States.

I. THE ARGUMENT IN SUPPORT OF THE DOCTRINE OF IMMUNITY

There are, in the main, five arguments which have been relied upon by those who contend for the retention of the rule of immunity of foreign States. In the first instance, it has been urged that the obligation of courts to decline jurisdiction over foreign Governments is firmly grounded in the principles of the independence, the equality, and the dignity of States; that the maxim *par in parem non habet imperium* follows directly from those principles; and that the assumption of jurisdiction over foreign States amounts to an exercise of *imperium* over them in disregard of the fundamental canons of international law. The accuracy of these propositions is discussed elsewhere in this article.[1]

Secondly, there have been some[2] who, while denying that the rule of immunity follows from any basic principle of the law of nations, have maintained that it has now become so by virtue of a customary rule of international law and that it is valid and binding as such. However, as will be shown here, it is a fact that the courts of a considerable majority of States have departed from that assumed rule of international law, at least to the extent of exercising jurisdiction over foreign States in matters *jure gestionis*, without, as a rule, giving occasion for protest on the part of the foreign States concerned. Accordingly, in so far as the actual practice of States may be said to be evidence of customary international law, there is no doubt that the principle of absolute immunity forms no part of international custom.

Thirdly, it has been suggested[3] that the preoccupation with the question of jurisdictional immunities by reference to the increased activities of the State in the economic sphere may not be wholly justified in view of the possibility that such activities may be only a passing phase in the life of States. Experience has not borne out that prediction. Independently of any retrogressive tendencies of totalitarianism, the welfare State has probably become, for the foreseeable future, a permanent feature of political organization.

Fourthly, those who still favour absolute immunity have often relied on the argument that as, according to existing law, no execution by way

[1] See below, pp. 322–8.

[2] See, for example, Anzilotti, in *Rivista*, 4 (1910), 477 *et seq.*

[3] See Fitzmaurice, in *B.Y.* 14 (1933), 106.

of seizure or otherwise can in any case be levied against a foreign State, the exercise of jurisdiction, even if limited to acts *jure gestionis*, must remain no more than a nominal gesture. Yet it is by no means certain that immunity from execution is an inevitable or universally recognized rule of international law.[1] Moreover, in countries which adhere to the rule of immunity from execution in respect of a foreign State, a judgment against that State may not be altogether without effect. This is so even if we assume – and it is doubtful whether we are entitled to make that assumption without qualifications – that the foreign State will simply ignore the judgment. Even if ignored, the latter may become the starting point for diplomatic action or, in suitable cases, for international judicial proceedings. There is no reason why the judgment should remain purely nominal in cases in which the defendant State possesses property within the jurisdiction. Also, the likelihood of the judgment being ignored depends on what is considered to be the accurate position of international law in the matter of jurisdiction over foreign States in general. So long as the view prevails that the exercise of such jurisdiction is not in accordance with international law, no moral opprobrium attaches to the refusal of a foreign State to pay attention to a judgment given against it, and instances of such refusal may be correspondingly frequent. The position is different if such exercise of jurisdiction is considered both lawful and proper.

Finally, the main argument in favour of absolute immunity from jurisdiction has been the view that what has been considered the only alternative to absolute immunity, namely, exercise of jurisdiction based on the distinction between acts *jure gestionis* and acts *jure imperii*, is impossible of definition and, therefore, of application. Apart from the fact that it disregards the third alternative, namely, the general abandonment of immunity, that argument appears to be, and probably is, decisive. Courts of different countries – and occasionally courts of the same country – have treated the same kind of activity in different ways. Thus the operation of railways by the State has been considered by some courts to be an activity of a public law character; it has been regarded by others as partaking of the nature of an undertaking of a private law nature. This, as between various countries, is hardly surprising seeing that while the Belgian law of 1869 declared that it is the duty of the State to provide rapid and easy communication for its citizens, the Belgian Court of Cassation held that Holland, acting in her capacity as the owner of a railway, acted as a *personne civile*.[2] Transactions connected with a tobacco monopoly were held by a

[1] See below, pp. 338, 339.

[2] *État néerlandais* v. *Société du chemin de fer Liègeois-Limbourgeois*; *Pasicrisie Belge*, 1 (1909), 294.

Roumanian court to be *jure gestionis* and as such subject to its jurisdiction.[1] An American court came to an opposite conclusion.[2] While the activities of a State calculated to promote immigration were held by a Belgian court to be an act *jure imperii*, an Italian court held otherwise.[3] Purchase of goods to be resold to nationals was held by one French court to be an act *jure gestionis*,[4] by another to be an act *jure imperii*[5] – though in the latter case the possible explanation may have been that the office established by Switzerland in France for the purpose of purchasing goods was set up in pursuance of a Swiss Decree 'concerning the measures necessary for assuring the security of the country and the maintenance of neutrality'. That explanation, however, may be contrasted with the Belgian decision in *Monnover* v. *État Français*[6] which treated as being *jure gestionis* the purchase of goods, by a French governmental agency, for the purposes of reconstruction of territory devastated by war. There has been a similar and clear divergence of practice with regard to State loans. The same applies to contracts relating to supplies for the army. Italian courts have held that a contract made by a foreign State for the purchase of shoes for its army was an act of a private law nature and therefore outside the principle of immunity.[7] A court in the United States decided that the same transaction constituted for the State 'the highest sovereign function of protecting itself against the enemies'.[8] The same view was expressed nearly a century before in a leading decision of the French Court of Cassation in the matter of the purchase of shoes for the Spanish army.[9] It is with reference to such and similar transactions, apparently of a purely private law nature, that in the course of the discussions in the League of Nations Committee of Experts for the Progressive Codification of International Law there were asked pertinent questions to which, in the nature of things, no conclusive answer was forthcoming. The French member of the Committee, while conceding that the purchase of a torpedo-boat was an act *jure imperii*, expressed doubts about the position with regard to the purchase of arms for manufacturing war material or of supplies for a powder factory.[10] The answer, of typically

[1] *Banque roumaine de commerce et de crédit de Prague* v. *État Polonais*; *Revue de droit international privé*, 19 (1924), 581.

[2] See below, pp. 326–7

[3] See below, p. 351.

[4] *État roumain* v. *Pascalet* (1924); *Dalloz hebd.* (1924), p. 260: *Annual Digest*, 2 (1923–4), 132.

[5] *Lakhowsky* v. *Swiss Federal Government*: *Annual Digest*, 1 (1919–22), 122.

[6] *Pasicrisie Belge*, 3 (1927), 129.

[7] *Governo Rumeno* v. *Trutta*; *Giurisprudenza Italiana*, 78 (1926), 1 (i), 774: *Annual Digest*, 3 (1925–6), 179.

[8] *Kingdom of Roumania* v. *Guaranty Trust Co. of New York*, 250 Fed. 2d. 341, 343.

[9] Sirey (1849), Part 1, p. 81; *Dalloz Pér.* (1849), vol. 1.

[10] Doc. C.P.D. 1/3 Session/P.V., pp. 55, 56.

limited usefulness, given by another member of the Committee, was that that question would have to be decided in accordance either with the law of the State engaged in the commercial transaction in question or the law of the State within whose jurisdiction it had taken place.[1]

Moreover, it is no longer generally accepted that the economic activities of the State – such as State management of industry, State buying, and State selling – are necessarily of a purely 'private law nature'; that they are '*jure gestionis*'; and that in engaging in them a State acts like a private person. In these and similar cases ostensibly removed from the normal field of its political and administrative activities, the State nevertheless acts as a public person for the general purposes of the community as a whole. This applies not only to States with a socialist economy where trading or management of industry have become a public function of the State. For the State always acts as a public person. It cannot act otherwise.[2] In a real sense all acts *jure gestionis* are acts *jure imperii*. When in *Berizzi Brothers* v. *Steamship Pesaro*[3] the Supreme Court of the United States refused to accept the existence of an 'international usage which regards the maintenance and advancement of the economic welfare of a people in time of peace as any less a public purpose than the maintenance or training of a naval force', it was expressing a view which, probably, is not far removed from reality – although it is not certain that the grant of immunity is the logical consequence of that opinion. For these reasons there is force in the view that, at least in modern conditions, the distinction between acts *jure gestionis* and acts *jure imperii* cannot be placed on a sound logical basis. French judicial practice has arrived at that conclusion after many years of painful experiment and has abandoned the traditional distinction, for the purposes of delimiting the competence of judicial and administrative tribunals, between *actes administratifs d'autorité* and *actes administratifs de gestion*.[4]

[1] It may be noted that Professor Niboyet, while approving, in Sirey (1930), Part I, p. 50, cols. 2, 3, a decision of the French Court in the latter sense, expressed the view that French courts have to consider as an emanation of the Russian State only such functions as according to French conceptions – a test in itself of considerable elasticity – have a public law character. De Praag (in *R.I.*, 3rd ser. 16 (1935), 124) expresses a contrary view.

[2] This aspect of the matter was presented forcibly and, it is believed, accurately, in 1893 by Chrétien in his *Principes de droit international public*. He said: 'L'État ne passe aucun acte, n'intervient dans aucun rapport juridique, sans que l'acte soit, directement ou indirectement, motivé par la nécessité de maintenir sa haute mission gouvernementale. . . . Il comprend bien ou mal sa mission; cela importe peu. Si l'on va au fond des choses, il ne peut jamais se présenter exclusivement comme personne privée.' Nys rejected for the same reason as being 'fantastic' the distinction between the two kinds of activities (Nys, II, 340 *et seq.*). For a lucid survey of the authorities on the subject see Fairman, in *A.J.* 22 (1928), 569–74.

[3] (1926), 271 U.S. 562: *Annual Digest*, 3 (1925–6), 186.

[4] For a survey of the French judicial practice in the matter see Duguit, *Traité de droit constitutionnel* (2nd ed. 1923), III, 39 *et seq.*

It is doubtful whether the most searching attempt yet made to solve the difficulty – an attempt made in 1923 by M. Weiss, for a time Judge of the Permanent Court of International Justice[1] – can be regarded as altogether successful. The gist of the theory propounded by him was that, in determining whether an act is *jure imperii* or *jure gestionis*, regard is to be had not to the object of the transaction but to its nature. The test, it is said, is not whether the transaction aimed at achieving an object directly connected with the political functions of the State as a sovereign entity, such as the provision, through purchase, of means for its defence or a public loan; the test is whether, irrespective of its object, the juridical nature of the transaction is such that it can be entered into by an individual. An individual can make a contract. That alone is decisive. The question as to what are the objects pursued by the contract is of no consequence. In the same line of argument it might be said that a tort – a libel or a trespass – can be committed by an individual. That gain is the determining factor. There is no immunity in such cases. On the other hand, according to that view, such acts as legislation, or the expulsion of an alien, or a denial of justice, cannot be performed by an individual acting in his own name. They can be performed only by the State acting as such. Such acts legitimately give rise to a claim to immunity. The criterion suggested would appear to be simple and easy of application. However, upon analysis, that test merely postpones the difficulty. To what extent is it true to say that contracts made by the State for the purchase of shoes for the army, or of a warship, or of munitions, or of foodstuffs necessary for the maintenance of the national economy, are not immune from the jurisdiction for the reason that they are *contracts* and that an individual can make a contract? For can it not be said that these particular contracts can be made by a State only, and not by individuals? Individuals do not purchase shoes for their armies; they do not buy warships for the use of the State; they are not, as such, responsible for the management of the national economy.

It may be contended that the difficulty of drawing the line is not confined or peculiar to the distinction between acts *jure gestionis* and acts *jure imperii* and that it is proper and feasible that, given the broad meaning of the distinction, the line should be determined in doubtful cases by the courts. In fact this is what the courts of a number of countries have been doing in the past. But the question still remains whether the uncertainty produced by their decisions, the inconsistencies, and the resulting absence of an ascertainable standard capable of

[1] 'Compétence ou l'incompétence des tribunaux à l'égard des États étrangers', in *Hague Recueil*, I (1923), 525.

general application ought to be perpetuated. There are persuasive reasons for the submission that the answer to that question must be in the negative and that the law on the subject should – and can – be placed on a footing different from either the existing doctrine of absolute immunity or the concession of immunity, by reference to the traditional distinction, in matters *jure imperii* as distinguished from those *jure gestionis*. For reasons already stated and for those which are elaborated below,[1] the objections to the doctrine of absolute immunity are, it is believed, decisive. It has been abandoned in most countries. It is productive of inconvenience, injustice, and resentment, which may be more inimical to friendly international intercourse than assumption of jurisdiction. It is unlikely that public opinion – and legal opinion – will continue to countenance its retention. There is evidence that enlightened Governments prefer not to appeal to it.[2] The fact that the other system – namely, that based on the distinction between acts *jure imperii* and *jure gestionis* – is open to serious and in the long run decisive objections does not mean that the principle of absolute immunity is the only alternative. There is another alternative which is consonant with the more recent developments in countries under the rule of law and which does away with a principle that places the sovereign State above the law. That alternative consists in making the foreign State accountable before otherwise competent courts in respect of claims put forward against it in the matter of both contract and tort in the same way as the domestic State is subject to the law administered by the courts.[3]

2. THE DOCTRINE OF IMMUNITY AND THE PRINCIPLES OF INTERNATIONAL LAW

The solution adumbrated in the preceding section, namely, the assimilation of the position of the foreign State to that of the organs of the domestic State in respect of the jurisdiction of the courts in countries under the rule of law, appears on the face of it to be far-reaching and drastic. In fact, although it implies a change in the law as hitherto acted upon by the courts of many countries, it is probably not contrary to any generally accepted principle of international law or to any

[1] See pp. 328–33.

[2] As is shown by the recent case of *The Ardennes* (*Owner of Cargo*) v. *The Ardennes* (*Owners*) [1950] 2 All E.R. 517, where the defendants, the shipowners, were the Belgian Government. Judgement was given against them.

[3] In the *Dollfus Mieg* case [1950] 1 Ch. 333, 360, Somervell L.J. drew attention to the American case, the *Tampico*, 16 Federal Reports, where the same principle, i.e. assimilation of the foreign State to the domestic State, was suggested. And see below, pp. 342–3.

uniform practice of States in the matter. Undoubtedly, it fully abandons the doctrine of absolute immunity. However, that doctrine has already been jettisoned by the majority of States. In view of recent experience, of the overwhelming consensus of legal opinion, of economic necessities, and of the general tendency to subject the State – the domestic State and the foreign State – to the rule of law in all its manifestations, it is difficult to assume that it will continue to form part of the law. The doctrine of absolute immunity has been replaced in many countries by the practice based on the distinction between acts *jure gestionis* and acts *jure imperii*. As shown, it is doubtful whether that distinction can accurately or profitably be accepted as the basis of future law. What is possible and desirable is to salvage from it that element which appears to be sound and practicable. This can probably be achieved by dint of an enumeration of some of the activities whose exemption from jurisdiction ought to continue and which have been included in the past within the notion of acts *jure imperii*, i.e. of acts of a public character in the strict sense of the word. The feasibility of an enumeration of that nature, which is intended to cover the exceptions from liability to jurisdiction, is examined in another part of this article.[1] These exceptions are of considerable scope and importance. They need not obscure the meaning of the wider change as here envisaged. That change, if accepted, would do away with the general immunity of foreign States in the matter of contract as well as of tort.

The question must accordingly be considered to what extent some such development implies a departure from any fundamental requirement of international law. Undoubtedly, it involves a departure from the existing practice of national courts or, what is the same thing, from the view which national courts have taken of the position of international law on the matter and their obligations thereunder. However, the time has come to inquire afresh whether there is in fact in existence a clear and categorical principle of international law which forbids the courts of a State to assume jurisdiction over another State. It is symptomatic of the existing position with regard to the entire subject of jurisdictional immunities that international practice shows no frequent instances of protests against assumption of jurisdiction, including execution, over foreign States. Governments occasionally communicate with one another in order to claim immunity in cases in which an attempt is made to bring them before a foreign court. Such communications are essentially in the nature of an appeal for intercession. They are not, as a rule, in the nature of protests. Neither are they followed by formal protests when the Government whose assistance is invoked refuses to act or when courts, in the free exercise of their judicial

[1] See below, pp. 334–5.

function, assume jurisdiction. When in the case of the *Attualità*, a vessel chartered by the Italian Government, the latter remonstrated in 1916 with the Government of the United States on account of assumption of jurisdiction over that ship by an American court, the remonstrance was based on the view that the assumption of jurisdiction in that case contravened the 'rules of international courtesy which are invariably observed when the sovereign rights of a foreign State are involved' and that it was 'inconsistent with the dignity of a sovereign State'.[1] There were no persistent protests when Italian and Belgian courts and the Mixed Courts of Egypt paved the way in assuming jurisdiction over foreign States in matters *jure gestionis*; when the courts of many countries followed suit; or even when the courts of some countries went to the length of assuming jurisdiction in the matter of execution. The fact that in some countries the grant of immunity from jurisdiction or execution has been made dependent upon reciprocity[2] shows, indirectly, that there is, in the view of these countries, no binding rule of international law on the subject. States do not make the observance of established rules of international law dependent upon reciprocity. Ordinarily, reciprocity is made to apply to concessions and privileges to which States are not entitled, or which they are not bound to grant, according to ordinary international law.

The view that there is at present no rule of international law which obliges States to grant jurisdictional immunity to other States is, admittedly, unorthodox and, being at variance with the view almost uniformly expressed in text-books, at first sight startling. This is so, in particular, if we contrast it with the opinion, again uniformly expressed by writers, to the effect that one of the consequences of the independence – or equality – of States is the duty of municipal courts to abstain from exercising jurisdiction over foreign States and that such duty is a rule of international law. That statement is now usually accompanied by the acknowledgment of the exception connected with acts *jure gestionis*. It is not explained why, if immunity from jurisdiction is a rule of international law, it should not apply to acts *jure gestionis*; or, assuming that absolute immunity from jurisdiction was originally a rule of international law, when and how States consented to a limitation of that rule in matters *jure gestionis*.

It is submitted that the view, so often expressed in text-books and elsewhere, that the immunity of foreign States and their property from the jurisdiction of the courts of foreign States follows from a clear principle of international law, namely, the principle of equality and independence of States, needs re-examination. It finds no support in

[1] Hackworth, II, 428.

[2] See below, p. 343.

classical international law. Grotius does not refer to it. Bynkershoek occasionally deprecates it: 'Principes dum contrahunt haberi privatorum loco'.[1] Vattel, after admitting it with regard to the person of the foreign Sovereign, is silent with regard to the position of foreign States as such.[2] It is rooted, to some extent, in the doctrine of the personal immunity of heads of States. It is with regard to these that the distinction between acts *jure imperii* and acts *jure gestionis* first attained prominence in Germany in the eighteenth century in the relations of the numerous German States and Principalities. Although in various decisions given in the nineteenth century on the subject much reliance was placed on the classical decision of Mr Justice Marshall in *Schooner Exchange* v. *MacFaddon*,[3] it is doubtful whether that decision can accurately be quoted as an authority in favour of the rigid principle of jurisdictional immunity of foreign States. It is clear from the language of that decision that the governing, the basic, principle is not the immunity of the foreign State but the full jurisdiction of the territorial State and that any immunity of the foreign State must be traced to a waiver – express or implied – of its jurisdiction on the part of the territorial State. Any derogation from that jurisdiction is an impairment of the sovereignty of the territorial State and must not readily be assumed. In fact it is not easy to see why the principle of independence and equality should preclude the courts of a State from exercising jurisdiction over another State and its property so long as the State exercising jurisdiction merely applies its ordinary law, including its rules of private international law, and so long as it applies it in an unobjectionable manner not open to the reproach of a denial of justice or of disregard of the legislative and administrative sovereignty of the foreign State. The principle of independence logically requires that the courts of a State should recognize as valid the legislative acts of another recognized State in so far as these are not contrary to international law and to fundamental principles of justice, so long as they do not require other States to enforce foreign public or fiscal law, and so long as they are not intended to have extraterritorial effect (to give them, as a matter of international duty, extraterritorial effect would be, once more, to admit the right of a State to reach out into the domain of the foreign State). Beyond this it does not go. Thus no legitimate claim of sovereignty is violated if the courts of a State assume jurisdiction over a foreign State with regard to contracts concluded or torts committed in the territory of the State assuming jurisdiction. On the contrary, the

[1] For a lucid analysis of Bynkershoek's views on the subject see Gmür, *Gerichtsbarkeit über fremde Staaten* (1948), pp. 38–43. See also Barbeyrac's translation of and notes on Bynkershoek's *De foro competente legatorum* (1723), pp. 43, 46.

[2] Vattel, book IV, ch. vii, p. 108.

[3] (1812), 7 Cranch's Reports, 116.

sovereignty, the independence, and the equality of the latter are denied if the foreign State claims as a matter of right – as a matter of international law – to be above the law of the State within the territory of which it has engaged in legal transactions or committed acts entailing legal consequences according to the law of that State.[1] The absence of any denial of independence or equality appears even more clearly when the State exercising jurisdiction over a foreign State submits itself, within the same sphere, to the full operation of its own law without claiming any privileged status or immunity.

A closer examination of the origin and of the development of the doctrine of immunity of foreign States from jurisdiction shows that it is perhaps not so much the principles of independence and equality which have nurtured the soil in which that doctrine has flourished, but factors of a different kind. These have been: (*a*) considerations of the dignity of the sovereign State and (*b*) the traditional claim, transposed into the international arena, of the sovereign State to be above the law and to claim, before its own courts, a privileged position compared with that enjoyed by the subject. Both these aspects may now be considered.

The view that the assumption of jurisdiction over foreign States is contrary to their dignity and as such inconsistent with international courtesy and the amity of international relations is a persistent theme of judicial decisions on the subject. In so far as the doctrine of immunity owes its acceptance to the decisions of the courts of the United States, it is explained to some extent by the fact that it was by reference to the dignity of the States of the Union that their immunity from suit was urged insistently and repetitiously. During the debates preceding the adoption of the Virginian Convention in 1788, John Marshall stressed the element of indignity inflicted upon a State by making it a defendant in an action.[2] In the leading case of *Chisholm* v. *Georgia* the main argument for the defendant State was that it was a 'degradation of sovereignty in the States to submit to the supreme judiciary of the United States'.[3] The courts of the United States have gone to the length of relying on the argument of dignity in the matter of immunity of foreign States from taxation. Thus we find the Court of Appeals of Kentucky saying in 1923 in the matter of taxation of tobacco owned by the French

[1] For a recent example of reliance on the sovereign equality of States as a reason for immunity from jurisdiction see the observations of Professor A. de Lapradelle in connection with the Report of M. Lémonon for the meeting of the Institute of International Law at Siena (1952). He says: 'L'égalité souveraine des États membres de la société internationale ne leur permet de venir ni en demande ni en défense devant les tribunaux d'un autre État.' He says with regard to the jurisdiction of municipal courts in the matter: 'Pour celle-ci, l'État, demandeur ou défendeur, est trop grand et cette justice trop petite' (*Annuaire*, 44 (1952) (1), 106, at p. 107).

[2] 3 Elliot, *Debates* (2nd ed. 1836), p. 555.

[3] 2 Dall. 419, 425 (U.S.), 1793.

Government: '. . . if one nation enters the territory of another with its consent, for the purpose of mutual intercourse, it does so with the implied understanding that it does not intend to degrade its dignity by placing itself or its sovereign rights within the jurisdiction of the other and we know of nothing more calculated to degrade the dignity of an independent nation than for another to attempt to exercise over it the sovereign right of taxation'.[1] Yet the courts of many countries have often given effect to the State's power of taxation in similar circumstances. In England 'dignity', coupled or identified with 'independence', played an important part as an explanation of the doctrine of immunity of foreign States. It did so in the *Parlement Belge*, where the Court said: 'From all these authorities it seems to us, although other reasons have sometimes been suggested, that the real principle on which the exemption of every sovereign from the jurisdiction of every court has been deduced is that the exercise of such jurisdiction would be incompatible with his regal dignity – that is to say, with his absolute independence of every superior authority.'[2] In the same case Brett L.J. referred variously to 'independence and dignity'[3] and to 'equality and independence'[4] as the basis of immunity. In the *Cristina* Lord Macmillan invoked 'dignity, equality and independence' of foreign States as the foundation of their immunity.[5] The part which considerations of dignity have played in the matter of award of costs against and to foreign States is referred to below.[6] There is a close similarity between the manner in which the 'dignity of the Sovereign' was used as a justification of sovereign immunity within the State and the way in which it was relied upon for the same purpose with regard to the jurisdictional immunities of foreign States.[7]

It is submitted that these strained emanations of the notion of dignity are an archaic survival and that they cannot continue as a rational basis of immunity.[8] This would be the case even if the level of

[1] *French Republic* v. *Board of Supervisors of Jefferson County* (1923), 200 Ky. 18; 252 S.W. 124.

[2] *Per* Esher L.J. (1880), L.R. 5 P.D. 197, 207.

[3] *Ibid.* at p. 214.

[4] *Ibid.* at p. 220.

[5] [1938] A.C. 485, at p. 498: *Annual Digest*, 9 (1938–40), 250.

[6] See below, p. 340.

[7] The doctrine that limitation of actions does not apply to the State – *nullum tempus occurrit regi* – is commonly stated to have been based on the view that the King was so occupied with the cares of government that he ought not to suffer from the negligence of his servants. But, in *Sir Edward Coke's* case, the argument of Hobart C.J. suggests that the maxim was accepted originally as required by the paramount dignity of the Sovereign. This was also, to some extent, the reason for immunity from estoppel and of the doctrine that laches do not apply against the State. In *Monckton* v. *Attorney-General*, 2 Mac. G. 402, Lord Cottenham explained the petition of right as existing 'only for the purpose of reconciling the dignity of the Crown and the rights of subjects. . . '. In *United States* v. *Lee* (1882), 106 U.S. 196, at p. 248, the Court justified the doctrine of immunity on grounds of 'sovereign dignity'.

[8] Yet it is of interest to note that van Praag, the most modern adherent of absolute immunity, supports it on the ground that assumption of jurisdiction over a foreign State is inconsistent with the respect due to it: *R.I.*, 3rd ser., 16 (1935), 100.

amenities of international intercourse – singularly lacking, in the relations of some States, in the traditional scrupulous respect for the dignity and the susceptibilities of foreign States – had not fallen below the standards punctiliously adhered to before the First World War. Such jurisdictional immunities as Soviet Russia may have enjoyed in 1951 in the United States were not due to considerations of the dignity of the Russian State. However, quite apart from what may be a passing phenomenon, any reconsideration of the question of immunity may well adopt a critical view of 'dignity' of States traditionally associated with the grant of immunity. A State does not derogate from the dignity of another State by subjecting it to the normal operation of the law under proper municipal and international safeguards and on a footing of equality with the State within which it concludes a contract or commits a tort. The dignity of foreign States is no more impaired by their being subjected to the law, impartially applied, of a foreign country than it is by submission to their own law. As English judges have occasionally observed, the dignity of a foreign State may suffer more from an appeal to immunity than from a denial of it.[1] In so far as the jurisdictional immunity of foreign States is assumed to be based on their dignity, the time has probably come for abandoning what is now no more than an incantation alien to the conception of the rule of law, national and international, and to the true position of the State in modern society.

3. JURISDICTIONAL IMMUNITY AND THE RULE OF LAW

Although reliance on 'dignity' has loomed large in judicial reasoning in connection with the doctrine of immunity of foreign States from jurisdiction, it is probable that a substantial explanation of that doctrine will be found in the traditional immunity of the sovereign State from suit in its own courts. The entire concept of State immunity – whether of the foreign State or of the territorial State – is a survival of the period when the Sovereign, if he did justice to the subject, did so as a matter not of duty but of grace. It is an inheritance, not as indirect as it may appear, of the principle that the personal Sovereign – and subsequently the State – is *legibus solutus*. It is one of the manifestations not so much of the Austinian as of the Hobbesian conception of the State – a conception to which Mr Justice Holmes gave expression in a frequently cited and often criticized passage in *Kawananakoa* v. *Polyblank*[2] in which he based the immunity of the State 'on the logical and practical ground that there can be no legal right as against the authority that

[1] See below, p. 346.

[2] (1907), 205 U.S. 349, 353.

makes the law on which the right depends'.[1] The philosophy of Mr Justice Holmes was not altogether in harmony with the contemporaneous developments in the law of the United States in the direction of limiting the immunity of the State.[2] But it gave expression to the original doctrine of the common law, taken over by the colonies, of the prerogative immunity of the Sovereign from suit. That inheritance explains to some extent – but only to some extent – what some regard as a juridical mystery inherent in the adoption of what was essentially an absolutist principle by a country which had risen in revolt against the unlimited sovereignty of the Crown.

A further explanation of the willing acceptance of that inheritance – an explanation which shows a direct connection of the American practice with the question of immunity of foreign sovereigns from suit – lies in the impact of the problems created by the mutual relations of the Federation and the member States. Hamilton's insistence, in the *Federalist*, on the imperative necessity of granting to member States immunity from suit, is most instructive on this point.[3] Subsequent to the decision in *Chisholm* v. *Georgia*[4] the fear of encroachment on the sovereignty of States by actions brought against them by individuals

[1] In the *Western Maid* (1921), 257 U.S. 419 – at a time when the State Department was, in a different sphere, embarking upon a policy of relaxing claims to immunity – Mr Justice Holmes was pursuing the same line of thought. As the United States had not consented to be sued in maritime tort, it could not, in any legal sense, have been guilty of a tort. The Sovereign, he said, is above the law which it applies to others; an act is a tort, in the legal sense, only because the State makes it so. These and similar pronouncements have proved, it may be added, one of the principal reasons for the criticism of Mr Justice Holmes' contribution to the development of the law: see Palmer, 'Hobbes, Holmes and Hitler', in *American Bar Association Journal*, 31 (1945), 569; Briggs, 'Justice Holmes was not a Ladder to Hitler', *ibid.* 32 (1946), 631; Palmer, *ibid.* 635. It is of interest to compare Mr Justice Holmes' explanation of the principle of immunity with that given by Cockburn C.J. in *Feather* v. *Reg.* (1865), 6 B. & S. 257, 295. He said: 'a petition of right in respect of a wrong, in the legal sense of the term, shews no right to legal redress against the Sovereign. For the maxim that the King can do no wrong applies to personal as well as to political wrongs; and not only to wrongs done personally by the Sovereign, if such a thing can be supposed to be possible, but to injuries done to a subject by the authority of the Sovereign. For from the maxim that the King cannot do wrong it follows, as a necessary consequence, that the King cannot authorize a wrong. . . As in the eye of the law no such wrong can be done, so, in law, no right to redress can arise.'

[2] See his observation, made in 1925, that 'public opinion as to the peculiar rights and preferences due to the sovereign has changed' (*Davis* v. *Pringle* (1925), 268 U.S. 315, at p. 316).

[3] No. 81. He wrote of immunity: 'It is inherent in the nature of sovereignty not to be amenable to the suit of an individual *without its consent.* This is the general sense and the general practice of mankind; and that exemption, as one of the attributes of sovereignty, is now enjoyed by the Government of every State in the Union. The contracts between a nation and individuals are only binding on the conscience of the Sovereign, and have no pretensions to a compulsive force. They confer no right of action independent of the sovereign will. To what purpose would it be to authorize suits against States for the debts they owe? How could recoveries be enforced? It is evident it could not be done without waging war against the contracting State; and to ascribe to the federal courts by mere implication, and in destruction of a pre-existing right of the State Governments, a power which would involve such a consequence would be altogether forced and unwarrantable.'

[4] 2 Dall. 419 U.S. 1793.

resulted in the 11th Amendment to the Constitution, which provided as follows: 'The judicial power of the United States shall not be construed to extend to any suit in law or equity commenced or presented against one of the United States by citizens of another State or by citizens or subjects of any foreign State.' That aspect of immunity has been fully maintained. It was emphatically reaffirmed in connection with a case in which a foreign State was the plaintiff.[1]

While the influence of the common law doctrine of the immunity of the Sovereign and the assumed necessity of safeguarding the position of the States of the Union explain the emphasis of the courts of the United States on State immunity in both the domestic and the international spheres, recent developments in that country have followed the general tendency to limit the claim to immunity as being inconsistent with the notion of a State under the rule of law. The changed attitude of the Supreme Court in the matter of jurisdictional immunities of foreign States is noted elsewhere in this article.[2] As to the immunities of the State in general, Mr Justice Frankfurter observed in 1939 in a leading case that 'the present climate of opinion . . . has brought governmental immunity from suit into disfavour'.[3] More recently, in 1949, in *Larson* v. *Domestic and Foreign Commerce Corp.*,[4] the Supreme Court gave some support to the argument that 'the principle of sovereign immunity is an archaic hangover not consonant with modern morality and that it should therefore be limited wherever possible'. The Court said: 'The Congress has increasingly permitted such suits to be maintained against the Sovereign and we should give hospitable scope to that trend.' In the field of legislation the setting up in 1885 of the Court of Claims, endowed with jurisdiction over claims against the United States founded upon 'any law of Congress or . . . upon any contract, express or implied', was followed by the Tucker Act of 1887 granting jurisdiction, in the matter of such claims, to federal district courts, by various enactments relating to other causes of action (such as the Statute of 1920 relating to federal liability for admiralty and maritime torts), and, finally, by the Federal Tort Claims Act.

In France the rigid limitation of the immunity of the State was not followed in the nineteenth century by a corresponding restrictive interpretation of immunities of foreign States. The probable explanation of that fact is that French courts have regarded matters pertaining to foreign affairs as being particularly within the domain of the executive and outside the province of the judiciary. They have done so, for

[1] *Monaco* v. *Mississippi* (1934), 292 U.S. 313: *Annual Digest*, 7 (1933–4), 166.

[2] See below, p. 369, for a comparison of the decisions in *The Pesaro* and *United States of Mexico* v. *Hoffmann*.

[3] *Keifer & Keifer* v. *Reconstruction Finance Corporation* (1939), 306 U.S. 381.

[4] 337 U.S. 682, 703.

instance, to the point of refusing to interpret treaties other than those regulating purely private interests of individuals. Foreign affairs constitute the most important part of *actes de gouvernement* which are not subject to review either by the courts or by the Conseil d'État. As Duguit put it in this connection, 'l'idée de souveraineté est restée plus vivante dans les relations extérieures des États que dans son activité intérieure'. 'Cette persistance', he added, 'n'est certainement pas étrangère au maintien de l'irresponsabilité de l'État en matière diplomatique.'[1] However, since the First World War – and even before that – French courts have been gradually abandoning the doctrine of the absolute immunity of foreign Governments.[2]

In Germany the Weimar Constitution laid down, in Article 131, the broad principle of the responsibility of the State for acts of its officials. In addition to the responsibility of the officials themselves, it provided expressly that recourse to the ordinary courts of justice shall not be excluded. Previously, the Roman law conception of the *fiscus*, although the question of its independent legal personality was a subject of controversy, paved the way for subordinating some – but only some – activities of the State to rules of private law.

It is probable that, as in the United States, so also in Great Britain, the somewhat rigid application of the doctrine of the absolute immunity of foreign Governments was not uninfluenced by the immunity of the Crown. In so far as the Crown Proceedings Act, 1947, has finally made available to the citizen the ordinary legal remedies against the Crown, it has cleared the path, also in relation to foreign States, for the completion of the development, which has been unmistakable in this and in other countries, in the direction of putting the State and the individual on a footing of equality before the law. As early as 1922 Professor Holdsworth noted the incipient tendency, in the matter of the rights of the subject against the Crown, to render the competence of courts, so far as possible, coextensive with the remedies available to one subject as against another.[3] But he observed that, at the time, the subject's rights against the Crown were, in general, still being governed by the rules of medieval common law.[4] That stage has now been overcome. In the internal sphere the law has curbed 'the chronic dislike of Sovereigns (however democratic) to pay for wrongs done'.[5] For, essentially, the immunities of foreign Governments are only one aspect of what is occasionally referred to as the dishonesty of sovereignties – a claim to a prerogative which the modern State inherited from its medieval predecessor.

It has been shown that no consideration essential to international

[1] *Traité de droit constitutionnel*, III, 475.

[2] See below, pp. 358–62.

[3] *L.Q.R.* 38 (1922), 296.

[4] *Ibid.* p. 295.

[5] Judge Hough in *H.L.R.* 37 (1924), 541.

law – such as the independence or the equality of States – stands in the way of its relinquishment in relation to foreign States. Its abandonment is required not only by the expansion of the activities of States and the injustice and inconvenience resulting from the disregard of these developments in relation to claims of individuals.[1] At a period in which in enlightened communities the securing of the rights of the individual, in all their aspects, against the State has become a matter of special and significant effort, there is no longer a disposition to tolerate the injustice which may arise whenever the State – our own State or a foreign State – screens itself behind the shield of immunity in order to defeat a legitimate claim. In a trenchant analysis Dr Allen has referred to the 'brutal cynicism' in the conduct of the litigation which resulted in the successful assertion of the immunity of the State of Kelantan, after it had previously agreed to arbitration, in the action brought against it by the Duff Development Company.[2] Without subscribing to the details, as there recounted, of the allocation of responsibility for the conduct of the proceedings in that case, it must be admitted that the charge adequately expressed what was the essence of the situation. That situation, in that and in most other cases of a claim to immunity, consists in an unwarranted – and often petty – refusal to satisfy what would otherwise be a good and enforceable legal claim. It amounts, in fact, to a denial of justice.[3] English, and other, courts have occasionally castigated in unmeasured terms the impropriety of such appeal to sovereign rights.[4] It is this essential incompatibility of the doctrine of jurisdictional immunity with the principle of the subjection of the sovereign State to the rule of law which explains the strength – we might say, the vehemence – of the opposition to the maintenance of that doctrine and the fact that only a diminishing minority of writers are willing to support it.[5] It is this factor rather than the expansion

[1] In the municipal sphere the extension of the activities of the Government was largely responsible, at the close of the nineteenth century, for the enlargement of the scope of remedies against the Crown in relation to colonial Governments (*Farnell* v. *Bowman* (1887), 12 App. Cases, at p. 649). It is with reference to this and similar cases that we find Maitland saying that 'it is a wholesome sight to see the Crown sued and answering for its torts' (*Collected Papers*, III, 263).

[2] *Bureaucracy Triumphant* (1931), p. 14. And see *Duff Development Co. Ltd.* v. *Government of Kelantan* [1924] A.C. 797: *Annual Digest*, 2 (1923–4), 124. For a recent affirmation of that decision see *Kahan* v. *Federation of Pakistan* [1951] 2 K.B. 1003, 1016: *I.L.R.* 18 (1951), 210.

[3] Sibert, I, 273, says with regard to the denial of the right of execution: 'L'attachement que de telles solutions entretiennent pour le *faux dogme de la souveraineté de l'État* aboutit à un véritable *déni de justice* et fait, là où elle est possible, de la poursuite de cet État étranger devant les tribunaux de l'autre État une manifestation illusoire.'

[4] See below, pp. 346, 371.

[5] That minority includes van Praag, in *R.I.* 3rd ser. 15 (1934), 652–82, and 16 (1935), 100–37; Provinciali, *L'Immunità giurisdizionale degli Stati esteri* (1933) (with some qualifications), see pp. 81 *et seq.*; Fitzmaurice, in *B.Y.* 14 (1933), 101–24. See, on the other hand, Weiss, in *Hague Recueil*, I (1923), 525–51; Ch. de Visscher, in *R.I.* 3rd ser. 3 (1922), 149–79,

of the activities of the State and the unfairness of its competition with the less privileged private individual that is the paramount feature of the situation.

4. ASSIMILATION OF JURISDICTIONAL IMMUNITIES OF FOREIGN STATES TO THOSE OF THE DOMESTIC STATE

The following conclusions may provisionally be drawn from what has been said in the three preceding sections of this essay : (1) the doctrine of absolute immunity of foreign States from jurisdiction has been largely abandoned by judicial practice ; (2) that doctrine has no foundation in the principles of international law ; (3) the same applies to the doctrine of limited immunity, as based on the distinction between acts *jure imperii* and acts *jure gestionis*, which is still adhered to by the courts of a large majority of States ; (4) the doctrine of limited immunity does not provide a workable basis for a regulation of the problem of jurisdictional immunities by reference to rules capable of general application ; (5) jurisdictional immunity of foreign States – either in its absolute form or when limited to so-called acts *jure imperii* – is, like the jurisdictional immunity of the domestic State, contrary to the wider principle which postulates the submission of the instrumentalities of the State to the ordinary operation of law as administered by courts.

The practical consequence necessarily following from these conclusions would seem to be the abolition, subject to specified safeguards and exceptions, of the rule of immunity of foreign States. That end can be achieved either by way of international agreement or by unilateral legislative action of States which have subjected their own governmental organs to the jurisdiction of their courts and which may decide to put on the same basis the position of governmental instrumentalities of foreign States. The merits and prospects of international regulation of abolition of jurisdictional immunities are discussed later in this essay.[1] So far as regulation, in that direction, by way of municipal legislation is concerned, reasons have been given why, subject to specified safeguards and exceptions, it can be achieved in full accord with the

300–35 ; Fensterwald, in *H.L.R.* 63 (1950), 614–42 ; Spruth, *Gerichtsbarkeit über fremde Staaten* (1929) ; Gmür, *Gerichtsbarkeit über fremde Staaten* (1948), and the same in the Swiss *Annuaire de droit international*, 7 (1951), 9–76. See also the comment to Article 11 of the Draft Convention on the subject of the Harvard Research Bureau of 1932 : 'National courts have been slow to break away from the traditional conceptions of State sovereignty, independence and equality, but gradually the demands of justice and the necessities of the situation have been reflected in a growing tendency in the jurisprudence of many countries to emphasize exceptions to State immunity rather than to emphasize the basic rule itself' (at pp. 473, 474). The Resolutions adopted in 1891 by the Institute of International Law went far in that direction : *Annuaire* (1891). See also Loewenfeld, in *Grotius Society*, 34 (1949), 111–26, and, in particular, Fairman, in *A.J.* 22 (1928), 566–89.

[1] See below, p. 344.

international obligations of the State. It may now be convenient to outline some of these principal safeguards and exceptions:

In the first instance, immunity must remain the rule with respect to the legislative acts of a foreign State and of measures taken in pursuance thereof. This would include, for instance, immunity of a foreign State – as distinguished from persons who acquire title from it – in respect of nationalization of property of aliens by virtue of a general statute or decree even if considered to be contrary to international law. It is true that a foreign State may be tempted to avoid its contractual obligations by enacting appropriate legislation. In that case, which cannot be regarded as typical, the remedy against the State itself would have to be of a diplomatic nature. Such immunity with regard to legislative acts would merely leave the foreign State in the same position as the domestic State which cannot be sued before its courts in respect of the acts of its legislature.

Secondly, there must be immunity from jurisdiction in respect of the executive and administrative acts of the foreign State within its territory, such as alleged unjustified expulsion or exaction of dues or wrongful imprisonment or, generally, denial of justice.[1] In particular, no action should lie with regard to torts committed by foreign States and their organs in their own territory. These must be left either to judicial remedies within that foreign State or to appropriate diplomatic action in accordance with the accepted practice of diplomatic protection of citizens abroad.[2]

Thirdly – to refer, by way of example, to the position under English law – the principle of immunity must continue with respect to contracts made with or by the foreign State, except contracts which have been concluded in the United Kingdom or which, though concluded abroad, contain elements which would cause an English court to apply to them rules of English law by virtue of rules of private international law as understood by English courts. For it must be of the essence of any comprehensive regulation of the subject that the general abolition of immunity should not place the foreign State in a position less advantageous than that of private individuals by submitting that State to jurisdiction in cases in which, by virtue of the operation of rules of

[1] With regard to immunity in respect of denial of justice in the strict sense of the word, i.e. at the hands of judicial authorities, it will be noted that in England the Crown enjoys that immunity under section 2 (5) of the Crown Proceedings Act of 1947 relating to the liability of the Crown in tort. A United States Statute of 1938 (52 Stat. 438) provides for a remedy against the State in cases of unjustified conviction or imprisonment.

[2] In the matter of torts the foreign State would thus be placed to some extent, as far as the United Kingdom is concerned, in a position of equality with the Crown. For although the latter can be sued for a tort committed abroad, it can – as would appear from the proviso to s. 2 (1) of the Crown Proceedings Act of 1947 – set up the defence of Act of State, a defence applicable to torts committed in relation to aliens abroad (see below, p. 342).

private international law, the courts would have no jurisdiction in a private action. On the other hand, it seems proper that English courts should have jurisdiction if the contract in question, though concluded abroad, is to be performed in England, or if it refers specifically to English law as the proper law of the contract, or if for any other reason, according to rules of private international law, an English court would hold it to be subject to English law.[1]

Fourthly, no action should lie or execution be levied against a foreign State contrary to the accepted principles of international law in the matter of diplomatic immunities. Neither should a man-of-war or a vessel assimilated thereto or an aircraft forming part of the armed forces of a foreign State be subject to an action *in rem*, seizure, or arrest.[2] Such exemption from liability to actions *in rem* and seizure would indirectly emphasize the liability of the foreign State for the contractual obligations undertaken on behalf of warships and for torts committed by those responsible for them. This, in general, must also be the position with regard to the contractual and tortious responsibility of a State in respect of its armed forces in a foreign country. Admittedly, the exception to be conceded in connection with diplomatic immunities is one of accommodation, calculated to soften the impact of a somewhat drastic innovation, rather than of principle. Courts of some countries have not hesitated, in appropriate cases, to assume jurisdiction over foreign States even when the subject matter of the action had some relation to diplomatic activities.[3] It is probable that, in modern conditions, the entire principle of diplomatic immunity may call for reconsideration. However, improvements in the content of international law are not made easier by being attempted simultaneously in various directions.

[1] In this connection the following question would require consideration, to take the United Kingdom as an example: If the position of foreign States is to be assimilated to that of the Crown, what shall be the extent of their immunities in respect of contracts of service concluded by them with their employees, whether their nationals or not, in the United Kingdom? In the United Kingdom the relation between the Crown and its servants is not of a contractual nature and therefore not subject to the ordinary jurisdiction of courts, especially with regard to dismissal, reduction of pay, and arrears of pay, although with regard to the latter s. 27 (1) of the Crown Proceedings Act has introduced an element of doubt. The courts of a number of countries, while assuming jurisdiction with regard to transactions of foreign State agencies on the ground that these are *jure gestionis*, have declined jurisdiction with regard to contracts of service made by these agencies on the ground that in entering into them the State acts *jure imperii* (see below, p. 357). As in the United Kingdom there may be, in this particular sphere and in other spheres, a difference between agencies which are identified with the Crown and corporations which are not, the question will arise to what extent are these differences applicable to foreign agencies.

[2] Such immunity attaches to British warships and aircraft under s. 29 of the Crown Proceedings Act. It will be noted that there is no immunity in the United Kingdom with respect to actions against the Crown arising out of damage caused by a warship except that the action must be brought within the period of one year fixed by the Limitation Act, 1939, for public authorities.

[3] See below, p. 341.

It is submitted that if a State were to adopt legislation on the lines indicated above – i.e. by placing, subject to specified safeguards and exceptions, foreign States in the same position of subjection to the jurisdiction of courts which it occupies in the matter of actions brought against itself – it would not be disregarding any clear or binding principle of international law. If, as the result of jurisdiction assumed in pursuance of such legislation, a foreign State were to bring a complaint before the International Court of Justice, it is unlikely that the Court would find that a rule of international law had been violated and that international responsibility had been incurred. It is very probable that the law of the countries, if any,[1] which still grant absolute immunity to foreign States, goes beyond the requirements of international law. The great majority of countries now decline to grant jurisdictional immunity to foreign States in what is described as acts *jure gestionis*. It is not contended by anyone that their attitude is contrary to international law. But does not the further development as here outlined go substantially beyond that? Does it not purport to confer upon national courts unlimited jurisdiction in matters usually described as being *jure imperii*? It is not believed that it does. The exceptions by which it is surrounded cover substantially what is generally intended to be included in the notion of acts *jure imperii* – save that, in particular, it specifically excludes from the scope of acts *jure imperii* contracts made and torts committed by a State outside its territory. Thus, if the cause of action arises out of a contract for the purchase of goods, there would be no room for immunity, regardless of whether the contract is for purchase of equipment for the army or whether it is made for the purpose of making a financial profit. To that extent the solution here outlined is based on a restricted interpretation of acts *jure imperii*. While not countenancing the assumption of jurisdiction in a way calculated to interfere with the sovereign rights of foreign States, that solution does not adopt as the basis of legislation the distinction, which experience has proved to be impracticable and productive of uncertainty, between acts *jure gestionis* and acts *jure imperii*.

The question of the conformity of the development as here envisaged with the principles of international law on the subject has been elaborated here in some detail for what appear to be cogent reasons. It is important, with regard to a problem which looms so large in decisions of courts of many countries and which has been so persistently, though inaccurately, related to the independence and the dignity of States, that nothing should be done which may seem to set aside any truly essential principle of international law or to be designed to meet some

[1] See below, pp. 368–71.

passing needs in relation to a particular State or groups of States. The problems involved are wider and more significant than the anomalies disclosed in any particular judicial decision specially offensive to public opinion or the more general phenomenon of the expanded activities of States in the economic and cognate fields. At the same time it is of importance to scrutinize any proposed change from the point of view not only of the existing law but also of convenience and of the requirements of friendly international intercourse. The normal exercise of jurisdiction of courts in actions against foreign States may in itself remove a frequent source of friction and resentment. From the point of view of securing a friendly atmosphere in international relations, judicial remedies against foreign States may be preferable to diplomatic action necessitated by the refusal of those States to submit to jurisdiction. It is well possible that, if absolute immunity ceases to be the rule, vexatious actions may be brought against foreign States with the view to embarrassing them. However – although this is not generally realized – even under a system of full jurisdictional immunity there is nothing to prevent a plaintiff from bringing such actions, with all the attendant publicity and inconvenience, until the courts have finally declared themselves incompetent. Moreover, courts may be trusted to discourage, by appropriate award of costs, any abuse of their process. In general, the assumption of jurisdiction over foreign States has not, in the past, given rise to international friction. The dangers, if any, lie not in the exercise of jurisdiction, but in the abuse of it by way of denial of justice through partiality, delay, or otherwise. No such dangers need be apprehended in countries under the rule of law. However, should a foreign State consider in any particular case that there has taken place a denial of justice or an assumption of jurisdiction in excess of the permissive provisions of the law, there is no reason why it should not have recourse to appropriate international remedies. There would be no difficulty in the matter in all cases in which the Optional Clause is effectively in operation in the relations of the States concerned. Moreover, it would be feasible and proper for a State when enacting legislation which might appear to some to be of a novel and drastic nature to declare that it would be ready to submit to the International Court of Justice, also in relation to countries with regard to which the Optional Clause was not effectively in operation, any complaints arising out of alleged improper application of such legislation.

5. SOME CONNECTED PROBLEMS

(1) *Seizure and execution*

There are a number of questions which will require consideration in connection with any modification or abolition of the rule of jurisdictional immunities of foreign Governments. In particular, the question would arise whether such reform should extend to seizure and execution. There seems to be no convincing reason why it should not. In England, under the Crown Proceedings Act, 1947, the Crown enjoys immunity from execution (though the Act provides for a process of certification of orders made against the Crown). This is so for the reason that there is no question of the Crown refusing to satisfy a judgment. That assurance does not exist in the case of foreign States - a consideration which provides an answer to the argument that as the State does not admit execution against itself it can hardly expect foreign States to submit to it.[1] However, does not immunity from seizure – whether by way of attachment or execution – constitute a rule of international law so generally accepted that any departure from it would constitute a most drastic innovation? In the matter of execution the courts of the majority of countries probably still adhere to the principle of absolute immunity – though recent developments have made inroads, also in that sphere, upon the established practice. Although Belgian courts for a time declined to go to the length of permitting execution,[2] the Civil Tribunal of Brussels in a recent decision containing a detailed discussion of the fundamental issues involved emphatically dissociated itself from the previous practice.[3] In the *Consular Premises* (*Greece*) case the Court of Athens observed that it was not necessary, in the case before it, to go into the question whether execution was admissible with regard to the acts of a foreign State of a private law nature seeing that 'one must assume that a foreign State will voluntarily submit to execution'.[4] A Greek law passed in 1938 permitted execution subject to the authorization of the Minister of Justice; that law was relied upon in a decision, given in 1949, of the Court of Appeal of Athens.[5] The frequently-changing practice of Dutch courts shows occasional examples

[1] See the observations of Madame Bastid to the Report of M. Lémonon for the meeting of the Institute of International Law in 1952, *Annuaire*, p. 49.

[2] See, for example, *West Russian Steamship Co.* v. *Captain Sucksdorff*: *Annual Digest*, 1 (1919–22), 152; *State of Portugal* v. *Sauvage*: *ibid.* p.154; and, in particular, *Brasseur and Associates* v. *Republic of Greece*: *ibid.* 6 (1931–2), 164.

[3] See the judgment of 30 April 1951, in *Société Commerciale de Belgique* v. *L'État Hellénique*, where the Court said: 'Le pouvoir d'exécution est la conséquence du pouvoir de jurisdiction' (*Clunet*, 79 (1952), 244).

[4] *Annual Digest*, 6 (1931–2), 338.

[5] See below, p. 354.

of execution against foreign States.[1] As shown below, the recent practice of Switzerland and France permits such execution.[2] With regard to the latter, the decision of the Court of Cassation in *Union of Soviet Socialist Republics* v. *Association France-Export*[3] bears directly upon the point. In Switzerland, a Decree of the Federal Court of 24 October 1939 made execution dependent upon the authorization of the Federal Council. It would appear that, apart from that Decree, the immunity of foreign States from execution, in Switzerland, depends upon reciprocity.[4] In Italy, according to a Law of 15 July 1926,[5] acts of execution and attachment in respect of the property of foreign States are permissible subject to authorization of the Minister of Justice. This appears also to be the position in Soviet Russia according to a Decree of 14 June 1929. The Mixed Courts of Egypt permitted execution in matters *jure gestionis*.[6] On the other hand, in the United States of America courts have affirmed immunity from execution even in cases in which they assumed jurisdiction on the merits.[7]

It is significant that States affected by measures of execution have not as a rule protested against it as being unlawful. In fact, it may be difficult to adduce reasons of principle which would require in the matter of execution a rule different from that obtaining in the matter of jurisdiction on the merits. Undoubtedly the question of execution can arise in practice only when the foreign State possesses property within the jurisdiction. But that is not a reason for dispensing with execution whenever practicable. At least in those cases there can be no valid reason for the objection that assumption of jurisdiction is a purely nominal gesture. On the other hand, there is room for a consideration

[1] See below, p. 362.

[2] See below, pp. 356, 360.

[3] *Annual Digest*, 5 (1929–30), 18.

[4] See Guggenheim, p. 177.

[5] Balladore Pallieri, *Diritto internazionale pubblico* (5th ed. 1948), p. 290.

[6] See *Egyptian Delta Rice Mills Co.* v. *Comisaría General etc.*: *Annual Digest*, 12 (1943–5), 103.

[7] See *Kunglig Jarnvagsstyrelsen* v. *Dexter & Carpenter Inc.*, as reported in Hackworth, II, 479. It will be noted that in various treaties connected with the activities of its Commercial Delegations the Soviet Union had agreed that execution may be levied against its property. Thus Article 5 (8) of the Temporary Commercial Agreement of 1934 with Great Britain provided that all property of the Soviet Union was subject to seizure, with the exception of property necessary for the exercise of diplomatic or consular functions in the United Kingdom (Treaty Series, no. 11 (1934), Cmd. 4567). In that Treaty the Soviet Union assumed liability on contracts concluded by the Commercial Delegation or other organizations guaranteed by it. Similarly, Article 7 of the Economic Agreement annexed to the Treaty between Germany and Soviet Russia of 12 October 1925 provided as follows: 'Legal acts of the Trade Delegation consummated in Germany which are binding on the U.S.S.R., and the economic effects of these acts, shall be subject to German law and German jurisdiction. Measures of compulsory execution may also be applied to the property of the U.S.S.R. in Germany, except in so far as regards objects which, according to the general rules of international law, are required for the exercise of sovereign rights or are intended for the use of diplomatic or consular representatives in their official capacity' (*L.N.T.S.* 53, 101). Similar treaties were concluded by Soviet Russia with Austria, Sweden, Denmark, and some other States.

of the safeguards which may be necessary in case execution against foreign States should become the general rule. In the first instance, execution cannot properly extend to warships and vessels assimilated thereto nor to diplomatic premises and to property placed there *bona fide*. Secondly, contingencies are conceivable in which seizure of the property or the assets of the foreign State might cause friction and raise issues likely to disturb in a serious way the friendly relations with the State concerned. Accordingly, if immunity from execution is abolished in principle, it may be considered whether, on the application of the foreign State concerned, one branch of the executive – such as the Minister of Foreign Affairs – should not be given the power to stay the execution. In that case provision would have to be made for indemnifying in some way the successful plaintiff.

(2) *Award of costs*

It would be in line with the abandonment of the principle of immunity that, in case the foreign State appears as plaintiff and judgment is given for the defendant, courts should have the power to award costs against the State concerned and that such order as to costs should be enforceable against it. In the past, with regard to heads of States, English courts have gone so far in respecting the dignity of foreign States as to decline to award costs in favour of the successful Sovereign on the ground that it would be a disparagement of his dignity to award costs to him[1] – though they have awarded costs when the successful plaintiff expressly asked for them.[2] However, it is probable that even under the existing law costs can be awarded against a foreign State. There are instances of courts ordering foreign States to deposit security for costs in cases in which they appear as plaintiffs.[3]

(3) *Immovable property*

There is uniform authority in support of the view that there is no immunity from jurisdiction with respect to actions relating to immovable

[1] *Hullet* v. *King of Spain* (Dow & Clarke's Rep., p. 169).

[2] *Monaco* v. *Monaco* (1937), 157 L.T.R. 231 : *Annual Digest*, 8 (1935–7), 23. In England, by the Administration of Justice (Miscellaneous Provisions) Act, 1933, s. 7, in any civil proceedings or arbitration to which the Crown is a party costs should be awarded in the same manner and on the same principles as in cases between subjects.

[3] *The Newbattle*, 10 P.D. 33 ; *Republic of Costa Rica* v. *Erlanger* (1876), 3 Ch.D. 62. In the case of *Dollfus Mieg* v. *Bank of England*, Wynn-Parry J. made an order for security for costs to be deposited by the United States and France, who asked to be joined as defendants : [1950] 2 All E.R. 60 : *Annual Digest*, 16 (1949), 103. This, it has been stated, is the normal practice. See also to the same effect *Fuchs* v. *Hertford Accident & Indemnity Co.*, decided by the United States District Court, S.D.N.Y. (1950), 93 F. Supp. 926, and *Republic of Roumania* v. *Constantinescu*, decided in 1951 by the High Court of the Canton of Zurich and reported in *A.J.* 45 (1951), 799.

property.[1] Most of the relevant judicial pronouncements are *obiter*, but – probably – that circumstance emphasizes the undoubted acceptance of the rule as stated.[2] In laying down in any particular case that the foreign State is entitled to immunity, courts consider it necessary to make an express reservation with regard to what they consider the obvious exception, namely, actions relating to immovable property.[3] However, that particular aspect of immunity is not altogether free of doubt – it is significant that there is no English decision directly supporting this exception from the principle of immunity – and its clarification would seem desirable.

(4) *Questions of procedure. Service of writ. Discovery. Act of State*

The assimilation of the immunities enjoyed by foreign Governments to those enjoyed by the domestic State would necessarily raise various connected questions of procedure. These cannot be discussed here in detail. They include, for instance, the question of the service of the writ. If, as in England, the governing principle is that the courts of a country have jurisdiction only over persons present within the jurisdiction, to what extent can the foreign State be deemed to be present as the result of the mere fact that it maintains a diplomatic or other representative in this country? If the diplomatic representative is to be the proper recipient of the writ in his capacity as the representative of

[1] It is not considered necessary to add to the length of this article by a quotation of legislative provisions and judicial decisions in support of that view. A considerable number of these will be found in the comment to Article 9 of the Harvard Research Draft on the Competence of Courts in regard to foreign States.

[2] As Professor Niboyet says in an article entitled 'Les immunités de juridiction, en droit français, des états étrangers engagés dans des transactions privées', in *R.G.* 43 (1936), at p. 534, 'La jurisprudence ne fournit pas de document, sans doute parce que tout le monde est d'accord'.

[3] The complete subjection of immovable property to the jurisdiction of the State has been regarded as subject to one limitation, namely, when the action concerns immovable property actually used for the purposes of the diplomatic mission. Thus in Czechoslovakia, after the Supreme Court gave judgment, in 1928, for the enforcement, in respect of a building used as the Hungarian legation, of an award of a Mixed Arbitral Tribunal rendered against Hungary, the Czechoslovak Ministry of Foreign Affairs formally gave a decision laying down that execution by means of a forced sale of the premises of a foreign legation was not in accordance with international law. The Supreme Court of Czechoslovakia gave effect to that ruling (*Immunity of Legation Buildings* case: *Annual Digest*, 4 (1927–8), 370). In the same category there may be included the decision of the Prussian Tribunal for Conflicts of Jurisdiction where the Court refused to entertain an action aiming at the removal of the insignia of the Polish State from a building occupied by the Polish vice-consul (*Halig* v. *Polish State*: *ibid.* p. 164). However, when in 1929 the Swedish ambassador in France invoked jurisdictional immunity and exemption from French legislation concerning tenancies in respect of property owned by the Swedish State and intended to be used for the purpose of the legation, the Court rejected the plea to the jurisdiction. It said: 'The acquisition of real property by a foreign State does not *ipso facto* invest that property with the privileges of exterritoriality; it is necessary that property be completely appropriated to the service of the embassy' (*Petrocchino* v. *Swedish State*: *ibid.* 5 (1929–30), 306). An account of a similar Italian case involving property to be used as an embassy is given below, p. 349.

the State, how can any such innovation be reconciled with the existing law prohibiting the service of a writ upon a foreign minister? To mention another example, to what extent ought foreign States, placed as they would be on a footing of equality with the domestic State, benefit from the privileges still enjoyed by the latter, as in the matter of discovery of documents or limitation of actions? It would follow from the principles of the reform here envisaged that foreign States would benefit from these privileges.[1] Consideration would also have to be given to the question of 'Acts of State'. If, to limit once more the example to the position in English law, 'Act of State' covers primarily acts done by the Crown in relation to aliens abroad,[2] if immunity in respect of 'Acts of State' is preserved by national legislation such as the Crown Proceedings Act, 1947, and if foreign States are to be placed in the same position as the Crown enjoys under the latter Act, then the result might be that the foreign State would enjoy immunity exactly in respect of the acts with regard to which it is intended to subject it to the jurisdiction of English courts, namely, acts done in this country in relation to British subjects. A further question which would require consideration would be that of admissibility, against foreign States, of declaratory judgments – for these may, in effect, be used as a substitute for an injunction or an order for specific performance.

(5) *Reciprocity as the basis of immunity*

The following are the reasons why the method of reciprocity cannot be considered as offering a satisfactory approach to the solution of the problem:

(1) In the first instance, it is probable that the adoption of the principle of reciprocity would result in a substantial degree of uncertainty in the administration of this branch of the law. Thus in order to determine whether a foreign State which has accepted, wholly or in part, the distinction between acts *jure imperii* and acts *jure gestionis* is entitled to immunity, it would be necessary to investigate the position

[1] In England, although discovery can be ordered against foreign States appearing as plaintiffs (*King of Spain* v. *Hullet*, 1 Cl. & F. 333; *Rothschild* v. *Queen of Portugal* (1839), 3 Y. & C. (Ex.) 594; *Prioleau* v. *United States* (1866), 2 Equity Cases 659) – and, probably, when submitting themselves to jurisdiction as defendants – such discovery may be subject to the exemptions provided for in respect of the Crown by the Crown Proceedings Act (s. 28) and the rule laid down in *Duncan* v. *Cammell Laird & Co.* [1924] A.C. 624.

[2] It has been suggested that *R.* v. *Bottrill* [1947] K.B. 41: *Annual Digest*, 13 (1946), 312; and *Netz* v. *Chuter Ede* [1946] 1 All E.R. 628, established the proposition that 'Act of State' can also be pleaded with regard to acts – detention and deportation, respectively, of enemy aliens – taking place in England. However, it is probable that the term 'Act of State' was used in these cases in its non-technical connotation. According to the United States Federal Tort Claims Act no action lies against the Government of the United States in respect of 'any claim arising in a foreign country'.

in that State. However, the law in most countries is far from being clear in this respect.[1] In most countries there are neither legislative provisions nor uniform or consistent judicial precedent on the subject.

(2) Secondly, if jurisdictional immunity is a principle which it is increasingly difficult to reconcile with modern developments, then the fact that the foreign State concerned grants immunity to other States would not be sufficient to justify the denial of a remedy to the individual plaintiff. The misgivings and the criticism to which the grant of jurisdictional immunity to foreign States occasionally gives rise are due not so much to any absence of reciprocity as to the fact that it is possible for a foreign State or its agency to disregard or invade with impunity rights otherwise protected by the law of the land. The adoption of the principle of reciprocity would accentuate – it would not remove – what is increasingly considered to be an undesirable situation.

(3) In so far as immunity represents a sound principle of international law – in particular in so far as it postulates that a State is not answerable to the jurisdiction of foreign courts in the matter of its legislation and similar acts of sovereignty – it must, in principle, continue to be given effect irrespective of reciprocity (though subject to the exercise of the right of retaliation in case of a violation of that principle by another State).

On general grounds reciprocity is probably an unsatisfactory instrument for securing the observance of ordinary rules of international law.[2] Courts do not, as a rule, make the granting of a remedy to one party conditional upon the observance by that party, on other occasions, of the legal rule *in pari materia*. Essentially, immunity from jurisdiction amounts to a denial of an otherwise available legal remedy. As such it is obnoxious. There is objection to a practice which in effect would make a court say to the plaintiff: 'We will deny you, as against a foreign State, a remedy to which you are otherwise entitled provided that the courts of the defendant State deny a remedy in similar circumstances as against our own State.'[3] There are only very few countries which have applied, in some respects, the principle of specific reciprocity to questions of immunity.[4]

[1] See above, p. 319.

[2] See, to the same effect, the observations of Lord Porter in *United States of America and Republic of France* v. *Dollfus Mieg et Cie and Bank of England* [1952] A.C. 582 : *I.L.R.* 19 (1952), 163.

[3] For an example of reciprocity in a different sphere see the United States Statute 28 U.S.C.A. 261 which provides as follows : 'Aliens who are citizens or subjects of any Government which accords to citizens of the United States the right to prosecute claims against such Government in its courts shall have the privilege of prosecuting claims against the United States in the Court of Claims, whereof such court, by reason of their subject matter and character shall have jurisdiction.'

[4] See above, p. 339, and below, p. 356, as to Switzerland and other countries in the matter of execution.

(6) *Availability of remedies within the State seeking immunity*

If the considerations adduced in this article as militating against the principle of jurisdictional immunity of foreign States are valid, then, it is submitted, their force is not decisively affected by the circumstance that the remedy sought by the plaintiff is available within the foreign State seeking immunity. Such remedy, which deprives the plaintiff of the natural and proper forum, may be for him costly and impracticable. It may, on occasions, be purely nominal or incomplete. The courts whose jurisdiction is sought would be burdened with the difficult task of determining the existence and the degree of reality of the purported remedy within the State claiming immunity.

6. ABOLITION OF IMMUNITY BY WAY OF INTERNATIONAL AGREEMENT

Reasons have been given why the solution of the problem of jurisdictional immunities of foreign States by way of assimilation of their position to that of States under the rule of law which have substantially renounced their own immunity before their courts would not be inconsistent with any basic principle of international law or with the requirements of friendly international intercourse. Moreover, a solution of that nature, circumscribed by clear and specified exceptions, would free international law of a subject matter which has occupied a large and disproportionate place in the activities of municipal courts and which, because of its essential insignificance, has tended to infuse an element of artificiality into international law. If that solution is adopted, it will no longer be necessary to give continued attention to such questions as the relevance of the peacefulness and legality of the possession exercised by the foreign State, the importance to be attached to the declaration by the foreign State as to the ownership or possession of the subject matter of the action, the intricate questions connected with the nature of possession, the subtleties of the relation of the State to its departments, the limits of waiver, and many others. It is a disquieting reflection upon the reality of the Law of Nations that in many countries most of the decisions of their courts relating to international law are concerned, in some form or other, with immunities of foreign Governments and their representatives.

However, while it is probable that the example of States which have abolished their own immunity within their borders may provide the initial impetus for freeing international law, by way of municipal legislation, of the shackles of an archaic and cumbersome doctrine of controversial validity and usefulness, it is clear that such unilateral method of reform cannot, in the long run, provide a final solution.[1] For the doctrine of jurisdictional immunity of foreign States has been generally considered – judicially and otherwise – to form part of international law. It is in the long run undesirable that the modification of such a doctrine should take place by way of national action which is unilateral, sporadic, and unco-ordinated. The resulting lack of uniformity would be bound to contribute to friction and confusion. For these reasons, the alternative of bringing about any reform in this field of international law by way of international agreement and concerted scientific effort, aiming at a codification of the subject, merits attention. The topic of jurisdictional immunities of States is among those which the International Law Commission has included within its programme of codification. A detailed study and discussion by that body may provide a much needed clarification of the subject by reference to the practice of Governments and courts. There is, in this matter, no such divergence of national interests or deeply rooted peculiarities or traditions of national jurisprudence as to hamper the Commission in the impartial, harmonious and effective fulfilment of its exploratory and codifying task.

It may be useful, at this stage, to emphasize these two aspects of the problem. In the first instance, it is becoming increasingly clear that the maintenance of immunity is not necessarily in the obvious interest of any particular State or group of States. There is probably no substance in the view – and in the fear – that once the restraints of the doctrine of immunity are abandoned States with world-wide interests may be confronted with a flood of petty and vexatious actions and extortions in foreign countries. The ordinary remedies of international law, including those of retaliation, as well as special remedies outlined elsewhere in this article,[2] may provide in most cases a substantial safeguard against any such possibility of abuse. It must also be borne in mind that States with wide commercial interests abroad are adversely affected, in the persons of their nationals, by the rule of immunity. This fact explains why government departments and organized economic interest of States whose courts still adhere to the rule of immunity have favoured its relinquishment. Moreover, the existing practice provides no firm safeguards against abuse. It is implicit in the still predominant distinction

[1] Reference may be made in this connection to a passage – which is illuminating by its very hesitation – in Professor Hyde's weighty treatment of the subject. He says: 'While the individual State may not by legislative enactment lessen the requirements of international law and thereby rid itself of an obligation to accord an exemption which the law prescribes, it may by such process not improperly express its own view concerning either what these requirements are or what they should be' (Hyde, II, 839).

[2] See above, p. 337.

between acts *jure gestionis* and acts *jure imperii* that it involves, in principle, the negation of the principle of immunity. For, in consequence of it, the State is submitted in the first instance to foreign jurisdiction which determines by reference to its own rules – for there are no rules of international law on the subject – whether the act in question is *jure imperii* or *jure gestionis*.

Secondly, care must be taken not to permit the inquiry to be stultified from the outset by the facile assumption – which international lawyers have occasionally been prone to make in other fields – that there is in this matter a clear division between two opposing systems or schools of jurisprudence: the 'Continental' (which has abandoned or is in the process of abandoning the principle of absolute immunity) and the 'Anglo-American' (said to adhere to it steadfastly). The survey attached as an appendix to this article shows that this is not the case. The courts of France, Holland, Germany, and other 'continental' countries have on occasions given their *imprimatur* to the doctrine of absolute immunity; according to some, they are still wedded to it. While in the United States and the United Kingdom the courts have adhered to the principle of absolute immunity with a certain rigidity, they have done so largely for reasons, the basis for which has disappeared, connected with the historic position of the executive and, in the United States, of States members of the Union. They have done so in opposition to the principle, which has gradually asserted itself in the domestic sphere, of the submission of the executive to the rule of law. As will be shown, there are clear indications in some recent decisions of American and English courts either of deliberate hesitation in applying the doctrine of immunity or of its indirect curtailment by way of circuitous avenues of the dialectics of the rules of possession and the like.[1]

[1] Sir Eric Beckett has stated, in connection with the examination of this subject by the Institute of International Law in 1951, that 'the amount of State immunity awarded by English courts at present is somewhat wider than is required by the principles of international law and is perhaps wider than is desirable' (*Annuaire* (1952)). With this there may be compared the following observation of Sir Robert Phillimore in the *Charkieh* (1873), L.R. 4 A. and E., at p. 99: 'No principle of international law, and no decided case, and no dictum of jurists of which I am aware has gone so far as to authorize a sovereign prince to assume the character of a trader, when it is for his benefit; and when he incurs an obligation to a private subject to throw off, if I may so speak, his disguise, and appear as sovereign, claiming for his own benefit, and to the injury of a private person, for the first time, all the attributes of his character.' That observation expressed the gist of Sir Robert Phillimore's judgment in that case. The same applies to his decision, overruled by the Court of Appeal, in the *Parlement Belge* (see below, p. 371). It is of interest to note that, at the time when the Court of Appeal in that case laid the foundations of the rigid doctrine of absolute immunity of foreign States in English law, the doctrine was repudiated, in judgments of great power and learning, by a judge who was the leading English international lawyer of his time. In comparison there is but limited persuasive force in the emphatic, though characteristically nebulous, references

Undoubtedly, the field to be surveyed is wide. The practice of some States is contradictory or inconclusive; that of others inarticulate or unrecorded. Around the problem of immunities there has accumulated a cobweb of phrases which have a powerful appeal inasmuch as they touch upon some apparently fundamental qualities of statehood and a seemingly well-established practice. On the other hand, there are but few subjects in which economic and social factors and the general progression towards the rule of law within the State provide a more compelling opportunity for a re-examination and eventual removal of what is widely and increasingly considered to be an anomaly. Even if the results of the work of the International Law Commission on the subject do not ripen into an international convention or conference, they are nevertheless bound to be of influence by throwing authoritative light on the question whether the doctrine of immunity of foreign States is an artificial encumbrance which has been thriving uneasily on a spuriously conceived notion of the dignity and independence of States or whether it corresponds to the practical needs of international society and to essential and inescapable legal qualities of its constituent members.

APPENDIX

JUDICIAL PRACTICE IN THE MATTER OF JURISDICTIONAL IMMUNITIES OF FOREIGN STATES

The purpose of this article has been to discuss the question of jurisdictional immunities of foreign States from the point of view of the legal possibility and desirability of the abolition, subject to specified exceptions and safeguards, of the principle of absolute immunity and its replacement by rules which are more in conformity with modern developments. The estimate generally accepted of judicial practice on the subject is that while in a small number of States courts have acted upon the distinction between acts *jure imperii* and acts *jure gestionis*, the courts of the majority of States are still wedded to the principle of absolute immunity.[1] That estimate is believed to be inaccurate.

of the judges of the Court of Appeal in the *Parlement Belge* to considerations of international comity and courtesy and independence, or equality or dignity – or all of them – as the basis of the doctrine of immunity.

[1] In many continental countries the distinction between the two kinds of acts has been familiar in constitutional law in connection with the question of judicial control over the executive. Thus in France, where the civil and tortious responsibility of the State and its servants is generally admitted, there was current for a prolonged period a legal doctrine according to which *actes de puissance publique* were subject to the jurisdiction of administrative tribunals while *actes de gestion* fell within the competence of ordinary courts. The determination of the border-line between these two categories of acts became subsequently the subject of controversy and of a conflicting practice of courts, with the result that it has now been abandoned, and the conception of *service publique* substituted for that of acts *jure imperii*. However, the original distinction was widely accepted for a time and that fact explains to some extent the ease with which it has been adopted in the altogether different sphere of the jurisdictional immunities of foreign States. This was also the case in Italy.

In England the distinction has been discussed by courts occasionally, though not *eo*

As will be shown in the survey which follows, in the great majority of States in which there is an articulate practice on the subject, courts have declined to follow the principle of absolute immunity. It is convenient to begin with the countries in which the distinction between acts *jure gestionis* and acts *jure imperii* has found unqualified acceptance in the sense that immunity is accorded in respect of the latter but denied in respect of the former. The following table may facilitate reference to the countries covered by this survey:

nomine, in connection with the question whether trading activities of foreign States are – or ought to be – entitled to the privileged treatment accorded to the activities of the State normally associated with its public functions as a sovereign State. In particular it was discussed in the *Cristina* [1938] A.C. 485: *Annual Digest*, 9 (1938–40), 250, where the immunity of foreign public vessels engaged in commerce was subjected to judicial criticism in a way which made it doubtful whether it would have been conceded in that case if the House of Lords had come definitely to the conclusion that the vessel in question was not *publicis usibus destinata.* It may be noted that, in a different sphere, English courts have considered a similar distinction with regard to the statutory duties of public corporations. Thus in *Bradford Corporation* v. *Myers* [1916] 1 A.C. 242, the House of Lords discussed the distinction, for the purposes of the Public Authorities Protection Act, 1893, between acts done in discharge of a public duty (or exercise of a public authority) and other transactions. They held that, while the supply of gas to the inhabitants of the district was an act in discharge of a public duty, the sale and supply of coke produced in the manufacture of the gas was not a transaction of that nature. In *Western India Match Co.* v. *Lock* [1946] K.B. 601 – a case arising out of the negligent unloading of a ship requisitioned by the Minister of War Transport and operated under charter to him – the Court discussed that distinction in relation to the question whether the case before it was in the nature of carriage of freight by way of a private contract or, as it eventually held, whether the Minister acted in the public interest. The distinction between actions brought against the King in his private and in his public capacity is still recognized in English law. The former is still governed by the rules of petition of right as they existed before the Petitions of Right Act, 1860 (see ss. 39 (1) and 40 (1) of the Crown Proceedings Act). American courts have had frequent occasion to invoke that distinction in connection with immunities of States members of the Union and otherwise. Thus, in *Bank of United States* v. *Planters' Bank of Georgia*, the Supreme Court said (significantly *per* Chief Justice Marshall, who used similar language in *The Schooner Exchange* v. *MacFaddon* when distinguishing between the private property of a Prince and 'any portion of that armed force which upholds his crown'): 'It is, we think, a sound principle, that when a Government becomes a partner in any trading company, it divests itself, so far as concerns the transaction of that company, of its sovereign character, and takes that of a private citizen' ((1824), 9 Wheaton 904). Similarly, in *South Carolina* v. *The United States*, the Supreme Court distinguished between State agencies 'of a strictly governmental nature' and those 'which are used by the State in the carrying on of an ordinary private business' ((1905), 199 U.S. 437). In the Massachusetts case of *Oliver* v. *Worcester*, Mr Justice Grey said: 'The distinction is well established between the responsibilities of towns and cities for acts done in their public capacity, in discharge of duties imposed upon them by the legislature for the public benefit, and for acts done in what may be called their private character, in the management of property or rights voluntarily held by them for their own immediate profit or advantage as a corporation, although inuring, of course, ultimately to the benefit of the public' (102 Mass. 488, 489).

Italy. Italy is foremost amongst the States which have acted upon the distinction between acts *jure imperii* and acts *jure gestionis.* A typical case illustrating the length to which Italian practice goes in this respect is the case, decided in 1925 by the Court of Cassation, of *Storelli* v. *Governo della Repubblica francese*[1] in which the Court assumed jurisdiction in an action by an Italian merchant against the French Government for goods sold and delivered to an aviation base maintained by that Government at Gallipoli (at that time Italian territory). The theory underlying the judgment of the Court was that of implied consent deduced from the fact of having entered into a series of transactions of a private law nature.

However, the Italian practice based on the distinction between acts *jure gestionis* and acts *jure imperii* – which is not necessarily identical with the fiction of implied consent – had been formulated, with some clarity, forty years before. That distinction was acted upon in 1886 when the Court of Cassation assumed jurisdiction in respect of an action concerning services rendered for the Bey of Tunis.[2] In the same year the Court of Cassation rejected the plea of State immunity put forward by the Greek Consul acting on behalf of his Government in a suit for the payment, in accordance with a contract made by the Consul, of the expenses of maintenance of a Greek subject in a municipal asylum. The Court said in that case:

> . . . No one can deny that the foundation of international law is [the principle of] the sovereignty and independence of States; and that in consequence of this principle each State, in the exercise of its powers, is exempted from the jurisdiction of other States. But the fallacy consists in considering the State exclusively and always as a body politic, although its activity as a civil entity cannot be gainsaid when it performs acts acquiring rights and assuming obligations in private relationships, like any other physical or juristic person being capable of exercising civil rights.[3]

In 1928 the Court of Cassation assumed jurisdiction in an action brought against the Mexican ambassador in connection with a contract for the purchase of property to be used as embassy buildings. It said:

> It seems quite arbitrary to derive a claim of jurisdictional immunity in favour of foreign States for all their activities in foreign territories from the fact that, to a certain extent, there exists a privilege of immunity in favour of their ambassadors or ministers plenipotentiary. For if it is true that the foreign States having a mission abroad can avail themselves of the privilege of exemption from the local jurisdiction with regard to matters of international relations of public law, it is similarly true that a foreign State cannot claim immunity from jurisdiction in another State when juridical relations have been created in the territory of that State which are in no way connected with the above-mentioned international relations in the domain of public law. Neither can immunity be claimed on account of the fact that the legal relations in respect of which immunity is claimed

[1] *Rivista*, 17 (1925), 236; *Annual Digest*, 2 (1923–4), 129.

[2] *Guttieres* v. *Elmilik*: *Foro Italiano* (1886), 1, 920, 922.

[3] *Typaldos, Console di Grecia* v. *Manicomio di Aversa*; *Giurisprudenza Italiana*, 48 (1886), Part 1, 228–9, as translated in the comment to Article 11 of the *Harvard Research Draft*, p. 623.

have been entered into by a person who at that time was exercising functions of diplomatic character.[1]

The Court of Cassation adopted the same attitude in relation to matters connected with the activities of the Russian Trade Delegation and, generally, of the commercial activities of the Russian State. Thus it assumed jurisdiction in an action brought by an Italian firm against the commercial representative of the Russian Government. The firm asked for an injunction restraining the commercial representative from disposing of silk cocoons forming the subject matter of a contract concluded between the parties. The Court rejected the plea of immunity put forward by the respondent. It did so by reference to the theory of implied waiver of immunity on the part of a State engaging in commercial activities in a foreign country.[2]

In 1936 the Court of Appeal, in the case of *De Semenoff* v. *Railway Administration of the Norwegian State*,[3] assumed jurisdiction in the matter of a contract of employment between the plaintiff and an agent of the Norwegian Railway Administration.

While Italian courts have assumed jurisdiction over foreign States in matters of a 'private law nature', they have declined to do so with respect to acts *jure imperii*. Thus in *Little* v. *Riccio*,[4] decided in 1934, the Court of Appeal and the Court of Cassation declined jurisdiction in an action for dismissal brought against a committee responsible for the maintenance of the British cemetery at Naples. In that case the British consul intervened on the ground that the cemetery was the property of the British Crown. It was held by the Court of Appeal that the 'cemetery was the property of the State of Great Britain, which desired to give protection to its subjects also after

[1] *Perrucchetti* v. *Puig y Cassauro*: *Foro Italiano* (1929), I, 112 ff.; *Rivista*, 20 (1928), 521–7; *Annual Digest*, 4 (1927–8), 365.

[2] *Rappresentanza commerciale dell'Unione delle repubbliche sovietiste socialiste* v. *Ditta Tesini e Malvezzi*: *Monitore dei Tribunali*, 66 (1925), 604; *Foro Italiano* (1925), I, 830, at pp. 833–4, 835.

[3] *Rivista*, 29 (1937), 224; *Annual Digest*, 8 (1935–7), 234. On the other hand, the Court of Cassation in 1933 declared Italian courts to be incompetent in an action for wrongful dismissal brought against the Russian Trade Delegation. It did so on the ground that 'trading abroad is regarded by the Russian State as a function of an essentially public character' and that 'it is so treated by the internal ordering of that State under which there is established in this respect, by the Constitution itself, a monopolistic régime, controlled by a People's Commissar' (*Russian Trade Delegation in Italy* v. *Kazmann*: *Annual Digest*, 7 (1933–4), 178). The somewhat contradictory practice of Italian courts in the matter of international contracts of service of public foreign corporations – for a summary of some of these cases see *ibid.* p. 179 – is of interest inasmuch as it indicates that such contracts may be considered as lying outside the scope of ordinary private law transactions. That, as is shown later, is the view of French courts. It is also in accordance with the view obtaining in England as to the nature of the employment of civil servants by the Crown. It is possible that, as indicated by the Rome Court of Appeal in the *De Semenoff* case, the refusal to assume jurisdiction in actions relating to the contracts of service of the Russian Trade Delegation was due to the fact that the Treaty of 1924 invested the Delegation with a diplomatic character. In general, however, Italian courts did not hesitate, apart from the provisions of the Treaty of 1924 which exempted from execution goods covered by transactions entered into with the Russian Trade Delegation, to subject to Italian jurisdiction contracts concluded by the Delegation. A detailed exposition of that view will be found in the decision of the Court of Cassation, given in 1935, in the case of *Russian Trade Delegation* v. *De Castro*: *ibid.*

[4] *Giurisprudenza Italiana*, 86 (1934), Part I, 976; *Annual Digest*, 7 (1933–4), 177.

their death by providing a place of burial according to their religion' and that 'this was surely a public law function, over the performance of which the Italian State could not exercise jurisdiction, as otherwise the political sovereignty of a foreign State would be infringed'. On further appeal the Court of Cassation held that the Italian courts had no jurisdiction. The cemetery, it held, was maintained by Great Britain *jure imperii* for the benefit of her nationals as such, and not for them as individuals.

Belgium. Belgian courts have consistently refused to grant immunity with regard to acts *jure gestionis*. They have declined to do so with regard to the operation of railways,[1] trading monopolies,[2] purchasing of arms and munitions,[3] and selling excess supplies.[4] That attitude found clear expression in 1879 when the Ghent Court of Appeal held that it had jurisdiction in a case involving the guano monopoly of Peru and in which the respondents were agents of Peru.[5] Belgian courts have gone to the length of assuming jurisdiction in acts connected with the issue of a public loan by the defendant State. Thus, in an action against a member State of the Federal State of Brazil, the Court of Appeal of Brussels said in 1907:

> Attendu que l'indépendance réciproque des États souverains exige, il est vrai, que l'acte souverain d'un État ne puisse être jugé par un autre; mais que cela revient à rechercher si l'acte, dont les conséquences sont soumises aux tribunaux, émane de la souveraineté de l'État étranger ou relève du droit civil, – s'il a été accompli par le souverain ou par une entité exerçant des droits privés.[6]

The most elaborate exposition, by reference to general and doctrinal considerations, of the reasons militating in favour of assumption of jurisdiction in matters *jure gestionis* will be found in the decision, given in 1903 by the Belgian Court of Cassation, in which, in setting aside the judgment of the Court of Appeal, it affirmed the jurisdiction of Belgian courts in an action against Holland in respect of work executed for the enlargement of a Dutch railway station.[7]

Belgian courts adopted the same attitude with regard to actions brought against the French Government and arising out of the sale of goods to a French governmental agency for the work of reconstruction in territory devastated by the war: *Société Monnoyer et Bernard* v. *État Français*.[8] The case is of special interest inasmuch as, having regard to the nature of the contract in question, there may have been some substance in the claim of the defendant State that the case was one of a transaction *jure imperii*. In holding that it had jurisdiction the Court said:

[1] *Société anonyme des chemins de fer Liègeois-Luxembourgeois* v. *État néerlandais*: *Pasicrisie Belge* (1903), I, 294.
[2] *Peruvian Guano Co.* v. *Dreyfus*: *Pasicrisie Belge* (1881), II, 313.
[3] *Société pour la fabrication des cartouches* v. *Col. M., Ministre de la Guerre de Bulgarie*: *La Belgique judiciaire* (1889), p. 383.
[4] *Gouvernement Ottoman* v. *Gaspary*: *Pasicrisie Belge* (1911), III, 104.
[5] *Rau, Vanden Abeele et Cie* v. *Duruty*: *Pasicrisie Belge* (1879), II, 175, 176.
[6] *Feldman* v. *État de Bahia*: *Pasicrisie Belge* (1908), II, 55, 57–8.
[7] *Société anonyme des chemins de fer Liégeois-Luxembourgeois* v. *État néerlandais* (*Ministère du Waetrstaat*): *Pasicrisie Belge* (1903), II, 294, 301–2.
[8] *Pasicrisie Belge* (1927), III, 129, 130; *Annual Digest*, 4 (1927–8), 177.

> Even if it were true that the French Government acted as a public organ when it assumed by the Act of 6 August 1917 the initiative towards industrial reconstruction in the invaded regions . . . nevertheless, in seeking to accomplish this end after the war, the French State was compelled to make purchases of raw materials, machinery, etc., . . . In transactions of this kind there can be no question of the power of a public organ, and the State can only act in the capacity of a private individual. And when, in this capacity, the State, after treating the other contracting party on an equal footing, wishes to have a dispute determined, or has itself been guilty of a breach of the contract, not coming within the head of public policy, a case exists raising questions of municipal law and solely cognizable by the courts in accordance with Article 92 of the constitution.

On the other hand, the Brussels Court of Appeal held, in 1937, that it had no jurisdiction in an action against the appellants against whom an action was brought in their capacity as agents of the Spanish Government which had requisitioned ships during the civil war. The Court said: 'Requisitions made by a Government in time of war are undoubtedly acts of a public character.'[1] Similarly, in 1934 a Belgian Court decided that it had no jurisdiction in an action brought against the Canadian Immigration Office at Antwerp for breach of a contract of employment. The Court held that the Immigration Office of Canada was a branch of public service, and that the Canadian Government in engaging the plaintiff as its employee was acting as a sovereign State and not as a subject of private law. Belgian courts had no jurisdiction over acts of foreign States of a political or governmental nature; in particular, they had no jurisdiction in respect of an action brought by an agent of a foreign Government for wrongful dismissal.[2] The position of Belgian courts in the matter of public bonds is clearly illustrated by the case of *Brasseur and Associates* v. *Republic of Greece*, decided in 1933 by the Court of Appeals of Brussels. This was an action by holders of the bonds of the Salonica–Monastir Railway Company against the Greek State in consequence of a Greek Decree cancelling 80,000 of the bonds which Greece had taken over in 1925. The Court declined jurisdiction inasmuch as it held that the cancellation of the bonds of the Salonica–Monastir Railway, which in 1917 were in the possession of German nationals, was a political act and that Belgian courts were not competent to examine its legality. On the other hand, the Court held that it had jurisdiction in so far as the action raised an issue *jure gestionis*, namely, in so far as the plaintiffs, without questioning the legality of the Decree cancelling the bonds, confined themselves to the assertion that their bonds did not fall within the scope of the Decree. In the view of the Court, the Greek Government, in denying the latter contention, was not acting as a political authority. It was merely expressing an opinion as to the application of a general order to a particular case and as to the existence or

[1] *Urrutia* v. *Martiarena*: *Annual Digest*, 8 (1935–7), 237.

[2] *Époux Perevostchikoff* v. *State of Canada*: *Pasicrisie Belge* (1936), III, 37; *Annual Digest* (1938–40), case no. 85. By way of contrast it may be noted that in 1960 an Italian Court assumed jurisdiction in an action brought against a State member of the Brazilian Federation and arising out of a contract for publishing a magazine for the purpose of promoting emigration to Brazil: *Somigli* v. *State of São Paulo of Brazil*: *Revue de droit international privé*, 6 (1910), 527.

non-existence of a debt for which it was liable *jure gestionis*. The Greek State 'was thereby acting like any private person who was called upon to pay a sum claimed in virtue of a bond entitling the holder to payment and who considered that he was under no obligation to pay the sum and defended the action brought against him'.[1]

Egyptian Mixed Courts. Although the Mixed Courts of Egypt came to an end in 1949, the consistent attitude of these Courts for nearly half a century, in assuming jurisdiction in actions *jure gestionis*, is of special interest in view of their international composition. Thus Egyptian Mixed Courts assumed jurisdiction in an action against the Palestine State Railways Administration notwithstanding the plea that it was a State organ and immune from liability. The Court held that in conducting a railway undertaking the Government of Palestine was performing an act of administration and not of sovereignty. By making the contract of carriage it had entered the sphere of private law; in view of the fact that the contract was to be performed in Egypt, the Mixed Courts had jurisdiction.[2] In 1943, in the case of *Egyptian Delta Rice Mills Co.* v. *Comisaría General de Madrid*, the Commercial Tribunal of Alexandria held that it had jurisdiction in an action arising out of a purchase of rice by what was described as an organ of the Spanish State. The reasoning of the Court, referring as it does to a transaction intended to secure the supply of food for a neutral State in time of war, is significant inasmuch as it refers both to the question of merits and to execution. The Court said:

> It is not contended in the present case that the rice in question was bought by the *Comisaría General* for the needs of the Spanish public services. On the contrary, it seems clearly established that the rice was bought for the feeding of the Spanish population during a difficult period. In negotiating this purchase herself, instead of leaving the matter to private enterprise, Spain proceeded in much the same manner as any other Spanish trader would have done who wanted to buy rice in Egypt: that is to say, she got it out of Egypt with the necessary permits and carried it to Spain in a Spanish ship in order to re-sell it on the usual commercial lines. This being so, the *Comisaría General* cannot claim immunity from jurisdiction, and the judgment entered against it must be confirmed.
>
> As regards the execution of the judgments, although a foreign State can claim immunity from execution, this immunity applies only where the execution takes place on the territory of that State or when the assets which it is proposed to attach are held by the State in virtue of its character as a public authority. On the other hand, where, as in the present case, the assets which are the object of the execution are on Egyptian territory and are in fact funds which belong to the *Comisaría General* not as a public authority but as the directing power over a group of undertakings, all of a commercial character, the execution must be authorized.[3]

[1] *Pasicrisie Belge* (1933), II, 197; *Annual Digest*, 6 (1931–2), 164.

[2] *Egyptian Government* v. *Palestine State Railways Administration*: *Annual Digest*, 11 (1919–42), 146.

[3] *Bulletin de législation et de jurisprudence égyptiennes*, 55 (1942–3), 114; *Annual Digest*, 12 (1943–5), 103.

The reasoning of the Mixed Court of Appeal in a case which raised the issue of jurisdiction, in the matter of a collision, against the captain of a Government-owned British ship was equally emphatic.[1]

On the other hand, the Mixed Courts of Egypt declined jurisdiction in cases clearly involving 'acts of sovereignty'. Thus, in 1948, the Mixed Court in Alexandria refused jurisdiction in an action against the Greek State for injuries sustained in a collision with a Greek army truck. The truck, the Court said, was operated by the State in its sovereign capacity: 'The theory and the practice of the Mixed Courts, adopting the modern tendency which limits the absolute immunity of States, . . . has always distinguished between acts of sovereignty or political acts and acts of commerce (*gestion*) or administration which relate to the private domain, retaining jurisdiction only in the latter instance.'[2] This was also the reasoning of the Court in *Hénon* v. *Egyptian Government and British Admiralty*, a case decided in 1947 by the Civil Tribunal of the Mixed Courts in respect of a villa requisitioned by the military governor of Cairo for the use of British forces in Egypt.[3]

Greece. Greek courts have assumed jurisdiction in actions involving State activities *jure gestionis*. Thus, in an action against the Soviet Government, the Court of Athens went to the length of upholding a distraint upon the property of the Russian Government. It said, in a decision given in 1928:

> . . . when the [Soviet] Union chooses to act as the vendor of goods, it assumes the character of an *entrepreneur*, undertakes an ordinary piece of civil business, and enters into a contract at municipal law. Its relations become then cognizable by the Greek courts, since the claimant is a Greek national invoking this jurisdiction to settle the question at issue. It must also be noted that by virtue of the contract the Union has voluntarily submitted to Greek jurisdiction.[4]

In 1931, while declining jurisdiction in a case of distress levied for rent of premises occupied by the British consul-general in Athens, the Court of Athens observed that a foreign State does not enjoy jurisdictional immunities with regard to acts of a private law nature such as contracts of sale, relations of landlord and tenant, lending of money, etc. However, it held that the renting of premises for the purposes of consular service was an act of a public character connected with the exercise of sovereign rights, and as such immune from jurisdiction.[5] In 1949 the Court of Appeals of Athens not only affirmed its jurisdiction in matters *jure gestionis*. It declared such jurisdiction to extend to execution, including – apparently – execution resulting in the expulsion of a diplomatic representative from premises occupied by him.[6]

[1] *Capitaine Hall* v. *Capitaine Zacarias Bengoa* (Cour d'appel mixte, Alexandria, 1920): *Bulletin de législation et de jurisprudence égyptiennes*, 33 (1920–1), 25, 26.

[2] *Aboutebout* v. *État Hellénique*, as reported in *A.J.* 44 (1950), 420.

[3] *Bulletin de législation et de jurisprudence égyptiennes*, 59 (1946–7), 225; *Annual Digest*, 14 (1947), 78.

[4] *Soviet Republic (Immunity in Greece)* case: *Thémis*, 40, 486; *Annual Digest*, 4 (1927–8), 172.

[5] *Consular Premises (Greece)* case: *Annual Digest*, 6 (1931–2), 338.

[6] Decision No. 1690/1949: reported in *Revue hellénique de droit international* (1950), p. 331.

Roumania. Prior to the Second World War the courts of that country were among those which assumed jurisdiction with regard to acts *jure gestionis.* Clear expression was given to that attitude in 1920 in a case, involving the supply of cigars, against the Polish Tobacco Monopolies administered by the Polish Ministry of Finance.[1]

Austria. Although for a short period Austrian courts declined to assume jurisdiction over foreign States in matters *jure gestionis,* that country must now be regarded as upholding the right to exercise such jurisdiction. Thus, in 1919, the Supreme Court assumed jurisdiction in a case by the Austrian-Hungarian Bank against Hungary. It said: 'It can be assumed that local jurisdiction may be invoked against a foreign State for the determination – and also for the enforcement – of such claims to be performed within the country concerning which the foreign State appears in consequence of a relationship of a purely private law nature.'[2] This was also the attitude of the Supreme Court in Civil Matters in a case decided in 1920 and arising out of an action against a foreign State, represented by its ambassador, in connection with contracts concluded by him for the execution of works in the embassy building.[3] A similar view was expressed, *obiter,* in the *Foreign States (Legation Buildings) Immunities* case, decided in 1928 by the Supreme Court, where the Court declined jurisdiction in an action against the Czechoslovak Republic in respect of an accident in the building of the Czechoslovak Legation in Vienna. The Court said:

> The Court is not prepared to accept the more extreme view that, having regard to the indivisibility of State sovereignty, a State can never be subjected to the jurisdiction of the foreign court, regardless of the fact whether the dispute arises out of the exercise of its sovereign rights or of its activity as the subject of private law, or whether it subjects itself expressly to the jurisdiction of the foreign court. However, in regard to the building in which the plaintiff met with an accident, the defendant State is subject to Austrian jurisdiction only in so far as the case affects the immovable property itself or any contract relating thereto.[4]

In 1950, in an elaborate judgment in the case of *Hoffmann* v. *Dralle,* the Austrian Supreme Court after reviewing at length the practice of Austrian and foreign courts as well as opinions of writers came to the conclusion that: '(1) foreign States are entitled, *according to international law,* to exemption

[1] The Court said: 'Considérant que tout État doit être considéré sous deux aspects comme conséquence de ses besoins et de ses obligations: (*a*) l'État qui fait des actes publics, des actes de souveraineté, de gouvernement, *jure imperii,* conséquence des besoins politiques et (*b*) l'État qui fait des actes civils, des actes de gestion, achète, vend, fait toute espèce de transactions *jure privato* comme conséquence des grandes attributions et des exigences de l'État moderne, cette dernière activité ayant pour effet que l'État ne se distingue pas d'un particulier; le critérium de la distinction de tels actes étant de les considérer d'après leur nature et non d'après le but qu'ils poursuivent'; *Banque roumaine de commerce* v. *État Polonais*: *Revue de droit international privé,* 19 (1924), 581.

[2] *Österreichisch-ungarische Bank* v. *Ungarische Regierung*: *Z.I.* 28 (1920), 506.

[3] *Immunities (Foreign State in Private Contracts)* case: *Annual Digest,* 1 (1919–22), 118.

[4] *Decisions of the Austrian Supreme Court in Civil and Administrative Matters,* 10 (1928), no. 177, pp. 427–9; *Annual Digest,* 4 (1927–8), 178.

from the jurisdiction of municipal courts only in respect of acts performed in the exercise of the sovereign power appertaining to them; (2) also, according to municipal law, foreign States are subject to national [Austrian] jurisdiction in all disputes arising out of private law relationships.'[1] In this case an injunction was sought and granted, in connection with certain patent rights, against the Czechoslovak State in respect of an industrial undertaking, a cosmetics factory, taken over and operated by that Government.

Switzerland. That country must be included among those which assume jurisdiction over foreign States with respect to acts *jure gestionis*. Such jurisdiction includes actions concerned with public loans. Thus in an action against the Austrian Treasury by a holder of Austrian treasury bonds, the Federal Court overruled a plea to its jurisdiction. In that case the Austrian Treasury had agreed to repay in Swiss currency bonds purchased by Swiss nationals in Switzerland. After reviewing the practice of the courts of various countries on the subject the Federal Court said: 'In view of this legal situation, the extension of Swiss jurisdiction over the facts in the instant case can unhesitatingly be affirmed. The legal relationship created between the Austrian States and the bondholders, through the issue of the treasury bonds in question, belongs to the domain of private law.'[2] Moreover, it appears that Swiss courts, acting in conformity with the relevant Swiss legislation,[3] admit execution against the property of foreign States. Thus in 1937 the Court of Zürich allowed the attachment of assets belonging to the Roumanian State and deposited with the Swiss National Bank. The attachment was ordered in execution of an award given by the German–Roumanian Mixed Arbitral Tribunal. The Higher Court of Zürich then issued a decree ordering the attachment and the summons for payment to be served upon the Roumanian Government through the diplomatic channel. The decision was reached after a detailed review of previous judicial pronouncements in the matter of execution against foreign States.[4]

In 1938 the Federal Tribunal dismissed an appeal against orders blocking assets of the Yugoslav State in various Swiss banks. The orders were issued at the instance of a holder of a number of bonds issued in 1895 by the Kingdom of Serbia. The appellants relied, *inter alia*, on the argument that Swiss courts had no jurisdiction for the reason that a loan floated by a State was in the nature of an act of sovereignty and not in the nature of a private law transaction. The Federal Court, while denying the absolute nature of immunity in respect of public loans of a State, dismissed the appeal on the ground that it was lodged too late.[5]

In yet another case, decided in 1940, the Higher Court of Zürich, although it revoked an order of attachment of the property of Austria (then repre-

[1] Judgment of 10 May 1950: Ob. 167/49; Ob. 171/50. The judgment is summarized by Dr Abel in *International Law Quarterly*, 3 (1950), 576–9.

[2] *K. k. Österreich. Finanzministerium* v. *Dreyfus*: *Entscheidungen des Schweizerischen Bundesgerichtes*, 44 (1918), 49, 54–5.

[3] See above, p. 339.

[4] *State Immunity* (*Switzerland*) (*No.* 1) case: *Blätter für Zürcherische Rechtsprechung*, 37 (1938), 319; *Annual Digest*, 10 (1941–2), 230.

[5] *Sogerfin* v. *State of Yugoslavia*: *Annual Digest*, 10 (1941–2), 232.

sented by Germany), laid down the principle that attachments of the property of foreign States were permissible if the claim arose out of transactions of a private law nature and if the place of performance was in Switzerland. While, in the view of the Court, the first condition was fulfilled in the case before it – the case arose out of certain transactions of the Austrian Tobacco Monopoly, which was a branch of the Austrian Treasury – the second condition was not.[1]

Eire. In the *Ramava*, a vessel apparently in the possession of the U.S.S.R., the High Court of Eire, after reviewing at length English and American cases, came to the conclusion, in 1941, that 'there was now no rule or usage of public international law granting immunity from process to State-owned trading vessels'.[2] Reference may also be made to the decision given in 1944 by the Supreme Court of Eire in *Saorstat and Continental Steamship Co.* v. *Rafael de las Morenas*, where the Court upheld its jurisdiction in an action brought against the defendant, a Colonel in the Spanish Army, who came to Eire as head of a commission appointed by the Spanish Government to purchase horses for the use of the Spanish Army. The Court said:

> The claim made on behalf of the plaintiff company is that the defendant, while in this country, entered into a contract with them, that he failed to carry out the terms of the contract, and that they, thereby, suffered loss and damage, and they sue him for damages for breach of the contract. They claim that the appellant is personally responsible to them, and they do not seek redress against any other person or persons. In these circumstances, and having regard to the nature and scope of the action, I am of opinion that there is no ground for the suggestion that the Government of Spain is being impleaded, either directly or indirectly, and no basis for the claim that the proceedings should be set aside.[3]

Russia. From the scant evidence available – a single decision given by the Russian State Council[4] in 1893 – it appears that the courts of pre-revolutionary Russia assumed jurisdiction in actions arising out of activities *jure*

[1] *State Immunity* (*Switzerland*) (*No.* 2) case: *Annual Digest*, 10 (1941–2), 235. The attitude of the Swiss courts found emphatic expression in the views submitted by the Swiss Government in 1928 in connection with the consideration of the matter by the League of Nations Committee of Experts on the Progressive Codification of International Law. It expressed the opinion that an international regulation of the subject in the direction of limiting the immunity of foreign States was desirable and that it did not present any insurmountable difficulty. It made constructive suggestions for overcoming what it considered the principal difficulty surrounding the matter, namely, the distinction between acts *jure gestionis* and *jure imperii*. It said: 'As regards the criteria to be employed in distinguishing between acts of sovereignty and acts of simple business administration in the event of jurisdictional immunity being recognized only for acts which are genuine manifestations of sovereignty, the solution most in harmony with the principles of judicial practice would be to conform entirely not to the definite purpose of the act but to its intrinsic nature. Before an act can have the character which confers full jurisdictional immunity upon it, it must be of such a nature that it cannot be performed by a private individual' (Doc. A. 15 (1928), v, 87).

[2] *The Irish Law Times*, 75 (1941), 153; *Annual Digest*, 10 (1941–2), 91.

[3] [1945] I.R. 291: *Annual Digest*, 12 (1943–5), 97.

[4] A semi-judicial body. For an account of the case see Allen, *The Position of Foreign States before National Courts* (1933), p. 293.

gestionis. In the case in question, arising out of negotiations between the plaintiff and the representative of the Italian Ministry of War concerning the laying out of a cemetery for the Italian dead in the Crimea, the Council declined jurisdiction on the ground that the Italian Government had acted *jure imperii*. No evidence as to the practice of Soviet Russia seems available except with regard to seizure of the property of foreign Governments. A Decree of 14 June 1929 provided that no seizure is permissible except with the authorization of the Council of People's Commissars. This applies only to States which grant reciprocal treatment to Soviet Russia.

Poland. The rare decisions of Polish courts before the Second World War show that they inclined to exercise jurisdiction in matters *jure gestionis*. In a decision given in 1926, in an action against the Czechoslovak Republic arising out of an injury inflicted by a car owned by Czechoslovakia, the Supreme Court declined jurisdiction on the ground that the action was directed against Czechoslovakia as a sovereign State.[1] However, in the case of *Russian Trade Delegation* v. *Fajana*,[2] the Supreme Court in assuming jurisdiction attached importance not only to the fact that by bringing proceedings the Soviet Union recognized the jurisdiction of Polish courts. The Court intimated that such submission may have taken place 'by the very fact of taking up commercial activities in Poland'. It appears from an observation made by the Polish representative at the meeting of the Committee of Experts for the Progressive Codification of International Law in 1927[3] that Polish courts assumed jurisdiction in an action against the United States Shipping Board. Similarly, in a case decided in 1937, in an action brought against the German State on account of illegal exaction of taxes, the Supreme Court, in declining jurisdiction, relied mainly on the fact that the action was not one *jure gestionis*. It also attached importance to the circumstance that as Germany in similar cases granted immunity the Polish courts were bound to do so by virtue of Article 5 of the Polish Code of Civil Procedure, which accepted the principle of reciprocity.[4]

France. France and Holland are occasionally referred to as countries in which courts grant jurisdictional immunity to foreign States irrespective of whether the activities in question are *jure imperii* or *jure gestionis*. That estimate is of doubtful accuracy. While for a prolonged period before the First World War French courts granted absolute immunity, there has been since then a tendency in the opposite direction. That tendency may be discerned even in those decisions in which the courts declined jurisdiction. Thus when in 1921 the Court of Appeal of Paris set aside a judgment for the respondent who sued the Swiss Government on a contract of shipment of goods to Switzerland in connection with the import of goods to that country during the First World War, it did so on the ground that the transactions in question

[1] *Czechoslovak Republic (Responsibility in Tort)* case (Supreme Court, 1926): *Orzecznictwa Sądów Polskich (Decisions of Polish Courts)*, 5, 440; *Zeitschrift für Ostrecht*, 1 (1927), 275; *Annual Digest*, 3 (1925–6), 180.

[2] *Ibid*. (1927–8), Case no. 108.

[3] 3rd Session, p. 53.

[4] *German Immunities in Poland* case, *Annual Digest*, 8 (1935–7), 239.

were not of a purely commercial character.[1] On the other hand, basing itself squarely on the distinction between acts *jure imperii* and acts *jure gestionis* and affirming the identity of the position of the foreign State and the French State acting in similar circumstances, the Court declined to grant immunity to the Roumanian Government in connection with a contract made by the latter for the sale of goods to be re-sold to Roumanian nationals. The Court said:

> . . . si la règle du droit des gens qui proclame l'indépendance des nations, découle du principe de leur souveraineté, elle est sans application, quand la souveraineté n'est pas mise en cause, lorsqu'il s'agit d'actes n'ayant pas le caractère d'actes de la puissance publique et qu'ainsi les États étrangers sont, en tant que personnes civiles et au même titre que les autres étrangers, justiciables des tribunaux français dans les conditions prévues par le Code civil, leur indépendance n'étant pas en jeu lorsqu'ils sont appelés en justice non pas comme pouvoir, mais uniquement par l'exercice ou la défense d'un droit privé. . . .[2]

The disinclination to grant immunity in matters *jure gestionis* found clear expression in cases relating to the commercial transactions of the Soviet Union in France. In 1926, in *Société le Gostorg et Union des Républiques Socialistes Soviétiques* v. *Association France-Export*, the Court of Paris held that the Soviet Commercial Delegation in France was subject to the jurisdiction of French courts, including the attachment of its property. It said: 'Transactions of a commercial character extending to all fields are only to be regarded as ordinary commercial transactions, having nothing in common with the principle of sovereignty of States.'[3] In 1937, in the case of *De Fallois* v. *Piatakoff*,[4] the Court of Cassation observed that, in the absence of special treaty provisions, the Soviet Commercial Agency 'even if in Soviet internal law it might be an integral portion of the diplomatic representation, had not as regards our institutions the like character – the manifestations of its character being merely commercial acts not affecting the principle of sovereignty of States'. In 1931 the Seine Civil Tribunal granted an application for the provisional attachment of the funds of the commercial representation of the Union of Soviet Socialist Republics in respect of debts of a Russian firm. It said: 'Attendu que la représentation commerciale de l'U.R.S.S. en France représente obligatoirement, aux termes de la législation soviétique, les sujets et les sociétés russes qui font du commerce à l'étranger; attendu, en outre, que l'État russe est pris en tant qu'État commerçant et non pas comme État souverain.'[5] Similarly, French courts assumed jurisdiction, coupled with execution, in *Union of Soviet Socialist Republics* v. *Association France-Export*,[6] decided in 1929 by the Court of Cassation, which allowed execution against the Soviet Trade Delegation. A recognized authority on

[1] *Lakhowsky* v. *Gouvernement fédéral suisse et Regnier* (Cour d'appel, Paris, 1921), *Clunet*, 48 (1921), 179, 180.

[2] *État Roumain* v. *Pascalet et Cie* (1924); *Dalloz hebd.* (1924), p. 260.

[3] *Annual Digest*, 3 (1925–6), 174.

[4] *Ibid.* 8 (1935–7), 223.

[5] *Magasins Universels de la R.S.F.S.R.* v. *Kahn*, *Clunet*, 58 (1931), 412.

[6] *Annual Digest*, 5 (1929–30), 18.

the subject considers that these cases of allowance of execution constitute significant precedents.[1]

In *Chaliapine* v. *Union of Soviet Socialist Republics*, in an action for damages for breach of copyright by selling in Paris an abridged and mutilated edition of an autobiography of the plaintiff, the Court of Cassation rejected, in 1936, the plea that the control exercised by the Soviet Government over the export of books made it an act of sovereignty as distinguished from a commercial transaction. It held that the facts alleged against the Commercial Agency did not relate to acts of sovereignty of the Russian State, but arose from commercial transactions. The Commercial Agency, which was responsible for those transactions, was not immune from the jurisdiction of the French courts. The Court said: 'This is not a question within the domain of political affairs, but of operations of a strictly commercial character which the courts can consider without any interference with Russian State administration. The publication of the memoirs of a singer is in no way a political act. . . .'[2]

In 1937 the Court of Appeal of Bordeaux assumed jurisdiction in an action against the Roumanian State as the universal legatee of a Roumanian subject who died in France. The Court said:

> This immunity from jurisdiction is absolute when applied to acts of an administrative or political order, seeing that the judge who decided these matters would be led to interfere with the exercise of a foreign sovereignty. It is otherwise when the dispute relates to civil interests properly so-called, when it affects the sphere of private relations. Thus a State which is the universal legatee of one of its nationals, relying on the universal succession which has fallen to it, acts in continuation of the personality of the testator. . . . At the same time it is bound by the obligations attaching to it; it is bound to respect particular legacies.[3]

In *Étienne* v. *Government of the Netherlands* the Tribunal Commercial de la Rochelle in 1947 declined jurisdiction in an action against a vessel requisitioned and operated by the Dutch Government in connection with activities which the Court considered to be *jure imperii*. It said:

> The Ambassador of the Netherlands in Paris contends, in a written declaration, that the steamer *Ittersum*, requisitioned and operated by his Government, was employed on a political, not a commercial venture. His testimony is confirmed by a declaration of the Ministry of Transport of the Netherlands. French courts have always held that ships employed by a foreign State for a political object are not subject to the common law or to the jurisdiction of French courts. This attitude has recently been endorsed by the Brussels Convention of 10 April 1926. The *Ittersum* proceeded to Sorel (Canada) in order to load wheat for the revictualling of

[1] Niboyet, in *R.G.* 43 (1936), 541–3.

[2] *Dalloz périodique* (1937), Part I, p. 63; Sirey (1937), Part I, p. 104; *Annual Digest*, 8 (1935–1937), 225.

[3] *Roumanian State* v. *Arricastre*: *Annual Digest*, 8 (1935–7), 232. But see below, p. 361, n. 4.

the Netherlands. That operation had no commercial or speculative character.[1]

When in 1919 the Court of Appeal of Rennes reversed a judgment of the Court below in the case of the *Angers* and the *Hungerford*, two vessels owned by the British Government and operated by a firm in Belfast, it did so on the ground that the vessels in question were not engaged in a private venture, but were acting in the national interest.[2]

In the *Vestwig* case, decided in 1946, the Court of Cassation held that there was no immunity when the foreign State acted as trustee of private property. In that case the plaintiffs brought garnishee proceedings in respect of moneys due to them and figuring in the accounts of the Norwegian State. The lower courts denied that the funds were immune, on the ground that the Norwegian Government was merely acting as a trustee on behalf of its national, and was therefore not impleaded. On the order of the Minister of Justice the *Procureur Général* at the Court of Cassation lodged an appeal against these decisions. He contended that if the immunity of foreign States were regarded as absolute, the courts had no power to inquire into the nature of the control of the Norwegian State over the funds in question. If, on the other hand, a distinction were drawn between acts of sovereignty and acts which did not have a political character, the Court of Cassation would uphold the decisions of the lower courts. The Court of Cassation held that the appeal had to be dismissed. The immunity of foreign States before French courts was based on their sovereignty. The sovereignty of the Norwegian State was not involved in the present case.[3] On the other hand, in *État Roumain* v. *Dlle Aricastre*, a case decided in 1950, the Court of Appeal of Poitier, departing from a decision given in the same case by another French Court of Appeals, declined jurisdiction in an inheritance action[4] over the State of Roumania acting as a legatee.

The cases in which the French courts declined jurisdiction have been mostly concerned with public loans issued by foreign States – such as the case of the Portuguese loan of 1832 the legality of which had apparently never been recognized by the Portuguese Government.[5] When in 1929 the Court of Appeal of Aix admitted, in a case concerning interest on bonds issued in 1904 by the Moroccan Government, the plea of immunity put forward by that Government, it did so on the ground that such loans were within the category of acts *jure imperii* and not *jure gestionis*.[6] In 1936 the *Tribunal Civil de la Seine* declared itself incompetent in an action against the Spanish National Tourist Office on the ground that it was 'a State organization without any commercial character'.[7] In the same year the Court of

[1] Transl. from *Annual Digest*, 14 (1947), 83; *Dalloz* (1948), p. 84.

[2] *Revue de droit international privé*, 18 (1922–3), 743.

[3] *Procureur Général* v. *Vestwig*: Sirey (1947), Part 1, p. 137; *Annual Digest*, 13 (1946), 78.

[4] Sirey (1950), Part 1, 2, p. 141. In a note to that case Professor Niboyet expressed doubts as to the authority of this case as a precedent. And see above, p. 360, n. 3.

[5] *Reilhac* v. *Comptoir National d'Escompte*, decided in 1895 by the Seine Civil Tribunal: as reported in Comment to Article 11 of the *Harvard Draft* (p. 636).

[6] *Gouvernement du Maroc et Maspéro* v. *Laurans et Autre*: *Gaz. Pal.* (1930), 1, 246; *La Semaine juridique* (1930), pp. 602, 605–6; *Annual Digest*, 5 (1929–30), 116.

[7] *Société Viajes* v. *Office National du Tourisme Espagnol*: *Annual Digest*, 8 (1935–7), 227.

Appeal of Paris, in an action against the American Battle Monuments Commission, declared that French courts had no jurisdiction.[1]

It appears from the above survey that France can no longer be included among countries which recognize an absolute immunity of foreign States from jurisdiction.[2]

Holland. Dutch practice on the subject has been hesitating and marked by an occasional discrepancy of views of the judiciary and the executive. In a series of cases before and during the First World War, Dutch courts not only assumed jurisdiction over foreign States, they also proceeded to attachment and execution. In 1900 they gave judgment in an action against the Belgian State in connection with an increase in railway fares on the part of a company operating under a concession from the Belgian State.[3] In 1904 the courts attempted to levy execution upon a Belgian State vessel used for training purposes.[4] In 1909 a court at Haarlem apparently authorized the seizure of a Swedish submarine in respect of a claim for assistance rendered to her.[5] Above all, in the well-known *De Booij* case, which occupied Dutch courts and the Dutch Foreign Office for a long period, they asserted jurisdiction, to the point of execution, with respect to what was in effect an act of the German forces in Belgium closely connected with military operations.[6] The executive successfully interposed in these cases by causing the enactment of special decrees. That new legislation was subsequently applied in a number of cases – including, in 1923, an action in tort against the Belgian State following upon a collision between the vessel owned by the plaintiff and a tug-boat owned by Belgium.[7]

Previously, in the case of *South Africa* v. *Herman Grote*, decided in 1921, the District Court of Amsterdam interpreted the relevant Dutch legislative provisions of 1829 and 1917 to the effect that, while limiting the jurisdiction of Dutch courts with respect to acts performed by foreign States *jure imperii*, they left open the question of their jurisdiction in other matters. The Court upheld the attachment of certain property of South Africa in respect of a claim for maritime assistance. It said:

> Article 12 (*a*) gives no specific list of the exceptions recognized by the Law of Nations, to which it refers. It may safely be said that with regard to *acta imperii*, either lawful or unlawful, whether acts of war or not, a

[1] *Lahalle and Levard* v. *The American Battle Monuments Commission*: *Annual Digest*, 8 (1935–7), 227.

[2] See Sibert, I, 271. See, however, Hamson in *B.Y.* 27 (1950), 292–331, for a somewhat different estimate of the French practice. Nevertheless, while denying that French courts have assumed jurisdiction over the foreign States as such, the learned writer admits that they have done so with regard to organized entities which are engaged in commercial or similar activities and which, according to French courts, are distinguishable from the foreign State as such. As in most matters of this nature States act through separate agencies created by them, the distinction, even if acceptable, seems to be devoid of practical importance.

[3] *De Belgische Staat* v. *Société du Chemin de Fer Internationale*: *Weekblad van het Recht* (1902), no. 7812.

[4] *Ibid.* (1904), no. 8010.

[5] *Ibid.* (1909), no. 8921.

[6] An account of this and the preceding cases will be found in Allen, *The Position of Foreign States before National Courts* (1933), pp. 103–8.

[7] *F. Advokaat* v. *I. Schuddinck & den Belgischen Staat* (*Arrond. Rechtbank* (Dordrecht, 1923)), *Weekblad van het Recht* (1923), no. 11088, 5 : 2.

State is not subject to the jurisdiction of the judiciary of another State. The intention of the new provision was clearly to sanction this principle. However, in enacting the new law, the legislature had not given any explicit decision with regard to cases in which foreign States are acting not in their capacity of sovereign Powers, but as ordinary persons. In cases where the judicial acts at issue have no connection whatever with the exercise of sovereign rights, the question ought to be decided in the sense that the foreign State is subject to the jurisdiction of Dutch courts.[1]

The principle of the absolute immunity of foreign States, regardless of the distinction between acts *jure gestionis* and acts *jure imperii*, was affirmed emphatically in 1942 by the Amsterdam Court of Appeal in the case of *Weber* v. *Union of Soviet Socialist Republics* – an action against the Union of Soviet Socialist Republics in respect of a contract concluded by one of its agencies.[2] In a note on this judgment contributed to the *Annual Digest and Reports of Public International Law Cases*, where the case is reported, the contributor, Professor Verzijl, says: 'It is of interest to observe that this judgment in favour of jurisdictional immunity of the Soviet Government was given by a Dutch court at the time of the occupation of Holland by German forces.' It is also of interest to note that in a subsequent judgment, given by the same Court in the same year, the relevance of the distinction between the two kinds of State activities was fully admitted. The case in question – *Poortensdijk Ltd.* v. *Soviet Republic of Latvia* – arose out of an action against a bank subsequently nationalized by the Soviet Latvian authorities. The Court held that that action had been performed *jure imperii*.[3] Previously, in the *Garbi*, a vessel requisitioned in 1937 by the Republican Spanish Government, the District Court of Middelburg admitted the existence of the distinction in question though it held it to be irrelevant for the purpose of the case before it.[4] In an earlier case, decided in 1932, the District Court of Amsterdam declined jurisdiction in an action against the Union of Soviet Socialist Republics for payment of the principal and interest of a debenture of the Russian consolidated public loan of 1880. The Court said: 'Although there is no unanimity on the question whether, in principle, a sovereign State may be subjected against its will to the jurisdiction of a tribunal of another State for *acta gestionis*, it is nevertheless almost universally taken for granted, though on different grounds, that no such subjection is possible in the case of a claim in regard to State loans raised by public subscription.'[5] The most recent decision (available to the writer) of a Dutch court fully affirms the distinction, for the purpose of immunity from jurisdiction, between acts *jure imperii* and acts *jure gestionis*. In the case of *Nederlandse Rijnbank, Amsterdam* v. *Mühlig Union*, decided in 1947 by the Council for the Restoration

[1] *Nederlandsche Jurisprudentie* (1921), p. 849; *Annual Digest*, 1 (1919–22), 22.

[2] *Ibid.* 11 (1919–42), Supplementary Volume, 140.

[3] *Annual Digest*, 11 (1919–42), Supplementary Volume, 142.

[4] *Ibid.* 155.

[5] *De Froe* v. *The Russian State*: *Annual Digest*, 6 (1931–2), 170. In a note to this case, contributed in 1938, Professor Verzijl stated that 'the question whether or not foreign States may be sued in Dutch Courts in respect of *acta gestionis* has not yet been definitely settled' (*ibid.* p. 17).

of Legal Rights (Division for Judicial Settlement), the Court held that it had jurisdiction notwithstanding the fact that the defendant company had been nationalized and merged into a public corporation under Czech law. The Court held that 'the principles of international law concerning the immunity of States from jurisdiction do not apply to State-conducted undertakings in the commercial, industrial, or financial fields'.[1]

It would appear, accordingly, that the balance of authority, so far as the judicial practice of Holland is concerned, is probably in favour of recognition of the distinction between acts *jure imperii* and acts *jure gestionis* and of the denial of absolute immunity of foreign States.

Scandinavian countries. While no direct information is available as to the position in Denmark or Norway, reference may be made to the two leading text-books in those countries. Professor Ross, in his *Text-book of International Law* (English translation, 1947), says that 'it must probably now be admitted that a change has taken place in the international view, the duty [of granting immunity] now only applying to the former cases [acts *jure imperii*]'.[2] Professor Castberg's view with regard to Norway is to the same effect.[3] In Sweden, the leading case of the *Rigmor*, decided in 1942 by the Supreme Court, although apparently based on the principle of absolute immunity is, in effect, inconclusive.[4] The judgment discusses in detail the limits of exemption from jurisdiction. The following passage may be noted:

> The modifications in the principle of immunity which in recent times have won recognition in different degrees in different parts of the world have been concerned solely with cases where the conflict in which the foreign State was involved has arisen out of facts which normally relate to the intercourse of private legal subjects with one another and are then covered by private law. On the other hand, the principle holds good unconditionally if the dispute relates to a situation which derives its character from an act of sovereignty on the part of the foreign State, as, for example, in the case of legal action for the vindication of a claim where the foreign State can justify its possession of the object of the claim on purely public law grounds, so long as these grounds can by their nature be recognized as legally valid within the territory of the country where the proceedings take place.[5]

[1] *Annual Digest*, 14 (1947), 77.

[2] At p. 190.

[3] *Folkerett*, pp. 70, 100. As to the tendency, in Scandinavian countries, to put restraints on State immunity, in particular in matters of commerce, see *Comité Maritime International, Bulletin*, no. 57, pp. 122 *et seq.*, 194.

[4] The judgment – fully reported in *Annual Digest*, 10 (1941–2), 240 – refers to the principle of absolute immunity as representing, prior to the passing of the law of 17 June 1928, the time-honoured view of Swedish law.

[5] As reported in *A.J.* 37 (1943), 141. It is also of interest to note, in this case, the attitude of the Swedish Supreme Court in relation to the question of immunity with regard to possession illegally obtained. The Court said: 'It does not follow from the above that under Swedish law executive interference with a foreign Power's factual possession of any moveable property is in all circumstances inadmissible, even where the possession can be justified by purely public law grounds. If, for example, possession has been acquired under compulsion, or in a manner involving arbitrary interference with previous possession within Swedish territory, there is no doubt but that the injured party ought to receive legal assistance from

On the whole, it seems doubtful whether Sweden can be regarded as adhering to the principle of absolute immunity. In its reply to the questionnaire sent out by the League of Nations Committee for the Progressive Codification of International Law, the Swedish Government drew attention to the tendency of Swedish courts to limit the jurisdictional immunities of foreign States in matters arising out of financial transactions. It pointed out that that was a natural attitude for Swedish courts to adopt seeing that in this respect the Swedish State was, so far as Swedish law was concerned, on a footing of complete equality with private individuals and that it could not refuse to appear before Swedish courts in connection with acts 'which concern the administration of business and are not acts of sovereignty'.[1] In general, the Swedish Government observed that the rules adopted in many countries and recognizing an extensive immunity of foreign States 'are becoming more and more unsatisfactory as States extend their activities in the industrial and commercial sphere and in that of transportation'.[2]

Latin-American countries. There is but scant evidence of practice from these countries, but such evidence as there exists tends in the direction of including these countries among that great majority of States which recognize affirmatively the distinction between acts *jure imperii* and acts *jure gestionis*. Thus Article 34 of the Argentine Civil Code gives Argentinian courts jurisdiction in actions against foreign States arising out of matters *jure gestionis*. From a decision given in 1937 by the Argentinian Federal Court of Appeal in the *Ibai* it appears that one of the reasons why the Court held that it had no jurisdiction in respect of a ship requisitioned by the Spanish Government was that the ship's voyage 'had nothing to do with speculation or gain, but was wholly prompted by the necessity of providing efficiently for the defence of the State'.[3] In 1924, in the *Cokato*, the Federal Court of Appeal of the Capital affirmed the jurisdiction of Argentinian courts over the United States Shipping Board Emergency Fleet Corporation.[4] Reference may also be made to the case of *Gobierno de Italia en Suc.* v. *Consejo Nacional de Educación*, decided in 1940 by the Camara Civil de la Capital, in which the Italian State was held, in its capacity as legatee, liable to taxation and other relevant provisions of the Argentinian law. The Court said: 'The fiscal law is to be applied to all entities which are persons, including the Italian State in its character as a juridical person.'[5] Accioly, the author of the leading Brazilian

the Swedish executive authorities to restore him to possession' (*Annual Digest*, 10 (1941–2), 240). Similarly, in the *Solgry*, decided in the same year, the following observation of the Court is relevant: 'The possession of the vessel, however, has been transferred on Swedish territory to that Government and the transfer has taken place without violence or any other arbitrary disturbance of the earlier possession' (*ibid.* 11 (1919–42), 153). However, in the absence of clear evidence of illegality in obtaining possession, immunity will be granted even if possession is not accompanied by ownership recognized by Swedish law (see *Russian Trade Delegation* v. *Carlbom*), where the Supreme Court affirmed, in 1944, the immunity of a ship in possession of Soviet Russia although it came to the conclusion, in a judgment given on the same day, that, as the Nationalization Decree in question had no extraterritorial effect, no property had been acquired over the ship: *ibid.* 12 (1943–5), 61 and 112.

[1] Doc. A. 15 (1928), v, 84.

[2] At p. 83.

[3] *Annual Digest*, 9 (1938–40), 293.

[4] *Ibid.* 2 (1923–4), 136.

[5] *Ibid.* 10 (1941–2), 196.

treatise on international law, gives no reference to the practice of his own or other Latin-American countries.[1] However, he expresses himself in favour of jurisdiction of municipal courts in cases in which such jurisdiction derives from the voluntary renunciation of immunity. Such renunciation must, he says, be implied, *inter alia*, 'quand il [the foreign State] fait des actes de commerce ou d'industrie en territoire étranger'. In the most recent Brazilian text-book on the subject Professor Podestà Costa gives reasons for limiting jurisdictional immunity with regard to transactions *jure gestionis*. He says: 'Y en cuanto a los contratos que el Estado realiza *jure gestionis* en el exterior, debe reconocerse que él tiene personalidad civil, aunque su ejercicio está subordinado a la jurisdicción local.'[2] The provisions of the so-called Bustamante Code of 1928, which has been accepted by a number of Latin-American States, are somewhat ambiguous.[3]

Germany. Although in 1921[4] the German Reichsgericht affirmed, not without some hesitation, the principle of absolute immunity, it is difficult to express an unqualified view as to the attitude of German courts in the matter. Prior to 1921, German courts assumed jurisdiction in a number of cases on the ground that the foreign State had acted *jure gestionis*. This was the view adopted in 1885 by the Bavarian Court of Conflicts of Jurisdiction in an action against the Austrian Government as the owner of a railway. The Court said in that case:

> The question must be considered whether the principle referred to would be applicable without exception also when the issue pertains to private law relationships. Such a critical distinction between the applicability of this premise in the domain of public law on the one hand, and private law on the other, seems the more justified since it was a generally recognized principle in Roman law, and one which has been consistently adhered to in modern legislation and, especially, in the Austrian civil law and public law, that the State assumes, as soon as it enters the domain of private law, the position to which a private law subject is entitled, with respect to its rights and obligations and with respect to judicial proceedings serving the protection of such rights.[5]

In 1920, in the case of the *Turkish Purchases Commission*, the Prussian Tribunal for Conflicts of Jurisdiction held that although, as a rule, submission to jurisdiction on the part of a foreign State did not imply submission to execu-

[1] *Traité de droit international public* (French transl. by Goulé, 1940), I, 214, 215.

[2] *Manual de derecho internacional público* (1947), p. 65.

[3] Article 333 provides that 'the judges and courts of each contracting State shall be incompetent to take cognizance of civil and commercial cases to which the other contracting States or their heads are contracting parties, if the action is a personal one, except in case of express submission or of counterclaims'. On the other hand Article 335 lays down that 'if the foreign contracting State or its head acted as an individual or private person, the judges or courts shall be competent to take cognizance of the cases where real or mixed actions are brought, if such competence belongs to them in respect to foreign individuals in conformity with this Code'. There appears to be some doubt as to the correct version of this article. See Hudson, *Legislation*, IV, 2328.

[4] See below, p. 367.

[5] *Heizer* v. *Kaiser-Franz-Joseph-Bahn A.-G.*, as reported in *Harvard Research Draft*, Comment to Article 7, p. 534.

tion, the position was different when, as in the case before the Court, submission to execution could be implied by conduct such as consisted in the opening, in Germany, of a special banking account for the satisfaction of the claims of the firm which had supplied Turkey with military material.[1]

On the other hand, in the *Ice King*, the Reichsgericht, in a detailed judgment given in 1921, assumed jurisdiction in an action for damages sustained in a collision with a vessel operated by the United States Shipping Board. It did so not without having considered the alternative solution. The Court said:

> . . . It cannot be denied that the efforts made particularly in writings on international law to remove or, at least, to restrict the international law principle of immunity regarding State property used for private purposes, especially in the field of international maritime law, have found more and more sympathy in competent circles. However, this development has not yet penetrated so generally in the practice of international intercourse that one can therefrom conclude a legally warranted change of the principle of international law. . . .[2]

The decision in the *Ice King* followed a series of decisions given by German courts in the first two decades of the twentieth century which affirmed the doctrine of absolute immunity – a development which was perhaps not unconnected with the emphasis on the sovereignty of the State, both domestic and foreign, in German legal and political thought of that period. Already in 1905 the Supreme Court held that German courts had no jurisdiction in an action against the Belgian Railway Administration. This was so, the Court said, although Belgian courts had adopted a different attitude.[3] In the well-known *Hellfeld* case, decided in 1910, the Prussian Court for Conflicts of Jurisdiction found that, regardless of the question whether German courts had jurisdiction on the merits, they had no power to order the attachment of the property of a foreign State.[4] In 1915 German courts declined jurisdiction in an action against the Russian Government in respect of work performed for it in connection with a fair exhibition at Leipzig. This was so although the decision was given at a time when a state of war existed between the two countries.[5]

The developments subsequent to the case of the *Ice King* do not bear out the view that German courts are committed to the principle of absolute immunity. Thus in an action decided in 1925 against the Finnish State Railway Administration, the Court, while granting immunity, attached importance to the fact that the place of performance of the contract was in Finland.[6] In the *Halig* case, jurisdiction was declined in an action aiming at the removal of the insignia of the Polish State from a building occupied by

[1] *Annual Digest*, 1 (1919–22), 114.

[2] *Gustaf Selling* v. *United States Shipping Board* (*Ice King*): *Entscheidungen des Reichsgerichts in Zivilsachen*, 103 (1922), 275, 276, 277; *Annual Digest*, 1 (1919–22), 150.

[3] *Entscheidungen des Reichsgerichts*, 62 (1906), 165.

[4] *A.J.* 5 (1911), 490.

[5] *Rechtssprechung des Oberlandesgerichts*, 31 (1915), 175.

[6] *Gehrckens* v. *Järnvägstyrelsen* (*Oberlandesgericht*, Hamburg, 1925): *Rechtssprechung des Oberlandesgerichts*, 45, 94; *Hanseatische Rechts-Zeitschrift*, 8 (1925), 904.

the Polish vice-consul. The decision was given on the ground that the case involved activities *jure imperii* on the part of a foreign State. The Court said:

> The placing of a coat of arms of a foreign State is an act of sovereignty and a foreign State can never be subject to local jurisdiction in respect of such an act. The independence and equality of sovereign States, recognized in international practice, does not permit their subjection to the jurisdiction of another State in respect of sovereign acts.[1]

The United States of America. It is doubtful to what extent the law of the United States continues to adhere rigidly to the doctrine of absolute immunity of foreign States. While the executive has expressly abandoned it, courts have continued to apply it – subject, however, to significant indications of a change. As in the United States the attitude of the executive in the matter of jurisdictional immunities is of considerable weight, in comparison with other countries,[2] it is useful to draw attention to this aspect of the legal position. As early as 1918 the Secretary of State addressed a communication to the Attorney General of the United States stating that 'where [Government-owned] vessels were engaged in commercial pursuits, they should be subject to the obligations and restrictions of trade, if they were to enjoy its benefits and profits'.[3] He explained the statement by reference: (1) to the soundness of the view that 'when a Sovereign enters into business, he submits himself to the conditions thereof'; and (2) to the consideration that 'if the claim of immunity were granted, American citizens as well as foreigners would be left without recourse in the Courts of such just claims as they might have against the vessels concerned' and 'their only means for obtaining satisfaction would be through political channels – either through Congress, or through diplomacy'. In 1921, in reply to a request of the Italian ambassador that steps be taken to prevent the arrest of the *Pesaro*, an armed merchant vessel of the Italian Government, the Department of State said: 'The Department is of the opinion that vessels owned by a State and engaged in commerce are not entitled, within the territorial waters of another State, to the immunity accorded vessels of war, and that notwithstanding such ownership these vessels are subject to the local jurisdiction to the same extent as other merchant vessels.'[4] Instructions to a similar effect were issued to American diplomatic and consular officers abroad.[5]

The attitude of the State Department as outlined above is not confined to State-owned ships engaged in commerce. Thus, when an action was brought by the United States in 1927 against the *Deutsche Kalisyndikat-Gesellschaft* in connection with the enforcement of anti-trust laws, the French ambassador informed the Department of State that the defendant corporation was an organization 'created and controlled by the French Republic' and that an action instituted against the corporation was, in fact, directed against the French State. In reply to an inquiry from the Attorney General of the United States as to the views of the Department of State regarding the matter, the

[1] *Halig* v. *Polnischen Staat*: *Z.V.* 15 (1929), 271, 275–6; *Annual Digest*, 4 (1927–8), 164.
[2] See Lyons, in *B.Y.* 24 (1947), 116–47.
[3] See Hackworth, II, 429.
[4] *Ibid.* 437.
[5] *Ibid.* 439–40.

latter stated that 'it has long been the view of the Department of State that agencies of foreign Governments engaged in ordinary commercial transactions in the United States enjoy no privileges or immunities not appertaining to other foreign corporations, agencies, and individuals doing business here, and should conform to the laws of this country governing such transactions'.[1] However, in the absence of an express legislative change, the courts did not consider themselves at liberty to depart from established judicial precedent wedded to the principle of absolute immunity. Thus, when in 1925 in connection with the proceedings against the *Pesaro*, an Italian Government-owned ship engaged in commerce, the Department of State declined to issue a certificate that the vessel was immune from process,[2] the Supreme Court, in the absence of a clear direction from the executive, proceeded to determine the issue. It did so by adopting, by a majority, the traditional view on the subject. It said : 'When, for the purpose of advancing the trade of its people or providing revenue for its treasury, a Government acquires, mans and operates ships in the carrying trade, they are public ships, in the same sense that war ships are. We know of no international usage which regards the maintenance and advancement of the economic welfare of a people in time of peace as any less a public purpose than the maintenance or training of a naval force.'[3] This view was reaffirmed by the Supreme Court in 1938 in the case of the *Navemar*,[4] and in other cases.

However, while it is probable that courts of subordinate jurisdiction in the United States would still deem themselves bound by the traditional doctrine of absolute immunity as reaffirmed by the Supreme Court, it is not certain what – in view of general developments in this sphere – may be the attitude of that high tribunal in the future. It is possible that instead of choosing the drastic method of a formal reversal of the established doctrine, it may proceed by way of a less direct approach, as it did twenty years later in *Mexico* v. *Hoffman*.[5] The vessel in question was owned by the Mexican Government and engaged in transportation of cargoes. The State Department declined to issue a certificate that she was entitled to immunity. The Court held that the vessel was not immune from jurisdiction. It did so on the ground that although owned by the Mexican Government the vessel was not actually in its possession. In an illuminating concurring opinion Mr Justice Frankfurter pointed to the tenuous nature of the notion of possession for the purpose of the distinction between vessels which are entitled to immunity and those which are not. He indicated the possibility of regarding the decision of the Court as 'an implied recession' from the decision in *Berizzi Brothers* v. *Steamship Pesaro* – which he subjected to strong criticism – and he urged that

[1] Hackworth, II, 481.

[2] When the case of the *Pesaro* first came before American courts, the State Department, in answer to an inquiry by Judge Mack, replied as follows : 'It is the view of the Department that Government-owned merchant vessels or vessels under requisition of Governments whose flag they fly employed in commerce should not be regarded as entitled to the immunities accorded public vessels of war. The Department has not claimed immunity for American vessels of this character' (*Pesaro*, 277 Fed. 473, 479–80, n. 3).

[3] 271 U.S. 562 : *Annual Digest*, 3 (1925–6), 186.

[4] 303 U.S. 68, 74.

[5] (1945), 324 U.S. 31 : *Annual Digest*, 12 (1943–5), 143.

its implications 'in the light of the important developments in the international scene that twenty years have brought, call for its reconsideration'. The probability of such reconsideration was clearly foreshadowed in the concluding passage of the opinion of the Court as delivered by Chief Justice Stone. He pointed to 'the duty of the courts, in a matter so intimately associated with our foreign policy and which may profoundly affect it, not to enlarge an immunity to an extent which the Government, although often asked, has not seen fit to recognize'. In view of the consistent policy of the Government of the United States in the matter of the activities of foreign States in the sphere of private law, the passage quoted may properly be considered as not irrelevant to the future attitude of the Supreme Court or, as shown in the case of the *Beaton Park*, perhaps even of other courts. The *Beaton Park* was decided by the United States District Court for the Western District of Washington, Northern Division, one year after the decision in *Mexico* v. *Hoffmann.* This was an action against the steamship *Beaton Park* for damages for personal injuries. The Canadian Government, owners of the vessel, entered a plea to the jurisdiction. It was held that the plea must be rejected and that a merchant vessel owned, but not possessed or operated, by a foreign Government was not entitled to immunity from jurisdiction. The Court said:

> Here it was not a Government function that was being pursued. It was merely an ordinary commercial operation of a merchant ship owned but not possessed or operated by the foreign Government, whereas in *Ervin* v. *Quintanilla* and in the *Pesaro* the vessel was both owned and possessed by the foreign Government. In the absence of statute or treaty, no sound principle of law or of international comity requires that the courts of this country treat a foreign Government more favorably as to sovereign immunity than our own Government is treated by the courts.[1]

In 1948 the Appellate Division of the New York Supreme Court, reversing the judgment of the Court below, declared that it had jurisdiction over the National Bank of Haiti, which was 'largely an instrumentality of the Republic of Haiti', in respect of conversion of securities of the plaintiff in pursuance of certain confiscatory Haitian decrees. These securities had been deposited with the defendants at the time when they were organized under the laws of Haiti as a commercial bank. Subsequently, all other stock was acquired by the Haitian Government. The Court rejected the view of the Court below that as the defendants acted under governmental orders their conduct did not amount to conversion. These orders, in the view of the Court, were purely confiscatory and, as such, void by the law of New York. Such confiscation, the Court said, 'has sometimes been compared, in its legal effects, to action by thieves or marauders'.[2] While this is merely an instance of assumption of jurisdiction over a foreign governmental agency with respect to obligations contracted by it at a time prior to its acquiring the character of such agency, the case is not without significance for the subject under review.

[1] 65 F. Supp. 213.

[2] *Plesch* v. *Banque Nationale de la République d'Haiti*, 77 N.Y.S. (2d) 41, 43 : *Annual Digest*, 15 (1948), 13.

The United Kingdom. In the United Kingdom, although the principle of absolute immunity has been applied with a consistency bordering on rigidity, without distinction between acts *jure gestionis* and acts *jure imperii*, amidst a consistent discouragement of any notion of implied waiver and regardless of the manner in which the foreign State obtained possession of the property, that practice has not been followed without some hesitation. That hesitation showed itself at the very inception of the adoption of the principle of absolute immunity, namely, in the *Parlement Belge*. There the judge of first instance[1] – Sir Robert Phillimore, an international lawyer of distinction – held that a State-owned vessel engaged in commercial ventures did not enjoy immunity. When in the *Porto Alexandre*[2] the Court acted on the principle of absolute immunity it did so not without an emphatic expression of its disapproval of the conduct of the foreign Government in question – a disapproval which vividly illustrates the implications of the general issue of the problem of jurisdictional immunities in modern circumstances.

When, in the *Cristina*, the House of Lords once more acted upon the law enunciated in the *Parlement Belge*, the effect of the observations of the majority of its members is such that it cannot be predicated with any assurance what may be the future attitude, in similar circumstances, of the highest tribunal of the realm. The main *ratio decidendi* in Lord Atkin's judgment was that the case was one 'of actual possession for public purposes'.[3] He admitted that 'there has been some difference in the practice of nations as to possible limitations of this second principle [immunity from seizure of property owned or in the possession of a foreign State] as to whether it extends to property only used for commercial purposes of the sovereign or to personal private property'. Lord Thankerton, after citing the relevant passage in the judgment of Brett L.J., stated that the decision in the *Parlement Belge* had reference to ships used for public purposes only, that there was therefore no reason why the Court in the *Porto Alexandre* should have considered itself bound by the *Parlement Belge*, and that he (Lord Thankerton) held himself free to reconsider the decision in the *Porto Alexandre*. Lord Macmillan was of the same view. Lord Maugham, after expressing agreement with the original judgment of Sir Robert Phillimore in the *Parlement Belge*, intimated his strong disapproval of the decision in the *Porto Alexandre* and gave expression, on grounds of justice, equity, and convenience, to the most pungent judicial criticism yet given of the rule of absolute immunity. Lord Wright – who alone subscribed without qualifications to the *Porto Alexandre* as expressing the correct rule of law – added: 'This modern development of the immunity of public ships has not escaped severe and in my opinion justifiable criticism on practical grounds of policy, at least as applied in times of peace.' In the *Dollfus Mieg* case[4] Evershed M.R. expressed agreement with Lord Thankerton's views in the *Cristina*.[5]

[1] (1879), 4 P.D. 129, 148. See also above, p. 346, n. 1.

[2] [1920] P. 30: *Annual Digest*, 1 (1919–22), 146.

[3] [1938] A.C. 485, at p. 492: *Annual Digest*, 9 (1938–40), 250.

[4] [1950] 1 Ch. 333: *Annual Digest*, 16 (1949), 103.

[5] The United Kingdom has not become a party to the Brussels Convention of 1926 on the Immunities of State-owned Ships Engaged in Commerce. It appears that that fact is attri-

While therefore some doubt must be deemed to exist as to the possible future attitude of the highest tribunal in the country in matters involving private law activities of a foreign State, English courts seem to adhere to the principle of immunity in other spheres. This was conspicuously so in *Krajina* v. *Tass Agency* – a case arising out of an alleged libel by an agency of a foreign State – although even in this case there were indications of the emergence of a different approach, inasmuch as the Court of Appeal examined in some detail the question whether the Tass Agency was an entity identical with the Russian State.[1] The same tendency manifested itself in the case of *Dollfus Mieg* v. *Bank of England*.[2] There the Court of Appeal, while affirming in principle the rule of immunity, in the result decided against it by reference to what has been described as 'the niceties of the English law of bailment'.[3] The House of Lords reversed, in effect, the decision of the Court of Appeal. It declined to withhold immunity by reference to a somewhat technical construction of the doctrine of possession. But it is significant that while in previous decisions English courts attached importance to emphasizing the necessity of giving a wide interpretation to the doctrine of immunity, in the *Dollfus Mieg* case in three out of the four judgments delivered in the House of Lords reference was made to the desirability, in the words of Lord Porter, that the doctrine of immunity of foreign States 'be narrowly watched'.[4] In *Sultan of Johore* v. *Abubakar*,[5] decided in 1952, Lord Simon, in delivering the opinion of the Judicial Committee of the Privy Council, attached importance to dispelling the view that there exists 'any absolute rule that a foreign independent sovereign cannot be impleaded in our courts in any circumstances'. He pointed out that if there existed such a rule 'there could have been no justification for reserving the case of a Sovereign's ship engaged in ordinary commerce – a reservation that was, in fact, made by the majority of the House of Lords in the *Cristina* case'. On the other hand, in *Kahan* v. *Federation of Pakistan*[6] the Court of Appeal fully adhered, as it was bound to do, to the judgment of the House of Lords in *Duff*

butable to certain constitutional reasons rather than objections of principle. In its reply to the questionnaire of the Committee for the Progressive Codification of International Law the British Government considered, in 1928, the question of the competence of the courts in regard to foreign States 'to be suitable for consideration by an international conference' (Doc. A (1928), v, 63). That cautious statement may be properly interpreted as meaning that already at that time the attitude of the British Government was not wholly adverse to the abandonment of the rigid principle of absolute immunity. This was also the attitude of the British member of the Committee (Dr Arnold D. McNair). He made the following proposal: 'That the Committee submit to the Council its opinion that, though difficult, it would be worth while making the attempt, by means of an international conference, to arrive at a general convention under which States would become subject to the jurisdiction of foreign States as regards their commercial or industrial enterprises and their *navires de commerce*' (Doc. C.P.D. 1/3rd Session/P.V. (1927), p. 54). Attention may be drawn in this connection to the resolution, on the same lines, of the Imperial Economic Conference with regard to taxation of foreign Government-owned trading enterprises (*Records of Proceedings* (H.M. Stationery Office, 1923), p. 22).

[1] [1949] All E.R. 774: *Annual Digest*, 16 (1949), 129.

[2] [1950] All E.R. 747.

[3] Johnson, in *B.Y.* 27 (1950), 461.

[4] *United States of America and Republic of France* v. *Dollfus Mieg et Cie and Bank of England* [1952] 1 All E.R. 572, at p. 585.

[5] [1952] 1 All E.R. 1268.

[6] [1951] 2 K.B. 1003, 1016.

Development Company v. *Government of Kelantan*[1] in requiring, in addition to initial renunciation of immunity, express submission to jurisdiction at every stage.

There are only a few instances of the judicial practice of the countries of the British Commonwealth of Nations on the subject. In general it may be considered to follow that of the United States of America and the United Kingdom.[2]

Conclusions

The preceding survey of judicial practice does not lend itself to a detailed summary by way of conclusions. Its object is to show the change which has occurred, in the practice of most countries, in the direction of the abandonment of the principle of absolute jurisdictional immunity of foreign States. What, in the past, has been considered to be an exception limited to a small number of countries, in particular to Italy and Belgium, assumes, with the increasingly precarious exceptions of the United States and the United Kingdom, the complexion of a general practice based on the distinction between acts *jure gestionis* and acts *jure imperii*. Both the limited degree of usefulness of that distinction for the future development of this branch of international law and its significance as implying the elimination of the principle of immunity as a general rule of international law have been indicated in the article above.

[1] See above, p. 332.

[2] As to Canada see, for example, the *Indochina* (*Annual Digest*, 1 (1919–22), Case no. 106) and *White* v. *The Ship Frank Dale* [1946] Ex C.R. 555 (*Annual Digest*, 13 (1946), Case no. 34). Both decisions adopt, with some hesitation, the principle of absolute immunity. But it is of interest to note that in the *India* the Supreme Court of South Africa, in holding that a vessel owned by the Portuguese Government and, apparently, operated by it was immune from seizure, attached importance to the fact that she was not used for purely commercial purposes. The Court said: 'The conclusion I have come to is that ships, the property of a foreign State and used for public purposes, are not subject to attachment under an order of the local court.... In my opinion any use of a vessel for the purpose of obtaining revenue for the State is a public purpose, just as its use for the protection of the State is public' (*per* Gardiner J. at p. 464; *Annual Digest*, 1 (1919–22), Case no. 105).

CHAPTER II

THE *CRISTINA*

Editor's note Lauterpacht wrote few case-notes. This analysis of the decision of the House of Lords in the *Cristina* [1938] A.C. 485 appeared in *L.Q.R.* 54 (1938), 339–44.

The *Cristina*[1] is one of the more interesting cases on international law decided in the last two years. Its interest lies not so much in the points of law which were laid down by the House of Lords and with regard to which there was no division of opinion among the five learned Lords, as in their discussion of matters which, admittedly, were not necessary for the decision and on which they clearly disagreed.

The facts of the case were simple enough. On 28 June 1937 the Spanish (Republican) Government issued a decree requisitioning all vessels registered in Bilbao. The *Cristina*, which at that time was not within the territorial jurisdiction of Spain, arrived in Cardiff on 8 July. On 14 July the Spanish consul, acting on behalf of the Spanish Government, went on board the *Cristina* and took possession of the vessel, after having a day before dismissed the captain by registered letter. It was conceded that there had been no breach of the peace and that the master and the crew from that time held themselves and the ship at the disposal of the Government. On 22 July the appellants issued a writ naming as defendants 'the steamship or vessel *Cristina* and all persons claiming an interest therein'. The respondent, the Spanish Government, entered a conditional appearance and on the same day lodged notice of a motion claiming that the writ be set aside on the ground that the *Cristina* was rightfully in possession of the Spanish Government, a Government of a foreign sovereign State, which was impleaded by the writ and which refused to sanction the proceedings.

Bucknill J. and the Court of Appeal granted the motion and set aside the writ. The House of Lords dismissed the appeal. Their Lordships held, in effect unanimously, that, in accordance with a principle of 'international law engrafted into our domestic law'[2], the courts: (*a*) will not exercise jurisdiction over a foreign Sovereign against his will; and (*b*) will not seize or detain property of which he is in possession or control. It appears from all the five judgments delivered in this case that the immunity of the foreign Government depends on its actually

[1] [1938] A.C. 485.

[2] *Per* Lord Atkin, at p. 490.

being in possession (as distinguished from a claim to possession of property in the hands of a third party) – a point which it was not necessary to decide expressly seeing that the Spanish Government was admittedly in possession of the ship.

It was not necessary to answer the question whether such possession must be rightfully obtained. Lord Maugham, who alone discussed this aspect of the matter, pointed out that, as diplomatic representations are often a doubtful weapon in these days, it is advisable to 'scrutinize with the greatest care' a claim to immunity in cases where possession had been obtained in this country 'without any shadow of right'.[1] However, in the course of his judgment he seems to have abandoned his doubts for he later states[2] that there is a valid claim to immunity whenever the foreign Government 'is, rightly or wrongly, in possession of [? movable] property in this country'.

All the learned Lords seem to have been agreed that as the ship was requisitioned in prosecution of the civil war it was *publicis usibus destinata*. And yet, the bulk of the report is devoted to the question as to what would have been the position if the *Cristina* had been a governmental ship used for commercial purposes. On this, hypothetical, question the House of Lords was clearly divided. Lord Atkin[3] was of the opinion that it is well settled that the immunity extends to property used for commercial purposes. Lord Wright, who dealt with the matter at length, was of the same view. That principle, he said, was laid down in the *Parlement Belge*;[4] it was rightly followed in the *Porto Alexandre*;[5] and it received persuasive approval by the Supreme Court of the United States in the *Pesaro*.[6] Lord Thankerton and Lord Maugham, on the other hand, thought that the *Parlement Belge* did not in fact lay down the principle contended for; that that case was wrongly interpreted in the *Porto Alexandre*; and that they therefore considered themselves at liberty to reconsider in the future the law followed in the latter case. Lord Macmillan, too, reserved his opinion on the question decided in the *Porto Alexandre*; but he based his view on considerations broader than adherence to precedent. After quoting the 'well-chosen' words of the judgment in *Mortensen* v. *Peters* laying down that 'It is a trite observation that there is no such thing as a standard of international law extraneous to the domestic law of a kingdom to which appeal may be made', he proceeded, somewhat unexpectedly, to investigate whether there existed in the matter an agreed rule of international law as evidenced by the accepted sources of the Law of Nations. He said: 'I

[1] At p. 515.
[2] At p. 517.
[3] At p. 490.
[4] (1880) 5 P.D. 197.
[5] [1920] P. 3: *Annual Digest*, 1 (1919–22), 146.
[6] (1925) 271 U.S. 562: *Annual Digest*, 3 (1925–6), 186.

confess that I should hesitate to lay down that it is part of the law of England that an ordinary foreign trading vessel is immune from civil process within this realm by reason merely of the fact that it is owned by a foreign State, for *such a principle must be an importation from international law, and there is no proved consensus of international opinion or practice to this effect.*'[1] He emphasized the fact that in view of the recent extension of the practice of State trading the circumstances which had originally led to the adoption of the principle of immunity had undergone substantial modifications.

The scope of this note permits comment on two points only: In the first instance, in view of the doubts which have been expressed, it may be stated that, as the law stands at present, a foreign recognized Government is entitled to immunity from jurisdiction in respect of property in its possession in this country regardless of whether it has gained possession by means or in a way of which the law approves. A foreign Government may have obtained possession in pursuance of a nationalization decree to which English courts deny, as a rule, any extraterritorial effect. Yet English courts will refrain from exercising jurisdiction against that Government in respect of such property so long – but not longer[2] – as it is in possession of that Government. The same applies probably to possession acquired by conduct constituting a tort or even a criminal act. This is so for the simple reason that if courts were competent to inquire into the legality of the acquisition of possession, the privilege of immunity might become nugatory. It is easy to criticize this aspect of jurisdictional immunity by pointing to its possible absurd consequences. What, for instance, would be the position if the representative of a foreign Government were to obtain by force possession in this country of a ship indisputably owned by a British subject? The answer is that such high-handed action may have the result of terminating abruptly the diplomatic or consular function of the person concerned (and of his successor persisting in the claim). As Lord Maugham said, diplomatic representations made to certain countries may be futile in these days. But so long as the abuse of the privilege of immunity takes place in this country, there is in drastic cases available the effective remedy of immediate diplomatic action in England. At a time when the authority of international law is exposed to considerable strain, it may not be desirable that courts should attempt to increase the efficacy of diplomatic efforts by a controversial interpretation of an accepted principle of the Law of Nations.

[1] At p. 498.

[2] A point well brought out by comparison of the *Jupiter* (*No.* 1) [1924] P. 231: *Annual Digest*, 3 (1925–6), 136; and the *Jupiter* (*No.* 2) [1925] P. 69: *Annual Digest*, 3 (1925–6), 136.

The same considerations apply to the question of jurisdictional immunities of foreign governmental vessels employed in commerce. A number of countries, including Italy, Switzerland and Belgium, have for a long time refused to recognize such immunity. In the Brussels Convention of 1926 for the Unification of Certain Rules Concerning the Immunities of Government Vessels – now ratified by various States, including Germany and Italy – the contracting parties renounced that immunity *inter se.* The exemption of such vessels from jurisdiction cannot, therefore, as Lord Macmillan said, be regarded as a generally-recognized principle of international law. However, prior to the *Cristina,* such exemption was generally regarded as part of international law as recognized by the courts of this country. Prior to the *Cristina,* the principle of the *Parlement Belge* as applied to commercial vessels and as followed in the *Porto Alexandre* was not seriously challenged as part of the law of the land – although doubts have been expressed as to its soundness in present conditions. Successive British Governments have so far declined to become a party to the Brussels Convention. That attitude may be explained on a number of grounds. Possibly it has been considered that any such renunciation of immunity ought to be preceded by a reform in English law in the matter of the immunity of the Crown from suit. For if Great Britain were at present to become a party to the Convention it might well happen that a subject of a foreign State would possess a remedy which the law denies to a British subject with regard to the same cause of action – unless, indeed, the Convention and the enabling Act of Parliament passed in pursuance thereof were made to operate as changing English law in relation to British subjects in respect of British ships covered by the Convention. Possibly it has occurred to some that the border-line between commercial and 'public' activities is not as rigid as is commonly assumed. Italian courts have held that the purchase of shoes for the army is an act of a private law nature and as such outside the principle of immunity.[1] In the United States the same transaction was held to constitute the exercise of the 'highest sovereign function of protecting itself against the enemies'.[2] Finally, it is possible that weight has been attached to the consideration, so eloquently expressed in the *Pesaro,* that commercial undertakings may be no less worthy of protection than other activities of the State.

These are not the views of the writer of this note, who confesses to a lack of sympathy with the continued immunity of governmental trading

[1] *Governo Rumeno* v. *Trutta*: *Guirispradenza Italiana* (1926), Part 1, 774; *Annual Digest,* 3 (1925–6), 179.

[2] *Kingdom of Roumania* v. *Guaranty Trust Co. of New York* (2nd), 250 Fed. 341, 343.

ships. Such exemption is not germane either to the original or to the proper purpose of jurisdictional immunity of foreign States; it tends to be unfair and unjust in its operation. But, here again, it is doubtful whether circumstances warrant a bold piece of judicial legislation adapting to changed conditions a rule of international law as understood by the courts of this country in the last fifty years. A similar problem arose not long ago in connection with the amalgamation of the diplomatic and consular services in some countries with the result that officials performing essentially consular functions were made to benefit from the immunities hitherto enjoyed by diplomatic representatives and their staff. But the case of *Engelke* v. *Musmann*,[1] although decided on a point of procedure, warrants the conclusion that the House of Lords did not consider themselves to be the proper organ to deal with the new situation. Similarly, in the matter of jurisdictional immunities of foreign ships engaged in commerce, the change, assuming that one is desirable, ought probably to come either by way of legislation or as the result of the adhesion of this country to the international convention which must have been for some time before the competent departments of the Crown.

[1] [1928] 1 K.B. 90; [1928] A.C. 433: *Annual Digest*, 4 (1927–8), 362.

PART IV

THE INDIVIDUAL IN INTERNATIONAL LAW

I

THE INDIVIDUAL AS A NATIONAL

CHAPTER 1

THE NATIONALITY OF DENATIONALIZED PERSONS

Editor's note Amongst Lauterpacht's papers there is an opinion of nineteen foolscap typed papers prepared at the request of the Intergovernmental Committee for Refugees on the effect of certain laws issued by the Allied Military Governments and by the Allied Control Council in Germany upon the status of persons, both in and outside Germany, who had been deprived of their German nationality by virtue of certain German laws and decrees passed during the National-Socialist régime. Although the opinion is undated, it appears from internal evidence to have been written during the first months of 1946. If Lauterpacht had not subsequently published the article of which the present chapter consists, it would have been appropriate to publish this opinion. However, as the ground covered by the two items is similar and the article is a fuller and more scholarly study, I have thought it reasonable to omit the opinion. Lauterpacht refers to the opinion in the final footnote of the chapter.

The article was published in the *Jewish Yearbook of International Law* (1948), pp. 164–185.

I

The present article is concerned with certain questions of nationality such as the rules of international law bearing upon the duty of a State to recognize the nationality laws of other States, the exceptions to that obligation in time of war, the right of a State to impose its nationality upon persons resident abroad, and the problem of the retroactive effect of legislation in matters of nationality. These are questions of limited compass. However, the circumstances preceding and accompanying the Second World War have imparted to them a complexion transcending any particular disputed question of international law in the matter of nationality. The issues which arose in this connection affected largely, though not exclusively, persons of the Jewish faith or race who had become victims of persecution at the hands of the National-Socialist State of Germany. Most of the consequences of that persecution – the most tragic and most cruel in the annals of history – are irretrievable. But some of them did lend themselves to remedial action by the Allied forces which occupied Germany. Such action was taken promptly and on a comprehensive scale. Yet such is the unavoidable generality of legal enactments that those very efforts brought about, in a disconcerting way, the contingency of the sufferings of some of the surviving victims of the persecution being aggravated rather than relieved by what was intended as an act of legality and justice. The issue thus raised became an instance of the complexities besetting the judicial function and a test of the application of international law and of general principles of law in a spirit consonant with international morality and with the international recognition of the rights of man.

On 18 September 1944 the Military Government of Germany (Supreme Commander's Area of Control) issued Law no. 1 which provided that 'in order to eliminate from German law and administration within the occupied territory the policies and doctrines of the National-Socialist Party and to restore to the German people the rule of justice and equality before the law', certain fundamental Nazi laws enacted since 30 January 1933, 'together with all supplementary or subsidiary carrying out laws, decrees or regulations whatsoever are hereby deprived of effect within the occupied territory'. Among the laws to be repealed was included the Reich Citizenship Law of 15 September 1935.[1] An identical Law was enacted on 20 September 1945, Law no. 1, by the Control Council. The reasons which prompted these measures of repeal were set forth in a succession of impressive declarations and pronouncements.[2]

The two principal Decrees enacted by the Reich in pursuance of the Citizenship Law were the Decree of 14 November 1935 and the Decree of 25 November 1941. The first Decree provided in effect that Jews may not be citizens of the Reich – a Reich citizen alone being 'the bearer of full political rights' who can exercise the right of voting in political matters and fill public office. Jews, however, continued to be 'nationals' of the Reich (*Staatsangehörige*) in the sense attached to the term by international law. The Decree of 25 November 1941 laid down: (1) that a Jew who has his ordinary place of residence abroad cannot be a German national; (2) that a Jew loses his German nationality either on the date of the issue of the Decree if on that date he has his ordinary residence abroad or, at a later date, when he transfers his ordinary residence abroad.[3] A considerable number of Jews lost their German nationality as the result of that Decree. The same Decree

[1] *Reichsgesetzblatt* (hereafter *RGBl.*), I, 1146.

[2] 'We shall overthrow the Nazi rule, dissolve the Nazi Party and abolish the cruel, oppressive and discriminating laws and institutions which the party has created' (Military Government Proclamation no. 1).

'No German law . . . shall be applied judicially or administratively within the occupied territory in any instance where such application would cause injustice or inequality . . . (*b*) by discriminating against any person by reason of his race, nationality, religious belief or opposition to the National Socialist Party or its doctrines' (Military Government Law no. 1, Article II).

[3] *RGBl.* I, 722.

provided for the confiscation of the property of Jews who had become stateless.

The Citizenship Law and the denationalization Decrees issued in pursuance thereof were one of the principal and most symbolic pieces of National-Socialist racial legislation, and it is not surprising that they should have been among the first selected for repeal. A cause of surprise lay elsewhere. It rested in the revelation of some of the consequences of a technical and literal interpretation of the repealing legislation. The result of that interpretation was to invest with German nationality persons of Jewish race who resided outside Germany and who had lost that nationality in consequence of German legislation. This is the interpretation adopted by the courts and administrative authorities of some countries. Its principal result is, in practice, that the persons in question are considered to have ceased to be stateless and to have re-acquired German nationality. As such, they are subject to the discriminatory, confiscatory, and repressive measures to which German nationals and their property are subjected abroad. The French Court of Cassation has given its great authority in support of that construction of the repealing legislation. In the case of *Kurzmann* v. *O'Rea*, decided on 28 November 1946,[1] it held that the plaintiff, who was a refugee in France since 1939 and who had been deprived of his German nationality by the German Decree of 25 November 1941, was to be considered a German and, therefore, enemy national, having regard to the repeal of the German Decree by the Allied authorities. In the opinion of the Court of Cassation the effect of the Allied legislation was 'not to give to the persons who had become stateless the right to regain German nationality, but to impose upon them that nationality'. As a result, the Court held that the plaintiff could not invoke the provisions of the Geneva Convention of 1938 which gave to stateless persons the right to equal treatment with other friendly aliens and that he could not, therefore, benefit from the French legislation providing for reinstatement of tenants dispossessed by the German occupation authorities.

It does not inevitably follow that the decision in the *Kurzmann* case is determining for all stateless Jewish refugees of German origin resident in France. The decisions of the French Court of Cassation are not absolutely binding, and it is significant that shortly afterwards, in February 1947, the Paris Court of Appeal in a reasoned decision arrived at conclusions diametrically opposed to that given by the Court of Cassation.[2] It declined to give to the Allied Law of 20 September 1945 an interpretation which would reduce it to a travesty of its

[1] No. 33,843 : see *Annual Digest*, 13 (1946), 136.
[2] *Terhoch* v. *Daudin* : see *ibid.* 14 (1947), 121.

liberating purpose. It is useful to quote verbatim the relevant part of the judgment:

The Law of 20 September 1945 must be interpreted in accordance with its purpose and the intention of the Control Council. That intention could not have been to impose German nationality upon persons who, after having fled from the persecution inflicted upon them by that State, have taken refuge abroad and have not returned to the country in relation to which they have ceased to have any relation of allegiance. The object aimed at by the Control Council is quite different. That object is stated in Law no. 1 of 20 September 1945 as being 'to eliminate from German law and public administration in occupied territory the policies and doctrines of the National-Socialist Party and to restore to the German people the rule of justice and equality before the law'. It is nowhere indicated that in order to achieve that result it is necessary to efface, for the past, the measures taken by Nazi laws and to compel those who have ceased to be German to become Germans once more against their will. While international law concedes to States the quasi-discretionary right to regulate questions of nationality, that right is limited in civilized States by the rights of human personality and by the free choice enjoyed by every person of age to re-acquire or to decline the re-acquisition of the nationality of which he has been deprived. Any other interpretation would have inadmissible results. The laws repealing Nazi legislation were intended, as stated above, to abolish the iniquities of the National-Socialist régime. These laws cannot result in an aggravation of the plight of the victims of that régime.

This part of the judgment has been reproduced here at some length not only as an instance of liberal interpretation in the best tradition of the French courts, but also because it states concisely and, it is believed, accurately the legal position on the subject. However, the decision of the Court of Cassation in the *Kurzmann* case calls for comment not on account of any persuasive cogency of its reasoning – the legal argument of the judgment is kept within the confines of a bare statement – but because of the high authority of the Court which rendered it and of the recurrent tendency shown by authorities in other countries to act on the view on which it is based. Moreover, the judgment raises significant issues of nationality and of the judicial approach to questions of the position of refugees. These issues are not limited to the effects of the repealing legislation of the Allied authorities in Germany. They arose, in a different form, in other countries. Thus English courts have been confronted, in a different way, with the question of the status of these persons. They have been called upon to decide, in effect, whether the individuals whom Germany purported to deprive of their nationality have actually, in the contemplation of English law, ceased to be German nationals. The Swiss Federal Court, in the case of *Madeleine*

Levita-Mühlstein v. *Federal Department of Justice*,[1] gave a reasoned judgment based on grounds different from those adduced by the Court of Cassation in the *Kurzmann* case but identical with it so far as the substantive result is concerned. It held that the person in question, the husband of the appellant, remained a German national on the double ground that the German denationalization Decree, being contrary to the Swiss conceptions of public policy, could not be recognized in Switzerland and also that, in view of the Allied legislation, he could effectively ask for re-instatement into German nationality.

Accordingly, the object of the present article is a threefold one. In the first instance, it is proposed to discuss briefly – for the matter is not one of international law, with which we are primarily concerned here – the question of the retroactivity of the Allied legislation repealing the discriminatory laws of National-Socialist Germany. Secondly, on the assumption – which is somewhat far-fetched – that the Allied measures of repeal were intended to re-invest German refugees abroad with German nationality, it is intended to examine the limits, under international law, upon the right of the State to impose its nationality upon persons resident abroad. Finally, in relation to the question which has arisen before English courts, we propose to enquire to what extent international law, principally as interpreted by British practice, imposes upon the State the duty to recognize the legislation of a foreign State in so far as it purports to deprive of their nationality individuals who hitherto were its citizens.

2. RETROACTIVITY OF LEGISLATION IN THE MATTER OF NATIONALITY

It is a general principle of law that legislation, unless it specially provides to the contrary or unless irresistible considerations of justice so require, is not retroactive. This is not a principle confined to the field of criminal law. Some systems of law, such as the French *Code Civil*, give specific expression to the prohibition of retroactivity.[2] In other systems of law that principle is an undisputed maxim of legislative policy. In so far as, in exceptional cases, the law is intended to be retroactive, it includes as a rule, in the interest of order and security, a detailed regulation of the incidence of its retroactive operation. Similarly,

[1] See below, p. 394.

[2] Article 2: 'La loi ne dispose que pour l'avenir; elle n'a point d'effet rétroactif' – a provision which follows closely the French Constitution of 1795. Article 2 of the Introductory Rules to the Italian Civil Code is to the same effect. And see generally Joseph-Barthélemy et Duez, *Traité Elémentaire de Droit Constitutionnel* (1926), pp. 588–91. See also Nipperdey, *Lehrbuch des Bürgerlichen Rechts* (13th ed. 1931), p. 57, on the identical position in German law.

the denial of retroactivity is a persistent feature of administrative law.[1] With regard to questions of status, the drawbacks of retroactivity are particularly apparent. For this reason, although the law of numerous countries provides for resumption of nationality, on application, in various contingencies – as in the case of nationality lost through marriage or by minors – no retroactive effect attaches to resumption of citizenship. Thus, when the British Nationality and Status of Aliens Act of 1933 provided – by repealing, in effect, what was the previous law on the subject – that a British woman marrying an alien shall not lose her British nationality unless she acquires at the same time the nationality of her husband, the new Act did not automatically restore British nationality to women who had lost their nationality as the result of the operation of the previous legislation. Occasionally, the absence of retrospective effect in the matter of repeal of legislation divesting persons of their nationality is expressly included in the statute. When the United States Statute of 13 July 1930,[2] repealed Section 3 of the Act of 1922 concerning the presumption of expatriation of an American married woman living abroad, it laid down that 'such repeal shall not restore citizenship lost under Section 3 before such repeal'.[3]

To that principle of non-retroactivity the laws promulgated in Germany by the Allied authorities with a view to abolishing discriminatory legislation provide no exception. In fact, reference to the various Articles of Law no. 1, issued on 18 September 1944, confirms that its purpose is not to prescribe any retroactive abolition of the effects of repealed laws, but to prevent their operation in the future. The Law as a whole is concerned with the administration of justice in Germany in the future; its purpose, unless specifically stated to the contrary, is not to undo the accomplished consequences of previous legislation. Thus Article II lays down that no German law shall be applied judicially or administratively so as to cause injustice or inequality by favouring persons because of their connection with the National-Socialist Party or by discriminating against persons for reasons of race, nationality, religion or opposition to the National-Socialist Party. Article III prohibits the interpretation and application of German laws in accordance with National-Socialist doctrines – a provision which does not affect the validity of rights previously acquired in accordance with such interpretation of German law. On the other hand, when the authors of Law no. 1 intended it to be retroactive, they stated so expressly. Thus

[1] See Gruia, 'De la Non-Rétroactivité des Actes Administratifs', in *Mélanges Paul Negulesco* (1935), pp. 343–412.

[2] 46 Stat. 854.

[3] It will be noted that, unlike the imposition of German nationality upon stateless refugees, in all these cases any retroactive effect of the repeal would not imply any hardship for the persons concerned.

Article III, which prohibits retroactive punishment, punishment for offences determined by analogy, as well as cruel or excessive punishment, lays down that all punishment imposed prior to the enactment of Law no. 1, and not yet carried out, shall be modified to conform to this Law or annulled.[1]

The purpose of the legislation enacted by the Allied authorities is to forbid the application in the future of the abolished Nazi laws. Its object is not to remedy the effect produced in the past by the enforcement of those laws. The legal effect, properly conceived, of the repeal of the Law of Citizenship of 1935 and of the Decree of 1941 is that in the future no German Jew shall lose his German nationality because of taking up habitual residence abroad. Its effect is not that the persons who lost their German nationality because of the operation of the Decree are automatically reinstated in German nationality. Any attempt to interpret the repeal of the National-Socialist legislation, in this and in other matters, as abolishing the legal effects already accomplished by the legislation which has been repealed and as restoring the *status quo ante*, would place the present administration and judiciary of Germany before perplexing and insoluble problems. Thus, as the result of the repealed legislation, in matters of nationality and otherwise the property of the denationalized persons was confiscated. But there is no suggestion that the abolition of the obnoxious legislation has the automatic effect of restoring property rights as they existed before. Any such result must be the subject of special legislation and arrangements in accordance with requirements of justice and economic conditions. Moreover, the problem is not limited to legislation concerning denationalization. Thus, for instance, Law no. 1 of the Control Council abolishes, among others, the Ordinance of 12 November 1938 for the Elimination of Jews from Economic Life and the Ordinance of 1 September 1941 concerning the Employment of Jews. Yet the object of the repealing Law is not to make the repeal retroactive in the sense of restoring to Jews the posts and businesses of which they had been deprived as the result of the discriminatory legislation. Moreover, in addition to the National-Socialist legislation in the economic sphere and in that of nationality, vast and numerous changes in status were brought about by direct anti-Jewish legislation or by interpretation of existing laws in the spirit of the National-Socialist State and ideology, for instance, in the field of marital relations. Thus, divorces were

[1] It must also be noted that, apart from any question of retroactivity, Law no. 1 provides expressly that it applies only within German territory. The wording of the introductory passage of Law no. 1 is as follows: '1. The following fundamental Nazi laws enacted since 30 January 1933, together with all supplementary or subsidiary carrying out laws, decrees or regulations whatsoever are hereby deprived of effect within the *occupied territory*.'

granted by German courts in pursuance of such legislation or of such judicial interpretation. But the repeal of the legislation in question cannot, by itself, have the result of validating marriages already dissolved, or of rendering subsequent marriages of the divorced persons bigamous, or of affecting the status of children born in the meantime. These are considerations *ab inconvenienti*. They are a specific illustration of the difficulties inherent in attempts to make repealing legislation retroactive. Non-retroactivity is a general principle of interpretation of statutes. As stated, it is a principle which may be overridden by the clearly expressed will of the legislator or, in extreme cases, by judicial construction intent upon avoiding a result patently inconsistent with justice. Neither of these contingencies applies to the case under discussion.[1]

3. TERRITORIAL LIMITS OF THE LEGISLATIVE COMPETENCE OF STATES

The laws of the Allied Military and Occupation Authorities repealing discriminatory German legislation in the matter of nationality cannot, having regard to their wording and purpose, be considered as endowed with the retroactive effect of restoring German nationality to persons previously deprived of it. No such result or intention can be attributed to them consistently with the general principles of law in the matter of the retroactive effect of legislation. There is a further reason why no such intention can be attributed or why, even if it were clear that such intention existed, it could not be given effect consistently with international law. That reason is that, according to international law, no law issued by the German State or by the authority substituted for the German State can properly impose German nationality upon persons who, according to German law, valid at the time of its promulgation, had ceased to be German nationals and are either stateless or have in the meantime acquired another nationality. For it may be assumed that the Control Council for the whole of Germany and the Military Govern-

[1] Under the provisions of a general German Law of 14 July 1933 (*RGBl.* I, no. 81, 480), a number of persons, Jews and others, both in Germany and abroad, were deprived of their German nationality by special decrees of the German Government. The Law, in addition to providing for the revocation of the German nationality of persons naturalized between 9 November 1918 and 15 July 1933 laid down that the Minister of the Interior may, in consultation with the Minister for Foreign Affairs, deprive of German nationality persons who reside abroad and who either injure the cause of the German Reich and people or who refuse to obey an order to return to Germany. That particular Law has not been repealed by the Allied authorities. It would appear, therefore, that the status of that considerable number of persons who were deprived of their German nationality by special decree applying to them individually under the Law of 1933 is in any case not affected by the repealing legislation of the Allied authorities in Germany.

ments for the various zones stand in the same position as the German State whose sovereignty is now suspended. If there were a German State with an independent Government in existence it would be, as a matter of law, quite incapable of imposing, by legislation or otherwise, German nationality upon persons who have been denationalized and who live outside its frontiers. There is no legal tie which connects these persons with Germany; any links which existed had been broken by their denationalization. Germany – or an authority acting in her place – may declare the original denationalization invalid, but such declaration, even if there were the intention to make it retroactive, has no binding effect upon the denationalized person abroad. He may avail himself of it if it is in his favour; he need not do so if he considers it contrary to his interest. He is under no legal obligation to, and has no legal relation with, the State of whose nationality he has been deprived. His relation with that State is a matter of history; it is no longer a source of rights or duties. Germany – or the authority substituted for her – might as well try to impose German nationality upon any other persons outside Germany who have never been German nationals.

There is, in law, no difference between the attempt by a State to impose its nationality upon persons resident abroad who were once its nationals and the endeavour compulsorily to confer its nationality upon persons resident abroad who have never possessed its nationality. An international court would hold either of these attempts to be illegal. It is true that international law concedes to States the right to regulate matters of nationality. But the discretion which a State enjoys in this matter is subject to general principles of law, to legitimate rights of other States, and to those rights of human personality which international law was increasingly recognizing even before the Charter of the United Nations gave recognition to fundamental human rights and freedoms. The Hague Convention on Certain Questions relating to the Conflict of Nationality Laws of 1930 laid down, in Article 1, that while it is for each State to decide under its own law what persons are its nationals, other States are under a duty to recognize such law only 'in so far as it is consistent with international conventions, international custom, and the principles of law generally recognized with regard to nationality'. In connection with the Hague Conference of 1930 a number of States gave expression to that inherent limitation of the rights of the State in matters of nationality. Thus, it was stated on behalf of the United States of America:

While . . . the Government of the United States has always recognized the fact that the acquisition or loss of the nationality of a particular State are matters which pertain primarily to domestic policy and are therefore determined by the domestic law of that State, it does not admit that a State is subject to no limitations in conferring its nationality on individuals. It has proceeded upon the theory, which is believed to be sound, that there are certain grounds generally recognized by civilized States upon which a State may properly clothe individuals with its nationality at or after birth, but that no State is free to extend the application of its laws of nationality in such way as to reach out and claim the allegiance of whomsoever it pleases. The scope of municipal law governing nationality must be regarded as limited by consideration of the rights and obligations of individuals and other States.[1]

Similar replies were given by other States, including Great Britain[2] and Germany.[3]

This generally acknowledged limitation of the right of the State in the matter of conferment of nationality has been asserted largely by reference to the interests of States affected by compulsory naturalization of their citizens. No State will lightly submit to the nationality of its citizens being adversely affected by arbitrary decrees of another State. However, there has also taken place an increasingly wide recognition of the view that the right of a State to impose its nationality is limited by the interests and the desires of the individuals concerned. The growing recognition of the right of option of nationality in cases of cession of territory – a practice which became almost universal in the last century – testifies to the vitality of the principle according to which individuals should not, if possible, be compelled to acquire or to retain a nationality against their will. Moreover, within the very institution of option there have taken place changes in the same direction. Thus, while previously option by the husband was decisive for the nationality of his wife, the Peace Treaties of 1947 have expressly abandoned that practice.[4] In a different sphere, the practice of the majority of States, including that of Great Britain, the United States, and France, has been that in case of annexation or cession individuals habitually resident outside the ceded or annexed territory do not against their will acquire the nationality of the new sovereign. Professor Westlake, a distinguished lawyer noted for restraint in expression, described as monstrous and inaccurate the notion that the successor State has the right to hold such persons to its nationality against their will.[5] The French Nationality Law of 19 October 1945 lays down, in Article 12, that when new territory is attached to the French State only persons retaining their domicile within the territory in question shall acquire

[1] Conference for the Codification of International Law, *Bases of Discussion*, 1, *Nationality* (1929), 16.

[2] *Ibid.* p. 17.

[3] *Ibid.* p. 13.

[4] See, for instance, Article 19 (2) of the Peace Treaty with Italy.

[5] Westlake, *Papers*, p. 487.

French nationality. In the case with which the present article is concerned the reasons why it is inadmissible to impose a nationality upon persons outside the territory are even more compelling. For the persons in question not only reside abroad; there is in respect of them no legal tie linking them in any way, through State succession or otherwise, with the nationality which they possessed prior to the denationalization.

There ought thus to be no doubt that, as a matter of international law, the State within whose territory such persons reside is *entitled* to refuse to give effect to an attempt to reimpose upon them the nationality of the State of whose nationality they had been previously deprived by an act valid according to the law of that State. Any such attempt is in violation of the territorial sovereignty of the foreign State in question and can be legitimately objected to and ignored. However, it is submitted that that foreign State and its judicial and administrative authorities are also *bound*, in law and in equity, to refuse to give effect to any such attempt to reimpose nationality upon persons resident abroad. That duty, which they may or may not owe to any particular State, is imposed upon them by the general principles of international law in the matter of nationality, which principles deny to a State the right to impose its nationality upon persons outside its territory. It is also imposed upon them by the as yet imperfect but increasingly recognized right of human personality not to be compulsorily afflicted with an odious nationality not based on residence.

In the particular case with which we are here concerned, that legal duty to refuse recognition to compulsory conferment of nationality upon persons resident abroad is reinforced by considerations of overwhelming cogency of international morality – considerations which cannot be divorced from the legal situation as a whole and which no international tribunal would deem itself free to leave out of account. The persons in question were originally deprived of their nationality in the course of a racial and religious persecution unprecedented in history. Their denationalization did not merely sever a formal tie with their country of origin. They were cut off, amidst calculated and prolonged indignities and humiliation, from any sort of community with the people of that country. Their livelihood and their property were destroyed and confiscated. Their relatives and co-religionists were subjected to a spiritual and physical persecution and extermination which shocked and outraged civilized mankind. The deprivation of nationality was a link in the chain of that ruthless persecution. However, in some ways that particular measure of oppression proved for those resident abroad a source of protection. During the War statelessness became for many of them a status preferable to that of the nationality of a belligerent

State. After Germany had been defeated, many of these remnants of the persecution regarded the condition of statelessness as a protection against the various measures of seizure and discrimination to which German nationals and their property abroad are exposed. The repealing legislation of the Allied authorities in Germany would, in a substantial respect, fail in its purpose if the victims of the persecution were, as the result of enactments intended to remove from them the burdens of discrimination, made to suffer from measures adopted against German nationals and intended as just compensation from and punishment of their persecutors. It is improbable that, in addition to the clear legal merits of the issue, these considerations of equity and morality would be disregarded by an international tribunal.

These considerations were referred to by the French Court of Cassation in a concluding passage of the judgment in the *Kurzmann* case.[1] The Court observed that if the existing law is not sufficiently clear so as to permit courts to include within the category of 'alien enemies' persons to whom, for reasons of equity and humanity, the executive wishes to accord the favourable treatment provided for in international conventions,[2] it is necessary to adopt a text which will put an end to uncertainty. It was open to the Court to resolve the existing doubts in favour of the refugee. It is not inconsistent with the proper exercise of the judicial function to take into account, in case of doubt, considerations of fairness and equity. This is especially so if we recall that the Paris Court of Appeal was subsequently able to arrive at a decision which runs clearly counter to that of the Court of Cassation.

This tendency, which on general grounds must give rise to apprehension, to adopt an interpretation of the law unfavourable to victims of persecution is apparent, even more emphatically, in the decision of the Swiss Federal Court of 14 June 1946, in the case of *Madeleine Levita-Mühlstein* v. *Federal Department of Justice and Police*.[3] In this case the Court held that a Swiss-born woman married to a German Jew affected by the German Denationalization Decree of 1941 had become a German national for the reason that the German Decree could not be recognized in Switzerland and that her husband therefore remained a German national. The Court declined to admit that she had become stateless. It based its decision, in the first instance, on the proposition that the German Decree, enacted in pursuance of a policy of racial discrimination, was so unjust and so offensive to the principle of human equality and of equality of citizens before the law as recognized by

[1] See above, p. 385.
[2] That is, the Convention on the Status of Refugees.
[3] *Arrêts du Tribunal Fédéral Suisse*, 72 (1946), I, 407: *Annual Digest*, 13 (1946), 133.

Switzerland that no effect could be given to it in that country. The second reason adduced by the Court was that, in view of the abolition by the Allied authorities of the German discriminatory legislation, it was open to the husband of the plaintiff to re-acquire German nationality (assuming that he had lost it previously). Both grounds of the judgment seem to be an innovation in relation to the previous decisions of Swiss and other courts, as well as to international practice, on the subject.[1] It is disquieting that the Court should have found it necessary to invoke considerations of justice and equality in order to reach a decision violative of both. The issue was not, it will be noted, confined to the case of a Swiss woman whom the Court held to be saddled with a nationality which was odious to her as much as to her husband and that she was to be henceforth subjected to the disadvantages attaching to German nationality and property in Switzerland. The Court must have been cognizant of the obvious implications of the decision to German denationalized persons at large. There was no warrant for the suggestion advanced by the Court that the Allied authorities in Germany, if called upon to declare themselves on the subject, would treat these persons as German nationals. As a matter of law – and of considerations of justice and equity – these authorities have treated such persons as stateless unless they express the desire to return to German nationality. Decisions such as those in the *Mühlstein* case invite criticism not only by reference to the relevant principles of law, but also by reference to that recognition of the dignity of the human person and fundamental human rights which is and will increasingly become a legitimate test of appropriateness of legislative, judicial and administrative[2] action.

It would thus appear not only that States outside Germany are under no obligation to act upon any decision to impose German nationality upon persons who had been previously deprived of their nationality as the result of German legislation. Even if there were an intention on the part of the Allied authorities to attach retroactive effect to their legislation – no such intention need or properly ought to be assumed – outside States would not be at liberty to act upon it. If their courts were to treat such persons as compulsorily restored to German nationality, they would not be acting in accordance with a

[1] See *Lempert* v. *Bonfol* (below, p. 399) and *Pauly* v. *Custodian of Enemy Property* (below, p. 401).

[2] Some Swiss authorities have adopted the view that the German Denationalization Decree did not of itself deprive the persons concerned of their nationality, but that a specific attestation by a competent German authority in every case was required – a proof which it is clearly difficult, if not impossible, to produce. This was the attitude of the Federal Department of Justice and Police in the *Madeleine Levita-Mühlstein* case. The judgment of the Federal Court seems to give countenance to that attitude.

clearly established rule of international law. The persons thus affected are, as a rule, stateless, and it would appear that they themselves have no international legal remedy. It does not follow that there do not exist alternative methods of ascertaining, in the international forum, the legality, from the point of view of international law, of the decisions of national courts and authorities in this matter.[1]

It remains to consider the effect of the repealing Law no. 1 upon denationalized persons who were in Germany at the time of the repeal (and continued to reside there) or who may return there in the future. With regard to persons denationalized in pursuance of the Decree of 1941, their position when residing or returning for residence in Germany would seem to be not essentially different from that of persons outside Germany. To both categories of individuals there applies the principle that the repealing laws of the Allied authorities are not and were not intended to be retroactive. On the other hand, there do not apply to these persons, with the same force, the more general considerations set forth above which, in conformity with an acknowledged principle of international law, prohibit a State from imposing its nationality upon persons not within its territory. No doubt, even with regard to persons within its territory the State's freedom of action is not, in this respect, unlimited. But such limits as there are, are largely, though not exclusively, determined by the interest of outside States and by their legal right to insist that their own nationals should not be arbitrarily converted into nationals of another State. Admittedly, the – so far imperfect – right of human personality not to be burdened by an unwelcome nationality is one enjoyed also by stateless persons, but it may not necessarily be improper for a State, or the authority acting on its behalf, to reimpose their former nationality upon stateless persons (as distinguished from those who have in the meantime acquired another nationality) who voluntarily enter its territory for permanent residence or who choose to remain there with that object in view. It follows that the Allied authorities in Germany might be justified in re-imposing, after a proper interval and subject to any contrary assurance given to the persons concerned, German nationality upon stateless former German nationals who return to Germany for permanent residence, or upon those already there who, though given effectively an opportunity to emigrate to another State, elect to remain in Germany.

[1] See below, pp. 402 *et seq.*

4. RECOGNITION OF FOREIGN DENATIONALIZATION DECREES

We have been examining so far the question of the effects, outside Germany, of the Allied enactments repealing, among others, German denationalization decrees. That question has been considered in relation to countries which had previously recognized the extra territorial effects of the German decrees. It has been submitted that these States and their courts are not at liberty to give retroactive effect to the repealing legislation, in the matter of denationalization, of the Allied authorities in Germany even if we assume – which we are not at liberty to do – that that repealing legislation was intended to be retroactive and to have effect outside Germany. We must now consider the position with regard to countries, such as Great Britain, which, having regard to the contingencies of the war, declined to give effect, during the war, to the denationalization decrees of Germany. Thus, English courts held that they will not in time of war recognize any change of nationality brought about by a decree of an enemy State which purports to turn any of its subjects into stateless persons or subjects of a neutral State. They held, in *Ex parte L. and Another*, that an alien enemy, who in consequence of such a decree had become a stateless person, still retained in the eyes of English law his enemy status, and if interned in Great Britain could not move a writ of *habeas corpus*.[1] The main reason given by the Court was that to recognize German denationalization decrees in time of war would mean to enable the enemy State to make use of agents whose potentiality for mischief is increased by the fact that they have been artificially divested of the status of enemy aliens.[2]

The judgment in the aforementioned case has been exposed to authoritative criticism on the grounds both of its unsoundness in law and of the inequitable consequences to which it is bound to lead.[3] With regard to the first, it has been pointed out that the Court confused the question of nationality with that of the procedural status of the persons in question and that, in particular, it was open to the Court to hold that, while they had become stateless persons by virtue

[1] *The King* v. *The Home Secretary, Ex parte L. and Another* [1945] 1 K.B. 7: *Annual Digest*, 12 (1943–5), 199.

[2] At the close of the Second World War there were present in Great Britain two categories of persons divested by German legislation of their German nationality: (1) those deprived of it before the war by virtue of individual denationalizations in accordance with the Law of 1933, which has not been repealed by the Allied Authorities: these persons were recognized as stateless and continue to be so. (2) Those divested of their German nationality by the Decree, now repealed, of 1941. These persons have been treated by British authorities and British courts as still possessing German nationality. The present article is concerned with the second category of persons.

[3] J. E. S. Fawcett, *B.Y.* 23 (1946), 378–81.

of the operation of the German decrees, they were liable to internment by virtue of the Royal prerogative. With regard to the second ground of criticism, the consequences of the decision have been described as 'inconvenient and unjust'. Thus, it has been pointed out, British-born women who married these persons after 1941 will be deemed to have married not stateless persons but enemy aliens; and further, these persons, who had been living domiciled in England under licence and free of restraint, would become liable to deportation to Germany and to a denial of certain property rights. To these weighty reasons the following considerations must be added: Even assuming that the judgment in *Ex parte L. and Another* was sound in law at the time when it was given, it is clear that the paramount reasons of military security which prevented the recognition of the persons concerned as stateless no longer exist in time of peace. If the matter were to come, in a different form, before an English court in time of peace, the considerations of military necessity which prompted a contrary view in 1944 could no longer be treated as decisive. There could, therefore, be no serious difficulty in adopting an attitude approximating to that of the American courts, according to which no reasons of public policy militated against the recognition of these persons as stateless.[1] Overwhelming considerations of fairness and equity demand that, in so far as the law allows, the victims of persecution should not be exposed to the hardships and losses attaching to a nationality of which they were deprived by a valid decree of the State responsible for the persecution. These considerations of fairness and equity are additional to the legal principles on which English courts, alongside those of other countries, have acted in the past.

In the first instance, it is a clear rule of English law, as laid down in *Stoeck* v. *Public Trustee*,[2] that the question 'whether a person is a national of a country must be determined by the municipal law of that country . . . There is not and cannot be such an individual as a German national according to English law'.[3] In expressly adopting the rule that the

[1] This was the view of the United States Circuit Court of Appeals, Second Circuit, in the case of *United States ex rel. Schwarzkopf* v. *Uhl, District Director of Immigration*, decided on 18 August 1943: 137 F. 2d 898: *Annual Digest*, 12 (1943–5), 188. The Court held that the appellant, interned as an alien enemy, must be released as his German citizenship, if any, was lost under the Decree of 1941 and that 'there is no public policy of this country to preclude an American court from recognizing the power of Germany to disclaim Schwarzkopf as a German citizen'. The decision was given at a time when the United States was at war, and the different result reached by an American court as compared with the decision arrived at in Great Britain is apparently due to the fact that in the latter, which was directly in the theatre of military operations, reasons of military necessity were of superior cogency.

[2] [1921] 2 Ch. 67: *Annual Digest*, 1 (1919–22), 224.

[3] In the same judgment the Court said: 'How could the municipal law of England determine that a person *is* a national of Germany? It might determine that for the purposes of English municipal law a person shall be deemed to be a national of Germany, or shall be

legislation of a State divesting its subjects of their nationality is decisive for determining their status abroad, the Court was giving expression to a generally recognized principle of international law. By denationalizing its subjects resident abroad, a State may be acting without due consideration for the interests of other States inasmuch as it may be depriving them of the possibility of deporting the persons in question. A special Protocol was adopted on 12 April 1930 at the Hague Codification Conference regulating this aspect of the matter.[1] However, whether such denationalization shows a sufficient degree of consideration for other States or not, it has full effect for the purpose of determining the status of the persons concerned. A striking illustration of the general adoption of that principle will be found in the decision of the Swiss Federal Tribunal given in June 1934 in the case of *Lempert* v. *Bonfol*. In that case the Court found that, notwithstanding the non-recognition, at that time, of the Soviet Government by Switzerland, it was bound to consider as stateless a person denationalized by a Soviet decree; this was so even if the issue of the decree was contrary to the international obligations of Soviet Russia.[2] Prior to the recognition of the Soviet Government by France in 1924 French courts considered denationalized Russians as still possessing Russian nationality. However, subsequent to the recognition these persons were treated as stateless both by the French courts and by the French administrative authorities.[3]

It is compatible with the principal rule laid down in *Stoeck* v. *Public Trustee* that, as a measure of public policy and having regard to the exigencies of war, no effect can be given during war to denationalization decrees of the enemy State. The reasons, connected with the safety of the realm, for that departure from the general rule were

treated as if he were a national of Germany; but that would not constitute him a national of Germany, if he were not such according to the municipal law of Germany.' Attention may be called in this connection to *In re Chamberlain's Settlement*, [1921] 2 Ch. 533, in which the Court followed closely the decision in *Stoeck* v. *Public Trustee* on the question of the exclusiveness of the law of the country of origin as determining personal status. In the former case it was held that as the relevant provision of the Treaty of Versailles referred to German 'nationals', the Court was bound to attach to that term the meaning which it had in German law, with the result that, although Chamberlain's naturalization in Germany in time of war was a mere nullity for the purposes of English law, in applying the Treaty the Court had to consider him a German national. The Court said: '... I do not think that there is anything incongruous in holding that the respondent is a German national within the meaning and for the purposes of the Treaty, although for all other purposes the Courts of this country would refuse to recognize his German nationality' (at p. 545). It is clear from the provisions of the British Nationality and Status of Aliens Act, 1933, with regard to the nationality of married women, that English statutory law recognizes the condition of statelessness. In *Stoeck* v. *Public Trustee* the Court expressly laid down that the law of England recognizes the condition of statelessness.

[1] Hudson, *Legislation*, v, 387.

[2] *Entscheidungen des schweizerischen Bundesgerichts*, 60, 67; *Annual Digest*, 7 (1933), 290.

[3] See *Clunet*, 19 (1924), 5 *et seq.*; *ibid.* 20 (1925) 318 *et seq.*, and 547 *et seq.*

stated in *Ex parte L. and Another* (although, as suggested above, the desired result could have been reached by distinguishing between nationality and procedural status). The same view was adopted by the British Government. On 30 July 1942 the Home Secretary, Mr Morrison, stated in the House of Commons that 'it would be contrary to public policy to recognize the power of an enemy State by its legislation in time of war to relieve persons who were its nationals at the outbreak of war from any disabilities, liabilities, or restrictions imposed by our law on aliens of enemy nationality'.[1] It will be noted that the modification in this matter of a general rule in deference to the exigencies of war is not an isolated event. Thus, although recent British practice fully recognizes the right of expatriation of British subjects by naturalization abroad, that right, so far as English law is concerned, is suspended during war. It is treason on the part of a British subject to attempt to become naturalized in an enemy country in time of war; nor will such naturalization be treated as valid for the purposes of English law.[2]

The reasons of public policy and national security which during the war prompted the refusal to recognize the German denationalization decrees – these being the reasons given in *Ex parte L. and Another* – do not obtain in time of peace. It might be argued that public policy demands that the Crown should be able to lay its hands on as much property as possible, but it is unlikely in the highest degree that an English court would lend its authority to such an interpretation of the conception of public policy in relation to the victims of persecution. Public policy, of which public morality is a not inconsiderable element, would seem to demand that the State should not identify itself with a measure of injustice inherent in the attempt to make the victims of the persecution pay for the policy and misdeeds of their persecutors.

It would appear, therefore, that the attitude of English courts on the subject is likely to be determined by two factors. The first is that in time of peace there is a natural tendency to relax the disinclination to regard former enemy nationals as divested of their national status. Thus, the case of *Stoeck* v. *Public Trustee*, decided after the First World War, indicated a change of emphasis in comparison with similar cases – which the Court 'distinguished'[3] – decided during that War: *Ex parte*

[1] *H.C. Deb.* 382, cols. 707–8.

[2] *R.* v. *Lynch* [1903] 1 K.B. 444. However, as has been rightly stated (see J. E. S. Fawcett, in *B.Y.*, 23 (1946), 379), there is a danger that the propositions in *R.* v. *Lynch* may be generalized to the point of irrelevancy. The issue in that case was one of *voluntary* naturalization abroad in time of war. Moreover, it was a question of nationality according to *English* law.

[3] One of the reasons for the 'distinction' was that the decision in the previous cases was to some extent based on inaccurate information supplied to the Court on the subject of the relevant German law.

Weber,[1] *Ex parte Liebmann*.[2] In these cases, in which the completeness of the loss of German nationality was at issue, the courts decided that, in the circumstances, the persons in question had not become 'for all purposes' divested of their German nationality and could not therefore be regarded as stateless. The Supreme Court of the Union of South Africa was even more emphatic in refusing to regard as relevant the decisions in *Ex parte Weber* and *Ex parte Liebmann*. The Court said: '. . . the fact that it [a State] confers upon its former nationals special facilities for regaining citizenship specially declared to have been lost does not seem to me to be a sufficient reason for holding that it was never lost at all'.[3] Similarly, after the First World War the courts of other countries frequently held, in situations analogous to that in the English cases referred to above, that there existed a condition of statelessness which exempted the persons concerned from measures of liquidation and sequestration to which the property of alien enemies was subject.[4]

The second factor is that, in so far as in the case of *Ex parte L. and Another* the Court departed from the established principle that the question whether a person possesses the nationality of a foreign State must be determined by the law of that State valid at the material time, that decision is unlikely to be followed; that the consequences of any change of status (as distinguished from status as such) must be judged by reference to public policy; and that no considerations of justice or public policy would impel – or permit – an English court to hold, in time of peace, that persons validly denationalized by German law in pursuance of a ruthless policy of persecution have retained their German nationality with the result of being exposed to repressive measures applied against former enemy nationals.

5

The legal problems raised in French and English courts in the matter of the nationality of denationalized persons are, in one sense, substantially different. French courts recognized the German denationalization decrees during the Second World War. Since the War the question before them has been to what extent the statelessness of the persons concerned was affected by the repealing legislation of the Allied forces of occupation. The English courts refused to recognize the German decrees of denationalization; they had, therefore, no

[1] [1916] 1 K.B. 280 n.; [1916] 1 A.C. 421. [2] [1916] 1 K.B. 268.

[3] *Pauly* v. *Custodian of Enemy Property* [1922] A.D. 161 : *Annual Digest*, 1 (1919–22), 225.

[4] See, e.g., the decision of the Belgian Court of Cassation of 10 January 1921 in *Procureur-Général* v. *Schneider* (*Annual Digest*, 1 (1919–22), 404)) and of the Court of Appeal of Ghent of 1 February 1924, in *Belgian State* v. *Haupert and de Vuyst* (*ibid.* 2 (1923–4), 258).

reason to consider the question of any retroactive effect of the Allied legislation. Yet, in one vital respect, the problem before the courts of both countries is the same: it is a question of restoring compulsorily to individuals or holding them against their will to a nationality of which they have been divested (or, at least, of which an attempt was made to divest them) and which has justly become abhorrent to them. It is at this point that questions of nationality and the rights of human personality converge in an interesting manner. The principles of law underlying the subject are sufficiently clear to warrant the hope that no judicial *imprimatur* will be given to a solution offensive alike to law and to justice. It is therefore on account of theoretical interest – which is considerable – rather than of practical necessity that the question will now be considered of the international legal remedies available to the persons concerned in case the substance of the decision of the Court of Cassation in the *Kurzmann* case or of the Divisional Court in *Ex parte L. and Another* should prove to be the fixed and final pronouncements of the highest tribunals in these – and other – countries. On the face of it there is no such remedy – whether these persons are deemed to be stateless or of German nationality. On neither hypothesis is there a State in existence able to take up their case and to bring about a judicial clarification of the issue. Actually, two possible remedies seem to be available.

In the first instance, refugees claiming the status of stateless persons may come within the orbit of the Convention of 10 February 1938 concerning Refugees coming from Germany. Any Signatory of that Convention has a legal right to intercede on behalf of a person who, in its view, is entitled to be treated as stateless in accordance with the terms of the Convention. Whether that right of intercession can be brought to the point of judicial determination of the contested legal issue would depend on the existence of a binding and effective instrument of arbitration or judicial settlement. Thus, for instance, assuming the existence of some such instrument between France and Belgium, the latter would be entitled to bring before the International Court of Justice a complaint, on the ground that France has refused to accord the status of stateless persons to persons rightly claiming it. It would not be necessary for the interceding State to show that the persons for whose benefit it is acting are its nationals. The rule as to nationality of claims does not, by definition, apply to the interpretation and application of a Convention concerned with persons who have no nationality. A Convention of this nature is in itself an illustration of the fact that the rule as to nationality of claims is not an absolute one. The issue thus brought before the Court would be one of those discussed in the present article. Thus, the Court would have to decide whether France is entitled to treat the repealing Allied legislation as having retroactive effect in France, or, if a complaint were brought against Great Britain, whether this country can consistently with international law decline to recognize the German denationalization decrees and to continue to treat the persons affected as German nationals. The circumstance that these persons are not nationals of the State asking for judicial determination of the issue would remove from the complaint any complexion of unfriendliness or partisan interest.[1]

The same applies to any similar attempt by the principal international agency entrusted with the protection of stateless and displaced persons, namely, the International Refugee Organization, which has taken over the functions of the Inter-governmental Committee for Refugees.[2] The problem raised by the germanization of stateless persons previously deprived of German nationality involves the issues of nationality and respect for human personality in a manner so compelling that the International Refugee Organization would be justified in an attempt to use the machinery of the United Nations and of the International Court of Justice in seeking to obtain an authoritative legal pronouncement on the subject. With this object in view it could avail itself of the provisions of the Charter of the United Nations and of the revised Statute of the International Court of Justice in the matter of advisory opinions. Article 65 of the Statute of the Court lays down that 'the Court may give an advisory opinion on any legal question at the request of whatever body may be authorized by or in accordance with the Charter of the United Nations to make such a request'. Article 96 of the Charter of the United Nations provides that 'the General Assembly or the Security Council may request the International Court of Justice to give an advisory opinion on any legal question' and that 'other organs of the United Nations and specialized agencies, which may at any time be so authorized by the General Assembly, may also request advisory opinions of the Court on legal questions arising within the scope of their activities'. The International Refugee Organization is a specialized agency in the sense of

[1] There may also be a possibility of the issue being raised by a State which is not a party to the Convention on Refugees. Thus, cases may arise in which a person who is compulsorily restored to German nationality has in the meantime acquired the nationality of another State. He may have become a naturalized citizen of the United States. In that case if another State were to attempt to treat that person as a German national by interfering with his property or otherwise, the United States would be entitled to take up the case of that person and to attempt to bring about an authoritative clarification of the issue.

[2] Part of the argument elaborated in the present article was submitted, in the form of an opinion, to the latter body, and I am indebted to the Director for permission to reproduce it in this form.

Article 96 of the Charter. However, it would be a matter for regret if any such resort to the International Court of Justice were to be proved necessary. For the legal issues involved, although of considerable general interest, hardly require clarification. It is to be hoped that after the initial interval of uncertainty occasioned by the transition from the turmoil of war to the condition of peace, municipal courts and authorities will uniformly apply the general principles of the law of nationality in a manner consistent with justice and with the dignity of man so as not to reimpose upon victims of persecution a nationality of which they were divested in circumstances which outraged the conscience of mankind.

II

THE INTERNATIONAL PROTECTION OF THE INDIVIDUAL

CHAPTER 2

AN INTERNATIONAL BILL OF HUMAN RIGHTS

Editor's note Reference has already been made, in the Editor's note to chapter 18 of volume 2 (p. 487) of these *Collected Papers*, to the evolution of Lauterpacht's work on the international protection of human rights from his original contribution in that field, in the shape of *The International Bill of the Rights of Man* (1945), to his second major work, *International Law and Human Rights* (1950). In fact, even before the original publication of the chapter just mentioned, Lauterpacht had delivered in 1943 a paper to the Grotius Society (subsequently published in *Grotius Society* 29 (1943), 1) on 'The law of nations, the law of nature and the rights of man'. Moreover in the period between the publication of the two volumes Lauterpacht also produced the following contributions:

'The International Protection of Human Rights', *Hague Recueil*, 70 (1947 – 1), 5;
'Human Rights, the Charter of the United Nations, and the International Bill of the Rights of Man', Report to the International Law Association, *Report of the Forty-third Conference of the International Law Association* (1948), p. 80 (reprinted in part in *O.Z.ö.R.* 3 (1949), 19);
'Human Rights', Statement at the Brussels Conference of the International Law Association, *ibid.* p. 29;
'The Universal Declaration of Human Rights', *B.Y.* 25 (1948), 354; and
'The proposed European Court of Human Rights', *Grotius Society*, 35 (1949) 25.

Because the material covered by these contributions is both substantial and is, for the most part, incorporated in *International Law and Human Rights*, I have not included them in these *Collected Papers*.

But Lauterpacht's interest in human rights may be represented by two lesser items – a letter to the Editor of *The Times* newspaper, published on 26 July 1947, which forms the present chapter, and a talk delivered on the Third Programme of the B.B.C. in October 1949, which constitutes the next chapter. A more substantial contribution, written in 1950, appears as chapter 4.

Although what has in practice turned out so far to be the most influential and effective instrument providing international protection for human rights, namely, the European Convention on Human Rights, was signed in 1950 and entered into force in 1953, and certainly owed much to Lauterpacht's earlier contributions (see *Grotius Society*, 35 (1949), 41), he appears to have written nothing about it save what appears at pp. 746–49 of the eighth edition of volume 1 of Oppenheim's *International Law*. The major step forward represented by the adoption in the United Nations of the International Covenants on, respectively, Economic, Social and Cultural Rights and Civil and Political Rights was only taken in 1966, six years after Lauterpacht died.

During the greater part of June a committee of the United Nations Commission on Human Rights were engaged in drafting an International Bill of Human Rights.

The present intention of the majority of the drafting committee seems to be that, after the Governments of all the United Nations have been given the opportunity to submit observations, a Declaration of Human Rights should be laid in 1948 for adoption by the General Assembly; that the declaration should be in the nature of a manifesto as distinguished from a binding and enforceable legal obligation; and that, if agreement can be reached at some future date, it should be followed by more specific conventions. I venture, Sir, to express the hope that careful consideration will be given to the matter before the organs of the United Nations commit themselves either to the substance of these proposals or to the date of their execution. It is doubtful whether an adequate Bill of Rights can be produced within the time contemplated. For this is not only a most difficult subject of codification of existing law. It is to a large extent a piece of international legislation. Unless the Bill is to be a mere statement of generalities or unless its clauses are to be reduced to the lowest common denominator, it must imply some changes, voluntarily consented to, in the law and practice of States.

The discussions held so far have revealed the vast complexity of the problems involved. There is agreement that the Bill must include personal rights of freedom and of equality before the law – such as security from arbitrary arrest, fair trial before independent courts, and freedom of speech, religion, association, and assembly. However, the extent to which most of these rights may be regarded as general principles of law is controversial. They all raise wider questions of jurisprudence and political philosophy, in particular the necessity of the limitation of all rights by the rights of other members of the community and by considerations of the welfare of the State, including the temporary suspension of the ordinary law. They also raise the question whether the Bill of Rights ought to remain a one-sided declaration of the claims of the individual without any reference to the duties which he owes to the State. These are not questions which can be rapidly solved by mere competence of drafting. They involve the weighty issue of the relation of man and State – the abiding problem of all law and government.

There is even less agreement with regard to another category of rights – the right to government by the consent of the governed, a right without which all others tend to become precarious and illusory. To what extent shall that right to political freedom be recognized and endowed with safeguards which, upon final analysis, amount to an international guarantee of constitutional government? The implications of a proposal of this kind are alarming, and many will dismiss it as wholly impracticable. Yet there are others who regard some such guarantee as the hard core of the Bill.

No less intricate are the problems raised by the economic and social rights. These include the right to work under proper conditions, to education, to equality of economic opportunity, and to social security. They are a subject of some novelty when contrasted with the French Declaration of 1789 or with the American Bill of Rights. But claims to 'freedom from want' are widely considered to be no less compelling than rights of personal freedom and of political liberty. The interest of Soviet Russia in the International Bill of Human Rights has been stated to lie particularly in this sphere. How far is it feasible to incorporate these claims in an enforceable Bill of Rights?

These questions cannot be readily solved by the art of skilful compromise at meetings of committees. The same applies to the no less crucial problem of enforcement. There will be objection in many quarters to the idea of fulfilling the promise of a Bill of Rights by means of a declaration binding only in the sphere of conscience. In so far as the existing provisions of the Charter amount to some – though controversial – measure of legal obligation and enforcement, a mere declaration of principles would be in the nature of a retrogression.

It is surely desirable that no attempt should be made, in this period of uncertainty and turmoil, to hasten unduly the drafting and the adoption of the Bill of Human Rights of Man and that ample time should be left for further discussion and study. This is pre-eminently an enactment in relation to which bodies other than Governments should be given the opportunity of forming and expressing their views. The Bill should be the product of the best efforts of statesmen and scholars in the fields of jurisprudence and of the political and social sciences. It might be greater in historic achievement if it materializes in 1950 rather than in 1948.

CHAPTER 3

TOWARDS AN INTERNATIONAL BILL OF RIGHTS

Editor's note In the note introducing Chapter 2 of this volume, some indication will be found of Lauterpacht's work in the field of human rights. The present chapter consists of a talk given on the Third Programme of the B.B.C. in October 1949. It was published in *The Listener*, vol. 42, no. 1084 (3 November 1949), at pp. 747–8.

It is not practicable within the compass of this talk to attempt a review, in the accepted sense of the word, of a collection of essays on one of the central issues of political science and jurisprudence, contributed by thinkers such as Jacques Maritain, Benedetto Croce, Don Salvador de Madariaga, Professor Laski and E. H. Carr. These essays[1] were written on the invitation of Unesco in connection with the drafting of what eventually became the Universal Declaration of Human Rights. That Declaration was adopted by the General Assembly of the United Nations in December 1948 without a dissenting vote and with nine abstentions – those of the Slav group of States, Saudi Arabia, Honduras and South Africa.

There ought to be no doubt as to the timeliness of these essays. It would be invidious to single out for discussion any of these weighty professions of faith or challenging statements of principle. But they provide a suitable occasion for surveying the position of the cause of human rights under the Charter of the United Nations and as the result of the Declaration adopted last year. The Declaration was intended by its authors, not as a final achievement but as the first instalment of a true and enforceable Bill of Human Rights conceived as part of the positive Law of Nations. The purpose of that Bill of Rights – which is now being prepared under the name of a 'Covenant' – is to define and to provide the necessary international guarantees for the observance of the legal obligations of the Charter in the matter of human rights and fundamental freedoms. These obligations are a solemn and constant theme of the Charter, which pledges the Members of the United Nations to joint and separate action on that behalf. These provisions of the Charter were not adopted as an afterthought or by way of embellishment. They were accepted after mature delibera-

[1] *Human Rights: Comments and Interpretations; a Symposium* (1949).

tion and full discussion in pursuance of repeated pledges and of a most compelling historic experience.

Yet I may have misled you – although I do not think I have – by saying that these clauses of the Charter are legal obligations binding upon the Members of the United Nations. The Charter does not expressly lay down that Members of the United Nations shall observe human rights and freedoms. It merely provides that they shall promote their observance. There are many – including the Governments of some of the leading Members of the United Nations – who are of the view that these provisions of the Charter are merely the expression of a social trend and of a noble ideal. In their opinion, to read a legal obligation into these clauses is to do violence to the clear wording of the Charter. That opinion is startling and bewildering, but it constitutes a widely accepted interpretation of the Charter. It explains the construction which the Commission on Human Rights, composed as it is of Governments, has so far put upon its jurisdiction. It has ruled that it has no power to take any action – not even action consisting of discussion, investigation and recommendation – in the matter of complaints of breaches of human rights brought before it either by States or by private persons and organizations. Some may be surprised to learn that, as the result of that interpretation, the members of the Commission are not entitled to have access to the original texts of the complaints of violations of human rights sent to the Secretary-General of the United Nations. They receive brief and confidential summaries, which do not disclose the names of the complainants. By a self-denying ordinance the Commission can take no action upon the complaints. This, then, is the present position with regard to the protection of the rights of man by the United Nations. We must not be deceived by spectacular debates in the General Assembly in such matters as the violation by Bulgaria and Hungary of their obligations as to human rights under the peace treaties or the refusal of the Russian Government to allow Russian-born wives of foreign citizens to leave the country. The Secretary-General of the United Nations, in the exercise of his right of independent initiative and criticism, has recently drawn the attention of the Commission of Human Rights to the urgent desirability of revising that negative estimate of its powers.

Has the Declaration of Human Rights made any difference in the situation? At the time when it was proclaimed by the General Assembly, in an apparent mood of exultation, the representatives of most Governments described it as one of the greatest achievements of the United Nations. Dr Evatt, a distinguished lawyer and statesman, who was President of the Assembly at that time, said: 'It [the Declaration] has the authority of the body of the United Nations as a whole, and millions of people, men, women and children all over the world, many miles from Paris and New York, will turn for help, guidance and inspiration to this document.' However, at the same time practically all Governments insisted that the Declaration about to be adopted was in no way legally binding upon them and that it was, in the words of its preamble, in the nature of a proclamation of a common standard of achievement. While proclaiming the rights of man, the Declaration scrupulously avoids any reference to the corresponding obligations of the State.

To a lawyer the enunciation of a right without the provision of a remedy is a juridical heresy. But then the Declaration was not intended to be – and is not – a legal instrument. Not having legal force, it cannot legitimately be resorted to for the purpose of interpreting the existing obligations of the Charter. At the time of the adoption of the Declaration there was no feeling of embarrassment at the incongruity between the enthusiastic acknowledgment of the fundamental character of the human rights proclaimed in the Declaration and the refusal to recognize them as a source of legal obligations binding in the sphere of conduct – a fact which in itself raises a cardinal issue of international morality. For that reason it may be difficult to brush aside with impatience the view which is held by some that the Declaration, which has been accepted by all – or nearly all – for the reason that it imposes obligations upon none, has only a very limited moral authority. There may be some force in the insistence that what is required at this juncture of history is not the recognition and not even the formulation of inalienable human rights but their effective protection, by an instrumentality higher than the State itself, against the arbitrariness of wilful men and against the complacent or selfish indolence of entrenched interests.

Yet the Declaration is the result of much arduous and devoted labour. It was intended by many of its authors as one of the great charters of liberty, such as the French Declaration of the Rights of Man and Citizen, of which Lord Acton said that it outweighed libraries and proved stronger than all the armies of Napoleon. Moreover, the authors of the Declaration did not regard it as the fulfilment of the promise of a true International Bill of Rights. On the contrary, the Commission on Human Rights is now engaged in drafting an instrument – a Covenant – which will be cast in the form of a treaty laying down legal obligations binding upon States and enforceable as such by their courts.

What are the problems confronting Governments and the Commission in framing the Covenant? It is intended that it shall include most of the safeguards associated with traditional Bills of Rights. However, there seems to be no intention to provide in the Covenant for the rights that loom so large in the essays which I am reviewing and which many regard as an essential condition of a Bill of Rights worthy of that name. In the first instance, in their view a Bill of Rights must recognize and secure the political right of men to government by consent. What is the value, they say, of personal rights of freedom from arbitrary arrest or of freedom of religion, of opinion, or association, if they are at the mercy of a tyrannical régime which is not accountable to and which cannot be replaced by a free electorate? Similarly, most of the authors of these essays would confess to incredulous amazement at a Bill of Rights which ignores the economic and social claims of man, such as the right to work, to fair and just conditions of employment, to security against sickness, old age, and undeserved want, to equality of educational opportunity and generally to a just share in social progress. What is the value of the political and personal rights of freedom to those whom the social order leaves insecure in their livelihood, starving or illiterate?

There is only one reply to all these questions. Yet the unanimity of the answer supplies no clue to the real difficulty: what shall be the international machinery for securing these rights after they have been recognized? These rights – political, social and economic – have all been acknowledged, generously and comprehensively, in the Declaration adopted last December. It was easy to recognize them in the Declaration, which is not binding except in the sphere of conscience. The Covenant which is now being prepared and which does impose legal obligations contains no reference to these rights. The reason is not far to seek. For the difficulties besetting the international supervision and enforcement of the right to government by consent and of social and economic rights are so great as to baffle imagination. They may seem to some to amount to an international guarantee of democratic rule and to a large measure of international government in most spheres of social and economic life. It is therefore not surprising that in the Covenant there is no mention of these rights at all. That negative solution will be regarded by many as proper and unavoidable. However, if adopted, it will mark the first stage only – and not the consummation – of a true Bill of Rights. In the long run the problem of protecting these rights can be solved only by constructive statesmanship differing in kind from a realism of short-cuts and resignation.

However, all this is only part of the problem. For how are we going to solve the question of the international guarantees of the non-controversial rights of freedom traditionally associated with Bills of Rights?

In what way and by what machinery should these be put under the shelter of the international community? How should they be made safe not only against the abuses of the executive, but also against the lawfully expressed sovereign will of parliamentary majorities? Shall we grant to the individual – the true beneficiary of the Bill of Rights – the effective right of petition to an international agency? Or shall we say that a Bill of Rights of Man signed by States is a matter for States only? If that is so, what assurance is there that the rights of man will not become the object of diplomatic bargaining and of political manoeuvres and that their protection will not be determined by the indifference or connivance of some Governments or the all too willing eagerness of others? At the same time there is room for the view that to admit the right of petition by private individuals may result in opening wide the floodgates of complaints. These may be petty, malevolent, or inspired by unfriendly Powers. They may render the work of the international authorities in question wholly impracticable. It is significant that at the session of the Human Rights Commission held last summer eight States expressed themselves in favour of the right of petition by private individuals and groups while the same number of States wished the procedure of implementing the Covenant to be confined to a confidential investigation of complaints brought by Governments only. The latter group included Soviet Russia, the United States and the United Kingdom – an interesting combination which reveals the complexity of the problem involved.

An effective and enforceable international Bill of Rights will be a decisive landmark in what Mr Churchill, in expounding in 1942 the major purposes of the war, described as the enthronement of the rights of man. It will open a new chapter in the constitutional law of mankind and in the relation of man and state. It will inevitably be a powerful contribution to international peace. That consummation cannot be achieved by verbal incantations and by elegant devices of diplomatic language. It cannot become a reality without States being willing to sacrifice some of their laws, practices and even constitutional principles.

These problems bring to mind the complexities of a Bill of Rights of a universal character as well as the alternative of some such compact as between a limited number of States bound together, in the words of the Statute of the Council of Europe, by the common heritage of the rule of law. We may recall in this connection the recommendation recently made by the European Assembly at Strasbourg for the establishment of a European Court of Human Rights. These possibilities cannot be discussed here. But they ought to be kept in mind. A substantial achievement on a narrower geographical basis may be preferable, for the time being, to a nominal solution of a universal character. In the meantime the Charter of the United Nations, when interpreted in good faith and in accordance with a vital purpose of its being, may be a potent instrument for the protection of human rights. A Bill of Rights is of the greatest importance – but it is not essential – for the fulfilment of that object. Enlightened public opinion may assist and encourage Governments in making the most of the instrument already at hand, namely, the Charter. For the United Nations and the Commission on Human Rights are only a name for the Governments who compose them.

CHAPTER 4

STATE SOVEREIGNTY AND HUMAN RIGHTS

Editor's note In 1950 Lauterpacht was invited to attend the celebrations in Jerusalem of the twenty-fifth anniversary of the foundation of the Hebrew University of Jerusalem and to deliver two guest lectures. One of these lectures, 'International Law after the Second World War', appears as chapter 7 of Part 1, printed at pp. 159–70 of volume 2 of these *Collected Papers*. The other lecture constitutes this chapter. This lecture was translated into Hebrew and was delivered by Lauterpacht in that language on 8 May 1950.

It is fitting that the second lecture in the field of international law which I have the honour to give in the Hebrew University on this auspicious occasion should be devoted to some aspects of the question of the international recognition and protection of the fundamental rights of man. There is not – and never has been – a nation which has suffered more frequently and more cruelly from a denial of these rights than the Jewish people. These inalienable human rights have now been recognized – and the way opened for the international supervision of their observance – largely as a reaction against the perversion and the magnitude of the contempt shown for them at the hands of the persecutors of the people of Israel. And Jews – individually and collectively – have played a leading rôle in making the natural rights of man part of the positive Law of Nations. This applies to the efforts of Jewish organizations at the Paris Peace Conference in 1919 and at the Conference at San Francisco. Of the individual efforts of Jewish lawyers. I may mention the untiring, prudent and not unsuccessful labours of Professor René Cassin, that great jurist and humanist who has represented the French Republic in the Commission on Human Rights. One of the most valuable scientific productions of Professor Feinberg, the present occupant of the Chair of International Law at the Hebrew University, has been his course of lectures, delivered at the Hague Academy of International Law, on the right of petition in international law. I am mentioning this not merely because it affords a welcome opportunity of paying a well-deserved tribute to Professor Feinberg's scholarship, but also because the right of petition is one of the central problems of the international protection of human rights. To that problem of the right of petition under the Charter and in connection with the proposed International Bill of Human Rights I propose to devote to a large extent this lecture on 'State Sovereignty and Human Rights'. For few matters shed so much instructive light on the relation of State sovereignty to human rights as the question of the effective right of international petition. I propose to devote the concluding observations of this lecture to a consideration of the more general question of the relation of sovereignty, federation and the rights of man.

The problem of human rights after the Second World War has centred round two questions: one of them has been the legal effect of the provisions of the Charter of the United Nations in the matter of human rights – a question the answer to which has had an indirect and inarticulate, but powerful influence on the treatment of the right of petition by the organs of the United Nations; the second question has been the proposed International Bill of Human Rights in which, once more, the matter of the right of petition has been most prominent.

At first sight it would appear to be an exaggeration to describe the recognition and protection of human rights under the Charter as implying a legal obligation. In so far as such protection signifies the safeguarding of these rights through a legally authorized and effective machinery of direct compulsion, it would seem that the authors of the Charter rejected the idea of a full guarantee thus conceived. From these limitations of the protection which the Charter affords to human rights and freedoms there may be drawn the easy – and inaccurate – conclusion that its provisions on the subject are a mere declaration of principle devoid of any element of legal obligation. Any such conclusion is no more than a facile generalization. The provisions of the Charter on the subject are its most constant theme. They figure prominently in the statement of the Purposes of the Charter. Members of the United Nations are under a legal obligation to act in accordance with these purposes. It is their legal duty not only to encourage and promote respect for these rights, but also to respect them. There is a distinct element of legal obligation in the undertaking expressed in Article 56 of the Charter in which 'all Members pledge themselves to take joint and separate action in co-operation with the Organization for the achievement of the purposes' of the Charter in this respect. The cumulative legal result of all these pronouncements cannot be ignored. The legal and binding character of these obligations of the Charter would remain even if the Charter were to contain no provision of any kind for their implementation. For, it must be noted, the Charter fails to provide for the enforcement of many of its other obligations the legal character of which is undoubted.

Neither is the legally binding effect of these provisions of the Charter impaired by the circumstance that it does not define in detail the rights and freedoms which the Members of the United Nations are bound to observe. Undoubtedly that defect impairs somewhat the juridical character of these obligations, inasmuch as a certain amount of clarity and precision is an important requisite of the law. This has been the reason for the importance justly attributed to an International Bill of Human Rights – although even in that instrument detailed definition is neither essential nor desirable.

Any construction of the Charter according to which Members of the United Nations are, in law, entitled to disregard – and to violate – human rights and fundamental freedoms is destructive of both the legal and the moral authority of the Charter as a whole. It runs counter to a fundamental principle of construction according to which treaties must be interpreted in good faith. The view, which I am here urging, that the provisions of the Charter in the matter of human rights are legally binding obligations rests not only upon the principle of interpretation according to which treaty provisions must be given effect in accordance with their avowed purpose. The International Court of Justice has repeatedly interpreted treaties in accordance with the principle that they must be construed so as to render them effective rather than ineffective. This is so notwithstanding the fact that the Court has occasionally given nominal approval to the rival view of restrictive interpretation of treaties limiting the sovereignty of States. Undoubtedly the principle of effectiveness, when applied to the exclusion of other considerations, is not free of doubt. International practice is often confronted with the positive intention of the parties to the treaty to deny it what would appear a natural degree of effectiveness. Unlike in the matter of contracts in the sphere of municipal law, treaties are often a political substitute rather than a legal expression of the agreement of the parties. Parties to treaties often wish their obligation to go so far and no further. They – or some of them – desire the treaty to be only partly effective. The intention of the parties must remain the governing consideration. But that intention must, in turn, be interpreted in accordance with requirements of good faith and of decency. It would be contrary both to these requirements and to the principle of effectiveness if the repeated and solemn provisions of the Charter in the matter of human rights and fundamental freedoms, coupled with the clear legal obligation to promote respect for them by joint and separate action, were interpreted as devoid of any obligation to respect them.

Admittedly, there is in the Charter no express provision by which the Members of the United Nations agree, *eis verbis*, to respect human rights and freedoms. But, it would be out of keeping with the spirit of the Charter and with the accepted canons of interpretation of treaties to attach decisive importance to that omission. It would have been otiose to the point of pedantry for the draftsmen of the Charter to incorporate an explicit provision of this nature in a document in which the principle of respect for and observance of these rights is one of the main pillars of the structure of the organization created by the Charter. This is a matter in which, perhaps more than in others, care must be taken not to permit the task of interpretation to degenerate into an attempt to derive the maximum advantage from the economy of expression of a basic international instrument.

It has been maintained that Members of the United Nations committed themselves to promote respect for and observance of human rights, but that they did not undertake the obligation to respect and observe them. There is no substance in that view. The legal duty to promote respect for human rights includes the legal duty to respect them. It comprises, in addition, the obligation of the United Nations as a whole to further the adoption of means and establishment of agencies for the effective international enforcement of these rights.

It may be said that States when signing or adhering to the Charter clearly did not intend to assume an absolute, literal and immediate legal duty to give effect to the most comprehensive obligation to respect human rights and fundamental freedoms without discrimination as to race, sex, language, or religion. It may be urged, for instance, that they did not assume a rigid obligation of this nature in respect of discrimination on account of sex – a subject which is admittedly of great complexity. However, like all provisions of international treaties so also the wide obligations of the Charter in this matter – covering as they do most comprehensively the relation of man and State – must be interpreted in a reasonable way. The obligation exists and it must be given effect in good faith, having regard to the circumstances and conditions of each State. Thus, although a reasonable interpretation of the Charter does not require that Members of the United Nations should henceforth with one stroke grant full equality to women in all respects, a State would no doubt act contrary to its obligations under the Charter if, under the impact of an anti-feminist régime, it were drastically to curtail the existing rights of women. A State would act contrary to its clear legal obligations under the Charter if it were to impose fresh discrimination on a religious, ethnical or racial group. And there would be, no doubt, a flagrant breach of its legal obligations if it were to embark upon active persecution of persons under its jurisdiction on account of their race, language or religion.

Why do I elaborate, on this occasion, this controversial problem of the Charter? The answer is not only because this is one of its two principal purposes, but also that it has influenced decisively the main aspect of the interpretation of human rights, namely, the effective right of international petition. It is the lack of appreciation of the momentous character of that achievement of the Charter – and of the terrible historic experience which led to it – which, coupled with considerations of national sovereignty, has led to the emaciation of the right of petition at the hands of the Commission on Human Rights, which is composed exclusively of representatives of States. In 1947 the Commission adopted a Resolution, subsequently confirmed by the Economic and Social Council, in which it recognized 'that it has no power to take any action in regard to any complaints concerning human rights'. There is nothing in the Charter which justifies such renunciation of one of the principal functions of the Commission – a renunciation which amounts to a denial of the right of international petition. Probably the Charter does not authorize the enforcement of its obligations in the matter of human rights through intervention conceived as dictatorial and direct interference. I say 'probably' because it is not certain that, having regard to the provisions of the Charter, human rights are now matters which are essentially within the domestic jurisdiction of States (and thus governed by the prohibition of intervention). But even if they are so governed, that fact does not deprive the organs of the United Nations of the right – nor release them of the duty – to make their contribution towards the implementation of the Charter by other means of considerable potency. Nothing in the Charter excludes either a general recommendation arising out of an individual complaint or a series of analogous complaints; or a specific recommendation addressed to a named State; or a request for information or comments on the subject of petitions received; or, with the consent of the State concerned, an investigation undertaken in its territory and with its co-operation; or, without the consent of the State in question, an investigation conducted outside its territory and not requiring its co-operation; or the initiation of a study, in fact indistinguishable from investigation, of the conditions underlying the complaint either in relation to the State concerned or to the general problem involved in the complaint; or the publication of the results of the investigation; or discussion of the specific and general aspects of the complaint. At present, as the result of the Resolution previously mentioned, members of the Commission are not entitled to read the actual complaints of violation of human rights. What they *are* entitled to is to receive a list of these complaints compiled by the Secretariat. Thus the basic source of information with regard to what on any reasonable interpretation of the Charter would appear to be the principal function of the Commission is consigned to the files of an official in the Division of Human Rights whose business it is 'to inform the writers of all communications concerning human rights . . . that their communications have been received and duly noted for consideration in accordance with the procedure laid down by the United Nations'. Yet, under the procedure adopted, there is no assurance that they will be considered or brought to the attention of the Commission or any of its members.

Undoubtedly, under a system of effective petition the United Nations and its organs may be burdened and embarrassed by communications which are malevolent, clearly unfounded, uninformed, or, while well-founded in law, petty and insignificant. Many of the petitions may imply an unjust affront to the dignity and good name of States. Yet it must become axiomatic that the sanctity of human rights and an effective system of petitions on their behalf are entitled to no less consideration than the dignity of sovereign States. A reconciliation of these two opposing considerations – assuming that there exists an inherent opposition between them – cannot be effected by a renunciation of the function of the United Nations in relation to a vital aspect of its purpose. The difficulties cannot be met by a self-imposed limitation on the part of the Commission on Human Rights. They can be solved only by the adoption of the twin principles that: (*a*) all communications and petitions, with the exception of those of an obviously frivolous character, must automatically – either in full or in a summary – reach all members of the Commission, and (*b*) that a procedure, semi-judicial and semi-administrative in character, must be devised for selecting such communications and petitions as call for full discussion and, generally, for further action by the Commission.

There is no prospect of the fulfilment of the purpose of the Charter in the matter of human rights and freedoms unless an effective right of petition is accepted as being of the essence of the system established by the Charter. The Charter does not refer to the right of petition as a safeguard of human rights and fundamental freedoms. Yet this is a right which must be held to be implied in the Charter as the very minimum of the means of its implementation. There was no mention of the right of petition in the system of mandates established after the First World War. That omission was not accidental, for proposals to that effect were submitted by Great Britain and the United States and considered by the Peace Conference. However, subsequent to the establishment of the Mandates Commission the right of petition was regarded as a natural concomitant of the system established by the Covenant.

No substantial opposition was encountered when, in July 1922, the British Government submitted detailed proposals on the subject – although care was taken to spare the susceptibilities and to ensure the full co-operation of the Mandatory Power. The receipt and examination of petitions became subsequently one of the main features of the system of mandates. In fact, the rules of procedure, ultimately adopted, concerning petitions did not differ substantially from those adopted in 1947 by the Trusteeship Council in pursuance of Article 87(b) of the Charter of the United Nations, which expressly envisaged the acceptance and examination of petitions in consultation with the administering authority.

Similarly, although under the system of protection of minorities within the framework of the League of Nations there was no provision in the various Minorities Treaties for the recognition of the full legal right of effective petition, that fact did not prevent the evolution of a procedure of petitions regulated in minute detail. Admittedly, the Council of the League adhered throughout to the view that petitions were primarily in the nature of a source of information enabling the members of the Council to fulfil their duties and that the procedure adopted did not confer legal rights upon the petitioners themselves. However, after a time, the procedure evolved by the Minorities Section of the Secretariat and the Minorities Committee of the Council provided for a full examination of the admissibility of the petitions and of the petitions themselves. The ultimate fate of petitions depended upon the action of the members of the Council, and this fact constituted the decisive weakness of the entire system. But the detail and the elaboration of the system which was actually in operation invite comparison with the rudimentary – in fact, nominal – procedure for the examination of and action upon petitions adopted by the Commission on Human Rights.

The same considerations apply to the question of the right of petition in any future International Bill of Human Rights. When the Third General Assembly of the United Nations discussed the right of petition, to national authorities or to the United Nations, as part of the proposed Universal Declaration of Human Rights, no majority could be secured for including the right of petition in an instrument which in any case was not considered legally binding. The proposal to that effect was opposed not only by Soviet Russia – on the ground that 'it would show disrespect for national sovereignty to permit individuals to petition the United Nations'. Many other States questioned the propriety of its inclusion in the Declaration. They were successful in their opposition. Yet the Resolution which recommended further study of the question was preceded by a Preamble laying down that 'the right of petition is an essential human right, as is recognized in the constitution of a great number of countries'. The minority of States which, in the Third Committee, opposed the Preamble included Soviet Russia (and her allies), Sweden, China, the United Kingdom, and the United States of America – a significant combination. Neither, it seems, is there at present a prospect of the recognition of the right of petition in the so-called 'Covenant' of human rights – an instrument the object of which is to lay down legally binding obligations of States. In the proposals put forward by some of the leading States, the right of bringing complaints is limited to Governments. However, it must become more generally recognized than it is at present that unless an effective right of petition – which means a right of petition coupled with the right to have the complaint investigated with a view to such action being taken upon it as is necessary and legally permissible – is granted to the individuals concerned or to the bodies acting on their behalf, any international remedy that may be provided will be deficient in its vital aspect. The denial, to the individuals affected, of the right of direct access to international agencies is tantamount to a withdrawal, to a large extent, of the principal benefit conferred by the Bill. It wholly disregards the enhanced stature of the individual which follows naturally from an enactment of that kind. It is rooted in the rigid notion of the individual conceived as a mere object of international law. Moreover, in so far as the object of that limitation is to safeguard the sovereignty and dignity of the States concerned, it is unlikely to achieve that object.

If the right of bringing complaints on account of the violation of the Bill of Rights is limited to States parties to the Bill of Rights, the individual will have no redress unless he petitions a foreign State and enlists its active support to the point of bringing a complaint against the offending State. In what ways and by what devious methods of persuasion shall he attempt to obtain the assistance of that foreign State or States? Are we entitled to exclude the possibility that their attention will be effectively solicited only when their interests are at stake – it being either some direct interest or the indirect interest of embarrassing a foreign Government? Or is it the underlying assumption of any such scheme that the interest of the foreign, friendly State or States ought to be enlisted only if the violations of the rights of the individual are on such a scale and of such enormity as to warrant the action of foreign States, and that single violations of individual rights, however outrageous, are of no consequence? If that is so, what becomes of the sanctity of the rights of the individual which the Covenant is supposed to uphold ? Are we to renounce the principle that a fundamental right of a single individual is as absolute and as sacrosanct as aggregates of rights of aggregates of persons ?

Neither is it easy to see how the sovereignty and dignity of the signatories of the Bill can be better safeguarded by the elimination of individual petition and the substitution for it of a procedure initiated by a State. In the case of a petition by an individual the complaint remains as a rule within the orbit of a grievance which can be redressed by appropriate judicial or administrative remedies. When the same case is taken up by a State, the complaint assumes immediately a political complexion. The original nature of the issue becomes obliterated by considerations and stratagems of international politics. Is it more conducive to the preservation of the sovereignty and dignity of a State if a complaint concerning the treatment of an individual or of a group of individuals is brought by a foreign State rather than by the person or persons concerned ? It may be argued that foreign States will refrain from pressing unduly numerous individual cases. That argument is controversial. Or is it to become a test of the friendliness of a signatory State whether it refrains from taking up charges of violation of the Covenant ? It is an illusion to assume that petty, ill-founded, or malevolent petitions can come only from individuals and not from Governments. Governments, if they are so minded, can press unfounded complaints with a frequency and persistency commensurate with the vastness of the resources available to the State. It would thus appear that the elimination of private petitions will not necessarily achieve the purpose of preventing complaints which are unfounded or malicious. On the other hand, in so far as it will accomplish the object of stifling – as the result of the connivance, complicity, servility or indifference of foreign Governments - such petitions as merit attention and examination, it will stultify the principle of implementation. The insistence on the right of the individual to lodge petitions is due to factors more real than any supposedly purely academic emphasis on the status of the individual as a subject of international law. It is due to a practical assessment of the merits of the procedure initiated by individuals as compared with that of governmental authorities. The organization of such a procedure raises issues of great complexity. Such issues are capable of a solution more reasonable, more just and in the long run more practicable than reliance upon the restrained attitude of friendly Governments.

Considerations connected with the dignity of sovereign States and the traditional conception of the inferior status of the individual have not been the only reason which has prompted the negative attitude of

Governments to the question of the right of petition by individuals. The other – and perhaps equally important – reason has been the apprehension that the international organ concerned, whether it be a court or other agency, would be flooded by a mass of petitions, some of them paltry, uninformed or malicious, with the result that its work would be made impracticable. These fears are largely hypothetical, exaggerated and probably unfounded.

The same considerations apply to the question of direct petitions by individuals before a judicial body. There is a possibility that an international court might be overwhelmed by a multitude of complaints coming from distant parts of the world. It might not be practicable for a strictly judicial body to devise machinery for examining in an informal manner complaints submitted to it with the view to eliminating cases which are frivolous, malicious, based on obviously deficient information as to the correct legal position, or otherwise not deserving of serious consideration. Yet such methods are possible. They have been resorted to by non-judicial bodies in connection with the protection of minorities, the system of Mandates, and the Trusteeship system. There seems to be no reason why an international court should not be able to devise some such preliminary procedure, for instance by deputing some of its members to examine complaints in the first instance and, with the consent of the President, to reject those which clearly do not call for consideration. Neither is it altogether certain that the availability of the international court – or of a non-judicial agency open to individuals – will open wide the flood-gates of petitions. The enforcement of the Bill of Rights must constitute, in the initial stages of its operation, a process of trial and error. It is difficult to foresee what will be the effect of a Bill of Rights, provided with instrumentalities of international supervision, upon the functioning of the international organs in question. It is not easy to forecast whether it will result in a flood of petitions and complaints, or whether the existence of the Bill will act as a restraining influence not only upon the conduct of States, but also upon the litigious propensities of individuals. There is nothing irrevocable in any machinery that may be adopted. Moreover, the constitution of the court – or of the non-judicial agency – may leave room for necessary adaptations, such as enlargement of the number of judges (or of members of the Human Rights Council), the setting up of additional chambers, or a regional subdivision of the work involved.

These aspects of the right of petition bring me to the concluding observations of this lecture. If the Bill of Rights is not to be a mere gesture, it cannot be brought about without the signatory States sacrificing some attributes, both substantive and formal, of their sovereignty. A Bill of Rights worthy of the name is not a consummation which can be achieved without some States giving up practices and constitutional principles in a way necessary to ensure an irreducible minimum standard of respect for fundamental human rights and of the requisite international guarantees. In current terminology, that consummation cannot be accomplished without some sacrifices of sovereignty not only in respect of the substance of the Bill but also of its enforcement. The essence of a Bill of the Rights of Man is that it implies a limitation upon the existing and the future powers of the State. There is no country so advanced or entitled to such absolute conviction of the excellence of its law and its institutions as not to be able to make a contribution to the common stock of a Bill of Rights by consenting to some change in its legal and constitutional system, or to the principle of international judicial or semi-judicial examination and review of its legislative, judicial and administrative conduct – including such examination and review in pursuance of petitions by private individuals.

In this connection it is fitting to draw attention, by way of general conclusion, to the intimate relation between the three central issues of international law and organization : the idea of sovereignty, the notion of the *civitas maxima* conceived as a world federation of States, and the international recognition and protection of the rights of man. It is the abiding lesson of history and a compelling postulate of reason that a world-embracing federation – of which regional federations may be a necessary stage – is, in the words of Immanuel Kant, the only means of attaining perfect internal government, which is, in turn, the essential condition of the realization of the moral and intellectual capacities of mankind. If that is so, then the idea of an all-embracing federation of States must be regarded not as an infinite ideal but as an object of a moral duty of positive action and as a practical standard of human endeavour.

However, it is unlikely that that consummation can be promoted by the determination to adhere in all respects to the accepted features of the federal system. For most of the federations, past and present, have not been associations of States differing in historic experience, language, culture, economic development, tradition and law. The rational solution of the problem of international organization will be hastened by the acceptance of the view that the differences between the typical forms of unions of States – such as federations and confederations – are to a large extent a matter of degree ; that no such solution is feasible in so far as it envisages the immediate and total disappearance of the international personality of States ; that, subject to that condition, there is no obstacle – certainly not in international law – to the gradual limitation of rights of sovereignty within an association of States based on the continued recognition of the distinct international personality of States; and that there is no contradiction between the notion of sovereignty, conceived as independence in relation to other States of the international society, and the gradual approximation to a federation of the world properly so-called.

In theory, a full-fledged federal system between the nations of the world would be more conducive to enhancing the stability of international peace, to the protection of the rights of man, and to reducing the evils and abuses of national power than a looser system of confederation based on the unrestricted sovereignty of its members. This may be admitted without conceding all the advantages claimed to be linked with the federal system. However, as it is highly controversial whether the political integration of mankind will – or can – be accomplished by the outright adoption of a world federal constitution, it is necessary to bear in mind the two typical characteristics of the federal system and to examine which of these is likely to offer more tangible prospects of realization.

The first of these features is, in the international sphere, the obliteration of the international personality of the member States and the substitution of that of the federation as such. This is one of the principal marks of the distinction between a Confederation and a federal State. It cannot be expected that Governments, or, indeed, the peoples whom they represent, will be willing to renounce the international personality of their States even in cases in which geographical propinquity seems to favour that course. Thus it may be impracticable to urge a form of European association in which Great Britain or France or Sweden will disappear as international units; in which they will be deprived of the right to send and receive diplomatic and consular representatives; in which, as in the case of member States of federal States, they will forfeit the jurisdictional immunities enjoyed by States in foreign courts; and in which they will not be permitted to conclude treaties either between themselves or with other States. It is irrelevant to point to the existing Federal States as showing that separate international personality of the member States is not essential and that its absence is borne with equanimity and without a sense of loss of a valuable attribute of statehood or of corporate dignity. For these member States were not, as a rule, international persons prior to having been linked by the bond of federal union. The importance, in the twentieth century, of the distinct international personality of States may be asserted without going to the length of the claim that, as at present constituted, they represent an enduring and indispensable form of political association.

In comparison, the second main distinguishing feature of the federal system, namely, the direct relation between the individual human being and the federation, offers possibilities which, being less drastic in nature, may become a factor of deep significance in the evolution of the federation of the world. That direct relation between the individual and the federation reveals itself in a variety of ways such as the operation of the federal law upon individuals and the participation of individuals in the creation of the federal legislative and other organs. It would manifest itself even more conspicuously through the recognition and protection, in relation to member States, of the fundamental rights of man. Inasmuch as such recognition and protection of the rights of man implies – as it clearly does – a restriction of their sovereignty in its vital aspect, it would add emphasis to the fact that no integration of international society is possible without far-reaching limitations of the sovereignty of its component units. At the same time such limitations of sovereignty, profound as they are, can be achieved without interference with their international personality and status.

It must be borne in mind, in this connection, that the idea and the historic experience of federations have, in a different way, tended to impair the authority of the notion of sovereignty conceived as the highest and indivisible source of authority. For it is not only that the phenomenon of the federal State was called in to show that a single and undivided sovereign will, as propounded in Austinian jurisprudence, is not essential to the State – where, it was asked, is the sovereign according to the constitution of the United States of America? The way in which writers, largely moved by political motives, juggled with the conception of sovereignty in order to find a solution suitable for their purposes has done much to demonstrate the relativity and divisibility of the rigid notion of an absolute, exclusive and sacrosanct 'competence to determine all competencies'. In the United States, the authors of the *Federalist*, anxious to smooth the path of the transition from a confederation to a federal State, developed the theory of the division of sovereignty between the union and the member States. De Tocqueville planted the doctrine in European soil. German writers, such as Waitz, adapted it for German consumption with the added embellishment of the distinction between the substance of sovereignty (which, they taught, was indivisible) and the attributes of sovereignty (which could be portioned out). That was a moderate theory when contrasted with that of Calhoun, the American protagonist of the right of secession, who insisted on the indivisibility of sovereignty but asserted that it was fully retained by the member States and not at all impaired by the delegation of some of its prerogatives to the federation. The other extreme was represented, in particular in Germany, by those believers in national unity who regarded sovereignty both as indivisible and as essential to the State, with the result that, in their view, the members of the union could not properly be regarded as States. The bitter pill was sweetened by writers such as Laband who served the causes both of the unity of the federation, which they considered to be exclusively sovereign, and of the separate individuality of the member States by means of the demonstration that sovereignty is not at all essential to statehood. They were supported by the high authority of Jellinek, who, while buttressing national unity by insisting on the complete subordination of the member States to the federation and on the absence of the right of secession, flattered the vanity of the member States by arguing that they took part in the life of the union in their capacity as States and that they were not without some status in international law. On the other hand, Duguit, while urging that the members of the federation are States as distinguished from decentralized provinces, insisted that statehood cannot be comprehended by reference to the traditional notion of sovereignty – in which fact he found yet another argument in support of his criticism of the accepted notion of the sovereign State. Similar consequences follow from the view that the essence of the federal system consists in the limitation of the competence – of the sovereignty – of the federation and of the member States to their respective spheres. It is that feature of the federal system which represents its principal contribution to the main theme of political thought and practice: the combination of self-government with the paramount necessity of order.

These, then, are some of the aspects of the inter-relation between the three central issues of international law: the political integration of mankind in the direction of the federation of the world, the curbing of the pretensions and aberrations of the doctrine of sovereignty, and the effective protection of human rights as part of the constitution of international society. The very idea of federation, inasmuch as it postulates a direct relation with the individual human being, receives a decisive accession of strength from the recognition, through effective institutions, of the rights of man. At the same time the notion and the experience of the federal system have acted as a powerful solvent of the doctrinal and political absoluteness of sovereignty. So have the ideas of the natural and inalienable rights of man which, when embodied in the safeguards and institutions of positive law – municipal and international – constitute a significant challenge to the unbridled sovereignty of the omnipotent State. In both senses – by their positive association with what is the essence of the federal system and by their negative effect on the mystic powers of sovereignty – the rights of man have played, and are increasingly bound to play, a significant part in the development towards a comprehensive federation of the States of the earth.

That advance towards the goal of federal integration can be visualized in accordance with two differing patterns of development. In the first instance, in terms of geography, it may be a combination of and a compromise between the essentially complementary principles of universality and regional association. The claim of the latter to moral authority increases in proportion as it is intended to serve or is capable of serving as a link in the chain of the evolution leading ultimately to a true federation of the world under the rule of law. Subject to that condition, regional organizations of States are justified and may be beneficent. This is so in particular in the sphere of protection of human rights in cases in which, within a limited number of States bound by an affinity of a geographical or other character, the respect for human rights and the rule of law based on the principle of government by consent have become part of the national heritage of the States in question not only in name but also in fact.

Secondly, the advance towards the final integration of international society can be accomplished not only by the formal and deliberate adoption of a comprehensive federal constitution. It can also be achieved by the gradual acceptance of institutions which are naturally congenial or essential to the federal system. Of these institutions the protection, within an association of a federal nature, of the rights of man, acknowledged and effectively guaranteed by the association, seems to offer more distinct prospects of realization than schemes based on the renunciation of the international personality of States. In so far as regional experience is a stage in the evolution towards the more complete integration of international society, such recognition and protection of human rights may in itself become a significant contributory factor in the consummation of the organized *civitas maxima*, with the individual human being in the very centre of the constitution of the world. To that development – it is to be hoped confidently and fervently – the State of Israel will contribute its proper and appointed share.

PART V

ORGANS OF INTERNATIONAL INTERCOURSE: DIPLOMATIC INTERCOURSE

CHAPTER I

IN RE SOLVAN VITIANU

Editor's note In 1949 Lauterpacht was asked by the Swiss Government for an opinion on the legality in international law of the arrest and trial by the Swiss authorities of Solvan Vitianu, a Roumanian national. Vitianu had, just prior to his arrest, been nominated by the Roumanian Government as economic counsellor to the Roumanian Legation at Berne. The appointment was notified to the Swiss Government but had not been accepted by it prior to Vitianu's arrest. The question was whether, in those circumstances, Vitianu was entitled to diplomatic immunity. Lauterpacht answered the question in the negative. But at the same time, in section 8 of the opinion, Lauterpacht observed that the manner in which the Swiss Government had acted could convey an impression of 'lack of respect' for 'the authority' of 'the principle of diplomatic immunity'; and he suggested that if Vitianu should be convicted 'the legal position of Switzerland . . . would not be prejudiced' if the Swiss authorities 'were to consider whether the circumstances of the case do not warrant a remission or mitigation of the sentence'.

On 24 June 1949 the Swiss Federal Tribunal upheld the conviction of Vitianu (see *Annual Digest*, 16 (1949), 281). Vitianu was sentenced to eighteen months' imprisonment (from which 238 days' detention pending trial was deductible) for usury, bribery and economic espionage. The other charges against him were dropped. He was also condemned to fifteen years' expulsion from Swiss territory.

The matter was referred to the Commission of Conciliation which had been established in the manner provided by the 1926 Treaty of Conciliation, Arbitration and Judicial Settlement between Switzerland and Roumania. Although summoned by its President to meet in the Hague on two occasions in July and August 1949, the Commission could not resolve the problem because on each occasion both the Commissioner appointed by Roumania and the Roumanian representative were absent.

Vitianu was deported from Switzerland on 5 December 1949, having been released from prison under Article 38 of the Swiss Criminal Code which entitles a prisoner to be freed for good conduct after serving two-thirds of his term.

The question involved in the *Vitianu* case is now regulated by Article 39 of the Vienna Convention on Diplomatic Relations, 1961.

I

1 I have been asked by the Swiss Government to give an opinion on the question of the legality under international law of the action of the Swiss authorities in arresting and continuing criminal proceedings

against Solvan Vitianu, a Roumanian national, whose appointment as economic counsellor to the Roumanian Legation at Berne had been previously notified to but never accepted by the Swiss Government. The present opinion is primarily intended for the guidance of the Swiss authorities, but I have informed them that there is no objection to their submitting the opinion – as a *consultation* (*Gutachten*) – to the Federal Court, or, indeed, to any arbitral or judicial body or conciliation commission which may be seized with the matter.

2 In the present opinion I am concerned only with the principal question as stated above. I do not propose to discuss the preliminary question as to whether the Swiss courts are bound to act upon the statement of or the attitude adopted by the Executive Department on the subject of the diplomatic status of the accused. I understand that in the view of the Swiss Government the judicial authorities have full jurisdiction to decide upon that issue.

3 In preparing the present opinion I have received considerable assistance from the opinions submitted on behalf of the accused by Professors Perassi and Merelli; by Professor Charles Rousseau; and, in particular, by Professor Hans Wehberg who has marshalled an imposing array of authorities, including those opposed to his thesis. I have also had the benefit of reading the observations submitted by Professor Paul Guggenheim for the use of the Swiss authorities.

2. THE FACTS

4 The question put to me is simplified by the circumstance that there is at present no dispute between the Swiss and the Roumanian Governments as to the principal facts underlying the controversy. These facts are, briefly stated, as follows: On 18 June 1948 the Roumanian Legation in Berne sent a communication to the Swiss Federal Political Department to the effect that M. Solvan Vitianu had been appointed, as from 15 June 1948, to the post of economic adviser (*conseiller economique*) of the Legation. M. Vitianu was at that time resident in Switzerland. According to information supplied to me by the Swiss Government he was since November 1947 under observation by the Swiss authorities in connection with alleged Communist activities and breaches of the criminal law of Switzerland. The Political Department refrained from acknowledging the communication of the Roumanian Legation of 18 June. On 25 June 1948 the Roumanian minister visited the Political Department in connection with a luncheon which the Legation was proposing to offer in honour of the chief of the Political Department. In connection with the suggestion, made by the

Roumanian minister, that M. Vitianu might participate in the function, the minister inquired as to the prospects of a speedy affirmative answer of the Political Department to the communication of 18 June 1948 concerning the appointment of M. Vitianu. He was informed that, as the appointment of a person already resident in the country was not fully in accordance with accepted usage, a delay in the Swiss answer was probable. (I note from the dossier that, in the subsequent correspondence, the Roumanian Legation has not referred to that interview. However, there seems to be no indication of any denial that the interview actually took place.) On 11 July 1948 a representative of the Roumanian Legation called once more at the Political Department in connection with the proposed luncheon and the list of the persons to be invited. As the proposed list included M. Vitianu, the chief of the Protocol of the Political Department declared that he would prefer that the name of M. Vitianu be omitted from the list in view of the fact that M. Vitianu's position had still to be clarified and that the matter would be the subject of an exchange of view between the chief of the Federal Political Department, M. Petitpierre (or the chief of the Department of Political Affairs). The representative of the Roumanian Legation declined to take note of that – in his view, unofficial – communication.

5 On 13 July 1948 M. Vitianu and his wife were arrested. Madame Vitianu was released on 12 August. M. Vitianu is still under arrest. They were both arrested on charges involving various violations of Swiss criminal law such as prohibited activities in favour of a foreign State (Article 271 of the Swiss Criminal Code), political espionage (Article 272) and economic espionage (Article 273). Subsequently further charges were brought against them for blackmail (Article 156), usury (Article 157), bribery (Article 228) and other offences.

6 On 15 July 1948 the Roumanian minister at Berne protested with the Swiss Political Department against the arrest of M. Vitianu and his wife. He described the action of the Swiss authorities as 'une violation inqualifiable des règles et usages habituels entre les Etats qui entretiennent des relations diplomatiques normales'. In a note of 16 July 1948 the Swiss Political Department denied that the appointment of M. Vitianu produced any legal effects in relation to Switzerland. It insisted that, in view of the absence of any acknowledgment of the notification of the appointment of M. Vitianu, that act remained a unilateral act of the Roumanian Legation. It was also pointed out that it was contrary to custom to appoint a person resident in the territory of the receiving State – in particular a person whose activities had drawn upon themselves the attention of the Swiss authorities and who was about to be arrested.

7 On 28 January 1949 the Roumanian Government informed the Swiss Federal Department that it invoked the procedure of conciliation provided for in the Treaty of Conciliation, Arbitration and Judicial Settlement signed by Switzerland and Roumania on 3 February 1926. In February 1949 the two States nominated members of the Commission of Conciliation as provided in the Treaty. On the 17 February 1949 the Roumanian Government demanded the immediate release of M. Vitianu. It relied on Article 18 of the above-mentioned Treaty which provided that pending the procedure of peaceful settlement as provided therein the parties shall refrain from steps calculated to prejudice the findings of bodies entrusted with conciliation, arbitration, or judicial settlement. On 18 March 1949 the Swiss Government denied that Article 18 of the Treaty obliged it to act in the manner suggested by the Roumanian Government and drew the attention of the latter to the fact that the case of M. Vitianu was to come before the Federal Court which alone was competent to decide on the question of the release of the accused. This was so in particular in view of Article 2 of the Treaty which laid down that local remedies must be exhausted before recourse is had to the procedure of pacific settlement provided for in the Treaty.

8 I understand that the case of M. Vitianu is due to come before the Swiss Federal Court in the course of June 1949.

3. THE CONTENTIONS OF THE SWISS AND ROUMANIAN GOVERNMENTS

9 The main issue between the Swiss and Roumanian Governments is a difference of opinion on a question of international law, i.e., whether the diplomatic status and the jurisdictional immunity of a subordinate member of the Legation are the result of a unilateral act of the sending State or whether acceptance, express or implied, by the receiving State is an essential condition for bringing about the diplomatic status and immunities of the official concerned. The view of the Swiss Government appears to be that the subordinate member of the diplomatic mission assumes his diplomatic status at the time when the notification of his appointment is accepted by the receiving State. Should the appointment be rejected then, in the view of the Swiss Government, the refusal to accept the individual in question is retroactive and there is no question of any diplomatic immunities having been acquired at all. The notification of rejection does not terminate an already existing status; it signifies that, so far as the receiving State is concerned, the appointment has never come into effect. In the pre-

sent case, in the view of the Swiss Government, the circumstances accompanying the absence of an express acceptance of the appointment of M. Vitianu clearly indicated the disinclination of the Swiss Government to commit itself to the acceptance of M. Vitianu. These circumstances included the fact that the customary prompt acknowledgment of the appointment, accompanied by the delivery of the appropriate document, did not take place; that the residence of M. Vitianu in Switzerland raised an additional point of difficulty; and that the attitude of the Swiss Government had been unofficially communicated to the Roumanian Legation.

10 In the view of the Roumanian Government a subordinate member of the Legation acquires diplomatic immunity as soon as notification of his appointment reaches the receiving State. It would appear that the Roumanian Government does not go to the extreme length of the view, adopted by some writers, that a State is under a duty to receive – or to agree to the appointment of – a subordinate member of the mission. But it does maintain: (*a*) that the unilateral act of appointment by the sending State creates diplomatic immunity and subjects the State where the mission operates to all the corresponding obligations; (*b*) that the diplomatic status subsists until the requested State has not expressly refused to accept the individual in question; and that even after the receiving State has expressly and officially declined to agree to the appointment of the person concerned his immunity is not terminated but he must be allowed to leave the country unmolested.

4. THE RULE OF INTERNATIONAL LAW

11 The legal position in the matter is clearly determined by considerations which the practice of States and the reason of the thing have evolved with regard to the reception of foreign diplomatic representatives. The receiving State cannot dictate to the sending State whom it shall appoint as the head of its diplomatic mission or as a member of it. To do so would mean a serious interference with the independence of the foreign State and with its freedom to conduct its foreign policy. It is generally regarded as contrary to usage and to good understanding between nations for one State to make even an unofficial intimation to the other as to whom it would like to receive as head of the mission or as a member of it.

12 However, the proposition that a State enjoys full freedom in determining the composition of its diplomatic personnel is true only in the sense that it cannot be compelled to select a person contrary to its wishes or interests. For the second guiding consideration governing this

branch of international law is that the receiving State cannot be forced to accept a person or a category of persons whose presence it considers either unnecessary, or inimical to the smooth conduct of diplomatic intercourse, or undesirable from the point of view of internal order and security. With regard to the latter it must be borne in mind that diplomatic immunity is the normal concomitant of diplomatic status. Diplomatic immunity is co-extensive with a corresponding limitation of the jurisdiction of the receiving State, and it is clear that no State can be compelled to assent to such limitation upon its jurisdictional rights without being entitled to refuse to accept a particular person or category of persons. For that reason the freedom of the State with regard to the acceptance of a person appointed by another State to diplomatic office is as absolute as its freedom to terminate it – subject to the safeguard of permitting unmolested departure – by a simple notification that the person in question had ceased to be a *persona grata* and that his recall is requested.

13 A reconciliation of these two apparently conflicting considerations – that of the freedom of the sending State to appoint its representatives and that of the right of the receiving State not to be burdened with individuals whose presence it considers unhelpful and undesirable – has found expression in the general acceptance of the principle of consent on the part of the receiving State, i.e., of the principle that effective diplomatic status is the result of a bilateral act analogous to offer and acceptance in the law of contract. That principle has been fully developed and endowed with a special degree of solemnity and deliberation with regard to the appointment of the head of the mission. The necessity of obtaining, through the so-called *agreatur*, the consent of the receiving State is universally recognized. The discretion of the receiving State in giving or refusing its consent to the proposed appointment is absolute. According to the better opinion and preponderant practice there is no legal obligation to give reasons why a person rejected is not considered to be *persona grata*. The same applies to the unilateral termination of an appointment already made. There is no legal sanction for any arbitrary refusal to accept a person designated as a diplomatic representative. Any arbitrary refusal to grant *agreatur* may be regarded as an unfriendly act calculated to give rise to similarly unfriendly acts of retorsion. Undoubtedly, the acceptance of a diplomatic representative may entail diplomatic status for persons with regard to whom no such acceptance has been expressed as is the case in respect of the wife and other members of the family of the person accepted, but any otherwise insoluble difficulties and inconveniences arising from that fact may be solved by the simple means of

withholding the *agreatur* or asking for the recall of the principal bearer of diplomatic immunity.

14 No different principle and practice obtain with regard to subordinate members of the mission. Undoubtedly, as the position of these persons is less important, there is less solemnity and deliberation about securing the consent of the State in which the diplomatic mission is placed. There is, as a rule, no previous inquiry as to the acceptability of the person in question. But the rule is not absolute. Thus, for instance, a number of States – such as Brazil, Argentine, France, Spain, Poland, Portugal, and some other countries – require preliminary consultation with regard to subordinate members of the mission whom it is intended to appoint as military or naval attachés. When in 1930, in pursuance of an Act of Congress, the Department of State of the United States decided to appoint 'agricultural attachés' as members of foreign diplomatic missions the United States asked for the preliminary consent of the foreign States concerned. That consent was given by a number of countries who informed the United States that they would be glad to grant to these categories of persons the customary privileges accorded to the members of diplomatic missions. (See Hackworth, 406.) When, however, a request was made in 1925 by the United States for similar recognition of certain treasury officials to be attached to American diplomatic missions abroad in the capacity of 'customs attachés' the requests for the recognition of such attachés 'were almost universally refused by the foreign Governments concerned' (*ibid.* p. 407). Some States demand a previous inquiry with regard to such persons as are their nationals. Others, as has been the occasional practice of the United States, require some such preliminary procedure with regard to subordinate members of the mission appointed at a time when they are already resident in the territory of the receiving State.

15 However, as a rule, in case of subordinate members of the mission the acceptance and the investigation which precede it take place subsequent to the appointment, namely, subsequent to the notification of the appointment in connection with the inclusion on the diplomatic list or in connection with the issue of the documents of identity certifying the diplomatic status of the person appointed. In the case of *agreatur* in respect of heads of the mission acceptance takes place prior to the appointment. Yet in both cases acceptance is decisive and essential. In the case of subordinate officials the investigation may be cursory, superficial or merely formal when no special circumstances call for detailed examination. But it is inaccurate to assume that it does not take place at all or that the procedure is purely automatic. There is hardly a State the Foreign Office of which would not reject with

impatience the view that the diplomatic status of a subordinate member of a foreign mission is conclusively decided by the unilateral act of appointment and notification. In the opinions submitted on behalf of the accused it is conceded that there is an undoubted right of investigation to determine whether the appointment is one genuinely pertaining to the exercise of diplomatic functions or whether it is an appointment made for extraneous purposes alien to the exercise of ordinary diplomatic activities. It is conceded that such appointment, especially if made *mala fide*, is null and void *ab initio* and incapable of producing diplomatic status and the privileges appertaining thereto. This very possibility implies the right of careful – and not merely casual – investigation and of eventual rejection of the appointment. A substantial portion of the history of the practice of English, and other, courts in the matter is the history of verification by the courts of the genuineness of the diplomatic function of the persons claiming immunity – this notwithstanding the fact that such examination has already taken place at the time of the inclusion in the list. At present, in the majority of States, courts fully rely upon the certificate, which they treat as conclusive, of the executive department as to the diplomatic status of the individual concerned. This is an additional reason for safeguarding the unimpeded right of the Foreign Offices to scrutinize the notifications of appointments and for insisting that no diplomatic status ensues independently of express acceptance.

16 The fact that the procedure of acceptance of subordinate members of the legation is less solemn than in the case of heads of the mission and that it takes place subsequent to and not before the appointment by the sending State, has led some writers to advance the view that the appointment is perfected when it is made by the sending State, but that the receiving State retains the right to decline to sanction it (though, it is maintained, such sanction must not be arbitrarily withheld). Thus Professor Verdross suggests that, with regard to subordinate members of the staff of the legation, 'the previous consent of the receiving State is not as a rule obtained', but that 'the latter is entitled not to admit individual persons for specific reasons and to decline to include them in the diplomatic list' (*Völkerrecht* (1937), p. 206). In so far as that statement implies that – unlike in the case of the head of the mission – the act of appointment does not require previous consent of the receiving State it is unobjectionable. In so far as it may be interpreted as meaning that no act of acceptance – however formal – is as a rule necessary, I do not consider it to be in conformity with practice and principle. Practice shows, with virtual uniformity, that such acceptance takes place and that it is preceded by appropriate

inquiry and investigation. It is that acceptance which completes the act of appointment and transforms it into a bilateral legal process. It is irrelevant that the confirmation of the appointment is occasionally couched in the form of a mere acknowledgment or transmission of the necessary documents of identity without express reference to the fact of acceptance. This, for instance, is the Swiss formula in acknowledging the receipt of the notification of acceptance. But it is inaccurate to deduce from the form of that acknowledgment that it follows as a matter of fact, that it is not preceded by appropriate examination, and that the Foreign Department of the receiving State is a mere registration office for the purpose. As is pointed out by the Colombian Foreign Office in reply to an inquiry made by the Swiss Government in connection with the present case, the acknowledgment of the notification

> implies the acceptance of the new official . . . If the ministry finds any objection to such appointment it will present it on that occasion. (Para que un funcionario adscrito a una Mision diplomática acreditada en Colombia y subalterno del Jefe de Mision sea reconocido con carácter diplomático y goce de las prerrogativas e inmunidades correspondientes se requiere que su nombramiento sea comunicado por el Jefe de la Mision diplomática y que el Ministerio de Relaciones Exteriores acuse recibo de tal comunicación expresando que ha tomado nota de ella, acto que implica la aceptación del nuevo funcionario. – Si el Ministerio tuviere alguna objeccion que hacer a tal nombramiento la presentara en esa ocasion.)

17 In the course of the exchange of views between the Swiss and Roumanian authorities following upon the arrest of M. Vitianu the Swiss Government advanced the view that it was contrary to international practice to appoint as a member of the diplomatic mission a person already resident in the country. I do not concur in that view. Some States – such as the United States – occasionally adopt a special procedure with regard to persons in that category, for instance, by requiring them to leave the country and enter it afresh prior to taking up the appointment. But that practice is certainly not general. On the other hand, the circumstance that the person appointed already resides in the country may justly be regarded as a reason for exercising care in the confirmation of the appointment. For instance, inquiries can reasonably be made as to the position of the person in question in matters of obligations of private – and, possibly – criminal law. Such inquiries may influence the decision as to acceptance or rejection of the designated person.

18 The scope of the present opinion does not permit a survey of the practice of various States – though I propose to consider later on in some detail the practice of Great Britain and of the United States. But

it may be sufficient to give an account of the conclusions of the legal position on the matter reached by the authors of the Harvard Draft Convention on Diplomatic Privileges and Immunities which was prepared in 1932 by the Harvard Law School Research in International Law and was based on a comprehensive survey of the practice of States. Article 8 of the Draft, entitled 'Selection of the Members of the Mission' provides as follows:

> A sending State may send as a member of its mission, other than the chief of mission, any person to whom no objection is made by the receiving State; provided, however, that a sending State may not send as a member of a mission a national of the receiving State without the express consent of the receiving State.

Thus, according to that Article in the case of a national of the receiving State the express consent of the receiving State is necessary before the appointment is made. In other cases no such previous consent is necessary but, subsequent to the appointment, the receiving State is entitled to withhold its consent and to reject the person appointed. The right of rejecting a person thus designated would have no meaning if he were held to acquire diplomatic status before the receiving State has been given the opportunity of examining the appointment and, if necessary, withholding its consent. The Comment appended to Article 8 by the authors of the Draft is instructive:

> That a State is, in general, free in the selection of the members and the personnel of its mission is believed to be a statement of an existing rule of international law.... In modern practice, however, this freedom of action on the part of the sending State is definitely limited for the purpose of assuring satisfactory diplomatic relations based on reciprocal advantage. Since no State is legally obligated to enter into diplomatic relations with another, it is not obliged to receive any designated individual as the envoy of a foreign State.

The Comment then proceeds as follows:

> That this refusal seldom occurs is not proof of the proposition that it would be contrary to international law. The receiving State may prefer to obtain the same end through action of the sending State itself, rather than to avail itself of a right whose exercise might endanger the cordial relations of the States concerned. Failure to exercise a right cannot of itself justify the conclusion that the right does not exist.

19 Some of the replies sent in about 1927 by various Governments in connection with the work of the Committee for the Progressive Codification of International Law throw further light in support of the view propounded in the present opinion of the substantive and not

purely nominal nature of the procedure of acceptance on the part of the receiving State. Thus the Swiss answer stressed that the inclusion of a person in the diplomatic list does not imply any legal consequences and that it is simply a formality '*connoting that the position claimed for the person concerned is recognised*' (League of Nations, Doc. C. 196, M. 70 (1927), V, 247). It will be noted that the reply refers to the position which is claimed and which must be recognized by the receiving State. The Egyptian Government considered that the possession of diplomatic privilege should be subject to the condition that a list containing the names of the officials of the mission should be officially communicated and that 'it should, of course, be possible to refuse such a list or to ask it to be altered' (*ibid.* p. 258). The Swedish Government insisted that the receiving State should be granted the right to refuse to admit an obviously exaggerated number of diplomatic agents (*ibid.* p. 235). This was also the view of the Czechoslovak Government (*ibid.* p. 255). It is clear that the right of rejection implies the right of preliminary investigation; it is inconsistent with the claim that the appointment is perfected by the unilateral action of the sending State. The German reply – probably prompted by the experience of the decision of the Darmstadt Court, discussed below in the present opinion, was emphatic with regard to this aspect of the question. It laid down that 'in any case, the principle should be laid down that the obtaining of prerogatives and privileges depends on consent – which, of course, will almost invariably be accorded by the State which receives' (*ibid.* p. 134). 'Consequently', it was added, 'no privileges of any kind could be claimed . . . for a person who . . . as the appointing State has in view of the circumstances good reason to suppose – is not *persona grata*, or who has not been attached to the mission *bona fide*' (*ibid.*). It will be noted that although the replies of the Government were given in connection with the proposed codification of international law on the subject, they were intended to give expression to what was believed to be the existing practice. They were not concerned primarily with suggestions *de lege ferenda*.

20 Brief reference may be made in this connection to the Resolution of the Institute of International Law adopted in 1929 on the subject of diplomatic immunities. Article 2 of the Resolution lays down that the diplomatic immunities provided therein shall apply: '. . . (2) aux membres de la mission officiellement reconnus comme tels' (*Annuaire*, II (1929), 307). Nothing in the discussion which preceded the adoption of this Article has led me to the conclusion that its carefully worded phrasing permits of any other than the natural interpretation of the

words 'officiellement reconnus'. The official recognition clearly refers to acceptance by the receiving State.

21 The British practice in the matter is particularly instructive having regard to the frequency with which English courts have been called upon to apply the law of diplomatic immunity and to the influence wielded by English practice since the historic – though in form declaratory – Act of Queen Anne of 1708. It is undoubted law that for a subordinate member of the diplomatic mission to be included in the diplomatic list it is necessary: (*a*) that his name be submitted by the head of the mission; (*b*) that he should be recognized and accepted as such by the British Government, i.e., the Secretary of State for Foreign Affairs. It is that acceptance which, so far as the receiving State is concerned, constitutes the basis of diplomatic status and immunity. The diplomatic list is merely evidence of such acceptance. The notification of the appointment is not followed by an automatic acceptance of the person nominated. It is followed by an acknowledgment of the communication coupled with an indication that the matter is receiving attention. (The Swiss Legation in London has supplied me, by way of example, with the original of the following communication from the Foreign Office:

> The Secretary of State for Foreign Affairs has the honour to acknowledge the receipt of the Swiss Chargé d'Affaires' Note no. IIk.16.1948 I of 9 February regarding appointment of Captain William Hurter and, in reply, begs leave to state that the matter is receiving attention. – Foreign Office, S.W.1 – 14 February 1948.)

The rule of English law on the subject is stated with clarity on page 135 of the sixth edition of Dicey's *Conflict of Laws*, published in 1949:

> The court is bound to take judicial cognisance of the status not only of an ambassador or chargé d'affaires, but also of members of his staff. Normally, a list of the staff is submitted to the Secretary of State for Foreign Affairs, who may refuse recognition to any person either because his claim to diplomatic status is dubious or the number of persons for whom status is claimed is excessive. If recognition is accorded, a statement by the Secretary of State is binding on the court, as it is a necessary part of the royal prerogative to accord or refuse recognition.

22 In *Engelke* v. *Mussmann*, one of the leading English cases on the subject of diplomatic immunities, the substantive nature of the act of recognizing and accepting the appointment of a subordinate member of the mission is expressed repeatedly and emphatically in passages which merit quotation in this connection. Thus in the House of Lords Lord Warrington of Clyffe said:

The Attorney-General states explicitly in para. 26 of his case that it is a necessary part of His Majesty's prerogative in his conduct of foreign affairs and his relations with foreign States and their representatives to accord or refuse recognition to any person as a member of a foreign ambassador's staff exercising diplomatic functions. The fact of recognition is of course peculiarly within the knowledge of the department according it, and a statement by or on behalf of the department that it has been accorded to any person must in my opinion come within the principles above referred to and be conclusive as to the status of that person.

It may be added that the Attorney-General states in his printed case that, for the purpose of obtaining recognition of the members of an ambassador's staff exercising diplomatic functions, a list of such members is furnished from time to time to the Secretary of State by every ambassador. The list is not accepted as of course on behalf of His Majesty, and after investigation it not infrequently happens that recognition is withheld from a person whose name appears upon the furnished list, either because his diplomatic status is in doubt, or because the number of persons for whom status is claimed appears to the Secretary of State to be excessive. ([1928] A.C., p. 457.)

Lord Phillimore said:

But just as the receiving State may intimate that a proposed ambassador will not be agreeable to it and will be refused, so, if the ambassador tenders a person as a domestic or domestic servant, the receiving State may refuse to accept and recognize the man as such, and when the person tendered is a subject of the receiving country conditions may be made. (*Ibid.* p. 450.)

Lord Buckmaster said:

Now the acceptance and recognition of persons who form the staff of an ambassador are matters which, having regard to the practice in the conduct of foreign affairs, are equally based on comity of nations and necessarily also within the cognizance of the Crown acting through the Foreign Office. They are in a position to know what are the duties performed and the persons who perform them, and it is plain that, though they trust the list put forward if it appears from their knowledge to be a list which might reasonably be accepted, yet the list itself is scrutinized, inquiries are made and, if necessary, persons are removed for sufficient reasons. (*Ibid.* p. 443.)

In *The Amazone* Mr Justice Langton said:

The list prepared under the Statute of 7 Anne, c. 12, as I understand it, is one which the Foreign Office prepares from names submitted by the members of the various diplomatic corps of those recognized by His Majesty as enjoying diplomatic immunity. It is, therefore, now beyond question that the defendant does enjoy full diplomatic immunity. ([1939], p. 325.)

I have quoted these passages at some length not because there is any doubt as to the British practice in the matter, but because they emphasize with abundant clarity that recognition and acceptance by the Foreign Office no less than appointment by the sending State are creative of diplomatic status and immunity.

23 The position in the United States is no less clear. The emphasis on acceptance as a condition of effective appointment in relation to the receiving State appears clearly from the following statement of Professor Hyde:

> A State is not obliged to accept or to permit to function as a part of, in connection with, a foreign diplomatic mission within its dominion, particular designated individuals, with or without diplomatic status, who are subordinate to the chief of the mission and to whom it may find reason to object. Again, a State may prescribe the conditions on which it will consent to the attachment of such mission of subordinates within particular enterprises. (Hyde, 2, 1243.)

The same emphasis on acceptance and recognition appears in the following statement made in 1931, by the Legal Adviser to the State Department in the matter of the Diplomatic List:

> Although there does not appear to be any statutory provision specifically directing that this Department publish a list of diplomatic officers duly accredited to it (the Government) by foreign Governments and *accepted* and *recognized* as such officers by this Government, the publication of such a list is a usual practice of nations in the conduct of foreign affairs. (Hackworth, 4, 429.)

It is explained, on the same page, that names of persons published in the diplomatic list are 'the names of members of foreign legations and foreign embassies in the United States entitled to diplomatic immunities, down to and including the grade of attachés' (*ibid.*). This function of 'recognizing and accepting' is not a mere formality. Thus in 1834 the Turkish embassy was informed, in respect of a particular inquiry, that the State Department would not permit the inclusion in the list of employees of a foreign mission of the name of a person engaged in practice outside the embassy or legation (*ibid.* p. 433). In 1933 the Venezuelan minister was informed that it was contrary to the practice of the Department of State to include in the Diplomatic List foreign diplomatic officers having merely an honorary status (*ibid.* p. 434).

24 I do not consider it necessary to survey, with any attempt at completeness, the literature of international law on the subject. As a rule text-books of international law concentrate on the question of the appointment and acceptance of the head of the mission. Neither do monographs throw illuminating light on the question – though attention may be drawn to the passage in Morton's valuable dissertation entitled 'Privilèges et immunités diplomatiques en Suisse' (1927) in

which he says: 'La qualité de membres d'une mission diplomatique en Suisse a pour origine l'agrément donné aux nominations par les autorités fédérales' (p. 164).

25 This opinion would be singularly incomplete without some reference to the outspoken assertion of the view which is contrary to that represented in the present opinion and which was advanced in 1926 by Professors Strupp and Giese (both printed in *Z.V.*, 13 (1926), Ergänzungsheft). That view received the support – though not the full support – of Professor Heyland (*ibid.*) and Professor Wehberg (*R.I.*, 3rd ser., 7, 300 *et seq.*). The views of Professors Strupp and Giese were expressed in opinions (*consultations*) submitted by them in defence of an accused member of the Persian embassy in the case decided by the *Oberlandesgericht* of Darmstadt in December 1926 and discussed below, in section 5 of the present opinion. According to Professors Giese and Strupp the valid appointment, with all the diplomatic privileges and immunities attaching thereto, is exclusively a matter for the sending State. The consent of the receiving State is not asked for and is irrelevant. Even if the sending State appoints a person fraudulently, *mala fide*, for purposes alien to the diplomatic mission, the rejection of that individual as a *persona non grata* by the receiving State is altogether irrelevant. The only remedy which the receiving State possesses in such cases is that of diplomatic protest and other appropriate action against what it considers to be an international delinquency of the sending State. I note that in the opinion submitted by Professor Wehberg in connection with the present case a similar, though slightly modified, view is expressed. He says (at p. 50):

> If the appointment takes place in the genuine intention to entrust the individual concerned with diplomatic functions, the fact that that person has already come into conflict with the laws of the receiving State merely gives the latter the right to demand his recall. In that case the person concerned enjoys, up to his recall, diplomatic immunity and a reasonable period must be granted to him for departure from the country subsequent to his recall.

26 These views have been reproduced here not only out of respect for the distinguished scholars who advanced them but also as showing the consequences to which they must necessarily lead. They are, it is submitted, contrary to elementary requirements of the sovereignty, of the dignity, and the security of the receiving State. They imply that a State may be saddled with individuals who have contracted civil obligations or who have committed offences against its criminal law and who, by the mere act of unilateral appointment, acquire immunity in respect of such acts – the only remedy available to the sending State

being that of request for recall coupled with an obligation to permit them to leave the country unmolested. As inquiries concerning their former activities may require considerable time, the further implication of that view would be that such persons would enjoy full immunity in respect of acts, however unlawful and prejudicial to the safety of the receiving State, committed since their appointment even if their recall is subsequently asked for. Any such views are alien to fundamental principles of diplomatic intercourse and, indeed, of common sense. With isolated exceptions they are at variance with the opinions expressed in the literature of international law. Above all, they are contrary to the practically uniform practice of States.

5. DIPLOMATIC IMMUNITY PRIOR TO ACCEPTANCE

27 The principle that acceptance – and acceptance only – of the receiving States completes the act of appointment of subordinate members of the mission supplies the answer to the question of their immunity from jurisdiction prior to acceptance by the receiving State. Once the appointment has thus been perfected immunity extends to all acts anterior both to acceptance and appointment. Prior to acceptance there is – with one probable exception referred to below – no immunity from jurisdiction. The position in the matter has been clarified by two judicial decisions bearing directly upon the point at issue.

28 The first is the case *In re Cloete* decided in 1891 by the English Court of Appeal (65 Law Times Reports (1891), p. 102). Cloete was a British subject who up to July 1890 had carried on business in London. In January 1891 he was appointed by the Persian ambassador an honorary attaché of the embassy. His name was sent to the Foreign Office as a member of the ambassador's suite. His appointment had in no way been recognized by the British Government. In bankruptcy proceedings which subsequently started against him he claimed immunity from civil process as a member of the Persian embassy. The Court of Appeal held that he was not entitled to immunity. The Court gave various reasons for its decision. But the following passages taken from the judgment of Lord Esher M.R. are relevant to the present issue:

> . . . He, having been at work for the Persian embassy, got his name put down as a member of the embassy in the way in which it has been done. He was never recognized as a member of the Persian embassy by the Foreign Office . . . Though his name does appear in this appointment as an honorary attaché of the embassy, he has done nothing to get himself recognized as a member of the embassy by the Foreign Office, which shows that he had not

any *bona fide* intention, in obtaining it, to be employed in the usual way in the service of the embassy. Therefore the privilege which he claims will not be allowed in an English court of law, and he has no protection against bankruptcy proceedings in this country. The receiving order was rightly made by the registrar, and this appeal must be dismissed.

Lord Justice Kay distinguished the present case (*In re Cloete*) from *Macartney* v. *Garbutt* (62 Law Times Reports, N.S., p. 656; 24 Q.B.D. 368) on which the appellant relied. He said that in *Macartney* v. *Garbutt* the defendant

proceeded expressly upon the ground that 'his name had been submitted to the Foreign Office in the usual way, and his position as a member of the embassy recognized without reservation or condition of any sort', whereas in this case there was nothing of that kind, for the debtor has not been received or recognized by the Foreign Office.

29 The second case which bears directly upon the question at issue is that decided on 20 December 1926 by the *Oberlandesgericht* of Darmstadt (reported in *Juristische Wochenschrift*, 56 (1927), 2324; *Z.I.* 39 (1928), 284; *Z.V.* 14 (1928), 594). Although some of the relevant facts in the report of that case are not stated with sufficient precision, the case is clearly one of assumption of criminal jurisdiction over a person whose appointment had been notified to the German Government but not accepted by it. The defendant in that case had been appointed honorary attaché to the Persian embassy. The German Government refused to accept him. When prosecuted for tax evasion he pleaded immunity. The Court found that it had jurisdiction. Pointing to the fact that, unlike in the case of heads of missions, no previous *agreatur* is required for the appointment of subordinate members of the mission, the Courts said: 'The reason for this lies solely in the lesser importance of these positions. But it must not be concluded from the practice described that the receiving state is legally obligated to accept every subordinate official and thereby to acknowledge him as exterritorial.'

30 Reference may now be made to what has been described above as the probable exception to the rule that acceptance – and acceptance alone – brings definitely into being the diplomatic status and the corresponding immunities of the persons appointed by the sending State. That exception consists in the rule – which is one of convenience – that once acceptance is given it dates retrospectively to the date of notification of the appointment. Once acceptance is given the person appointed enjoys immunity as from that date. This is the sense of the observation made by Sir Cecil Hurst: 'Dans le cas de membres subalternes de la suite, *l'immunité* date du moment ou leur nomination

est notifiée au ministère des Affaires etrangères' (*Hague Recueil* (1926) (ii), p. 237). It will be noted that Sir Cecil Hurst refers to the date of the commencement of *immunity*. In view of the clear British practice in the matter it cannot be assumed that that distinguished lawyer who at that time was Legal Adviser to the Foreign Office would have intended to say that the mere act of appointment brings into being the diplomatic status of the designated person regardless of the acceptance by the receiving State. Moreover, with regard to persons already resident in the receiving State Sir Cecil Hurst says expressly:

> Dans le cas ou une personne qui habite déjà le territoire est nommée agent diplomatique d'un autre pays, elle aura droit aux immunités et aux exemptions reconnues dès le moment ou sa nomination est notifiée au gouvernement auprès duquel elle est accreditée et acceptée par celui-ci.

It is clear from the context that by 'agent diplomatique' Sir Cecil Hurst understands both the head of the mission and subordinate members of it.

6. THE QUESTION OF IMPLIED ACCEPTANCE

31 I can now deal, very briefly, with the question whether the silence – the official silence – of the Swiss Political Department following upon the notification of the appointment of M. Vitianu did not amount to an implied acceptance of the appointment. In my view no such implied acceptance took place. Neither, in the circumstances of the case, does it appear that the Roumanian authorities would have been justified in assuming that such implied acceptance occurred. In the present case it was clear almost from the very outset that there was no disposition on the part of the Swiss Government to accept the designated person as a matter of course. According to the established Swiss practice – which must have been known to the Roumanian Legation – the acknowledgment of the notification of the appointment of the subordinate member of the mission and the issue of the necessary documents do not involve a prolonged procedure. The unusual delay, in the present case, in sending the usual acknowledgment, was therefore not without significance. Moreover, the unofficial communications made by the Swiss authorities and received by the Roumanian Legation showed clearly that, at least for the time being, there was no intention to grant recognition of the appointment. The fact that the Head of the Swiss Foreign Department refused to take part in a social function, if attended by M. Vitianu, could bear only one interpretation. It might not have been altogether unreasonable for the Swiss authorities to assume that the Roumanian Legation would draw the necessary

conclusions from these unofficial intimations – at least to the extent of assuming that no acceptance of M. Vitianu had taken place. In some matters it is convenient and reasonable to act on the principle acted upon by the Permanent Court of International Justice in the case of the Mavrommatis Palestine Concessions (Judgment no. 2, series A, no. 2, p. 15) and insisting on the 'flexibility which ought to characterize international relations'.

32 Above all, there obtains in this matter – as in weightier matters, such as recognition of States and Governments – the governing principle that implied consent must not be rashly assumed; that it must not be assumed in cases, like the present, in which practice postulates a formal act of acceptance; and, above all, that there is no room at all for implied acceptance or recognition of status when it is clear from the circumstances that there is no intention to grant it.

7. ABUSE OF RIGHTS AND THE INITIAL NULLITY OF THE APPOINTMENT

33 In the present opinion I am advising the Swiss Government to the effect that the diplomatic status of a person appointed as a member of the subordinate staff of the Legation depends upon his acceptance by the receiving State; that, while the effects of such acceptance in respect of diplomatic immunity may date back to the time of appointment, they do not arise independently of such acceptance; that the acceptance is an act entirely within the discretion of the receiving State; and that the sanction of any arbitrary or negligent exercise of that discretion is of a political – and not of a legal – nature.

34 In view of the above conclusions I do not find it necessary to discuss in detail the question whether the appointment of M. Vitianu was not in itself tainted with nullity for the alleged reason that it resulted from an abuse of a right of appointment by the Roumanian Government. There would be a clear abuse of a right if the appointment had been of fraudulent nature, that is to say, if it had been made in order to shield M. Vitianu from civil or criminal jurisdiction of Swiss courts or if his appointment had nothing to do with the fulfilment of diplomatic functions proper. The effect of such fraudulent appointment, if proved conclusively, might be, in addition to engaging the international responsibility of the Roumanian State, that a court of law would regard the appointment as null and void *ab initio* and decline to grant jurisdictional immunities in respect of acts committed or obligations incurred during the tenure of the appointment thus fraudulently made even if the appointment had been accepted by the Political

Department. The prohibition of abuse of rights is a generally recognized principle of law and may be held to be part of international law. I do not propose to add to the length of the present opinion by citing the relevant decisions and the literature on the subject. These are contained in the eighth edition of volume I of Oppenheim (p. 313), in the chapter on the Doctrine of Abuse of Rights in my book *The Function of Law in the International Community* (1933), pp. 286–306 and in the concluding part of Professor Guggenheim's opinion. The principle that no legal rights arise from an illegality – *ex injuria jus non oritur* – is equally a general principle of law. The matter is discussed in detail in my book on *Recognition in International Law* (1948), pp. 420–27.

35 In fact, the freedom of courts to refuse legal effect to an appointment effected by way of an abuse of rights in violation of international law might be in many cases the only remedy consistent with justice and with respect for international law. For although the Political Department might terminate the appointment by requesting the recall of the person concerned as a *persona non grata*, such termination would not in itself produce results with regard to acts prior to the termination of the appointment. It would be for the courts, in the legitimate exercise of their function of administering international law in good faith, to treat such appointment as invalid from the outset and decline to grant jurisdictional immunities to the person concerned notwithstanding his previous acceptance by the Political Department. This is the natural and inescapable limit to the conclusiveness of the acceptance, or certification, by the Political Department or of the inclusion in the Diplomatic List. Occasionally Governments of unimpeached record in the matter of diplomatic immunities, have taken it upon themselves to remedy the consequences of diplomatic appointments brought about in a manner admitting of doubt as to the *bona fides* of the appointment. Thus in the case of Wolf von Igel, an attaché of the German embassy, the Government of the United States claimed, in 1916, the right to proceed criminally against him in respect of acts committed prior to his appointment. The Secretary of State said on that occasion in an official communication addressed to the German Ambassador:

> In the case of von Igel, however, I do not think that Your Excellency's Government can legally claim for him diplomatic immunity since the nature of the crimes with which he is charged is so grave and since the crimes were committed before he was notified to the Department of State to be an attaché of your embassy. Manifestly it would be contrary to the usage of nations and to rules which govern their intercourse to permit diplomatic immunity to be thrown about a person in these circumstances in order to save him from the consequences of his act. (24 April 1916, *U.S. For. Rel.* (1916), Suppl. p. 810.)

No opinion is here expressed as to the validity of the contention put forward by the Secretary of State. In the present case the Swiss Government has expressly disclaimed any intention of invoking a rule according to which a State is entitled to assume jurisdiction over members of the diplomatic mission with regard to offences committed prior to the effective commencement of diplomatic status. Its view of the legal position is that M. Vitianu had never assumed diplomatic status. But the incident may be noted as an example of the consequences, if unchecked by courts, of the abuse of international rights in this matter.

36 For the above reason, should the Federal Court, or an international tribunal, hold, contrary to the view expressed in the present opinion, that mere appointment by the sending State – or appointment not followed by immediate and unequivocal rejection by the receiving State – brings about diplomatic status, it will still be open to the Swiss Government to submit evidence showing that the appointment, being fraudulent and by way of an abuse of a right, was void in law and incapable of producing results in the field of diplomatic immunity. However, according to the view adopted in the present opinion, it is not essential for the Swiss Government to rely, in the first instance, on the submission that the appointment, having been effected *mala fide* – in order to shield from the jurisdiction of Swiss courts a person accused of a serious violation of Swiss criminal law and in order to enable him to pursue activities contrary to the laws and interests of Switzerland – was null and void. Neither is it necessary for it to adduce these circumstances as a justification of its refusal to accept the accused. For it had the right to refuse its consent by dint of the mere intimation that M. Vitianu was a person *non grata*. The Swiss Government is fully entitled to maintain that even if the Roumanian Legation and the Roumanian Government had acted in perfect good faith it would still have the right to act as it did, namely, to decline to accept an individual whom it believed to be objectionable.

37 I am not suggesting that evidence – as to the substance of which I am unable to pronounce a view – of the alleged criminal activities of the accused is altogether irrelevant with regard to the aspect of the case with which the present Opinion is concerned. For such evidence may be helpful as showing: (*a*) that the delay, on the part of the Swiss authorities, in unequivocally rejecting the appointment of M. Vitianu, was neither arbitrary nor grossly negligent; and (*b*) that the Roumanian Legation, assuming that they had knowledge of the nature of the activities or the character of M. Vitianu, could have no reasonable doubt as to the true and probable attitude of the Swiss Political Department. However, although such evidence may be helpful, I do not

consider it essential for the success of the main thesis of the Swiss Government, namely, that the accused having never been accepted by it as member of a diplomatic mission never acquired diplomatic status and the diplomatic immunities appertaining thereto.

38 In connection with the question of abuse of rights I wish to advise that should the judgment of the Federal Court substantiate the allegations of the Swiss Government in the matter and should the present case come before the International Court of Justice or an arbitral tribunal by way of agreement of the parties or by unilateral request, the Swiss Government ought to insist that the Court (or the tribunal) should be asked to answer the separate question whether the Roumanian Government committed a violation of international law and an international delinquency towards Switzerland by appointing M. Vitianu member of the diplomatic mission of Roumania in Switzerland in a manner amounting to an abuse of a right.

8. THE ATTITUDE OF THE SWISS GOVERNMENT AND THE PRINCIPLES OF INTERNATIONAL COMITY IN THE MATTER OF DIPLOMATIC IMMUNITY

39 The main conclusion of the present opinion is that inasmuch as there had been no express or implied acceptance by the Swiss Government of the notification of the appointment of M. Vitianu as member of the Roumanian Legation the action of the Swiss authorities in denying to him jurisdictional immunity was in accordance with international law. At the same time I feel bound to attempt to answer the question whether the manner in which the Swiss authorities exercised their undoubted legal right was not such as to affect the legal position in the matter. International law knows of situations in which, though a State may be entitled to adopt certain measures, the manner in which it exercises its right may engage its responsibility or constitute an unfriendly act. Thus although a State may expel aliens at discretion the manner in which that right is exercised is not wholly irrelevant; the same applies to the way in which a State uses its undoubted right of excluding certain categories of aliens from admission into its territory. The answer to the question whether in any particular instance the manner in which a State has availed itself of its rights constitutes an abuse of a right and, consequently, an international delinquency or whether it is merely an offence against international comity and good neighbourliness must depend upon the circumstances of each individual case.

40 The question which, with regard to the unfortunate incident

with which the present opinion is concerned, requires consideration is whether, although the Swiss Government was entitled to deny diplomatic immunities to a person whom it had never accepted as a member of the diplomatic mission, its conduct was not in some way prejudicial to the authority and sanctity of one of the oldest and most universally recognized institutions of international law – the principle of diplomatic immunity. Undoubtedly the sacrosanctity of that principle is not absolute. Courts, while anxious to respect and to maintain it, have safeguarded its usefulness by curtailing its abuses and exaggerations. Occasionally, they have distinguished between activities which can validly be covered by the principle of immunity and those which must be left outside it. They have often and implicitly discouraged reliance on diplomatic immunity for purposes alien to its true function. But, by and large, they have treated it as a venerable international institution the history of which goes back to antiquity. So has the practice of States notwithstanding the fact that recent developments in communications and transmission of news have affected some aspects of the diplomatic function and although the general deterioration of international relations and modern practices of propaganda have prompted some States to use diplomatic privilege for purposes inimical to the security and interests of the receiving State.

41 While bearing all these considerations in mind I am unable to say that the conduct of the Swiss authorities in this matter – although justified in law – was fully in keeping with the general authority of diplomatic privilege which States ought to respect even if confronted with conduct over which they rightly feel indignant. Undoubtedly, the outright rejection of M. Vitianu might have been inconvenient inasmuch as it might have provided him with a warning and – by prompting him to leave the country – might have interfered with the course of justice. It is possible that at the time of the notification of his appointment no sufficient proof was yet available of his alleged criminal activities. But it is clear from the material supplied to me by the Swiss authorities that there was sufficient evidence justifying his rejection as a *persona non grata* – assuming that much justification is necessary at all. What the Swiss authorities did – apparently with the object of gaining time – was to keep the Roumanian Legation in suspense as to their final intentions. As the result, although M. Vitianu had certainly no reason to assume that his appointment had been accepted, he had no definite indication that it would be rejected. In thus acting, the Swiss authorities made the operation of diplomatic immunity the object of a delaying device. They laid themselves open to the reproach of a questionable practice in a matter of fundamental significance in international

law. There is a substantial gap between ostensible signs of hesitation in accepting a designated member of a diplomatic mission and arresting him without having previously taken the obvious step of expressly rejecting him. Diplomatic privilege is one of the bulwarks of traditional international law. Greatest care must be exercised to avoid any appearance of lack of respect for its authority even in cases when the receiving State is acting in accordance with its strict legal right.

42 The Swiss Government may maintain that they owed no moral or other duty of punctilious consideration to a mission and to a Government which, in their view, outrageously abused the facilities of diplomatic intercourse. I do not feel called upon to pronounce on any such contention. But I submit respectfully that some such duty was owed, generally, to the principle of diplomatic immunity as such and to the generality of States interested in it. In so far as the accused suffered from a disregard by the Swiss Government of these considerations I submit that in case the Federal Court should find him to be subject to its jurisdiction, and sentence him after conviction, the legal position of Switzerland thus authoritatively ascertained would not be prejudiced if the executive or legislative authorities of Switzerland to whom the constitution of the country has entrusted the prerogative of pardon were to consider whether the circumstances of the case do not warrant a remission or a mitigation of the sentence. This they may feel at liberty to do after the Swiss highest tribunal, justly renowned for an impartial administration of international law, has pronounced upon the legal position and after the Swiss authorities have so vigorously asserted the principle that they would not tolerate the abuse of diplomatic immunity. The Swiss authorities may feel inclined, by a statesmanlike act of clemency, to terminate an incident in which they successfully asserted the correct legal position in circumstances which may have given rise to plausible criticism of the manner in which they exercised their juridical right. In so far as the manner of the exercise of an international right has a bearing on the general authority of the principles on which it is based and on international comity I feel that advice of this nature is not altogether outside the province of a legal opinion. Possibly the Swiss Government or Parliament might be more inclined to act in the way suggested if the Roumanian Government, in their turn, were willing to offer some satisfaction for appointing a person by way of a clear abuse of the right of diplomatic appointment – assuming that the evidence before the Court shows that an abuse of a right had in fact taken place. However, I venture to submit that even in the absence of some such satisfaction on the part of the Roumanian

Government, the Swiss authorities might properly consider action of the kind intimated above.

9. CONCLUSIONS

I I am of the opinion that, in assuming criminal jurisdiction over a person appointed as a subordinate member of the Roumanian Legation but not accepted as such by Switzerland, the Swiss authorities have not acted contrary to international law. Swiss Courts are entitled to exercise criminal jurisdiction over M. Vitianu.

II I am of the opinion that, in the eventuality envisaged in section 8 of the present opinion, it would be proper for the competent authorities of Switzerland to consider the adoption of a course of action which may commend itself to them owing to the circumstances and the manner in which they exercised their undoubted right under international law.

PART VI

LAW OF INTERNATIONAL GOVERNMENT, ADMINISTRATION AND CO-OPERATION

CHAPTER I

THE PRINCIPLES OF INTERNATIONAL ORGANIZATION

Editor's note This chapter is full of interest to the historian of international law and organization. It consists of an essay on the principal problems affecting the drafting of the constitution of a new general international organization to replace the League of Nations. So far as can be ascertained, the piece has not previously been published, though some signs of the thinking that went into it may be perceived in the section on 'The Principles of International Organization' which introduces the chapter on 'The Legal Organization of the International Community' in the eighth edition of volume I of Oppenheim's *International Law* (1955), pp. 370–80.

The present chapter must be ranked as one of the most practical in Lauterpacht's writing. For one thing, the directness and comparative simplicity of the style will be noted. For another, Lauterpacht here shows a very real sense of what is called for and what is capable of achievement – particularly in his emphasis on universality, on the prohibition of recourse to force, on the enforcement of that prohibition by common action and on the need for majority voting. He identified too, though not in terms which would have withstood the vast expansion during the later 1950s and the 1960s of the membership of the international community, the essential need to provide for peaceful change in the content of the law.

The copy of the essay found in Lauterpacht's papers bears the heading 'British Committee for the Consideration of the Principles of International Law and Organization'. Of whom this Committee consisted; what it did; when it functioned – all these are questions to which it has not been possible to find an answer. The Committee appears to have left no printed record of its existence. Otherwise, one might have expected to find some mention of it in, for example, a footnote in Oppenheim, I. Thus it is impossible to determine with full confidence when Lauterpacht's undated memorandum was prepared.

In contrast with Lauterpacht's other writings, this one contains neither footnotes nor references to any other contemporary materials except the League of Nations *Statistical Yearbook 1940–1941*. The only helpful clue is in the footnote where he refers to 'the document prepared by the American Committee' and to 'consultation with our American colleagues'. Clearly, at the time when Lauterpacht wrote, 'the American document' – if it had indeed even been prepared – was not yet available, for, if it had been, Lauterpacht would undoubtedly have referred to it. So even the identity of the American document and the American Committee is uncertain. But we do know that Lauterpacht was in the United States in the autumn of 1941 and the early months of 1942. In a long letter to Sir Stephen Gaselee, the

Librarian of the Foreign Office, dated 30 March 1942 reporting on his activities in the United States, Lauterpacht mentioned that he had taken part in the Conference on legal studies of post-war problems convened in Atlantic City at the end of February, 1942 by the International Law Division of the Carnegie Endowment for International Peace. Although this meeting is not expressly mentioned in the Preparatory Note to 'The International Law of the Future – Postulates, Principles and Proposals' which was published by the Carnegie Endowment on 1 January 1944 (reprinted in *A.J.* 38 (1944), Supplement, pp. 44–139), it seems likely that the meeting was one at which some consideration was given to this subject. There is, therefore, a distinct possibility that on his return to England in March 1942 Lauterpacht began to work independently, but on the same subject, as his American colleagues and that his reference in the final note of his essay to the work of the American Committee is in fact a reference to the work which was evolving in the United States during 1942 and 1943. It is interesting too, that this American publication was one of the only two productions of a private organization referred to in Oppenheim 1, 402, n. 1, where Lauterpacht writes about the evolution of the Charter of the United Nations. The other was the work of the Commission to study the Organization of Peace.

There is another possible explanation of the reference to 'the American Committee'. In the early part of 1942 the United States Department of State established an Advisory Committee on Post-War Foreign Policy. This set up a Sub-committee on Political Problems which, in its turn, established a special sub-committee on international organization. By 14 July 1943 this sub-committee had produced a 'draft constitution of international organization' (see Department of State, *Postwar Foreign Policy Preparation 1939–1945* (1949), pp. 71, 96, 108 and 472). But the likelihood of this explanation being correct is small, if only because the work of this official group appears to have received virtually no publicity at the time.

Thus we are led to the general conclusion that Lauterpacht's memorandum was probably written in the second half of 1942 or sometime in 1943, before he had any opportunity to see the drafts prepared by either of the groups, official and unofficial, working in the United States.

The present statement of principles is not intended as a detailed scheme of the future international organization. Its purpose is to formulate and discuss the principles on which the international political organization of States ought to be based. For this reason, it must be made clear at the outset that what follows is not an exposition of the existing law on the subject. In its essential aspects it is a proposal for far-reaching changes in the law. But a correct appreciation and understanding of the existing law is a necessary condition of the satisfactory fulfilment of any such task. The formulation and consideration of proposals for a future international organization must therefore be regarded as being properly within the province of international lawyers.

It is convenient to set forth at the beginning of the present document the proposed principles of international organization. The term 'society of nations' is used provisionally as denoting the future political international organization of States; the terms 'General Council' and 'General Assembly' are used as referring to its two principal organs.

1. *Universality*

Organized international society must be established on the basis of universality. Its membership must be compulsory for all independent States, including those defeated in the [Second World] War. Within a universal international organization bearing effective responsibility for the preservation of peace in all parts of the world there is no room, save in a transitional period pending the firm establishment of the new international system, for regional groupings and alliances of States set up for the sole purpose of acting as a parallel and supplementary agency for maintaining and ensuring peace.

2. *Continuity*

The future international organization must make the fullest use of the experience and the institutions of the League of Nations. It must be a matter for consideration whether the interests of the society of nations will be best served if it is made to function as a continuation of the League of Nations, with a radically amended Covenant, or whether an entirely new international organization is set up with a constitution of its own.

3. *Prohibition of war and of armed force*

The unqualified prohibition of recourse to war and other forms of armed force for giving effect to claims, legal or otherwise, must form an integral part of the constitution of the Society of Nations.

4. *Obligatory rule of law*

The principle of the rule of law in international society implies that there can be no limit to the obligatory jurisdiction of international tribunals save that inherent in the nature of their judicial function, namely, in their duty to apply existing law. That principle excludes reservations either of a specific character or in the form of the traditional distinction between justiciable and non-justiciable disputes. At the same time, that principle is not inconsistent with the exclusion from the purview of compulsory judicial settlement of disputes arising out of the conduct of belligerent operations or of claims to territory which has been subject to the sovereignty of a State for a prolonged period of time.

5. *Collective security and enforcement of the law*

Collective security, conceived as the enforcement by common action of the prohibition of aggressive war and of decisions of international courts and tribunals, must constitute the principal aim of the society of nations. Collective security in that sense must include the legal obligation of its members to participate in military and economic measures prescribed by the society of nations and the legal power of its highest organs to initiate and to direct such common action. The problem of an international police force and of the limitation of armaments must be viewed in the light of the system of collective security thus instituted.

6. *Peaceful change and international legislation*

It is essential for the satisfactory working and development of the international system and of international law, as well as for the observance and the enforcement of the obligations of judicial settlement and of the prohibition of resort to force, that there should exist an effective procedure for the peaceful change of the existing law as part of a more comprehensive machinery of international legislation. The latter must be limited to matters of international concern. Questions relating to the territorial integrity of States and to their exclusive right to regulate the admission of aliens must remain outside the province of international legislation.

7. *The principle of majority rule*

The abandonment of the principle of unanimity in matters of international legislation and otherwise and its replacement by a flexible system of qualified and simple majorities is an indispensable condition of a sound international order and of satisfactory international government. The abandonment of the principle of unanimity is, in turn, conditioned by the relinquishment of that aspect of the doctrine of equality of States which expresses itself in equality of voting power and of representation.

8. *International recognition and protection of the rights of man*

The international recognition and effective protection of fundamental human rights, either through an international Bill of the rights of man forming part of the constitution of the society of nations or in some other manner, is an important condition of international peace, of social progress upon which peace depends, and of the moral authority of international organization and law.

9. *Co-ordination of international administration*

The effective co-ordination of autonomous organs of international administration set up on a functional basis under the aegis of the society of nations and within the framework of international government must form part of the constitution of the society of nations.

10. *The constitution of the international organization and the peace settlement*

While the society of nations ought to be established concurrently with the peace settlement, after adequate preparation in the period between the armistice and the conclusion of peace, it must be independent of any peace treaties terminating the Second World War and free of responsibility for ensuring the execution of any of their specific clauses.

I. UNIVERSALITY

Organized international society must be established on the basis of universality. Its membership must be compulsory for all independent States, including those defeated in the [Second World] War. Within a universal international organization bearing effective responsibility for the preservation of peace in all parts of the world there is no room, save in a transitional period pending the firm establishment of the new international system, for regional groupings and alliances of States set up for the sole purpose of acting as a parallel and supplementary agency for maintaining and ensuring peace.

1 The question of universality is one of the fundamental problems of international organization. It is of a significance transcending the necessity of securing effective collective action for enforcing the obligations of pacific settlement and of international law in general. It was largely from this latter point of view that the question of the universality of the League of Nations was discussed, in particular in connection with the work of the Committee appointed by the Council to consider the means for amending the Covenant and rendering it more effective. Thus conceived, the discussion tended to terminate in a deadlock inasmuch as it led to two equally discouraging alternatives: a League apparently effective because of the fullness and the clarity of the obligation to enforce peace but depleted and weakened by the absence of States unwilling to subscribe to its far-reaching obligations; or a League approaching universality because rendered acceptable to all – or almost all – States on account of the limited character of its obligations, but for that very reason doomed to ineffectiveness in the fulfilment of its major purpose.

2 It is probable that an international organization comprising an overwhelming majority of the Great Powers would be able, even without being universal, to act successfully as an agency for enforcing peace and securing international co-operation. The absence of universality in the League of Nations was often adduced as a reason for its inability to apply the sanctions of the Covenant with a full measure of effectiveness, but it may be doubted whether there was substance in that particular explanation. The fact is that for the first fifteen years of its existence the overwhelming majority of States was represented in the League and – if the Covenant had contained binding obligations to that effect and if there had been a determination to act upon those obligations – the League would have been in a position to bring a decisive accumulation of power to bear upon a Covenant-breaking State. No such accumulation of power is probable under an international system in which the responsibility for maintaining and enforcing the peace is made to rest upon regional groupings and alliances. For this reason the necessity for full effectiveness and certainty in the enforcement of peace is not so much an argument in favour of universality as one against a regional organization of peace.

3 In fact, the argument in support of the universality of the future international organization of States rests upon considerations weightier than the effectiveness of collective action in the military and economic spheres. In the first instance, any international system which is regional in character is by this very fact a potential danger to peace. Large groupings of States, unless operating under the shelter and regulative power of a world-embracing rule of law, are in themselves a likely source of inter-regional strife and conflict.

4 This negative, though not unimportant, aspect of the problem is of comparatively minor significance when related to the fact that international peace, the securing of which is the primary purpose of all international organization, is in a fundamental sense indivisible and that its enforcement must therefore rest on the basis of universality. The indivisibility of peace has been denied by a school of thought which styles itself realist, on the ground that States cannot be expected to undertake and fulfil the ultimate obligations of collective security where their vital interests are not at stake; and it has been frequently assailed by apologists of aggressive States bent on piecemeal conquest. The indivisibility of peace must nevertheless be regarded as axiomatic and, with it, the universality of international organization as an expression of the universality of the interest in the maintenance of peace. The triumphant assertion of force in one part of the world results in a weakening of the authority of the law everywhere. Successful lawless-

ness is infectious and is an encouragement to aggression. Moreover, there is no psychological or political limit to the mentality of conquest. The aggressor will in due course turn to further conquests in other regions in order to make secure those already accomplished.

5 From a wider point of view, the universality of the political organization of States would give expression to – as on any rational principle it follows from – the interdependence of the world and the unity of the human race. A regional grouping for the purpose of preserving peace is, in essence, an alliance. It is a political device not grounded in any moral appeal transcending the interests of the parties thereto. An international system built on any principle other than that of universality would be deprived of a vital element of authority, dignity and inspiration. It would negative one of the most significant and persistent aspirations of mankind.

6 At the same time, those who urge the desirability of a universal society of nations must realize the revolutionary nature of the innovation which it would introduce into international law. For the universality of international organization is more than a question of comprehensiveness and accessibility. A universal organization is not only one which is open to all States which desire to enter it and from which no State can be excluded as a punishment either for previous misdeeds or, after admission, for non-fulfilment of its obligations. A universal international organization is one which all States are compelled to join and from which no withdrawal is legally possible. If the universal organization thus created did not imply any additional obligations; if it had no power of decision over its members; and if its action depended invariably upon their unanimous consent – the derogation of sovereignty implicit in such compulsory membership would still be considerable. But a compulsory universal organization which has the ultimate power to decide disputes between its members; which implies the prohibition (and the enforcement of that prohibition) of recourse to war and armed force between them; which can revise treaties; which can alter the legal rights of its members by legislative processes either incidental to the settlement of disputes or independently of it – and, as is submitted later in this draft, no satisfactory international organization can be conceived which does not wield these powers – such a compulsory international organization constitutes a stupendous and, in theory, irrevocable limitation of sovereignty.

7 A compulsory universal organization of States which all must enter, from which no one is allowed to secede, and from which no one can be expelled, is no longer a mere compact of sovereign States. It is a union exercising effective authority over its members, a union more

integrated than a mere confederation of States, a union indissoluble by any legal means except, possibly, the amendment of its constitution. The fact is that once a State has assumed membership of a wider society from which no withdrawal is legally possible and which has been endowed with legislative powers, it has thereby irrevocably consented to a fundamental limitation of its sovereignty. As a matter of legal theory, it is doubtful whether the extent of that limitation can be circumscribed with finality in the original constitution – even if, on the analogy of some federal constitutions, there is adopted as part of the fundamental charter of the society of nations a definite barrier to the legislative competence of the international organization. The States of the American Union are sovereign States. The Constitution guarantees to them certain rights and reserves certain matters to their exclusive jurisdiction. But that sovereignty and those guarantees are subject to the measureless possibilities of constitutional amendment and to the less conspicuous but in the long run equally effective levelling processes of judicial interpretation.

8 These are the possible consequences of the principle of universality of the international organization. Some of them are to a large extent in the domain of theoretical contingencies – just as the repeal of the Statute of Westminster and the reassertion by the Imperial Parliament of its former supremacy are a theoretical possibility of negligible political importance. But other consequences of the principle of universality are less theoretical, and it is proper that they should be clearly stated and carefully considered. They do not in any way impair the conclusion here adopted that the future international organization must be erected on the basis of universality in the full meaning of the term. But it is imperative to face at the outset the difficulties and the problems involved in the principle of universality.

9 The same applies to the question as to the means by which universality, conceived as compulsory membership, should be given effect. The answer to this question is comparatively simple. The principle of compulsory membership would have to be adopted concurrently with the decision to establish an international organization. The adoption of that principle would be in the nature of a legislative act of international policy of the very highest order. But, once adopted, it would automatically assume as existing the membership of all States and subject them to all the obligations of the constitution of the international organization, including those relating to obligatory judicial settlement of disputes and pacific settlement in general. The question of compelling States to accept membership would not arise. Membership would be assumed and declared to exist. The only question would be that of

enforcing the obligations of membership. It would be a matter for a recalcitrant State to consider to what extent it should avail itself of the rights and benefits accruing from membership of the organization.

10 It is implied in the principle of universality that the constitution of the society of nations must exclude expulsion as a means of punishment. Other methods of punishment, more direct and effective and more in keeping with the nature and purpose of the society of nations, must be adopted. Neither can there be room for withdrawal. The experience of the League of Nations has shown how the membership of what was at the outset an almost universal organization can be whittled down by withdrawal resorted to for petty or unworthy reasons.

11 For these reasons the society of nations must demand and acquiesce in the membership of Germany, Italy and Japan and of their minor satellites. It would run contrary to the purpose of the organization and seriously impair its moral authority if, even if only for a transitional period, it were to be limited to what are often described as the 'peace-loving nations'. Such discrimination against the defeated States as may be dictated by considerations of justice and expediency can properly take place within the framework of the society of nations.

12 In connection with the universality of the future international organization, there must be considered the problem of regional groupings within the society of nations. There would in any case appear to be no inconsistency between the character and purposes of the society of nations and the existence of particular associations in the form of federal States or other unions of States, like the British Commonwealth of Nations, organically bound together for a variety of objects including that of external defence. On the contrary, within the comprehensive system of a universal association of States such groupings established on a federal or similar basis would fulfil the incidental but significant function of providing a working example of a more integrated international organization. Neither would it be inconsistent with the purposes of a universal international organization to encourage regional or similar groupings for administrative, economic or cultural co-operation, like the Pan-American Union as at present constituted. But regional groupings or alliances intended as an auxiliary instrument of security and of enforcement of peace are in a different category. After the universal international organization has become a firmly established and well-tried instrument of peace, supplementary agencies would become unnecessary. They might constitute a source of danger and an inducement for the international organization to divest itself of its responsibilities. For this reason, there ought to be no room in the

constitution of the society of nations for an unqualified provision such as is contained in Article 21 of the Covenant of the League of Nations. On the other hand, it must be borne in mind that in its initial stages the international organization will be an untried instrument. It would be contrary to the duties of wise statesmanship and to the best interests of the world to rely on it as the sole safeguard of peace. This means that during a transitory period, which may last one or two generations, alliances, regional and others, of separate and independent States for the purpose of securing peace might properly be declared to be consistent with the objects of the society of nations.

2. THE PRINCIPLE OF CONTINUITY

The future international organization must make the fullest use of the experience and the institutions of the League of Nations. It must be a matter for consideration whether the interests of the society of nations will be best served if it is made to function as a continuation of the League of Nations, with a radically amended Covenant, or whether an entirely new international organization is set up with a constitution of its own.

13 Ought the future international organization to be, in law, a continuation of the League of Nations, or ought it to be based on an entirely new compact between States and a newly devised machinery? The problem is one of a significance deeper than mere expediency. The argument in favour of the second alternative has been repeatedly stated: the League of Nations failed because of its inherent shortcomings, and this is in itself a sufficient and cogent reason why any association with it must be abandoned. The answer often given to this manner of reasoning is well known. It is that the failure of the League was due neither to the excessively ambitious scope of the Covenant, as maintained by some, nor to the insufficiency of the obligations which it imposed upon its Members, as asserted by others, but to the failure of Governments to implement the law of the Covenant. The correct appreciation of that fact is, according to the last-mentioned view, of an importance transcending that of mere historic accuracy. On that view it would be disastrous for the future of mankind if peoples could divest themselves of responsibility – be it only moral responsibility – for their actions by attaching blame to the inadequacy of institutions which they themselves created. To jettison the League on account of a failure which was due to 'it' and which can be remedied by the creation of a new organization, would mean to forgo a most important lesson of experience. On that view, in so far as the fate of the League was due to the imperfections of its Covenant, the remedy would lie in the

amendment of that instrument. In so far as its failure was due to causes outside its Covenant, the creation of a new organization would be clearly in the nature of a *non sequitur*.

14 This manner of assessing the experience of the League of Nations and its lesson for the future international organization is, it is believed, entitled to respect. At the same time, it must be borne in mind that what is often described as the failure of the members of the League to implement the Covenant was not a persistent refusal to give effect to clear legal obligations. For, in the main, the Covenant imposed no clear obligations either with regard to the duty not to resort to war or, in particular, with regard to the obligation to suppress unlawful use of force. Thus, for instance, in the course of the Manchurian dispute, the crucial event in the history of the League, the Members of the League by abstaining from finding – as they were entitled to abstain – that there had been 'resort to war' on the part of Japan, escaped any legal obligation to apply the sanctions of Article 16. Even in cases where resort to war (or force) was clearly unlawful and was found to be so, the Members of the League were under no positive obligation to suppress by military force the violation of the Covenant – though the latter *authorized* them to act in that capacity. The failure of the Members of the League to act on that authorization may have been politically and morally reprehensible. For it was a failure to act on an authorization of the Covenant to coerce the aggressor by swift and overwhelming force with a probability of success approaching certainty and with a determination commensurate with the challenge thrown out to the new international system and to the best hopes of mankind. It is true that on occasion there was a failure to fulfil a clear legal obligation. There was, for instance, no warrant in the Covenant itself – as distinguished from the Resolutions of the Assembly adopted in 1921 – for the modified, gradual and devitalized application of economic sanctions against Italy in 1935 and 1936. However, it is doubtful whether economic sanctions, even if fully applied, would have had the effect of decisively influencing the conduct of an aggressor.

15 The Covenant of the League of Nations introduced significant and, in a sense, revolutionary innovations consisting in the limitation of the right of war (though not necessarily of force short of war), in the right of intervention by the League in disputes between its Members, and in the principle of enforcing the obligations of the Covenant in the matter of pacific settlement. But otherwise it was deficient in vital respects. It did not prohibit altogether recourse to war. Even the limitation of the right of war was rendered uncertain inasmuch as it did not necessarily extend to resort to force. The Covenant failed to recognize

the principle of obligatory judicial settlement of disputes. Partly as a consequence of that omission, it transformed the Council into the main agency for settling disputes between the Members of the League. The result, paradoxical and disastrous, was that the principal organ of the League was deflected from devoting most of its energies to the creative tasks of international administration and initiation of international legislation. The Covenant rendered the enforcement of the obligations of pacific settlement largely illusory by confining any legal duty in this respect to economic sanctions, for the effective organization of which it contained no provision. There is no escape from the fact that in the Covenant the concessions which sovereign States made to the principle of order and subjection to law were hesitating and, in the result, inconsiderable; that no determined attempt was made to break away from some of the most retrogressive principles of international law, like the admissibility of war and the absence of a duty to resort to the compulsory process of law; and that in these and other respects the authors of the Covenant failed to capitalize the general sentiment of the world at the end of the First World War and the lessons of the period which preceded it. The Covenant adhered fully to the disintegrating and essentially unworkable principle of unanimity. It took over, to a large extent, the obsolete and obstructive doctrine of equality of States. It failed to provide for international legislation. Its provisions as to peaceful change were nominal in the extreme. There was no room in it for the protection, through an international guarantee of the rights of man, of those principles of democracy which by common consent were deemed essential to the peace of the world. The question must be faced as to how far – if at all – it is desirable to build the future international organization on the basis of a constitution so defective in vital respects.

16 There is an additional factor of importance which must be taken into account. The Covenant was, as pointed out, deficient in vital respects. Some of its unsatisfactory features were clearly expressed and impervious to any ameliorative interpretation. On the other hand, some of its principal provisions were sufficiently elastic to render possible a progressive construction favourable to the requirements of peace and order. Of these, Article 11 – a provision of great potentialities – afforded an instructive example. The Council of the League interpreted it as requiring the absolute unanimity of all its Members, including the vote of the State charged with a violation of the Covenant, for the legal validity of decisions taken by the Council in pursuance of its duty to take steps deemed wise and effectual for maintaining the peace of the world. That interpretation did not follow inevitably from

the terms of the Covenant; in the view of many it was contrary to an accepted principle of jurisprudence. In an analogous situation the Permanent Court of International Justice held, in the advisory opinion concerning the *Mosul Boundary*, that the jurisprudential principle which demands that no one can be judge in his own cause applied to the function of the Council as an arbitrator notwithstanding the provisions of the Covenant in the matter of unanimity. The fact is that in the two decades which followed the World War the elasticity of the Covenant, which some considered to be one of its chief merits, worked in one way only, namely, in the direction of stressing the freedom of action of the Members of the League and of restricting the effective authority of the League of Nations. The conservative manner in which the Council of the League interpreted the general guarantee of the Minorities Treaties, in the sense of excluding any permanent machinery of supervision, is another example of the same process. In that atmosphere a body of law, in the form of the decisions and the practice of the organs of the League, was engrafted upon the Covenant which in the eyes of many has still further reduced its usefulness and authority. To neutralize the effect of that practice, interpretative amendments of the Covenant would be necessary. Thus the question arises whether it is practicable to continue on the basis of a Covenant abounding not only in inherent shortcomings of its own but burdened with the *damnosa heredita*s of a timid and sterile interpretation in a period of retrogression.

17 There is a still further difficulty in the way of proceeding on the basis of the Covenant. The backbone of the Covenant is the machinery for settling disputes between the Members of the League and for preserving the peace. But that machinery was built on the assumption that war, subject to procedural restraints, continued to be a legal right of States; that resort to force, though possibly limited, was not prohibited; and that there existed, in principle, no obligation to resort to courts for the purpose of settling disputes. These features of the Covenant explain the multiplicity and the elaborate nature of its articles relating to the settlement of disputes. They also explain why the Council, the principal organ of the League, instead of remaining free to devote itself fully to the tasks of international government and legislation as well as to the executive enforcement of peace, was saddled – and mostly occupied – with the function of settling disputes. From this point of view it is questionable whether the existing structure of the Covenant is an adequate basis for an international organization built on more advanced principles.

18 There is no doubt that the existing Covenant could be amended to include the desired fundamental changes. There is room for the

view that even after these drastic alterations have been effected, the retention of the Covenant as such, far from being a mere formality, would have the advantage of preserving the continuity of the greatest political advance made by the society of nations in the direction of securing international peace and order. However, any such continuity would probably be merely symbolic.

19 In fact, the principle of continuity in relation to the League of Nations may mean either formal continuity in relation to the Covenant of the League and its institutions or substantive continuity with the idea of the League as the first historic attempt to set up on the basis of universality an association of States for the purpose of maintaining and enforcing the peace of the world. If continuity in the first sense may not be feasible in its entirety owing to the undoubted necessity of far-reaching changes in the existing constitution of the League, the second may not be altogether without significance. The continuity thus conceived would be, in a sense, a negative one. The Covenant of the League would live in the constitution of the society of nations by dint of that very advance which it failed to achieve but which its experience showed to be imperative. Finally, a most substantial element of continuity could – and ought to – be achieved in any case by incorporating into the structure of the new international organization those institutions of the League in the field of economic co-operation, communications and transit, health, mandatory government, regulation of the use of narcotics and dangerous drugs, and scientific and intellectual co-operation, whose record has been one of unchallenged utility and success.

20 The decision as to which line of continuity is to govern the form and the substance of the future international organization is essentially a political one. That decision need not be exclusively determined either by the view that the League of Nations must be discarded because it 'failed' or that the existing Covenant provides the only or the most satisfactory basis for continuing the advance, begun by the League, towards the political integration of mankind.

3. PROHIBITION OF WAR AND OF ARMED FORCE

The unqualified prohibition of recourse to war and other forms of armed force for giving effect to claims, legal or otherwise, must form an integral part of the constitution of the society of nations.

21 The prohibition of war as a legal institution and the enforcement of that prohibition must be regarded as the primary purpose of all political organizations of States. The Covenant of the League of

Nations stopped short of depriving its Members of the right, the unlimited right, which they enjoyed under international law to have recourse to war. It restricted that right by imposing upon the Members of the League the obligation to resort to the machinery of pacific settlement prescribed in the Covenant. In particular, the Members of the League undertook not to go to war against a State complying with a unanimous recommendation under Article 15. But otherwise the Covenant envisaged war as legally permissible not only as a measure of self-defence and of collective enforcement of the Covenant, but also in other cases. War was permissible when one or both parties to a dispute declined to comply with the terms of a unanimous report; when there was a failure to reach a unanimous report; when one or both disputants refused to abide by a judicial decision or arbitral award given in pursuance of Article 12; when the Council declined to act in a dispute held to involve a matter within the exclusive domestic jurisdiction of one party to the dispute; and in other instances. Subsequently, practically all the Members of the League accepted the obligations of the General Treaty for the Renunciation of War. These obligations signified, notwithstanding the express or implied reservation of self-defence, the elimination of war as an independent right of sovereign States. Attempts were made to bring the Covenant into harmony with the General Treaty for the Renunciation of War, but these efforts had not been brought to fruition at the time of the outbreak of the Second World War.

22 The reasons why the authors of the Covenant omitted to incorporate the full prohibition of war as a fundamental principle of the League have never been satisfactorily explained. The failure to effect that change in international law derogated from the moral authority of the League and was inconsistent with the proclamation of the rule of law under the Covenant. There ought to be no hesitation in adopting to its full extent the law laid down in the Pact of Paris as an integral part of the constitution of the future organization of States as well as of the municipal law of the individual States.

23 In connection with the prohibition of war, the so-called reservation of self-defence must be given a clear and authoritative answer. That reservation, even if not expressed, necessarily underlies all renunciation of war or of force. The State which deems itself menaced in its existence as the result of an actual attack upon its territory or its armed forces must judge for itself whether circumstances require action in self-defence. But that judgment cannot claim finality. The legitimacy of armed action claimed to have been taken in self-defence must in case of doubt be subject to the final determination of an impartial authority.

That determination will be aided by the express adoption of the principle that the test of aggression is intrinsically simple and that only actual invasion of territory or actual attack upon the armed forces of the State can be regarded as justifying recourse to force in self-defence. There cannot be room for the refinements which underlay some of the definitions of aggression in the past, such as the toleration of armed bands threatening to invade the territory of a neighbouring State. Neither can the anticipation of what a State believes to be an impending attack be allowed to confuse a clear and working test of self-defence. Protection against any such dangers and illegalities must be sought in the ordinary judicial and political remedies available under the constitution of the Society of Nations.

24 The international organization of the future must go beyond both the Covenant and the Pact of Paris by prohibiting not only recourse to war but recourse to force generally. The authors of the Covenant deliberately - but, as subsequent experience showed, with fatal results - limited the obligations of the Covenant in this matter to recourse to war. The Committee of Jurists appointed subsequent to the Italian attack on Corfu - an event which thrust the thin end of the wedge of disintegration into the edifice of the League - expressed the view that recourse to measures of force short of war may or may not be inconsistent with the obligations of the Covenant and that it was for the Council in each case to decide, having regard to the circumstances of the situation, whether the measures of force ought to be maintained, modified or withdrawn. The improvement resulting from that interpretation was insignificant. There is no reason of sufficient importance why international society should prohibit recourse to formal war in its technical sense but stop short of forbidding resort to armed force short of war. Any such differentiation is unreal and threatens to frustrate the major purpose of eliminating war as an actual occurrence in the relations of States.

25 Moreover, it must remain a matter for consideration whether, in an international system of which the principle of obligatory judicial settlement of disputes and of enforcement of decisions given in pursuance thereof forms an integral part, there is room for reprisals even if they do not involve the use of force. The *raison d'être* of the institution of reprisals is the assumption that in the absence of remedies for a violation of a legal right the injured State must take the law into its own hands by committing an otherwise illegal act. That assumption disappears once the duty of judicial settlement and of compliance with decisions given in pursuance thereof is adopted as a general principle. It must be for the international authority and not the injured State to

draw the necessary consequences from a failure to comply with that duty.

4. THE OBLIGATORY RULE OF LAW

The principle of the rule of law in international society implies that there can be no limit to the obligatory jurisdiction of international tribunals save that inherent in the nature of their judicial function, namely, in their duty to apply existing law. That principle excludes reservations either of a specific character or in the form of the traditional distinction between justiciable and non-justiciable disputes. At the same time, that principle is not inconsistent with the exclusion from the purview of compulsory judicial settlement of disputes arising out of the conduct of belligerent operations or of claims to territory which has been subject to the sovereignty of a State for a prolonged period of time.

26 The principle of the rule of law in international society implies that the lawfulness of any claim put forward by one State against another is subject to the compulsory jurisdiction of international tribunals and that international society assumes responsibility for the enforcement, if need be, of decisions given by these tribunals. This principle has not so far formed part of international law. The Covenant of the League of Nations did not adopt it – although, according to some, it came near to recognizing it with regard to the comprehensive, though vague, classes of dispute enumerated in Article 13. Subsequently, the obligations of compulsory judicial settlement between Members of the League reached substantial proportions through the Optional Clause and various treaties. All these instruments were concluded for a limited period of years, and this fact, as well as the far-reaching reservations usually attaching to them, emphasized the absence in international society of a principle universally operative within the State. It is significant that the majority of the judgments of the Permanent Court of International Justice have been concerned with a plea to the jurisdiction of the Court on the part of the defendant State.

27 The rule, which is still part of international law, that every State is, in principle, entitled to be judge in its own cause and to refuse to another State which puts forward a claim the benefit of a judicial determination of its legal validity, must be abandoned expressly and emphatically. Its relinquishment must form an integral part of the basic constitutional instrument of international society.

28 The fundamental change inherent in the adoption of the principle of the obligatory jurisdiction of international tribunals would be inconsistent with the maintenance of the practice of reservations as such

or under the guise of the traditional distinction between so-called legal and so-called political disputes. That distinction has been widely – almost universally – adopted in instruments of pacific settlement. It has acquired the character of a sound and obvious limitation of the jurisdiction of international tribunals. In fact, however, the only proper limitation upon the jurisdiction of international tribunals – as, indeed, of all judicial tribunals – consists in the fact that they administer law and must not administer anything else. But this is not a limitation which can be safeguarded by a legal proviso or a technique of reservations – just as judicial impartiality cannot be secured by such means. Both are inherent and of necessity assumed in the judicial function. Undoubtedly, a tribunal cannot *settle* a dispute arising out of a claim which is unsupported by law – if to settle a dispute means to reach a solution which is satisfactory to both parties or which is desirable politically irrespective of its legal merits. What a tribunal can do is formally to dismiss such a claim and to divest it of any pretence of legality. Such adjudication by a tribunal need not preclude the subsequent examination of the dispute by a political organ.

29 It must also become axiomatic that the jurisdiction of international tribunals applying law cannot be limited by reference to the importance of the subject matter of the dispute. The only limitation that seems to be admissible is that grounded in the unsuitability of any particular category of disputes, defined with scrupulous precision, to be the subject matter of judicial decision for the reason that with regard to that category of disputes there exists such a pronounced and generally acknowledged absence of agreement as to what constitutes the law as to negative the existence of a body of rules which a tribunal could apply without endangering its authority as an impartial judicial organ. This applies in particular to disputes arising out of belligerent operations, especially at sea. It was that category of disputes which was largely responsible for the comprehensive and vague reservation of 'past disputes' in the Optional Clause and elsewhere. A specific reservation of these disputes could be generally declared without jeopardizing the effectiveness and the authority of the principle of compulsory adjudication of disputes. It would find sufficient explanation in the fact that, in the matter of the law of the sea, the divergencies of principle and of practice are such as to preclude the existence of a working body of substantive rules which an international tribunal could apply in the normal exercise of its judicial function. There is, accordingly, no necessity for a sweeping and, essentially, arbitrary, reservation of 'past disputes' to cover a definite category of disputes which, having regard to the position of international law on

the subject and to the best interests of international courts, ought to be excluded from the province of compulsory juridical settlement.

30 The same applies to another group of differences which in the past has been responsible for the insistence on the reservation of 'past disputes'. These are controversies concerning territory over which a State has exercised sovereignty for a considerable period of time and the fate of which it is unwilling to submit to a judicial decision pronouncing upon the legality of the original title. There is room for the view that compulsory judicial settlement ought not to be used as a weapon for challenging long-established titles of this nature. Here, too, the reservation of 'past disputes' is too comprehensive an instrument for achieving the desired object. With regard to territories over which the defendant State has exercised jurisdiction for a considerable period, the intended result could be achieved by a declaration, on the lines of the arbitration agreement preceding the *British Guiana* arbitration, to the effect that undisturbed occupation of territory and exercise of normal attributes of sovereignty therein for a period of fifty years shall, regardless of the mode or circumstances of the original acquisition, constitute a good legal title.

31 These two qualifications – the one relating to belligerent measures, the other to the operation of prescription with regard to acquisition of territorial title – would not in any way impair the principle of obligatory arbitration, which must be considered as an obvious and indispensable part of any international system worthy of the name. It is idle to speculate which is more essential to the existence of a legal order: the obligatory jurisdiction of courts or the enforcement of the law, including the enforcement of the obligation of pacific settlement and of prohibition of war. It is equally irrelevant to consider whether, in the absence of adequate machinery for peaceful change, law in itself is sufficient to secure peace. Even if it were not sufficient it would still be indispensable – although it must be admitted that the degree of its usefulness would be dependent on the rate of parallel progress in other fields, in particular in that of collective security and of the provision of effective machinery for changing the existing law.

32 If and when the principle of compulsory judicial settlement is adopted as an integral part of international law and organization, it will probably become necessary to consider the resulting desirability of changes in the organization of the international judicial system. One of the consequences of compulsory juridical settlement will be an increase in the volume of judicial business, which might impose an undue strain upon the Permanent Court of International Justice as hitherto constituted. There is room for the view that in addition to the

existing Permanent Court of International Justice of fifteen judges, there should be created sub-divisions of that Court located in the principal regions of the world and operating, with the agreement of the parties and subject to a right of appeal to the full Court, as courts of first instance. It might be provided that with regard to some categories of claims, for instance those arising out of alleged injuries to the life and property of aliens, these courts should act as compulsory tribunals of first instance.

5. COLLECTIVE SECURITY AND ENFORCEMENT OF THE LAW

Collective security, conceived as the enforcement by common action of the prohibition of aggressive war and of decisions of international courts and tribunals, must constitute the principal aim of the society of nations. Collective security in that sense must include the legal obligation of its members to participate in military and economic measures prescribed by the society of nations and the legal power of its highest organs to initiate and to direct such common action. The problem of an international police force and of the limitation of armaments must be viewed in the light of the system of collective security thus instituted.

33 The prohibition of resort to war and of force generally, as well as the obligatory jurisdiction of tribunals, have little meaning unless enforced, when necessary, by collective action of the society of nations. In the Covenant of the League of Nations the most significant innovation was the recognition of the principle of the collective enforcement, as against sovereign States, of what was considered to be the fundamental law of the Covenant, namely, its obligations of pacific settlement. The collective enforcement of at least that aspect of the law – including the duty of compulsory juridical settlement and of observance of decisions given in pursuance thereof – must be an essential feature of the future international order.

The Covenant of the League was no less instructive in its positive achievement in laying down the principle of the collective enforcement of the law against sovereign States, than in its failure to make that principle fully effective. The shortcomings of the Covenant in this respect are well known. In the first instance, the Covenant did not confer upon the Assembly or the Council or any other organ of the League the power to declare, with an effect binding upon all Members of the League, whether a State had resorted to war in violation of its obligations. Each Member of the League retained the right to determine for itself whether the conditions of fact giving rise to the duty to apply coercive measures had arisen. The exercise of that right was neither optional nor arbitrary. Members of the League were bound to exercise it, and they were under a duty to exercise it in good faith having regard to the general purpose of the Covenant. But the gist of the legal situation was that the possibility of collective action was to a large extent rendered nominal at the very outset by the absence of any authoritative machinery for finding whether the legal duty had arisen to set it in motion.

34 For these reasons, in the future organization of collective security the highest executive agency must be given the power of finding, by an appropriate majority and with an effect binding on all, whether unlawful resort to war or force has taken place. It must be a matter for consideration whether machinery could be devised for making such a finding subject to confirmation by – or open to appeal before – a judicial body acting with an expedition commensurate with the urgency of the situation. Such confirmation could be dispensed with in cases where the finding of the international authority is unanimous.

35 The second lesson of the Covenant in this respect is that the measures which the members of the society of nations ought to be under a duty to apply as a matter of legal obligation must include armed force. No such duty exists under the Covenant. The limitation of the obligation to apply economic sanctions was the result both of an exaggeration of the effectiveness of the economic weapon and of reluctance, which expressed itself in other Articles of the Covenant, to assume commitments of a far-reaching nature. Experience has shown that economic sanctions are inadequate as a means of coercing an aggressor, especially if the latter is a powerful State attacking a weak neighbour. The unlawful design will be accomplished long before economic pressure has seriously inconvenienced the aggressor. Neither is the economic weapon in the long run a substitute for armed force. When used against a powerful aggressor the economic measures will be tolerated by him only so long as they do not impede his military effort. Thus economic sanctions must either be ineffective or lead to hostilities. As against a small State, military repressive force is the most efficacious and in the long run the most merciful means of coercion. But these considerations, however cogent, shrink into insignificance when related to the fact that it is utterly inconsistent with the notion of a political society under law that an attempt upon the very life of any of its members should be met by any means other than immediate and total application of all available resources of direct and most effective physical force.

36 Thirdly, it follows from what has been said above that not only

must there exist a duty of the members of the society of nations to employ their military forces for the purpose of protecting its fundamental law in face of armed aggression against any of its members. The international authority must be given the power to organize and, by an appropriate majority, to order – and not merely to recommend – the military measures to be taken against the aggressor. No such power was conferred in the Covenant upon any organ of the League.

37 The adoption of the principles outlined above – the right of the international authority to determine the cause of aggression, the duty of the members to apply military force against the aggressor, and the power of the international authority to organize the necessary military action – would provide a substantive solution of the problem of an international police force. For there would then exist an international police force whenever circumstances should call for its being brought into action. There would still remain the question of the desirability of a permanent international police force as well as the further question whether it should be composed of units contributed from the armed forces of the member States or whether it should be recruited by the international authority independently of the armed forces of the member States. These and other questions may be a proper subject of study in the period following the establishment of the new international authority. They would not present a problem of pressing urgency whose solution might complicate or retard the setting up of the international organization.

38 The problem of the limitation of armaments must be viewed in the light of these developments. In the Covenant of the League of Nations the limitation of armaments was linked with and made conditional upon 'the enforcement by common action of international obligations'. The close connection between the maintenance of adequate armed forces by States and the fulfilment of their obligations to enforce peace was abundantly demonstrated in the interval between the two World Wars. It is probable that at the time of the establishment of the League and in the period which followed it the importance of armaments as a psychological cause of and incentive to war was considerably exaggerated, as were the economic causes of war. Some of the most potent causes of war have been its admissibility as a legal institution, the refusal to recognize the obligatory jurisdiction of international tribunals, the absence of effective enforcement of pacific settlement, and the imperfections of the international legislative procedure for amending the existing law. With radical improvements in all these spheres and with the unilateral disarmament, for a considerable period, of States which experience has shown to be a danger to peace,

the armed forces of States will, in essence, constitute the required international police force. This being so, it will be preferable, for an extended transitional period, to leave the problem of limitation of armaments outside the scope of binding legal obligations or even of any urgent concern of the society of nations. After that, it ought to be a matter for consideration to what extent there ought to be created, under the aegis of the international organization, machinery of consultation and information with the view to such progressive reduction of armaments as may be found feasible in the light of the general stabilization of the peace of the world and the increase of confidence and mutual relations of its members.

39 International society must go beyond enforcing that part of international law which prohibits unlawful resort to war and force. It must give effect to all claims based on law and found by an international tribunal to be so based. There must be an enforceable remedy for every injury done without lawful cause. The prohibition of war and other forms of physical force must, in the long run, become unreal if international society does not itself assume ultimate responsibility for giving effect to claims based on law and found to be so. The principle of obligatory judicial settlement has little meaning unless the concomitant principle is adopted that every decision of an international tribunal will be enforced, if need be, by international action. Under a system of obligatory judicial settlement this would signify effective redress for every illegal injury and satisfaction for every claim supported by law. That principle was to some extent recognized in Article 13 of the Covenant, in which Members of the League agreed that they would carry out in full good faith any award that might be rendered by a tribunal and which provided that 'in the event of any failure to carry out such an award or decision, the Council shall propose what steps should be taken to give effect thereto'. The Covenant, it will be noted, spoke of the Council 'proposing' the necessary steps. In an orderly international society the highest executive authority must have the power and the duty to enjoin the measures necessary to give effect to decisions of courts, in the same way as in the case of suppression of unlawful recourse to war and other forms of force. This must be one of the proper and normal tasks of the highest executive organ of the society of nations. Its Executive Council ought not to devote the bulk of its energies to settling disputes. Its proper function is in the realms of co-ordination of international administration, of initiation of and participation in international legislation, and of enforcing international law in general and the obligations of pacific settlement in particular.

6. PEACEFUL CHANGE AND INTERNATIONAL LEGISLATION

It is essential for the satisfactory working and development of the international system and of international law, as well as for the observance and the enforcement of the obligations of judicial settlement and of the prohibition of resort to force, that there should exist an effective procedure for the peaceful change of the existing law as part of a more comprehensive machinery of international legislation. The latter must be limited to matters of international concern. Questions relating to the territorial integrity of States and to their exclusive right to regulate the admission of aliens must remain outside the province of international legislation.

40 The experience of the League of Nations has shown that the principle of the rule of law through obligatory judicial settlement and of enforcement of the prohibition of resort to war are subjected to dangerous strain as the result of the absence of effective provisions for the peaceful change of conditions and obligations resulting both from treaties and from customary international law. Public opinion has shown itself to be sensitive to the anomaly of the situation in which international tribunals are endowed with compulsory jurisdiction to render decisions which, while fully in conformity with existing law, may be inconsistent with considerations of equity, with the requirements of international progress and, ultimately, with international peace itself. The same applies to the enforcement of the obligations of pacific settlement against a State which has resorted to force rather than abide by an intolerable and unalterable *status quo*. The view has been repeatedly expressed that so long as there exists no effective machinery for changing the existing law, the prohibition of war, obligatory judicial settlement and the enforcement of pacific settlement are premature and in the long run deceptive.

41 The school of thought which has been conspicuous in stressing the necessity for machinery of peaceful change and which has explained the failure of the League of Nations by reference to the absence of such machinery, has been open to criticism on two grounds. In the first instance, it has often combined insistence on the necessity for peaceful change with opposition, so long as that machinery did not exist, to progressive developments in the field of collective security and obligatory judicial settlement. To that extent its attitude has been illogical and retrogressive. The advantages of the normal operation of the law through tribunals and agencies enforcing the law outweigh the disadvantages of such injustice as results from the absence of effective machinery for changing the law. Secondly, many advocates of peaceful change have seldom, if ever, been prepared to face or give their consent

to the implications of 'peaceful change' as an effective legal institution. 'Peaceful change' does not mean the willingness of States to agree peacefully to an abandonment of their rights. Neither does it signify machinery of mere consultation and discussion, with that object in view. Ample provision was made for the latter in Article 19 of the Covenant. What it implies is the existence of the institutions by means of which States may be compelled to acquiesce in changes, including the alteration and the impairment of their rights, decreed by an international authority. This is the crucial difficulty of the problem of peaceful change. Peaceful change as an institution of international society is tantamount to international legislation in its most controversial and acute aspect. There has so far been no general disposition to face this dilemma squarely in all its implications. Without such willingness, insistence on 'peaceful change' has little meaning.

42 Effective organs of peaceful change are indispensable to the satisfactory functioning of any political society, including that of the society of nations. But 'peaceful change' is only one aspect of the more general and more significant problem of international legislation. Are sovereign States willing to confer upon an international authority the power to decree changes not only with regard to specific rights which a State enjoys under international law and which have become the subject matter of a dispute, but with regard to needs and situations existing independently of any particular dispute and relating to the general good of the world at large? No substantial and sustained progress in the legal organization of international society and of international peace is likely unless States agree to international legislation thus conceived and implying a limitation of sovereignty more considerable than the principle of obligatory judicial settlement or renunciation of the right to resort to war or armed force.

43 For these reasons, no scheme of international organization can be regarded as adequate which does not include constructive provisions for effective machinery for peaceful change as well as for international legislation in general. Neither can any such scheme be regarded as adequate if, though apparently providing for international legislation, it uses that term in its loose and metaphorical connotation as is the case when unanimity of all or some of the legislative organs is postulated as a condition of valid legislation.

44 Any scheme, however drastic, of effective international legislation will be unreal unless it faces and attempts to solve two major difficulties involved in any such fundamental departure in international constitutional law. The first difficulty is the question of the limits of international legislation. It is the question whether it is possible to

confine its limits in advance, so as to exclude from it matters which ought intrinsically to remain outside international legislation or to the inclusion of which Governments are likely to offer insurmountable resistance. There would, of course, be nothing new in limiting, however drastically, the legislative powers of the international authority. The delimitation of the respective legislative competencies of a federation and of its member States is a constant feature of federal constitutional practice. Admittedly, the legislative sovereignty of the members of the society of nations would have to be safeguarded more rigidly than that of the members of a federation. In theory, that safeguard cannot be absolute. In a universal organization in which membership is compulsory and in which the constitution may be amended by a procedure not requiring unanimity, there is no absolute legal protection against further restriction of the legislative sovereignty of the member States. But there exists a *substantial* legal safeguard in the requirement of a qualified majority approaching 'unanimity' in the procedure of amendment. There exists an even more powerful political safeguard in the fact that any attempt to alter in this respect the original basis of the compact of the society of nations would amount to an attempt, revolutionary in character, to amend its fundamental constitution in a manner contrary to the spirit of the original compact.

45 What, then, shall be the matters which ought to be exempted from the legislative competence of the international authority ? These comprise, in the first instance, the right of every State to the maintenance of its territorial integrity. No State ought to be divested of its territory, against its consent, by any act of international legislation. The constitution of the United States offers an instructive instance in this respect. Closely – and inseparably – connected with the right of the State to the maintenance of its territorial integrity is its right to regulate the admission of aliens. Without it, the exclusive right to territorial integrity becomes illusory.

46 Secondly, international legislation must be governed by the principle that only such matters as are of international concern are within its legitimate province. This is a limitation which is of a general character and which it is not possible to define in advance. Thus legislation in the sphere of public health is and must remain an internal matter, but the already existing international machinery on the subject shows that some of its important aspects are of international concern. Criminal law is clearly a matter which must remain within the province of domestic legislation, but some of its aspects – like extradition or the question of criminal jurisdiction over aliens with regard to crimes committed abroad – are a suitable subject matter of international regula-

tion. The vast field of international labour conventions offers another instructive example.

47 For these reasons, the best method of circumscribing the limits of international legislation would be, after excluding from it clearly defined subjects like integrity of territory and admission of aliens, to adopt the principle that it should be confined to matters of international concern. The test thus adopted would admittedly be an elastic one, but it is a test preferable to an unworkable catalogue. The dangers of elasticity can to a considerable extent be met by further safeguards specially appropriate to the case of international legislation. These are the exacting requirements of a qualified majority, differentiation in voting power, the necessity of joint action by both the General Assembly and the Council of the society of nations, the judicial determination of matters of international concern, and the devolution of non-political aspects of international legislation.

(*a*) *The requirement of a qualified majority*

The transition to international legislation must be gradual. There must be a transitory stage between the present entire absence of international legislation and its adoption on the basis of a simple majority (assuming that legislation by a simple majority can ever be advisable or practicable in the international sphere). That transition must be found in the adoption of the principle of a qualified majority. Under that system the kind of qualified majority required would vary with the subject matter of legislation, ranging from a qualification approaching unanimity in matters of high political import to a less exacting majority with regard to other matters.

(*b*) *The differentiation in voting power*

This subject is referred to more conveniently below in connection with the general problem of unanimity and majority.

(*c*) *Concurrent legislative action of the General Assembly and the Council*

It follows from the importance attaching to the legislative function that it ought to be exercised by both the Council and the General Assembly of the society of nations. The reasons which have prompted the retention of the system of two chambers as constituent parts of the legislative procedure in practically all countries apply with special weight in the international sphere. The powers of the Council, with the predominant influence and voting strength of the Great Powers, must in this matter be the same as those of the general representative body.

(*d*) *Judicial determination of matters of international concern*

It would have to be a subject for consideration whether, as a further safeguard against any unwarranted encroachment of international legislation, the Permanent Court of International Justice should not be given the power to decide, at the request of one or, preferably, a number of States, whether a matter which it is sought to regulate by way of international legislation is of sufficient international concern to warrant interference with the internal autonomy of States.

(*e*) *Devolution of non-political aspects of international legislation*

The danger of the international authority interfering unduly by legislative action with matters of internal jurisdiction may be considerably reduced by the devolution of non-political aspects of international legislation upon representative organs set up on a functional basis and endowed with legislative powers which they do not at present possess. Thus, for instance, the entire field of international labour legislation could be left within the province of the International Labour Organization. Legislation in the field of health or communications could be reserved to the international representative bodies directing international co-operation and administration in these matters. The so-called unions of States, almost universal in scope, which have been or may be set up for these and similar matters would be the proper instruments for that purpose. Their legislative activity would be entirely non-political in nature and to that extent rendered more acceptable. Moreover, their functional and non-political character would render feasible the elimination of unanimity and equality in representation and voting power – a development which some of these bodies have already achieved to a considerable extent.

48 The above somewhat detailed elaboration of the question of international legislation may create an impression of unreality. But that impression must be viewed and assessed in the light of the fact that, by general admission, international legislation and the effective provision of peaceful change are essential links in the structure of obligatory judicial settlement, of the elimination of war and, generally, of an orderly working of international society. Hitherto, the problem of international legislation and of effective peaceful change has often been raised mainly as an argumentative starting point against the principle of compulsory judicial settlement and the prohibition of war as a legal institution. Those who have thus argued have found it superfluous to give detailed consideration to the difficulties involved in international legislation and to means calculated to overcome them. But once the

view is adopted that effective institutions of peaceful change, conceived as one aspect of international legislation in general, are an essential condition of a working international order, there is no option but to probe the details of this most difficult aspect of international constitutional law.

49 Undoubtedly, the limitation – such as envisaged here – of international legislation in consequence of the exclusion from its province of matters relating to territorial integrity and to the admission of aliens is open to the objection that it ignores matters which in the past have been among the most potent sources of conflict between States. These limitations are at present believed to be unavoidable. They do not rule out altogether active international interest or influence. Territorial problems can be alleviated by international action and co-operation in the field of access to raw materials and tariffs. Rights of transit and provision of bases, not involving changes in territorial sovereignty, might still be a proper subject of international legislation. With regard to dependent States and territories under Mandatory and colonial government, the international concern in their gradual advance to self-government and, eventually, to independence – a concern which constitutes one aspect of the international recognition and protection of the rights of man (see below, section 8) – would prevent this feature of the territorial *status quo* from acquiring the character of stagnation and immobility. In the matter of admission of aliens means may be found which, though not as directly effective as international regulation of immigration, may go a long way towards alleviating the real difficulties of this problem. These means may include international assistance for undeveloped territories, with a view to making possible the admission of immigrants, and the regulation by the States concerned of the increase of their population.

50 The fact is that matters which prudence and necessity alike exclude from the province of international legislation touch only the fringe of its potentialities. Thus, to give one instructive example, under a system of international legislation in the true sense of the word the codification of international law – not confined to the somewhat artificial category of 'matters ripe for codification' but embracing the entirety of the international law of peace – would become a practical possibility. The idea of codification of international law has become somewhat discredited in the eyes of many as the result of the experience of codification conferences operating on the basis of unanimity and, in consequence, either failing in their efforts or producing results which have been nominal or retrogressive. But there ought to be no doubt as to the beneficence and the urgency of the need for codification,

conceived as a truly legislative process, of international law. International legislation in the true sense of the word means, in this connection as in others, legislation dispensing with the requirement of unanimity. Such legislation would bring into relief the intrinsic insignificance of the reasons which, in a situation where no national interest of any importance was involved, produced the category of subjects 'not ripe for codification'.

51 The legislative function of the international authority will thus spring from two sources. One will originate in disputes between States in which a specific claim is put forward by one State against another. Any such dispute must be brought in the first instance for a judicial decision defining the existing legal position with all requisite clarity. Should one of the parties wish to press its claim on an other than legal basis with a view to having the situation remedied by international legislative action, machinery ought to be provided for the claim to be investigated by an advisory though authoritative standing organ, whose function would be to transmit its recommendation or opinion, not based on law, for further action by the legislative authority. But for the fact that the recommendation of that standing body would not be binding and that appearance before it would not be compulsory, it might be described as an Equity Tribunal. One of the reasons for its existence would be to prevent the contentious procedure of actual disputes from being a drain upon the energies of the highest organs of the international authority. Under the proposed procedure, after the Equity Tribunal has referred the matter to the Council with an affirmative recommendation, the business before the latter will no longer be primarily the settlement of a dispute between two States. For the Council will then be confronted with a recommendation, in the legislative province, for action which although arising out of a particular claim or situation is in essence of general application.

52 The second source of the legislative action of the international authority would be independent of any particular dispute. It would lie in the responsibility of the highest organs of the society of nations for initiating legislation for promoting the general good of the international community. The legislative authority might properly be assisted by a standing legislative committee composed of statesmen, officials and jurists of distinction and charged with the task of reporting to the legislative authority on proposals for legislation brought before the latter and of drawing, on its own initiative, the attention of the Council to matters requiring international legislative action.

53 In this connection the Permanent Court of International Justice or other judicial organs might perform a useful function not inconsistent

with their judicial character. They could be specifically authorized to avail themselves of the power, which they probably possess without special authorization, to express an opinion on the necessity for remedial legislative action in matters of general international law covered by or incidental to the judicial decision. Municipal courts often express opinions of this nature. Similarly, international tribunals ought to be given the power to express an opinion that a treaty, which they have been unable to declare invalid on account of the operation of the doctrine of *rebus sic stantibus*, has become so unduly onerous as to call for modification or abrogation by agreement of the parties or by international legislation. (There may also be room for consideration whether the doctrine of *rebus sic stantibus*, i.e. the doctrine of frustration on account of a vital change in circumstances, ought not, in relation to international treaties, to be subject to a less rigid interpretation than that adopted by the Permanent Court of International Justice.)

7. THE PRINCIPLE OF MAJORITY RULE

The abandonment of the principle of unanimity in matters of international legislation and otherwise and its replacement by a flexible system of qualified and simple majorities is an indispensable condition of a sound international order and of satisfactory international government. The abandonment of the principle of unanimity is, in turn, conditioned by the relinquishment of that aspect of the doctrine of equality of States which expresses itself in equality of voting power and of representation.

54 Most of the principles of international organization here put forward, such as those with regard to the international legislative process or the effective enforcement of the obligation of pacific and judicial settlement, are based on the view that the existing law in relation to unanimity and equality of representation must be abandoned. In general, order and organization, conceived as institutions of the law, and the principle of unanimity are contradictory notions. Order and organization imply a possibility of action independent of unanimous agreement on any particular issue. From this point of view unanimity, which is the principle of *liberum veto*, is a manifestation of anarchy. It is an extreme assertion of sovereignty. For while it makes it lawful for one State to resist the will of the overwhelming majority, it submits that overwhelming majority to the will of the isolated dissentient in all matters in which unanimity is postulated as a condition of positive action.

55 There is little substance in the view that the necessity for unanimity is conducive to compromise while majority rule makes it

possible for the majority to ride roughshod over the wishes and interests of the minority without endeavouring to seek and to find a reasonable reconciliation of conflicting interests. The tendency and readiness to compromise must be sought in an attitude of accommodation and in an existing or gradually evolving sense of community. It cannot be found in the mechanical operation of the principle of unanimity. For the compromise arrived at under the impact of the requirement of unanimity tends to be one of evasion, of inaction, of artificiality, and of retrogression.

56 The governing principle in international organization must be that of a majority vote, ranging from an ordinary majority in matters of procedure and purely administrative and technical questions not involving political and economic interests of significance to a highly qualified majority of four-fifths in such matters as determination and suppression of aggression or some of the more important subjects of international legislation. The kind of majority required in each particular case must be determined in the constitution of the society of nations – a matter which, once the principle of unanimity has been discarded, is unlikely to cause insurmountable difficulty. While the Covenant of the League of Nations lays down the general principle of unanimity 'unless otherwise provided', the future constitution of international society must adopt the principle of a simple majority unless otherwise provided. Cases in which a qualified majority may be required will and ought to be frequent – although in no case ought it to be so exacting as to approach complete unanimity. But there is a fundamental difference between accepting a simple majority as the normal procedure and making it an exception.

57 The abandonment of the principle of unanimity and the adoption of majority rule – simple or qualified – can have useful application only if the future international organization is successful in discarding that aspect of the doctrine of equality of States which expresses itself, among other things, in equality of voting power. The right of every member of the Council or of the General Assembly of the international organization to have one vote of identical weight is an innocuous rule of controversial attractiveness so long as unanimity is the rigid principle. It is of no consequence whether unanimity is frustrated by one dissenting vote or twenty. The position is altogether different when a majority, simple or qualified, becomes the governing principle. When that happens, equality of voting power may mean that a majority of small or diminutive States, representing an insignificant fraction of the population or of the surface of the world, may be in a position to impose their will upon three or four Great Powers representing the bulk of the

population of the world and of its resources. It may mean that a minority of small or diminutive States may, when a qualified majority is required, prevent measures of vital importance and urgency to international society.

58 In these and similar cases, the offensive paradox of the doctrine of equality of States reveals itself in a striking manner. Common sense and justice require a close parallelism between the actual degree of responsibility and the power to determine the nature of the decisions likely to call that responsibility into play. It is impracticable and intolerable that a State which will have an insignificant share in carrying out a decision should have a vote equal to that of the States upon which will fall the major responsibility in the matter. In the Covenant of the League the paradox of the doctrine of equality of States thus conceived was, in a sense, rendered inconspicuous because of the operation of the principle of unanimity. If unanimity is the rule, if one vote can prevent the legal validity of a decision, then differentiation in voting power serves no purpose. Once the principle of unanimity is abandoned, the doctrine of equality of States conceived as equality of voting power and of representation ceases to be innocuous and becomes mischievous.

59 The doctrine of equality of States originated in a period in which the absence of any effective international security rendered valuable to small States such legal and moral safeguards as could be derived from the fiction of equality. At that time it served a useful purpose. In an international society organized or about to be organized on the basis of the effective rule of law and security, it becomes a serious check upon international progress. It is said occasionally that at least that aspect of the doctrine of equality of States ought to be maintained which secures to all States, small and great, equal protection, before international tribunals and otherwise, of such rights as they possess under international law. However, such equality of protection of legal rights has only a slight connection, if any, with the doctrine of equality of States. It is the consequence, or the expression, of the principle of equality before the law.

60 For these reasons it must be recognized that the doctrine of equality of States conceived as equality of representation and voting power is incompatible with the requirements of an effective and progressive international organization. It has already been abandoned to some extent in a number of technical international organizations established on a functional basis. Whenever such a functional approach to international organization proves practicable, the departure from mechanical equality will be prompted by such obvious considerations

of reasonableness and convenience that its abandonment is not likely to cause undue difficulty. Inasmuch as a substantial part of international legislation and administration can be delegated to such bodies, there is a good prospect of removing in this way much of the existing anomaly. But no such functional basis is feasible with regard to the political aspects of international organization. In this respect the sharp knife of policy must accomplish a change which by general assent is an important condition of progress in the field of international organization.

61 Even after the necessity for differentiation in voting power has been admitted in principle, the exact definition of voting strength will present serious difficulties, in addition to those of novelty and prestige. For the test to be adopted must be a cumulation of factors defying exact measurement and assessment. These include the size of population; the extent of territory; political importance in terms, among others, of past contributions to international co-operation; military strength; industrial, agricultural and commercial development; standard of cultural achievement; extent of financial contribution to the expenses of international organization. The task of expressing these often intangible factors in terms of figures will be both invidious and delicate. But it is a task which must be faced. It is proper that any person or group who propose a significant and difficult innovation of this nature should not shrink from applying the principle in detail and from incurring criticism, which can supply a useful basis of study and discussion, of an unorthodox proposal. What follows is therefore an attempt to translate the general principle of differentiation in voting power into a table showing the proposed voting strength of each State.

62 The abandonment of the doctrine of equality of States cannot be limited to the adoption of the principle of differentiation in voting power. It implies also the relinquishment, whenever necessary, of equality in the matter of representation. The view that in all international bodies every State is entitled to equal representation, although not as mischievous as the principle of equality of voting power, is nevertheless indefensible. The Covenant of the League, in providing for a permanent seat on the Council for some States, expressly abandoned, in one important aspect, the principle of equality of representation. So did the constitution of the International Labour Organization, in making provision for the representation on the governing body of the International Labour Office of the eight most important industrial States. The system of permanent representation, in the highest executive organ of the international society, of the Governments of the most important States must be maintained wherever desirable. (It

Table showing the proposed voting strength in the Council and the General Assembly

(The figures in brackets indicate the population of each State as given in the League of Nations Statistical Yearbook, 1940–1941)

12 votes		3 votes (*cont.*)	
United States of America	(131,416,000)	Iran	(15,000,000)
Great Britain	(47,735,000)	Ireland	(2,946,000)
Soviet Russia	(172,000,000)	New Zealand	(1,642,000)
10 votes		Norway	(2,937,000)
China	(450,000,000)	Peru	(7,000,000)
France	(41,950,000)	Portugal	(7,620,000)
Germany	(69,317,000)	Venezuela	(3,650,000)
8 votes		2 votes	
Brazil	(40,900,000)	Afghanistan	(7,000,000)
Italy	(43,864,000)	Bolivia	(3,400,000)
Japan	(72,520,000)	Cuba	(4,253,000)
6 votes		Ecuador	(3,000,000)
Poland	(35,090,000)	Ethiopia	(5,500,000)
Spain	(26,000,000)	Guatemala	(3,260,000)
Turkey	(17,620,000)	Iraq	(3,700,000)
5 votes		Thailand	(15,600,000)
Argentine	(13,132,000)	1 vote	
Australia	(6,997,000)	Albania	(1,064,000)
Belgium	(8,396,000)	Costa Rica	(639,000)
Canada	(11,368,000)	Dominican Republic	(1,650,000)
Czechoslovakia	(15,239,000)	El Salvador	(1,745,000)
Mexico	(19,038,000)	Esthonia	(1,122,000)
Netherlands	(8,834,000)	Haiti	(2,600,000)
Sweden	(6,341,000)	Honduras	(1,090,000)
4 votes		Iceland	(120,000)
Austria	(6,650,000)	Latvia	(1,951,000)
Greece	(7,201,000)	Liberia	(2,500,000)
Hungary	(13,500,000)	Luxemburg	(301,000)
Roumania	(13,300,000)	Nepal	(5,600,000)
South Africa	(10,251,000)	Nicaragua	(883,000)
Switzerland	(4,206,000)	Panama	(570,000)
Yugoslavia	(15,703,000)	Paraguay	(970,000)
3 votes		Saudi Arabia	(4,500,000)
Bulgaria	(6,620,000)	Uruguay	(2,147,000)
Chile	(4,940,000)	Yemen	(3,500,000)
Colombia	(8,986,000)	1 joint vote	
Denmark	(3,825,000)	Liechtenstein	(12,000)
Egypt	(16,680,000)	Monaco	(24,000)
Finland	(3,684,000)	San Marino	(15,000)

must be a matter for consideration to what extent that system of permanent representation of Great Powers may make it possible to abstain from introducing differentiation in voting strength in some cases. Thus in the Council, whose members may, in a sense, be regarded as the representatives of the General Assembly and not of their States – though this was not the theory of the Covenant – no differentiation in voting strength may be required so long as the principle of the absolute numerical preponderance of the Great Powers is adhered to. It may be argued that if the proportion of Great Powers to small States were that of three to one and if thus the danger were eliminated of the former being outvoted by a majority of small States, the variation in voting strength could be dispensed with. However, the calculation may be a deceptive one. For there would still remain the possibility of a minority of the Great Powers on the Council joining with the small Powers in order to force a decision upon the majority of the permanent members.)

63 The introduction of the principle of differentiation in voting power in the General Assembly may render equality of representation in that body acceptable to all and desirable from many points of view. The drawbacks of equality of representation are negligible in so far as international bodies serve the purpose of deliberation and expression of opinion. It is of the essence of the democratic principle that every State, however small, should be in a position to make its voice heard and to give utterance to its opinions and its needs. It is mainly where equality of representation, resulting in numerically unwieldy executive or judicial organs, impairs the efficiency of international bodies that it ought to be modified or jettisoned altogether.

64 There is a further reason in favour of not limiting the representation to the General Assembly and of making it possible for every State to send to it an adequate number of representatives. That reason lies in the possibility of the gradual acceptance of the principle that the delegates to the General Assembly ought to be the representatives not only of their Government but also of the nation at large – a principle which has found expression, in a modified form, in the Constitution of the International Labour Organization. In the evolutionary progress of the society of nations to a true Parliament of Man – a consummation which ought not to be lost sight of in any scheme of international organization – such a reform would be of far-reaching significance. The actual exercise of the vote would have to be confined to the representatives of the Governments, but there would still be a purpose in the innovation whereby the delegation of each State would consist, in addition to the representatives of the Government, of persons appointed by the Government on the nomination of the two largest political parties. The presence of the latter in the delegation would not only tend to impart to the policy of States in the international organization an impressive element of continuity and authority. It would also have the effect of acting as a check upon any tendencies to laxity in the fulfilment of obligations.

65 With regard to the composition of the Permanent Court of International Justice, the question of equality of representation ought, in principle, to be irrelevant for the reason that the judges must be

assumed to represent not their States but the impersonal interests of justice. Accordingly, it would not be proper to ensure, through express constitutional provision, that the Court should include nationals of the Great Powers. However, the voting strength of the Great Powers both in the Council and in the General Assembly may be relied upon to safeguard that result within the framework of the existing Statute of the Court.

8. INTERNATIONAL RECOGNITION AND PROTECTION OF THE RIGHTS OF MAN

The international recognition and effective protection of fundamental human rights either through an International Bill of the Rights of Man forming part of the constitution of the society of nations or in some other manner, is an important condition of international peace, of social progress upon which peace depends, and of the moral authority of international organization and law.

66 The international recognition and protection of the fundamental rights of man – in the words of Mr Churchill 'the enthronement of the rights of man' – has been repeatedly declared, in authoritative pronouncements of leading statesmen and in international instruments, to constitute one of the major purposes of the Second World War. Wide sections of public opinion have viewed the objects of the War in that light. The same purpose, expressed as the determination 'to make the world safe for democracy', loomed large in the declarations of peace aims during the First World War.

67 The necessity of making the protection of the fundamental rights of man part of the positive law of the society of nations is grounded in considerations weightier than pronouncements of statesmen or agreements made during the War. Inasmuch as the denial of the right of man to freedom and equality is identical with or results in tyranny and dictatorship, it has proved and is bound to be a danger to international peace. The entire fabric of international law and organization must derive its moral authority from the notion that the individual human being is the ultimate subject of all law; that the purpose of the law is to secure the welfare of the individual and the respect of the sanctity of human personality; that the State, far from being an end unto itself, is the trustee of that purpose; that it is accountable to international society for the proper fulfilment of that task; and that international law and international organization must include appropriate safeguards on that behalf. Finally, the intimate connection between international peace and social justice and progress throws into

relief, from a different angle, the international recognition and protection of the rights of man.

68 The achievement of that task by means of the adoption of international obligations and appropriate institutions is fraught with immense difficulties. These consist, in the first instance, in reaching agreement concerning the substance of the human rights which are to form the object of international protection. For these must include not only the rights of freedom in the accepted sense, like freedom from arbitrary arrest and freedom of speech, of opinion, and of association, and equality before the law. They must comprise what is the essence of the democratic principle, namely, the right of self-government, i.e. the right of man to be governed by rulers chosen by and accountable to him. Moreover, the same principle demands the concession of that right to peoples in dependent States and to populations of territories at present under colonial and mandatory government. But these would not be the only difficulties. There would remain not only such controversial questions as the equality of the sexes or the right of every person to a nationality, but the much wider problem of recognizing as falling within international concern what has been described as freedom from want, namely, the right to work, to proper conditions of employment, to social security and to equal opportunity of education.

69 There would be little difficulty in expressing recognition of these and similar 'rights' – and any agreement as to their substance and extent – in an international instrument if it were to be a mere statement of lofty principle and a mere declaration of intention unaccompanied by provisions for their observance, supervision and enforcement. But an instrument thus conceived would not further any of the objects which render the international protection of the rights of man desirable and imperative. The insignificance of the achievement, when related both to the magnitude of its declared purpose and to the need which gave rise to it, would amount, in effect, to a retrogressive step. On the other hand, the international implementation and enforcement of an International Bill of the Rights of Man raise problems of unprecedented complexity. While the system of international judicial review of municipal legislation and jurisprudence from the point of view of their compatibility with an International Bill of the Rights of Man is theoretically possible, it is in fact impracticable. The alternative machinery would have to consist in a delicately balanced combination of the political, judicial and diplomatic method of supervision and eventual enforcement – a combination requiring the highest degree of statesmanship and impartiality. A system of this nature is believed to be practicable and to afford a prospect of successfully accomplishing the

required fundamental advance in the constitutional law of States and of mankind.

70 The relation of man to the State, the protection of his inherent rights against the State, and the utmost development of his human faculties within the State, are an enduring problem of law and politics. That problem cannot be solved by a mere gesture or by means of arrangements which, although constituting an advance, do not go to the root of the matter. Such partial advance would consist, for instance, in the adoption in a revised Covenant of the League of Nations or in any other basic international document, of a provision of broad generality laying down that with regard to all persons within its jurisdiction the State shall respect the inherent rights of man to freedom and to equality before the law and that the observance of that fundamental obligation shall be a matter of concern for the international organization. A provision of this nature would amount to the solemn international recognition of the rights of man and would elevate to the authority of a rule of law the principle of collective intervention whenever these are violated on a scale warranting international action. But any such innovation would suffer from most of the traditional drawbacks of political intervention; it would be called into being only in extreme cases while leaving outside international supervision the normal observance of the principle of respect for the rights of man; and it would be, in any case, concerned only with the fringe of the notion of the rights of man by leaving on one side the political right to self-government and the wide range of rights in the social and economic sphere.

71 For these reasons it is believed that the constitution of the society of nations, while proclaiming in general terms the principle of the international protection and recognition of the rights of man, ought at the same time to adopt as an integral part an International Bill of the Rights of Man to be framed and adopted concurrently with or subsequently to the acceptance of the basic instrument of the society of nations. In laying down the foundations of international order we must not avoid the solution of a problem which is vitally connected with international peace and with the enduring purpose of all law and government.

72 In comparison with this issue, little significance attaches to a reform which has loomed large in the discussions of international lawyers and which is directly connected with the international position of the individual, namely, the question of direct access of individuals to international tribunals. Once the principle of the obligatory jurisdiction of international tribunals is accepted, the way will be open for all

claims of individuals – except those of stateless persons – against foreign States being sponsored by their own States. Reasons of political difficulty and delicacy which have occasionally militated against a State taking up a legitimate claim of its national will disappear when, under the régime of obligatory judicial settlement, the sponsoring of a claim by a State will become a normal occurrence not implying any litigious spirit of unfriendliness. That development will be assisted if, within the system of obligatory jurisdiction of international tribunals and subject to the ultimate right of appeal to the Permanent Court of International Justice, there are established subsidiary courts of first instance, possibly on a regional basis, to entertain claims of this character. It will also be noted that the conferment upon aliens of the right of direct access to international tribunals would be a one-sided reform if unaccompanied by the conferment of a similar right upon individuals as against their own State.

73 Should the international protection of human rights through an International Bill of the Rights of Man fail to secure acceptance, it will be imperative to continue the more limited protection afforded to groups of persons in certain countries bound by Minorities Treaties and similar instruments concluded in 1919 and in the following years. The fact that these treaties failed, to a large extent, to fulfil their purpose was due not so much to their inherent shortcomings as to the circumstance that they shared inevitably in the breakdown of the general international system of which they were intended to form a part. The abandonment of the Minorities Treaties not accompanied by their replacement by a wider system of protection of human rights would constitute a retrogressive step impairing the moral authority of any international system that may be set up.

9. CO-ORDINATION OF INTERNATIONAL ADMINISTRATION

The effective co-ordination of autonomous organs of international administration set up on a functional basis under the aegis of the society of nations and within the framework of international government must form part of the constitution of the society of nations.

74 An international organization of States based upon the principle of universality and compulsory membership must assume general responsibility for the co-ordination of the manifold organs of international co-operation and administration. Article 24 of the Covenant of the League of Nations provides that all international bureaux already established by general treaties shall be placed under the direction of the League if the parties to these treaties consent, and that all international

bureaux and all commissions for the regulation of matters of international interest constituted after the establishment of the League shall be placed under its direction. The great potentialities of that provision remained unfulfilled, mainly owing to the actual absence of universality in the League. With the establishment of a truly universal organization of States there will be removed the principal difficulty in the way of ensuring the necessary measure of co-ordination and co-operation in international administration and government.

75 The co-ordination of international administration need not and ought not to be identical with centralization. In particular, it ought not to interfere with the organization of international co-operation on a functional basis. Thus, for instance, international co-operation and government in the spheres of health or communications can and ought to continue in the form of the existing international unions of States exercising powers both of administration and of legislation. The non-political character of these functional units of international government will facilitate the solution of the problems of unanimity and equality of voting as a factor in the legislative process. These considerations apply with special force to the International Labour Organization which, while remaining an organ of the society of nations for the fulfilment of one of its vital purposes, must at the same time continue to enjoy the highest possible degree of autonomy and initiative.

10. THE CONSTITUTION OF THE INTERNATIONAL ORGANIZATION AND THE PEACE SETTLEMENT

While the society of nations ought to be established concurrently with the peace settlement, after adequate preparation in the period between the armistice and the conclusion of peace, it must be independent of any peace treaties terminating the Second World War and free of responsibility for ensuring the execution of any of their specific clauses.

76 There are reasons of obvious cogency why the setting up of the society of nations should not be delayed beyond the conclusion of the Treaty of Peace. The intervening period, which may extend for a number of years, between the armistice and the conclusion of peace ought to be used, among other things, for the purpose of a thorough preparation of the constitution of the international organization. That task ought to be entrusted to an authoritative and representative body appointed by Governments before or after the signing of the armistice.

77 During that period, it will be the duty of statesmen and of those called upon to form public opinion to keep alive among the peoples of the world the conviction that any peace settlement not accompanied by

the establishment of a universal and effective organization of States for ensuring peace, for promoting international government and for securing the international protection of the rights of man will be deficient in its vital purpose. It will terminate the War without laying the foundations of peace. Power, however essential as an element of order, cannot alone supply that foundation. But such has been the ascendancy and the menace of aggressive power before and during the Second World War and such is the exertion of force necessary to overcome them, that the emphasis upon power, unredeemed by the transcending aim of a 'universal dominion of right', threatens to acquire a hold over the consciousness of nations. That tendency must be resisted. Similarly, while the continued existence of sovereign and independent States must for a long time to come continue to be the basis of world order, it is of importance that the advance which political and legal science has achieved in the present generation in their criticism of some aspects of sovereignty should not be lost. The fact is that sovereignty conceived as the ultimate and uncontrollable force is a menace both to civilization and to the survival of the State itself. There is a danger that the benefits of that advance may be lost as the result of a reaction to the mortal danger to which the sovereignty of some States has been exposed and of the excessive emphasis on the element of power. It is imperative that, in the intervening period when and while the constitution of the society of nations is forged, nations should regain the right historic perspective on these vital issues.

78 While it is of importance that the establishment of the international organization of States should take place simultaneously with the conclusion of the peace treaty, it is no less important that the society of nations thus established and its constitution should be independent of and separate from the Treaty of Peace. Considerations of principle and the experience of the League of Nations counsel that course. Neither ought the society of nations to be entrusted with any share in the execution of specific clauses of the Treaty of Peace. The society of nations will owe its existence to the victory of the United Nations. But this cannot in the long run be a sufficient reason why it should become an instrument for serving their particular interests. However closely that victory may be identified with the common good of international society, it is desirable that such identity should manifest itself not in the clauses of the Treaty of Peace but in the enduring law of the fundamental charter of the society of nations.

NOTE

If this Statement of the Principles of International Organization is agreed upon by the Committee, it ought, it is believed, to conclude with two appendices:

(1) One appendix ought to contain two drafts of the constitution of the future international organization: one being an adaptation of the existing Covenant of the League of Nations to the principles agreed upon; the other being a draft of an entirely new constitution of the society of nations incorporating these principles.

(2) The other appendix ought to contain comment on and a comparison with the Document prepared by the American Committee. Assuming that the British Committee can produce an agreed Statement of Principles and that that document is intended to be of practical value, consultation with our American colleagues and, if possible, a joint expression of views, might be practicable and desirable.

CHAPTER 2

THE UNITED NATIONS GENERAL ASSEMBLY–VOTING AND COMPETENCE IN THE PALESTINE QUESTION

Editor's note This chapter consists of an opinion prepared by Lauterpacht for the Jewish Agency for Palestine. The opinion was requested on 23 October 1947 and was delivered two days later on 25 October 1947. The urgency of the matter arose from the fact that the General Assembly, having convened for its second session, had established at its ninetieth meeting on 23 September 1947 an *ad hoc* Committee on Palestine to which there had been referred, *inter alia*, the Report of the United Nations Special Committee on Palestine (UNSCOP). The *ad hoc* Committee set up two sub-committees, of which the first, charged with drawing up a detailed plan for Palestine based on the majority proposals of UNSCOP, held its first meeting on 23 October and concluded its work in time to place its report before the Special Committee on 19 November 1947. On the basis of the report then adopted by the Special Committee, the General Assembly on 29 November 1947 adopted by a vote of 33 to 13 with 10 abstentions Resolution 181 (II)A on the future government of Palestine. In fact, no question arose in the General Assembly regarding voting on this Resolution.

The first question put to me is 'whether a two-thirds majority is inherently essential for the Assembly's recommendation on the future government of Palestine and which organ of United Nations is competent to decide this point'.

There seems to me no warrant for any emphatic assertion that a majority of two-thirds of the members of the General Assembly is required for a recommendation of this nature. It has been widely assumed in the press and elsewhere that a two-thirds majority is necessary in this connection, but there is no reason why – should the necessity arise – the Jewish Agency should not put forward the view that, as a matter of a clear interpretation of the Charter and of sound legal principle, a simple majority is sufficient. The terms of Article 18(2) and Article 18(3) of the Charter are explicit on the subject. Article 18(2) lays down that 'decisions of the General Assembly on important questions shall be made by a two-thirds majority of the members present and voting'. The same paragraph then proceeds to lay down what shall be included among 'important questions'. These are: 'recommendations with respect to the maintenance of international peace and security, the election of the non-permanent members of the Security Council, the election of the members of the Economic and Social Council, the election of members of the Trusteeship Council in accordance with paragraph 1 (c) of Article 86, the admission of new Members to the United Nations, the suspension of the rights and privileges of membership, the expulsion of Members, questions relating to the operation of the trusteeship system, and budgetary questions'.

The question of the future status and government of Palestine cannot be regarded as included within these categories. Neither can the question of Palestine as submitted to the General Assembly be regarded as coming within the scope of 'recommendations with respect to the maintenance of international peace and security'. The British Government, in submitting the question of Palestine to the United Nations on 2 April 1947, did not submit it as a matter 'affecting international peace and security'. Neither, unless it is decided to apply to Palestine the Trusteeship system under a trusteeship agreement, is a two-thirds majority required on account of the penultimate phrase of the second paragraph of Article 18.

Admittedly, the enumeration of 'important questions' in Article 18(2) is not final. But the matters there enumerated are not listed by way of mere illustration. The enumeration is exhaustive so far as Article 18(2) is concerned – though that Article leaves open the possibility of extending the list through the application of Article 18(3). That Article provides for the possibility of other categories of 'important questions' being added to those requiring a two-thirds majority. But unless a question, however seemingly important, is covered by the enumerative list of Article 18(2) or unless, in pursuance of Article 18(3), it has been expressly included within a category of important questions requiring a two-thirds majority, it is subject to recommendations by a simple majority.

It is clear, therefore, that it is not enough for a question to be 'important' to fall within the requirement of a two-thirds majority. It must either fall within the enumeration of Article 18(2) or it must belong to a category which by an express decision under Article 18(3) has been elevated to the category of questions requiring a two-thirds majority. No other matter is covered by the requirement of two-thirds majority. It follows that, unless the question of Palestine as submitted to the General Assembly is declared by an ordinary majority of the General Assembly to require a two-thirds majority, a recommendation adopted by an ordinary majority will constitute a valid recommendation of the General Assembly.

This result may appear startling to those who have given a hasty reading to Article 18(2), but it is a result which follows inevitably from the clear wording of the Charter and which, on consideration, is perfectly sound in law. To say that every matter which seems 'important' is automatically covered by the requirement of a two-thirds majority is to put forward a proposition which is meaningless in itself and which renders both Article 18(2) and Article 18(3) meaningless. The answer to the question whether a matter is 'important' in the contemplation of Article 18 or not, is not automatic; a matter may appear important to some, but not to others. It is possible to think of a multitude of subjects of the very greatest importance which, unless specially made so by a decision under Article 18(3), are not covered by the requirement of a two-thirds majority. (That contingency is not as startling as appears at first sight, for the simple reason that decisions of the General Assembly are not, as a rule, binding and do not produce immediate legal results formally obligating the Members of the United Nations except when otherwise provided by the Charter, such as in the matter of elections to the Security Council, the Trusteeship Council or the Economic and Social Council, or admission or expulsion of Members. Their legal effect is to provide legal authorization for action. Inasmuch as they are, in substance, an expression of the opinion and of the moral judgment of the world, it is clear that, in certain circumstances, a recommendation adopted by a simple majority – including the Great Powers – may be more representative than one reached by a two-thirds majority which does not include the votes of the permanent members of the Security Council.) Unless a subject is covered by the clear enumeration of Article 18(2), it must, in order to be brought within the two-thirds rule, be made the subject of a special decision under Article 18(3). If it were otherwise, Article 18(3) would serve no purpose whatsoever.

For these reasons there is little persuasive force in the possible argument that as Article 18(2) refers generally to 'important' questions and as the enumeration which follows seems to be purely illustrative ('these questions shall include'), other important questions, not specifically enumerated, may fall within the scope of that paragraph. Admittedly, the enumeration of Article 18(2) is not exhaustive. But the only source from which it can be amplified is in Article 18(3), namely, an express decision of the General Assembly to that effect. The enumeration contained in Article 18(2) is not a vague list of examples of important questions. It is a mandatory provision removing questions there enumerated from the discretion left to the General Assembly under Article 18(3).

These considerations, and the terms of Article 18(3), supply an answer to the second part of the first question, namely, who is competent to decide whether an ordinary or a two-thirds majority of the General Assembly is required for a recommendation in the matter of Palestine. As a general principle the interpretation of the Charter is a matter for the organ of the United Nations charged, within the sphere of its competence, with the application of the Charter on any given question. That organ, when in doubt, may ask for the assistance of the International Court of Justice by way of an advisory opinion. It need not do it. It may itself resolve the issue by adopting a legal interpretation of the Charter of its own. The General Assembly has on previous occasions interpreted Article 18. This means that it will be for the General Assembly to decide whether the question of Palestine is covered by the two-thirds requirement of Article 18(2). The answer to that question must, it is believed, be in the negative. The Assembly *may* then by an ordinary majority decide that although the question of Palestine does not come within the requirement of a two-thirds majority under Article 18(2), it shall be so treated by virtue of the authorization of Article 18(3). The legal propriety of any such decision could perhaps be challenged on the grounds that Article 18(3) permits the application of the requirement of a two-thirds majority to 'categories of questions' as distinguished from individual questions.

The latter consideration is also relevant to the question whether the General Assembly ought not, as a matter of interpretation in good faith of the provisions of the Charter, to avail itself of its power of declaring, under Article 18(3), that the problem of Palestine is 'important' within the meaning of Article 18(2). In the first instance, as submitted, it is doubtful whether any particular matter can be described and treated as a 'category'. Secondly, there can be no question of the General Assembly being, in any circumstances, under a *legal duty* to act upon the authorization contained in Article 18(3). Thirdly, as a matter of propriety and good faith, there may be cases in which the importance of the subject matter will be recognized more effectively by the refusal to subject it to the requirement of a two-thirds majority. This contingency will arise in cases in which a two-thirds majority may justly be considered as less representative than is indicated by its numerical appearance and in which a vote of the majority, which includes all or most of the Great Powers, may fairly be held to represent more adequately and more faithfully the moral judgment and the political strength of the international society. Of such a contingency the problem of Palestine in the circumstances of the Second General Assembly is a fit illustration.

2

The second question on which I am asked to advise is 'what are the best legal grounds for refuting the suggestion that the General Assembly has no legal competence to partition Palestine?'

1 The answer to that suggestion is, in the first instance, that a power of that nature – i.e. the power to recommend a solution of the Palestine question and the steps to put it into effect – has been recognized by all the interested parties as being within the competence of the United Nations:

(*a*) It has been recognized by Great Britain which, as the Power effectively exercising sovereignty over Palestine, has requested the United Nations to pronounce a finding upon the question of Palestine and its political future in all its aspects. The successive declarations of the British Foreign Minister and of other members of the British Government – which ought to be set out in full in any pleadings by the Jewish Agency – leave no room for uncertainty on this matter. The significance of this fact is not impaired by the circumstance that His Majesty's Government have declined to commit themselves to an unqualified acceptance of the Recommendation of the General Assembly in all its aspects (see below, section 2).

(*b*) The power of the General Assembly to make recommendations as to the future of Palestine in all its aspects has been recognized, in addition to Great Britain, by the other Allied and Associated Powers of the First World War which can now speak effectively in the international sphere. (In Article 40 of the Peace Treaty of 10 February 1947 Italy renounced all her rights derived from the Mandates system; the rights of Japan must be regarded as extinguished.) This fact is particularly relevant seeing that, assuming that the residuary (i.e. ultimate) sovereignty over Palestine is not vested in the United Nations, such sovereignty must, according to some, be deemed to reside in – or, on the demise of the League of Nations, be considered as having reverted to – the Allied and Associated Powers.

(*c*) The unrestricted powers of the General Assembly to recommend the solution of the problem of Palestine must be considered to have been recognized by the Members of the United Nations who, apparently without reservations, concurred in the summoning of the Special General Assembly to consider the question of Palestine for the comprehensive purposes indicated in the British request.

(*d*) In particular, the wide powers of the General Assembly in the matter must be considered to have been recognized by the Arab States which formally requested, on 21 and 22 April 1947, that the question of 'the termination of the Mandate over Palestine and the declaration of its independence' be put on the agenda of the General Assembly. If the powers, thus conceded, of the General Assembly include the right to decree the cessation of the present sovereignty over Palestine, there is no reason why they should not cover the competence to lay down the political status and the division of territories detached from the present sovereign. It is not open to a State to maintain that the General Assembly has the power to decree the independence of the whole of Palestine, but that it is not entitled to decide that Palestine should be constituted into two independent States. There is no legal substance in the assertion that the General Assembly is entitled to proceed to a fundamental and drastic solution of one kind, but that it has no power to decree a solution of a different kind. The Arab request of 21 and 22 April 1947 can properly be construed as an admission that, as a matter of law, the residuary sovereignty over Palestine is vested with the United Nations with the resulting power to declare the independence of Palestine. The limits, if any, of that power are a matter for determination by the General Assembly. There is little doubt that the International Court of Justice would hold that the Arab States are, by their conduct, estopped from questioning the right of the General Assembly to decree the independence of two Palestinian States instead of one.

(*e*) The power of the General Assembly to deal with the question of Palestine comprehensively and subject to such limitations only as are implicit in the Charter must be deemed to have been recognized by the final Resolution of the League of Nations of 17 April 1946 in the matter of the Mandated territories. The relevant passages of that Resolution are as follows:

> The Assembly . . .
>
> 3. Recognizes that, on the termination of the League's existence, its functions with respect to the Mandated territories will come to an end, but notes that chapters XI, XII and XIII of the Charter of the United Nations embody principles corresponding to those declared in Article 22 of the Covenant of the League;
>
> 4. Takes note of the expressed intentions of the Members of the League now administering territories under mandate to continue to administer them for the well-being and development of the peoples concerned in accordance with the obligations contained in the respective Mandates, until other arrangements have been agreed between the United Nations and the respective Mandatory Powers.

The first legal effect of that Resolution is to maintain, pending the conclusion of new arrangements with the United Nations, the general principles and the régime of the Mandatory system as it existed at the time of the dissolution of the League of Nations. While noting the fact that the Charter contains principles corresponding to those of Article 22 of the Covenant and the declared intention of the Mandatory Powers to continue to administer the Mandated territories in accordance with the existing obligations, the Resolution states as a matter of fact that with the termination of the existence of the League its functions in the matter of Mandates have come to an end. It is only the functions of the League which, on the cessation of its existence, have come to an end – not the régime and the obligations of the Mandatory system. When the final Resolution was voted the Egyptian delegate added a reservation to the effect that as, in his view, the régime of Mandates had terminated with the dissolution of the League, Palestine should not be included within the proposed system of Trusteeship. That reservation secured no support. The absence of a legal gap between the Mandatory system and the future arrangements in the matter of the territories concerned was emphasized by the Australian representative who acted as rapporteur of the League Assembly. While thus the supervisory functions of the League of Nations had ceased, there was – and is – no question of the cessation of the residuary power, vested in the organized international community, in the matter of the territories in question. (It is irrelevant whether these residual powers are referred to by the name of legal sovereignty, as distinguished from the exercise of sovereignty, or by any other name.) That organized international community is now represented by the United Nations.

The second effect of the final Resolution of the League of Nations is to establish a legal link between the Mandatory system and the future régime of the territories hitherto placed under Mandatory government. The Resolution not only notes the close correspondence between the relevant principles of the Covenant and of the Charter; it puts formally on record the expressed intention of the Mandatory Powers to effect future arrangements by agreement with the United Nations. The ultimate jurisdiction of the United Nations must thus be considered to have been recognized as a consequence of and as incidental to the cessation of the functions of the League of Nations. (This aspect of the legal position can be asserted with confidence without it being necessary to elaborate the point whether the United Nations is in this respect the full successor of the League of Nations. It may be noted that in October 1947 the Syrian representative on the Trusteeship Council advanced the proposition that the United Nations had become heir, in every sense of the term, to the League of Nations and that, for that reason, South Africa was bound to submit a Trusteeship agreement. The attitude of the United Nations in the matter of the legal duty of former Mandatories to submit Trusteeship agreements indicates that according to the general view on the subject – the Resolution in the matter of the incorporation of South-West Africa was adopted by 39 votes to 0 – the reversionary rights of the League are vested in the United Nations.)

2 The following considerations must be added in elaboration of what has been said above under 1(*a*): Palestine is not at present an independent State. There is no Palestinian State in which the sovereignty over the country is vested. While it may be a matter of theoretical controversy where at present is the exact legal situs of ultimate sovereignty, it is undisputed that its actual exercise rests with the Government of Great Britain. In fact, such uncertainty as exists, in the present period of transition, in the matter of residual sovereignty over Palestine emphasizes the legal importance of the position of the Administering Power as the trustee of the international community. It is also clear that international law cannot admit or tolerate a legal hiatus and that there must exist an ultimate legal authority vested with the power of decision as to the future of Palestine. In view of this it is highly relevant that the Administering Power has handed over for advice and action by the General Assembly the exercise of the main prerogative of sovereignty, namely, the determination of the political status and the political future of Palestine. This is so even if it were admitted – no such admission is called for – that the United Nations is not the general successor of the League of Nations in the matter of the Mandated territories.

3 There is recorded evidence of the attempts of Arab States, both at the San Francisco Conference and on the occasion of the dissolution of the League of Nations, to limit in advance the freedom of the United Nations with regard to its final disposition of the Palestine issue. There is similarly recorded evidence – which ought to be adduced in full – of the repeated rejection, on the part of the overwhelming majority of the United Nations, of those attempts by the Arab States. This circumstance is of direct legal relevance in relation to the issue under discussion.

4 It is not denied by the Arab States and their supporters – it is conceded by them – that the United Nations is entitled to effect a fundamental decision of one kind in the matter of Palestine, namely, to alter its present legal status by proclaiming it an independent State. Unless they now withdraw that recognition of the powers of the United Nations, their present opposition would appear to question the legal right of the General Assembly to effect a *particular* kind of decision, namely, the decision to partition the country. Any such distinction between the powers of the United Nations in fact asserts that the United Nations is entitled to decree a solution favourable to the Arabs but that it is not entitled to adopt a solution with which the Arab States are in disagreement. It is a distinction which is wholly arbitrary and legally

untenable. An attempt may be made on the Arab side to support that proposition by the argument that, as a matter of law, Mandated territory must be treated as a whole and that it is not, in law, a proper object of division or cession. The history of Mandatory government contradicts that assertion – the only legal limitation being that the Mandatory Power is not entitled to dispose of or change the boundaries of the territory without the consent of the authority on behalf of which the territory is administered. Secondly, an attempt may be made to support the Arab proposition by reference to the general principles of the Charter (such as the right of self-determination) and to considerations of justice. The Jewish Agency may be safely left to reply to this particular argument.

5 There is a further reason which militates in favour of the view that a power of decision in the matter of Palestine must be considered to be vested in the General Assembly. In the final Resolution of the League of Nations on the subject of Mandates note was taken of the undertaking of the Mandatory Powers that they would continue to discharge their obligations until such time as agreement for a change in the régime of the territories concerned has been reached between them and the United Nations. Such agreement implies a power of decision on the part of the United Nations. The United Nations must be able to decide, so far as it is concerned, on the terms of the agreement. To deny to it that power would amount to rendering impossible the termination of the Mandate – unanimously recommended by the United Nations Palestine Commission – in conformity with the undertaking recorded in the Resolution of the League of Nations.

6 The argument may be put forward on behalf of the Arab States that the General Assembly lacks the power to 'decide' on the partition of Palestine for the reason that its recommendations, being merely 'recommendations', are not binding. Undoubtedly, unlike the decisions of the Security Council under chapter VII of the Charter, the recommendations of the General Assembly are not, as a rule, binding. This does not mean that they have no legal force or validity and that their effect is limited to the moral sphere. Although recommendations of the General Assembly do not impose the obligation of positive action, they constitute a powerful legal authority which can be relied upon by the Members of the United Nations willing to act in conformity with a recommendation validly adopted. (The position is in some respects similar to that obtaining with regard to the recommendations of the Security Council under chapter VI and in some cases, chapter VII of the Charter. These recommendations are not, in law, binding upon the parties to the dispute. But they may, in due course, provide a starting

point for action, of an imperative and enforcing character, by the Security Council.) This means that any State or group of States acting in pursuance of a valid recommendation of the General Assembly would be able to invoke the legal authority of a Recommendation of the General Assembly on a subject with regard to which the United Nations has been called upon to act by the State directly concerned and with regard to which it has agreed to act by a practically unanimous vote of its Members other than the Arab States. The Recommendation, although not binding upon individual States, would also provide legal authority for any action of the United Nations as a whole. There would thus appear to be no force in the argument that the partition of Palestine is outside the powers of effective decision on the part of the United Nations for the reason that recommendations are not binding.

7 If necessary, the Jewish Agency will be in a position, in due course, to advance the argument that the Recommendation is not only a valid source of legal authority for action by the United Nations and its Members, but also that it is more generally a binding pronouncement of the United Nations. For this is not a case of a recommendation within the ordinary province of the activities of the Organization. There is conferred in the case upon the United Nations a power of determination, in what is in effect partly an arbitral and partly a legislative capacity, of a concrete issue. A higher decree of force and finality must attach to a determination of this nature.

8 Finally, it may be necessary to answer the objection that the General Assembly is not entitled to decree the contested legal issues involved in partition without asking for an Opinion of the International Court of Justice. There is no substance in that objection. The General Assembly (as well as other organs of the United Nations) has repeatedly interpreted its legal powers on disputed issues and controversial points of procedure without reference to the Court. The General Assembly may ask for an opinion of the Court if it so desires. But it is axiomatic that the General Assembly is the primary organ for the interpretation of the Charter in matters which come before it.

CHAPTER 3

VOTING PROCEDURE IN THE GENERAL ASSEMBLY

Editor's note The title of this chapter is a convenient abbreviation of the full heading given by the International Court of Justice to its advisory opinion of 7 June 1955 (on *Voting Procedure on questions relating to Reports and Petitions concerning the Territory of South-West Africa, I.C.J. Reports* 1955, p. 67).

The questions put to the Court were as follows:

(*a*) Is the following rule on the voting procedure to be followed by the General Assembly a correct interpretation of the advisory opinion of the International Court of Justice of 11 July 1950: 'Decisions of the General Assembly on questions relating to reports and petitions concerning the Territory of South-West Africa shall be regarded as important questions within the meaning of Article 18, paragraph 2, of the Charter of the United Nations'?

(*b*) If this interpretion of the advisory opinion of the Court is not correct, what voting procedure should be followed by the General Assembly in taking decisions on questions relating to reports and petitions concerning the Territory of South-West Africa?

Lauterpacht, who had taken his place as a judge of the Court in February 1955, agreed with the unanimous conclusion of the Court but delivered (at pp. 90–123) the separate opinion which is printed as this chapter. The considerations which have led to the reprinting at the relevant places in these *Collected Papers* of Lauterpacht's separate and dissenting opinions as a judge of the International Court have been set out in the Preface to this volume.

This opinion has played a considerable part in subsequent discussion of the rôle and effect of resolutions of the General Assembly.

In the present case the General Assembly has asked the Court for an advisory opinion on the question whether the special Rule F, which, on 11 October 1954, the Assembly adopted with regard to the voting procedure to be followed by it in taking decisions on questions relating to reports and petitions concerning the Territory of South-West Africa, is a correct interpretation of the opinion of the Court given in 1950 on the International Status of South-West Africa. Rule F laid down that such decisions shall be regarded as important questions within the meaning of Article 18(2) of the Charter, that is to say, that a majority of two-thirds shall be required for their adoption. In the Preamble to its request the General Assembly drew special attention to certain passages of the opinion of 1950. These passages are referred to below.

I have considered it incumbent upon me to append the present separate opinion for, while I concur in the unanimous opinion of the Court inasmuch as it gives an affirmative answer to the question put to it, I do so on grounds and by a method substantially different – and differing – from those on which that opinion is based. On the subject of method I find it necessary to devote some preliminary observations to the question as to the legal issues which ought to find an answer in the opinion of the Court. This matter raises the more general question of the character of the function of the Court and the nature of its judicial pronouncements.

The present opinion can be decided, in addition to what may be described as the method of pure construction, by exclusive reference to any of the following three legal questions:

(1) Inasmuch as the main issue arises from the contention of South Africa that absolute unanimity was required for the decisions of the Council of the League of Nations acting as a supervisory organ of the Mandates system, the opinion could be based on the rejection of that contention as being unfounded in law. In that case it might be said – though, as will be seen, not quite accurately – that questions (2) and (3) do not arise.

(2) It is possible to base the opinion of the Court on the view adopted by the Court that whatever may be the answer to the other two questions the General Assembly is absolutely prevented from acting by a method of voting other than that laid down in Article 18 of the Charter, and that for that reason it must be held, in adopting Rule F, to have complied 'as far as possible' with the opinion of the Court given in 1950. If that view is adopted, it might be said that questions (1) and (3) need not be answered.

(3) It is possible to base the opinion of the Court on the view that as, unlike the decisions of the Council of the League, the decisions of the General Assembly are not legally binding, Rule F clearly does not imply any excess of supervision as compared with that of the Council of the League and that therefore neither question (1) nor question (2) need be answered.

Finally, and this is substantially the method followed by the Court, it is possible to answer the question put to the Court without primary reference to any of these questions but merely on the basis of a construction of the relevant passages of the opinion of the Court of 1950.

In my view it is essential, having regard both to the circumstances of the case and to the objects of the judicial function of the Court in general, that its opinion should contain an answer to the legal issues relevant to the case, especially when relied upon by the Members of the General Assembly, including South Africa.

Thus with regard to question (1) – namely, that arising out of the contention of South Africa that the absolute unanimity of the Members of the Council of the League was required for its Resolutions relating to Mandates – although the Court has come to the conclusion that the relevant passage of its opinion of 1950 does not apply to the voting procedure, I consider that that argument of South Africa ought to be answered in all requisite detail. It ought not to be disregarded on the ground that it is irrelevant for the reason that it is ruled out by what is described as the ordinary and natural meaning of the words of the opinion of 1950. For this was the main argument put forward by South Africa in the course of the discussions before the General Assembly and its Committees. It was the question of the justification of that contention which exercised Members of the General Assembly, which troubled their consciences, and which was largely responsible for the request for the present opinion. The circumstances of the case are such that full consideration ought to be given to the principal legal argument of the State which, as a Mandatory, has put itself in opposition to the repeatedly expressed judgment of the United Nations and whose conduct has been the object of wide disapproval. For this reason, although I do not accept this particular contention of the Government of South Africa, I must consider it in detail.

The same considerations apply to what may be called the constitutional issue as expressed in question (2). The opinion of the Court is based on the view that the General Assembly is absolutely precluded from acting by a voting procedure other than that laid down in the Charter and that for that reason Rule F complies with the opinion of the Court, given in 1950, which laid down that the procedure of the General Assembly must approximate to that of the Council of the League 'as far as possible'. It is possible to dispose of the entire issue by reference to the simple proposition that the provisions of the Charter in the matter of voting are mandatory and peremptory and that any modification of the voting procedure of the General Assembly, designed to meet the circumstances of the case, would constitute a violation of the Charter or, more emphatically, that it would constitute a juridical impossibility. But that proposition is controversial. Some previous practice, to which reference will be made later, suggests the permissibility of a different voting procedure if an extraneous instrument so provides – although the Court seems to have accepted the view that there is no such instrument in the present case seeing that the powers of the General Assembly are, it is said, derived from the Charter and not from an extraneous instrument. That, too, is controversial. Above all, it appears that the constitutional problem as stated underlay a great deal of the debate before the General Assembly and that most of its Members – as indeed does the opinion of the Court – were prepared to regard the constitutional objection as decisive and sufficient. This being so, it seems to me desirable that the solution of that aspect of the matter should not be taken for granted or as being self-evident. For this reason, having regard to conflicting considerations of principle and to divergence of practice, I believe it to be my duty to examine fully that aspect of the matter.

The same considerations apply, once more, to question (3) – a question by reference to which it may be possible to dispose of the issue before the Court on the ground that the decisions of the General Assembly are of no legal effect or of more limited effect than those of the Council of the League. It is a ground by reference to which – and mainly to which – it may be thought, as I do in the present opinion, that an affirmative answer can be given to the question put by the General Assembly. For this reason I am not at liberty to disregard that issue on account of any difficulties or complications inherent in it. The absence, in general, of full legal binding force in the Resolutions of the General Assembly is a proposition so fundamental and so rudimentary that an attempt to apply and to circumscribe it need not be regarded as dangerous or unhelpful. I cannot disregard that aspect of the matter on the alleged ground that the Court cannot answer this – or any other legal question – incidental to the opinion, seeing that the General Assembly has not specifically asked for an answer to these questions. The General Assembly has asked only one substantive question; that issue, and that issue only, is answered in the operative part of the unanimous opinion of the Court. Clearly, in order to reply to that question, the Court is bound in the course of its reasoning to consider and to answer a variety of legal questions. This is of the very essence of its judicial function which makes it possible for it to render judgments and opinions which carry conviction and clarify the law.

For these reasons I cannot attach prominent – and certainly not exclusive – importance to what may be described as the 'mere construction' point of view, such as that implied in the argument that the question of voting is not at all germane to either of the two crucial passages of the opinion of the Court of 1950, namely, those relating to 'degree of supervision' and 'procedure' of the Council of the League. It is possible to hold the view that there is an implied reference to voting procedure in both these expressions; it may be held that such reference is implicit only in one or only in the other of these expressions; and there is room for the view, which finds some support in the opinion of the

Court, that neither of these expressions contains any reference to voting. This diversity of construction provides some illustration of the unreliability of reliance on the supposed ordinary and natural meaning of words.

Neither, having regard to the integrity of the function of interpretation, is it desirable that countenance be given to a method which by way of construction may result in a summary treatment or disregard of the principal issue before the Court. Thus it may be said that, as according to the opinion of the Court given in 1950, the General Assembly, acting under Article 10 of its Charter, is to be responsible for the task of supervision, it cannot fulfil that function otherwise than in accordance with its own procedure and that by applying its voting procedure, deemed unalterable, it approximates 'as far as possible' to the procedure of the Council of the League. However, this – the 'constitutional' issue – is one of the principal questions before the Court. I would not feel justified in answering it – without adequate examination of available practice – by reference to assumed logical impossibility.

These considerations I believe to be in the highest interest of the authority of international justice. They do not exclude the necessity of basing the opinion of the Court on, *inter alia*, a construction of the texts before it.

Do the expressions 'degree of supervision' and 'procedure of the Council of the League' refer to voting procedure?

One of the main passages of the opinion of 1950 which the Court is now requested to interpret lays down two directives: (1) that the degree of supervision to be exercised by the General Assembly should not exceed that which applied under the Mandates system, and (2) that it should conform as far as possible to the procedure followed in this respect by the Council of the League of Nations.

The expression 'degree of supervision' has two meanings: it signifies primarily the means of supervision. Thus it is clear that the place assigned to periodic missions or to petitions in the system of Trusteeship exceeds the degree of supervision adopted in the Mandates system and that that means of supervision by the United Nations cannot, without the consent of the Government of the Union of South Africa, be applied to the Mandated Territory of South-West Africa. This is a question of means of supervision in their wider sense. The Court, whose opinion is requested on the question of voting, is not concerned with them. However, the term 'degree of supervision' covers also the methods of ensuring compliance with the means thus adopted and, in particular, the method of deciding whether the administering authority has complied with them and what steps it ought to take with that object in view. If the General Assembly were to be enabled to take binding decisions on petitions and reports subject to voting requirements less stringent than those obtaining in the Council of the League of Nations – such decisions including request for further information, expression of regret at or disapproval of the action or inaction of the Administering Authority, and call for the cessation of the action disapproved of – then the innovation thus effected would appear to amount to a degree of supervision exceeding that previously in force. This is so although on occasions such decisions may amount to an approval or support of the action of the Administering State – in which case it might be argued that the less exacting vote implies a relaxation of the degree of supervision. However, the State subject to supervision is primarily concerned with the potential interference with its freedom of action by the supervisory organ. Thus viewed, the less exacting method of voting adds to the stringency and the degree of supervision – just as a change of the procedure of voting may add to the extent of the obligations. If I agree to accept the obligation to pay taxes in pursuance of unanimous decisions of a committee, then my obligation is increased if the committee, by changing its procedure, can impose taxation by a majority vote. This seems to be a proposition of common sense.

My view, as expressed below, is that Rule F does not result in an excess of supervision for the reason that the decisions of the Council of the League did not require absolute unanimity and that, in any case, the decisions of the General Assembly are not of the same legal authority as the decisions of the Council of the League. But I am not of the view that the opinion of the Court ought to base the answer to the question put to it on the ground that the degree of supervision has no relation to the question of voting. The procedure of voting determines the degree of supervision. For even if we do not go to the length – to the unwarranted length – of conceding that a valid decision of the Council of the League of Nations acting as the supervisory organ of the Mandates system could be prevented by a veto of the Mandatory States, the fact remains that, according to the contemplated Rule F, for the otherwise unanimous decisions of the Council which included all the principal Powers that were Members of the League, there is to be substituted a decision of two-thirds of the General Assembly which may or may not include the vote of any permanent Member of the Security Council, which may represent less than one-fourth of the budgetary contributions or less than one-fourth or one-fifth of the total population of the Members of the United Nations, and which acts by methods different from those which characterized the Council of the League which, in turn, in conformity with the entire political climate of the League, tended to proceed, ultimately, by agreement rather than by counting of votes. Neither is it altogether irrelevant that on the Council of the League of Nations that unanimity or quasi-unanimity had the additional safeguard of being influenced by the reports and the point of view of a commission of experts – for the Mandates Commission was a commission of experts – of high standing and independent of Governments. The decisions of the General Assembly, which will be reached according to the contemplated Rule F, will be formed under the impact of the Committee on South Africa – a body whose devotion and disinterestedness must not be questioned but which is of different composition.

These factors are directly relevant to the question of the 'degree of supervision'. This is not inconsistent with the fact that the second part of the passage ('and should conform as far as necessary to the procedure followed by the Council of the League of Nations') also, and more directly, refers to voting. Accepted usage includes voting within matters of procedure. It is probable that, while the first part of the passage refers to the major principle of not exceeding the degree of supervision hitherto obtaining, the last quoted passage is directed to the more specific problem of the approximation, as far as possible, of that procedure to that obtaining under the Council of the League of Nations. For these reasons I am reluctant to admit that the ordinary and natural meaning of words excludes the method of voting from the notion of degree of supervision. There is no ordinary and natural meaning of the term 'degree of supervision' in the abstract. Its meaning is not something which appears on the surface; it is relative to the situations and problems with which the Court is concerned. Moreover, it is relative to the legal issues directly connected with the situation. Thus, assuming that the main South African contention on the question of unanimity is correct, it would be reasonable to assume that the expressions used by the Court with regard both to 'degree of supervision' and 'procedure' were not used with the intention of ignoring the legal position thus established. It may not be profitable to regard the entire issue as non-existing on the ground that the words used have a meaning which is fixed, certain and immutable.

It is, of course, possible that the question of voting was not before the mind of the Court when it gave the Opinion in 1950. This does not mean that the procedure of voting is not an essential element in the situation. On the contrary, it is for this Court, confronted as it is with an apparent gap in the opinion of the Court of 1950 with respect to a situation which calls for clarification, to fill the lacuna by all available means of interpretation. These do not include the knowledge of any particular member of the present Court as to the state of his – or his colleagues' – minds at the time when the advisory opinion was rendered in 1950.

* * *

It is of importance, in this connection, to bear in mind the relation between the two passages here discussed. In my view, of the two conditions there prescribed, the first, relating to the degree of supervision, is the governing directive of a substantive character; the second, which is qualified by the words 'as far as possible', is, in terms, procedural. The question is whether the opinion of 1950 can be properly interpreted in a way which would subject the substantive rule to considerations of procedural conformity and convenience. The question is whether such considerations can properly be permitted to affect or impair the governing principle laid down by the Court in 1950 according to which, in the absence of agreement on the part of the Union of South Africa, the degree of supervision by the United Nations must not exceed that exercised by the Council of the League of Nations.

There is room for the view that the Union of South Africa is legally entitled to resist any attempted extension of the scope of its accountability and of the corresponding degree of scrutiny, interference and supervision by the United Nations, even if such extension is of a procedural nature, for instance, by way of a particular system of voting, so long as no conclusive proof has been adduced that such extension is unavoidable on account of an imperative necessity of relying on the procedure in force in the General Assembly and unalterable in any circumstances.

The system of trusteeship under the United Nations has not replaced the Mandates system; the latter remains in force so far as South-West Africa is concerned. As repeatedly stated in the opinion given in 1950 the continued exercise of the Mandate must be subject to supervision surrounded by the same, but not greater, obligations and safeguards as those which existed under the League of Nations. Now the obligations of a country can be decisively influenced by the voting procedure in respect of the decisions which interpret and apply those obligations. When the opinion of 1950 said, and reiterated, that the obligations of the Mandatory remained unaltered, it did not mean only that South Africa continued to be bound by these obligations and that she must not subtract from them; it meant also that these obligations ought not to be increased. The continuation of the obligation must in all fairness be held to work both ways. This seems to me to be the governing consideration. In relation to it, the interpretation, however necessary, of the terms 'degree of supervision' and 'as far as possible' seems almost to assume the complexion of a technicality. In relation to it, exclusive reliance on the supposed ordinary and natural meaning of the expression 'degree of supervision' as bearing no relation to the voting procedure would seem to me highly questionable.

As I see it, the words 'as far as possible' do not mean that the unqualified injunction against exceeding the degree of supervision under the League of Nations is in fact qualified by the obligation to follow 'as far as possible' – and only as far as possible – the procedure of the Council of the League of Nations and that if such approximation to that procedure is not possible having regard to the voting procedure of the General Assembly of the United Nations as laid down in Article 18 of the Charter, then the degree of supervision must unavoidably be exceeded. The opinion of the Court rendered in 1950 did not say that the degree of supervision as it existed under the Mandates system must not be exceeded *provided* that that is possible under the then existing voting procedure of the General Assembly. On the face of it, the words 'as far as possible' may be interpreted as meaning that, within the framework of compliance with the overriding prohibition of exceeding the degree of supervision of the League of Nations and if there is a variety of procedures available, that procedure must be followed which corresponds more closely to that of the Council of the League of Nations. For reasons stated elsewhere in this opinion, I cannot accept the view that the words 'as far as possible' contained an implied and imperative reference to an existing and unalterable procedure of the General Assembly and that any such interpretation has the legitimate effect of overriding the basic prohibition of extending the degree of supervision under the League of Nations by dint of the statement that by adopting the rule of two-thirds majority the General Assembly went 'as far as possible', i.e. as far as is legally permissible under the Charter. That statement must be proved by a rigorous and searching examination. Such examination may show, as suggested in another part of this separate opinion, that it was legally possible for the General Assembly to go somewhat further than does Rule F in complying with the direction to approximate 'as far as possible' to the procedure of the Council of the League.

My own conclusions with regard both to construction and the three main questions as formulated above are such that it is not necessary for this Court to adopt an interpretation of the opinion given in 1950 which in my view would amount to saying that in that opinion the Court laid down, as the result of an oversight or otherwise, two mutually contradictory directives, and that, by way of an implied reference to an unalterable voting procedure of the General Assembly, it reduced to meagre proportions the essence of its substantive ruling on one of the principal aspects of its advisory opinion on the International Status of South-West Africa.

Question 1: '*Did the rule of absolute unanimity obtain in the Council of the League acting as a supervisory organ of the Mandates system?*'

I now come to the first of the three principal legal issues with which the Court must properly be deemed to be confronted in the present case: Does the contemplated Rule F correctly interpret the opinion of the Court inasmuch as it replaces by a less stringent system the rule of absolute unanimity which, according to the contention of the Government of South Africa, obtained in the Council of the League of Nations in respect of its supervisory functions under the Mandates system? Did any such rule obtain in the Council of the League of Nations?

With regard to this question, I am unable to accept the contention advanced by the Government of the Union of South Africa that there is an inconsistency between the proposed Rule F and the procedure followed by the Council of the League of Nations for the alleged reason that the latter was based on the rule of absolute unanimity, including the vote of the Mandatory State concerned. This has been the principal view put forward by the Government of South Africa in the matter. I have given reasons why it was desirable that the Court should examine it in all its aspects.

Admittedly, the procedure of the Council of the League of Nations was governed by the principle of unanimity not only of the Members of the Council but of States who, though not ordinarily Members thereof, were invited to sit at its table in connection with a matter under its consideration – a rule which applied also to the representatives of the Mandatory State invited to take part in the proceedings of the Council. However, having regard both to principle and practice, as I interpret them, the ruling of the Court given in its Twelfth Advisory Opinion on the *Interpretation of the Treaty of Lausanne* must be held to apply also to the question with which the Court is now concerned. In that case, the Court held that the principle which was enshrined in Article 15 of the Covenant and which excluded the vote of the parties to the dispute from the requirement of unanimity as a condition of the validity of a recommendation made by the Council, was of general application in so far as it embodied the 'well-known rule that no one can be judge in his own suit'.[1] That 'well-known rule', henceforth sanctioned by a pronouncement of the Permanent Court of International Justice, must be held to

[1] *P.C.I.J.* Series B, no. 12, p. 32.

apply to the case in which an international organ, even when acting otherwise under the rule of unanimity, judges in a supervisory capacity the legal propriety of the conduct of a State administering an international Mandate or Trust. The supervisory organ may do so either directly by pronouncing a verdict upon the conformity of the action of the administering State with its international obligations or indirectly by calling upon it to adopt – or desist from – a certain line of action.

In the absence of cogent proof to the contrary, there is no justification for rendering legally permissible a situation in which a State, bound by virtue of solemn international obligations to observe a definite rule of conduct and to submit to the international supervision of its observance, is at the same time entitled to render, by its adverse vote, such supervision nominal and ineffective. Undoubtedly, international practice knows instances of States reserving for themselves the right to determine the extent of their own obligation and, in a sense, to remain judges in their own case. However, unless such right is reserved in explicit terms, States which thus attempt to avail themselves of their contractual capacity for purposes alien to its primary purpose – which is the creation of binding obligations – act at their peril. Such express reservation of this exceptional right, obnoxious to legal principle and to tenets of good faith, cannot be conclusively inferred from the mere fact that the basic instrument provides for the rule of unanimity. It could not, in particular, be inferred from the rigid wording of Article 5 of the Covenant, which laid down that, unless expressly provided to the contrary, the rule of unanimity should obtain. For, in the absence of a clear provision to the contrary, that rule is in itself qualified by the principle laid down by the Permanent Court of International Justice in the advisory opinion on the *Interpretation of the Treaty of Lausanne*. In that opinion the Court considered this rule to be of general application for the decisions of the Council when acting in a judicial or arbitral capacity. Its ruling was not limited to cases brought before it by virtue of an extraneous treaty.

It must be conceded that the application of the principle *nemo judex in re sua* to what is in essence a controversy between the mandatory and the otherwise unanimous Council constitutes an extension of that principle as laid down by the Court. However, the extension is more apparent than real. For the reasons stated above, there does not seem to exist any solid ground for distinguishing between decisions taken in pursuance of the supervisory functions of an international organ and decisions of a judicial or arbitral nature such as that with which the Council of the League was confronted in the matter of the determination of the boundary between Turkey and Iraq. In all cases in which there is a difference of opinion, brought to the point of a formal discordant vote, between the supervising organ and the administering authority as to the conformity of the conduct of the latter with its international obligations, such difference has the essential elements of a dispute as to the application of a binding international instrument. In any such controversy the principle that no one is judge in his own cause must be deemed to apply. To put it differently, there is no valid reason for distinguishing, in connection with the applicability of the principle that no one is judge in his own cause, between the judicial and the supervisory organs. Both administer, in different ways, a system of binding rules of conduct.

* * *

I will now turn from principle to practice. The practice, as I read it, of the League of Nations, does not conclusively support the view that there was an invariable, or even predominant, tendency – in cases in which a Member of the Council was itself a party to the dispute – to attach literal importance to the seemingly rigid or exhaustive provisions of Article 5 of the Covenant in the matter of unanimity. On occasions, the principle of absolute unanimity, including the votes of the parties to the dispute, was acted upon with some rigidity. This occurred in two cases in connection with the application of Article 11 of the Covenant, namely, in the dispute between Poland and Lithuania in 1928,[1] and, in particular, in the course of the Sino-Japanese dispute in 1931.[2] In both cases a resolution of the Council, assented to by all its Members save one of the parties to the dispute, was formally stated not to be binding. It may be observed that with regard to the latter case, Professor Brierly, a writer of authority noted for his restraint, stated that the interpretation of Article 11 then adopted was 'unexpected and doubtfully correct'.[3] Apart from these rare cases, the tendency was either in the direction of an express amendment of these provisions of the Covenant which, on the face of it, left room for the frustration of an otherwise unanimous decision by a vote of an interested party or in the direction of regarding such amendment as unnecessary and of acting on the view that the principle *nemo judex in re sua* was already an integral part of the Covenant. Thus, in 1921, the Assembly recommended that, pending the ratification of an express amendment of the Charter to that effect, the votes of the parties to the dispute should be excluded in the voting on the question whether a Member of the League had gone to war in breach of the Covenant.[4] In 1922, the Council seems to have proceeded in two cases on the view that when acting in an arbitral or semi-judicial capacity it

[1] *Official Journal of the League of Nations* (1928), p. 896.
[2] *Ibid.* (1931), p. 2358.
[3] *The Covenant and the Charter* (1947), p. 15.
[4] *Records of the Second Assembly, Plenary Meeting*, p. 806.

was bound to exclude the votes of the parties for the purpose of ascertaining the unanimity required by the Covenant. The first of these cases concerned the claim of India to be included among the eight States of chief industrial importance in connection with representation on the Governing Body of the International Labour Organization. In that case, the Council endorsed and acted on the legal opinion submitted to it by the Secretariat to the effect that 'the Council would act in this affair as arbitrator, and that India could not be both judge and party to the case'.[1] The case is of special importance in the present connection inasmuch as the Council acted in an administrative rather than judicial capacity. In the acute Greco-Bulgarian dispute in 1925, the Council, acting in a private meeting in the absence of the representatives of the two parties, prepared what was described as a 'dictatorial request' for acceptance by the parties who declared themselves ready to accept the *decision* of the Council thus subsequently sanctioned by a unanimous vote.[2] In the same year, in the Hungarian Optants dispute between Hungary and Roumania, which came before it under Article 11, paragraph 2, of the Covenant, the Council accepted a recommendation by a unanimous vote exclusive of the representatives of the parties after the President of the Council stated that, in inviting the Council to pronounce itself on the recommendation contained in the report, he 'deliberately excepted two members of the Council who are parties to the dispute'.[3]

It would thus appear that the Twelfth Advisory Opinion of the Court, in addition to being based on a general principle of law of cogent application, was not without support in the practice of the League, both prior and subsequent to the time when it was rendered. It may be useful in this connection to draw attention to the official publication of the Secretariat of the League of Nations, entitled *The Council of the League of Nations, 1920–38*, in which, on page 69, according to the view of the Secretariat, on the question of the inclusion of the votes of the parties in determining unanimity 'there is a certain division of opinion as to whether the votes of the parties should or should not be counted'.

It has been maintained that whatever may have been the practice of the Council of the League of Nations in the matter of international disputes, in other spheres it strictly adhered to the principle of absolute unanimity. From this the conclusion is drawn that the Mandatory State enjoyed a power of veto with regard to the supervisory function of the Council. I am not persuaded of the accuracy either of what is supposed to be the factual premise or of the conclusion which is being drawn from

[1] *Official Journal* (1922), p. 1160.
[2] *Ibid.* (1925), p. 1700.
[3] *Ibid.* (1927), p. 1413.

it. An account of some of the practice of the Council in this sphere is given in a paper prepared by the Secretariat of the United Nations for the working group of the Committee on South Africa and included as no. 39 in the file of documents put at the disposal of the Court. There are other cases to which reference will be made presently. My reading of the practice as recorded is that, while there is no instance of a resolution of the Council being formally declared adopted as against the opposing vote of the Mandatory State, there is, on the evidence, no authentic and recorded instance of a contemplated resolution of the Council being frustrated as the result of the adverse vote of the Mandatory State. A study of these cases, which were concerned with the Mandated Territory of South-West Africa, shows that while in no instance a resolution was adopted contrary to the express attitude of the Government of South Africa, this was not necessarily so because of any threatened exercise of the power of veto. In some of these cases, that Government, after having stated its doubts or objections, did not insist on them; in two other cases the Council modified an alternative text submitted by the representative of South Africa; in the sixth case the Government of South Africa eventually decided not to be represented at the resumed discussion of the issue in question. The same solution was adopted by the South African Government in some other cases, of which one relating to the status of the South African Mandate calls for special mention. In its Report, made in 1935, the Mandates Commission noted that it had been informed by the Mandatory Power that the latter had appointed a special Committee to study certain constitutional problems raised by a motion of the Legislative Assembly of the territory aiming at its incorporation as 'a fifth province of the Union'. The Report concluded with the following passage:

> As the guardian of the integrity of the institution of Mandates, the Commission therefore expects to be informed of the Mandatory Power's views on the question, which it will not fail to subject to that careful examination that its international importance demands. The Commission wishes, on this occasion, to draw attention to the Mandatory Power's fundamental obligation to give effect, not only to the provisions of the Mandates, but also to those of Article 22 of the Covenant.[1]

The Report of the Commission on this and other matters was adopted by the Council which instructed the Secretary-General to communicate to the Mandatory Powers the observations of the Commission and to request them to take the action asked for by the Commission.[2] The Government of South Africa informed the Secretary-General that it would not be represented at the meeting of the Council. It may or may

[1] *Official Journal* (1935), p. 1235.

[2] *Ibid.* p. 1148.

not be profitable to inquire into the reasons which prompted abstention from participation in a decision which had a distinct bearing on an important issue touching upon an essential aspect of the rights and duties of the mandatory. At least on six other occasions the Government of South Africa was not represented at meetings of the Council at which Resolutions were adopted or discussions took place concerning South-West Africa.

The fact which thus emerges with some clarity from a survey of the practice of the Council of the League of Nations on the subject is that it supplies no conclusive or convincing evidence in support of the view that as a matter of practice the rule of unanimity operated and was interpreted in a manner substantiating any right of veto on the part of the Mandatory Power. It would probably be more accurate to say that, assuming that it existed during the initial period of the functioning of the League, that right fell into desuetude and lapsed as the result. Undoubtedly, importance was attached to securing the concurring vote of the Mandatory Power by patient efforts at compromise and accommodation, especially with respect to the language of the Resolutions of the Council. It is therefore probable that a case, repeatedly – though rather vaguely – referred to in the argument of the Government of South Africa before the United Nations, in which the Council of the League of Nations desisted in deference to the attitude of South Africa from a proposed course of action, is not wholly apocryphal. There were bound to be a number of cases of that nature. However, these do not tell the whole story. In other – and probably more frequent – cases unanimity was achieved for the reason that the Mandatory Power adapted its attitude to the general sense of the Council, or, in some cases, for the reason that it decided not to participate in the meeting at which the Council accepted the Resolution. It is probable – we cannot put it higher than that – that it adopted that course because it deemed it preferable to open disagreement with an otherwise unanimous Council or to a public debate before an antagonistic and practically unanimous Assembly. From this point of view there is a distinct measure of unreality in the insistence on the absolutely unanimous vote in the Council. The Council was not a mere voting machine.

It is of interest to note that Professor Quincy Wright, in the most exhaustive treatise on the subject of Mandates, comes to the following conclusion:

> Thus it is possible that a resolution dealing with a particular Mandatory might be effective over the adverse vote of that Mandatory. On the other hand, it may be thought that the Council in dealing with Mandates acts in an administrative rather than a quasi-judicial character, in which case

absolute unanimity might be required. It is probable that the character of the particular question before the Council would determine the matter but up to date there has always been absolute unanimity.[1]

However, as already suggested, the Council, in passing resolutions on Mandates, acted essentially in a quasi-judicial capacity. Apart from procedural safeguards, there is probably no basic difference between the judicial and the administrative application of the law. As shown, the circumstance that resolutions had in fact been accepted by absolute unanimity throws no decisive light on the legal position here examined. When Professor Wright stated – a statement subsequently repeated by other well-informed commentators[2] – that as a matter of fact decisions of the Council in the matter of Mandates were unanimous, the statement, if we disregard the occasional abstention of the Mandatory Power from participation in the meetings, was on the face of it correct. But, as shown, it was clearly intended only as a statement of fact, not of law. That fact is open to varying – and divergent – legal construction.

There is thus in the practice of the Council no conclusive factor which is apt to override the basic legal considerations to which I have referred above, namely, that in an instrument such as the Covenant of the League of Nations the general requirement of unanimity is not in itself sufficient to displace the principle that a party cannot be judge in its own case; that the requirement of unanimity, however expressly stated, is implicitly qualified by the latter principle; and that nothing short of its express exclusion is sufficient to justify a State in insisting that it should, by acting as judge in its own case, possess the right to render inoperative a solemn international obligation to which it has subscribed. This principle ought to be kept prominently in mind when it is a question of the supervised State claiming the right to frustrate by its own vote the legal efficacy of the supervision. The effectiveness of international obligations may not be the only governing consideration in the interpretation of treaties seeing that the parties occasionally intend to render them less effective than is indicated by their apparent purpose. But it is a consideration which cannot be ignored. In so far as the principle *nemo judex in re sua* is not only a general principle of law, expressly sanctioned by the Court, but also a principle of good faith, it is particularly appropriate in relation to an instrument of a fiduciary character such as a Mandate or a Trust in which equitable considerations acting upon the conscience are of compelling application. This, too, is a general principle of law recognized by civilized States. There is therefore

[1] *Mandates under the League of Nations* (1930), p. 132. A similar view is expressed on p. 522.
[2] Hall, *Mandates, Dependencies and Trusteeship* (1948), p. 175.

no sufficient reason for assuming that if the Permanent Court of International Justice had been called upon to apply its ruling in the Twelfth Advisory Opinion to the question of unanimity in connection with the supervisory function of the Council in the matter of Mandates, it would have abandoned the principle there enunciated. It may be strange that ten years after the dissolution of the League this Court should be confronted with the same question, but this is not a valid ground for departing from that principle. There is, it may be added, no reason why the Court should not interpret the Covenant of the League as it existed in 1945. The determination of rights validly acquired under treaties or statutes which have lapsed is a frequent occurrence in judicial practice. There is no occasion for any excess of judicial caution in this respect. Moreover, in the present case the Court interprets primarily the Mandate which, as it repeatedly stated in its opinion of 1950, continues to exist.

I cannot say that I have arrived without hesitation at my conclusion on this aspect of the question or that I would have been prepared to base my affirmative answer to the question put by the General Assembly solely on this ground. I am impressed by the doubts voiced in this connection by Judge Klaestad in his separate opinion. For we ought to attach due weight to the general rule of unanimity in the Covenant and the fact that there is no explicit case on record in which the Council affirmed its right to give a valid decision in face of a formal objection of the interested Mandatory State. At the same time, I must attach equal – and, I believe, decisive – weight to the general principle as here outlined and as acted upon by the Court itself in the Twelfth Advisory Opinion; to the preponderant practice of the Council of the League in a sphere not confined to the settlement of disputes; and, above all, to the custom – to what in English practice is referred to as a constitutional convention – according to which the Mandatory States never in fact exercised any right of veto. Also, I have some doubts as to the existence of any vested right of South Africa to an immutable system of voting in face of actual or potential changes in the practice of the League of Nations on the subject of the voting procedure. There is no doubt that, in the course of time and without any formal amendment, the rule of absolute unanimity ceased to be a factor to which there was invariably attached decisive importance. This, in addition to the practice outlined above, is shown by the gradual adoption of such practices as passing of resolutions by way of a *voeu* or recommendation by simple majority; by treating some substantive matters as being questions of procedure; by considering abstention as absence; and by the practice of majority voting in Committees. When in 1937 Members of the League of Nations expressed their view as to whether absolute unanimity of the Council was required for a request for an advisory opinion, a large majority of those who formulated their attitude denied the existence of any such requirement. This was so although in this case there were reasons of some cogency for maintaining the rule of absolute unanimity having regard to the principle that States cannot be compelled, directly or indirectly, to bring their disputes before the Court. A proper interpretation of a constitutional instrument must take into account not only the formal letter of the original instrument, but also its operation in actual practice and in the light of the revealed tendencies in the life of the Organization. This being so, although I am not prepared to say that the main contention of South Africa was wholly unfounded, I cannot accept it as being legally correct.

For these reasons, my conclusion is that the proposed Rule F is not inconsistent with a correct interpretation of the opinion of the Court of 1950 inasmuch as it is based on the view that the opposing vote of the Mandatory State could not in all circumstances adversely affect the required unanimity of the Council of the League of Nations.

Question 2: 'Has the General Assembly the power to proceed by a voting procedure other than that laid down in Article 18 of the Charter?'

Although the Court has decided that it is not necessary for it to consider the South African contention in so far as it is based on the notion that the absolute unanimity of the Council of the League was required for the validity of its decisions. it has not thereby disposed of the issue before it. For there remains the possibility, foreshadowed in the request for the present opinion, of alternative voting procedures other than absolute unanimity or the two-thirds majority of Rule F. The General Assembly expressly asked the Court to indicate what other voting procedure should be followed in case it finds that Rule F is inconsistent with its opinion of 1950. There may be a qualified unanimity (i.e. one not including the vote of the Administering State), or some kind of majority half-way between unanimity and two-thirds such as a majority of three-fourths or four-fifths, or any kind of majority which includes certain States or groups of States such as the States represented on the Trusteeship Council or such of these States as administer Trust territories. Can it be said that all these procedures, as well as that of absolute unanimity, are ruled out for the reason that they are constitutionally inadmissible having regard to the Charter of the United Nations and the fact that the only voting procedure permitted to the General Assembly is that of simple majority or of a two-thirds majority? Is it legally possible for the General Assembly, in any circumstances, to adopt a voting procedure different from that laid down in the Charter, namely, simple majority or a two-thirds majority? Is it legally possible for it to determine that a certain type of question shall be decided in the future by any of the alternative voting procedures as outlined above? If it is legally possible for the General Assembly to adopt any of these voting systems and if Rule F, which replaces the unanimity rule by a two-thirds majority, is not, upon examination, shown to represent the closest possible approximation to the procedure of the Council of the League of Nations, then there arises in an acute form the question of its compatibility with the opinion of the Court given in 1950. What is the answer to these questions?

To put it in different words, must Rule F be regarded as approximating 'as far as possible' to the procedure of the Council of the League for the reason that under the voting system of the Charter no other voting procedure save that of simple majority or a two-thirds majority is possible or permissible? Did the Court have that limitation in mind when it used the expression 'as far as possible'? That this was so was repeatedly asserted during the debates in the General Assembly and in the Committee for South-West Africa. It is a problem which is essential to the whole question. Its examination – and an answer to it – cannot be avoided on the ground that a positive answer constitutes a juridical impossibility. The General Assembly did not consider it in that light for, as stated, it specifically asked the Court to say what should be its alternative voting procedure in case the Court should give a negative answer to the main question put to it. Neither can the answer to the constitutional aspect of the question be taken as self-evident by way of 'construction' in the sense that as the Court held that the supervision must lie with the General Assembly, the General Assembly can resort for that purpose to a procedure no other than that laid down in the Charter, and that by adopting Rule F it followed the procedure of the Council of the League as far as possible. To do so is to beg the question. Neither do I think it permissible to avoid it because of the difficulty raised by a baffling practice and by conflicting considerations of principle.

Principle would seem to suggest that it is not legally possible for the General Assembly to decide – whether by an ordinary majority or a two-thirds majority – that any question or category of questions, or all questions, shall be in the future decided by a majority of three-fourths or four-fifths or by a unanimous vote. The reasons for that view are persuasive. If the General Assembly were to make any such decision, it would be depriving some, as yet undetermined, Members of the General

Assembly of the right, safeguarded by the Charter, to have a matter determined by a two-thirds majority in which they participate. If that is so, then it would appear that the General Assembly is not legally in the position to adopt any such special procedure of voting even in pursuance of an advisory opinion of the Court. Any such change must be the result of an amendment of the Charter. This view is strengthened by jurisprudential considerations of obvious cogency:

The size of the majority required for the validity of the decisions of a corporate political body is not a mere matter of technical convenience or mathematical computation. It is expressive of the basic political philosophy of the organization. A study of the preparatory work of the Conference of San Francisco, including that of the Dumbarton Oaks proposals, shows that the adoption of the existing system of voting was the result of prolonged deliberation. In any case it now forms part of the law of the Charter. Unlike in the League of Nations, the basic philosophy of the Charter of the United Nations is, to put it in a negative form, that of the rejection of the rule of unanimity. There is not a single provision of the Charter which prescribes or authorizes for voting in the General Assembly the requirement of unanimity or any kind of majority other than a simple or two-thirds majority (although, significantly, there is in Articles 108 and 109 a provision for a majority which must include Permanent Members of the Security Council). It is outside the purpose of this opinion to inquire into the reason and objects of that system of voting based on the rejection of unanimity or anything approaching it. It suffices to say that the system as adopted is in accordance with the structure of the United Nations conceived as an entity existing, as it were, independently of its Members and endowed with a personality of its own – one aspect of which is vividly illustrated by the opinion of the Court in the *Injuries* case – as distinguished from the League of Nations which in acting, by virtue of the principle of unanimity, by agreement rather than by majority, bore the character of an association of a different character.

Principle would seem to demand that whenever the basic instrument of a corporate political body prescribes the manner in which its collective will is to be formed and expressed, that basic instrument is in this respect paramount and overriding and nothing save a constitutional amendment as distinguished from legislative action can authorize an alternative procedure of voting. On that view it would not seem to matter, in the case of the United Nations, whether the action is taken in pursuance of the objects of organization, or in pursuance of a function accepted under some extraneous instrument such as a treaty. Such function must in any case lie within the orbit of its competence as laid down in the Charter. For the organization cannot accept the fulfilment of a task which lies outside the scope of its functions as determined by its constitution. Thus, for instance, if two or more States were to confer by treaty upon the General Assembly certain functions in the sphere of pacific settlement – e.g. by appointing an arbitration commission or by deciding itself the disputed issue – and if the treaty provided that these functions shall be fulfilled by a three-fourths or four-fifths majority or qualified unanimity, principle would seem to suggest that the General Assembly cannot act in that way. It cannot override a seemingly mandatory provision of the Charter by the device of accepting a task conferred by a treaty. It might otherwise be possible to alter, through extraneous treaties, the character of the Organization in an important aspect of its activity.

These were probably the reasons – although they do not seem to have been expressed in articulate language – which made some Members of the United Nations insist that in giving its opinion in 1950 the Court must have envisaged the voting procedure of the General Assembly such as it is and must have ruled out the possibility of its being adapted to the governing requirement that the degree of supervision must not exceed that under the system of Mandates. In doing so, they were able to point to the Advisory Opinion no. 12 on the *Interpretation of the Treaty of Lausanne* in which the Court appeared to have laid down the principle that a political body entrusted with a decision by virtue of an extraneous instrument can proceed in the matter only in accordance with its own procedure of voting. If that view, so cogently supported by principle and, apparently, by the Court, is correct, then, clearly, Rule F cannot be challenged on the ground that it is tainted by an avoidable failure to approximate to the voting procedure of the Council of the League. It means, to put it in different words, that Rule F is a correct interpretation of the opinion of 1950 for the reason: (*a*) that the absolute unanimity rule, even if it were correct, could not be given effect having regard to the binding character of the voting procedure of the Charter; and (*b*) that, for the same reason, it was not legally possible for the General Assembly to contemplate or to adopt any alternative procedure falling short of absolute unanimity.

* * *

However, although the view as here outlined seems to be supported by principle and practice, there are opposing considerations both of practice and principle. In fact, the Permanent Court of International Justice, after enunciating in Advisory Opinion no. 12 the rule which seems to go one way, qualified it in the same opinion in the opposite direction. It began by rejecting the view, put forward by Great Britain, that the unanimity rule as laid down in Article 5 of the Covenant. contemplated only the exercise of powers granted in the Covenant itself, It said: 'The fact that the present case concerns the exercise of a power outside the normal province of the Council, clearly cannot be used as an argument for the diminution of the safeguards with which, in the Covenant, it was felt necessary to surround the Council's decision.'[1] It thus seems to have adopted the view, which I have described as seemingly being in accordance with principle, that a political body can act only in accordance with the procedure as laid down in its constitution. However, after having said that, the Court proceeded to qualify the apparent general rule. It said: 'On the other hand, no one denies that the Council can undertake to give decisions by a majority in specific cases, if express provision is made for this power by treaty stipulations.'[2] Again, after referring to the binding character of the voting procedure of a 'body already constituted and having its own rules of organization and procedure', it qualified that statement by adding: 'unless a contrary intention has been expressed'.[3]

In thus qualifying the major principle which it enunciated and on which it acted, the Court was in fact able to rely on – although it did not refer to – some substantial practice of the League of Nations. Of that practice the Rules of Procedure adopted by the Assembly and the Council of the League provide a significant example. Article 5(1) of the Covenant laid down as follows: 'Except when otherwise provided in this Covenant or by the terms of the present treaty, decisions of any meeting of the Assembly, or of the Council, require the agreement of all the Members represented at the meeting.' However, the Rules of Procedure, subsequently framed with respect to both the Assembly and the Council, effected in this matter an important – though at first sight inconspicuous – change. In Rule 19(1) of the Rules of Procedure of the Assembly the words of Article 5, paragraph 1, of the Covenant were reproduced with a significant modification. In place of the words 'by the terms of the present treaty' there were substituted the words 'of *a* treaty'. Article 8, paragraph (1), of the Council's Rules of Procedure made the same change. In the Rules of Procedure of the Council, adopted on 26 May 1933, this aspect of the matter was expressed even more clearly. Article 9 of the revised Rules provided as follows: 'Except where otherwise expressly provided by the Covenant, or by the terms of any other instrument which is to be applied, decisions at any meeting of the Council require the agreement of all the Members of the League represented at the meeting.'

[1] *P.C.I.J.* Series B, no. 12, p. 30. [2] At p. 30. [3] At p. 31.

Moreover, in a large number of treaties adopted subsequent to the Peace Treaties and in some cases expressly accepted by the Council, provision was made for voting by some kind of majority as distinguished from unanimity. This applied in particular to the 'Minorities Treaties' which all contained provisions allowing the Council to proceed by a majority of votes in proposing modifications to these treaties. Similar provisions were incorporated in some other instruments such as Article 4 of the Declaration of 9 November 1921, of the Principal Allied Powers concerning Albania; Article 15 of the second Geneva Protocol of 14 March 1924, concerning the economic rehabilitation of Hungary; Article 14 of Annex 2 and Article 4 of Annex 3 of the Memel Agreement of 8 May 1924, between the Principal Allied Powers and Lithuania; Article 9 of the Financial Agreement of 9 December 1927, between Bulgaria and Greece; Article 7 of the Agreement of 20 October 1921, concerning the non-militarization and neutralization of the Aaland Islands; Article 8 of the Locarno Pact of 16 October 1925; Article 28(3) of the Agreement on Financial Assistance of 2 October 1930. And, of course, there were numerous provisions to that effect in the various Peace Treaties to which, as stated, express reference was made in the Covenant. There was no disposition among authors who commented in detail upon the amended Rules of Procedure and the provisions of these treaties to question their propriety in any way.[1]

Having regard to the practice of the League of Nations and to the important qualification of the apparent major principle expressed by the Court in Advisory Opinion no. 12, as well as to considerations of a practical character, it cannot be said, by way of an absolute rule, that in no circumstances may the General Assembly act by a system of voting other than that laid down in the Charter. There is no room for any emphasis of language suggesting that any such modification of the voting procedure is a juridical impossibility. Frequent practice of the League of Nations accomplished that juridical impossibility and the Court expressly gave it its approval. On the other hand, in view of the persuasiveness of the contrary considerations outlined above, it does not seem to me permissible to go as far as the Rules of Procedure of the Assembly or the Council of the League – or, indeed, the Court itself in Advisory Opinion no. 12 – went in this respect and to hold that a modification of the system of voting is permitted every time when the organization acts under a treaty other than its own constitutional Charter. The correct rule seems to lie half-way between these two solutions. The available practice and considerations of utility point to the justification

[1] See Schücking-Wehberg, *Die Satzung des Völkerbundes* (3rd ed. 1931), I, 517, 521; Ray, *Commentaire du Pacte de la Société des Nations* (1930), pp. 226, 227; Stone, in *B.Y.* 14 (1933), 33–5.

of a rule which recognizes in this matter a measure of elasticity not inconsistent with the fundamental structure of the Organization. Within these limits, it is in my view a sound legal proposition that such modification is permissible under the terms of a general treaty, in the general international interest, and in relation to institutions and arrangements partaking of an international status – in particular, in cases in which the General Assembly acts in substitution for a body which has hitherto fulfilled the functions in question. This is the position in the present case. While the powers of the General Assembly in the matter are to be exercised primarily in pursuance of the Charter as interpreted by the Court in its opinion rendered in 1950, and in particular of Articles 10 and 80, they are also to be exercised in pursuance of the continuing system of Mandates whose obligations were declared by the Court to be binding upon the Union of South Africa in respect of the territory which continues to be held under the international Mandate assumed by her in 1920. In view of this, there is room, as a matter of law, for the modification of the voting procedure of the General Assembly in respect of a jurisdiction whose source is of a dual character inasmuch as it emanates both from the Charter and the Mandate. In so far as considerations of international interest constitute a legitimate factor in the situation, they do so with much cogency in a situation which concerns the exercise of an international trust in respect of a territory which is endowed with an international status, which is the subject of an opinion of this Court, and which has been the cause of international friction.

The question which calls for an answer is whether in the present case there exists a treaty of a character as described above. The words of the opinion of 1950 seem to suggest a negative answer inasmuch as the opinion lays down that 'the competence of the General Assembly of the United Nations to exercise such supervision and to receive and examine reports is derived from the provisions of Article 10 of the Charter'.[1] However, the passage must be read not in isolation but in the general context of the Opinion and in the light of the dual character of the source of the supervisory function of the General Assembly. The true meaning of the passage in question is that Article 10 of the Charter confers upon the General Assembly the competence to fulfil the functions as derived from the international instrument which establishes the international status of the territory in question, namely, the Mandate. It is the Mandate which is the original source of the powers of the General Assembly. The competence to apply the Mandate is derived from Article 10.

It follows from what has been said above that there is no warrant for

[1] *I.C.J. Reports*, p. 137.

considering as a dogma, for which no proof is required and with regard to which any contrary evidence can be ignored, the rule that under no circumstances may the General Assembly act under a voting procedure other than that laid down in Article 18. This being so, what are the modifications of the voting procedure of the General Assembly which may properly be contemplated in this connection? It is clear that any application of the principle of absolute unanimity – which in any case would be ruled out by virtue of the answer given above to question 1 – is inadmissible under the legal principle here formulated for the reason that it offends against a fundamental tenet of the constitution of the United Nations, namely, the abandonment of the doctrine of unanimity. For the same reason there would seem to be no room for a system of qualified unanimity not including the vote of the Administering State – a system which would be open to the additional objection that it would place South Africa in some ways in a better position than that obtaining under the procedure of the Council of the League. For the number of States required for unanimity in the General Assembly is about four times as large as in the Council of the League.

Yet there was – and there is – room for exploring the practicability of voting procedures lying half-way between qualified unanimity and a two-thirds majority. This opinion is not the appropriate occasion for an examination of these solutions. There may be an element of artificiality in some of them inasmuch as they must of necessity leave out of account the differences in the composition of the General Assembly and the Council of the League. The discussions on the General Assembly show a somewhat disturbing absence of attempts to explore some of the more practicable possibilities – though this fact may perhaps be explained by the repetitive and rigid adherence on the part of the Government of South Africa, an adherence unrelieved by alternative proposals, to the notion of absolute unanimity. In particular, there is room for the consideration of a solution consisting, on the analogy of Articles 108 and 109 of the Charter, in qualifying the requirement of a two-thirds majority, as laid down in Rule F, by the additional requirement that it must include either all the Members of the Trusteeship Council other than South Africa or all its Members other than South Africa administering Trust territories. I am not prepared to say that some such solution, couched in the very language of Article 18 of the Charter, would be inconsistent with it. There is only limited merit in a judicial interpretation intent upon extracting every ounce of rigidity from a written constitution or in simplifying the issue by concentrating exclusively on extreme solutions. Thus, while unanimity, absolute or qualified, may be entirely alien to the spirit of the Charter and as such inconsistent with it, this does not apply to alternative solutions falling short of unanimity. In particular, when the General Assembly takes over functions from a body whose procedure it is enjoined to follow as far as possible, it seems to me reasonable to explore, in a spirit of accommodation free from exaggerations of language, other solutions appropriate to the situation and not basically inconsistent with the Charter.

Accordingly, in so far as Rule F fails to provide for practicable modifications of the voting procedure of the General Assembly, not inconsistent with the fundamental principles of the Charter of the United Nations on the subject, I might, if not prevented by my answer to question 3, feel bound to hold that Rule F does not approximate as far as possible to the voting procedure of the Council of the League and that in so far as it involves a higher degree of supervision it fails to conform with the opinion rendered in 1950. However, I cannot so hold for the reason that my answer to question 3 is that, as the decisions of the General Assembly are not of a legal effect equal to that of the decisions of the Council of the League, Rule F does not involve a degree of supervision exceeding that in force under the Mandates system and that it therefore constitutes a correct interpretation of the opinion rendered by the Court in 1950.

Question 3 : 'Do the decisions of the General Assembly possess the same legal force in the system of supervision as the decisons of the Council of the League of Nations?'

The final, and in my view, decisive question is whether it cannot correctly be said that Rule F is in accordance with the opinion of the Court rendered in 1950 for the reason that what South Africa is now asked to accept are majority decisions which are not binding or not fully binding in place of decisions which were binding — which means in effect that she is asked to accept a system of supervision which, far from being more exacting, is much less so. Even if it is assumed that she was not bound by decisions of the League Council to which she did not agree and that she could prevent any such decision from coming into force, can it not be said that she is not bound or not fully bound by the decisions of the General Assembly for the simple reason that these are not binding or not fully binding ? If the Court were to accept that argument, it would have to reject the assertion that Rule F implies a degree of supervision in excess of that obtaining under the system of Mandates. There would be such excess of supervision if the decision of the General Assembly reached by a two-thirds majority had the same legal and binding force as unanimous resolutions of the Council of the League of

Nations. On the other hand, if the position is in fact that, while the supervision by the General Assembly exceeds that of the Council of the League of Nations inasmuch as it is exercised by a majority vote of two-thirds and thus deprived of the safeguards of unanimity, it is at the same time less exacting inasmuch as it is exercised by means of decisions of a character less binding than those of the Council of the League of Nations – if that is the position, can it not be fairly held that there is established a rough equivalence of supervision which brings Rule F within the terms of the ruling of the Court in its advisory opinion rendered in 1950? My view is that that contention is fully relevant to the present case and that it is substantially correct.

Although decisions of the General Assembly are endowed with full legal effect in some spheres of the activity of the United Nations and with limited legal effect in other spheres, it may be said, by way of a broad generalization, that they are not legally binding upon the Members of the United Nations. In some matters – such as the election of the Secretary-General, election of members of the Economic and Social Council and of some members of the Trusteeship Council, the adoption of rules of procedure, admission to, suspension from and termination of membership, and approval of the budget and the apportionment of expenses – the full legal effects of the Resolutions of the General Assembly are undeniable. But, in general, they are in the nature of recommendations and it is in the nature of recommendations that, although on proper occasions they provide a legal authorization for Members determined to act upon them individually or collectively, they do not create a legal obligation to comply with them. This is so although Rule F and the General Assembly's request for the present opinion both refer to 'decisions' which, in ordinary connotation, signify binding expressions of will. In fact, the request of the General Assembly and the special Rule F, in referring to 'decisions', contemplate decisions in their wider, somewhat non-technical, sense as used in Article 18 of the Charter of the United Nations. The intended reference is to Resolutions generally, a generic term which, although it does not occur in the Charter, has found an accepted place in the practice of the United Nations. Now 'resolutions' cover two distinct matters: They cover occasionally decisions which have a definite binding effect either in relation to Members of the United Nations or its organs or both, or the United Nations as a whole. But normally they refer to recommendations, properly so called, whose legal effect, although not always altogether absent, is more limited and approaching what, when taken in isolation, appears to be no more than a moral obligation.

This, in principle, is also the position with respect to the recommendations of the General Assembly in relation to the administration of Trust territories. The Trusteeship agreements do not provide for a legal obligation of the Administering Authority to comply with the decisions of the organs of the United Nations in the matter of Trusteeship. Thus there is no legal obligation, on the part of the Administering Authority, to give effect to a recommendation of the General Assembly to adopt or depart from a particular course of legislation or any particular administrative measure. The legal obligation resting upon the Administering Authority is to administer the Trust Territory in accordance with the principles of the Charter and the provisions of the Trusteeship agreement, but not necessarily in accordance with any specific recommendation of the General Assembly or of the Trusteeship Council. This is so as a matter both of existing law and of sound principles of government. The Administering Authority, not the General Assembly, bears the direct responsibility for the welfare of the population of the Trust Territory. There is no sufficient guarantee of the timeliness and practicability of a particular recommendation made by a body acting occasionally amidst a pressure of business, at times deprived of expert advice and information, and not always able to foresee the consequences of a particular measure in relation to the totality of legislation and administration of the Trust Territory. Recommendations in the sphere of Trusteeship have been made by the General Assembly frequently and as a matter of course. To suggest that any such particular recommendation is binding in the sense that there is a legal obligation to put it into effect is to run counter not only to the paramount rule that the General Assembly has no legal power to legislate or bind its Members by way of recommendations, but, for reasons stated, also to cogent considerations of good government and administration.

In fact States administering Trust territories have often asserted their right not to accept recommendations of the General Assembly or of the Trusteeship Council as approved by the General Assembly. That right has never been seriously challenged. There are numerous examples of express refusal on the part of the Administering Authority to comply with a recommendation. This occurred, for instance, with regard to the recommendation of the Trusteeship Council at its Third Session,[1] which considered that the existing tribal structure in Tanganyika is an obstacle to the political and social advancement of the indigenous inhabitants – a recommendation which the Administering Authority rejected on the ground that 'the great mass of the people everywhere are strongly attached to their tribal institutions and in most cases offer

[1] *Official Records of the General Assembly*, Third Session, Supplement no. 4 (A/603), p. 31.

strong resistance to any suggestions of serious modification'.[1] When the Trusteeship Council recommended that consideration be given to the introduction of a system of universal suffrage applicable to all inhabitants of Western Samoa,[2] the Administering Authority informed the Council that 'it would be entirely wrong to force on the Samoans any radical change in their customs since the introduction of universal suffrage at this stage would be incompatible with that respect for Samoan culture to which it and the Government of Western Samoa are equally urged by the Trusteeship Council'.[3] When the Trusteeship Council recommended in respect of Nauru that the long-term royalty investment funds should not necessarily be limited to Australian Government securities, but should be invested freely in the best interest of the Nauruans, the Administering Authority explained why it was unable to act upon the recommendation.[4] When the Trusteeship Council recommended the reconsideration of the head tax in the Pacific Islands, the Administering Authority explained why in its opinion this was a satisfactory and desirable form of tax under the economic and political conditions prevailing in the Trust Territory.[5]

* * *

I have elaborated at what may appear to be excessive length a point which seems non-controversial, namely, that recommendations of the General Assembly are not binding. I have done it by reference to recommendations which are relevant to the issue now before the Court, namely, the recommendations with respect to Trust territories. They are so relevant although, of course, the territory of South-West Africa is not a Trust Territory. However, unless adequately explained and qualified, this statement of the legal position is bound to be incomplete to the point of being misleading. For reasons stated at the end of this opinion, although I am basing my answer to this question on the view that the decisions of the General Assembly do not possess the same legal value as those of the Council of the League, I consider it essential to explain and to qualify this aspect of the present separate opinion. It is one thing to affirm the somewhat obvious principle that the recommendations of the General Assembly in the matter of trusteeship or otherwise addressed to the Members of the United Nations are not legally binding upon them in the sense that full effect must be given to them. It is another thing to give currency to the view that they have no force at all whether

[1] *Report for 1948*, p. 52.
[2] *Official Records of the General Assembly*, Fourth Session, Supplement no. 4 (A/933), p. 58.
[3] *Ibid.* (A/1903/Add. 2), p. 9.
[4] *Ibid.* (A/933), p. 77; Fifth Session, Supplement no. 4 (A/1306), p. 134.
[5] *Reports of the Trusteeship Council to the Security Council* (5/1358), p. 13, (S/1628), p. 15.

legal or other and that therefore they cannot be regarded as forming in any sense part of a legal system of supervision.

In the first instance, not all the resolutions of the General Assembly in the matter are in the form of recommendations addressed to the Administering Authority. They are often, in form and in substance, directives addressed to the organs of the United Nations such as the Trusteeship Council or the Secretary-General. As such, they are endowed with legal validity and effect. They are measures of supervision of a force comparable with the legal effects of such acts of the General Assembly as the election of members of the Trusteeship Council or the confirmation of the Trusteeship agreements. A survey of the resolutions passed by the General Assembly in the sphere of Trusteeship shows the frequency of this aspect of the supervisory function of the General Assembly.

However, even in relation to the Administering Authority the question of the effect of the decision of the General Assembly cannot accurately be answered by the simple statement that they are not legally binding. In general it is clear that as the General Assembly has no power of decision – as distinguished from recommendation – imposing itself with binding force upon the substantive action of the Member States, its Resolutions have *per se* no binding force in relation to the Administering State. Thus that State is not bound to comply with any specific Resolution recommending it to undertake or to abstain from any particular legislative or administrative action. As stated, no considerations of practical persuasiveness permit any different interpretation of the existing law on the subject. I have referred to cases in which the Administering Authority has expressly declined to act upon the recommendation addressed to it. Its right to do so has never been challenged. What has been challenged – and, I believe, properly challenged – is its right simply to ignore the recommendations and to abstain from adducing reasons for not putting them into effect or for not submitting them for examination with the view to giving effect to them. What has been questioned is the opinion that a recommendation is of no legal effect whatsoever. A Resolution recommending to an Administering State a specific course of action creates *some* legal obligation which, however rudimentary, elastic and imperfect, is nevertheless a legal obligation and constitutes a measure of supervision. The State in question, while not bound to accept the recommendation, is bound to give it due consideration in good faith. If, having regard to its own ultimate responsibility for the good government of the territory, it decides to disregard it, it is bound to explain the reasons for its decision. These obligations appear intangible and almost nominal when, compared with the ultimate discretion of the Administering Authority. They nevertheless constitute an obligation; they have been acknowledged as such by the Administering Authorities. This appear swith some clarity from the searching discussion at the Sixth General Assembly in 1952 which followed upon the presentation by the Secretary-General, in pursuance of a previous recommendation of the General Assembly, of a series of documents entitled *Information on the Implementation of Trusteeship Council and General Assembly Resolutions relating to Trust Territories.*[1] (In Resolution 436 (V) of 2 December 1950 the General Assembly requested the Secretary-General to report to it on the measures taken by the Administering Authorities to implement the Resolutions of the General Assembly and the Trusteeship Council and if there had been no action on the part of an Administering Authority in respect of any particular Resolution to set forth the reasons given concerning that matter.) While pointing to the difficulties in the way of giving effect to some of the recommendations and while affirming their own final responsibility and their own right of ultimate decision, various delegations of the Administering States made no attempt to assert that these recommendations were *bruta fulmina* devoid of any element of legal obligation. Thus at the Sixth General Assembly, in the course of the debate of the Trusteeship Committee, the representative of the United Kingdom stated as follows: 'The United Kingdom considered that, in cases where the Trusteeship Council and the General Assembly had adopted Resolutions concerning the Trust territories, they were perfectly entitled to be informed of the decisions taken by the Administering Authorities in regard to them.'[2] Although, as stated, the Trusteeship agreements do not provide for a legal obligation of the Administering Authority to comply with the decisions of an organ of the United Nations, they are not in this respect devoid of an element of legal obligation. In practically all of them the Administering Authority undertakes to collaborate fully with the General Assembly and the Trusteeship Council in the discharge of their functions, to facilitate periodic missions, and the like. Such collaboration, which is a matter of legal duty, is initiated by decisions of the organs of the United Nations.

Both principle and practice would thus appear to suggest that the discretion which, in the sphere of the administration of Trust territories or territories assimilated thereto is vested in the Members of the United Nations in respect of the Resolutions of the General Assembly, is not a discretion tantamount to unrestricted freedom of action. It is a discretion to be exercised in good faith. Undoubtedly, the degree of applica-

[1] A/1903; A/1903/Add. 1; A/1903/Add. 2 (October 1952).

[2] 245th Meeting, 12 January 1952, Fourth Committee, *Sixth General Assembly*, p. 295.

tion of good faith in the exercise of full discretion does not lend itself to rigid legal appreciation. This fact does not destroy altogether the legal relevance of the discretion thus to be exercised. This is particularly so in relation to a succession of recommendations, on the same subject and with regard to the same State, solemnly reaffirmed by the General Assembly. Whatever may be the content of the recommendation and whatever may be the nature and the circumstances of the majority by which it has been reached, it is nevertheless a legal act of the principal organ of the United Nations which Members of the United Nations are under a duty to treat with a degree of respect appropriate to a Resolution of the General Assembly. The same considerations apply to Resolutions in the sphere of territories administered by virtue of the principles of the system of Trusteeship. Although there is no automatic obligation to accept fully a particular recommendation or series of recommendations, there is a legal obligation to act in good faith in accordance with the principles of the Charter and of the system of Trusteeship. An Administering State may not be acting illegally by declining to act upon a recommendation or series of recommendations on the same subject. But in doing so it acts at its peril when a point is reached when the cumulative effect of the persistent disregard of the articulate opinion of the Organization is such as to foster the conviction that the State in question has become guilty of disloyalty to the principles and purposes of the Charter. Thus an Administering State which consistently sets itself above the solemnly and repeatedly expressed judgment of the Organization, in particular in proportion as that judgment approximates to unanimity, may find that it has overstepped the imperceptible line between impropriety and illegality, between discretion and arbitrariness, between the exercise of the legal right to disregard the recommendation and the abuse of that right, and that it has exposed itself to consequences legitimately following as a legal sanction.

Moreover – and for similar reasons – even if the view is adopted that the effect of a decision of the General Assembly is no greater than its moral force, a decision thus conceived still constitutes a measure of supervision. A system of supervision devoid of an element of legal obligation and legal sanction can nevertheless provide a powerful degree of supervision because of the moral force inherent in its findings and recommendations. It will be noted – and the matter is not without significance – that the advisory opinion of 1950 lays down not only that the new system must not add to the legal obligations of South Africa; it says that the degree of supervision must not exceed that obtaining under the League of Nations. The phrase 'degree of supervision' used in the advisory opinion of 1950 does not refer necessarily or exclusively to supervision exercised by means of legally binding or enforceable pronouncements. Moral reprobation following upon non-compliance with a valid recommendation adopted in conformity with the Charter may provide a means of supervision as potent as or more potent than a legal sanction.

This absence of a purely legal machinery and the reliance upon the moral authority of the findings and the reports of the Mandates Commission were in fact the essential feature of the supervision of the Mandates system. Public opinion – and the resulting attitude of the Mandatory Powers – were influenced not so much by the formal Resolutions of the Council and Assembly as by the reports of the Mandates Commission, which was the true organ of supervision. In legal theory the Mandates Commission was no more than a subsidiary and expert organ of the Council which received and approved its reports and which occasionally softened their impact by the use of diplomatic language intent upon not offending the susceptibilities of the Mandatory Power. The Commission could not communicate directly with the Mandatory Powers and was often reminded of the limitations of its authority. Its representatives who appeared before the Council often acknowledged those limitations and deprecated any intention of exceeding them. But it was a fact which was generally recognized and of which judicial notice must be taken that the actual scrutiny of the conduct of the Mandatory Power rested with the Mandates Commission. Yet no legal sanction was attached to non-compliance with or disregard of the recommendations, the hopes and the regrets of the Commission. The legal sanction of the judicial supervision by the Permanent Court of International Justice, although forming part of all Mandates, was never invoked. The occasional public and detailed discussions before the General Assembly and the Council, which influenced powerfully public opinion and the conduct of the Mandatory, were in pursuance of the reports of the Mandates Commission.

There are two reasons why I have considered it essential to elaborate the point – which in a sense seems to put in doubt the grounds of my own final conclusion – that decisions of the General Assembly in the matter of territories administered under the principles of Trusteeship have, after all, some legal and certainly some moral effect and that they may therefore be regarded as a factor in the legal system of supervision in which the system of voting is relevant:

In the first instance, the preceding observations show that I have not reached the final conclusion without some hesitation and without having fully weighed the correctness of an opposite conclusion, which is that although the decisions of the General Assembly have no full legal effect they are nevertheless a weighty factor in the system of supervision and that therefore the procedure of the voting by which they are reached is decisive for the purpose of the opinion of the Court.

The second reason is that, after full allowance has been made for the necessity of stating what is the inexorable legal position resulting from the very nature of 'recommendations', it is not admissible to give currency to an interpretation, without qualifying it in all requisite details, which gratuitously weakens the effectiveness of the Charter. It would be wholly inconsistent with sound principles of interpretation as well as with highest international interest, which can never be legally irrelevant, to reduce the value of the Resolutions of the General Assembly – one of the principal instrumentalities of the formation of the collective will and judgment of the community of nations represented by the United Nations – and to treat them, for the purpose of this opinion and otherwise, as nominal, insignificant and having no claim to influence the conduct of the Members. International interest demands that no judicial support, however indirect, be given to any such conception of the Resolutions of the General Assembly as being of no consequence.

These considerations, as well as actual practice, prevent me from basing my conclusion on the proposition that the decisions of the General Assembly have no binding effect at all. However, there is no escape from the fact that they are of a legal potency lower than that implicit in the Resolutions of the Council of the League. To that fact I must attach decisive importance. It is unreasonable to claim that decisions of distinctly more limited legal value than that inherent in the decisions of the Council of the League of Nations must be reached by the same exacting and rigid system of voting. The fact that some resolutions of the General Assembly in the matter of Trusteeship and elsewhere have a definite legal effect does not alter decisively the normal situation. This being so, I come to the conclusion, with regard to question 3, that Rule F constitutes a correct interpretation of the opinion of the Court given in 1950.

* * *

Accordingly, while I have reached the final result on grounds different from those underlying the opinion of the Court, I concur in its operative part for the reason:

(1) that, in so far as the doubts as to the correctness of Rule F were prompted by the contention that the vote of the General Assembly on reports and petitions from South Africa is subject to the rule of absolute unanimity on the ground that this was the rule obtaining in the Council

of the League of Nations, there is doubt whether such rule can correctly be held to have been in actual operation at the time of the dissolution of the League in the Council of the League acting as the supervisory organ of the Mandates system;

(2) that, in so far as it is contended that the vote of the General Assembly on these questions might be subject to some other procedure of voting more exacting than a two-thirds majority, though falling short of absolute unanimity, Rule F is nevertheless in accordance with a correct interpretation of the opinion of the Court given in 1950. This is so for the reason that the decisions of the General Assembly in the meaning of Rule F do not possess a degree of legal authority equal to that of the decisions of the Council of the League of Nations. In view of this, although adopted through a less stringent voting procedure, they cannot be held to involve a degree of supervision exceeding that which obtained under the Mandates system. These considerations would also apply if, contrary to the conclusion (1), it could be held that the decisions of the Council of the League on the subject required absolute unanimity.

CHAPTER 4

ADMISSIBILITY OF HEARINGS OF PETITIONERS

Editor's note On 1 June 1956 the International Court of Justice gave an advisory opinion on *Admissibility of Hearings of Petitioners by the Committee on South-West Africa* (*I.C.J. Reports* 1956, p. 23). The question put to the Court was:

> Is it consistent with the advisory opinion of the International Court of Justice of 11 July 1950 for the Committee on South-West Africa, established by General Assembly resolution 749A (VIII) of 28 November 1953, to grant oral hearings to petitioners on matters relating to the Territory of South-West Africa?

The Court, by eight votes to five, answered the question in the affirmative. Lauterpacht concurred in the operative part of the Court's opinion, but gave the separate opinion reprinted here (see *I.C.J. Reports* 1956, pp. 35–59).

While I am in general agreement with the opinion of the Court, I have concurred in it subject to reservations both with regard to the scope of the operative part of the opinion and the reasons adduced in support of it. Moreover, I feel it my duty to elaborate in more detail certain questions relating to the main problem confronting the Court.

I

There arises in the present case a preliminary issue which is to a large extent responsible for the division of the Court and which is connected in a significant manner with the exercise of its advisory function.

The request for the present advisory opinion of the Court is stated in apparently general terms. It runs as follows: 'Is it consistent with the advisory opinion of the International Court of Justice of 11 July 1950 for the Committee on South-West Africa, established by General Assembly Resolution 749A (VIII) of 28 November 1953, to grant oral hearings to petitioners on matters relating to the Territory of South-West Africa?' Thus put, the question does not seem to refer to any specific situation. In view of this, it has been suggested – a suggestion to which the Court, rightly in my view, has declined to accede – that the reply of the Court must be of a general character unrelated to the events and providing no answer to the difficulty which underlay the request for the opinion. Yet it is clear from the documents transmitted to the Court by the Secretary-General that in asking the Court for an opinion on the question whether oral hearings of petitioners on matters relating to the Territory of South-West Africa are consistent with the opinion of the Court of 11 July 1950, the General Assembly was referring not to this question in general but to one aspect of that question as it results from a particular situation. The gist of that situation is that, while the General Assembly has with practical unanimity approved the opinion of the Court of 11 July 1950, the Union of South Africa has declined to accept it as expressing the correct legal position and that it has refused to comply with its principal obligations in respect of the supervision of the legal régime of the Mandated Territory of South-West Africa as ascertained by the Court in its opinion of 11 July 1950. In particular, it has declined to provide the supervising authority with annual reports and to lend its assistance by forwarding, commenting upon, or participating in the examination of written petitions submitted to the Committee on South-West Africa. It is on account of that situation that the Court has been requested to give the present advisory opinion. So far as I am aware, no suggestion has been made from any quarter that the Committee on South-West Africa is or should be entitled to grant oral hearings even if the Union of South Africa fulfils her obligations as Mandatory in the matter of annual reports and petitions. It cannot be reasonably assumed that in framing its request the General Assembly intended no more than to obtain the confirmation of a proposition which has not been disputed and which is not at issue. The General Assembly could not have intended to confine the task of the Court to an academic exercise not requiring any notable display of judicial effort.

This being so, the Court cannot answer the question put to it without direct reference to a situation of which a complete picture is presented in the documents which have been sent to it by the Secretary-General and of which it must also otherwise take judicial notice. Moreover, that particular situation is set out in the very terms of the request for an advisory opinion. The request expressly refers to Resolution 749A (VIII) of 28 November 1953 which, in its recitals, includes an account of the attitude adopted by the Union of South Africa. Even if the Court were to ignore the official documents, minutes and reports submitted to it by the Secretary-General, the wording of the request, in embodying Resolution 749A (VIII), must be held to give, in considerable detail, a picture of the problem confronting the General Assembly. It is clear, therefore, that there is no warrant in the present case for extracting from the wording of the request for the opinion of the Court all possible element of generality and abstraction with the object of producing an answer which is entirely academic in character.

There occurs in the advisory opinion of 28 May 1948 on the *Conditions of Admission of a State to Membership in the United Nations* a passage which, when read in isolation, seems to give support to a view contrary to that here advanced. In that case the Court said: 'It is the duty of the Court to envisage the question submitted to it only in the abstract form which has been given to it; nothing which is said in the present opinion refers, either directly or indirectly, to concrete cases or to particular circumstances.'[1] That passage seems to lend colour to the suggestion that the Court ought also in the present case to answer the question put to it without reference to the circumstances which prompted the General Assembly to make the request. However, on reading the relevant paragraph as a whole it is clear that the passage quoted is not germane to the present issue. The Court was on that occasion concerned with the objection that 'the question put [to it] must be regarded as a political one and that, for this reason, it falls outside the jurisdiction of the Court'. The Court rejected that contention on the ground that it 'cannot attribute a political character to a request which, framed in abstract terms, invites it to undertake an essentially judicial task, the interpretation of a treaty provision' and that 'it is not concerned with the motives which may have inspired this request, nor with the considerations which, in the concrete cases submitted for examination to the Security Council, formed the subject of the exchange of views which took place in that body'. There followed the sentence quoted at the beginning of this paragraph. It will thus be seen from this bare recital that the passage in question is not relevant to the issue now before the Court.

At the same time, while I am in agreement with the present opinion of the Court as to this aspect of the matter, I do not consider that the question put to it by the General Assembly can accurately be answered by way of a simple affirmative. The difficulty arises from the fact that the General Assembly, although actually desirous of an answer of the Court bearing upon a specific situation, cast its request in an apparently general form unrelated to that situation. This being so, a bare affirmative answer does not seem to me to meet the exigencies of the case. It is a matter of common experience that a mere affirmation or a mere denial of a question does not necessarily result in a close approximation to truth. The previous practice of the Court supplies authority for the proposition that the Court enjoys considerable latitude in construing the question put to it or in formulating its answer in such a manner as to

[1] *I.C.J. Reports* 1947–8, p. 61.

make its advisory function effective and useful. Thus, for instance, in the *Jaworzina* case[1] the Court amplified the question submitted to the Court. Although the request for an advisory opinion in that case seemed to be confined to the frontier region of Spisz, the Court came to the conclusion that it must express an opinion on the other parts of the frontier in so far as the delimitation of the frontiers in the entire region may be interdependent. In the case concerning the *Competence of the International Labour Organization*, it restated and limited the question put to it.[2] In the advisory opinion on the *Interpretation of the Greco-Turkish Agreement*, the Court held that as the request for its opinion did not state exactly the question upon which the opinion was sought, 'it is essential that it should determine what this question is and formulate an exact statement of it'.[3] In the field of the contentious procedure the previous jurisprudence of the Court as formulated in its Judgment no. 11 on the *Interpretation of Judgments nos. 7 & 8*[4] contains authority for the proposition that the Court, for the purpose of the interpretation of its judgments – a matter of some importance for the purposes of the present advisory opinion designed to interpret a previous opinion – does not consider itself as bound simply to reply 'yes' or 'no' to the propositions formulated by the parties and that 'it cannot be bound by formulae chosen by the parties concerned, but must be able to take an unhampered decision'.

Undoubtedly it is desirable that the request for an advisory opinion should not, through excess of brevity, make it necessary for the Court to go outside the question as formulated. Reference may be made in this connection to suggestions bearing upon possible developments in the procedure followed by the General Assembly in making requests for an advisory opinion of the Court.[5] However, the absence of the requisite degree of precision or elaboration in the wording of the request does not absolve the Court of the duty to give an effective and accurate answer in conformity with the true purpose of its advisory function. For these reasons I consider that, having regard to the apparently general form in which the request for the opinion is framed, the opinion of the Court in the present case could not properly be couched in terms of 'yes' or 'no' but ought to have been given in relation both to the specific situation underlying the request for the advisory opinion and to the powers of the Committee on South-West Africa irrespective of that situation. An answer which concentrates on only one of these two aspects may well be such as either to ignore the true issue before the Court or to open the door for yet another interpretative opinion.

[1] *P.C.I.J.* Series B, no. 8, p. 50.
[2] *Ibid.* Series B, no. 3, p. 59.
[3] *Ibid.* Series B, no. 16, p. 14.
[4] *Ibid.* Series A, no. 11, p. 4.
[5] See Sir Gerald Fitzmaurice, in *Grotius Society*, 38 (1952), 139.

It may be convenient if, in order to illustrate the above aspect of the present Separate Opinion, I reverse the customary order and give my own version as to what ought to be the answer of the Court in the present case:

(1) It may or may not be consistent with the advisory opinion of 11 July 1950 for the Committee on South-West Africa to grant oral hearings to petitioners on matters relating to the territory of South-West Africa.

(2) In circumstances in which there is present the requisite co-operation on the part of the Mandatory complying with his obligation to send reports and transmit petitions to the supervising authority as envisaged in the opinion of 11 July 1950, it is not consistent with that opinion to grant oral hearings to petitioners.

(3) It is consistent with the advisory opinion of 11 July 1950 for the Committee on South-West Africa to grant oral hearings to petitioners from that territory whenever, and so long as, owing to the absence of such co-operation on the part of the Mandatory, the Committee feels constrained, in order to fulfil the duty entrusted to it by the General Assembly, to use sources of information other than those which would be normally available to it if the Mandatory were willing to assist the Committee in obtaining information in accordance with the procedure as it existed under the League of Nations.

It will be seen that on the main issue, as formulated under (3), my view is substantially identical with that of the operative part of the opinion of the Court. I differ from it inasmuch as, in consequence of the generality of its answer, the latter may be interpreted as meaning that the Committee on South-West Africa is entitled to grant oral hearings even if there is present the necessary co-operation on the part of the Union of South Africa. Any such finding would, in my view, be unwarranted and inconsistent with the opinion of 11 July 1950.

2

I now propose to examine the main substantive question which is relevant to the answer of the Court, namely, whether oral hearings are consistent with that qualifying clause of its opinion of 11 July 1950 which laid down that 'the degree of supervision to be exercised by the General Assembly should not . . . exceed that which applied under the Mandates system, and should conform as far as possible to the procedure followed in this respect by the Council of the League of Nations'. That qualifying clause was in the nature of an elaboration – a necessary elaboration – of the governing consideration which underlay that opinion, namely, that in the absence of a new arrangement agreed to by the Union of South Africa her obligations and her position in the matter of supervision were, in principle, to continue unaltered. No other object can properly be attributed to that qualifying clause. In particular, no intention can reasonably be imputed to the Court to crystallize in absolute terms and in every detail the degree of supervision and the procedure obtaining under the Mandates system. The object was to preserve the degree and the procedure of supervision not as an end in itself or because of any immutable virtue inherent in it, but merely as a means of obviating an extension or diminution of the obligations of the Union of South Africa as a Mandatory. If, as I believe to be the case, the grant of oral hearings does not, upon examination of the entire position ensuing from the attitude of the Union of South Africa, result in any addition to its obligations, then the issue of crystallizing the degree and procedure of supervision cannot properly be deemed to arise.

So far as the language of the above-mentioned qualifying clause is concerned, I have come to the conclusion that normally, i.e. so long as there are available the regular sources of information through annual reports and petitions transmitted by the Union of South Africa in accordance with the opinion of 11 July 1950, the grant of oral hearings to petitioners would exceed the degree of supervision which applied during the Mandates system and that it would not conform to the procedure followed in this respect, i.e. in the matter of supervision, by the Council of the League of Nations. Obtaining of information through oral hearings results in a degree of supervision more stringent than that implied in the system of written petitions. Oral hearings were not permitted under the system applied by the Council of the League of Nations. They were expressly disallowed by it on repeated occasions. As will be submitted later on, that attitude of the Council must be viewed in the light of the circumstances which explained its refusal to authorize oral hearings. However, these circumstances, although they are relevant to the more general issue now before the Court, do not alter the fact that oral hearings found no place in the procedure of supervision as applied under the Mandates system. I have little doubt that this would have been the answer – in the nature of a simple and obvious *constatation* – if that question had been asked during the existence of the League of Nations, at the time of its formal demise in 1946, or when the advisory opinion of the Court was given in 1950.

Neither have I found it possible to rely to any substantial extent on the view that although the Council of the League did not permit and that although it expressly rejected the procedure of oral hearings, it was *entitled* to grant oral hearings by virtue of its inherent powers in the matter of supervision and that these powers passed from the Council of the League of Nations to the General Assembly of the United Nations in conformity with the opinion of the Court of 11 July 1950. Any devolution of powers in this respect could take place only subject to the governing rule as laid down in that opinion, namely, that the degree of supervision by the General Assembly should not exceed that applied under the Mandates system. I find it difficult to accept as a substantial ground for the present opinion of the Court an interpretation which construes that qualifying rule as referring not necessarily to the system which actually applied but to one which could or might have been applied in certain circumstances. The doctrine of implied powers of the Council might, if resorted to, render meaningless – to a large extent – the rule that there must be no excess of supervision. As the Council of the League, in the exercise of its alleged inherent powers, could introduce any means of supervision not patently inconsistent with the Mandate, no means of supervision thus introduced by the General Assembly could conceivably be in excess of the supervision 'applied' under the Mandates system. I cannot accept any such interpretation of the advisory opinion of 1950 which may go a long way towards reducing its principal qualifying provision to a mere form of words. The word 'applied' in the qualifying passage, quoted above, of the opinion of 1950 means 'actually' (and not 'potentially') applied just as the words 'procedure followed in this respect by the Council' mean the procedure as actually followed and not as it might have been followed.

It may also be borne in mind that there is a distinct element of unreality in relying, in this and in other matters, on the inherent powers of the Council of the League. Such powers, if any, were powers not of an ordinary legislature or executive proceeding by a majority vote. They were powers of a body acting under the rule of unanimity scrupulously observed. There was, as a matter of reasonable estimate, little prospect of the Council, which included the principal Mandatory Powers as its Members, decreeing by a unanimous vote the authorization of oral hearings which encountered the emphatic opposition of these Powers. There is accordingly no persuasive merit in the argument which relies on inherent powers whose exercise hung on the slender thread of unanimity in circumstances such as these.

* * *

While I am of the view that in normal circumstances the grant of oral hearings to petitioners would result in exceeding the degree of supervision as actually applied under the Mandates system and that it would not conform with the procedure followed in this respect by the Council of the League, I believe that both the excess and the departure are of limited compass. This fact, although it does not affect my answer to the more limited aspect of the question here examined, has a bearing upon what I consider to be the proper basis of the opinion of the Court.

With regard to degree of supervision, it is difficult to deny that oral hearings, as compared with written petitions, result to some extent in exceeding the degree of supervision obtaining under the League of Nations. In so far as oral hearings accompanied by a detailed examination of petitioners add to the reality and the effectiveness of the scrutiny of the conduct of the administering authority – and it is difficult to deny that they do so – they increase the degree of supervision as compared with a system which knows of no oral hearings of petitioners. It has been suggested that as oral hearings may disclose the spurious or fraudulent nature of some petitions, such hearings are to the advantage of the Mandatory and that they do not therefore increase his obligations in the matter of supervision. This argument I find unconvincing. It assumes that fraudulent petitions are the rule, and not the exception.

Similar considerations apply to the question whether oral hearings constitute a departure from the procedure obtaining under the League of Nations. By and large, oral hearings before the Mandates Commission were not admissible under the procedure of the League of Nations and, in fact, they were never resorted to. On the face of it, recourse to oral hearings would therefore constitute a departure from the procedure of the Mandates Commission and the Council of the League of Nations.

* * *

Admittedly, the above findings ought to be qualified by reference to certain factors which suggest that the departure consisting in the admission of oral hearings is – although real – less radical than appears at first sight. In the first instance, although the Mandates Commission, in compliance with the attitude of the Council of the League, did not grant oral hearings, that practice was not expressive of its view of the usefulness and of the necessity, in some cases, of relying on that procedure. The record shows that the Mandates Commission felt itself free to approach the Council on future occasions with a view to obtaining a modification of its attitude. Secondly, although the Commission as such did not grant oral hearings, its members and its Chairman, in their individual capacity, did in fact grant oral hearings to petitioners in private interviews outside the meetings of the Commission. Although subsequently some fine psychological distinctions were made between the minds of the members of the Commission as influenced outside its meetings and as formed inside the Commission, the reality of that distinction is limited. Thirdly, the refusal of the Council of the League of Nations to authorize oral hearings did not bear any mark of finality. In stating repeatedly that there was no reason, on the occasions before it, to depart from the previous practice, the Council left the door open for a modification of its practice in exceptional circumstances. It is not certain to what extent such possible modifications included the admissibility of oral hearings. In the report accompanying the Resolution approved by the Council on the last occasion when it declined to authorize oral hearings, it was stated that if in any particular circumstances it should be impossible for all the necessary information to be secured with the assistance of the Mandatory Power, the Council could 'decide on such exceptional procedure as might seem appropriate and necessary in the particular circumstances'.[1] It is possible – we cannot put it higher than that – that, having regard to the circumstances which brought about the Resolution, the Council, in referring to 'such exceptional procedure', was referring to oral hearings. The particular situations, referred to in the Resolution, may fairly be assumed to arise when, owing to an attitude of total non-co-operation on his part, no assistance whatsoever is forthcoming from the Mandatory. Fourthly, it appears from the replies which the Mandatory Powers gave in 1926 and in which they rejected the principle of oral hearings that one of the main reasons for their attitude was the assumption of the continuing co-operation and assistance on the part of the Mandatory. It is noteworthy that throughout the existence of the League of Nations there were no instances of a Mandatory Power refusing to supply information with regard to a complaint brought before the Mandates Commission. (In the case of the Bondelzwarts rebellion, which has been referred to as an instance of that nature, although the Government of South Africa refused to accept and comment on a report of a local commission of inquiry, the South African administrator of the territory in question was questioned at length by the Mandates Commission in the presence of the South African representative and submitted a detailed memorandum on the subject of the complaint.[2])

When, therefore, it is said that oral hearings did not exist under the League and that recourse to them by the Committee on South-West Africa would be a departure from that practice, this statement – although strictly true – is a simplification of the situation. This is so not only because the exclusion of the oral hearings was less rigid than cursory examination seems to indicate. This is so mainly because the

[1] Report approved on 7 March 1927.

[2] *Permanent Mandates Commission, Minutes of Third Session* (1923).

exclusion of oral hearings was a practice adopted within the orbit of the normal operation of other aspects of the machinery of supervision. These have now ceased to operate in consequence of the attitude adopted by the Union of South Africa. To put it in different words, the departure from the legal procedure involved in the system of oral hearings is substantial only if viewed against the background of the situation as it obtained during the existence of the League when reports and petitions were regularly transmitted by the Mandatory. The departure is less drastic when viewed in the light of the cessation of that system as the result of the attitude of non-co-operation as adopted by South Africa. For this reason there is no warrant for treating the practice under the League of Nations as being so unequivocal and decisive as to rule out all other factors of a legal or practical nature.

* * *

The above considerations do not decisively affect my answer to the general question whether oral hearings are consistent with the Court's opinion of 1950. That question, when answered in the abstract – i.e. without reference to the existing situation underlying the request for the advisory opinion – must be answered in the negative. However, as already explained, it is not open to the Court to confine itself to an answer in the abstract. For this reason these considerations are of some indirect importance for the specific question as to whether oral hearings are consistent with the opinion of 1950 having regard to the actual situation in respect of the Territory of South-West Africa.

3

As stated, if the Court were not confronted with a situation created by the attitude of the Government of South Africa and if it were merely called upon to reply in the abstract to the question put to it, I would feel bound to answer that the grant of oral hearings constitutes a sufficient addition to the degree of supervision and that it departs sufficiently from the procedure obtaining under the League of Nations to bring it within the two restrictive clauses, referred to above, of the opinion of 11 July 1950. However, this is not the situation with which the Court is faced. The Court is now called upon to answer not an abstract question, but – primarily – the question as to the consistency of oral hearings with its opinion of 11 July 1950 in a situation in which the two positive dispositions of that opinion for securing the international supervision of the territory have become inoperative. These are the provisions, repeatedly affirmed in the opinion, referring to the obligation of the

Mandatory Power to submit annual reports and to transmit petitions from the inhabitants of the Mandated Territory. They are the basic provisions whose place as such must be kept in mind. For this reason any preoccupation with the two limitative clauses of the opinion ought not to be allowed to overshadow its main purport. There has been a tendency to describe these limitative clauses as the basic provisions of the opinion of 11 July 1950. Any such emphasis distorts that opinion.

* * *

It is submitted that in answering the question put to it against the background of the fact that the two basic provisions of the operative part of its opinion of 1950 are in abeyance owing to the attitude adopted by the Union of South Africa, the Court must be guided by established principles of interpretation and the applicable general principles of law.

In the first instance, in accordance with a recognized principle of interpretation, its opinion of 11 July 1950 must, like any other legal text, be read as a whole. It must be read as a comprehensive pronouncement providing for the continuation of the administration and the continued supervision, by the United Nations, of the administration of South-West Africa as a Mandated territory. All other dispositions, injunctions and qualifications of the opinion of 11 July 1950 must be regarded as subservient to that overriding purpose. The principal means for fulfilling that purpose – namely, annual reports supplied by the Mandatory and written petitions transmitted, commented upon and explained by him before the supervising body – which were in operation under the Mandates system are now in abeyance owing to the attitude adopted by the Union of South Africa. If the opinion of 11 July 1950 is read as a whole, then it is impossible, without destroying its effect, to maintain fully and literally provisions qualifying the operation of a system whose main characteristics have become inoperative. It seems unreasonable to uphold fully and literally the limitations of a rule after the possibility of giving effect to the rule itself has disappeared. To do that is to elevate the exception into a rule and to reduce the governing rule to a nullity. A court of law cannot give its sanction to any such simplification of logic. Neither can it avoid its judicial duty by declaring that only a political or legislative body is competent to resolve the conflict which has arisen, as the result of the action of a party, between the overriding purpose of the instrument and its individual provisions and limitations. To resolve that conflict, in the light of the instrument as a whole, is an essential function of a judicial tribunal.

In particular, if we act on the principle that the opinion of 11 July 1950 must be read and interpreted as a whole, then it is necessary to apply that principle to the interpretation of that clause of that opinion which lays down that the degree of supervision must not exceed that obtaining under the Mandates system. That clause, properly interpreted, does not rigidly and automatically apply to each and every aspect of supervision. If, owing to the attitude of the Government of South Africa, the degree of supervision as applied under the Mandates system is in danger of being severely reduced with regard to the principal aspects of its operation, it is fully consistent with the opinion of the Court of 11 July 1950 that in some respects that supervision should become more stringent provided that it can be said, in reason and in good faith, that the total effect is not such as to increase the degree of supervision as previously obtaining. It is in accordance with sound principles of interpretation that the Court should safeguard the operation of its opinion of 11 July 1950 not merely with regard to its individual clauses but in relation to its major purpose. That is, in the present context, the meaning of the principle that that opinion must be interpreted as a whole. The question is not whether the admission of oral hearings of petitioners implies an excess of supervision with regard to this particular means of supervision. The decisive question is whether, owing to the situation brought about by the Union of South Africa, oral hearings of petitioners would result in an excess of supervision as a whole. It may be admitted that the procedure of oral hearings of petitioners connotes in itself a degree of supervision of a stringency greater than that obtaining in the matter of petitions under the Mandates system. But if, as the result of the attitude of the Union of South Africa, the degree of supervision is substantially reduced in other respects, then the total effect of the departure here contemplated will not be such as to result in exceeding the degree of supervision as a whole. On the contrary, however effective oral hearings of petitioners may be, they are unlikely to restore to the procedure of supervision the effectiveness of which it is being deprived as the result of the attitude of non-co-operation on the part of the Union of South Africa. Thus viewed, the authorization of oral hearings is no more than a specific application of the principle that a legal text must be interpreted as a whole.

* * *

The second principle of law of general import in the present case is connected with the nature of the régime of the Territory of South-West Africa as declared in the opinion of 11 July 1950. Inasmuch as that opinion laid down, by reference to the Covenant of the League of

Nations and the Charter of the United Nations, the status of South-West Africa – a régime in the nature of an objective law which is legally operative irrespective of the conduct of the Union of South Africa – that status must be given effect except in so far as its application is rendered impossible, in terms of its general purpose, having regard to the attitude adopted by the Union. To that extent there are permissible such modifications in its application as are necessary to maintain – but no more – the effectiveness of that status as contemplated in the Court's opinion of 1950. It is a sound principle of law that whenever a legal instrument of continuing validity cannot be applied literally owing to the conduct of one of the parties, it must, without allowing that party to take advantage of its own conduct, be applied in a way approximating most closely to its primary object. To do that is to interpret and to give effect to the instrument – not to change it.

Consequently, there can be no question here of the Union of South Africa having been divested, owing to the attitude adopted by her, of any safeguards which the opinion of 11 July 1950 provided in her interest as the Mandatory with the view to not increasing her obligations. No countenance can be given to the suggestion that, as the result of the attitude adopted by South Africa, the régime as established by that opinion of the Court is liable to changes – except in pursuance of the principle that that régime as a whole must be and remain effective. The opinion of 11 July 1950 has been accepted and approved by the General Assembly. Whatever may be its binding force as part of international law – a question upon which the Court need not express a view – it is the law recognized by the United Nations. It continues to be so although the Government of South Africa has declined to accept it as binding upon it and although it has acted in disregard of the international obligations as declared by the Court in that opinion.

* * *

At the same time, and for the same reasons, in so far as the opinion of 1950 is relied upon for the purpose of upholding literally all the safeguards and restrictions formulated in the interest of the Mandatory, it must, like any other legal instrument, be interpreted reasonably and in accordance with legal principle. The jurisprudence of the Court in the matter of treaties and otherwise provides by analogy some useful instruction in this respect. In the Fifteenth Advisory Opinion on the *Jurisdiction of the Courts of Danzig*, the Court formulated the principle that a State cannot avail itself of an objection which would amount to relying on the non-fulfilment of an obligation imposed on it by an international engagement.[1] It is not suggested that these principles are directly germane or applicable to the present case. For this is not the case of a treaty – although the opinion of 11 July 1950 did no more than to formulate a régime resulting from two multilateral conventional instruments, namely, the Covenant of the League of Nations and the Charter of the United Nations. Neither do I suggest that this is technically a case of estoppel – though there is a measure of contradiction, reminiscent of situations underlying estoppel, in the fact that an instrument repudiated by a Government is being invoked for the benefit of that Government. (While the Government of South Africa did not participate in the present proceedings before the Court, in the Fourth Committee of the General Assembly of 1955 it opposed oral hearings in reliance on the advisory opinion of 11 July 1950.[2]) Finally, I do not attach any decisive importance to the possible submission that this is an instance of a Government claiming to benefit from its own wrong by declining to supply and transmit information which, according to the opinion of 11 July 1950, it is legally bound to supply and transmit and at the same time resisting the contemplated effort to obtain alternative information. For it may not be easy to characterize precisely in legal terms a situation in which South Africa declines to act on an advisory opinion which it was not legally bound to accept but which gave expression to the legal position as ascertained by the Court and as accepted by the General Assembly.

Nevertheless, the above considerations are not wholly extraneous to the case now before the Court. For these are not technical rules of the law of contract or treaties. They are rules of common sense and good faith. As such they are relevant to all legal instruments, of whatsoever description, inasmuch as their effect is not to permit a party which repudiates an instrument to rely literally on it – or have it invoked for its benefit – in a manner which renders the fulfilment of its purpose impossible. In particular, these principles are relevant to the question – which ought not to remain unanswered – as to the legal basis of a judicial decision which by way of interpretation substitutes a measure of supervision or an act of performance for one repudiated or frustrated by the party affected by the instrument in question. What, apart from the general principles of interpretation as set out above, is the authority for the proposition that the Court may replace one means of supervision by another, not previously authorized – nay, expressly disallowed ? This, it may be objected, is not the way in which courts normally proceed in the matter of contracts between individuals (though in many countries

[1] *P.C.I.J.* Series B, no. 15, p. 27.
[2] Fourth Committee, 500th Meeting, 8 November 1955, *Official Records*, p. 182.

courts, when confronted with a situation in which a substantive provision of the instrument governing succession is in danger of being frustrated owing to an obscurity of expression or an event subsequently arising, will vary the original disposition in such a way as to make it approximate so far as possible to the general intention of its author. It will be noted that the supervision by the United Nations of the Mandate for South-West Africa constitutes the most important example of succession in international organization).

However, this is not a case of a contract or even of an ordinary treaty analogous to a contract. As already pointed out, this is a case of the operation and application of multilateral instruments, as interpreted by the Court in its opinion of 11 July 1950, creating an international status – an international régime – transcending a mere contractual relation.[1] The essence of such instruments is that their validity continues notwithstanding changes in the attitudes, or the status, or the very survival of individual parties or persons affected. Their continuing validity implies their continued operation and the resulting legitimacy of the means devised for that purpose by way of judicial interpretation and application of the original instrument. The unity and the operation of the régime created by them cannot be allowed to fail because of a breakdown or gap which may arise in consequence of an act of a party or otherwise. Thus viewed, the issue before the Court is potentially of wider import than the problem which has provided the occasion for the present advisory opinion. It is just because the régime established by them constitutes a unity that, in relation to instruments of this nature, the law – the existing law as judicially interpreted – finds means for removing a clog or filling a lacuna or adopting an alternative device in order to prevent a standstill of the entire system on account of a failure in any particular link or part. This is unlike the case of a breach of the provisions of an ordinary treaty – which breach creates, as a rule, a right for the injured party to denounce it and to claim damages. It is instructive in this connection that with regard to general texts of a law-making character or those providing for an international régime or administration the principle of separability of their provisions with a view to ensuring the continuous operation of the treaty as a whole has been increasingly recognized by international practice. The treaty as a whole does not terminate as the result of a breach of an individual clause. Neither is it necessarily rendered impotent and inoperative as the result of the action or inaction of one of the parties. It continues in being subject to adaptation to circumstances which have arisen.

[1] *I.C.J. Reports* 1950, p. 132.

4

It is now necessary to inquire to what extent the situation with which the General Assembly – and the Court – are confronted call for and permit the application of the principles of law as here outlined. To what extent has the refusal of the Union of South Africa to submit annual reports and to transmit and comment on written petitions in conformity with the obligations established in the opinion of 11 July 1950, created a gap so serious in the system there contemplated as – in conformity with these principles – to render legitimate alternative sources of information not exceeding the total degree of supervision envisaged in that opinion? These principles are that the opinion of 1950 must be read as a whole; that it cannot be deprived of its effect by the action of the State which has repudiated it; and that the ensuring of the continued operation of the international régime in question is a legitimate object of the interpretative task of the Court.

Having regard to the non-co-operation of the Mandatory, what is the position in the matter of the sources of information available to the supervising agency and indispensable for the proper working of the system of supervision and the implementing of the opinion of the Court of 11 July 1950?

In the first instance, the annual report of the Mandatory, as provided by the opinion of the Court of 1950 and as forming an integral part of the procedure of the League of Nations, has disappeared. It has been replaced by a conscientious and well-documented volume prepared by the Secretary-General and entitled *Information and Documentation in respect of the Territory of South West Africa.*[1] That volume provides, to a considerable extent, the substance of the report which the Committee on South-West Africa submits to the General Assembly. But this is not a document in the same category as a report submitted by the Mandatory and explained by it point by point, if necessary, at the meetings of the Committee. The supervising authority is thus deprived of an authentic source of information which is one of the two main pillars of the system of supervision. There is a gap here and a resulting diminution of the degree of supervision as previously existing and as envisaged by the Court in its opinion of 1950. It is consistent with that opinion to interpret it in a manner which authorizes the filling of that gap – provided that the result is not to increase the total degree of supervision of the system as a whole.

The second main source of information which forms an important part of the system of supervision and to which the opinion of the Court

[1] Such as in Doc. A/AC 73 L3; Doc. A/AC 73/L7.

of 1950 refers in passages of particular emphasis are petitions sent by the inhabitants of the administered territory. Under the League of Nations only petitions in writing were admissible. These, when supplemented by the observations of the Mandatory and the explanations supplied by him in the course of the proceedings of the supervising organ, are a weighty instrument of supervision and an important factor in the formation of the judgment of the supervising authority. As the result of the attitude of non-co-operation adopted by the Union of South Africa, the efficacy of that source has been substantially reduced. The Mandatory, who is absent from the meetings of the Committee, provides no comment of his own and does not assist the supervisory body by explanations supplied at its request during or subsequent to its meetings. Moreover, the Mandatory has declined to transmit petitions submitted by the inhabitants of the administered territory. If the procedure of the Mandates Commission were adhered to in this respect, it is difficult to see how written petitions from the inhabitants of the territory could come at all before the Committee on South-West Africa. That Committee has now adopted a deliberate change in the procedure obtaining under the Mandates system. The rules of procedure as adopted in 1923 by the League of Nations provided that petitions by communities or sections of the population of Mandated territories shall be sent to the Secretariat of the League through the Mandatory Governments concerned and that any petitions received by the Secretary-General of the League through any channel other than the Mandatory Government should be returned to the signatories with the request that they should re-submit the petitions in accordance with the above procedure. As the Government of South Africa has refused to transmit the petitions thus received, the Committee on South-West Africa has provided in its Provisional Rules of Procedure – Rule 26 – that on receipt of a petition the Secretary-General shall request the signatories to submit the petition to the Committee through the Government of South Africa but that if, after a period of two months, the petition has not been received through the Government of South Africa, the Committee shall regard the petition as validly received. It is also provided that the Committee shall subsequently notify the Government of South Africa as to the conclusions it has reached on the petition. It does not appear that objection has been raised against that particular – and important – departure from the procedure obtaining under the Mandates system.

However, although thus made available to the supervising organ, the written petition no longer fulfils the same function and no longer partakes of the same effectiveness as written petitions examined in the presence and with the co-operation of the Mandatory. It is in the nature of *ex parte* information which may or may not be capable of verification. This does not mean that the written petition examined without the assistance of the Mandatory is without value or that it can never provide a basis for the conclusions of the supervising Committee. But it is clear that it is not the same thing as and that it is a lesser thing than written petitions within the framework of a machinery operating with the participation of the Mandatory.

* * *

The interpretation, in this matter, of the opinion of the Court of 11 July 1950 is thus confronted with the fact that owing to the attitude of South Africa the potency of the two principal instruments of supervision is substantially reduced and that other means, not fundamentally inconsistent with that opinion, must be found in order to give effect to its essential purpose. The crucial question which the Court has now to answer is: Are oral hearings one of these means? Are they truly necessary and effective for filling the gap that has arisen? Do they secure the reality of the task of supervision otherwise reduced below the level contemplated by and underlying the opinion of 1950? I am of the view that, in the circumstances, they fulfil that purpose. Oral hearings contribute one of the tangible elements of supervision which otherwise – i.e. in the absence of other means of supervision – operates in an atmosphere of unreality. Undoubtedly, the information received through oral hearings may be exaggerated, false and misleading. Oral hearings may be abused by fanatics and seekers for self-advertisement. But these difficulties and dangers are also present, and less capable of correction, in the case of written petitions – especially when examined in the absence of the Mandatory. Moreover, it is clear that the importance of oral hearings increases in proportion as the effectiveness of the other instruments of supervision has been reduced as the result of the attitude of the Union of South Africa. If the United Nations were not confronted with the refusal of the Union of South Africa to abide by its obligations as a Mandatory in conformity with the opinion of the Court of 1950 and if there remained, in their full effectiveness, the other instruments of supervision, therein provided, then the advantages of oral hearings, considerable as they may be and though being, according to some, in keeping with the recognition within the United Nations of the right of oral hearing as a corollary of the fundamental right of petition, would be no more than an improvement on the existing machinery of supervision. They would not be essential to it. In fact, being in the nature of an excess of supervision as it existed under the League of Nations, they would be contrary, on that account, to the opinion of 1950. But this is not the position with which the Court is confronted. The Court is not here called upon to express a view on the controversial question of the merits of oral hearings in general. The question before it is the necessity for oral hearings in a situation amounting to a substantial drying up of other sources of information.

There is therefore little force in the argument that, after all, oral hearings are not the only source of information. Admittedly, they are not. There are other sources. In particular, written petitions are still available. However, if the effectiveness of these available means has become drastically reduced owing to the attitude of the Mandatory, then it is open to the Committee on South-West Africa, as a matter of effectiveness of the instrument which it has to apply, to fulfil that duty by other means.

It may be objected that oral hearings in the absence of the Mandatory are a procedure which amounts to passing of judgment in default upon that authority in its absence and that for that, if no other, reason it constitutes a particularly flagrant excess of supervision. But is that so? When the Committee on South-West Africa examines written petitions in the absence of the Mandatory, that procedure may also be said to amount to passing of judgment by default. The Committee simply informs the Government of South Africa of its conclusions. But it has not been denied that the Committee is entitled to do so and that the rule of procedure which it has adopted for that purpose is in accordance with the opinion of the Court of 11 July 1950. Moreover, when the supervising authority hears petitioners in person it has the opportunity of checking and verifying their statements by a direct and efficacious method which is not available when written petitions are examined in the absence of their authors.

This, then, is the principal question before the Court. Is the need for oral hearings real? If permitted, would they, in the situation before the Court, contribute to exceeding the total degree of supervision as circumscribed in the opinion of the Court of 1950? For it is only under the following two conditions that oral hearings of petitioners can be held to be consistent with that opinion: the need for them must be real in terms of implementing the two basic provisions of that opinion of the Court; secondly, they must not add to the degree of supervision in such a way that in the aggregate it becomes more stringent than under the League of Nations. Oral hearings of petitioners would not be permissible if they were attempted not because of that real need but as an expression of the disapproval of the attitude of South Africa. Any such innovation implying that the opinion of 1950 has lost its regulating and restraining force would not be permissible. The opinion of 1950 is not a treaty whose provisions can be discarded for the reason that South Africa has declined to comply with them. It gives expression to an objective legal status recognized by the United Nations and it must be acted upon. But it must be acted upon in a reasonable – and not in a one-sided and literal – manner.

My conclusion is, therefore, that there is a true need for oral hearings in order to supplement sources of information which have become incomplete in consequence of the attitude of the Union of South Africa and that, if adopted, they would not result in exceeding the total degree of supervision as laid down in the opinion of 11 July 1950. This being so, they must be held to be consistent with that opinion. They would be so consistent even if the opinion of 11 July 1950 were in absolute terms, namely, if it did not contain the qualification 'as far as possible'.

5

In view of the preceding observations I need only refer briefly to the second qualifying clause of the opinion of 11 July 1950, namely, that 'the degree of supervision . . . should conform as far as possible to the procedure followed in this respect by the Council of the League of Nations'. The expression 'as far as possible' is a form of words of pronounced elasticity. Its interpretation is a matter of degree. It is 'possible' for a system of supervision to continue without reports of the Mandatory, without written petitions accompanied by his comments and explanations, without the representatives of the latter being present at the meetings of the supervisory organ, and without oral hearings filling the gap which has thus arisen. But that would not be a supervision as contemplated by the opinion of 1950. It would be a supervision falling short not only of the assumption of effectiveness which underlay that opinion of the Court, but also of what must be regarded as a reasonable measure of effectiveness. It has been suggested that the Committee would meet with no difficulty if it were to abstain from oral hearings of petitioners. Admittedly, there is as a rule no difficulty encountered by doing nothing or little, but this is hardly a reasonable standard by which to gauge the fulfilment of the task of the supervising authority. There is no occasion to go to the extreme length in thus interpreting away the requirements of satisfactory supervision in deference to a persistent attitude of non-co-operation on the part of the Mandatory. There is no general interest involved in weakening the system of supervision so considerably below the level contemplated in the opinion of 1950. For these reasons I find no difficulty in accepting the view that the saving expression 'so far as possible' can properly be relied upon in this case so as to permit oral hearings of petitioners. I cannot accept the argument that the expression 'as far as possible' should be reduced to insignificance for the reason that the opinion of 1950 intended to crystallize the substantive and procedural *status quo* as it then existed. Reasons have been given above why there is no merit in the view that the Court ought to lend its authority to the continued and unaltered maintenance of that *status quo* by upholding the two qualifying clauses of its opinion of 1950 after the two basic provisions which it thus qualified have ceased to be operative as the result of the attitude of the Mandatory.

* * *

There is one point which requires some explanation in this connection. In its opinion of 7 June 1955 on the *Voting Procedure*, the Court, in explaining the expression 'as far as possible' as being 'designed to allow for adjustments and modifications necessitated by legal or practical considerations'[1] – an explanation which fully covers the issue now before the Court – seemed to give a restricted scope to that expression. It explained that phrase as 'indicating that in the nature of things the General Assembly, operating under an instrument different from that which governed the Council of the League of Nations, would not be able to follow precisely the same procedures as were followed by the Council'.[2] It might thus appear that the Court was limiting the operation of the 'as far as possible' principle to the exigencies of the Charter and of the procedure of the General Assembly. It is not believed that this is so. In the case of the *Voting Procedure* the Court was concerned with this particular aspect of the question and it was therefore natural that its reasoning should have concentrated on that issue. There is no reason to assume that it intended to limit generally the apparent comprehensiveness of the clause 'as far as possible'. Similar considerations apply to those passages of the opinion of 1955 in which the Court attached importance to stating that the expression 'degree of supervision', inasmuch as it related to the 'measure and means of supervision' and to 'the means employed by the supervisory authority in obtaining adequate information', should not be interpreted as relating to procedural matters.[3] The correct view is that the issue of oral hearings is both a question of substantive supervision and of procedure. It is clear that a procedural measure may decisively affect the rights and obligations of the parties. There would be a disadvantage in basing the judgments and opinions of the Court not on legal considerations of

[1] *I.C.J. Reports* 1955, p. 69, at p. 77.
[2] *Ibid.*
[3] *Ibid.* p. 72.

general application but on controversial technicalities and artificial classifications.

6

There remains the question whether, assuming that there has been created a real gap in the system of supervision and that oral hearings may be instrumental to some extent in filling that gap, the consistency of oral hearings with the opinion of 11 July 1950 can be ascertained by way of judicial interpretation or whether it can only be decreed, by way of legislative change, by the General Assembly. This question, it is believed, must be answered affirmatively in the light of the general legal considerations outlined above.

There are three possible methods of approach for a court of law confronted with a situation such as the present, namely, that of a party refusing to recognize or to act upon a legal instrument which purports to express the legal obligations of that party and whose validity must, as in the present case, be regarded as continuing:

(1) It is possible to hold that, even if that party refuses to be bound by any of the obligations or limitations of the legal instrument in question, the other party – in this case the United Nations and the Committee on South-West Africa are the other party – must fulfil literally and abide by all the restraining provisions enacted for the benefit of the recalcitrant party even if such one-sided application results in reducing substantially the effectiveness of the instrument. Any such method I consider to be unsound.

(2) The second method is to assert that, as the legal instrument in question has been repudiated by one party, a new factual and legal situation has arisen in which the other party is free to act as it pleases and to disregard all the restraints of the instrument. This, I believe, is not the view which the Court can properly adopt. The opinion of 1950 continues to be the law. It established – or recognized – a legal status of the territory. It is the law binding upon the Committee for South-West Africa.

(3) The third possibility, which appears to me most appropriate as a legal proposition and in accordance with good faith and common sense, is to interpret the instrument as continuing in validity and as fully applicable subject to reasonable re-adjustments calculated to maintain the effectiveness, though not more than that, of the major purpose of the instrument.

Similarly, it is in the light of the general principle as thus stated that there must be considered the contention that if as the result of the attitude of South Africa and the situation which has thus arisen it is necessary to effect changes in the opinion of the Court of 11 July 1950, such changes must be accomplished by the General Assembly and not by the Court. For it would appear that that argument begs the question. The Court, in finding that oral hearings are consistent with its opinion of 11 July 1950, is not changing the law as laid down in that opinion. It interprets it in accordance with good sense and sound legal principle. This in fact was the method which the Court followed in its opinion of 11 July 1950, when it was called upon to interpret the relevant clauses of the Covenant of the League of Nations and of the Charter of the United Nations. In answering the question as to the existing international legal position of South-West Africa it applied the relevant international instruments in so far as this was possible. It did not change the law as contained therein. The essence of that opinion was that the Court declined to apply literally the legal régime which it was called upon to interpret. It declined to admit that the continuity of the Mandatory system meant necessarily that only the League of Nations – and no one else – could act as the supervising authority. On the face of it, the opinion, inasmuch as it held that the United Nations must be substituted for the League of Nations as the supervisory organ, signified a change as compared with the letter of the Covenant. Actually, the opinion did no more than give effect to the main purpose of the legal instruments before it. That is the true function of interpretation. The opinion gave effect to the existing law in a situation in which otherwise its purpose, as the Court saw it, would have been endangered. This is essentially the situation with which the Court is confronted in the present case.

There is one further consideration which must be borne in mind in relation to the suggestion that although the Court cannot declare oral hearings of petitioners to be consistent with its opinion of 1950, the General Assembly – and the General Assembly only – has the power to do so. The Preamble to the request for the present opinion begins as follows: 'The General Assembly, having been requested by the Committee on South-West Africa to decide whether or not the oral hearing of petitioners on matters relating to the Territory of South-West Africa is admissible before that Committee . . .' The Court is requested to advise the General Assembly whether, as a matter of law embodied in the opinion of the Court of 11 July 1950, the General Assembly is entitled to decide that oral hearings are admissible. In view of this, it is hardly possible for the Court to give a negative answer to the question put to it and to say – or imply – that if any change is required as the result of the attitude of South Africa then that change must be effected by the General Assembly and not the Court. For this is the very question which the Court has been asked to answer. It is not possible for the

Court to say that it would be contrary to the opinion of 11 July 1950 for the General Assembly to authorize oral hearings and at the same time to say, or imply, that the General Assembly may do it. If the General Assembly had felt at liberty to authorize oral hearings regardless of whether such authorization is consistent with the opinion of 11 July 1950 or not, it would have hardly found it necessary to request the Court to give the present advisory opinion. This being so, the Court could not, in the present case, renounce its legitimate function on the ground that the appropriate result can be achieved by the legislative action of the political organ. Reluctance to encroach upon the province of the legislature is a proper manifestation of judicial caution. If exaggerated, it may amount to unwillingness to fulfil a task which is within the orbit of the functions of the Court as defined by its Statute. The Court cannot properly be concerned with any political effects of its decisions. But it is important, as a matter of international public policy, to bear in mind the indirect consequences of any pronouncement which, by giving a purely literal interpretation of the opinion of 11 July 1950, would have rendered it impotent in face of obstruction by one party.

In fact, from whatever angle the request for the present advisory opinion is viewed, a substantive answer to it seems indicated by reference to general legal considerations such as outlined in this and in the preceding parts of this separate opinion. This applies also to that part of the opinion in which I have come to the conclusion that oral hearings of petitioners would – apart from the situation actually confronting the United Nations – be inconsistent with the opinion of 11 July 1950 inasmuch as they depart from the system which obtained under the League of Nations. But, as explained, that system was predicated on the fulfilment by the Mandatory of his obligations in the matter of reports and petitions. As the result of the attitude now adopted by the Union of South Africa, that assumption no longer applies. The maxim *cessante ratione cessat lex ipsa* is a trite legal proposition. This circumstance does not affect the propriety and the necessity of its judicial application.

* * *

It is necessary in this connection to refer to the apparent inconsistency between the view which is put forward in this separate opinion (and which in effect underlies the present opinion of the Court) and that on which the Court seems to have based its opinion of 18 July 1950 on the *Interpretation of the Peace Treaties* (*Second Phase*). In the latter case the Court declined to hold that the failure, contrary to their international obligations, of certain States to appoint representatives to the Commissions provided by the treaties in question for settling disputes justified some alternative method of appointment not contemplated by these treaties. As in the present case, the conduct of the States in question had thus created a gap – in fact, a breakdown – in the operation of the system of supervision contemplated by the treaties. Yet the Court refused to admit the legality of an alternative method designed to remedy the situation. It said:

> The failure of machinery for settling disputes by reason of the practical impossibility of creating the Commission provided for in the Treaties is one thing; international responsibility is another. The breach of a treaty obligation cannot be remedied by creating a Commission which is not the kind of Commission contemplated by the Treaties. It is the duty of the Court to interpret the Treaties, not to revise them.[1]

The resemblance of the two cases is as striking as the apparent discrepancy between the present opinion of the Court and that in the case of the *Interpretation of the Peace Treaties.* In view of this it is appropriate and desirable to state the reasons, if any, for this seeming departure from a previous opinion. Without expressing a view as to the merits of the opinion of the Court on the *Interpretation of the Peace Treaties,* I consider that, in fact, the two cases are dissimilar in a vital respect. The clauses of the Peace Treaties of 1947 relating to settlement of disputes were, as shown in their wording and the protracted history of their adoption, formulated in terms which clearly revealed the absence of agreement to endow them with a full measure of effectiveness – including safeguards to be resorted to in the event of the failure of one of the parties to participate in the procedure of settlement of disputes. This was a case in which the application of the principle of effectiveness in the interpretation of treaties found, in the view of the Court, a necessary limit in the circumstance that the parties had failed – not accidentally, but by design – to render them fully effective. This is not the position in the present case when the Court is confronted with the interpretation of provisions concerning a régime in the nature of an international status of established and continuous operation; provisions in relation to which the Court, in the opinion of 11 July 1950 and that of 5 June 1955 on *Voting Procedure,* affirmed in emphatic language the necessity of securing the unimpeded and effective application of the system of supervision in accordance with the fundamental provisions of the Covenant and the Charter; and with regard to which it qualified the notion of any literal and rigid continuity of the Mandates system by making it obligatory only 'so far as possible' – an expression expressly

[1] *I.C.J. Reports* 1950, p. 229.

'designed to allow for adjustments and modifications necessitated by legal or practical considerations.'[1]

This being so, the present advisory opinion of the Court seems to be fully in accordance with its previous practice of interpreting treaties and other international instruments in a manner calculated to secure their effective operation. For this reason, subject to some doubts as to the formulation of the operative part of the opinion and as to some aspects of its reasoning such as the extent of the reliance on the implied powers of the Council of the League of Nations, I have no hesitation in concurring in the opinion of the Court.

[1] *I.C.J. Reports* 1955, p. 77.

CHAPTER 5

THE LEAGUE OF NATIONS

Editor's note This chapter consists of the text of an address delivered to the Cambridge University League of Nations Union on 16 November 1938. It has not previously been published.

I must apologize for reading this address from the manuscript. It is not my custom, and it is not the custom of these meetings. But the League of Nations is a subject on which some of us may feel too strongly to entrust to the freely spoken word our anxiety about the future of the League, our impatience with the attempts to adapt it to the shifting needs of a period of retrogression, and our profound faith in its ultimate success. Possibly as a jurist I am particularly apprehensive lest my caution as a lawyer should run away with my sentiment as a citizen. In any case, it is advisable to speak of these matters with a restraint and deliberation appropriate to a subject which is both the central theme of the history of mankind and, in the long run, one of the decisive factors of our personal fate. I hope therefore that you will bear with me if I give up at the very outset the attempt to enliven a dull performance by an attempt at oratory.

I have given to this address the pretentious title of 'The League of Nations', for, like many of us, I have felt that we have reached a stage in which what is at issue is not any particular question or problem, but the League as such. It has now become a commonplace to say that the League has reached the lowest point of failure. That trite saying is nevertheless profoundly true. One glaring instance of recent date will illustrate the position. On previous occasions, like the invasion of China and the annexation of Abyssinia, the Members of the League who were the victims of aggression at least invoked the provisions of the Covenant and put their trust in the League. They were cruelly deceived, but their action testified to the vitality of the Covenant. But when recently Czechoslovakia was confronted by far-reaching territorial demands on the part of Poland and Hungary, two fellow-Members of the League, she thought it expedient to disregard altogether the prospect of assistance by the protectors of her independence and integrity. And in one case she concurred in the selection of two States, priding themselves on their antagonism to the League, as arbitrators to assist in the amputation of her territory.

Our first duty is to obtain a clear notion of the extent of the frustration of the principal purpose of the League as intended by the statesmen who founded it and, in particular, by public opinion which, more than statesmen and Governments, was responsible for its establishment. For public opinion, the League to be established was to be a league to enforce peace by providing security from and a deterrent against aggression. If at that time the vast body of people for whom the League was the main outcome of the World War, had been told that twenty years hence we shall be content, as some do now, to advocate a League whose object is confined to being a meeting ground for statesmen and a centre of efficient administration in various branches of international co-operation, and that we shall at the same time insist on calling these the League of Nations, they would have regarded this as a corruption of language and as a challenge to their faith. It is true that the Covenant in its preamble refers to international co-operation as one of the objects of the League. There is no doubt that in the field of humanitarian, economic and scientific collaboration the League has shown notable achievements and has revealed unexpected potentialities. But these activities were intended to be and, on any rational analysis are, a superstructure which, without the foundations of a secured rule of law, is as unstable and unreal as is life itself in a pure state of nature – a life of which Hobbes said that it is solitary, poor, nasty, brutish and short. In its principal object the League has failed, and in comparison with the extent and the persistency of that failure its successes, both administrative and political, fade into insignificance.

However, the moment calls for even greater frankness. The frustration of the overriding object of the Covenant has gone so far that it is no longer merely a political fact constituting a regrettable departure from the law. That failure has now become part of the law; or, to put it in different words, the Covenant of the League is now, in law, no longer what it was in 1919. Law, it is true, is stronger than isolated breaches of its rule. But the cumulative effect of the position repeatedly taken up by those who had bound themselves to uphold the Covenant against violation and of the general situation brought about by that conduct is such as to amount to a change in the law.

One of these changes, never formally adopted but now no longer in doubt, is the fate of Article 10 of the Covenant – the guarantee Article. To give a concrete example taken from recent history – one of the not least significant features of the events leading to the dismemberment of Czechoslovakia was that Great Britain insisted in good faith and in all sincerity and without contradiction that, unlike France, she had no commitments towards Czechoslovakia. France, it was said, had a Treaty of Defensive Alliance with that country; Great Britain had none. But if words mean anything, Great Britain, together with the other members of the League, undertook in Article 10 of the Covenant to preserve Czechoslovakia, as indeed any other Member of the League, from external aggression by any other State. That obligation has never been expressly abrogated. But the process of emaciation of Article 10 began soon after the establishment of the League. It went far in that direction in 1924 when, but for the dissenting voice of Persia, the Assembly would in effect have declared that every Member of the League is legally entitled to determine for itself the extent to which it is bound to fulfil the obligation of the guarantee. Since then, on a number of obvious occasions which even the interpretative resolution of 1924 could not have taken out of the orbit of an imperative obligation of assistance, Article 10 has been treated as devoid of legal force. This is not a case of an ambiguity in a legal instrument; it is a case of a continuous and uniform non-observance of the letter as well as of the spirit of a still valid undertaking which was repeatedly described by leading lawyers as the backbone of the Covenant. It is no longer possible to ignore the legal outcome of this history of non-fulfilment.

The same applies, less conspicuously but with the same final result, to Articles 16 and 17 of the Covenant, in which Members of the League undertook to apply immediately most comprehensive measures of economic and financial pressure against members of the League and others resorting to war in disregard of the obligations or the machinery of the Covenant. These obligations, if adhered to, would have indirectly achieved the object of the guarantee contemplated in Article 10. But they, too, have been allowed to fall into desuetude. The elastic language of the Covenant, the natural inclination of lawyers not to assume lightly the intention to break the law, and their desire to save as much as possible from the wreckage of a constructive principle of order, have tended to obscure what must now be regarded as a fact, namely, that the obligations of that article have not been fulfilled. They were not complied with in the case of Manchuria, although a semblance of legality was preserved by the device of Members of the League choosing not to go to the length of considering the Japanese action as resort to war in the meaning of the Covenant. In the case of Abyssinia Members of the League had no option but to decide that the hostilities did constitute resort to war on the part of Italy, but they failed to bring into force immediately and to their full extent the measures of pressure authorized and enjoined by the Covenant which, if so applied, would have successfully vindicated the authority of the law. The sanctions were applied as a manifestation of moral disapproval, not as an instrument for coercing the will of the aggressor. When in September of this year [1938] China requested that in conformity with Article 17 sanctions should be applied against Japan, the Assembly, while affirming the continued legal validity of the principle involved, declared that in the existing conditions it could not be regarded as effectively operative. In doing so the Assembly gave clear and, I believe, accurate, expression to one aspect of the legal position.

That position is that the binding force of the fundamental provisions of the Covenant – the realization of the law by the joint effort of the community – is no more. It may be a matter of discussion whether the last spark of legal validity has now departed from it or whether its operation is merely suspended so that it will automatically revive with a change of conditions. But the essence of the matter cannot be disputed. There is, first, the cumulative result of the failure to observe the Covenant. The law is not affected by isolated acts of lawlessness; but its impotence when repeated, tolerated and willed, must tell in the end; its continued futility ceases to be a disappointment of legitimate expectations. Secondly, there has in the meantime disappeared the necessary presupposition of the principle of the collective enforcement of the law. That presupposition is that force wielded against the law-breaker is paramount force applied by an overwhelming majority of the members of the community with an authority and a prospect of success comparable to the irresistible action of the law within the State. This is no longer the case. Because the League has ceased to be anything like universal, there has, for the time being, disappeared a vital condition of the obligation of collective security. The Covenant is a treaty, and it is consistent with good faith to interpret it in this way.

It is supremely important, for various reasons, that we should know what the legal position is. In the first instance, law, properly ascertained, is part of existing international relations. We ought not to shut our eyes to any part of that political reality. Secondly, it is undesirable that we should aggravate an unsatisfactory situation and add to the demoralization of international relations by, in the future, charging Governments with ignoring obligations whose force is no longer what it was. Thirdly, it is desirable that we should know the exact position so that we can aim at a re-enactment or confirmation of principles to which we attach importance and which have ceased to be effective law.

Finally, it is only by realizing that the law has been abrogated in one sphere that we shall be able to understand and draw comfort from its continued validity in another. For we must not be misled into thinking that the whole fabric of the fundamental law of the League has gone by the board. What was and is still revolutionary in the Covenant is not only the duty to repress unlawful recourse to war but also the obligations not to go to war in disregard of its provisions. Those obligations have restricted the sovereignty of States in its most vital aspect. They have never ceased to be the law of the League. They are as fully valid as they were in 1919. They have been violated, but there has never been a general acquiescence in or condonation of their breach. Italy and Japan and Paraguay left the League after their action had been condemned and declared unlawful. While the duty to enforce the peace has thus lapsed, at least temporarily, the obligation to observe the peace is still a prominent feature of the Covenant and is of undiminished vitality. Moreover, that charter of peace has remained legally unimpaired not only in respect of the duty not to resort to war but also in the matter of the positive procedure for pacific settlement and – another radical innovation of the Covenant – with regard to the right of intervention of the League as a whole in disputes between Members of the League. Finally, although the duty to enforce peace may now be regarded as legally obsolete – or at least in abeyance – there still remains fully intact the right to act in that capacity. The Covenant is still a valid and solemn legal authorization to repress aggression – a power from which restraining and coercive action may well spring.

However, while not everything has succumbed to the onslaught of retrogression, we must not be easily comforted. We must not lose sight of the fact that the principal object of the Covenant has disappeared as a political and legal reality. This being so, we should be failing in our duty if we were to give up the attempt to understand the cause of the defeat of the most significant attempt ever made to introduce the effective reign of reason and order into the mutual relations of independent States. We must dismiss, without argument, the metaphysical explanation in terms of philosophy of history – the explanation, that is to say, that there is no progress in the history of mankind, that events move in circles, spirals or zigzags, and that therefore what has happened to the League was rational because inevitable in the pre-ordained scheme of things. We must dismiss as economically and historically inaccurate the view that it was the defection of the United States which, by depriving the League of its universality, divested it of the power to enforce the Covenant (for this argument is often put forward by the same persons who, in order to secure the membership of the United States in the League, would dispense with sanctions altogether). And we must reject an interpretation of events which connects the defeat of the League with its association with the Treaty of Versailles. The Corfu incident, the invasion of Manchuria, Abyssinia and China as a whole, and the attack upon the independence of Spain, had no connection with the iniquities or the justice of the Treaty of Versailles. Nor can we accept the somewhat uncritically repeated explanation that the setback to the League was due to the absence in its constitution of effective provisions for the peaceful change of the existing law. Such effective provisions, if enacted, would amount to endowing the League with legislative powers of an overriding nature; they would transform the League into the much dreaded super-State – a consummation which those critics of the League would reject with scorn and horror. Undoubtedly a system which enjoins the observance of the peace without providing means for altering conditions which make peace intolerable is an unsatisfactory and in the long run unworkable system. And it would have been better if the authors of the Covenant had faced that problem squarely and courageously. At the same time it is a fact, as shown by the cases of China and Abyssinia, that the most glaring instances of the successful violation of the Covenant were not due to that defect in its constitution. They were the result of a wanton and lawless will for conquest pure and simple – a will which just concessions would not have appeased and which a law-abiding society would have curbed with exemplary determination.

But there are three sets of causes without the appreciation of which we shall find it difficult to understand the failure of the League as an instrument to preserve the peace and to prevent war. The first is that, in establishing the League, Governments, in their wisdom and their caution, fell short of their own professions made during the World War and the expectations of large sections of their peoples. As an instrument for the legal organization of peace the League was defective from the very beginning. Those who framed the Covenant were deliberately obscure in their prohibition of war, and by limiting it to 'resort to war' left the door wide open for abuse and confusion. While introducing the principle of collective enforcement of peace, they limited its obligations to economic action and refrained from providing for the jurisdiction of the League as a whole both to determine the case of aggression and to direct authoritatively the course of collective action aiming at the suppression of aggression. They declined to sanction the principle of obligatory judicial settlement even with regard to disputes which they described as generally suitable for such settlement. They carefully preserved their full freedom of action with regard to any procedure calculated to change the legal *status quo* by common action of the League. Sovereignty, formally enshrined in the rigid principle of unanimity, was made to permeate even the machinery of pacific settlement. The result of that combination of far-reaching restrictions with the maintenance of sovereignty was a flexible instrument of great elasticity – an instrument which, because of this quality, has often been described by adherents of the League as the best instrument that could be devised for the purpose for which it was intended. This would have been so if the circumstances had been favourable. But they were not. In consequence, the elasticity of the Covenant has worked one way only. Its potential strength has been allowed to remain in the background; but Governments have often appealed to those of its provisions which left them complete freedom of action and which reduced the Covenant to a mere declaration of principles. This brings us to the second cause.

The idea of collective security – and the Covenant is in its origin and its purpose primarily a system of collective security – is one which requires on the part of the Governments and peoples concerned a sacrifice of immediate benefits, including the benefits of peace, for the sake of larger future interests. It is in the nature of an insurance, and may demand the payment of costly premiums; it requires a long-range policy of principle; it disdains opportunism; it scorns instantaneous success, even if that success be immediate peace. Like other institutions of civilized life, it demands temporary sacrifices as a condition of making sure of the final good. It is not unnatural that when the sacrifice demanded is that of peace, the man in the street, unless guided, will shrink from the logic of a principle which only a day before he cherished as rational and obvious. For peace is a precious thing – as precious as life itself; and war is ghastly and incalculable. If the necessity of that risk and of that sacrifice is to assert itself against the overwhelming appeal of peace and immediate safety then it must be imposed upon the mass of the people by persuasive national leadership conscious of the essential continuity of national life beset by the danger of a disorganized world. But Governments composed of statesmen and politicians directly dependent on popular approval are inclined to favour success which is near at hand – and when that success assumes the form of avoiding war or the danger of a war, the call is practically irresistible. This is why Governments, constituted as they are, must act fully on the words of the prayer: Give us peace in our time, O Lord. Yet it is of the essence of collective security that we may have to sacrifice our own peace in order to save from utter destruction those who will come after us – or even ourselves in the day after tomorrow. The clash between public and private morality thus manifests itself in a novel form. Democratic statesmen agree that they must not act on Machiavellian principles and that they must not do the wicked thing they would be ashamed to do as private individuals for the protection of their private interests. But they do maintain that they are trustees not of their private consciences but of the interests – and lives – of others; they sincerely believe that they must not sacrifice or endanger these for the sake of untried principles, however lofty.[1]

The third cause of the fate which has befallen the League, namely, the emergence of dictatorships on a scale unprecedented in history, was an event to which the League – perhaps inevitably – could not accommodate itself. When founded, the League was conceived as a League of democratic States. The cry about making the world safe for democracy was not a desperate device of war propaganda. When in 1795 Kant formulated the articles of a federation of peoples for the mutual guarantee of independence and the preservation of peace, he regarded it as essential that the member-States should possess a democratic constitution. The League was conceived as a League of democratic States because it was thought that democracies are essentially peaceful while dictatorships, for a variety of reasons, tend to regard war, be it by arms or by revolutionary propaganda, not only as a means of achieving political ends but also as part and parcel of the national conception of life.

Secondly, what are now called ideological differences may be a bad reason for international enmity and strife; but ideological affinity, i.e. a community of views on things essential in man's social and political life, was and is not unnaturally regarded as the indispensable condition of a system in which one nation may have to sacrifice what is best and most precious in it in defence of another. We may have to ally ourselves temporarily with a State whose conceptions of social justice and morality we abhor and whose actions within its borders call forth our indignation and, even in a decadent age, our passionate protest. But to be wedded to it permanently, for good or for evil, for the defence of its inferior statehood is to embark on an artificial and, in the long run, intolerable relationship.

Finally, it was also assumed, as part of the same philosophy, that neither peace nor international law, whose firm establishment was described as one of the principal objects of the League, can become a reality until we have recognized the individual human being as the ultimate beneficiary of the law and the ultimate unit of human progress, to be protected by international action, if necessary, from the power of the omnipotent State. The provisions as to mandates, as to minorities, and as to the protection of labour, and the vast scope of humanitarian action envisaged by the League, bore witness to the view that the general good of the international community cannot be achieved except by the effective acknowledgment of the sanctity of human personality as

[1] At this point there is a gap of about nine lines in the typescript which renders meaningless the following seven lines. They are therefore also omitted (Editor).

the final unit of all society. This is not a philosophy congenial to the totalitarian conception of the State.

For this and other reasons it is true to say that much of the spirit of the League departed from it when it retained the membership of the totalitarian States of Italy and Germany and when it acquiesced in the adhesion of Soviet Russia. In the eyes of many the League could put up with the membership of these States – but only as a rump of its spiritual self.

These are the causes which in their cumulative result have contributed to the failure of the principal object of the League. No one of these causes need in itself be decisive; it is their combination that has been disastrous. Neither are these causes necessarily permanent. Some of them may be gradually overcome by the education both of public opinion and of Governments in democratic countries. Others have been brought about by human agencies and may be modified by them. There must always remain, as a matter of moral duty, the hope that the true spirit of man will assert itself in the long run.

But what have we to do in the meantime? Ought we to abandon the League and start afresh as soon as the obstacles disappear? Ought we to maintain it and to adapt it to the needs of a retrogressive period? Ought we to pursue the ideal of universality by reforming the League so as to make it acceptable to everyone? Ought we to admit that if peace cannot be achieved by collective effort, there are other good things that can be achieved through it? These and many other similar questions must necessarily occur to us. There is no simple answer to them – certainly not one which partakes of the simplicity of the advice which a member of Parliament gave us the other day in the House of Commons: 'Let us trust Germany and keep our powder dry.' But there are two major considerations on which, I submit, it is right to rely.

The first is that the League of Nations, as an attempt to realize part of the ideal of the political organization of mankind, is a creation much greater than the product of the experience of the World War – a no mean experience in itself. The League of Nations is even more than an expression of the physiological, moral and economic unity and interdependence of mankind. In the terminology of Emmanuel Kant – perhaps the greatest philosopher of all ages – it embodies the idea of a world federation as the only means of attaining perfect internal government, which in turn is the absolute condition for the realization of the moral and intellectual capacities of mankind. As such, it is the abiding political ideal of humanity. It is the culmination of the political and philosophical systems of leading thinkers of all ages, as it is the final vision of prophets of religion. This being so, it is absolutely proper that we should approach the subject of the League of Nations with a sense of sincere humility, of deep suspicion of our ingenuity in devising new plans, and of a determination not to judge a League of Nations, once established, by reference to the brief span of our personal experience in a short period of adversity.

The second guiding consideration is that in a League of Nations, thus understood as an enduring object of human endeavour, collective security is the most essential element. Collective security is not a controversial political slogan discredited by disloyalty and failure. Neither is it a luxury or an unnecessary refinement. If law means prevention by the community of unlawful violence – and that is the primary function of any law worthy of the name – then collective security is merely another name for law and order. It was for a good reason that Dr McNair, a teacher distinguished for his scholarship both in international and in English law, gave only two years ago to his inaugural lecture as Professor of International Law in this University the title of 'Collective Security'. Without that foundation, other things in the League are unreal and deceptive – they are a dangerous superstructure of pretentious activity which lulls our consciences and conceals the utter precariousness of our effort. Without that foundation – or at least without a sense of its inherent rationality and an active conviction of its final triumph, however shaken it may be at a time of stress – universality is mere decoration. Without that foundation, efficiency of international administration – in itself a highly desirable object – is a very small matter. International co-operation on a substantial scale in technical, humanitarian and economic matters existed before the establishment of the League and has continued largely independently of it in the last twenty years. It would be a tragedy if the administrative potentialities of the League were to be used as a convenient screen for a painless liquidation of the major purpose for which it was set up. Neither need we seriously entertain the offensive suggestion that we ought to retain the League somehow in order to find a use for its splendid edifice. It is futile to expect that co-operation in practical matters of small compass will contribute to the growth of the law-abiding spirit in matters of significance. There is no gradual transition – there is an unbridgeable gap – between anarchy and the supremacy of the law. Those, therefore, who urge the retention of the League subject to the elimination from the Covenant of the obligations to enforce peace by collective action merely use decorous language calculated to conceal the suggestion that we abandon the object for which the League was created and without which the name 'League of Nations' is a travesty of its essential purpose.

If we keep in mind these two guiding considerations – that the League of Nations is a manifestation of the highest political ideal of humanity and that of this ideal collective security forms the vital part – we shall not find ourselves forlorn and perplexed in working out the right course of action in a period of uncertainty. We may, and we are bound to, admit that the obligations to enforce peace by collective action – i.e. the obligations of Articles 10, 16 and 17 – have for the time being lost their legal validity. But while admitting that, we ought to insist that we regard the setback as merely temporary; that our conviction of the soundness and wisdom of the principle of collective security remains unshaken; that we must accordingly keep intact the structure of the Covenant; that we regard as fully subsisting in law our right to suppress aggression against any member of the League; and that, in our view, collective security as expressed in the guarantee of territorial integrity and in the obligation to suppress aggression must once more become part of the law binding those nations which wish to be bound by it in the future. This, in fact, was declared at the Assembly of the League of Nations in September 1938 to be the policy of His Majesty's Government.

The task of enlightened public opinion – and particularly of the League of Nations Union – is: (*a*) to defend that policy and those principles against the impatience of wise people of much self-assurance for whom the short span of totalitarian ascendancy of force is a compelling reason for throwing overboard principles which they, in common with us, have hitherto regarded as obvious and unassailable; (*b*) to defend that policy and those principles against the danger of degenerating into a diplomatic euphemism and a meaningless phrase unaccompanied by positive action.

As to the first, namely, as to those who, rendered wise by the experience of a decade, tell us simply that 'Articles 10, 16 and 17 must go: let us go back to the nineteenth Century', nothing more need be said except that it seems pessimistic and unreasonable to exchange the wider experience of history for the disillusionment and the fears and the little stratagems of the moment. There is all the difference between the suggestion that these Articles ought to be abandoned and the view that, although their legal force is now largely spent, their purpose is sound and that we ought to aim at reviving them as soon as conditions permit.

As to the second, it is fervently to be desired that His Majesty's Government will bear in mind that the League of Nations not only still continues to be a potential instrument of value for resisting the forces of lawlessness and aggression. It is for many a great spiritual heritage of the past, distant and immediate, and a starting point of constructive action as soon as the flow of progress has once more emerged into the daylight; it embodies for many a hope of a rational order of things and an indispensable condition of lifting social consciousness from the depth of cynicism and materialism into which it is being plunged. If those who think so were in a minority it would still be consistent with that spirit of consideration and compromise which is of the essence of democracy if, for their sake, the Government were to lend to the League that support which it clearly can give it without jeopardizing the success of its policy of peace through other agencies. But we know that those who think so are not in a minority. This being so, although collective security as laid down in the Covenant is legally in abeyance, States so disposed may find many ways of showing attachment to the principles of the League by themselves observing the obligations of pacific settlement and lending their authority to the full use of its machinery; by subscribing without stint to the principle of compulsory arbitration; by extending whenever possible the activities of the International Labour Organization; by treating the League with reverence and its institutions with studious respect; by adopting towards its budget an attitude of open-minded generosity as distinguished from petty economy which, on any hypothesis, is inexcusable and vicious; by giving to its officials that large measure of encouragement and support of which, in these times, they are so much in need; and by using every opportunity for enlarging the sphere of its action in so far as this is not made impossible by the necessity of the co-operation of non-member States.

Moreover, the principle of collective security can be kept alive not only by words and professions. It can be gradually resuscitated by political action. It can be revived as between groups of nations, Members of the League, of a sufficient community of outlook and interest. The members of such groups could not only re-affirm their obligation not to resort to war against one another; they could also undertake, this time expressly and unequivocally, that they will suppress unconditionally and in all circumstances, whether foreseen or not, the violation of that duty. There would thus exist, as between those States, a complete system of collective security. It would not be unreasonable if the States thus united were to pledge themselves to defend one another against aggression by other States who are not Members of the association. It would further be in accordance with the lessons of experience if the States in question were to lay down as between themselves the foundations of a more organic Commonwealth by undertaking not only the obligation to respect the existing law, but also the duty to abide by the changes in the law, as between themselves, decreed by a competent legislative organ of the Commonwealth. A community both of outlook and of interest must, it has been suggested, be the indispensable basis of that close association of collective security. At the same time a substantial measure of co-operation could be maintained with nations which, while adhering to principles of government and of political morality different from our own, are interested in the maintenance of peace and in prevention of aggression. Conversely, the fact that the articles imposing the duty to enforce the provisions of the Covenant are no longer fully valid may make feasible the enlargement of the membership of the League by the adherence of those nations which, like the United States, consider sanctions to be obnoxious. There would thus be room in the League for two kinds of membership: the first for those who regard as sufficient the assumption of a duty to observe the peace and the participation in the persuasive and consultative processes of peaceful settlement; the second for those for whom the enforcement of peace and the principles of collective security are ideas of permanent value which they are content to practise as between themselves and to hope that others will adopt them in due course.

If we make ourselves responsible for urging this course of action and, above all, if we succeed in making ourselves and public opinion conscious of the reasons which ought to prompt it, we shall be making sure of not losing the historic perspective and of upholding a sustaining sense of purpose in the difficult times in which we live and which lie ahead of us. They are difficult not only because of their political uncertainty. They are a period in which progress in things essential has been arrested and the clock turned back. How immeasurably far backwards do we seem to have travelled from those days of unbounded optimism born of a sense of reality of progress in the international sphere, the days of the great International Exhibition in London when the Prince Consort used these words: 'Nobody who has paid any attention to the peculiar features of our present era will doubt for a moment that we are living at a period of most wonderful transition which tends rapidly to accomplish that great end to which indeed all history points – the realization of the unity of mankind.' This was said in 1851. The magnitude of the present reversal of progress may not be a reason for deep despondency for those for whom, as a matter of ethical theory, a happy and satisfied life consists in doing the good thing, or showing pity and compassion; for these are utterly independent of circumstances. But for the vast majority of thinking persons the meaning of life and the only possible hypothesis on which evil and suffering are bearable consist in the assumption that the human race, by dint of its own efforts, is destined to progress in capacity and well-being. For that vast majority the almost tangible reality of the present retrogression and frustration of hopes must, but for one thing, be a personal tragedy. But for one thing: we may decide to forge our lives, consciously and actively and defiantly, into a link in the chain of that perennial though unsteady course of progress in relation to which the present misfortune is no more than an episode. I have submitted that in the affairs of man an indispensable condition of that progress is the integration of the human society into a federation of States under an enforceable and enforced rule of law – into a League of Nations. If this be so, then this League of Nations Union stands for a purpose whose appeal, I firmly believe, will in the long run prove stronger than the discouragement of a temporary relapse.

CHAPTER 6

CREDENTIALS OF THE ABYSSINIAN DELEGATION

Editor's note The note which forms this chapter appeared in *B.Y.* 18 (1937), 184–6.

The Seventeenth Assembly of the League of Nations was confronted, in September 1936, with a problem which the framers of the Covenant did not foresee and could not properly have attempted to foresee. That problem was the continued right of representation in the Assembly of a State whose territory has been invaded, occupied and formally annexed by a fellow Member of the League in indisputable breach of the Covenant. On 2 May 1936 the Emperor of Abyssinia, confronted by an overwhelming force, left his country. On 5 May Italian troops entered the capital of Abyssinia. On 9 May an Italian Royal Decree purported to place Abyssinia under Italian sovereignty. On 16 September the Abyssinian Legation in London issued a statement to the effect that there existed in the west of Abyssinia a regular Government exercising normal functions of administration under the authority and in accordance with the instructions of the Emperor of Abyssinia. On the same day the Abyssinian Legation in London announced that Abyssinia was sending a delegation to the forthcoming session of the Assembly. It soon became known that, while Italy did not intend to raise the question of the status of Abyssinia at the Assembly, she would regard the admission of the Abyssinian delegation as a ground for not sending her own. The Credentials Committee of the Assembly was thus confronted with a task of the utmost delicacy, and there was accordingly some difficulty in inducing the representatives of the various Governments to serve on the Committee. The Committee as eventually chosen was composed of the representatives of the following States: France, Great Britain, Peru, the Soviet Union, the Netherlands, Czechoslovakia, New Zealand, Greece, and Turkey.

In dealing with the question of Abyssinia the Committee was guided by Article 5 of the rules relating to the procedure of the Assembly, which provides as follows:

1. Each Member shall communicate to the Secretary-General, if possible one week before the date fixed for the opening of the session, the names of its

representatives, of whom there shall not be more than three. The names of substitute representatives may be added.

2. The full powers of the representatives shall be delivered to the Secretary-General, if possible, one week before the date fixed for the opening of the session. They shall be issued either by the head of the State or by the Minister for Foreign Affairs.

3. A Committee of nine Members for the examination of the credentials shall be elected by the Assembly on the proposal of the President. The Committee shall report without delay.

4. Any representative to whose admission objection has been made shall sit provisionally with the same rights as other representatives, unless the Assembly decides otherwise.

The Committee, after having discarded the suggestion that the Permanent Court of International Justice might be asked to give an advisory opinion on the question whether the representatives of Abyssinia were entitled to sit at the Assembly, recommended the admission of the Abyssinian delegation. It is convenient to quote the crucial passages of the Committee's Report relating to the credentials of the Abyssinian delegation:

Its credentials are derived from the same authority as had more than once in the past issued the full powers of the Ethiopian delegation to previous sessions of the Assembly. On the dates on which they were issued (14 and 19 September), however, the situation in Ethiopia had greatly changed in various respects. The head of the State is in a foreign country; the Government is no longer in the capital; according to some of the documents submitted, a governmental authority is stated to be established in another part of the country. It seems exceptionally difficult to judge of the nature and extent of the power of that authority, and of the strength of the connections still existing between it and the head of the State. The question that accordingly presented itself to the Committee was whether the head of the State from whom the credentials under examination emanate was exercising his legal title effectively enough to make those credentials perfectly in order . . . the best solution would be to propose that the Assembly should consider the credentials submitted by the Ethiopian delegation, despite the doubt as to their regularity, as sufficient to permit that delegation to sit at the present session.[1]

It pointed out that in situations like that with which the Committee was confronted 'the delegation in question should have the benefit of the doubt' and that 'by the adoption of the solution indicated, which holds good only for the present session, nothing is done to prejudice the future'.

This Report, which was adopted by the Assembly on 23 September, seems to have dealt with the difficulty on the purely factual basis of the

[1] League of Nations Doc. A. 41 (1936). Reprinted in *Documents on International Affairs, 1935*, ed. Heald, p. 545.

effectiveness of the power of the lawful Government in some parts of Abyssinia. It is a fair implication from the Report that should it become definitely established that there no longer exists an organization meriting the designation of an independent Government and exercising authority on behalf of the Emperor of Abyssinia, the Assembly might refuse to recognize the continued validity of the credentials of a delegation appointed by the Emperor of Abyssinia.

It may be a matter of dispute how far the Assembly is entitled, by laying down the conditions of effectiveness of the administration on the part of the Government concerned, to question the legality of credentials regularly issued by the lawful Sovereign of a recognized State, a member of the League. However that may be, the decision of the Assembly is probably not relevant to the question of membership. Even if the Assembly were at some future date to decide that the credentials issued by the Emperor of Abyssinia can no longer be recognized, that decision would not affect the question of the Abyssinian membership of the League. Abyssinia would continue as a member of the League so long as the League as a whole or the substantial majority of its Members have not *de jure* recognized the annexation of Abyssinia by Italy, or so long as its membership of the League has not terminated as the result of expulsion under Article 16(4) or voluntary withdrawal under Article 1(3). The refusal to recognize the validity of the credentials issued by the lawful Sovereign of a State would mean in practice a suspension from the exercise of rights of membership of the State concerned, with the concomitant provisional cessation of its duties, financial and otherwise, to the League. The same result might be brought about if the Emperor of Abyssinia were to inform the League that, in view of the occupation of Abyssinia by a hostile army and the cessation of normal governmental functions, he does not propose for the time being to be represented at the Assembly and, generally, in the activities of or conferences convened under the auspices of the League. A step of that nature, while fully safeguarding the ultimate interests of Abyssinia, might well obviate the necessity of or inducement to decisions prejudicial to the cause of the League and to the authority of international law.

CHAPTER 7

RESURRECTION OF THE LEAGUE

Editor's note This chapter consists of a review article of Lord Cecil's autobiography, *A Great Experiment* (1941). The review was published in *The Political Quarterly*, 12 (1941), 121–33.

The appearance of Lord Cecil's autobiography, in terms, largely, of the history of the League of Nations, marks an event of significance for political thought in the sphere of international relations. The book does not herald or invite a new movement of opinion. But it is likely to lend powerful and authoritative support to a trend well under way. For Lord Cecil's autobiography appears at a period of the War when there has already begun to take place a visible change in the general attitude towards the League of Nations. The future historian will be able to state with substantial accuracy that, when in the second year of the Second World War the problem of post-war international reconstruction became a subject of study and discussion, there was no longer a tendency to view the League of Nations as a pathetic and grotesque heap of ruins to which it had been reduced by totalitarian force. The League of Nations was becoming once more what it was in 1919 to enlightened public opinion, namely, an expression of the highest political aspiration of humanity. When founded in 1919, the League was more than the sequel of the experience of the World War and of the period of international anarchy which preceded it – a no mean experience in itself. There was then a willingness – inarticulate in some, but active in most – to accept the basic philosophy of the League in terms which underlay Kant's explanation of a World Federation : The purpose of man is to progress in well-being towards the development of his intellectual and moral capacities ; such progress is conditioned by the attainment of perfect internal government ; the possibility of such government is, in turn, dependent on the establishment of an international system for securing the peace of the world. Thus conceived, a League of Nations must be regarded as the abiding political ideal of mankind. It was realized that its future achievements and failures must be viewed from that wider perspective, and that there was a duty not to judge it by reference to any passing period of adversity.

That attitude suffered a setback in the decade preceding the Second World War. The successful assertion of power politics and of defiance of international law and morality lent a touch of plausibility to attempts to revitalize the teachings of Frederick the Great, of Hegel and of Treitschke under the attractive guise of a realist science of international relations. In that science power was once more acclaimed as the primary and enduring factor in the relations of States; human beings organized as sovereign States were once more declared to be outside those moral restraints and incapable of that intelligence benefiting from experience which, within the State, have lifted the individual from barbarism to civilization; and the schemes of international organization which, to the glory of the human spirit, have been successively put forward by constructive thinkers of all ages were represented as subtle devices of ingenious nationalism bent on perpetuating the advantages of the national *status quo* at any particular period. That facile perversion of realism was in itself a melancholy reminder of the corrupting power of force. There were many who, while denouncing and condemning violence, were unable to escape the influence of its glamorous successes. However, the attraction of that rationalization of physical force in the field of social science was naturally shortlived. It did not survive the revolt of civilized society against organized lawlessness. In 1941 there was a growing realization that the fact and the magnitude and the appraisal, by the remaining neutrals, of the meaning of the war waged by the Allies were a proper measure of the essential reality of the ideals of the League of Nations. That enduring significance of the League of Nations was becoming clear in proportion as it was generally acknowledged that the discussion and study, on the part of those suitably situated, of the problem of the future organization of the world, was a proper and legitimate pre-occupation in time of war. Statements, which were formerly apt to be brushed aside with impatience, like 'if the League did not exist, it would be necessary to invent it' or 'what else can you put in its place?' acquired a new and affirmative meaning. The League had become once more the anchor sheet of constructive thought in the matter of international organization. There was a feeling of embarrassment at the thought that during a transient period of retrogression so many should have yielded so readily to the temporary triumphs of force as to embrace or treat seriously a recrudescence of realism which political science and ethics had agreed in regarding as utterly discredited. In the second year of the Second World War this kind of realism had become largely a matter of the past. The feeling was growing that, in addition to any possible schemes of regional federation, the continuance of a strengthened League of Nations as a universal system for the purpose of securing peace by the collective effort of States was an essential part of the ultimate war aim. To that growing consciousness Lord Cecil's book is bound to give a powerful impetus.

There are two special reasons why the personality of the author of this unorthodox biography counts for so much in this connection. The first is that he has never wavered in his adherence to the essential principles of the League. This can be said of very few only – even of those whose devotion to the idea of the League has been beyond cavil. Ardent believers in collective security and leaders of the League of Nations movement were ready, on strategic and other grounds, to justify the attitude of the British and French Governments at the time of the invasion of Manchuria. After the annexation of Abyssinia by Italy many supporters of the League emphasized the wisdom of recognizing facts as well as the duty of remembering that, after all, Great Britain had been responsible for similar actions in the past. Statesmen, who in 1919 regarded physical sanctions for coercing and penalizing the aggressor as of the essence of the League, in 1936 deprecated the idea of compulsion and spoke of the League as being exclusively an organ of conciliation and co-operation. Lord Cecil is one of the few whose course has not been subject to any such vacillations. As the official representative of successive Governments at the Assembly and in the Council he was often compelled to give effect to decisions of which he did not approve. On such occasions he refrained as a rule from an eloquent justification of a course of action which appeared to him distasteful. On crucial occasions his manner was one of a dignity and a determination which succeeded in rescuing what could be saved from the wreckage of opportunism or obstructive caution. There are many who will not share Lord Cecil's view that the League emerged successfully from the Corfu incident when Italy bombarded and occupied the island as a reprisal against the murder of an Italian general in Greek territory. There are many who believe that that incident was the thin edge of disintegration thrust into the structure of the League. But it is difficult to deny that Lord Cecil's bearing at the Assembly did much to offset the damage. In answer to the contention of the Italian delegates that the matter was one touching the sovereignty of the Italian State and, as such, beyond the jurisdiction of any outside body, Lord Cecil, at a meeting of the Assembly unprecedented in dramatic tension and in the realization of the significance of the event with which it was confronted, asked the Secretary-General to read out aloud the relevant articles of the Covenant as a clear and solemn answer to the Italian claim.

And yet, although the book tells the story of one who has adhered unflinchingly to the major principles of the Covenant, the reader is far from gathering the impression that that consistency was one of a fanatic or of a doctrinaire. In the cumulative light of post-war history the book is one of a realist statesman in the true meaning of the word. It shows how the maintenance and the collective enforcement of international peace constitute a major national interest – an interest in the long run as tangible as that involved in a direct attack upon national territory.

The second reason for the importance of Lord Cecil's book is the fact that it is based on the experience of one who can truly say of himself *pars maxima fui*. As such it is full of instruction on the vital question of the reasons of the failure of the League in the second decade of its existence. The predominant impression with which the reader is left is that that failure was due to deficiencies of leadership, to its ignorance and its shortsightedness. In fact, there runs through the book an accusing note which is not devoid of bitterness. Lord Cecil is of the view that 'if the League has failed in some respects, it is because the Governments or some of them actively or passively desired that it should fail' (p. 80). He believes that Mr Baldwin and other Conservative leaders regarded the League 'as a kind of excrescence which must be carefully prevented from having too much influence on our foreign policy' and that 'Geneva, to them, was a strange place in which a new-fangled machine existed in order to enable foreigners to influence our international action' (p. 146). His view of most Conservative politicians is that 'not only did they reject in their hearts the League of Nations, but they did not propose to take any steps for getting rid of war' (p. 189). He thinks that in 1933 'one of the chief objects of the British Government seemed to be to lessen the prestige and authority of the League' (p. 245). He recalls that at the Assembly of the League following upon the Lytton Report, the British delegate, Sir John Simon, 'made a forensic defence of Japan, and, according to the account of some of those present, was formally thanked by M. Matsuoka, the Japanese delegate' (p. 234). And there are other, even more pronounced, passages which hardly substantiate the publisher's view that Lord Cecil 'scarcely blames' and that he 'rarely criticizes'. But we still may agree, with affection and respect for one who has beneficently dedicated his life to the greatest of all causes, that 'Lord Cecil writes as he has lived, as a gentleman'. For there is no trace in his narrative of personal attack or of imputation of motives. It is an accusation of the shortsightedness of the leaders of a world empire who, in the author's view, embraced a parochial realism ignoring the essential interdependence of the world. It is an accusation of leadership which sheltered itself behind the doubtful expediency of the refusal to undertake commitments covering unforeseeable contingencies. The fact is that the security of civilized life consists in framing laws and accepting obligations for future contingencies which cannot be foreseen in all their implications. The possible – in fact, the inevitable – measure of resulting injustice is preferable to the insecurity and precariousness of anarchy. This is a truth which applies to States no less than to individuals. The verdict of history will probably support Lord Cecil's view that successive Governments were ill-advised in their refusal to agree to the extension or definition of their obligations in the matter of collective security. In the end, they were driven to give far-reaching undertakings in circumstances which were politically and otherwise open to question.

There will probably be less agreement with Lord Cecil's strictures on the disarmament policy of British Governments. There is warrant for the view that they bore a share of responsibility for the disintegration of the League by their laxity in the fulfilment of existing obligations and by their refusal to support effectively the cause of international security and arbitration. These contributions to international peace could have been made, without stint, consistently with the true interests of Great Britain and of the Empire. However, given the situation created by the refusal to contribute more effectively to the cause of international arbitration and security, it was difficult to expect a more drastic policy of limitation of armaments than that actually followed by the British Governments. Very few will agree with Lord Cecil that the Treaty of Versailles, when read in conjunction with the Covenant, imposed upon the Allies the absolute legal duty of limitation of armaments consequent upon German disarmament. Neither was such duty imposed by the Covenant. Disarmament, when unaccompanied by parallel progress in the sphere of security and arbitration, was not a programme which could be urged consistently with national and international security. Politically, it is not easy to acquiesce in the opinion that if the Allies had disarmed, the principal German grievance would have disappeared and with it the main cause of the rise and growth of the Nazi régime.

There will probably be agreement – and there must be agreement unless we abandon ourselves to the view that in the international sphere events are impervious to human will and intelligence – that the collapse of collective security was the consequence of the absence of far-sighted and courageous leadership. It may, of course, be said that the absence of such leadership was due to the fact that there was no public opinion sufficiently determined and sufficiently endowed with a sense of historic continuity. But these are not usual qualities of the collective mind. However, it is a mistake to identify this failure of leadership with the shortcomings or defection of one particular party. It is possible that some such error may be the result of the emphasis which Lord Cecil places on the circumstance that the League gained a new and continuing accession of power with the advent of the Labour Government in 1929 and that some of the Conservative leaders exhibited an uninformed and petty dislike of the League and of its ideals. The fact is that it is by no means certain that if a Labour Government had been in power in the course of the Manchurian dispute in 1931 or during the Italo-Abyssinian war in 1935, the British attitude would have been radically different from what it was. It is probable that the roots of the evil go much deeper and that they are intimately connected with the entire problem of the conduct of foreign affairs in democracies in relation to collective security. Democratic Governments are composed of statesmen and politicians who, for various reasons, are subject to the overwhelming desire to avoid trouble and to preserve peace even if such peace means a precarious war for the next generation or even for their own on the day after tomorrow. They are inclined to act literally on the words of the prayer: Give us peace in our day, O Lord. But the obligations of collective security are in the nature of an insurance which requires the payment of costly premiums. Like other institutions of civilized life, it may demand the sacrifice of immediate interests – including the immediate interest of peace – for the sake of a wider future good. It must be a matter for most serious consideration and for future study how best to ensure the continuity and effectiveness of the foreign policy of democracies, especially in the field of national and collective security, irrespective of ephemeral exigencies of internal politics. When Mr Baldwin, in his capacity as Prime Minister, revealed that his Government refrained from proceeding with the task of rearmament on the ground that a disclosure of its necessity would have seriously endangered the electoral chances of his party, he was drawing attention to a problem of a gravity transcending the immediate issue with which he was concerned.

However, the failure of the League of Nations is not attributable to any single cause. In particular, it is impossible to evade the question as to how far this result was due to the absence of a sufficiently large measure of restriction upon the legal freedom of action of the members of the League. It is not altogether clear what is Lord Cecil's final answer to this question. Occasionally he expresses the view that the very existence of clear-cut obligations for the collective enforcement of peace is in itself a powerful factor in the promotion of peace and security. Thus he is 'morally certain' that if the Treaty of Mutual Assistance had been in operation 'the Italian invasion of Abyssinia and the German invasions of Czechoslovakia and Poland would never have taken place' (p. 158). He often deplores the unwillingness of Great Britain to undertake definite commitments, and it is obvious that he sees in that disinclination a major factor in the post-War retrogression. At the same time he is emphatic that there is nothing inherently wrong in the existing provisions of the Covenant and that if interpreted loyally and in good faith they would have proved adequate for the purpose for which they were designed. There is no doubt that he would have preferred a more pronounced limitation of the sovereignty of the Members of the League. But he explains in various parts of his autobiography that any limitation of sovereignty beyond that actually achieved in the Covenant was impossible in 1919 at the Peace Conference. There was, he says repeatedly, a marked opposition against anything in the nature of a super-State. 'Nothing can be more certain than that any attempt to erect a super-State would have failed' (p. 71). There will be many who will be inclined to join issue with Lord Cecil on that question. There is a *via media* between what is popularly regarded as a super-State and the rigid principle of unanimity under the Covenant. There is also abundant evidence in Lord Cecil's own book that it was not inevitable that the League of Nations should have been exclusively the work of the politicians and the diplomats assembled at the Peace Conference. The establishment of the League was to a large extent the result of the insistence of wide masses determined to prevent a repetition of the cataclysm of another World War. Lord Cecil admits that the great mass of the peoples was ready to make great sacrifices to secure peace. So real was that pressure from below that any of the delegates determined to represent effectively popular feeling would have been in a strong position.

Undoubtedly, the Covenant of the League is an example of an unparalleled and truly revolutionary limitation of the sovereignty of its Members. For no other designation can properly be given to the enactment of the collective right of intervention on the part of the League in disputes between its Members, to the most drastic limitation of the right of war, and to the recognition of the principle of coercive sanctions against sovereign States. At the same time it is true that in the Covenant, both as adopted and as interpreted in practice, these limitations did not go far enough and that, apart from other reasons which may well have proved superior to any purely legal obligation, however rigid and far-reaching, the effective reservation of freedom of action was one of the principal causes of the collapse of the collective system set up in the Covenant. In establishing the League, Governments fell short of their own professions made during the World War and of the expectations of large sections of their peoples. As an instrument for the legal organization of peace, the Covenant was defective from the very beginning. Those who framed it were deliberately obscure in the matter of prohibition of war, and by limiting it to 'resort to war', as distinguished from resort to force, left the door wide open for abuse and confusion. While introducing the principle of collective enforcement of peace, they limited its obligations to economic action and refrained from providing for the jurisdiction of the League as a whole both to determine the case of aggression and to direct the course of collective action aiming at its suppression. They declined to sanction the principle of obligatory judicial settlement even with regard to disputes which they themselves described as generally suitable for such settlement. Sovereignty, formally enshrined in the rigid principle of unanimity, was made to permeate even the machinery of pacific settlement. The result of that combination of far-reaching restrictions with the maintenance of sovereignty was a flexible instrument of great elasticity – an instrument which, because of its elasticity, has often been described by friends of the League as the best instrument that could be devised for the purpose for which it was intended. This would have been so if the circumstances had been favourable. But they were not. In consequence, the elasticity of the Covenant has worked one way only. Its potential strength has been allowed to remain in the background; but Members of the League have often appealed to those of its provisions which left them complete freedom of action and which reduced the Covenant to a mere declaration of principle.

While, therefore, any argument based on the use of the term 'super-State' is bound to be of limited advantage in the discussion, it is probable that a further surrender of sovereignty within a reformed League of Nations will be recognized to be a necessary condition of its usefulness as an instrument of peace. This applies in particular to the question of the peaceful change of treaties and of customary international law – a matter which is generally regarded as one of the crucial problems of international peace and organization. There are many who believe that the failure of the post-War system as set up in the Covenant of the League was due to the fact that it did not provide effective means for changing conditions which, in the language of the Covenant, have become dangerous to the peace of the world. It is possible to argue – and Lord Cecil does not altogether seem to disapprove of the argument – that even the existing Article 19 which lays down that the Assembly may recommend the reconsideration of treaties and conditions calling for a change would have been adequate for the purpose of instituting responsible discussion and of mobilizing public opinion in support of a change. However, as in the matter of enforcing the law so also with regard to changing it, public opinion, when relied upon as the chief instrumentality, is a deceptive weapon. It is therefore somewhat perturbing to find that in his scheme of an International Authority, printed as an appendix at the end of the book, Lord Cecil's solution does not differ radically from that adopted in the Covenant. He proposes that if the recommendation for a change is agreed upon unanimously, except for the votes of States immediately interested, it should be binding on all State members, and that if it is adopted by a majority it should bind those who voted in the majority. The proposed departure from the existing Covenant is not, it is true, a negligible one. Qualified unanimity – i.e. one in which the votes of the interested parties are not counted – is substituted for the principle of absolute unanimity. The history of the League has shown that on important occasions it was possible to achieve such qualified unanimity. But there were occasions which admitted of no element of doubt – as in the case of the Italian invasion of Abyssinia – and in which no qualified unanimity could be achieved. The very requirement of qualified unanimity may act as an invitation to obstruction, as an inducement to secure a subservient satellite, or as a means of devitalizing the proposed change.

The problem of peaceful change cannot be solved on any other than legislative basis, i.e. by way of decisions of an international organ endowed with effective authority in law and in fact to impose its decrees upon a dissenting minority. Such an authority may, perhaps not inaccurately, invite the charge of constituting a super-State. Whatever name we choose to give to the organ entrusted with such powers, it is the only instrument capable of a true solution of the problem of peaceful change. The question of the size of the majority required for legislative action of this nature must remain a matter of study and discussion. There will be general agreement that no State should be required to give up its legal rights unless in pursuance of a decision of an overwhelming majority of the members of the League. To be real and acceptable, any such addition to the competence of the League must be accompanied by a substantial modification of the present rights of its members in the matter of voting and representation. The rigid principle of abstract equality, in addition to being morally objectionable, is not compatible with the existence of a League entrusted with the solution of this and other crucial problems of international order. Any revision of the Covenant in the matter of equality in representation and in voting power is admittedly fraught with difficulties. But it is better to face squarely the immensity of the problem in all its ramifications than to adopt solutions which leave matters substantially as they were before. An ineffective solution is, in its results, almost as reprehensible as the flippancy of the realist who concedes that the question of peaceful change is the central problem of international relations; who admits that its effective solution is impossible short of a limitation of sovereignty implied in the power of an international authority to impose changes by a majority vote; who denies that States will ever consent to any such limitation; and who resigns himself to the conviction that the problem of change in the relations of States is in essence one of power and to the hope that such power may exert its influence by way of peaceful persuasion and a precarious interplay of threats and pressure short of war rather than through its more natural manifestations.

In the matter of the recent schemes of federation, Lord Cecil is distinctly critical insofar as such schemes are put forward as alternatives to the League of Nations. But he is in favour of confederations within the framework of the League, established on the basis of geographical propinquity and endowed with organs of their own. There is no reason why such confederations should not be thought of in terms of the federal principle proper, subject to the retention of separate international personality by the Member States. For it is probable that the progression of mankind towards a politically integrated international society conceived as a true federation of the world will proceed on two parallel lines: horizontally, as it were, by way of a gradual development of the existing confederation of States, namely, the League of Nations, in the direction of a federation through the slow process of progressive limitations of the sovereignty of its Members; vertically, as it were, by way of geographically limited federations in the full sense of the word, established on the basis of affinity of culture, of language, of tradition, and of political ideas. Any such schemes must be regarded as a proper subject of serious and unprejudiced study. They may supplement, with great advantage, the development resulting from the rebirth of a reformed and strengthened League of Nations. But the latter must remain the starting point of political thought and action in the field of international reconstruction. Without the unifying and restraining influence of a League of Nations universal in its potential membership, any such limited federations may well become a source of regional friction and far-flung wars. Without the League of Nations – every consideration of dignity and perspective impels us to retain its very name – we must see ourselves deprived of that beacon of historic continuity, of universality, and of the unity of the human race without which all schemes of international organization must remain mere constitution mongering.

INDEX

INDEX

Made in the USA
Monee, IL
14 September 2026

63198316R00374